BEST ROAD TRIPS

EUROPE

-------------→

ESCAPES ON THE OPEN ROAD

Isabel Albiston, Oliver Berry, Stuart Butler, Jean-Bernard Carillet, Fionn Davenport, Marc Di Duca, Belinda Dixon, Peter Dragicevich, Duncan Garwood, Anthony Ham, Paula Hardy, Catherine Le Nevez, John Noble, Sally O'Brien, Josephine Quintero, Kevin Raub, Daniel Robinson, Brendan Sainsbury, Regis St Louis, Andy Symington, Ryan Ver Berkmoes, Kerry Walker, Nicola Williams, Neil Wilson

SYMBOLS IN THIS BOOK

Top Tips	📖 History & Culture	📷 Essential Photo
🅢 Link Your Trips	🚶 Family	🏃 Walking Tour
💬 Tips from Locals	🍷 Food & Drink	🍴 Eating
🔁 Trip Detour	🌳 Outdoors	🛏 Sleeping

📞 Telephone Number	@ Internet Access	📖 English-Language Menu
🕐 Opening Hours	📶 Wi-Fi Access	👪 Family-Friendly
🅿 Parking	🥗 Vegetarian Selection	🐾 Pet-Friendly
🚭 Nonsmoking		
❄ Air-Conditioning	🏊 Swimming Pool	

MAP LEGEND

Routes

- Trip Route
- Trip Detour
- Linked Trip
- Walk Route
- Tollway
- Freeway
- Primary
- Secondary
- Tertiary
- Lane
- Unsealed Road
- Plaza/Mall
- Steps
-)= = Tunnel
- Pedestrian Overpass
- Walk Track/Path

Boundaries

- – – – International
- – – – – State/Province
- Cliff
- Wall

Population

- ✪ Capital (National)
- ◉ Capital (State/Province)
- ● City/Large Town
- ● Town/Village

Transport

- ✈ Airport
- +⊕+ Cable Car/Funicular
- 🅟 Parking
- +⊕+ Train/Railway
- Ⓣ Tram
- Ⓜ Underground Train Station

Trips

- 1 Trip Numbers
- 9 Trip Stop
- 🏃 Walking tour
- 🔁 Trip Detour

Route Markers

- E44 E-road network
- M100 National network

Hydrography

- River/Creek
- Intermittent River
- Swamp/Mangrove
- Canal
- Water
- Dry/Salt/Intermittent Lake
- Glacier

Areas

- Beach
- Cemetery (Christian)
- × × Cemetery (Other)
- Park
- Forest
- Urban Area
- Sportsground

PLAN YOUR TRIP

ON THE ROAD

CONTENTS

Ireland p297

Great Britain p203

Germany p487

Austria p567

France p117

Switzerland p537

Italy p25

Portugal p445

Spain p369

Contents

COVID-19

We have re-checked every business in this book before publication to ensure that it is still open after the COVID-19 outbreak. However, the economic and social impacts of COVID-19 will continue to be felt long after the outbreak has been contained, and many businesses, services and events referenced in this guide may experience ongoing restrictions. Some businesses may be temporarily closed, have changed their opening hours and services, or require bookings; some will unfortunately have closed their doors permanently. We suggest you check with venues before visiting for the latest information.

WELCOME TO
EUROPE

Europe has an embarrassment of riches. To incomparable art and architecture, add a vivid past. To spectacular scenery and vibrant cities add the finest food and wine. It's a place that helps you do and be what you've always wanted. Hike mountain passes. Savour wine beside sun-ripened vines. Tour *palazzi* and *pueblos*. Linger over lunchtime people watching. Feel you belong.

These riches are best by far discovered by car. And the countless stops we've crafted into 41 road trips are your key to unlocking those experiences. Grip the wheel in white-knuckle mountain routes. Cruise along coast roads. Drive historical timelines. Trace gourmet and vineyard trails.

Trips packed with culture, cities, history, mountains, food, beaches, wine and art – they're all waiting to be discovered and our routes will guide you every stop of the way.

St Peter's Basilica, Rome

EUROPE HIGHLIGHTS

35 Romantic Rhine
The majestic river winds past medieval villages, vineyards and castles. **5–7 DAYS**

8 Essential France
This grand tour visits some of France's most unmissable sights. **21 DAYS**

17 The Historic South
Rich in nautical, archaeological and architectural heritage. **9–11 DAYS**

19 Royal Highlands
Imposing mountains, emerald green glades and glinting lochs. **4–5 DAYS**

14 Châteaux of the Loire
Austere medieval fortresses to ostentatious royal pleasure palaces. **5 DAYS**

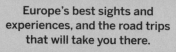

Europe's best sights and experiences, and the road trips that will take you there.

EUROPE
HIGHLIGHTS

Italian Lakes

Italy's northern lakes are simply sublime. The most picturesque and least visited is Lago di Como (Lake Como), which is a highlight of **Trip 2: The Graceful Italian Lakes**, a scenic jaunt around Lakes Maggiore, Orta and Como. Set in the shadow of the Rhaetian Alps, Lago di Como's banks are speckled with Liberty-style villas and fabulous landscaped gardens that burst into blushing colour in April and May.

Trip

Varenna Scenic view of Lake Como

Paris The city's iconic skyline

Paris

What is there to say about the City of Light that hasn't been said a thousand times before? Quite simply, this is one of the world's essential cities: sexy, suave and sophisticated. There's a lifetime of experiences here, from the treasures of the Louvre to the cafes of Montmartre – encounter them on **Trip 8: Essential France**, which steers you all the way from the chic capital to the glistening Med.

Trip 8

Amalfi Coast

The quintessential Mediterranean shoreline, the Amalfi Coast – detailed in **Trip 4: Amalfi Coast** – curves sinuously along the coast, taking you from one steeply stacked town to another. All around, sheer cliffs drop down into sparkling blue waters, lemons grow on hillside terraces, and towering *fichi d'India* (prickly pears) guard silent mountain paths.

Trip 4

Scottish Highlands

Scotland's wild places abound in breathtaking vistas: imposing mountains, emerald green glades, glinting lochs – the scenery here is truly awe-inspiring. Drive right into the views on **Trip 19: Royal Highlands & Cairngorms**, which delivers castles, peaks and wildlife galore – and the chance to explore the Royal family's summer holiday haunts.

Trip 19

Loire Valley Chateau de Villandry

BEST ROADS FOR DRIVING

SS163 The 'Nastro Azzurro' weaves along the precipitous Amalfi Coast. **Trip** 4

Col d'Aubisque A route through the craggy Pyrenees; more like flying than driving **Trip** 11

The São Vicente Coast Road Cliff tops en route to Europe's southwestern-most tip. **Trip** 33

A939 Scottish Highlands Motor beside ski slopes at rollercoaster Lecht Pass. **Trip** 19

Silvretta High Alpine Road Brave 34 white-knuckle-switchbacks 2500m high in the Austrian Alps. **Trip** 40

Châteaux of the Loire

For sky's-the-limit extravagance, don't miss **Trip 14: Châteaux of the Loire**. Constructed by France's aristocratic elite between the 15th and 17th centuries, these lavish mansions were designed to show off their owners' wealth – something they manage to achieve in spectacular fashion. Chambord is the jewel in the crown, but on this trip you'll see plenty of sparkling gems.

Trip 14

13

England Stonehenge

Stonehenge

Mysterious and compelling, Stonehenge is Great Britain's most iconic ancient site. People have been drawn to this myth-laden ring of bluestones for the last 5000 years, and we still don't know quite why it was built. Come up with your own theories while gazing at these massive megaliths.

Trips

BEST SIPPING & SUPPING

Castello di Verrazzano Sample Chianti Classico and olive oil at this ancient Italian castle. **Trip** 3

Épernay Explore bottle-packed cellars in the French town dubbed the capitale du champagne. **Trip** 13

Quinta do Crasto Spectacular, terraced vineyards on a ridge above the Río Douro. **Trip** 32

Rioja Trek Tour a vineyard; sup in a bodega; make your own wine. **Trip** 31

Engelszell Visit a 13th century abbey to taste monk-made cheese and beer. **Trip** 41

HIGHLIGHTS

★

Kandersteg Oeschinensee

Florence Duomo

La Rioja Wine Country

La Rioja is the sort of place where you could spend weeks meandering along quiet roads searching out the finest drops. Bodegas offering wine-tastings and villages that shelter wine museums are the mainstay in this region. Aside from scenery and fine quaffs, you'll find plenty of surprises (such as a Frank Gehry–designed masterpiece in a tiny village).

Trip **31**

Florence

From Brunelleschi's red-capped Duomo to Michelangelo's *David* and Botticelli's *The Birth of Venus*, Florence (Firenze) boasts priceless masterpieces and a historic centre that looks much as it did in Renaissance times. Art aside, the city is perfect for al fresco dining and relaxed wine drinking.

Trip **5**

Swiss Alps

You'd think after motoring through 537km of mind-blowing Alpine scenery on **Trip 38: The Swiss Alps** that you've seen it all. Wrong. After a relentless succession of dramatic green peaks, Alpine lakes, glacial ravines and other hallucinatory natural landscapes, you pull into your final destination: Zermatt, an Alpine resort built around the incomparable Matterhorn.

Trip **38**

Algarve Beaches

Beach-lovers have much to celebrate on a drive along Portugal's southern coast. Sandy islands, cliffs and shore set the stage for memorable backroad explorations on **Trip 33: Alentejo & Algarve Beaches**. After a day spent surfing or frolicking in the sea, you can roll up to a beautifully sited restaurant for a seafood feast overlooking the crashing waves.

Trip

The Giant's Causeway

The grand geological flourish of the Giant's Causeway is Northern Ireland's most popular attraction and one of the world's most startling natural wonders. Here, you can clamber over some of the 40,000 unique hexagonal basalt columns that trail off into the sea. Discover the rich legends that surround them on **Trip 23: The Long Way Round**; as you circumnavigate enchanting Ireland's entire shore.

Trips

(left) **Portimão** Beach in the Algarve region;

(below) **Ireland** Giant's Causeway

Romantic Rhine

The Rhine has long mesmerised artists, as is illustrated by the 19th-century paintings in Koblenz on **Trip 35: Romantic Rhine**. From Düsseldorf and Cologne, the majestic river snakes through churning whirlpools, medieval villages, vineyards and castle-capped cliffs. Your trail mirrors it, leading to forests and fortresses, and to evenings sipping rieslings under chestnut trees.

Trip 35

BEST CITIES

London Theatre, history, art, food: Britain's capital excels at them all. **Trips** 15 17

Rome Unique, exquisite, romantic; the one-time capital of the world remains unmissable **Trips** 1 5

Dublin Georgian charm in a vibrant, contemporary city. Plus 1000-plus pubs **Trips** 22 23

Barcelona Playful, historic and flush with unique art. The Spanish city of your dreams **Trip** 27

19

Portsmouth Historic HMS Victory flagship

Architecture

Boasting an unparalleled architectural legacy, Europe is home to some of the world's most celebrated masterpieces in building design. Romanesque cathedrals, baroque palaces, Georgian cities, chalet farmsteads, ancient monuments, cutting-edge creations – the wealth of buildings so clearly in evidence here will be a memorable part of your trip.

14 Châteaux of the Loire Resplendent châteaux line the banks of the Loire, each one more extravagant than the last.

17 The Historic South Three of England's most spectacular cathedrals, plus London and Bath's Georgian city-scape.

29 Northern Spain Pilgrimage Showcasing both a string of ancient chapels and Bilbao's modern Guggenheim Museum.

Great Views

Awe-inspiring mountains, sun-kissed shores, majestic river valleys, vine-etched hills – Europe can claim superb landscapes linked by ribboning roads. These are truly unforgettable drives.

4 Amalfi Coast Italy's most celebrated shore is a classic Mediterranean pin-up – with simply sublime views.

38 The Swiss Alps All the big names are here: Matterhorn, Eiger, Jungfrau, Schilthorn, Titlis and Mönch.

24 Ring of Kerry Virtually every corner on this iconic Irish drive reveals a vista worthy of a postcard.

19 Royal Highlands & Cairngorms A sweep of majestic mountains and pine forests encircles the Queen's Scottish summer home.

Art

Renaissance glories, Impressionist masterpieces, modernist marvels, landmark museums – Europe's astonishing artistic legacy is guaranteed to linger long in the memory after you get home. From Michelangelo to Picasso, Europe is a sheer indulgence for art-lovers and a feast for the eyes.

1 Grand Tour Take in Leonardo's *The Last Supper*, Botticelli's *The Birth of Venus*, Michelangelo's *David* and so much more.

27 Mediterranean Meander See artwork by Spanish greats, from Picasso in Malaga to Catalan giants in Barcelona.

39 Geneva to Zürich Rich and diverse art collections dot this mountainous route – encompassing everything from the Renaissance to Cubism.

Austria The serpentine Grossglockner Road

Outdoors

Europe is an adventure playground extraordinaire. Here you can break free of the schedule and revel in landscapes that make pretty much any activity possible. Hike mountain trails, surf gorgeous beaches, go summer-time skiing, windsurfing and white-water rafting – our adrenaline-laced trips enable it all.

40 Grossglockner Road
A feat of 1930s Austrian engineering, this road swings giddily around 36 switchbacks – opening up mountain activities galore.

16 Britain's Wild Side
A fresh-air fuelled tour of Britain's best wilderness spots, including eight gloriously diverse National Parks.

33 Alentejo & Algarve Beaches Portugal's south coast stunner, offering cliff-backed shores, seaside villages and great surf.

History

In Europe the past is ever present. Everywhere lies evidence of an enthralling heritage stretching back thousands of years – from stone circles and Greek temples to battlefields, chateaux, cathedrals and castles.

5 World Heritage Wonders Rome's Colosseum and Verona's Arena; a classic cross-country drive.

17 The Historic South
Britain's Stonehenge, Unesco-listed city Bath, sublime cathedrals, Napoleonic-era ships.

9 D-Day's Beaches
The events of D-Day still resonate along Normandy's shores; the museums and memorials explain why.

6 Wonders of Ancient Sicily Sicily's ancient Greek temples are the best you'll see outside of Greece.

Food

With its superb produce and culinary traditions, Europe is a food- and wine-lover's dream destination. Here you can dine al fresco in a medieval piazza, feast on seafood in a historic port, or nibble on cured meats in a Spanish bodega. Handily, top foodie hotspots tend to congregate in incomparable wine regions.

13 Champagne Taster
Chefs cook up a storm while cellars echo to the sound of popping corks.

3 Tuscan Wine Tour
Savour fine dining in Chianti's picturesque vineyards.

31 Roving La Rioja Wine Region Bodegas, quality eateries and vineyards to the horizon.

32 Douro Valley Vineyard Trails Northern Portugal's culinary corner boasts sublime views and red wines.

EUROPE
BY REGION

These nine glorious countries have dramatically different characters – each as irresistible and as exciting as the next. What to do and where to go? Here's your guide to getting the very best experiences from each country.

Ireland

Ireland is chock full of charm. The Emerald Isle delivers picture-postcard views that are brooding, dramatic and delightful in turn. It's a place to revel in scenery, history, music-filled pubs and the stillness of village life.

Portugal

Portugal's mix of the medieval and the maritime makes touring a real treat. The legacy of a sometimes turbulent past includes medieval castles, vine-lined terraces and captivating cities. Meanwhile, the pounding Atlantic has sculpted a coast of glorious sandy bays.

Spain

Passionate, sophisticated and devoted to living the good life, Spain ensures your expectations are met. Showcasing sun-baked plains and glittering shores, it also enables leisurely discoveries of heritage, food, wine and art.

Great Britain

Great Britain overflows with unforgettable experiences and memorable sights. From cliff-backed shores and quaint villages, to historic monuments and wild, wild moors. Then there's the string of vibrant cities boasting everything from Georgian architecture to 21st-century art.

France

France seduces with a somehow familiar culture woven around cafe terraces, village-square markets and lace-curtained bistros where the *plat du jour* is chalked up outside. Here too find world-class art, architecture and delightfully scenic drives.

Germany

Germany offers soul-stirring scenery, spirit-lifting culture, big-city beauties, romantic palaces and half-timbered towns. Here the majestic Rhine snakes through churning whirlpools, vast vineyards and medieval villages. And all around storybook castles crown jagged cliffs.

Austria

Buckle up for some exhilarating, roller-coaster drives. White-knuckle Alpine passes usher in a wealth of adrenaline sports, from year-round skiing to windsurfing and white-water rafting, while pretty castles and dense forests frame the majestic, mighty Danube.

Switzerland

Switzerland is simply spectacular, with dazzling scenery at every turn: pristine lakes, lush meadows, snow-dusted Alps. Add cosmopolitan cities and you have a country making it easy to drive deep into its heart.

Italy

Epicentre of the Roman Empire and birthplace of the Renaissance, this sun-kissed virtuoso serves up sublime music, food and wine.

Italy

FEW COUNTRIES CAN RIVAL ITALY'S WEALTH OF RICHES. Its historic cities boast iconic monuments and masterpieces at every turn, its food is imitated the world over and its landscape is a majestic patchwork of snow-capped peaks, plunging coastlines, lakes and remote valleys. And with many thrilling roads to explore, it offers plenty of epic driving.

The trips outlined in this section run the length of the country, leading from Alpine summits to southern volcanoes, and from hilltop towns in Tuscany to fishing villages on the Amalfi Coast. They take in heavyweight cities and little-known gems, and cover a wide range of experiences. So whether you want to tour gourmet towns and historic vineyards, idyllic coastlines or pristine national parks, we have a route for you.

Syracuse View of the Ortygia cityscape

Italy

200 miles
400 km

GERMANY

AUSTRIA

Innsbruck

SWITZERLAND

Bolzano

Tarvisio

SLOVENIA

Monte
Bianco
(4810m)

Locarno
Verbania

Ortles
(3905m)

Marmolada
(3343m)

LJUBLJANA

Como

Bergamo

Lago di
Como

Trento

Aosta

Lago
Maggiore

Milan

Brescia

Lago di
Garda

Verona

Padua

Venice

Trieste

Rijeka

Turin

Asti

Piacenza

Monte
Viso
(3841m)

Alessandria

Modena

Valle di
Comacchio

Körner
Gulf

CROATIA

FRANCE

Ventimiglia

Genoa

Monte
Croce
(1314m)

Bologna

MONACO

MONACO

Pisa

Florence

SAN
MARINO

Ancona

Montepulciano

Monte Amiata
(1736m)

Lago di
Bolsena

Perugia

Lago
Trasimeno

Ascoli
Piceno

Adriatic
Sea

Viterbo

L'Aquila

Corno Grande
(2912m)

ROME

Frosinone

Monte Cavo
(949m)

Monte Amaro
(2795m)

Vieste

FRANCE

Santa
Teresa di
Gallura

Olbia

Sassari

Nuoro

Oristano

Punta
La Marmora
(1834m)

Iglesias

Cagliari

Tyrrhenian
Sea

Naples

Ischia

Capri

Vico Equense

Golfo di
Salerno

Mt Vesuvius
(1281m)

Salerno

Potenza

Monte Pollino
(2248m)

Foggia

Bari

Taranto

Lecc

Gallipoli

Cosenza

Crotone

Vibo
Valentia

Messina

Trapani

Palermo

Mt Etna
(3340m)

Taormina

Ionian Sea

Marsala

Pizzo
Carbonara
(1979m)

Catania

MEDITERRANEAN
SEA

Agrigento

Ragusa

Syracuse

1 **Grand Tour 12–14 Days**
The classic cultural tour – part pilgrimage, part rite of passage.

2 **The Graceful Italian Lakes 5–7 Days**
The destination of choice for Goethe, Hemingway and George Clooney.

3 **Tuscan Wine Tour 4 Days**
Red wine fuels this jaunt around historic Chianti vineyards and Tuscan cellars.

4 **Amalfi Coast 7 Days**
A stunning coastline of vertical landscapes and chic resort towns.

5 **World Heritage Wonders 14 Days**
Discover the Unesco-listed treasures of Italy's art cities.

6 **Wonders of Ancient Sicily 12–14 Days**
Unearth Sicily's ancient Greek temples, Byzantine treasures and bewitching baroque towns.

7 **Italian Riviera 4 Days**
Seaside bastions, palm-fringed promenades, belle-époque villas.

 DON'T MISS

Scrovegni Chapel
See the Renaissance blossoming through the tears in Giotto's moving frescoes for the Cappella degli Scrovegni in Padua on Trip **1**

Montalcino
Crowned by a 14th-century fort, this hilltop town produces one of Italy's top red wines. Indulge yourself on Trip **3**

Vietri sul Mare
Bring back a piece of the Amalfi Coast from this seaside centre, renowned for its bright-hued ceramics, on Trip **4**

Noto
Stroll one of Italy's most beautiful town centres, admiring golden baroque buildings in the southern Sicilian sun on Trip **6**

Grand Tour

Taking in Italy's greatest hits, the Grand Tour was the gap-year trip of its day, a liberating search for art and enlightenment, adventure and debauchery.

TRIP HIGHLIGHTS

555 km

Venice
Marvel at marble palaces and gold mosaics

START
Turin

Genoa

710 km

Florence
Enjoy the world's greatest Renaissance hits

Viterbo

FINISH

Rome
Catch up on 2000 years of Western history

1070 km

Naples
Ponder the fallen in Pompeii and the treasures they left behind

1390 km

12–14 DAYS
1390KM / 865 MILES

GREAT FOR...

BEST TIME TO GO
Spring (March to May) is perfect for urban sightseeing.

ESSENTIAL PHOTO
Florence's multicoloured, marble *duomo* (cathedral).

BEST FOR HISTORY
Rome, the repository of over 2500 years of European history.

Florence *David*, Galleria dell'Accademia

1 Grand Tour

From the Savoy palaces of Turin and Leonardo's *Last Supper* to the disreputable drinking dens of Genoa and pleasure palaces of Rome, the Grand Tour is part scholar's pilgrimage and part rite of passage. Offering a chance to view some of the world's greatest masterpieces and hear Vivaldi played on 18th-century cellos, it's a rollicking trip filled with the sights, sounds and tastes that have shaped European society for centuries.

❶ Turin

In his travel guide, *Voyage through Italy* (1670), travel writer and tutor Richard Lassels advocated a grand cultural tour of Europe, and in particular Italy, for young English aristocrats, during which the study of classical antiquity and the High Renaissance would ready them for future influential roles shaping the political, economic and social realities of the day.

First they travelled through France before crossing the Alps at Mt Cenis and heading to Turin (Torino), where letters of introduction admitted them to the city's agreeable Parisian-style social whirl.

Today Turin's tree-lined boulevards retain their elegant, French feel and many gilded cafes, such as **Caffè Al Bicerin** (www.bicerin.it; Piazza della Consolata 5; ⊘8.30am-7.30pm Thu-Tue, closed Aug), still serve its signature coffee and chocolate drink – as it has since the 1760s.

Like the Medicis in Florence (Firenze) and the Borghese in Rome (Roma), Turin's Savoy princes had a penchant for extravagant architecture and interior decor. You suspect they also pined for their hunting lodges in Chambéry, France, from where they originated, as they invited André le Nôtre, Versailles landscaper,

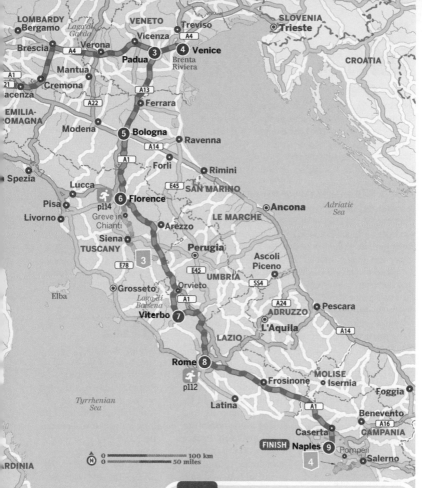

to design the gardens of **Palazzo Reale** (www.museireali.beniculturali.it; Piazza Castello; adult/reduced €15/2, 1st Sun of month free; ☉10am-7pm Tue-Sun) in 1697.

✗ p40

The Drive ›› The two-hour (170km) drive to Genoa is all on autostrada, the final stretch twisting through the mountains. Leave Turin following signs for

§ **LINK YOUR TRIP**

3 Tuscan Wine Tour

Linger in the bucolic hills around Florence and enjoy fine gourmet dining and world-renowned wine tasting.

4 Amalfi Coast

Play truant from high-minded museums and head south from Naples for the Blue Ribbon drive on the Amalfi Coast.

ITALY **1** GRAND TOUR

DETOUR: MILAN

Start: ❶ Turin

No Grand Tour would be complete without a detour up the A4 to Milan (Milano) to eyeball Leonardo da Vinci's iconic mural **The Last Supper** (Il Cenacolo; ☎02 9280 0360; www.cenacolovinciano.net; Piazza Santa Maria delle Grazie 2; adult/reduced €15/2, plus booking fee €2; ⏱8.15am-7pm Tue-Sun; Ⓜ Cadorna). Advance booking is essential.

From his *Portrait of a Young Man* (c 1486) to portraits of Duke Ludovico Sforza's beautiful mistresses, *The Lady with the Ermine* (c 1489) and *La Belle Ferronière* (c 1490), Leonardo transformed the rigid conventions of portraiture to depict highly individual images imbued with naturalism. Then he evolved concepts of idealised proportions and the depiction of internal emotional states through physical dynamism *(St Jerome)*, all of which cohere in the masterly *Il Cenacolo*.

While you're here, take some time to walk around other parts of the city too.

---

the A55 (towards Alessandria), which quickly merges with the A21 passing through the pretty Piedmontese countryside. Just before Alessandria turn south onto the A26 for Genoa/Livorno.

---

❷ Genoa

Despite its superb location, mild microclimate and lush flora, Genova has a dubious reputation. Its historic centre was a warren of dark, insalubrious *caruggi* (alleys), while the excessive shrewdness of the Genovese banking families earned them a reputation, according to author Thomas Nugent, as 'a treacherous and over-reaching set of people'.

And yet with tourists and businesspeople arriving from around the world, Genoa was, and still is, a cosmopolitan place. The **Rolli Palaces**, a collection of grand mansions originally meant to host visiting popes, dignitaries and royalty, made Via Balbi and Strada Nuova (now Via Giuseppe Garibaldi) two of the most famous streets in Europe. Visit the finest of them, the **Palazzo Spinola** (www.palazzospinola.beniculturali.it; Piazza Superiore di Pellicceria 1; adult/reduced €6/2; ⏱8.30am-7.30pm Tue-Sat, 1.30-7.30pm Sun) and the **Palazzo Reale** (☎010 271 02 36; www.palazzore

alegenova.beniculturali.it; Via Balbi 10; adult/reduced €6/2; ⏱9am-6.30pm Tue-Fri, 1.30-7pm Sat & Sun). Afterwards stop for sweets at **Pietro Romanengo fu Stefano** (www.romanengo.com; Via Soziglia 74r; ⏱3.15-7.15pm Mon, 9am-1pm & 3.15-7.15pm Tue-Sat).

 p40

The Drive » This 365km drive takes most of the day, so stop for lunch in Cremona. Although the drive is on autostrada, endless fields of corn line the route. Take the A7 north out of Genoa and at Tortona exit onto the A21 around industrial Piacenza to Brescia. At Brescia, change again onto the A4 direct to Padua.

---

❸ Padua

Bound for Venice (Venezia), Grand Tourists could hardly avoid visiting Padua (Padova), although by the 18th century international students no longer flocked to **Palazzo Bo** (☎049 827 39 39; www.unipd.it/en/guidedtours; Via VIII Febbraio 2; adult/reduced €7/3; ⏱see website for tour times), the Venetian Republic's radical university where Copernicus and Galileo taught class.

You can visit the university's claustrophobic, wooden **anatomy theatre** (the first in the world), although it's no longer de rigueur to witness dissections on the average tourist itinerary. Afterwards don't forget to pay your respects to the skulls of noble professors who donated themselves for dissection because of the difficulty involved in acquiring fresh corpses. Their skulls are lined up in the graduation hall.

Beyond the university the melancholy air of the city did little to detain foreign visitors. Even Giotto's spectacular frescoes in the **Cappella degli Scrovegni** (Scrovegni Chapel; ☑049 201 00 20; www.cappelladegliscrovegni. it; Piazza Eremitani 8; adult/reduced €14/10, night ticket €8/6; ◷9am-7pm, night ticket 7-9.20pm), where advance reservations are essential, were of limited interest given medieval art was out of fashion, and only devout Catholics ventured to revere the strange relics of St Anthony in the **Basilica di Sant'Antonio** (Il Santo; ☑049 822 56 52; www.ba silicadelsanto.org; Piazza del Santo; ◷6.20am-7.45pm).

The Drive » Barely 40km from Venice, the drive from Padua is through featureless areas of light industry along the A4 and then the A57.

- - - - - - - - - - - - - - -

TRIP HIGHLIGHT

❹ Venice

Top of the itinerary, Venice at last! Then, as now, La Serenissima's watery landscape captured the imagination of travellers. At **Carnevale** (www.car nevale.venezia.it) in February numbers swelled to 30,000; now they number in the hundreds of thousands. You cannot take your car onto the lagoon islands so leave it in a secure garage in Mestre, such as **Garage Europa Mestre** (☑041 95 92 02; www.garageeuropamestre. com; Corso del Popolo 55; per day €15; ◷8am-10pm), and hop on the train to Venice Santa Lucia where water taxis connect to all the islands.

Aside from the mind-improving art in the **Gallerie dell'Accademia** (☑041 522 22 47; www. gallerieaccademia.it; Campo de la Carità 1050; adult/reduced €12/2; ◷8.15am-2pm Mon, to 7.15pm Tue-Sun; ⛴Accademia) and extraordinary architectural masterpieces such as the **Palazzo Ducale**, the **Campanile**, Longhena's **Chiesa di Santa Maria della Salute** and the glittering domes of the **Basilica di San Marco** (St Mark's Basilica; ☑041 270 83 11; www.basilicasanmarco.it; Piazza San Marco; ◷9.30am-5pm Mon-Sat, 2-5pm Sun mid-Apr–Oct, to 4.30pm Sun Nov–mid-Apr; ⛴San Marco), Venice was considered an exciting den of debauchery. Venetian wives were notorious for keeping handsome escorts *(cicisbeo)*, and whole areas of town were given over to venality. One of Venice's best restaurants, **Antiche Carampane** (☑041 524 01 65; www.antichecarampane. com; Rio Terà de le Carampane 1911; meals €55-63; ◷12.45-2.15pm & 7.30-10pm Tue-Sat; ⛴San Stae), is located in what was once a den of vice, so called because of the notorious brothel at Palazzo Ca'Rampani.

Eighteenth-century tourists would inevitably have stopped for coffee at the newly opened **Caffè Florian** (☑041 520 56 41; www.caffeflorian.com; Piazza San Marco 57; ◷9am-midnight Apr-Oct, shorter hours in winter; ⛴San Marco) and paid a visit to the opera house, **Teatro La Fenice** (☑041 78 66 54; www.teatrolafenice.it; Campo San Fantin 1965; tickets €15-380; ⛴Giglio), to hear groundbreaking concerts now being revived by the **Venice Music Project** (☑345 791 1948; www.ven icemusicproject.it; St George's Anglican Church, Campo San Vio; tickets €15-50; ◷Mar-Jun & Sep-Nov; ⛴Accademia).

✗ 🍴 p40, p87

The Drive » Retrace your steps to Padua on the A57 and A4 and navigate around the ring road in the direction of Bologna to pick up the A13 southwest for this short two-hour drive (154km or so). After Padua the autostrada dashes through wide-open farmland and crosses the Po River, which forms the southern border of the Veneto.

- - - - - - - - - - - - - - -

❺ Bologna

Home to Europe's oldest university (established in 1088) and once the stomping ground of Dante, Boccaccio and Petrarch, Bologna had an enviable reputation for courtesy and culture. Its historic centre, complete with 20 soaring towers, is one of the best-preserved

WHY THIS IS A GREAT TRIP
DUNCAN GARWOOD,
WRITER

Inspired by the 18th-century Grand Tour, this timeless route retraces the footsteps of the trailblazing tourists who set off for Italy in search of sun, culture and perhaps a little illicit adventure. Covering the country's show-stopping cities, it offers travellers a view of Italy's very best art, architecture and antiquities, while transporting them from snow-capped Alpine peaks to sun-kissed southern shores.

Above: Teatro San Carlo, Naples
Left: Palazzo Reale, Genoa
Right: Canal, Venice

medieval cities in the world. In the **Basilica di San Petronio** ([☎]051 23 14 15; www.basilicadisanpetronio. org; Piazza Maggiore; photo pass €2; [⌚]7.45am-1.30pm & 2.30-6.30pm Mon-Sat, 7.45am-1.30pm & 2.30-7pm Sun), originally intended to dwarf St Peter's in Rome, Giovanni Cassini's sundial (1655) proved the problems with the Julian calendar, giving us the leap year, while Bolognesi students advanced human knowledge in obstetrics, natural science, zoology and anthropology. You can peer at their strange model waxworks and studiously labelled collections in the **Palazzo Poggi** (www.sma.unibo.it/it/ il-sistema-museale/museo-di -palazzo-poggi; Via Zamboni 33; adult/reduced €5/3; [⌚]10am-4pm Tue-Fri, 10am-6pm Sat & Sun).

In art as in science, the School of Bologna gave birth to the Carracci brothers, Annibale and Agostino, and their cousin Ludovico, who were among the founding fathers of Italian baroque and were deeply influenced by the Counter-Reformation. See their emotionally charged blockbusters in the **Pinacoteca Nazionale** (www.pinacotecabologna. beniculturali.it; Via delle Belle Arti 56; adult/reduced €6/2; [⌚]8.30am-7.30pm Tue-Sun Sep-Jun, 8.30am-2pm Tue &

Wed, 1.45-7.30pm Thu-Sun Jul & Aug).

 p40

The Drive » Bologna sits at the intersection of the A1, A13 and A14. From the centre navigate west out of the city, across the river Reno, onto the A1. From here it's a straight shot into Florence for 100km, leaving the Po plains behind you and entering the low hills of Emilia-Romagna and the forested valleys of Tuscany.

TRIP HIGHLIGHT

❻ Florence

From Filippo Brunelleschi's red-tiled dome atop Florence's **Duomo** (Cattedrale di Santa Maria del Fiore; ☎055 230 28 85; www.museumflorence.com; Piazza del Duomo; ☉10am-5pm Mon-Wed & Fri, to 4.30pm Thu & Sat, 1.30-4.45pm Sun) to Michelangelo's and Botticelli's greatest hits, *David* and *The Birth of Venus,* in the **Galleria dell'Accademia** (☎055 098 71 00; www.galleriaaccademiafirenze.beniculturali.it; Via Ricasoli 58/60; adult/reduced €12/2; ☉8.15am-

6.50pm Tue-Sun) and the **Galleria degli Uffizi** (Uffizi Gallery; ☎055 29 48 83; www.uffizi.it; Piazzale degli Uffizi 6; adult/reduced Mar-Oct €20/2, Nov-Feb €12/2; ☉8.15am-6.50pm Tue-Sun), Florence, according to Unesco, contains the highest number of artistic masterpieces in the world.

Whereas Rome and Milan have torn themselves down and been rebuilt many times, incorporating a multitude of architectural whims, central Florence looks much as it did in 1550, with stone towers and cypress-lined gardens.

 p41, p63, p86

The Drive » The next 210km, continuing south along the A1, travels through some of Italy's most lovely scenery. Just southwest of Florence the vineyards of Greve in Chianti harbour some great farm stays, while Arezzo is to the east. Exit at Orvieto and follow on the SR71 and SR2 for the final 45km into Viterbo.

❼ Viterbo

From Florence the road to Rome crossed the dreaded and pestilential *campagna* (countryside), a swampy, mosquito-infested low-lying area. Unlike now, inns en route were uncomfortable and hazardous, so travellers hurried through Siena, stocking up on wine for the rough road ahead. They also stopped briefly in medieval Viterbo for a quick douse in the thermal springs at the **Terme dei Papi** (☎0761 35 01; www.termedeipapi.it; Strada Bagni 12; pool weekday €12, Sat & Sun €18, Sat night €20; ☉pool 9am-8pm Wed-Mon summer, to 7pm winter, 9.30pm-1am Sat year-round), and a tour of the High Renaissance gardens at **Villa Lante** (☎0761 28 80 08; www.polomusealelazio.beniculturali.it; Via Barozzi 71, Bagnaia; adult/reduced €5/2; ☉8.30am-1hr before sunset Tue-Sun).

The Drive » Rejoin the A1 after a 28km drive along the rural SS675. For the next 40km the A1 descends through Lazio, criss-crossing the Tevere River and keeping the ridge of the Apennines to the left as it darts through tunnels. At Fiano Romano exit for Roma Nord and follow the A1dir and SS4 (Via Salaria) for the final 20km push into the capital.

TRIP HIGHLIGHT

❽ Rome

In the 18th century Rome, even in ruins,

✓ TOP TIP: JUMP THE QUEUE IN FLORENCE

In July, August and other busy periods such as Easter, long queues are a fact of life at Florence's key museums. For a fee of €4 each, tickets to the Uffizi and Galleria dell'Accademia (where *David* lives) can be booked in advance. Book online or by phone through **Firenze Musei** (Florence Museums; ☎055 265 43 21; www.firenzemusei.it).

was still thought of as the august capital of the world. Here more than anywhere the Grand Tourist was awakened to an interest in art and architecture, although the **Colosseum** (Colosseo; [🎫]06 3996 7700; www.parcocolosseo.it; Piazza del Colosseo; adult/reduced incl Roman Forum & Palatino €16/2, with arena & SUPER sites €22/2, 1st Sun of month Oct-Mar free; [🕐]8.30am-1hr before sunset, last entry 1hr before closing; [Ⓜ]Colosseo) was still filled with debris and the **Palatino** (Palatine Hill; Via di San Gregorio 30, Piazza di Santa Maria Nova; [Ⓜ]Colosseo) was covered in gardens, its excavated treasures slowly accumulating in the world's oldest national museum, the **Capitoline Museums** (Musei Capitolini; [🎫]06 06 08; www.museicapitolini.org; Piazza del Campidoglio 1; adult/reduced €11.50/9.50; [🕐]9.30am-7.30pm, last entry 6.30pm; [🚌]Piazza Venezia).

Arriving through the Porta del Popolo, visitors first espied the dome of **St Peter's Basilica** (Basilica di San Pietro; [🎫]06 6988 3731; www.vatican.va; St Peter's Sq; [🕐]7am-7pm Apr-Sep, to 6.30pm Oct-Mar; [🚌]Piazza del Risorgimento, [Ⓜ]Ottaviano-San Pietro) before clattering along the *corso* to the customs house. Once done, they headed to **Piazza di Spagna** ([Ⓜ]Spagna), the city's principal meeting place where Keats

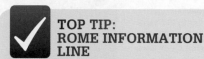

TOP TIP: ROME INFORMATION LINE

The Comune di Roma (Rome city council) runs a **phone line** ([🎫]06 06 08; www.060608.it; [🕐]9am-7pm) providing info on sights, events, transport and accommodation. You can also book theatre, concert, exhibition and museum tickets. Staff speak English, as well as French, Spanish, German and Japanese. Its website is also a good source of up-to-date information.

penned his love poems and died of consumption.

Although the **Pantheon** (www.pantheonroma.com; Piazza della Rotonda; [🕐]8.30am-7.30pm Mon-Sat, 9am-6pm Sun; [🚌]Largo di Torre Argentina) and **Vatican Museums** (Musei Vaticani; [🎫]06 6988 4676; www.museivaticani.va; Viale Vaticano; adult/reduced €17/8, free last Sun of the month; [🕐]9am-6pm Mon-Sat, to 2pm last Sun of month, last admission 2hr before close; [🚌]Piazza del Risorgimento, [Ⓜ]Ottaviano-San Pietro) were a must, most travellers preferred to socialise in the grounds of the **Borghese Palace** ([🎫]06 3 28 10; http://galleriaborghese.beniculturali.it; Piazzale del Museo Borghese 5; adult/reduced €13/2 plus €2 booking fee, free some Sun & every 2nd Wed of the month; [🕐]9am-7pm Tue-Sun; [🚌]Via Pinciana).

Follow their example and mix the choicest sights with more venal pleasures such as fine dining at **Aroma** ([🎫]06 9761 5109; www.aromarestaurant.it; Via Labicana 125; meals €120-130, 7-course tasting

menu €180; [🕐]12.30-3pm & 7-11.30pm; [🚌]Via Labicana) and souvenir shopping at antique perfumery **Officina Profumo Farmaceutica di Santa Maria Novella** ([🎫]06 687 96 08; www.smnovella.com; Corso del Rinascimento 47; [🕐]10am-7.30pm Mon-Sat; [🚌]Corso del Rinascimento).

[🍴][🛏] p41, p86

The Drive » Past Rome the landscape is hotter and drier, trees give way to Mediterranean shrubbery and the grass starts to yellow. Beyond the vineyards of Frascati, just 20km south of Rome, the A1 runs 225km to Naples (Napoli), a two-hour drive that can take longer if there's heavy traffic.

- - - - - - - - - - - - - - - - - -

TRIP HIGHLIGHT

❾ Naples

Only the more adventurous Grand Tourists continued south to the salacious southern city of Naples. At the time Mt Vesuvius glowed menacingly on the bay, erupting no less than six times during the 18th century and eight times in the 19th century. But Naples was the home of opera and *commedia dell'arte* (improvised comedic drama satirising stock social stereotypes), and singing lessons and seats at **Teatro San Carlo** (☎box office 081 797 23 31; www.teatrosancarlo.it; Via San Carlo 98f; ⊗box office 10am-9pm Mon-Sat, to 6pm Sun; ☐R2 to Via San Carlo, Ⓜ Municipio) were obligatory.

Then there were the myths of Virgil and Dante to explore at Lago d'Averno and **Campi Flegrei** (the Phlegrean Fields). And, after the discovery of **Pompeii** (☎081 857 53 47; www.pompeiisites.org; entrances at Porta Marina & Piazza Anfiteatro; adult/reduced €16/2; ⊗9am-7.30pm Mon-Fri, from 8.30am Sat & Sun, last entry 6pm Apr-Oct, 9am-5.30pm Mon-Fri, from 8.30am Sat & Sun, last entry 3.30pm Nov-Mar; ☒Circumvesuviana to Pompei Scavi–Villa dei Misteri) in 1748, the unfolding drama of a Roman town in its death throes drew throngs of mawkish voyeurs. Then, as now, it was one of the most popular tourist sights in Italy and its priceless mosaics, pornographic frescoes and colossal sculptures filled the **Museo Archeologico Nazionale** (☎848 800288; www.museoarcheologiconapoli.it; Piazza Museo Nazionale 19; adult/reduced €18/2; ⊗9am-7.30pm Wed-Mon; Ⓜ Museo, Piazza Cavour).

✕ ⛺ p41

Rome St Peter's Basilica

Eating & Sleeping

Turin ❶

🍷 Fiorio   Cafe €

(www.caffefiorio.it; Via Po 8; ☉8am-midnight
Mon-Thu, to 1am Fri & Sat, 8am-9pm Sun) Garner
literary inspiration in Mark Twain's old window
seat as you contemplate the gilded interior of a
cafe where 19th-century students once plotted
revolutions and the Count of Cavour deftly
played whist. The bittersweet hot chocolate
remains inspirational.

Genoa ❷

✗ Trattoria Rosmarino   Trattoria €€

(☎010 251 04 75; www.trattoriarosmarino.it;
Salita del Fondaco 30; meals €28-34; ☉12.30-
2.30pm & 7.30-10.30pm Mon-Sat) Rosmarino
cooks up the standard local specialities, yes,
but the straightforwardly priced menu has
an elegance and vibrancy that sets it apart.
With two nightly sittings, there's always a nice
buzz (though there are also enough nooks and
crannies that a romantic night for two isn't out
of the question). Call ahead for an evening table.

Cremona ❷

✗ Hosteria 700   Lombard €€

(☎0372 3 61 75; www.hosteria700.com; Piazza
Gallina 1; meals €33-40; ☉noon-2.45pm Wed-
Mon, 7-11pm Wed-Sun) Behind the dilapidated
facade lurks a diamond in the rough. Some of
the vaulted rooms come with ceiling frescoes,
dark timber tables come with ancient wooden
chairs, and the hearty Lombard cuisine comes
at a refreshingly competitive cost.

Venice ❹

🍷 Grancaffè Quadri   Cafe €

(☎041 522 21 05; www.alajmo.it; Piazza San
Marco 121; ☉9am-midnight; 🚤San Marco)
Powdered wigs seem appropriate inside this
baroque bar-cafe that's been serving happy
hours since 1638. During Carnevale, costumed

Quadri revellers party like it's 1699 – despite
prices shooting up to €15 for a *spritz*. Grab a
seat on the piazza to watch the best show in
town: the basilica's golden mosaics ablaze in
the sunset.

✗ CoVino   Venetian €€

(☎041 241 27 05; www.covinovenezia.com; Calle
del Pestrin 3829; fixed-price menu lunch €27-38,
dinner €40; ☉12.45-2.30pm & 7pm-midnight
Thu-Mon; 🤳; 🚤Arsenale) Tiny CoVino has only
14 seats but demonstrates bags of ambition
with its inventive, seasonal menu inspired by
the Venetian terroir. Speciality products are
selected from Slow Food Foundation producers,
and the charming waiters make enthusiastic
recommendations from the wine list. Only a
three-course set menu is available at dinner;
however, you can choose from two fixed-price
options at lunch.

🛏 Locanda Fiorita   Boutique Hotel €€

(☎041 523 47 54; www.locandafiorita.com;
Campiello Novo 3457a; d €80-180; 🅿🤳; 🚤San
Samuele) Few budget digs can match this smart
10-room hotel with flower-draped terraces
and dreamy views of Chiesa di Santo Stefano
from its rooms. Petite bedrooms offer a chic,
updated take on Venetian style, with Rubelli-
style fabrics and period furnishings. Room 10
has a private terrace. Head out for *aperitivo* on
the roof terrace of adjoining B&B Bloom (same
management) and breakfast in Campiello Novo.

Bologna ❺

✗ All'Osteria Bottega   Osteria €€

(☎051 58 51 11; Via Santa Caterina 51; meals
€36-41; ☉12.30-2.30pm & 8-10.30pm Tue-Sat)
At Bologna's temple of culinary contentment,
owners Daniele and Valeria lavish attention
on every table between trips to the kitchen for
astonishing plates of *culatello di Zibello* ham,
tortellini in capon broth, Petroniana-style veal
cutlets, off-menu speciality pigeon and other
Slow Food delights.

🛏 Bologna nel Cuore   B&B €€

(☎329 2193354; www.bolognanelcuore.it; Via
Cesare Battisti 29; s €90-120, d €125-150, apt

€140-145; [P] [❄] [📶]) This centrally located, immaculate and well-loved B&B features a pair of bright, high-ceilinged rooms with pretty tiled bathrooms and endless mod cons, plus two comfortable, spacious apartments with kitchen and laundry facilities. Owner and art historian Maria generously shares her knowledge of Bologna and serves breakfasts featuring jams made with fruit picked near her childhood home in the Dolomites.

Florence ❻

✖ Trattoria Mario　　　　　Tuscan €

([☎]055 21 85 50; www.trattoria-mario.com; Via Rosina 2r; meals €25; [🕐]noon-3.30pm Mon-Sat, closed 3 weeks Aug; [❄]) Arrive by noon to ensure a spot at this noisy, busy, brilliant trattoria – a legend that retains its soul (and allure with locals) despite being in every guidebook. Charming Fabio, whose grandfather opened the place in 1953, is front of house while big brother Romeo and nephew Francesco cook with speed in the kitchen. No advance reservations; cash only.

🛏 Hotel Davanzati　　　　Hotel €€

([☎]055 28 66 66; www.hoteldavanzati.it; Via Porta Rossa 5; s/d from €140/229; [❄] [@] [📶]) Twenty-six steps lead up to this family-run hotel. A labyrinth of enchanting rooms, frescoes and modern comforts, it oozes charm. Rooms come with a mini iPad (meaning free wi-fi around town), direct messaging with the hotel, handy digital city guide and complimentary access to a nearby gym.

Rome ❽

✖ Salumeria Roscioli　　　Deli €€€

([☎]06 687 52 87; www.salumeriaroscioli.com; Via dei Giubbonari 21; meals €55-60; [🕐]12.30-4pm & 7pm-midnight Mon-Sat, open Sun in Dec; [🚇]Via Arenula) The name Roscioli has long been a byword for foodie excellence in Rome, and this deli-restaurant is one of a clutch of venues the family operates near the Campo de' Fiori. The produce here is top-notch and the wine list is marvellous, but the surroundings are cramped and noisy.

🛏 Residenza Maritti　　Guesthouse €€

([☎]06 678 82 33; www.residenzamaritti.com; Via Tor Dè Conti 17; s €100, d €130-180, tr €150-200, q €170-210; [❄] [📶]; [M]Cavour) Boasting stunning views over the nearby forums and Vittoriano, this hidden gem has 13 rooms spread across three floors. Some are bright and modern while others are more cosy with antiques, original tiled floors and family furniture. There's a fully equipped kitchen and a buffet breakfast is served in the bistro next door.

Naples ❾

✖ Concettina Ai Tre Santi　　Pizza €

([☎]081 29 00 37; www.pizzeriaoliva.it; Via Arena della Sanità 7; pizzas from €5; [🕐]noon-midnight Mon-Sat, to 5pm Sun; [📶]; [M]Piazza Cavour, Museo) Head in by noon (or 7.30pm at dinner) to avoid a long wait at this hot-spot pizzeria, made famous thanks to its young, driven *pizzaiolo* Ciro Oliva. The menu is an index of fastidiously sourced artisanal ingredients, used to top Ciro's flawless, wood-fired bases. Traditional Neapolitan pizza aside, you'll also find a string of creative seasonal options.

🛏 Hotel Piazza Bellini　　　Hotel €€

([☎]081 45 17 32; www.hotelpiazzabellini.com; Via Santa Maria di Costantinopoli 101; d €90-190; [❄] [@] [📶]; [M]Dante) Only steps from the bars and nightlife of Piazza Bellini, this sharp, hip hotel occupies a 16th-century *palazzo* (mansion), its pure-white spaces spiked with original majolica tiles, vaulted ceilings and *piperno*-stone paving. Rooms are modern and functional, with designer fittings, fluffy duvets and chic bathrooms with excellent showers.

The Graceful Italian Lakes

2

Writers from Goethe to Hemingway have lavished praise on the Italian Lakes, dramatically ringed by snow-powdered mountains and garlanded by grand villas and exotic, tropical flora.

TRIP HIGHLIGHTS

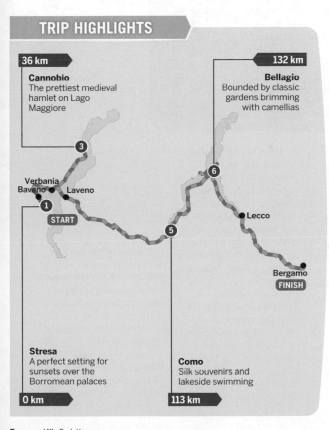

36 km

Cannobio
The prettiest medieval hamlet on Lago Maggiore

③

132 km

Bellagio
Bounded by classic gardens brimming with camellias

⑥

Verbania
Baveno ● Laveno

①

START

● Lecco

⑤

Bergamo ●
FINISH

Stresa
A perfect setting for sunsets over the Borromean palaces

0 km

Como
Silk souvenirs and lakeside swimming

113 km

5–7 DAYS
213KM / 132 MILES

GREAT FOR...

BEST TIME TO GO
April to June, when the camellias are in full bloom.

  ESSENTIAL PHOTO
The cascading gardens of Palazzo Borromeo.

 BEST FOR GLAMOUR
Touring Bellagio's headland in a mahogany cigarette boat.

2 The Graceful Italian Lakes

Formed at the end of the last ice age, and a popular holiday spot since Roman times, the Italian Lakes have an enduring natural beauty. At Lake Maggiore the palaces of the Borromean Islands lie like a fleet of fine vessels in the gulf, while the siren call of Lake Como draws Arabian sheikhs and James Bond location scouts to its discreet forested slopes.

TRIP HIGHLIGHT

❶ Stresa

More than Como and Garda, Lake Maggiore has retained the belle-époque air of its early tourist heyday. Attracted by the mild climate and the easy access the new 1855 railway provided, the European *haute bourgeoisie* flocked to buy and build grand lake-side villas. The best of them are paraded in the small but select lakeside town of Stresa.

From here it's a short punt to the palace-punctuated Borromean Islands (Isole Borromee), Maggiore's star attractions. **Isola Bella** took the name of Carlo III's wife, the *bella* Isabella, in the 17th century, when its centrepiece, **Palazzo Borromeo** (📞0323 93 34 78; www.isoleborromee.it; Isola Bella; adult/child €17/9, incl Palazzo Madre €24/10.50; 🕙9am-5.30pm Apr-Sep, short-er hours rest of year, closed 2 Nov-19 Mar), was built. Construction of the villa and gardens was thought out in such a way that

the island would have the appearance of a vessel, with the villa at the prow and the gardens dripping down 10 tiered terraces at the rear. Inside, you'll find the work of countless old masters.

By contrast, **Isola Madre** (📞0323 93 34 78; www.isoleborromee.it; adult/child €13.50/7, incl Palazzo

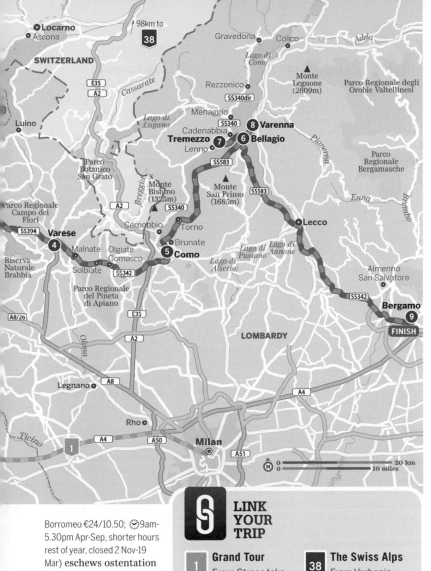

Borromeo €24/10.50; ⊙9am-
5.30pm Apr-Sep, shorter hours
rest of year, closed 2 Nov-19
Mar) eschews ostentation
for a more romantic,
familial atmosphere. The
16th- to 18th-century
Palazzo Madre includes
a 'horror' theatre with a
cast of devilish mari-
onettes, while Chinese

LINK YOUR TRIP

1 Grand Tour

From Stresa take
the A8 to Milan (Milano)
and the A4 on to Turin
(Torino), from where you
can commence your own
Grand Tour of Italy.

38 The Swiss Alps

From Verbania
head northeast for the
greatest of the great
outdoors: perfect peaks,
gorgeous glaciers,
verdant valleys.

DETOUR:
LAGO D'ORTA

Start: ❶ Stresa

Separated from Lake Maggiore by Monte Mottarone (1492m) and enveloped by thick, dark-green woodlands, Lago d'Orta would make a perfect elopers' getaway. At 13.4km long by 2.5km wide you can drive around the lake in a day. The focal point is the captivating medieval village of **Orta San Giulio**, which sits across from Isola San Giulio, where you'll spy the frescoed, 12th-century **Basilica di San Giulio** (Isola San Giulio; ⏱9.30am-6pm Tue-Sun, 2-5pm Mon Apr-Sep, 9.30am-noon & 2-5pm Tue-Sun, 2-5pm Mon Oct-Mar). Come during the week and you'll have the place largely to yourself.

---

pheasants stalk the English gardens.

🍴 p53

The Drive » Leave Stresa westwards on the Via Sempione (SS33), skirting the edge of the lake for this short, 14km drive. Pass through Baveno and round the western edge of the gulf through the greenery of the Fondo Toce natural reserve. When you reach the junction with the SS34, turn right for Verbania.

---

❷ Verbania

There are two Verbanias: Pallanza, a waterside maze of serpentine streets that serves as an embarkation point for the Borromean Islands, and Intra, the broader, newer ferry port. Between them sits the late-19th-century **Villa Taranto** (📞0323 55 66 67; www.villataranto.it; Via Vittorio Veneto 111, Verbania Pallanza; adult/child €11/5.50; ⏱8.30am-6.30pm Apr-Sep, shorter hours rest of year, closed Nov-Feb; 🅿). In 1931,

royal archer and Scottish captain Neil McEacharn bought the villa from the Savoy family and started to plant some 20,000 species. With its rolling hillsides of purple rhododendrons and camellias, hectares of tulip flowers and hothouses full of equatorial lilies, it is considered one of Europe's finest botanical gardens. During the last week in April, **Settimana del Tulipano** takes place, when tens of thousands of tulips erupt in magnificent multicoloured bloom.

🍴 p53

The Drive » Pick up the SS34 again, continuing in a northeasterly direction out of Verbania, through the suburbs of Intra and Pallanza. Once you've cleared the town the 20km to Cannobio are the prettiest on the tour, shadowing the lake shore the entire way with views across the water.

TRIP HIGHLIGHT

❸ Cannobio

Sheltered by a high mountain and sitting at the foot of the Cannobina valley, the medieval hamlet of Cannobio is located 5km from the Swiss border. It is a dreamy place. **Piazza di Vittorio Emanuele III**, lined with pastel-hued houses, is the location of a huge **Sunday market** that attracts visitors from Switzerland.

You can hire SUP boards, canoes and small sailing boats from **Tomaso Surf & Sail** (📞333 7000291; www.tomaso.com; Via Nazionale 7; ⏱9.30am-7pm Jun-Sep, 11am-5.30pm Oct-May) next to the town lido. A good boat excursion is to the ruined **Castelli della Malpaga**, located on two rocky islets to the south of Cannobio. In summer it is a favourite picnic spot.

Alternatively, explore the wild beauty of the Valle Cannobina. Trails begin in town and snake alongside the surging Torrente Cannobino into the heavily wooded hillsides to Malesco. Just 2.5km along the valley, in Sant'Anna, the torrent forces its way powerfully through a narrow gorge known as the **Orrido di Sant'Anna**, crossed at its narrowest part by a Romanesque bridge.

The Drive » The next part of the journey involves retracing the previous 22km drive to Verbania-Intra to board the cross-lake ferry to Laveno. Ferries run every 20 minutes (one-way tickets cost €7.80 to €12.80 for cars and driver). Once in Laveno pick up the SP394dir and then the SP1var and SS394 for the 23km drive to Varese.

❹ Varese

Spread out to the south of the Campo dei Fiori hills, Varese is a prosperous provincial capital. From the 17th century onwards, Milanese nobles began to build second residences here, the most sumptuous being the **Palazzo Estense**, completed in 1771 for Francesco III d'Este, the governor of the Duchy of Milan. Although you cannot visit the palace you are free to wander the vast Italianate **gardens** (open 8am to dusk).

To the north of the city sits another great villa, **Villa Panza** (☎033228 39 60; www.fondoambiente. it; Piazza Litta 1; adult/reduced €15/7; ⊙10am-6pm Tue-Sun), donated to the state in 1996. Part of the donation was 150 contemporary canvases collected by Giuseppe Panza di Biumo, mostly by post-WWII American artists. One of the finest rooms is the 1830 **Salone Impero** (Empire Hall), with heavy chandeliers and four canvases by David Simpson (b 1928).

The Drive ⟫ The 28km drive from Varese to Como

isn't terribly exciting, passing through a string of small towns and suburbs nestled in the wooded hills. The single-lane SS342 passes through Malnate, Solbiate and Olgiate Comasco before reaching Como.

- - - - - - - - - - - - - - - - - - - -

TRIP HIGHLIGHT

❺ Como

Built on the wealth of its silk industry, Como is an elegant town and remains Europe's most important producer of silk products. The **Museo della Seta** (Silk Museum; ☎031 30 31 80; www.museosetacomo.com; Via Castelnuovo 9; adult/reduced €10/7; ⊙10am-6pm Tue-Sun) unravels the town's industrial history, with early dyeing and printing equipment on display. At **A Picci** (☎031 26 13 69; Via Vittorio Emanuele II 54; ⊙3-7.30pm Mon, 9am-12.30pm & 3-7.30pm Tue-Sat) you can buy top-quality scarves, ties and fabrics.

After wandering the medieval alleys of the historic centre take a stroll along **Passeggiata Lino Gelpi**, where you pass a series of water-

front mansions, finally arriving at **Villa Olmo** (☎031 25 23 52; www.villaolmocomo.it; Via Cantoni 1; gardens free, villa entry varies by exhibition; ⊙villa 10am-6pm Tue-Sun during exhibitions, gardens 7am-11pm Apr-Sep, to 8pm Oct-Mar). Set grandly facing the lake, this Como landmark was built in 1728 by the Odescalchi family, related to Pope Innocent XI, and now hosts blockbuster art shows. On Sundays you can continue your walk through the gardens of **Villa del Grumello** and the **Villa Sucota** on the so-called *Chilometro della Conoscenza* (Kilometre of Knowledge).

On the other side of Como's marina, the **Funicolare Como–Brunate** (☎031 30 36 08; www.funicolarecomo.it; Piazza de Gasperi 4; one-way/return adult €3.10/5.70, reduced €2.10/3.30; ⊙half-hourly departures 6am-midnight summer, to 10.30pm winter) whisks you uphill to the quiet village of **Brunate** for splendid views across the lake.

LAGO MAGGIORE EXPRESS

The **Lago Maggiore Express** (☎091 756 04 00; www.lagomaggioreexpress.com; adult/child 1-day tour €34/17, 2-day tour €44/22) is a picturesque day trip you can do without the car. It includes train travel from Arona or Stresa to Domodossola, from where you get the charming *Centovalli* train, crossing 100 valleys, to Locarno in Switzerland and a ferry back to Stresa. The two-day version is perhaps better value if you have the time.

WHY THIS IS A GREAT TRIP
BRENDAN SAINSBURY, WRITER

Maggiore has always been my favourite Italian lake, where you can escape into the quiet woods of the Valle Cannobina and convalesce afterwards in a history-evoking belle-époche cafe in Stresa. And who doesn't have a soft spot for Como, where history buffs can vicariously become Napoleon, or James Bond in a gilded lakeside villa? Away from the water, Bergamo continues the classic theme, but with a little less pretension.

Above: Isola Bella, Stresa
Left: Gardens at Villa Taranto, Verbania
Right: Basilica di Santa Maria Maggiore, Bergamo

✕ 🛏 p53

The Drive » The 32km drive from Como to Bellagio along the SS583 is spectacular. The narrow road swoops and twists around the lake shore the entire way and rises up out of Como giving panoramic views over the lake. There are plenty of spots en route where you can pull over for photographs.

- - - - - - - - - - - - - - - - - -

TRIP HIGHLIGHT

⑥ Bellagio

It's impossible not to be charmed by Bellagio's waterfront of bobbing boats, its maze of stone staircases, cypress groves and showy gardens.

Bellagio is a place best absorbed slowly on your own. You can pick up three self-guided walking tour brochures from the **tourist office** (📞031 95 02 04; www.bellagiolakecomo.com; Piazza Mazzini; ⊘9.30am-12.30pm & 1-5.30pm, shorter hours winter). The longest three-hour walk takes in neighbouring villages, including **Pescallo**, a small one-time fishing port about 1km from the centre, and **Loppia**, with the 11th-century Chiesa di Santa Maria, which is only visitable from the outside.

The walk to one of Como's finest mansions, **Villa Melzi d'Eril** (📞333 4877427; www.giardinidivillamelzi.it; Lungo Lario Manzoni; adult/reduced €6.50/4; ⊘9.30am-6.30pm Mar-Oct), heads south along the lake shore from the Bellagio ferry jetties, revealing views of ranks of gracious residencies stacked up on the waterside hills. The grounds of the neoclassical Villa Melzi run right down to the lake and are adorned with classical statues couched in blushing azaleas.

For on-the-lake frollics, **Barindelli's** (☎338 2110337; www.barindellitaxiboats.it; Piazza Mazzini; tours per hr €220) operates slick, mahogany cigarette boats in which you can tool around the headland on a sunset tour.

🛌 p53

The Drive ≫ The best way to reach Tremezzo, without driving all the way around the bottom of the lake, is to take the ferry from Piazza Mazzini. One-way fares cost €4.60 and the journey takes 10 minutes, but for sightseeing you may want to consider the one-day central lake ticket (€15) covering Bellagio, Varenna, Tremezzo and Cadenabbia.

- - - - - - - - - - - - - - - - - -

❼ Tremezzo

Tremezzo is high on everyone's list for a visit to the 17th-century **Villa Carlotta** (☎0344 4 04 05; www.villacarlotta.it; Via Regina 2; adult/reduced €12/6; ⊙9am-6.30pm Mar-Sep, shorter hours rest of year), whose botanic gardens are filled with orange trees knitted into pergolas and some of Europe's finest rhododendrons, azaleas and camellias. The villa, which is strung with paintings and fine alabaster-white sculptures (especially lovely are those by Antonio Canova),

Bellagio On the banks of Lake Como

SEAPLANES ON THE LAKE

For a touch of Hollywood glamour, check out **Aero Club Como** (☎031 57 44 95; www.aeroclubcomo.com; Viale Masia 44; 30min flight per person €120), which has been sending seaplanes out all over the lakes since 1930. A 30-minute flight from Como to Bellagio and back costs €240 for two people. Longer excursions over Lake Maggiore are also possible. In summer you need to reserve at least three days in advance.

takes its name from the Prussian princess who was given the palace in 1847 as a wedding present from her mother.

The Drive » As with the trip to Tremezzo, the best way to travel to Varenna is by passenger ferry either from Cadenabbia (1.3km north of Tremezzo's boat dock) or Bellagio.

----

⑧ Varenna

A mirror image of Bellagio across the water, Varenna is a beguiling village bursting with florid plantlife, narrow lanes and pastel-coloured houses stacked up on mountain slopes that defy the laws of physics.

You can wander the flower-laden pathway from Piazzale Martiri della Libertà to the gardens of **Villa Cipressi** (☎0341 83 01 13; www.hotel villacipressi.it; Via IV Novembre 22; adult/child €8/3; ☀10am-7.30pm May-Jun & Sep, to 8pm Jul & Aug, shorter hours rest of year), now a luxury hotel, or undertake a 40-minute walk up to the 13th-century **Castello di Vezio** (☎333 4485975; www.

castellodivezio.it; Vezio, near Varenna; adult/reduced €4/3; ☀10am-7pm Mon-Fri, to 8pm Sat & Sun Jun-Aug, to 6pm Mar-May, Sep & Oct), high above the terracotta rooftops of Varenna. The castle was once part of a chain of early-warning medieval watchtowers. These days it hosts alfresco temporary exhibitions of avant-garde art and holds falconry displays in the afternoons – daily except Tuesdays and Fridays. There's also a small cafe.

The Drive » Departing Bellagio, pick up the SS583, but this time head southeast towards Lecco down the other 'leg' of Lake Como. As with the stretch from Como to Bellagio, the road hugs the lake, offering spectacular views the whole 20km to Lecco. Once you reach Lecco head south out of town down Via Industriale and pick up the SS342 for the final 40km to Bergamo.

----

⑨ Bergamo

Although Milan's skyscrapers are visible on a clear day, historically Bergamo was more closely associated with Venice (Venezia). The Venetian-style architecture can be

seen in **Piazza Vecchia** and, more stridently, in the Unesco-listed **City Walls**.

Behind this secular core sits the **Piazza del Duomo** with its modest baroque cathedral. A great deal more interesting is the **Basilica di Santa Maria Maggiore** (www.www.fondazionemia.it; Piazza del Duomo; ☀9am-12.30pm & 2.30-6pm Mon-Fri, 9am-6pm Sat & Sun Apr-Oct, shorter hours Nov-Mar) next door. To its whirl of frescoed, Romanesque apses, begun in 1137, Gothic touches were added, as was the Renaissance **Cappella Colleoni** (Piazza del Duomo; ☀9am-12.30pm & 2-6.30pm Mar-Oct, to 4.30pm Tue-Sun Nov-Feb), the mausoleum-cum-chapel of the famous mercenary commander Bartolomeo Colleoni (1696–1770). Demolishing an entire apse of the basilica, he commissioned Giovanni Antonio Amadeo to create a tomb that is now considered a masterpiece of Lombard art.

Also like Venice, Bergamo has a grand art academy. The seminal **Accademia Carrara** (☎035 23 43 96; www.lacarrara.it; Piazza Carrara 82; adult/reduced €10/8; ☀9.30am-5.30pm Wed-Mon) is both school and museum, its stunning collection of 1800 Renaissance paintings amassed by local scholar Count Giacomo Carrara (1714–96).

✕ 🛏 p53

Eating & Sleeping

Stresa ❶

✕ Ristorante Il Vicoletto Ristorante €€

(☎0323 93 21 02; www.ristorantevicoletto.com; Vicolo del Pocivo 3; meals €32-38; ⊘noon-2pm & 7-10pm Fri-Wed) One of Stresa's most gourmet restaurants doesn't advertise itself from its modest perch up a narrow side street. Local word of mouth means the small interior is often full, with diners spilling out onto a heated front patio. Walk by and you'll see them demolishing cod carpaccio, saffron, asparagus and anchovy risotto, and lamb stewed in Nebbiolo wine.

Verbania ❷

✕ Ristorante Milano Modern Italian €€€

(☎0323 55 68 16; www.ristorantemilano lagomaggiore.it; Corso Zanitello 2, Verbania Pallanza; meals €68-80; ⊘noon-2pm & 7-9pm Wed-Mon; ✿) Milano directly overlooks Pallanza's minuscule horseshoe-shaped harbour, with a scattering of tables sitting on lakeside lawns amid the trees. It's an idyllic if pricey spot to enjoy lake fish, local lamb and some innovative Italian cuisine.

Como ❺

✕ Osteria del Gallo Italian €€

(☎031 27 25 91; www.osteriadelgallo-como.it; Via Vitani 16; meals €26-32; ⊘12.30-3pm Mon-Sat, 7-9pm Tue-Sat) An ageless osteria (casual tavern) that looks exactly the part. In the wood-lined checker-clothed dining room, wine bottles and other goodies fill the shelves, and diners sit at small timber tables to tuck into traditional local food.

🛏 Avenue Hotel Boutique Hotel €€

(☎031 27 21 86; www.avenuehotel.it; Piazzolo Terragni 6; d €165-210, ste €250-290; 🅿✿📶) An assured sense of style at this à la mode boutique hotel sees ultramodern, minimalist rooms team crisp white walls with shots of purple or fuchsia pink. Unusual art (two giant zebras in the breakfast room) melds with unusual design (square toilets) to leave a memorable impression, lent weight by warm but discreet service and fun extras (you can borrow bikes gratis).

Bellagio ❻

🛏 Hotel Silvio Hotel €€

(☎031 95 03 22; www.bellagiosilvio.com; Via Carcano 10; d €75-115, apt from €110; 🅿✿📶🏊) Located above the fishing hamlet of Loppia a short walk from the village, this family-run hotel is one of Bellagio's most relaxing spots. Here you can wake up in a contemporary Zen-like room and gaze out over the gardens of some of Lago di Como's most prestigious villas, then spend the morning at Bellagio's lido (free for hotel guests).

Bergamo ❾

✕ La Tana Italian €€

(☎035 21 31 37; www.tanaristorante.it; Via San Lorenzo 25; meals €32-42; ⊘noon-2.30pm & 7-10pm Wed-Sun, 7-10pm Tue) In the upper town, tucked close to the Venetian walls, La Tana remains exceptionally popular for painstakingly prepared Bergamesque dishes served in a sun-drenched interior of exposed brick and colourful artwork, or out on the small front terrace.

✕ Vineria Cozzi Italian €€

(☎035 23 88 36; www.vineriacozzi.it; Via Bartolomeo Colleoni 22, Città Alta; meals €37-45; ⊘10.30am-3pm & 6.30pm-midnight) Things have changed little since the original wine dealer started here in 1848. Elegant tables with delicate wrought-iron-backed chairs, globe lamps and red-and-white-checked floors make a charming setting for bruschetta with goat cheese and smoked aubergine, or homemade ravioli with bacon, butter and sage.

🛏 Agriturismo Casa Clelia Agriturismo €

(☎035 79 91 33; www.casaclelia.com; Via Corna 1/3, Sotto il Monte Giovanni XXIII; s/d €60/100; 🅿📶) Barely a 10-minute stroll from the centre of Sotto il Monte Giovanni XXIII, and 20km west of Bergamo, this working farm offers 10 spacious, beautiful rooms in the carefully restored 16th-century main farmhouse set amid pretty gardens. Exposed stone and brick, timber beams and dark-wood furniture characterise the rooms.

Tuscan Wine Tour

Tuscany has its fair share of highlights, but few can match the indulgence of a drive through its wine country – an intoxicating blend of scenery, acclaimed restaurants and red wine.

3

TRIP HIGHLIGHTS

34 km

Greve in Chianti
Taste Tuscany's best at Greve's vast cellar

START
Florence

4 **3**
● Panzano in Chianti

● Radda in Chianti

Badia a Passignano
Idyllically located wine estate and medieval abbey

41 km

6
67 km

Castello di Ama
Enjoy modern art and excellent Chianti Classico

● Siena

FINISH
Montepulciano

138 km

7

Montalcino
A fortified hill town, home of Brunello di Montalcino

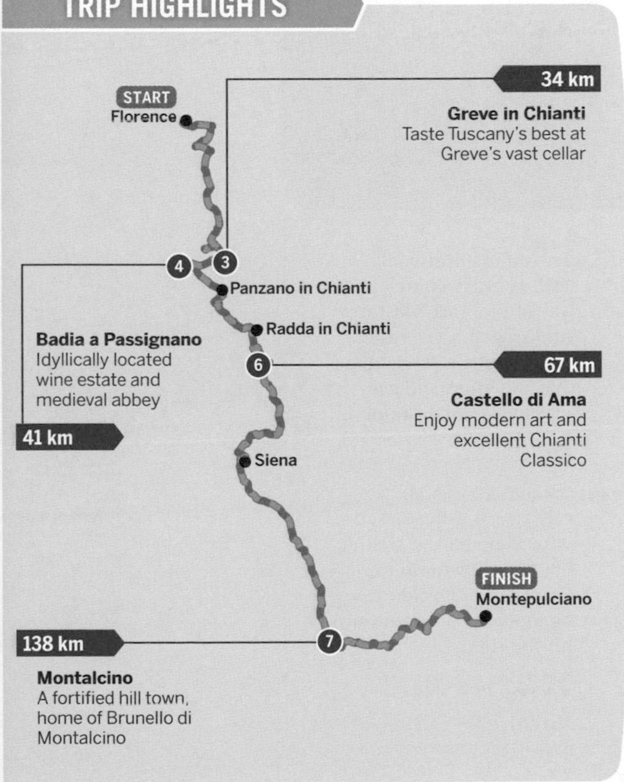

**4 DAYS
185KM / 115 MILES**

GREAT FOR...

BEST TIME TO GO
Autumn (September to November) for earthy hues and the grape harvest.

ESSENTIAL PHOTO
Val di Chiana and Val d'Orcia panoramas from Montepulciano's upper town.

BEST FOR GOURMETS
Tuscan *bistecca* (steak) in Panzano in Chianti.

Val d'Orcia A Tuscan vineyard

START
Florence ①
A1
p114

SR222

Castello di Verrazzano ②
Badia a Passignano ④
③
Greve in Chianti SP118
Panzano in Chianti ⑤

Riserva
Naturale
Alto Merse

E78

N 0 ——————— 10 km
  0 ——————— 5 miles

3 Tuscan Wine Tour

Meandering through Tuscany's bucolic wine districts, this classic Chianti tour offers a taste of life in the slow lane. Once out of Florence (Firenze), you'll find yourself on quiet back roads driving through wooded hills and immaculate vineyards, stopping off at wine estates and hilltop towns to sample the local vintages. En route, you'll enjoy soul-stirring scenery, farmhouse food and some captivating hilltop towns.

❶ Florence

Whet your appetite for the road ahead with a one-day cooking course at the **Cucina Lorenzo de' Medici** (☏334 3040551; www.cucinaldm.com; Piazza del Mercato Centrale, Mercato Centrale), one of Florence's many cookery schools. Once you're done at the stove, sneak out to visit the **Chiesa e Museo di Orsanmichele** (www.bargel lomusei.beniculturali.it; Via dell'Arte della Lana; ☉church 10am-4.50pm daily, closed Mon Aug, museum 10am-4.50pm Mon, 10am-12.30pm Sat), an inspirational 14th-century church and one of Florence's lesser-known gems. Over the river, you can stock up on Tuscan wines and gourmet foods at **Obsequium** (☏055 21 68 49; www.obsequi um.it; Borgo San Jacopo 17/39; ☉11am-9pm Mon-Sat, from noon Sun), a well-stocked wine shop on the ground floor of a medieval tower. Or, explore the old town on foot (p114) before you hit the road.

✕ p41, p63, p86

The Drive 》 From Florence it's about an hour to Verrazzano.

Head south along the scenic SR222 (Via Chiantigiana) towards Greve. When you get to Greti, you'll see a shop selling wine from the Castello di Verrazzano and, just before it, a right turn up to the castle.

❷ Castello di Verrazzano

Some 26km south of Florence, the **Castello di Verrazzano** (☎0558 5 42 43; www.verrazzano.com; Via Citille 32a, Greti; tours €22-68; ◷9.30am-6pm Mon-Sat, 10am-1pm & 3-6.30pm Sun) lords it over a 230-hectare estate where Chianti Classico, Vin Santo, grappa, honey, olive oil and balsamic vinegar are produced. In a previous life, the castle was home to Giovanni di Verrazzano (1485–1528), an adventurer who explored the North American coast and is commemorated in New

LINK YOUR TRIP

1 Grand Tour
From Florence head either north or south to embark upon your own Grand Tour of Italy.

5 World Heritage Wonders
From Florence pick up the A1 to Siena and towards Rome, for Unesco-listed beauties.

57

WINE TASTING GOES HIGH TECH

One of Tuscany's biggest cellars, the **Enoteca Falorni** (📞0558 54 64 04; www.enotecafalorni.it; Piazza delle Cantine 6; tastings by glass €0.60-30; ⊙11am-5pm Mon, Thu & Fri, to 7pm Sat & Sun) in Greve in Chianti stocks more than 1000 labels, of which around 100 are available for tasting. It's a lovely, brick-arched place, but wine tasting here is a very modern experience, thanks to a sophisticated wine-dispensing system that preserves wine in an open bottle for up to three weeks and allows tasters to serve themselves by the glass. Leave your credit-card as a guarantee or buy a nonrefundable prepaid wine card (€5 to €100) to test your tipples of choice at the various 'tasting islands' dotted around the cellar. Curated tastings are also available.

York by the Verrazzano-Narrows Bridge linking Staten Island to Brooklyn.

At the *castello,* you can choose from a range of guided tours, which include a tasting and can also include lunch with the estate wines. Book ahead.

The Drive >> From the *castello* it's a simple 10-minute drive to Greve in Chianti. Double back to the SR222 in Greti, turn right and follow for about 3km.

- - - - - - - - - - - - - - - -

TRIP HIGHLIGHT

❸ Greve in Chianti

The main town in the Chianti Fiorentino, the northernmost of the two Chianti districts, Greve in Chianti has been an important wine centre for centuries. It has an amiable market-town air, and several eateries and *enoteche* (wine bars) that showcase the best Chianti food and drink. To

stock up on picnic supplies, head to **Antica Macelleria Falorni** (📞0558 5 30 29; www.falorni.it; Piazza Giacomo Matteotti 71; ⊙9am-1pm & 3-7pm Mon-Sat, from 10am Sun), an atmospheric butcher's shop–cumbistro that the Bencistà Falorni family have been running since the early 19th century and which specialises in delicious *finocchiona briciolona*

(pork salami made with fennel seeds and Chianti wine). The family also run the Enoteca Falorni, the town's top cellar, where you can sample all sorts of local wine.

The Drive >> From Greve turn off the main through road, Viale Giovanni di Verrazzano, near the Esso petrol station, and head up towards Montefioralle. Continue on as the road climbs past olive groves and through woods to Badia a Passignano, about 15 minutes away.

- - - - - - - - - - - - - - - -

TRIP HIGHLIGHT

❹ Badia a Passignano

Encircled by cypress trees and surrounded by swaths of olive groves and vineyards, the 11th-century **Chiesa di San Michele Arcangelo** (Abbey of Passignano; Via di Passignano; ⊙10am-noon & 3-5pm Mon-Wed, Fri & Sat, 3-5pm Sun) at Passignano sits at the heart of a historic wine estate run by the Antinoris, one of Tuscany's oldest and most

TOP TIP: DRIVING IN CHIANTI

To cut down on driving stress, purchase a copy of *Le strade del Gallo Nero* (€2.50), a useful map that shows major and secondary roads and has a comprehensive list of wine estates. It's available at the tourist office in Greve and at **Casa Chianti Classico** (📞0577 73 81 87; www.casachianticlassico.it; Monastery of Santa Maria al Prato, Circonvallazione Santa Maria 18; self-guided tour with glass of wine €7; ⊙tours & tastings 11am-5pm Thu-Sat, to 3pm Sun Mar-Oct), the headquarters of the Consorzio di Chianti Classico in Radda.

TUSCAN REDS

Something of a viticultural powerhouse, Tuscany excites wine buffs with its myriad of full-bodied, highly respected reds. Like all Italian wines, these are classified according to strict guidelines, with the best denominated *Denominazione di Origine Controllata e Garantita* (DOCG), followed by *Denominazione di Origine Controllata* (DOC) and *Indicazione di Geografica Tipica* (IGT).

Chianti
Cheery, full and dry, contemporary Chianti gets the thumbs up from wine critics. Produced in eight subzones from Sangiovese and a mix of other grape varieties, Chianti Classico is the best known, with its Gallo Nero (Black Cockerel) emblem, which once symbolised the medieval Chianti League. Young, fun Chianti Colli Senesi from the Siena hills is the largest subzone; Chianti delle Colline Pisane is light and soft in style; and Chianti Rùfina comes from the hills east of Florence.

Brunello di Montalcino
Brunello is among Italy's most prized wines. The product of Sangiovese grapes, it must be aged for a minimum of 24 months in oak barrels and four months in bottles, and cannot be released until five years after the vintage. Intense and complex with an ethereal fragrance, it is best paired with game, wild boar and roasts. Brunello grape rejects go into Rosso di Montalcino, Brunello's substantially cheaper but wholly drinkable kid sister.

Vino Nobile di Montepulciano
Prugnolo Gentile grapes (a clone of Sangiovese) form the backbone of the distinguished Vino Nobile di Montepulciano. Its intense but delicate nose and dry, vaguely tannic taste make it the perfect companion to red meat and mature cheese.

Super Tuscans
Developed in the 1970s, the Super Tuscans are wines that fall outside the traditional classification categories. As a result they are often made with a combination of local and imported grape varieties, such as Merlot and Cabernet. Sassacaia, Solaia, Bolgheri, Tignanello and Luce are all super hot Super Tuscans.

prestigious winemaking families. The estate offers a range of guided tours, tastings and cookery courses. Most require prior booking, but you can just turn up at the estate's wine shop, **La Bottega** (☑055 807 12 78; www.osteriadipassignano. com; Via di Passignano 33; ◷10am-7.30pm Mon-Sat), to taste and buy wines and olive oil.

✗ ⭢ p63

The Drive » From Badia a Passignano, double back towards Greve and pick up the signposted SP118 for a pleasant 15-minute drive along the narrow tree-shaded road to Panzano.

- - - - - - - - - - - - - - -

⑤ Panzano in Chianti

The quiet medieval town of Panzano is an essential stop on any gourmet's tour of Tuscany. Here you can stock up on meaty picnic fare at **L'Antica**

Macelleria Cecchini (☑0558 5 20 20; www.dari ocecchini.com; Via XX Luglio 11; ◷9am-4pm), a celebrated butcher's shop run by the poetry-spouting guru of Tuscan meat, Dario Cecchini. Alternatively, you can eat at one of his three eateries: the **Officina della Bistecca** (☑0558 5 20 20; www. dariocecchini.com; Via XX Luglio 11; set menu adult/child under 10yr €50/25; ◷ sittings 1-1.30pm & 8-8.30pm), which serves a simple set

WHY THIS IS A GREAT TRIP
DUNCAN GARWOOD, WRITER

The best Italian wine I've ever tasted was a Brunello di Montalcino. I bought it directly from a producer after a tasting in the Val d'Orcia and it was a revelation. It was just so thrilling to be drinking wine in the place it had been made. And it's this, combined with the inspiring scenery and magnificent food, that makes this tour of Tuscan wineries so uplifting.

Above: Montepulciano
Left: Window detail in Chiesa di San Michele Arcangelo, Badia a Passignano
Right: Brunello di Montalcino wine, Montalcino

menu based on *bistecca;* **Solociccia** (☎0558 5 27 27; www.dariocecchini.com; Via XX Luglio; set meat menu adult/child under 10yr €30/15; ✿ sittings 1-1.30pm, 8pm & 9pm), where guests share a communal table to sample meat dishes other than *bistecca;* and **Dario DOC** (☎0558 5 21 76; www. dariocecchini.com; Via XX Luglio 11; burgers €10 or €15 Mon-Fri, €15 Sat, meat sushi €20; ✿ noon-3pm Mon-Sat), a casual daytime eatery. Book ahead for the Officina and Solociccia.

The Drive » From Panzano, it's about 20km to the Castello di Ama. Strike south on the SR222 towards Radda in Chianti, enjoying views off to the right as you wend your way through the green countryside. At Croce, just beyond Radda, turn left and head towards Lecchi and San Sano. The Castello di Ama is signposted after a further 7km.

TRIP HIGHLIGHT

❻ Castello di Ama

To indulge in some contemporary-art appreciation between wine tastings, make for **Castello di Ama** (☎0577 74 60 69; www.castellodiama.com; Località Ama; guided tours adult/ child under 16yr €25/free; ✿ enoteca 10am-7pm, tours by appointment) near Lecchi. This highly regarded wine estate produces a fine Chianti Classico and has an original sculpture park showcasing 14 site-specific works by artists including Louise Bourgeois, Chen Zhen,

Anish Kapoor, Kendell Geers and Daniel Buren. Book ahead.

The Drive » Reckon on about 1½ hours to Montalcino from the castello. Double back to the SP408 and head south to Lecchi and then on towards Siena. Skirt around the east of Siena and pick up the SR2 (Via Cassia) to Buonconvento and hilltop Montalcino, off to the right of the main road.

- - - - - - - - - - - - - - - -

`TRIP HIGHLIGHT`

❼ Montalcino

Montalcino, a pretty medieval town perched above the Val d'Orcia, is home to one of Italy's great wines, Brunello di Montalcino (and the more modest, but still very palatable, Rosso di Montalcino). There are plenty of *enoteche* where you can taste and buy, including one in the **Fortezza** (📞0577 84 92 11; Piazzale Fortezza; ramparts adult/reduced €4/2, courtyard free; ⏰9am-8pm Apr-Oct, 10am-6pm Nov-Mar), the 14th-century fortress that dominates the town's skyline.

For a historical insight into the town's winemaking past, head to the **Museo della Comunità di Montalcino e del Brunello** (📞0577 84 11 11; www.fattoriadeibarbi.it/museo-del-brunello; Fattoria dei Barbi, Località Podernovi

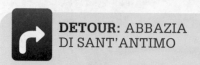

DETOUR: ABBAZIA DI SANT'ANTIMO

Start: ❼ Montalcino

The striking Romanesque **Abbazia di Sant'Antimo** (📞0577 28 63 00; www.antimo.it; Castelnuovo dell'Abate; ⏰10am-7pm Apr-Oct, to 5pm Nov-Mar) lies in an isolated valley just below the village of Castelnuovo dell'Abate, 10.5km from Montalcino.

According to tradition, Charlemagne founded the original monastery in 781. The exterior, built in pale travertine stone, is simple but for the stone carvings, which include various fantastical animals. Inside, look for the polychrome 13th-century *Madonna and Child* and 12th-century *Crucifixion* above the main altar. The abbey's church, crypt, upper loggia, chapel, pharmacy and garden can be visited with a rented video guide (€6).

170; adult/reduced €5/3; ⏰10am-12.30pm & 2.30-6pm Thu-Tue Easter-late Nov), a small museum at the Fattoria dei Barbi wine estate, one of the oldest in the region.

🍴 p63

The Drive » From Montalcino, head downhill and then, after about 8km, turn onto the SR2. At San Quirico d'Orcia pick up the SP146, a fabulously scenic road that weaves along the Val d'Orcia through rolling green hills, past the pretty town of Pienza, to Montepulciano. Allow about an hour.

- - - - - - - - - - - - - - - -

❽ Montepulciano

Set atop a narrow ridge of volcanic rock, the Renaissance centre of Montepulciano produces the celebrated red wine Vino Nobile. To sample it, head up the main street, called in stages Via di Gracciano nel Corso, Via di Voltaia del Corso and Via dell'Opio nel Corso, to the **Enoliteca Consortile** (www.enolitecavinonobile.it; Fortezza di Montepulciano, Via San Donato 21; ⏰11am-7pm), a modern tasting room operated by local wine producers. Housed on the ground floor of the town's Medicean fortress, it offers over 70 wines for tasting and purchase.

🍴🛏 p63

Eating & Sleeping

Florence ❶

✖ Il Santo Bevitore   Tuscan €€

(📞055 21 12 64; www.ilsantobevitore.com; Via di Santo Spirito 64-66r; meals €40; ⏱12.30-2.30pm & 7.30-11.30pm, closed Sun lunch & Aug) Reserve or arrive right on 7.30pm to snag the last table at this ever-popular address, an ode to stylish dining where gastronomes eat by candlelight in a vaulted, whitewashed, bottle-lined interior. The menu is a creative reinvention of seasonal classics: pumpkin gnocchi with hazelnuts, coffee and green-veined *blu di Capra* (goat's-milk cheese), *tagliatelle* with hare *ragù*, garlic cream and sweet Carmignano figs.

✖ All'Antico Vinaio   Osteria €

(📞349 3719947, 055 238 27 23; www.allanticovinaio.com; Via de' Neri 65r; tasting platters €10-30; ⏱10am-4pm & 6-11pm Tue-Sat, noon-3.30pm Sun) The crowd spills out the door of this noisy Florentine thoroughbred. Push your way to the tables at the back to taste cheese and salami in situ (reservations recommended). Or join the queue at the deli counter for a well-stuffed *schiacciata* (a type of focaccia) to take away – the quality is outstanding.

Badia a Passignano ❹

✖ L'Antica Scuderia   Tuscan €€

(📞055 807 16 23, 335 8252669; www.ristorolanticascuderia.com; Via di Passignano 17; meals €45, pizza €10-18; ⏱12.30-2.30pm & 7.30-10.30pm Wed-Mon; 🖼🛜🚗) The large terrace overlooks one of the Antinori vineyards and is perfect for summer dining. In winter, the elegant dining room comes into its own. Lunch features antipasti, pastas and traditional grilled meats, while dinner sees plenty of pizza-oven action. Huge wine list.

🛏 Fattoria di Rignana   Agriturismo €€

(📞0558 5 20 65; www.rignana.it; Via di Rignana 15, Rignana; d from €100; ⏱Apr-Nov; 🅿@🛜🚗🏊) The historic *fattoria* (farmhouse) of this wine estate has its very own chapel and bell tower, which reveal themselves

after you brave a long, rutted access road. You'll also find glorious views, a large swimming pool and a nearby eatery. Sleep in rustic en suite rooms in the *fattoria*. Find it 4km from Badia a Passignano.

Montalcino ❼

✖ Re di Macchia   Tuscan €€

(📞0577 84 61 16; redimacchia@alice.it; Via Soccorso Saloni 21; meals €35, set menus €35; ⏱noon-2pm & 7-9pm Fri-Wed; 🍴) Husband-and-wife team Antonio and Roberta run this relaxed eatery in the centre of town with great aplomb. Roberta's cooking is much more sophisticated than the Tuscan average but retains the usual laudable focus on local, seasonal produce. Antonio's excellent and affordable wine list is one of the best in town. The four-course set menus (one vegetarian) offer excellent value.

Montepulciano ❽

✖ La Dogana   Italian €€

(📞339 5405196; www.ladoganaenoteca.it; Strada Lauretana Nord 75, Valiano; 4-course set lunch €35, meals €34; ⏱11am-3.30pm & 6-10pm Wed-Mon, closed Jan) This chic *enoteca* overlooks the Palazzo Vecchio Winery, 13km northeast of Montepulciano. Windows frame vistas of vines and cypress trees, but the best seats in the house are on the grassed rear terrace. The casual menu showcases seasonal produce (much of it grown in the kitchen garden).

🛏 Locanda San Francesco   B&B €€€

(📞0578 75 87 25; www.locandasanfrancesco.it; Piazza San Francesco 5; r from €176; ⏱closed mid-Jan–early Feb; 🅿🖼@🛜) The only downside to this four-room luxury B&B is that once you check in, you might never want to leave. The feel is elegant but also homey: refined furnishings meet well-stocked bookshelves; restrained fabrics are teamed with fluffy bathrobes. The best room has superb views over the Val d'Orcia on one side and Val di Chiana on the other. Excellent breakfast.

Amalfi Coast

4

Not for the fainthearted, this trip along the Amalfi Coast tests your driving skill on a 100km stretch, featuring dizzying hairpin turns and pastel-coloured towns draped over sea-cliffs.

TRIP HIGHLIGHTS

20 km

Sant'Agata sui Due Golfi
The region's most panoramic views

75 km

Ravello
Romantic gardens and ethereal coastal views

FINISH
Vietri sul Mare

START
Vico Equense

9

8

5

Praiano

3

Marina del Cantone

68 km

Amalfi
Sun-filled piazzas and a cosmopolitan cathedral

Positano
One of Italy's chicest, most photogenic coastal towns

53 km

7 DAYS
100KM / 62 MILES

GREAT FOR...

BEST TIME TO GO
June or September for beach weather without the peak summer crowds.

ESSENTIAL PHOTO
Positano's vertiginous stack of pastel-coloured houses cascading down to the sea.

BEST FOR OUTDOORS
Hiking Ravello and its environs.

Amalfi Cattedrale di Sant'Andrea

4 Amalfi Coast

This trip is all about dramatic landscapes, taking you where mountains plunge seaward in a stunning vertical landscape of precipitous crags, forests and fabled fishing towns. Stops include the celebrated coastal resorts of Positano and Amalfi, as well as serene, mountain-top Ravello, famed for its gardens and views. Cars are useful for inland exploration, as are the walking trails that provide a wonderful escape from the built-up coastal clamour.

22km to
1

Castellammare di Stabia
Stabiae

Golfo di Napoli

SS145   SP366

Pimonte

Monte Faito
(1131m)▲

Vico Equense   START
1   Massaquano   SP366

Moiano   Mt Sant'Angelo
a Tre Pizzi
(1443m)
▲   Agérola

Santa Maria
del Castello   p68 Montepertuso   Bomerano

SS145   Meta   Nocelle   Conca dei
Marini

Marina
di Puolo   Sant'Agnello   **Positano** **5**   **Marina di**
Furore **7**
SS145   SS163

Marina
della
Lobra   **2** **Sorrento**   SS163   SS163   SS163
6

SS145   **3** **Sant'Agata**   **Praiano**
sui Due Golfi

Termini   Nerano

4 **Marina del**
Cantone

❶ Vico Equense

The Bay of Naples is justifiably famous for its pizza, invented here as a savoury way to highlight two local specialities: mozzarella and sun-kissed tomatoes. Besides its pretty little *centro storico* (historic centre), this little clifftop town overlooking the Bay of Naples claims some of the region's top pie, including a by-the-metre version at cult-status **Ristorante & Pizzeria da Gigino** (☎081 879 83 09; www.pizzametro.it; Via Nicotera 15; pizza per metre €28-38; ⏰noon-1.30am; 🛜🅿).

The Drive » From Vico Equense to Sorrento, your main route will be the SS145 roadway for 12km. Expect to hug the sparkling coastline after Marina di Equa before venturing inland around Meta.

❷ Sorrento

On paper, cliff-straddling Sorrento is a place to avoid – a package-holiday centre with few sights, no beach to speak of, and a glut of brassy English-style pubs. In reality, it's strangely appealing, its laid-back southern Italian charm resisting all attempts to swamp it in souvenir tat and graceless development.

According to Greek legend, it was in Sorrento's waters that the mythical sirens once lived. Sailors of antiquity were powerless to resist the beautiful song of these charming maidens-cum-monsters, who would lure them to their doom.

✕ 🛏 p73

The Drive » Take the SS145 for 8km to Sant'Agata sui Due Golfi. Sun-dappled village streets give way to forest as you head further inland.

TRIP HIGHLIGHT

❸ Sant'Agata sui Due Golfi

Perched high in the hills above Sorrento, sleepy

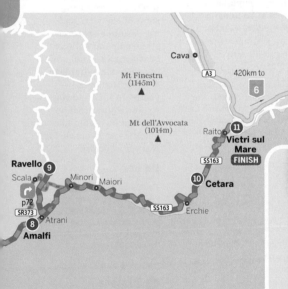

Cava

Mt Finestra (1145m)

A3 420km to **6**

Mt dell'Avvocata (1014m)

Raito

Vietri sul Mare FINISH

SS163

Ravello ❾

Scala   Minori   Maiori

p72

SR373   ❿ **Cetara**

❽ Atrani   SS163   Erchie

Amalfi

Golfo di Salerno

Ⓝ 0 — 5 km
0 — 2.5 miles

LINK YOUR TRIP

1 Grand Tour
It's a short hop north to Naples, from where you can start your search for enlightenment and adventure.

6 Wonders of Ancient Sicily
While you're in the south, why not head to Sicily for Arab treasures and Greek splendours?

Sant'Agata sui Due Golfi commands spectacular views of the Bay of Naples on one side and the Bay of Salerno on the other (hence its name, Saint Agatha on the Two Gulfs).

The best viewpoint is the **Convento del Deserto** (Monastero di San Paolo; 081 878 01 99; Via Deserto; grounds 8am-7pm, viewpoint 10am-noon & 5-7pm summer, 10am-noon & 3-5pm winter), a Carmelite convent 1.5km uphill from the village centre. It's a knee-wearing hike, but make it to the top and you're rewarded with fabulous 360-degree vistas.

The Drive » From Sant'Agata sui Due Golfi to Marina del Cantone it's a 9km drive, the last part involving some serious hairpin turns. Don't let the gorgeous sea views distract you.

❹ Marina del Cantone

From **Nerano**, where you'll park, a beautiful hiking trail leads down to the stunning Bay of Ieranto and one of the coast's top swimming spots, Marina del Cantone. This unassuming village with its small pebble beach is a lovely, tranquil place to stay as well as a popular diving destination. The village also has a reputation as a gastronomic hotspot and VIPs regularly catch a boat over from Capri to dine on superlative seafood at **Lo Scoglio** (081 808 10 26; www.hotelloscoglio. com; Piazza delle Sirene 15; meals €60; 12.30-5pm & 7.30-11pm).

The Drive » First, head back up that switchback to Sant'Agata sui Due Golfi. Catch the SS145 and then the SS163 as they weave their way along bluffs and cliff sides to Positano. Most of the 24km offer stunning sea views.

TRIP HIGHLIGHT

❺ Positano

The pearl in the pack, Positano is the coast's most photogenic and expensive town. Its steeply stacked houses are a medley of peaches, pinks and terracottas, and its near-vertical streets (many of which are, in fact, staircases) are lined with voguish shop displays, elegant hotels and smart restaurants. Look closely, though, and you'll find reassuring signs of everyday reality – crumbling stucco, streaked paintwork and occasionally a faint whiff of problematic drainage.

John Steinbeck visited in 1953 and was so bowled over that he wrote of its dream-like qualities in an article for *Harper's Bazaar*.

p73

The Drive » From Positano to Praiano it's a quick 6km spin on the SS163, passing Il San Pietro di Positano at the halfway point, then heading southeast along the peninsula's edge.

❻ Praiano

An ancient fishing village, a low-key summer resort and, increasingly, a popular centre for the arts, Praiano is a delight. With no centre as such, its whitewashed houses

DETOUR: NOCELLE

Start: ❺ Positano

A tiny, still relatively isolated mountain village above Positano, Nocelle (450m) commands some of the most memorable views on the entire coast. A world apart from touristy Positano, it's a sleepy, silent place where not much ever happens, nor would its few residents ever want it to. If you want to stay, consider delightful **Villa della Quercia** (089 812 34 97; www. villalaquercia.com; Via Nocelle 5; d €80-90; Apr–mid-Oct;), a former monastery with spectacular vistas. Nocelle lies eight very winding kilometres northeast of Positano.

pepper the verdant ridge of Monte Sant'Angelo as it slopes towards Capo Sottile. Exploring involves lots of steps and there are several trails that start from town, including the legendary **Sentiero degli Dei**.

For those who'd rather venture below sea level, **La Boa** (☎089 81 30 34; www.laboa.com; Marina di Praia; 1 dive without/with equipment €60/100) runs dives that explore the area's coral, marine life and grottoes.

The Drive » From Praiano, Marina di Furore is just 3km further on, past beautiful coves that cut into the shoreline.

7 Marina di Furore

A few kilometres further on, Marina di Furore sits at the bottom of what's known as the fjord of Furore, a giant cleft that cuts through the Lattari mountains. The main village, however, stands 300m above, in the upper Vallone del Furore. A one-horse place that sees few tourists, it breathes a distinctly rural air despite the presence of colourful murals and unlikely modern sculpture.

The Drive » From Marina di Furore to Amalfi, the sparkling Mediterranean Sea will be your escort as you drive eastward along the SS163 coastal road for 6km. Look for Vettica Minore and Conca dei Marini on the way, along with fluffy bunches of fragrant cypress trees.

WALK OF THE GODS

Probably the best-known walk on the Amalfi Coast is the three-hour, 12km **Sentiero degli Dei**, which follows the high ridge linking Praiano to Positano. The walk commences in the heart of **Praiano**, where a thigh-challenging 1000-step start takes you up to the path itself. The route proper is not advised for vertigo sufferers: it's a spectacular, meandering trail along the top of the mountains, with caves and terraces set dramatically in the cliffs and deep valleys framed by the brilliant blue of the sea. You'll eventually emerge at Nocelle (p68), from where a series of steps will take you through the olive groves and deposit you on the road just east of **Positano**.

TRIP HIGHLIGHT

8 Amalfi

It is hard to grasp that pretty little Amalfi, with its sun-filled piazzas and small beach, was once a maritime superpower with a population of more than 70,000. For one thing, it's not a big place – you can easily walk from one end to the other in about 20 minutes. For another, there are very few historical buildings of note. The explanation is chilling – most of the old city, along with its populace, simply slid into the sea during an earthquake in 1343.

One happy exception is the striking **Cattedrale di Sant'Andrea** (☎089 87 35 58; Piazza del Duomo; adult/reduced €3/1 between 10am-5pm; ◷7.30am-8.30pm, closed Nov-Mar), parts of which date from the early 10th century. Between 10am and 5pm

THE BLUE RIBBON DRIVE

Stretching from Vietri sul Mare to Sant'Agata sui Due Golfi near Sorrento, the SS163 – nicknamed the Nastro Azzurro (Blue Ribbon) – remains one of Italy's most breathtaking roadways. Commissioned by Bourbon king Ferdinand II and completed in 1853, it wends its way along the Amalfi Coast's entire length, snaking round impossibly tight curves, over deep ravines and through tunnels gouged out of sheer rock. It's a magnificent feat of civil engineering – although it can be challenging to drive – and in certain places it's not wide enough for two cars to pass.

WHY THIS IS A GREAT TRIP
CRISTIAN BONETTO, WRITER

From Richard Wagner to Gore Vidal, the Amalfi Coast has bewitched some of the world's most illustrious figures. This is Italy's most arresting coastline, with a natural beauty that borders on the ethereal. While this trip takes in the fabled, sun-drenched towns the Amalfi Coast is famous for, it also sees you hitting the sleepy, hike-friendly hills above, where the views demand a symphony.

Above: Boats, Praiano
Left: Ceramic plate, Positano
Right: Villa Rufolo, Ravello

entrance to the cathedral is through the adjacent **Chiostro del Paradiso** (☎089 87 13 24; Piazza del Duomo; adult/reduced €3/1; ⊕9am-7.45pm Jul & Aug, shorter hours Sep-early Jan & Mar-Jun, closed early Jan & Feb), a 13th-century Moorish-style cloister.

Be sure to take the short walk around the headland to neighbouring **Atrani**, a picturesque tangle of whitewashed alleys and arches centred on a lively, lived-in piazza and popular beach.

✕ ⊨ p73

The Drive ≫ Start the 7km trip to Ravello by heading along the coast to Atrani. Here turn inland and follow the SR373 as it climbs the steep hillside in a series of second-gear hairpin turns up to Ravello.

- - - - - - - - - - - - - - - - - -

TRIP HIGHLIGHT

❾ Ravello

Sitting high in the hills above Amalfi, polished Ravello is a town almost entirely dedicated to tourism. Boasting impeccable artistic credentials – Richard Wagner, DH Lawrence and Virginia Woolf all lounged here – it's known today for its ravishing gardens and stupendous views, the best in the world according to former resident Gore Vidal.

To enjoy these views, head south of Ravello's cathedral to the 14th-century tower that marks the entrance to

Villa Rufolo (☎089 85 76 21; www.villarufolo.it; Piazza Duomo; adult/reduced €7/5; ⏰9am-9pm summer, reduced hours winter, tower museum 10am-7pm summer, reduced hours winter). Created by Scotsman Scott Neville Reid in 1853, these gardens combine celestial panoramic views, exotic colours, artistically crumbling towers and luxurious blooms.

Also worth seeking out is the wonderful **Camo** (☎089 85 74 61; www.museo delcorallo.com; Piazza Duomo 9; ⏰10am-noon & 3-4pm Mon-Sat). Squeezed between tourist-driven shops, this very special place is, on the face of it, a cameo shop. And exquisite they are too, crafted primarily out of coral and shell. But don't stop here; ask to see the treasure trove of a museum beyond the showroom.

 �p73

The Drive » Head back down to the SS163 for a 19km journey that twists and turns challengingly along the coast to Cetara. Pine trees and a variety of flowering shrubs line the way.

---

⑩ Cetara

Cetara is a picturesque, tumbledown fishing village with a reputation as a gastronomic delight. Since medieval times it has been an important fishing centre, and today its deep-sea tuna fleet is considered one of the Mediterranean's most important. At night, fishermen set out in small boats armed with powerful lamps to fish for anchovies. No surprise then that tuna and anchovies dominate local menus, including at **Cetara Punto e Pasta** (☎089 26 11 09; Corso Garibaldi 14; meals €25; ⏰noon-4pm & 7-11.30pm Mon, Wed, Thu & Sun, 11.30am-midnight Fri & Sat), a sterling seafood restaurant near the small harbour.

The Drive » From Cetara to Vietri sul Mare, head northeast for 6km on the SS163 for more twisting, turning and stupendous views across the Golfo di Salerno.

---

⑪ Vietri sul Mare

Marking the end of the coastal road, Vietri sul Mare is the ceramics capital of Campania. Although production dates back to Roman times, it didn't take off as an industry until the 16th and 17th centuries. Today, ceramics shopaholics can get their fix at the **Ceramica Artistica Solimene** (☎089 21 02 43; www.ceramicasolimene. it; Via Madonna degli Angeli 7; ⏰9am-8pm Mon-Fri, 9am-1.30pm & 4-8pm Sat, 9am-1.30pm & 4-7pm Sun), a vast factory outlet with an extraordinary glass and ceramic facade.

For a primer on the history of the area's ceramics, seek out the **Museo della Ceramica** (☎089 21 18 35; Villa Guariglia, Via Nuova Raito; ⏰9am-3pm Tue-Sat, 9.30am-1pm Sun) in the nearby village of Raito.

DETOUR: RAVELLO WALKS

Start: ⑨ **Ravello**

Ravello is the starting point for numerous walks that follow ancient paths through the surrounding Lattari mountains. If you've got the legs for it, you can walk down to **Minori** via an attractive route of steps, hidden alleys and olive groves, passing the picturesque hamlet of **Torello** en route. Alternatively, you can head the other way, to Amalfi, via the ancient village of **Scala**. Once a flourishing religious centre with more than a hundred churches and the oldest settlement on the Amalfi Coast, Scala is now a pocket-sized, sleepy place where the wind whistles through empty streets, and gnarled locals go patiently about their daily chores.

Eating & Sleeping

Sorrento ❷

✗ Soul & Fish   Seafood €€

(☎081 878 21 70; www.soulandfish.com; Via
Marina Grande 202; meals €38-46; ⏱noon-
2.30pm & 7-10.30pm, closed Nov-Easter; 🐾)
Soul & Fish has a hipper vibe than Marina
Grande's no-nonsense seafood restaurants.
Your bread comes in a bag, your dessert might
come in a Kilner jar and your freshly grilled
fish with a waiter ready to slice it up before
your eyes. The decor is more chic beach shack
than sea-shanty dive bar, with wooden decks,
director chairs and puffy cushions.

🛏 Palazzo Marziale   Boutique Hotel €€€

(☎081 807 44 06; www.palazzomarziale.com;
Largo San Francesco 2; d/ste from €220/455;
❄🐾) From cascading vines, Chinese porcelain
urns and Persian rugs in the lobby lounge,
to antique furniture, objets and artworks in
the hallways, and inlaid wood in the lift, this
sophisticated, 11-room hideaway is big on
details. The family's elegant tastes extend to the
rooms, resplendent with high ceilings, chaises
longues and classy mattresses and linens.

Positano ❺

🛏 Albergo California   Hotel €€

(☎089 87 53 82; www.hotelcaliforniapositano.
it; Via Cristoforo Colombo 141; d €160-250;
⏱Mar–mid-Oct; 🅿❄🐾) If you were to choose
the best place to take a quintessential Positano
photo, it might be from the balcony of this hotel.
But the view isn't all you get. The rooms in the
older part of this grand 18th-century palace
are magnificent, with original ceiling friezes
and decorative doors. New rooms are simply
decorated but tasteful, spacious and minimalist.

Amalfi ❽

✗ Le Arcate   Italian €€

(☎089 87 13 67; www.learcateatrani.it; Largo
Orlando Buonocore, Atrani; pizzas from €6,

meals €30; ⏱12-3.30pm & 7-11pm daily Jul &
Aug, closed Mon Sep-Jun; 🐾) If you've had it
with the tourist tumult of Amalfi, try temporarily
relocating to its quieter cousin Atrani to eat
al fresco at one of its traditional restaurants.
Arcate is right on the seafront with huge
parasols shading its sprawl of tables, and a
dining room in a stone-walled natural cave.

🛏 Hotel Luna Convento   Hotel €€€

(☎089 87 10 02; www.lunahotel.it; Via
Pantaleone Comite 33; d from €340; ⏱mid-
Mar–Dec; 🅿❄@🐾🏊) This former convent
was founded by St Francis in 1222 and has
been a hotel for some 170 years. Rooms in the
original building are in the former monks' cells,
but there's nothing poky about the bright tiles,
balconies and seamless sea views. The newer
wing is equally beguiling, with religious frescoes
over the beds. The cloistered courtyard is
magnificent.

Ravello ❾

✗ Da Salvatore   Italian €€

(☎089 85 72 27; Via della Repubblica 2; meals
€38-45, pizzas from €5; ⏱12.30-3pm & 7.30-
10pm Tue-Sun Easter-Nov) Da Salvatore doesn't
merely rest on the laurels of its spectacular
terrace views. This is one of the coast's best
restaurants, serving arresting dishes that
showcase local produce with creativity, flair and
whimsy; your pre-meal benvenuto (welcome)
may include an aperitivo of Negroni encased in a
white-chocolate ball.

🛏 Villa Casale   Apartment €€

(☎340 9479909; www.ravelloresidence.it;
Via Orso Papice 4; apt €99-206, ste €179-280;
❄🐾🏊) Practically next to the Villa Rufolo and
enjoying the same glamorous view, Villa Casale
consists of a handful of elegant suites and
apartments arranged around a large pool. Top
billing goes to the suites, graced with antiques
and occupying the original 14th-century
building. All come with a self-contained kitchen
and the property has tranquil terraced gardens.

World Heritage Wonders

From Rome to Venice, this tour of Unesco World Heritage Sites takes in some of Italy's greatest hits, including the Colosseum and the Leaning Tower of Pisa, and some lesser-known treasures.

5

TRIP HIGHLIGHTS

738 km

Verona
Experience opera, history and drama in romantic Verona

FINISH

Padua

6

8

870 km

Venice
Lose your heart in Italy's unique canal city

● Modena

Florence

Pisa ●

240 km

Siena
A gorgeous medieval city in the heart of Tuscany

2

0 km

Rome
Legends, history and masterpieces in the Eternal City

1

START

14 DAYS
870KM / 540 MILES

GREAT FOR...

BEST TIME TO GO
April, May and September for ideal sightseeing weather and local produce.

ESSENTIAL PHOTO
Roman Forum from the Palatino.

BEST FOR ART
Florence's Galleria degli Uffizi.

5 World Heritage Wonders

Topping the Unesco charts with 54 World Heritage Sites, Italy offers the full gamut, ranging from historic city centres and human-made masterpieces to snow-capped mountains and areas of outstanding natural beauty. This trip through central and northern Italy touches on the country's unparalleled artistic and architectural legacy, taking in ancient Roman ruins, priceless Renaissance paintings, great cathedrals and, to cap it all off, Venice's unique canal-scape.

TRIP HIGHLIGHT

Rome

An epic, monumental metropolis, Italy's capital is a city of thrilling beauty and high drama. Its historic centre, which according to Unesco boasts some of antiquity's most important monuments, has been a World Heritage Site since 1980, and the **Vatican**, technically a separate state but in reality located within Rome's city limits, has been on the Unesco list since 1984.

Of Rome's many ancient monuments, the most iconic is the Colosseum (p37), the towering 1st-century-CE amphitheatre where gladiators met in mortal combat and condemned criminals fought off wild beasts. Nearby, the Palatino (p37) was the ancient city's most exclusive neighbourhood, as well as its oldest – Romulus and Remus supposedly founded the city here in 753 BCE. From the Palatino, you can stroll down to the skeletal ruins of the **Roman Forum** (Foro Romano; ☏06 3996 7700; www.parcocolosseo.it; Largo della Salara Vecchia, Piazza di Santa Maria Nova; adult/reduced incl Palatino & SUPER sites €16/2, incl Colosseum & Palatino €16/2, incl Colosseum, Palatino & SUPER sites €22/2,

1st Sun of month Oct-Mar free; ☺8.30am-1hr before sunset; SUPER ticket sites Tue, Thu, Sat & afternoon Sun only, last entry 1hr before closing; 🚍Via dei Fori Imperiali), the once-beating heart of the ancient city. All three sights are covered by a single ticket.

To complete your tour of classical wonders search out the Pantheon (p37), the best preserved of Rome's ancient monuments. One of the most influential buildings in the world, this domed temple, now a church, is an extraordinary sight with its vast columned portico and soaring marble-clad interior.

🍴 🛏 p41, p86

The Drive » The easiest route to Siena is via the A1 autostrada (about 230km). Join this from the Rome ring road, the GRA (Grande Raccordo Anulare), and head north, past Orvieto's dramatic clifftop cathedral,

LINK YOUR TRIP

2 **The Graceful Italian Lakes**

Branch off at Verona and take the A4 for some refined elegance and mountain scenery.

3 **Tuscan Wine Tour**

From Florence head south to Tuscany's Chianti wine country to indulge in some wine tasting at the area's historic vineyards.

to the Valdichiano exit. Take this and follow signs onto the Raccordo Siena-Bettolle (E78) for the last leg into Siena.

TRIP HIGHLIGHT

② Siena

Siena is one of Italy's most enchanting medieval towns. Its walled centre, a beautifully preserved warren of dark lanes, Gothic *palazzi* (mansions) and pretty piazzas, is centred on **Piazza del Campo** (known as Il Campo), the sloping shell-shaped square that stages the city's annual horse race, Il Palio, on 2 July and 16 August.

On the piazza, the 102m-high **Torre del Mangia** (0577 29 26 15; ticket@comune.siena.it; Palazzo Pubblico, Piazza del Campo 1; adult/family €10/25; 10am-6.15pm Mar–mid-Oct, to 3.15pm mid-Oct–Feb) **soars** above the Gothic **Palazzo Pubblico** (Palazzo Comunale), home to the city's finest art museum, the **Museo Civico** (Civic Museum; 0577 29 26 15; Palazzo Pubblico, Piazza del Campo 1; adult/reduced €10/9, with Torre del Mangia €15, with Torre del Mangia & Complesso Museale di Santa Maria della Scala €20; 10am-6.15pm mid-Mar–Oct, to 5.15pm Nov–mid-Mar). Of Siena's churches, the one to see is the 13th-century **Duomo** (Cattedrale di Santa Maria Assunta; 0577 28 63 00; www.operaduomo.siena.it; Piazza Duomo; Mar-Oct €5, Nov-Feb free, when floor displayed €8; 10.30am-7pm Mon-Sat, 1.30-6pm Sun Mar-Oct, 10.30am-5.30pm Mon-Sat, 1.30-5.30pm Sun Nov-Feb), one of Italy's greatest Gothic churches. Highlights include the remarkable white, green and red facade, and, inside, the magnificent inlaid marble floor that illustrates historical and biblical stories.

 p86

The Drive » There are two alternatives to get to Florence. The quickest, via the fast RA3 Siena–Firenze Raccordo, takes about 1½ hours (73km). But if you have the time, we recommend the scenic SR222, which snakes through the Chianti wine country, passing through quintessential hilltop towns and vine-laden slopes. Reckon on at least 2½ hours for this route.

---

③ Florence

Cradle of the Renaissance and home of Michelangelo, Machiavelli and the Medici, Florence (Firenze) is magnetic, romantic, unique and busy. A couple of days is not long here but it's enough for a breathless introduction to the city's top sights, many

---

↱ DETOUR: SAN GIMIGNANO

Start: ② Siena

Dubbed the medieval Manhattan thanks to its 14 11th-century towers, San Gimignano is a classic hilltop town and an easy detour from Siena.

From the car park next to Porta San Giovanni, it's a short walk up to **Palazzo Comunale** (0577 28 63 00; www.sangimignanomusei.it; Piazza del Duomo 2; combined Civic Museums ticket adult/reduced €9/7; 10am-7.30pm Apr-Sep, 11am-5.30pm Oct-Mar), which houses the town's art gallery, the **Pinacoteca**, and tallest tower, the **Torre Grossa**. Nearby, the Romanesque basilica, known as the **Collegiata** (Duomo; Basilica di Santa Maria Assunta; 0577 28 63 00; www.duomosangimignano.it; Piazza del Duomo; adult/reduced €4/2; 10am-7.30pm Mon-Fri, to 5.30pm Sat, 12.30-7.30pm Sun Apr-Oct, shorter hours Nov-Mar), boasts some remarkable Ghirlandaio frescoes.

Before leaving town, be sure to sample the local Vernaccia wine at the **Vernaccia di San Gimignano Wine Experience** (0577 94 12 67; www.sangimignanomuseovernaccia.com; Via della Rocca 1; 11.30am-7.30pm Apr-Oct, to 6.30pm Nov & Mar, closed Dec-Feb) next to the Rocca (fortress).

San Gimignano is about 40km northwest of Siena. Head for Florence on the RA3 until Poggibonsi and then pick up the SS429.

WORLD HERITAGE SITES

With 55 World Heritage Sites, Italy has more than any other country. But what exactly is a World Heritage Site? Basically it's anywhere that Unesco's World Heritage Committee decides is of 'outstanding universal value' and inscribes on the World Heritage List. It could be a natural wonder such as the Great Barrier Reef in Australia or a human-made icon such as New York's Statue of Liberty, a historic city centre or a great work of art or architecture.

The list was set up in 1972 and has since grown to include 1121 sites from 167 countries. Italy first got in on the act in 1979 when it successfully nominated its first entry – the prehistoric rock drawings of the Valcamonica valley in northeastern Lombardy. The inscription process requires sites to be nominated by a country and then independently evaluated. If they pass scrutiny and meet at least one of 10 selection criteria, they get the green light at the World Heritage Committee's annual meeting. Once on the list, sites qualify for management support and access to the World Heritage Fund.

Italian nominations have generally fared well and since Rome's historic centre and the Chiesa di Santa Maria delle Grazie in Milan were inscribed in 1980, many of the nation's greatest attractions have made it onto the list – the historic centres of Florence, Naples, Siena and San Gimignano; the cities of Venice, Verona and Ferrara; the archaeological sites of Pompeii, Paestum and Agrigento; as well as natural beauties such as the Amalfi Coast, Aeolian Islands, Dolomites and Tuscany's Val d'Orcia.

of which can be enjoyed on foot (p114).

Towering above the medieval skyline, the Duomo (p36) dominates the city centre with its famous red-tiled dome and striking facade. A short hop away, **Piazza della Signoria** opens onto the sculpture-filled **Loggia dei Lanzi** and the **Torre d'Arnolfo** above **Palazzo Vecchio** (☑055 276 85 58; www.musefirenze.it; Piazza della Signoria; adult/reduced museum €12.50/10, tower €12.50/10, museum & tower €17.50/15, museum & archaeological tour €16/13.50, combination ticket €19.50/17.50; ☺museum 9am-11pm Fri-Wed, to 2pm Thu Apr-Sep, 9am-7pm Fri-Wed, to 2pm Thu Oct-Mar, tower 9am-9pm Fri-Wed, to 2pm Thu Apr-Sep, 10am-5pm Fri-Wed, to 2pm Thu Oct-Mar), Florence's lavish City Hall.

Next to the *palazzo,* the Galleria degli Uffizi (p36) houses one of the world's great art collections, including works by Botticelli, Leonardo da Vinci, Michelangelo, Raphael and many other Renaissance maestros.

✗ ⊨ p41, p73, p86

The Drive » From Florence it's about 88km to Pisa along the A11 autostrada or just over an hour using the speedy, toll-free FI-PI-LI (SS67) linking the two cities. At the end of either route, follow signs to Pisa centro.

- - - - - - - - - - - - - - - - -

❹ Pisa

Once a maritime republic to rival Genoa and Venice, Pisa now owes its fame to an architectural project gone horribly wrong. The **Leaning Tower** (Torre Pendente; ☑050 83 50 11; www.opapisa. it; Piazza del Duomo; €18; ☺8.30am-10pm mid-Jun–Aug, 9am-8pm Apr–mid-Jun & Sep, to 7pm Oct & Mar, to 6pm Nov–Feb) is an extraordinary sight and one of Italy's most photographed monuments. The tower, originally erected as a *campanile* (bell tower) in the late 12th century, is one of three Romanesque buildings on the immaculate lawns of **Piazza dei Miracoli** (also known as Campo dei Miracoli or Piazza del Duomo).

The candy-striped **Duomo** (Duomo di Santa Maria Assunta; ☑050 83 50 11;

WHY THIS IS A GREAT TRIP
DUNCAN GARWOOD, WRITER

Every one of the towns and cities on this drive is special. The great treasures of Rome, Florence and Venice are amazing but, for me, it's the lesser-known highlights that make this such an incredible trip – Siena's Gothic Duomo, Modena's stunning Romanesque cathedral, the Cappella degli Scrovegni in Padua, and Verona's gorgeous medieval centre.

Above: Duomo, Siena
Left: Cappella degli Scrovegni, Padua
Right: Verona

www.opapisa.it; Piazza del Duomo; ◷10am-8pm Apr-Oct, to 6pm or 7pm Nov-Feb), **begun in 1063, has a graceful tiered facade and cavernous interior, while to its west, the cupcake-like Battistero** (Battistero di San Giovanni; ☏050 83 50 11; www.opapisa.it; Piazza del Duomo; €5, combination ticket with Camposanto or Museo delle Sinopie €7, Camposanto & Museo delle Sinopie €8; ◷8am-8pm Apr-Oct, 9am-6pm or 7pm Nov-Mar) **is something of an architectural hybrid, with a Pisan-Romanesque lower section and a Gothic upper level and dome. End your Piazza dei Miracoli foray with a saunter atop the city's old medieval walls, Mura di Pisa** (☏050 098 74 80; www.muradipisa.it; Piazza del Duomo; adult/reduced €3/2; ◷9am-7pm Apr-May & Sep, 9am-7pm Mon-Thu, to 9pm Fri-Sun Jun-Aug, shorter hours rest of year; ♿).

✕ p87

The Drive » It's a 2½-hour drive up to Modena from Pisa (210km). Head back towards Florence on the A11 and then pick up the A1 to Bologna. Continue as the road twists and falls through the wooded Apennines before flattening out near Bologna. Exit at Modena Sud (Modena South) and follow signs for the centro.

----

❺ Modena

One of Italy's top foodie towns, Modena boasts a stunning medieval centre and a trio of Unesco-listed sights. First up is the gorgeous **Duomo** (Cattedrale Metropolitana di Santa Maria Assunta e San Geminiano; www.duomodimodena.it; Corso Duomo; ⊙7am-12.30pm & 3.30-7.30pm Mon, 7am-7pm Tue-Sat, 7.30am-7pm Sun), which is widely considered to be Italy's finest Romanesque church. Features to look out for include the Gothic rose window and a series of bas-reliefs depicting scenes from Genesis.

Nearby, the 13th-century **Torre Ghirlandina** (www.unesco.modena.it; Corso Duomo; adult/reduced €3/2; ⊙9.30am-1pm & 3-7pm Tue-Fri, 9.30am-7pm Sat & Sun Apr-Sep, to 5.30pm Oct-Mar), an 87m-high tower topped by a Gothic spire, was named after Seville's Giralda bell tower by exiled Spanish Jews in the early 16th century. The last of the Unesco threesome is **Piazza Grande**, just south of the

ITALIAN ART & ARCHITECTURE

The Ancients
In pre-Roman times, the Greeks built theatres and proportionally perfect temples in their southern colonies at Agrigento, Syracuse and Paestum, while the Etruscans concentrated on funerary art, creating elaborate tombs at Tarquinia and Cerveteri. Coming in their wake, the Romans specialised in roads, aqueducts and monumental amphitheatres such as the Colosseum and Verona's Arena.

Romanesque
With the advent of Christianity in the 4th century, basilicas began to spring up, many with glittering Byzantine-style mosaics. The Romanesque period (c 1050–1200) saw the construction of fortified monasteries and robust, bulky churches such as Bari's Basilica di San Nicola and Modena's cathedral. Pisa's striking *duomo* (cathedral) displays a characteristic Tuscan variation on the style.

Gothic
Gothic architecture, epic in scale and typically embellished by gargoyles, pinnacles and statues, took on a more classical form in Italy. Assisi's Basilica di San Francesco is an outstanding early example, but for the full-blown Italian Gothic style check out the cathedrals in Florence, Venice, Siena and Orvieto.

Renaissance
From quiet beginnings in 14th-century Florence, the Renaissance erupted across Italy before spreading across Europe. In Italy, painters such as Giotto, Botticelli, Leonardo da Vinci and Raphael led the way, while architects Brunelleschi and Bramante rewrote the rule books with their beautifully proportioned basilicas. All-rounder Michelangelo worked his way into immortality, producing masterpieces such as *David* and the Sistine Chapel frescoes.

Baroque
Dominating the 17th century, the extravagant baroque style found fertile soil in Italy. Witness the Roman works of Gian Lorenzo Bernini and Francesco Borromini, Lecce's flamboyant *centro storico* (historic centre) and the magical baroque towns of southeastern Sicily.

Neoclassicism
Signalling a return to sober classical lines, neoclassicism majored in the late 18th and early19th centuries. Signature works include Caserta's Palazzo Reale and La Scala opera house in Milan. In artistic terms, the most famous Italian exponent was Antonio Canova.

cathedral. The city's focal square, this is flanked by the porticoed **Palazzo Comunale**, Modena's elegant town hall.

 p87

The Drive ≫ From Modena reckon on about 1¼ hours to Verona, via the A22 and A4 autostradas. Follow the A22 as it traverses the flat Po valley plain, passing the medieval town of Mantua (Mantova; worth a quick break) before connecting with the A4. Turn off at Verona Sud and follow signs for the city centre.

TRIP HIGHLIGHT

❻ Verona

A World Heritage Site since 2000, Verona's historic centre is a beautiful compilation of architectural styles and inspiring buildings. Chief among these is its stunning Roman amphitheatre, known as the **Arena** (⌨045 800 51 51; www.arena. it; Piazza Brà 1; adult/reduced €10/7.50; ☺8.30am-7.30pm Tue-Sun, 1.30-7.30pm Mon). Dating to the 1st century CE, this is Italy's third-largest amphitheatre after the Colosseum and Capua amphitheatre, and although it can no longer seat 30,000, it still draws sizeable crowds to its op-era and music concerts.

But Verona isn't simply a relic of the past. A thriving regional city, it also hosts a fantastic modern art gallery, **Galleria d'Arte Moderna Achille Forti** (Palazzo della Ragione; ⌨045 800 19 03; https://gam.comune.verona.it;

Cortile Mercato Vecchio; adult/reduced €4/2.50, incl Torre dei Lamberti €8/5; ☺10am-6pm Tue-Fri, 11am-7pm Sat & Sun), with a fabulous collection of under-appreciated Italian modernists such as Felice Casorati and Angelo Zamboni. It's also packed with excellent contemporary restau-rants like **Locanda 4 Cuochi** (⌨045 803 03 11; www.locanda4cuochi.it; Via Alberto Mario 12; meals €40, 5-course set menu €43; ☺12.30-2.30pm & 7.30-10.30pm, closed lunch Mon & Tue; 📶) and wine bars, such as **Antica Bottega del Vino** (⌨045 800 45 35; www.bottegavini.it; Vicolo Scudo di Francia 3; ☺noon-2.40pm & 7-11pm), showcas-ing regional wines.

 p87

The Drive ≫ To Padua it's about an hour from Verona on the A4 Venice autostrada. Exit at Padova Ovest (Padua West) and join the SP47 after the toll booth. Follow this until you see, after a road bridge, a turn-off signposted to the centro.

----

❼ Padua

Travellers to Padua (Padova) usually make a beeline for the city's main attraction, the **Cappella degli Scrovegni** (Scrovegni Chapel; ⌨049 201 00 20; www.cappelladegliscrovegni. it; Piazza Eremitani 8; adult/reduced €14/10, night ticket €8/6; ☺9am-7pm, night ticket 7-9.20pm), but there's more to Padua than Giotto frescoes and

it's actually the **Orto Botanico** (⌨049 827 39 39; www.ortobotanicopd.it; Via dell'Orto Botanico 15; adult/reduced €10/8, with Padova Card €5; ☺9am-7pm Tue-Sun Apr-Sep, to 6pm Oct, to 5pm Nov-Mar) that represents Padua on Unesco's list of World Heritage Sites. The oldest botanical garden in the world, this dates to 1545 when a group of medical students planted some rare plants in order to study their medicinal properties. Discover Padua's outsized contribution to science and, in particular, medi-cine at the fascinating **Museum of Medical His-tory** (Musme; www.musme. it; Via San Francesco 94; adult/reduced/child €10/8/6; ☺2.30-7pm Tue-Fri, 9.30am-7pm Sat & Sun), housed in what was ostensibly the world's first hospital where medical students learnt clinical practice at a patient's bedside.

The Drive ≫ Traffic permitting, it's about 45 minutes from Padua to Venice, along the A4. Pass through Mestre and over the Ponte della Libertà bridge to Interparking Venezia Tronchetto on the island of Tronchetto.

TRIP HIGHLIGHT

❽ Venice

The end of the road, quite literally, is Venice (Venezia). Of the city's many must-sees the most famous are on Piazza San Marco, including the Basilica di San Marco (p33), Venice's great showpiece church. Built originally to house the bones of St Mark, it's a truly awe-inspiring vision with its spangled spires, Byzantine domes, luminous mosaics and lavish marble work. For a bird's-eye view, head to the nearby **campanile** (www.basilicasanmarco.it; Piazza San Marco; adult/reduced €8/4; ☺8.30am-9pm mid-Apr-Sep, 9.30am-5.30pm Oct-Mar, shorter hours rest of year; 🚏San Marco).

Adjacent to the basilica, the **Palazzo Ducale** (Ducal Palace; 📞041 271 59 11; www.palazzoducale.visitmuve.it; Piazzetta San Marco 1; adult/reduced incl Museo Correr €25/13, with Museum Pass free; ☺8.30am-9pm Mon-Thu, to 11pm Fri & Sat Apr-Oct, 8.30am-7pm Nov-Mar; 🚏San Zaccaria) was the official residence of Venice's doges (ruling dukes) from the 9th century. Inside, its lavishly decorated chambers harbour some seriously heavyweight art, including Tintoretto's gigantic *Paradiso* (Paradise) in the Sala del Maggiore Consiglio. Connecting the palace to the city dungeons, the **Ponte dei Sospiri** (Bridge of Sighs; 🚏San Zaccaria) was named after the sighs that prisoners – including Casanova – emitted en route from court to cell. If you're hungry, hit the streets on foot to get a real taste of the city.

✗ 🛏 p40, p87

KAVALENKAVA/SHUTTERSTOCK ©

Venice View over the entry to the Grand Canal

Eating & Sleeping

Rome ❶

✗ La Ciambella
Italian €€

(📞06 683 29 30; www.la-ciambella.it; Via dell'Arco della Ciambella 20; meals €35-45; 🕐noon-11pm Tue-Sat, to 10pm Sun; 🚇Largo di Torre Argentina) Near the Pantheon but as yet largely undiscovered by the tourist hordes, this friendly restaurant beats much of the neighbourhood competition. Its handsome, light-filled interior is set over the ruins of the Terme di Agrippa, visible through transparent floor panels, setting an attractive stage for interesting, imaginative food.

✗ Flavio al Velavevodetto
Trattoria €€

(📞06 574 41 94; www.ristorantevelavevodetto.it; Via di Monte Testaccio 97-99; meals €30-35; 🕐12.30-3pm & 7.45-11pm; 🚇Via Galvani) This cavernous trattoria is celebrated locally for its earthy, no-nonsense *cucina romana* (Roman cuisine). Antipasti and pastas are very good and the wine list is extremely well priced, but mains and desserts are often disappointing and foreigners are often relegated to the worst tables in the house – if you don't like where you've been seated, ask to move.

🛏 Arco del Lauro
Guesthouse €€

(📞06 9784 0350; www.arcodellauro.it; Via Arco de' Tolomei 27; r €110-145; ❄ @ 🛜; 🚇Viale di Trastevere, 🚇Viale di Trastevere) Perfectly placed on a peaceful cobbled lane on the 'quiet side' of Trastevere, this ground-floor guesthouse sports six gleaming white rooms with parquet floors, a modern low-key look and well-equipped bathrooms. Guests share a fridge, a complimentary fruit bowl and cakes. Breakfast (€5) is served in a nearby cafe. Daniele and Lorenzo, who run the place, could not be friendlier or more helpful.

Siena ❷

✗ Ristorante Enzo
Tuscan €€€

(📞0577 28 12 77; www.daenzo.net; Via Camollia 49; meals €52; 🕐noon-2.30pm & 7.30-10pm Tue-Sun) The epitome of refined Sienese dining, Da Enzo, as it is popularly called, welcomes guests with a complimentary glass of prosecco (sparkling wine) and follows up with Tuscan dishes made with skill and care. There's plenty of fish on the menu, as well as excellent handmade pasta and nonstandard meat dishes. The setting is equally impressive, with quality napery and glassware.

Florence ❸

✗ Il Teatro del Sale
Tuscan €€

(📞055 200 14 92; www.teatrodelsale.com; Via dei Macci 111r; brunch/dinner €20/30; 🕐noon-2.30pm & 7-11pm Tue-Fri, noon-3pm & 7-11pm Sat, noon-3pm Sun, closed Aug) Florentine chef Fabio Picchi is one of Florence's living treasures who steals the Sant'Ambrogio show with this eccentric, good-value, members-only club (everyone welcome, membership €7) inside an old theatre. He cooks up brunch and dinner, culminating at 9.30pm in a live performance of drama, music or comedy arranged by his wife, artistic director and comic actress Maria Cassi.

✗ Essenziale
Tuscan €€€

(📞055 247 69 56; www.essenziale.me; Piazza di Cestello 3r; 6-/8-course tasting menu €65/80; 🕐7-10pm Tue-Sat; 🛜) There's no finer showcase for modern Tuscan cuisine than this loft-style restaurant in a 19th-century warehouse. Preparing dishes at the kitchen bar in rolled-up shirt sleeves and navy butcher's apron is dazzling young chef Simone Cipriani. Order one of his tasting menus to sample the full range of his inventive, thoroughly modern cuisine inspired by classic Tuscan dishes.

🛏 Hotel Scoti
Pension €€

(📞055 29 21 28; www.hotelscoti.com; Via de' Tornabuoni 7; d/tr €140/165; 🛜) Wedged between designer boutiques on Florence's smartest shopping strip, this hidden *pensione* is a fabulous mix of old-fashioned charm and value for money. Its traditionally styled rooms are spread across the 2nd floor of a 16th-century *palazzo;* some have lovely rooftop views. Guests can borrow hairdryers, bottle openers etc and the frescoed lounge (1780) is stunning. Optional breakfast €5 extra.

Pisa ❹

✖ Osteria dei Cavalieri   Tuscan €€

(📞050 58 08 58; www.osteriacavalieri.pisa.it;
Via San Frediano 16; meals €25-30; ⊙12.30-
2pm & 7.45-10pm Mon-Fri, 7.45-10pm Sat)
When an *osteria* cooks up a tripe platter for
antipasto, bone marrow with saffron-spiced
rice as *primo* and feisty T-bone steaks as
secondo, you know you've struck Tuscan
foodie gold. A trio of inspired *piatti unico*
(single dishes) promise a quick lunch, or linger
over themed multi-course menus (including,
unusually, a vegetarian menu) packed with
timeless Tuscan faves.

Modena ❺

✖ Trattoria Ermes   Trattoria €

(📞059 23 80 65; Via Ganaceto 89; meals €20;
⊙noon-2.30pm Mon-Sat) In business since
1963, this fabulous, affordable little lunch spot
is tucked into a single wood-panelled room
at the northern edge of downtown Modena.
Gregarious patron Ermes Rinaldi runs the place
with his wife Bruna: she cooks, he juggles plates
and orders while excessively bantering with the
customers, though these days he often sits out
for health reasons.

🛏 Hotel Cervetta 5   Hotel €€

(📞059 23 84 47; www.hotelcervetta5.com;
Via Cervetta 5; s €80-104, d €120-150; ❄🕸)
Cervetta is about as hip as Modena gets
without pandering to the convention crowd.
Adjacent to the intimate Piazza Grande, it has
quasi-boutique facilities, including rooms that
complement the wonderfully soothing, candlelit
lobby with rustic-chic additions like African iron
light covers, unfinished concrete bathrooms
and roped Edison lighting.

Verona ❻

✖ Café Carducci   Bistro €€

(📞045 803 06 04; www.cafecarducci.it; Via
Carducci 12; meals €25-45; ⊙8am-3pm &
6-10pm Mon-Sat; ❄) A charming 1920s-style
bistro where stylish diners relax in the mirror-
lined interior at linen-topped tables set with
candles and plates of exquisitely sweet salami
and local cheeses. The menu is as classic as the
surroundings, offering risotto in an Amarone
reduction and black rice with scallops. In cherry
season, don't miss the cream gelato with
Bigarreau cherries doused in grappa.

Venice ❽

✖ All'Arco   Venetian €

(📞041 520 56 66; Calle de l'Ochialer 436;
cicheti €2-2.50; ⊙9am-2.30pm Mon-Sat;
🚤Rialto Mercato) Search out this authentic
neighbourhood bar for some of the best
cicheti (Venetian tapas) in town. Armed with
ingredients from the nearby Rialto Market,
father-son team Francesco and Matteo serve
miniature masterpieces to the scrum of eager
patrons crowding the counter and spilling out
onto the street. Even with copious prosecco,
hardly any meal here tops €20.

🛏 Novecento   Boutique Hotel €€€

(📞041 241 37 65; www.novecento.biz; Calle del
Dose 2683/84; d from €190; ❄🕸; 🚤Giglio)
Run by the Romanelli family for more than 50
years, this hotel is a home away from home.
Nine individually designed rooms are inspired
by designer Mario Fortuny and come finished
with Turkish kilim pillows, velvet draperies and
carved bedsteads. You can mingle with creative
fellow travellers around the honesty bar, while
the garden is a lovely spot in which to linger over
breakfast.

Wonders of Ancient Sicily

More than a trip around la bella Sicilia, this is also a journey through time, from spare Greek temples to Norman churches decked out with Arab and Byzantine finery.

6

TRIP HIGHLIGHTS

82 km

Segesta
A huge 5th-century-BCE Greek temple amid desolate mountains

664 km

Taormina
Marvel at the ancient Greek theatre suspended between sea and sky

START
● Palermo

Trapani
2

FINISH **14**

●Catania

8

12

● Ragusa

318 km

Agrigento
Pay homage to this mesmerising complex of five Doric temples

545 km

Syracuse
Extraordinary tapestry of Graeco-Roman ruins, baroque piazzas and medieval streets

12–14 DAYS
664KM / 412 MILES

GREAT FOR...

BEST TIME TO GO
Spring and autumn are best. Avoid the heat and crowds of high summer.

ESSENTIAL PHOTO
Mt Etna from Taormina's Greek theatre.

BEST FOR HISTORY
Exploring layers of Sicily's past in Syracuse.

Agrigento Tempio della Concordia

6 Wonders of Ancient Sicily

A Mediterranean crossroads for 25 centuries, Sicily is heir to an unparalleled cultural legacy, from the temples of Magna Graecia to Norman churches made kaleidoscopic by Byzantine and Arab craftsmen. This trip takes you from exotic, palm-fanned Palermo to the baroque splendours of Syracuse and Catania. On the way, you'll also experience Sicily's startlingly diverse landscape, including bucolic farmland, smouldering volcanoes and long stretches of aquamarine coastline.

❶ Palermo

Palermo is a fascinating conglomeration of splendour and decay. Unlike Florence or Rome, many of its treasures are hidden rather than scrubbed up for endless streams of tourists. The city's cross-cultural history infuses its daily life, lending its dusty backstreet markets a distinct Middle Eastern feel and its architecture a unique East-meets-West look.

A trading port since Phoenician times, the city, which is best explored on foot, first came to prominence as the capital of Arab Sicily in the 9th century CE. When the Normans rode into town in the 11th century, they used Arab know-how to turn it into Christendom's richest and most sophisticated city. The **Cappella Palatina** (Palatine Chapel; ☎091 705 56 11; www.federicosecondo.org; Piazza del Parlamento; adult/reduced incl Appartamenti Reali €9.50/7.50; ⊗8.15am-5.40pm Mon-Sat, to 1pm Sun) is the perfect expression of this marriage, with its gold-inflected Byzantine mosaics crowned by a honeycomb *muqarnas* ceiling – a masterpiece of Arab craftsmanship.

For an insight into Sicily's long and turbulent past, the **Museo Archeologico Regionale Antonio Salinas** (☎091 611 68 07; www.regione.sicilia.it/bbccaa/salinas; Piazza Olivella 24; €3; ⊗9am-6pm Tue-Sat, to 1.30pm Sun) houses some of the island's most valuable Greek and Roman artefacts.

✕ 🏠 p98

The Drive » From Palermo the 82km trip to Segesta starts along the fast-moving A29 as it skirts the mountains west of Palermo, then runs along agricultural plains until reaching the hills of Segesta. The Greek ruins lie just off the A29dir.

LINK YOUR TRIP

1 Grand Tour
Head north to Naples where you can start your search for enlightenment and adventure.

4 Amalfi Coast
Don't miss this week-long adventure of hairpin turns and vertical landscapes amid the world's most glamorous stretch of coastline.

TRIP HIGHLIGHT

❷ Segesta

Set on the edge of a deep canyon in the midst of desolate mountains, the 5th-century-BCE ruins of **Segesta** (☎0924 95 23 56; Contrada Barbaro, SR22; adult/child €6/free; ⊗9am-7.30pm Apr-Sep, to 6.30pm Mar & Oct, to 5pm Nov-Feb) are a magical site. The city, founded by the ancient Elymians, was in constant conflict with Selinunte, whose destruction it sought with dogged determination and singular success. Time, however, has done to Segesta what violence inflicted on Selinunte; little remains now, save the theatre and the never-completed Doric temple. The latter dates from around 430 BCE and is remarkably well preserved. On windy days its 36 giant columns are said to act like an organ, producing mysterious notes.

The Drive » Keep heading along A29dir through a patchwork of green and ochre fields and follow signs for the 40km to Trapani. As you reach its outskirts, you'll head up the very windy SP31 to Erice, with great views of countryside and sea.

❸ Erice

A spectacular hill town, Erice combines medieval charm with astounding 360-degree views from atop the legendary **Mt Eryx** (750m) – on a clear day, you can see as far as Cape Bon in Tunisia. Wander the medieval streets interspersed with churches, forts and tiny cobbled piazzas. Little remains from its ancient past, though as a centre for the cult of Venus, it has a seductive history.

The best views can be had from the **Giardino del Balio**, which overlooks the rugged turrets and wooded hillsides down to the saltpans of Trapani and the sea. Adjacent to the gardens is the Norman **Castello di Venere** (Castle of Venus; 📞329 7823035; www.fondazione ericearte.org/castello divenere.php; Via Castello di Venere; adult/reduced €4/2; 🕐10am-8pm Aug, to 7pm Jul & Sep, to 6pm Apr-Jun & Oct, 10am-1pm Sat & Sun Nov-Mar), built in the 12th and 13th centuries over the ancient Temple of Venus. And while Venus may be the goddess of love, Erice's goddess of all things sweet is Maria Grammatico, whose eponymous **pasticceria** (📞0923 86 93 90; www.mariagrammatico.it; Via Vittorio Emanuele 14; pastries from €2; 🕐9am-midnight May-Sep, to 9pm Oct-Apr) is revered around the globe. Don't leave town without savouring one of her *cannoli* (pastry shells with a sweet filling) or lemon-flavoured *cuscinetti* (small fried pastries).

The Drive >> For the 12km to Trapani, it's back down the switchbacks of the SP31.

----

❹ Trapani

Once a key link in a powerful trading network that stretched from Carthage to Venice, Trapani occupies a sickle-shaped spit of land that hugs its ancient harbour. Although Trapani's industrial outskirts are rather bleak, its historic centre is filled with atmospheric pedestrian streets and some lovely churches and baroque buildings. The narrow network of streets remains a Moorish labyrinth, although it takes much of its character from the fabulous 18th-century baroque of the Spanish period. Make time for the **Chiesa Anime Sante del Purgatorio** (📞329 7078896; Via San Francesco d'Assisi; by donation; 🕐7.45am-noon & 4-7pm Mon-Sat, 10am-noon & 4-7pm Sun), home to the 18th-century *Misteri,* 20 life-size effigies depicting the Passion of Christ.

🍴 🛏 p98

The Drive >> For the 33km trip from Trapani to Marsala, head south on the SS115. Small towns alternate with farmland until you reach Marsala on Sicily's west coast.

----

❺ Marsala

Best known for its eponymous sweet dessert wines, Marsala is an elegant town of stately baroque buildings within a perfect square of city walls. Founded by Phoenicians escaping Roman attacks, the city still has remnants of the 7m-thick ramparts they built, ensuring that it was the last Punic settlement to fall to the Romans.

Marsala's finest treasure is the partially reconstructed remains of a Carthaginian *liburna* (warship) – the only remaining physical evidence of the Phoenicians' seafaring superiority in the 3rd century BCE. You can visit it at the **Museo Archeologico Baglio Anselmi** (📞0923 95 25 35; Via Lungomare Boeo 30; adult/reduced €4/2; 🕐9am-6.30pm Tue-Sat, to 1.30pm Sun).

🍴 p98

The Drive >> For this 52km leg, once again head down the SS115, passing through farmland and scattered towns until you reach the A29. Continue on the autostrada to Castelvetrano, then follow the SS115 and SS115dir for the last leg through orchards and fields to seaside Selinunte.

----

❻ Selinunte

Built on a promontory overlooking the sea, the Greek **ruins of Selinunte** (Selinunte Archaeological Park; 📞0924 4 62 77, 334 6040459; https://en.visitselinunte.com/archaeological-park/; Via Selinunte, Castelvetrano; adult/reduced €6/3; 🕐9am-6pm Mar-Oct, to 5pm Nov-Feb) are among the most impressive in Sicily, dating to around the 7th century BCE. There are few historical records of the city, which was once one of the world's most powerful, and even the names of the various temples have been forgotten and are now identified by letters. The most impressive, **Temple E**, has been partially rebuilt, its columns pieced together from their fragments with part of its tympanum. Many of the carvings, which are on a par with the Parthenon marbles, particularly those from **Temple C**, are now in Palermo's archaeological museum.

The Drive » Head back up to the SS115 and past a series of hills and plains for the 37km trip to Sciacca.

❼ Sciacca

Seaside Sciacca was founded in the 5th century BCE as a thermal resort for nearby Selinunte. Until 2015, when financial woes forced the spa to shut down indefinitely, Sciacca's healing waters continued to be the big drawcard, attracting coachloads of Italian tourists who came to wallow in its sulphurous vapours and mineral-rich mud. Spas and thermal cures apart, it remains a laid-back town with an attractive medieval core and some excellent seafood restaurants.

The Drive » Continue eastwards on the SS115 as it follows the southern coast onto Porto Empedocle and then, 10km inland, Agrigento's hilltop centre. In all, it's about 62km.

TRIP HIGHLIGHT

❽ Agrigento

Seen from a distance, Agrigento's unsightly apartment blocks loom incongruously on the hillside, distracting

attention from the splendid Valley of Temples below. In the Valley, the mesmerising **ruins** (Valle dei Templi; ☎0922 183 99 96; www.parcovalledeitempli.it; adult/reduced €12/7, incl Museo Archeologico €15.50/9, incl Museo Archeologico & Giardino della Kolymbetra €17/11; ◷8.30am-8pm, to 11pm mid-Jul–mid-Sep) of ancient Akragras claim the best-preserved Doric temples outside of Greece.

The ruins are spread over a 13-sq-km site which is divided into eastern and western halves. Head first to the eastern zone, where you'll find the three best temples: the **Tempio di Hera**, the **Tempio di Ercole**, and, most spectacularly, the **Tempio della Concordia** (Temple of Concord). This, the only temple to survive

relatively intact, was built around 440 BCE and was converted into a Christian church in the 6th century.

Uphill from the ruins, Agrigento's **medieval centre** also has its charms, with a 14th-century cathedral and a number of medieval and baroque buildings.

 p98

The Drive » For this 133km leg head back to the SS115, which veers from inland farmland to brief encounters with the sea. Past the town of Gela, you will head into more hilly country, including a steep climb past Comiso, followed by a straight shot along the SP52 to Ragusa.

❾ Ragusa

Set amid the rocky peaks northwest of Modica,

DETOUR: VILLA ROMANA DEL CASALE

Start: ❽ **Agrigento**

Near the town of Piazza Armerina in central Sicily, the stunning 3rd-century Roman **Villa Romana del Casale** (☎0935 68 00 36; www.villaromanadelcasale.it; adult/reduced €10/5, combined ticket incl Morgantina & Museo Archeologico di Aidone €14/7; ◷9am-11.30pm Apr-Oct, to 5pm Nov-May) is thought to have been the country retreat of Diocletian's co-emperor Marcus Aurelius Maximianus. Buried under mud in a 12th-century flood, the villa remained hidden for 700 years before its floor mosaics – considered some of the finest in existence – were discovered in the 1950s. Covering almost the entire villa floor, they are regarded as unique for their range of hues and natural, narrative style.

WHY THIS IS A GREAT TRIP
DUNCAN GARWOOD, WRITER

Sicily claims some of the most spectacular artistic and archaeological treasures you've never heard of. The great Greek ruins of Agrigento and Syracuse might be on many travellers' radars but what about Palermo's Cappella Palatina or Noto's flamboyant baroque streets? These masterpieces are all the more rewarding for being so unexpected, and make this round-island trip an unforgettable experience.

Above: Catania
Left: *Cannoli* (pastry shells with a sweet filling)
Right: Cappella Palatina, Palermo

KIEVVICTOR/SHUTTERSTOCK ©

Ragusa has two faces. Atop the hill sits **Ragusa Superiore**, a busy town with all the trappings of a modern provincial capital, while etched into the hillside is **Ragusa Ibla**. This sloping area of tangled alleyways, grey stone houses and baroque *palazzi* (mansions) is Ragusa's magnificent historic centre.

Like other towns in the region, Ragusa Ibla collapsed after the 1693 earthquake. But the aristocracy, ever impractical, rebuilt their homes on exactly the same spot. Grand baroque churches and *palazzi* line the twisting, narrow lanes, which then open suddenly onto sun-drenched piazzas. Piazza del Duomo, the centre of town, is dominated by the 18th-century baroque **Duomo di San Giorgio** (Ragusa Ibla; ⊘10am-1pm & 3-6.30pm Apr-Oct & Dec, shorter hours rest of year), with its magnificent neoclassical dome and stained-glass windows.

The Drive » Follow the SS115 for this winding, up-and-down 15km drive through rock-littered hilltops to Modica.

⑩ Modica

Atmospheric Modica recalls a *presepe* (traditional nativity crib), its medieval buildings climbing steeply up either side of a deep gorge. But unlike some of the other Unesco-listed cities in the area, its treasures aren't packaged into a single easy-to-see street or central piazza: rather, they are spread around the town and take some discovering. Its star attraction is the baroque **Duomo di San Giorgio** (☐0932 94 12 79; Corso San Giorgio, Modica Alta; ☺8am-12.30pm & 3.30-7pm), which stands in isolated splendour atop a majestic 250-step staircase.

The city's nerve centre is Corso Umberto. A wide avenue flanked by graceful palaces, churches, restaurants and bars, the thoroughfare is where the locals take their evening *passeggiata* (stroll). Originally a raging river flowed through town, but after major flood damage in 1902 it was dammed and Corso Umberto was built over it.

🛏 p99

The Drive ≫ Head back onto the SS115, which becomes quite curvy as you close in on Noto, 40km away.

- - - - - - - - - - - - - - - - - -

⓫ Noto

Flattened by the 1693 earthquake, Noto was rebuilt quickly and grandly, and its golden-hued sandstone buildings make it the finest baroque town in Sicily, especially impressive at night when illuminations accentuate its intricately carved facades. The pièce de résistance is **Corso Vittorio Emanuele**, an elegantly manicured walkway flanked by thrilling baroque *palazzi* and churches.

Just off Corso Vittorio Emanuele, the **Palazzo Castelluccio** (☐0931 83 88 81; http://palazzocastelluccio. it; Via Cavour 10; adult/child €12/free; ☺11am-7pm, closed Mon & Tue winter) reveals the luxury to which the local nobility were accustomed. Its suite of lavish rooms are awash

with murals, evocative paintings, gilded settees, and worn glazed floors revealing the paths of long-gone servants.

The Drive ≫ The 39km drive to Syracuse from Noto takes you down the SP59 and then northeast on the A18/E45, past the majestic Riserva Naturale Cavagrande del Cassibile as you parallel Sicily's eastern coast.

- - - - - - - - - - - - - - - - - -

TRIP HIGHLIGHT

⓬ Syracuse

Syracuse is a dense tapestry of overlapping cultures and civilisations. Ancient Greek ruins rise out of lush citrus orchards, cafe tables spill out onto baroque piazzas, and medieval lanes meander to the sea. Your visit, like the city itself, can be split into two easy parts: one dedicated to the archaeological site, the other to Ortygia, the ancient island neighbourhood connected to the modern town by bridge.

It's difficult to imagine now but in its heyday Syracuse was the largest city in the ancient world, bigger even than Athens and Corinth. The **Parco Archeologico della Neapolis** (☐0931 6 62 06; Viale Paradiso 14; adult/reduced €10/5, incl Museo Archeologico €13.50/7; ☺8.30am-1hr before sunset) is home to well-preserved Greek (and Roman) remains, with the remarkably intact **Teatro Greco** – constructed in the 5th century BCE and rebuilt

EARTHQUAKE

On 11 January 1693, a devastating, 7.4-magnitude earthquake hit southeastern Sicily, destroying buildings from Catania to Ragusa. The destruction was terrible, but it also created a blank palette for architects to rebuild the region's cities and towns out of whole cloth, in the latest style and according to rational urban planning – a phenomenon practically unheard of since ancient times. In fact, the earthquake ushered in an entirely new architectural style known as Sicilian baroque, defined by its seductive curves and elaborate detail, which you can see on display in Ragusa, Modica, Catania and many other cities in the region.

two centuries later – as the main attraction. In the grounds of Villa Landolina, about 500m east of the archaeological park, is the exceptional **Museo Archeologico Paolo Orsi** (📞0931 48 95 11; www.regione.sicilia.it/beni culturali/museopaoloorsi; Viale Teocrito 66; adult/reduced €8/4, incl Parco Archeologico €13.50/7; ☻9am-6pm Tue-Sat, to 1pm Sun).

Compact, labyrinthine **Ortygia** encompasses 25 centuries of history. At its heart, the city's 7th-century **Duomo** (adult/reduced €2/1; ☻9am-6.30pm Mon-Sat Apr-Oct, to 5.30pm Nov-Mar) lords it over Piazza del Duomo, one of Italy's most magnificent squares. The cathedral was built over a pre-existing 5th-century-BCE Greek temple, incorporating most of the original Doric columns in its three-aisled structure. The sumptuous baroque facade was added in the 18th century.

✗ 🛏 p99

The Drive ≫ From Syracuse to Catania, it is a 66km drive north along the A18/E45. This is orange-growing country and you will see many orchards, which can be gorgeously fragrant when in bloom.

⑬ Catania

Gritty, vibrant Catania is a true city of the volcano, much of it constructed from the lava that poured down on it during Mt Etna's 1669 eruption. The baroque centre is lava-black in colour, as if a fine dusting of soot permanently covers its elegant buildings, most of which are the work of Giovanni Battista Vaccarini. The 18th-century architect almost single-handedly rebuilt the civic centre into an elegant, modern city of spacious boulevards and set-piece piazzas.

Long buried under lava, the submerged stage of a 2nd-century Roman theatre and its small rehearsal theatre, part of the **Parco Archeologico Greco Romano** (📞095 715 05 08; Via Vittorio Emanuele II 262; adult/reduced incl Casa Liberti €6/3; ☻9am-7pm), remind you that Catania's history goes back much further. Picturesquely sited in a crumbling residential area, the ruins are occasionally brightened by laundry flapping on the rooftops of vine-covered buildings that appear to have sprouted organically from the half-submerged stage.

 p99

The Drive ≫ The 53km drive to Taormina along the A18/E45 is a coast-hugging northern run, taking in more orange groves as well as glimpses of the sparkling Ionian Sea.

⑭ Taormina

Over the centuries, Taormina has seduced an exhaustive line of writers and artists, from Goethe to DH Lawrence. The main reason for their infatuation? The perfect horseshoe-shaped **Teatro Greco** (📞0942 2 32 20; Via Teatro Greco; adult/reduced €10/5; ☻9am-1hr before sunset), a lofty ancient marvel looking out towards mighty Mt Etna and the Ionian Sea. Built in the 3rd century BCE, the *teatro* is the most dramatically situated Greek theatre in the world and the second largest in Sicily (after Syracuse).

The 9th-century capital of Byzantine Sicily, Taormina also boasts a well-preserved, if touristy, **medieval town**, its chi-chi streets dotted with fashionable cafes and bars perfect for a glamorous wrap-up toast to your journey.

✗ 🛏 p99

ITALY **6** WONDERS OF ANCIENT SICILY

Eating & Sleeping

Palermo ❶

✕ Aja Mola — Seafood €€

(☎091 611 91 59, 334 1508335; www.
ajamolapalermo.it; Via Cassari 39; meals €35-40;
⏱12.30-3pm & 7.30-11pm Tue-Sun; 🛜) On-
point Aja Mola is among Palermo's top seafood
eateries. The interior's smart, subtle take on a
nautical theme is reflected in the open kitchen,
which eschews stock-standard cliches for
modern, creative dishes. The result: appetite-
piquing options like teriyaki-style tartare with
caperberries, or surf-turf *tagliolini* pasta with
succulent shrimps and pork jowl. Bar seating
available; ideal for solo diners. Book ahead.

🛏 Butera 28 — Apartment €€

(☎333 3165432; www.butera28.it; Via Butera
28; apt per day €85-265, per week €570-1780;
🅿 ❀ 🛜) Delightful multilingual owner
Nicoletta rents 12 apartments in the 18th-
century Palazzo Lanzi Tomasi, the last home of
Giuseppe Tomasi di Lampedusa, author of *The
Leopard*. Graced with family antiques, the units
range from 30 to 180 sq metres, most sleeping
a family of four or more. Five apartments face
the sea and all feature laundry facilities, well-
equipped kitchens and soundproofed windows.

Trapani ❹

✕ La Bettolaccia — Sicilian €€

(☎0923 2 59 32; www.labettolaccia.it; Via Enrico
Fardella 25; meals €35-45; ⏱12.45-3pm &
7.45-11pm Mon-Fri, 7.45-11pm Sat) Unwaveringly
authentic, this on-trend Slow Food favourite,
squirrelled away down a sleepy side street, is
the hotspot to feast on spicy couscous with
fried fish or mixed seafood, *caponata* (eggplant
and sun-dried tomatoes with capers in a
sweet-and-sour sauce), the catch of the day, and
other traditional Trapanese dishes in a sharp,
minimalist white space. Reservations essential.

🛏 La Gancia Residence — Hotel €€

(☎0923 43 80 60; www.lagancia.com; Piazza
Mercato del Pesce; d €110-170, tr €200, q €189-
280; ⏱reception 7am-midnight; ❀ 🛜) Spoon
yourself a jelly sweet out of the huge sweetie jar

at reception, admire the soaring centuries-old
ceiling and chic Moorish-styled lounge, and
congratulate yourself on landing a room at one
of the most beautiful spots in town, practically
on the water. Sea views from many rooms
could not be bolder or more romantic, and the
breakfast terrace is a dream.

Marsala ❺

✕ Quimera — Sandwiches €

(☎349 0765524; www.facebook.com/
quimerapub; Via Sarzana 34-36; sandwiches &
salads from €5; ⏱noon-3pm & 6.30pm-2am
Mon-Sat, 6.30pm-2am Sun) Smack in the heart
of Marsala's pedestrianised centre, this buzzy
eating-drinking hybrid is the local hotspot for
artisanal craft beers, gourmet sandwiches
and meal-sized salads – all served with a big
smile and bags of charm by the friendly young
owners. Linger over a shared cutting board of
cheeses or salami, or agonise over the choice of
creatively filled *panini* and *piadine* (wraps).

Agrigento ❽

✕ Kalòs — Sicilian €€

(☎0922 2 63 89; www.ristorantekalos.it;
Piazzetta San Calogero; meals €35-45; ⏱12.30-
3pm & 7-11pm Tue-Sun) For fine dining, head to
this restaurant just outside the historic centre.
Tables on little balconies offer a delightful
setting to enjoy homemade *pasta all'agrigentina*
(with fresh tomatoes, basil and almonds), grilled
lamb chops or *spada gratinata* (baked swordfish
in breadcrumbs). Superb desserts, including
homemade *cannoli* and almond *semifreddi* (a
light frozen dessert), round out the menu.

🛏 PortAtenea — B&B €

(☎349 0937492; www.portatenea.com;
Via Atenea, cnr Via Cesare Battisti; s/d/
tr €50/70/90; ❀ 🛜) This five-room B&B
wins plaudits for its panoramic roof terrace
overlooking the Valley of the Temples, and its
super-convenient location at the entrance to
the old town. Best of all is the generous advice
about Agrigento offered by hosts Sandra and

Filippo (witness Filippo's amazing Google Earth tour of nearby beaches!).

Modica 🔟

🛏 Masseria Quartarella   Agriturismo €

(📞360 654829; www.quartarella.com; Contrada Quartarella Passo Cane 1; s €40, d €75-80, tr €85-100, q €90-120; 🅿 ❄ 🛜 🛍) Spacious rooms, welcoming hosts and ample breakfasts make this converted farmhouse in the countryside south of Modica an appealing choice for anyone travelling by car. Owners Francesco and Francesca are generous in sharing their love and encyclopaedic knowledge of local history, flora and fauna and can suggest a multitude of driving itineraries in the surrounding area.

Syracuse 12

✖ Il Pesce Azzurro   Seafood €€

(📞366 2445056; Via Cavour 53; meals €30-35; 🕐noon-3.30pm & 6.30-10.30pm) Seafood-loving locals swear by this easy-to-miss *osteria* (casual tavern), its white-and-blue interior somewhat reminiscent of a Greek-island taverna. The menu favours simplicity and top-notch produce, whether it's sweet, succulent Mazara shrimps drizzled in lime juice, plump *vongole* (clams) paired with spaghetti and garlic, or tender *polpo* (octopus) served *alla luciana* (in a rich tomato and onion sauce). Honest, flavour-packed goodness.

🛏 Hotel Gutkowski   Hotel €€

(📞0931 46 58 61; www.guthotel.it; Lungomare Vittorini 26; d €90-150, tr €150, q €160; ❄🛜) Book well in advance for one of the sea-view rooms at this stylish, eclectic hotel on the Ortygia waterfront, at the edge of the Giudecca neighbourhood. Divided between two buildings, its rooms are simple yet chic, with pretty tiled floors, walls in teals, greys, blues and browns, and a sharply curated mix of vintage and industrial details.

Catania 13

✖ Pescheria Fratelli Vittorio   Seafood €€

(📞339 7733890; Via Dusmet 1; meals €25-40; 🕐11.30am-3.30pm & 7pm-midnight Tue-Sun, closed Sun dinner Nov–mid-May) Cats would kill for a table at Fratelli Vittorio, a cult-status eatery whose counter glistens with Catania's freshest fish and seafood. It's not surprising given that co-owner Giovanni is a fishmonger, handpicking the best ingredients from the nearby market. For an overview, order the *degustazione di antipasti del giorno,* or feel the love in the generous *zuppa di pesce* (seafood soup).

Taormina 14

✖ Osteria Nero D'Avola   Sicilian €€

(📞0942 62 88 74; www.facebook.com/osterianerodavola; Piazza San Domenico 2b; meals €40-50; 🕐7-11pm daily mid-Jun–mid-Sep, noon-2.30pm & 7-11pm Tue-Sun rest of year; 🛜) Owner Turi Siligato fishes, hunts and forages for his smart *osteria,* and if he's in, he'll probably share anecdotes about the day's bounty and play a few tunes on the piano. This is one of Taormina's top eateries, where seasonality, local producers and passion underpin outstanding dishes, such as grilled meatballs in lemon leaves, and fresh fish with Sicilian pesto.

🛏 Hotel Villa Belvedere   Hotel €€€

(📞0942 2 37 91; www.villabelvedere.it; Via Bagnoli Croce 79; d €120-680, ste €390-890; 🕐Mar-late Nov; ❄ @ 🛜 🛍) Built in 1902, the distinguished, supremely comfortable Villa Belvedere was one of Taormina's original grand hotels. Well positioned with fabulous views, luxuriant gardens and wonderful service, its highlights include plush, communal lounge areas and a swimming pool complete with a century-old palm. Neutral hues and understated style typify the hotel's 55 rooms, with parking costing an extra €20 per day.

Italian Riviera

Curving west in a broad arc, backed by the Maritime Alps, the Italian Riviera sweeps down from Genoa through ancient hamlets and olive groves to the French border at Ventimiglia.

7

TRIP HIGHLIGHTS

107 km

Alassio
The preferred holiday spot of presidents and artists

0 km

Genoa
For big-city grit and glamour

START

● **Savona**

3

4

● **Cervo**

Taggia

6

Ventimiglia
FINISH

San Remo
Italy's wannabe Monte Carlo

165 km

Finale Ligure
Provides a sandy shore nestled between two rivers

74 km

---

4 DAYS
214KM / 133 MILES

GREAT FOR...

BEST TIME TO GO
April, May and June for flowers and hiking; October for harvest.

ESSENTIAL PHOTO
Cascading terraces of exotic flowers at Giardini Botanici Hanbury.

BEST FINE DINING
Purple San Remo prawns on the terrace of San Giorgio.

Genoa Old-town architecture

7 Italian Riviera

The contrast between sun-washed, sophisticated coastal towns and a deeply rural, mountainous hinterland, full of heritage farms, olive oil producers and wineries, gave rise to the Riviera's 19th-century fame, when European expatriates outnumbered locals. They amused themselves in lavish botanical gardens, gambled in the casino of San Remo and dined in style in fine art-nouveau villas, much as you will on this tour.

❶ Genoa

Like Dr Jekyll and Mr Hyde, Genoa is a city with a split personality. At its centre, medieval *caruggi* (narrow streets) untangle outwards to the **Porto Antico** and teem with hawkers, merchants and office workers. Along Via Garibaldi and Via XXV Aprile is another Genoa, one of Unesco-sponsored palaces, smart shops and grand architectural gestures like **Piazza de Ferrari** with its monumental fountain, art-nouveau **Palazzo**

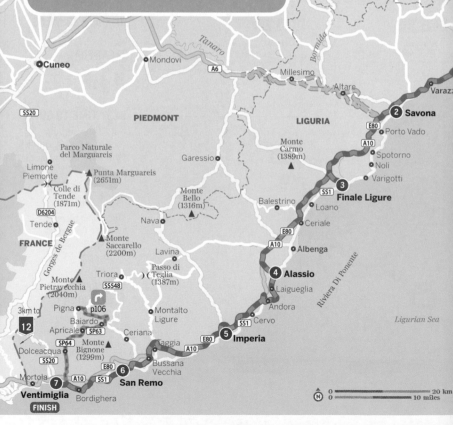

Borsa (once the city's stock exchange) and the neoclassical **Teatro Carlo Felice** (☎010 58 93 29; www.carlofelice.it; Passo Eugenio Montale 4).

Join the well-dressed *haute bourgeoisie* enjoying high-profile art exhibits in the grand Mannerist halls of the **Palazzo Ducale** (www.palazzoducale.genova.it; Piazza Giacomo Matteotti 9; price varies by exhibition; ☺hours vary), then retire to sip a *spritz* amid 17th-century frescoes at **Les Rouges** (☎329 3490644; www.lesrouges.it; 1st fl, Piazza

Golfo di Genova (Gulf of Genoa)

Campetto 8a; ☺6-11.45pm Sun-Thu, to 12.45am Fri & Sat).

 p107

The Drive » Exit Genoa westward, through a tangle of flyovers and tunnels, to access the A10 for the first 56km drive to Savona. Once out of the suburbs the forested slopes of the Maritime Alps rise to your right and sea views peep out from the left as you duck through tunnels.

TRIP HIGHLIGHT

➋ Savona

Don't be put off by Savona's horrifying industrial sprawl; the Savonesi were a powerful maritime people and the town centre is unexpectedly graceful. Standing near the port are three of the many medieval towers that once studded the cityscape. Genoa's greatest rival, the town was savagely sacked in 1528, the castle dismantled and most of the population slaughtered, but somehow the **Fortezza del Priamàr** (www.museoarcheosavona.it; Corso Mazzini 1; ☺9am-6.30pm

mid-Sep–mid-Jun, to midnight mid-Jun–mid-Sep) and the **Cattedrale di Nostra Signora Assunta** (Piazza del Duomo; ☺7.30am-7.30pm) survived.

But you're not here for the architecture – you're here for the food. The covered **market** (Via Pietro Giuria 64r; ☺6.30am-1.30pm Mon-Thu, 6.30am-1.30pm & 4.30-7.30pm Fri & Sat Jun-Oct, shorter hours Nov-May) is crammed with fruit-and-veg stalls and fish stands stacked with salt cod. **Grigiomar** (Via Pietro Giuria 42r; ☺7.15am-1pm Mon-Sat) salts its own local anchovies. Then there are the local specialities like the addictive *farinata di grano* (wheat-flour flat bread) at **Vino e Farinata** (www.vinoefarinata.it; Via Pia 15; meals €18-28; ☺noon-2pm & 6.30-9.30pm Tue-Sat).

The Drive » Rejoin the A10 and leave the industrial chimneys of Savona behind you. For the first 13km the A10 continues with views of the sea, then at Spotorno it ducks inland for the final 15km to the Finale Ligure exit. Descend steeply for 3km to the Finale hamlets on the coast.

 LINK YOUR TRIP

2 **The Graceful Italian Lakes**

Heading north from Genoa you're soon in the land of refreshing lakes and mountains.

12 **Riviera Crossing**

Roll right on into France for more beaches, glam cities and glittering seascapes.

TRIP HIGHLIGHT

③ Finale Ligure

Finale Ligure comprises several seaside districts. The marina is narrow and charming, spreading along the sandy shore between two small rivers, the Porra and the Sciusa. A good place to pick up some picnic fare is **Salumeria Chiesa** (☎019 69 25 16; Via Pertica 15; small plates from €6; ⊙11am-2.30pm & 6-8.30pm May-Oct, closed Sun Nov-Apr), a delicatessen with a huge array of seafood salads, salamis, cheeses and gnocchi with pesto, of course.

Around 1.5km north of the seaside, **Finalborgo** is the old medieval centre. Its cobblestone streets are ripe for exploring, and you can stop for a meal or a pick-me-up at one of many charming restaurants with outdoor tables on the pavement. Each year in March, Finalborgo's cloisters are home to the **Salone dell'Agroalimentare Ligure**, where local farmers hawk seasonal delicacies and vintages.

On Thursday it's worth driving 9km up the coast to picturesque **Noli** for the weekly outdoor market on Corso d'Italia.

✕ ⌂ p107

The Drive » Once again take the high road away from the coast and follow the A10 for a further 35km to Alassio. Near

Albenga you'll cross the river Centa and the broad valley where dozens of hothouses dot the landscape.

TRIP HIGHLIGHT

④ Alassio

Less than 100km from the French border, Alassio's popularity among the 18th- and 19th-century jet set has left it with an elegant colonial character. Its pastel-hued villas range around a broad, sandy beach, which stretches all the way to **Laigueglia** (4km to the south). American president Thomas Jefferson holidayed here in 1787 and Edward Elgar composed *In the South,* inspired by his stay in 1904. **Il Muretto**, a ceramic-covered wall, records the names of 550 celebrities who've passed through.

Follow the local lead and promenade along Via XX Settembre or the unspoilt waterfront. Take coffee at **Antico Caffè Pasticceria Balzola** (www.balzola1902.com; Piazza Matteotti 26; pastries from €1.50; ⊙9am-10pm Tue-Sun) and enjoy gelato on the beach beneath a stripy umbrella.

⌂ p107

The Drive » If you have time take the scenic coast road, SS1 (Via Roma), from Alassio through Laigueglia and Marina di Andora to Imperia. It is a shorter and more scenic jaunt when traffic is light. The

alternative, when traffic is heavy, is to head back to the A10.

⑤ Imperia

Imperia consists of two small seaside towns, Oneglia and Porto Maurizio, on either side of the Impero river.

Oneglia, birthplace of Admiral Doria, the Genoese Republic's greatest naval hero, is the less attractive of the two, although **Piazza Dante**, with its arcaded walkways, is a pleasant place to grab a coffee. This is also where the great olive oil dynasties made their name. Visit the **Museo**

San Remo View over the Mediterranean

dell'Olivo (www.museo dellolivo.com; Via Garessio 13, Imperia; adult/reduced €5/2.50; ⊘9am-12.30pm & 3-6.30pm Mon-Sat), housed in a lovely art-nouveau mansion belonging to the heritage Fratelli Carli factory. The museum is surprisingly extensive and details the history of the Italian Riviera industry from the 2nd century BCE. Buy quality oil here or anywhere in town.

West of Oneglia is pirate haven **Porto Maurizio**, perched on a rocky spur that overlooks a yacht-filled harbour.

The Drive ≫ Rejoining the A10 at Imperia, the landscape begins to change. The olive terraces are dense, spear-like cypresses and umbrella pines shade the hillsides, and the fragrant maquis (Mediterranean scrub) is prolific. Loop inland around Taggia and then descend slowly into San Remo.

SAN GIORGIO

Cult restaurant **San Giorgio** (📞0183 40 01 75; Via A Volta 19, Cervo; meals €45-65; ⊘12.30-2pm & 7.30-10pm Wed-Mon, closed Jan) has been quietly wowing gourmets with its authentic Ligurian cooking since the 1950s when mother-and-son team Caterina and Alessandro opened the doors of their home in the *borgo* (medieval hamlet) of **Cervo Alta**.

Dine out on the bougainvillea-draped terrace in summer, or in intimate dining rooms cluttered with family silverware and antiques in winter. Below the restaurant, in an old oil mill, is the less formal wine bar and deli **San Giorgino**.

105

⑥ San Remo

San Remo, Italy's wannabe Monte Carlo, is a sun-dappled Mediterranean resort with a grand belle-époque **casino** (www.casinosanremo.it; Corso degli Inglesi 18; ☺10am-2.30am Sun-Thu, to 3.30am Fri & Sat) and lashings of Riviera-style grandeur.

During the mid-19th century the city became a magnet for European exiles such as Czar Nicolas of Russia, who favoured the town's balmy winters. They built an onion-domed **Russian Orthodox church** (Via Nuvoloni 2; €1; ☺9.30am-12.30pm & 3-6.30pm) reminiscent of Moscow's St Basil's Cathedral, which still turns heads down by the seafront. Swedish inventor Alfred Nobel also maintained a villa here, the **Villa Nobel** (Corso Felice Cavallotti 112), which now houses a museum dedicated to him.

Beyond the waterfront, San Remo hides a little-visited old town, a labyrinth of twisting lanes that cascade down the Italian Riviera hillside. Curling around the base is the **Italian Cycling Riviera**, a path that tracks the coast as far as Imperia. For bike hire, enquire at the **tourist office** (📞0184 58 05 00; Corso Giuseppe Garibaldi; ☺9.30am-1pm daily, plus 3-6.30pm Tue & Thu-Sat).

✖ 🛏 p107

The Drive » For the final 17km stretch to Ventimiglia take the SS1 coastal road, which hugs the base of the mountains and offers uninterrupted sea views. In summer and at Easter, however, when traffic is heavy, your best bet is the A10.

⑦ Ventimiglia

Despite its enviable position between the glitter of San Remo and the Côte d'Azur, Ventimiglia is a soulful but disorderly border town, its Roman past still evident in its bridges, amphitheatre and ruined baths. Now it's the huge **Friday market** (Lungo Roja Rossi; ☺6am-6pm Fri May-Oct, to 5pm Fri Nov-Apr) that draws the crowds.

If you can't find a souvenir here then consider one of the prized artisanal honeys at **Apicoltura Ballestra** (📞333 7337412; www.mielleriedelaroya.com; Lungo Roja Rossi 5; ☺9am-12.30pm & 3.30-7pm Tue-Sat), which has hives in the hills above the Valle Roya. There are over a dozen different types.

To end the tour head over to the pretty western suburb of Ponte San Ludovico to the **Giardini Botanici Hanbury** (www.giardinihanbury.com; Corso Montecarlo 43, La Mortola; adult/reduced €9/7.50; ☺9.30am-6pm Mar–mid-June, to 7pm mid-Jun–mid-Oct, to 5pm mid-Oct–Feb, closed Mon Nov-Feb), the 18-hectare estate of English businessman Sir Thomas Hanbury; he planted it with an extravagant 5800 botanical species from five continents.

✖ p107

DETOUR: L'ENTROTERRA

Start: ⑦ **Ventimiglia**

The designation 'Riviera' omits the pleated, mountainous interior – *l'entroterra* – that makes up nine-tenths of the Italian Riviera. Harried by invasions, coast-dwellers took to these vertical landscapes over a thousand years ago, hewing their perched villages from the rock face of the Maritime Alps. You'll want to set aside two extra days to drive the coiling roads that rise up from Ventimiglia to **Dolceacqua**, **Apricale** and **Pigna**. If you do make the effort, book into gorgeous boutique hotel **Apricus Locanda** (📞339 6008622; www.apricuslocanda.com; Via IV Novembre 5, Apricale; d from €110; 🅿🐾); it's worth it for the breakfast and see-forever panoramas.

Eating & Sleeping

Genoa ❶

✖ Il Marin — Seafood €€€

(Eataly Genova; ☎010 869 87 22; www.eataly.
net; Porto Antico; meals €50-60, 8-course menu
€75; ☾12.30-3pm & 7.30-10.30pm Wed-Mon)
Eating by the water often means a compromise
in quality, but Eataly's 3rd-floor fine-dining
space delivers both panoramic port views
and Genoa's most innovative seafood menu.
Rustic wooden tables, Renzo Piano–blessed
furniture and an open kitchen make for an easy,
relaxed glamour, while dishes use unusual
Mediterranean-sourced produce and look
gorgeous on the plate. Book ahead.

⌁ Palazzo Grillo — Design Hotel €€

(☎010 247 73 56; www.hotelpalazzogrillo.it;
Piazza delle Vigne 4; d €130-300; ✳🛜) In a
once derelict *palazzo*, Genovese locals Matteo
and Laura have created the extraordinary place
to stay that Genoa has been crying out for.
Stunning public spaces are dotted with spot-on
contemporary design pieces, character-filled
vintage finds and – look in any direction –
original 15th-century frescoes. Rooms are
simple but superstylish with Vitra TVs and high
ceilings.

Finale Ligure ❸

✖ Osteria ai Cuattru Canti — Osteria €€

(☎019 68 05 40; Via Torcelli 22; meals €25-35;
☾noon-2pm & 7.30-10pm Tue-Sun) Simple and
good Ligurian specialities are cooked up at this
rustic place in Finalborgo's historic centre.

⌁ Valleponci — Agriturismo €

(☎329 3154169; www.valleponci.it; Val Ponci 22,
Localita Verzi; d €80-100, apt €165) Only 4km
from the beach, Val Ponce feels deliciously wild,
tucked away in a rugged Ligurian valley. Horses
graze, grapevines bud and the restaurant turns
out fresh Ligurian dishes, with vegetables
and herbs from a kitchen garden. On weekend
evenings and Sunday lunch, there's live music

or classic vinyl. Rooms are simple but show the
keen eye of the Milanese escapee owners.

Alassio ❹

⌁ Villa della Pergola — Boutique Hotel €€€

(☎0182 64 61 30; www.villadellapergola.com;
Via Privata Montagu 9/1, Alassio; d €270-900;
P ✳🛜🏊) Sitting in a tropical garden with
sea views, this luxury hotel was one of the
homes of eminent Victorian, General McMurdo.
Built in 1875, the villa is in the then vogue
Anglo–Indian style with large airy rooms, broad
verandahs and cascading terraces. Some suites
are furnished accordingly, while others take
more contemporary cues.

San Remo ❻

✖ A Cuvèa — Italian €

(Corso Giuseppe Garibaldi 110; meals €15-30;
☾noon-2.45pm & 7.15-9.45pm) This cosy,
warmly lit place lined with wine bottles
overflows with locals tucking into homemade
traditional dishes such as *tagliolini* with seafood
or *zimino di seppie* (cuttlefish stew); it also has
the most genial host in town. The set menus
(€28) are a fabulous deal, available at lunch
and dinner.

Ventimiglia ❼

✖ Pasta & Basta — Ligurian €€

(☎0184 23 08 78; www.pastaebastaventimiglia.
com; Via Marconi 20a; meals €25-40; ☾noon-
3pm & 7.30-10pm Tue-Sun) Near the seafront
on the border side of town (overlooking the
new marina) you'll find elegant Pasta & Basta.
Various house-made fresh pasta can be mixed
and matched with a large menu of sauces,
including a good pesto or *salsa di noci* (walnut
puree), and washed down with a carafe of pale
and refreshing Pigato, a local white.

NEED TO KNOW

Climate

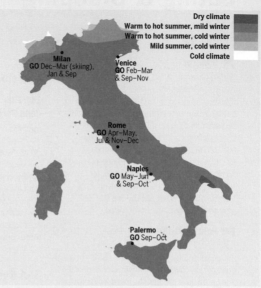

Dry climate
Warm to hot summer, mild winter
Warm to hot summer, cold winter
Mild summer, cold winter
Cold climate

Milan
GO Dec–Mar (skiing), Jan & Sep

Venice
GO Feb–Mar & Sep–Nov

Rome
GO Apr–May, Jul & Nov–Dec

Naples
GO May–Jun & Sep–Oct

Palermo
GO Sep–Oct

When to Go

High Season (Jul & Aug)
» Queues at big sights and on the road, especially in August.

» Prices also rocket for Christmas, New Year and Easter.

» Late December to March is high season in the Alps and Dolomites.

Shoulder (Apr–Jun & Sep–Oct)
» Good deals on accommodation, especially in the south.

» Spring is best for festivals, flowers and local produce.

» Autumn provides warm weather and the grape harvest.

Low Season (Nov–Mar)
» Prices up to 30% lower than in high season.

» Many sights and hotels closed in coastal and mountainous areas.

» A good period for cultural events in large cities.

Your Daily Budget

Budget: Less than €100
» Dorm bed: €20–35

» Double room in a budget hotel: €60–110

» Pizza or pasta: €6–15

Midrange: €100–250
» Double room in a hotel: €110–200

» Local restaurant dinner: €25–45

» Museum admission: €4–18

Top end: More than €250
» Double room in a four- or five-star hotel: €200 plus

» Top restaurant dinner: €45–150

» Opera ticket: €40–210

Eating

Trattoria Informal, family-run restaurant cooking up traditional regional dishes.

Ristorante Formal dining, often with comprehensive wine lists and more sophisticated local or national fare.

Vegetarians Most places offer good vegetable starters and side dishes.

Price ranges indicate the cost of a two-course meal with a glass of house wine and *coperto* (cover charge).

€	< €25
€€	€25–45
€€€	> €45

Sleeping

Hotels From luxury boutique palaces to modest family-run *pensioni* (small hotels).

B&Bs Rooms in restored farmhouses, city townhouses or seaside bungalows.

Agriturismi Farm stays range from working farms to luxury rural retreats.

Room Tax A nightly occupancy tax is charged on top of room rates.

Price ranges indicate the cost of a double room with private bathroom (breakfast included) in high season.

€	< €110
€€	€110–200
€€€	> €200

Arriving in Italy

Rome Fiumicino
Rental cars Agencies are located near the multilevel car park.

Trains €14; run frequently from 6.23am to 11.23pm.

Buses €5.50–7; take an hour and operate at least hourly 24 hours per day.

Taxi Set fare to centre €48; 45 to 60 minutes.

Milan Malpensa
Rental cars Agencies in the Arrivals halls.

Trains €13; every 30 minutes from 5.43am to 10.27pm.

Buses €8; every 30 minutes from 5am to 1.20am.

Taxis Set fare €95; 50 minutes.

Naples Capodichino
Rental cars Contact agencies in the Arrivals hall.

Buses €5; run frequently between 6am and 11.20pm.

Taxis Set fares €18–27; 20 to 35 minutes.

Mobile Phones

Local SIM cards can be used in European, Australian and some unlocked US phones. Other phones must be set to roaming.

Internet Access

Free wi-fi is available in most hotels, hostels, B&Bs and *agriturismi,* and in many bars and cafes.

Money

ATMs are widespread in Italy. Major credit cards are widely accepted, but some smaller shops, trattorias and hotels might not take them.

Tipping

Not common; you may round up the bill or leave a euro or two for excellent service.

Useful Websites

Lonely Planet (lonelyplanet.com/italy) Travel tips, accommodation, recommendations and more.

ENIT (www.italia.it) Official Italian-government tourism website.

Language

Italian sounds can all be found in English. If you read our coloured pronunciation guides as if they were English, you'll be understood. Note that ai is pronounced as in 'aisle', ay as in 'say', ow as in 'how', dz as the 'ds' in 'lids', and that r is strong and rolled. If the consonant is written as a double letter, it's pronounced a little stronger, eg *sonno* son·no (sleep) versus *sono* so·no (I am). The stressed syllables are indicated with italics.

BASICS

Hello.	*Buongiorno.*	bwon·*jor*·no
Goodbye.	*Arrivederci.*	a·ree·ve·*der*·chee
Yes./No.	*Sì./No.*	see/no
Excuse me.	*Mi scusi.*	mee *skoo*·zee
Sorry.	*Mi dispiace.*	mee dees·*pya*·che
Please.	*Per favore.*	per fa·*vo*·re
Thank you.	*Grazie.*	*gra*·tsye

You're welcome.
Prego. — *pre*·go

Do you speak English?
Parli inglese? — *par*·lee een·*gle*·ze

I don't understand.
Non capisco. — non ka·*pee*·sko

How much is this?
Quanto costa questo? — *kwan*·to *kos*·ta *kwe*·sto

ACCOMMODATION

Do you have a room?
Avete una camera? — a·*ve*·te *oo*·na *ka*·me·ra

Want More

For in-depth language information and handy phrases, check out Lonely Planet's *Italian Phrasebook*. You'll find it at **shop.lonelyplanet.com**.

How much is it per night/person?
Quanto costa per una notte/persona? — *kwan*·to *kos*·ta per *oo*·na *no*·te/per·*so*·na

DIRECTIONS

Where's ...?
Dov'è ...? — do·*ve* ...

Can you show me (on the map)?
Può mostrarmi (sulla pianta)? — pwo mos·*trar*·mee (*soo*·la *pyan*·ta)

EATING & DRINKING

What would you recommend?
Cosa mi consiglia? — *ko*·za mee kon·*see*·lya

I'd like ..., please.
Vorrei ..., per favore. — vo·*ray* ... per fa·*vo*·re

I don't eat (meat).
Non mangio (carne). — non *man*·jo (*kar*·ne)

Please bring the bill.
Mi porta il conto, per favore? — mee *por*·ta eel *kon*·to per fa·*vo*·re

EMERGENCIES

Help!
Aiuto! — a·*yoo*·to

I'm lost.
Mi sono perso/a. (m/f) — mee *so*·no per·*so*/a

I'm ill.
Mi sento male. — mee *sen*·to *ma*·le

Call the police!
Chiami la polizia! — *kya*·mee la po·lee·*tsee*·a

Call a doctor!
Chiami un medico! — *kya*·mee oon *me*·dee·ko

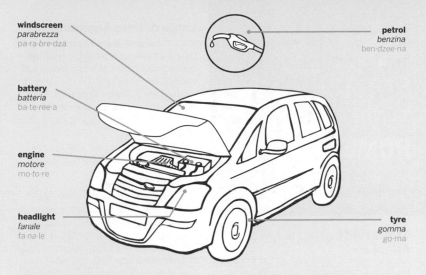

windscreen
parabrezza
pa·ra·*bre*·dza

petrol
benzina
ben·*dzee*·na

battery
batteria
ba·te·*ree*·a

engine
motore
mo·*to*·re

headlight
fanale
fa·*na*·le

tyre
gomma
go·ma

ON THE ROAD

I'd like to hire a/an ...	*Vorrei noleggiare ...*	vo·*ray* no·le·*ja*·re ...
4WD	*un fuoristrada*	oon fwo·ree·*stra*·da
automatic/ manual	*una macchina automatica/ manuale*	oo·na *ma*·kee·na ow·to·*ma*·tee·ka/ ma·noo·a·le
motorbike	*una moto*	oo·na *mo*·to

How much is it ...?	*Quanto costa ...?*	*kwan*·to *kos*·ta ...
daily	*al giorno*	al *jor*·no
weekly	*alla settimana*	a·la se·tee·*ma*·na

Does that include insurance?
E' compresa l'assicurazione?
e kom·*pre*·sa la·see·koo·ra·*tsyo*·ne

Signs

Alt	Stop
Dare la Precedenza	Give Way
Deviazione	Detour
Divieto di Accesso	No Entry
Entrata	Entrance
Pedaggio	Toll
Senso Unico	One Way
Uscita	Exit

Does that include mileage?
E' compreso il chilometraggio?
e kom·*pre*·so eel kee·lo·me·*tra*·jo

What's the city/country speed limit?
Qual'è il limite di velocità in città/campagna?
kwa·le eel *lee*·mee·te dee ve·lo·*chee*·ta een chee·*ta*/kam·*pa*·nya

Is this the road to (Venice)?
Questa strada porta a (Venezia)?
kwe·sta *stra*·da *por*·ta a (ve·*ne*·tsya)

(How long) Can I park here?
(Per quanto tempo) Posso parcheggiare qui?
(per *kwan*·to *tem*·po) *po*·so par·ke·*ja*·re kwee

Where's a service station?
Dov'è una stazione di servizio?
do·ve oo·na sta·*tsyo*·ne dee ser·*vee*·tsyo

Please fill it up.
Il pieno, per favore.
eel *pye*·no per fa·*vo*·re

I'd like (30) litres.
Vorrei (trenta) litri.
vo·*ray* (*tren*·ta) *lee*·tree

Please check the oil/water.
Può controllare l'olio/ l'acqua, per favore?
pwo kon·tro·*la*·re *lo*·lyo/ *la*·kwa per fa·*vo*·re

I need a mechanic.
Ho bisogno di un meccanico.
o bee·*zo*·nyo dee oon me·*ka*·nee·ko

The car/motorbike has broken down.
La macchina/moto si è guastata.
la *ma*·kee·na/*mo*·to see e gwas·*ta*·ta

I had an accident.
Ho avuto un incidente.
o a·*voo*·to oon een·chee·*den*·te

STRETCH YOUR LEGS
ROME

Start/Finish: Largo di Torre Argentina

Distance: 1.7km

Duration: 2 hours

Rome's historic centre, much of which is closed to unauthorised traffic, is best explored on foot. Park near Stazione Termini, then hop on a bus to the *centro* where you'll discover picturesque cobbled lanes, showboating piazzas, basilicas and ancient ruins.

Take this walk on Trips

Largo di Torre Argentina

Start in **Largo di Torre Argentina**, a busy transport hub set around the remains of four temples dating to between the 2nd and 4th centuries BCE. On the square's western flank, **Teatro Argentina**, Rome's premier theatre, stands near the spot where Julius Caesar was assassinated in 44 BCE.

The Walk ≫ From the square, head east along Corso Vittorio Emanuele II to Piazza del Gesù.

Chiesa del Gesù

The landmark **Chiesa del Gesù** (✆06 69 70 01; www.chiesadelgesu.org; Piazza del Gesù; ⊙7am-noon & 4-7.30pm, St Ignatius rooms 4-6pm Mon-Sat, 10am-noon Sun; ◻Largo di Torre Argentina) is Rome's most important Jesuit church. Behind its imposing facade is an awe-inspiring baroque interior. Headline works include a swirling vault fresco by Il Baciccia and Andrea del Pozzo's opulent tomb for Ignatius Loyola, the Jesuits' founder.

The Walk ≫ Cross Corso Vittorio Emanuele II and follow Via del Gesù north. Then turn left onto Via Santa Caterina da Siena.

Basilica di Santa Maria Sopra Minerva

Trumpeted by Bernini's much-loved **Elefantino** statue, this **basilica** (www.santa mariasopraminerva.it; Piazza della Minerva 42; ⊙6.50am-7pm Mon-Fri, 10am-12.30pm & 3.30-7pm Sat, 8am-12.30pm & 3.30-7pm Sun; ◻Largo di Torre Argentina) is Rome's only Gothic church. Little remains of the original 13th-century structure and these days the main drawcard is a minor Michelangelo sculpture and its art-rich interior.

The Walk ≫ From the basilica, it's an easy stroll up Via della Minerva to Piazza della Rotonda.

Pantheon

A 2000-year-old temple, now a church, the **Pantheon** (www.pantheonroma.com; Piazza della Rotonda; ⊙8.30am-7.30pm Mon-Sat, 9am-6pm Sun; ◻Largo di Torre Argentina) is the best preserved of Rome's ancient monuments. Built by Hadrian over Marcus Agrippa's earlier 27 BCE temple,

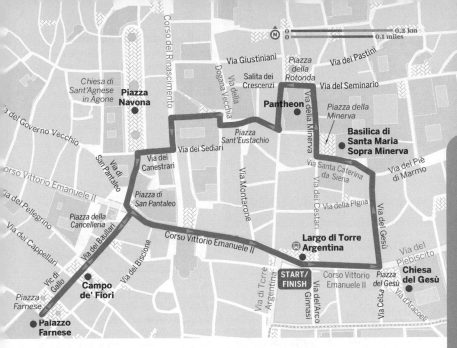

it has stood since around 125 CE. It's an exhilarating experience to go in and gaze up at the largest unreinforced concrete dome ever built.

The Walk » Follow the signs to Piazza Navona, stopping en route for a quick coffee at Caffè Sant'Eustachio.

Piazza Navona

With its showy fountains, baroque *palazzi* (mansions) and colourful cast of street artists, hawkers and tourists, **Piazza Navona** (🚇Corso del Rinascimento) is central Rome's elegant showcase square. Its grand centrepiece is Bernini's **Fontana dei Quattro Fiumi**, a flamboyant fountain featuring personifications of the Nile, Ganges, Danube and Plate rivers.

The Walk » Exit the piazza to the south, cross Corso Vittorio Emanuele II and continue up Via dei Baullari.

Campo de' Fiori

Colourful and always busy, **Il Campo** (🚇Corso Vittorio Emanuele II) is a major

focus of Roman life: by day it hosts one of the city's best-known markets; by night it heaves with tourists and young drinkers. Amid the chaos look out for the sinister statue of philosopher Giordano Bruno who was burned for heresy here in 1600.

The Walk » Head up to Piazza Farnese, a matter of metres away.

Palazzo Farnese

Palazzo Farnese (www.inventerrome.com; Piazza Farnese; tours €9; 🕑guided tours 3pm, 4pm & 5pm Mon, Wed & Fri; 🚇Corso Vittorio Emanuele II) is one of Rome's finest Renaissance buildings. Home to the French Embassy, it can only be visited on a guided tour, but it's worth it to see Annibale Carracci's frescoes that are said by some to rival Michelangelo's in the Sistine Chapel.

The Walk » To get back to Largo di Torre Argentina, double back to Corso Vittorio Emanuele II and head east.

STRETCH YOUR LEGS
FLORENCE

Start/Finish: Galleria dell'Accademia

Distance: 2.5km

Duration: 1 day

To get the best out of Florence (Firenze) park your car at Piazza della Libertà, and head into the city's historic centre on foot. This tour provides a great introduction to the city, passing through its headlining piazzas, basilicas and galleries.

Take this walk on Trips

Galleria dell'Accademia

Before heading into the heart of the historic centre, take time to salute Florence's fabled poster boy. Michelangelo's *David* (1504) stands in all his naked glory in the **Galleria dell'Accademia** (☑055 098 71 00; www.galleriaaccademiafirenze. beniculturali.it; Via Ricasoli 58/60; adult/reduced €12/2; ⊕8.15am-6.50pm Tue-Sun). He originally guarded Palazzo Vecchio but was moved here in 1873.

The Walk ≫ From the gallery, head south along Via Ricasoli, past the Carabé gelateria, down to Via de' Pucci. Turn right, skirting past Palazzo Pucci, as you continue on to Piazza San Lorenzo.

Basilica di San Lorenzo

A fine example of Renaissance architecture, the **Basilica di San Lorenzo** (☑055 21 40 42; www.operamedicealaurenziana.org; Piazza San Lorenzo; €7, with Biblioteca Medicea Laurenziana €9.50; ⊕10am-5.30pm Mon-Sat) is best known for its Brunelleschi-designed **Sagrestia Vecchia** (Old Sacristy). Around the corner, at the rear of the basilica, the **Museo delle Cappelle Medicee** (Medici Chapels; ☑055 064 94 30; www.bargello musei.beniculturali.it/musei/2/medicee; Piazza Madonna degli Aldobrandini 6; adult/reduced €9/2; ⊕8.15am-2pm, closed 2nd & 4th Sun, 1st, 3rd & 5th Mon of month) has some exquisite Michelangelo sculptures.

The Walk ≫ From Piazza Madonna degli Aldobrandini, head down Via de' Conti and its continuation Via F Zanetti to Via de' Cerretani. Hang a left and soon you'll see Piazza del Duomo ahead.

Duomo

Florence's 14th-century **Duomo** (Cattedrale di Santa Maria del Fiore; ☑055 230 28 85; www.museumflorence.com; Piazza del Duomo; ⊕10am-5pm Mon-Wed & Fri, to 4.30pm Thu & Sat, 1.30-4.45pm Sun) is the city's most iconic landmark with its pink, white and green marble facade and red-tiled **dome** (adult/reduced incl baptistry, campanile, crypt & museum €18/3; ⊕8.30am-7pm Mon-Fri, to 5pm Sat, 1-4pm Sun). Nearby, you can climb the **campanile** (⊕8.15am-7pm) and admire the bas-reliefs on the 11th-century **Battistero**

(Baptistry; ⊘8.15-10.15am & 11.15am-7.30pm Mon-Fri, 8.15am-6.30pm Sat, 8.15am-1.30pm Sun).

The Walk » It's a straightforward 400m or so down Via dei Calzaiuoli to Piazza della Signoria.

Piazza della Signoria

This lovely cafe-lined piazza is overlooked by the **Torre d'Arnolfo**, the high point of **Palazzo Vecchio** (⌖055 276 85 58; www.musefirenze.it; Piazza della Signoria; adult/reduced museum €12.50/10, tower €12.50/10, museum & tower €17.50/15, museum & archaeological tour €16/13.50, combination ticket €19.50/17.50; ⊘ museum 9am-11pm Fri-Wed, to 2pm Thu Apr-Sep, 9am-7pm Fri-Wed, to 2pm Thu Oct-Mar, tower 9am-9pm Fri-Wed, to 2pm Thu Apr-Sep, 10am-5pm Fri-Wed, to 2pm Thu Oct-Mar), Florence's medieval City Hall. It still houses the mayor's office but you can visit its lavish apartments.

The Walk » To get to the Galleria degli Uffizi takes a matter of seconds, although we can't vouch for how long it'll take to get inside. The gallery is just off the piazza's southeastern corner, in a grey porticoed palazzo.

Galleria degli Uffizi

The **Galleria degli Uffizi** (Uffizi Gallery; ⌖055 29 48 83; www.uffizi.it; Piazzale degli Uffizi 6; adult/reduced Mar-Oct €20/2, Nov-Feb €12/2; ⊘8.15am-6.50pm Tue-Sun) boasts one of Italy's greatest art collections. The highlight is the stash of Renaissance art, including Botticelli's *La nascita di Venere* (Birth of Venus) and Michelangelo's *Tondo doni* (Holy Family).

The Walk » Pick up Via Lambertesca, over the way from the gallery entrance, and follow it to Via Por Santa Maria. Go left and it's a short hop to the river.

Ponte Vecchio

Florence's celebrated bridge has twinkled with the wares of jewellers since the 16th century. The bridge as it stands was built in 1345 and was the only one in Florence saved from destruction by the retreating Germans in 1944.

The Walk » To get back to the Galleria dell'Accademia, pick up bus C1 from Lungarno Generale Diaz and head up to Piazza San Marco.

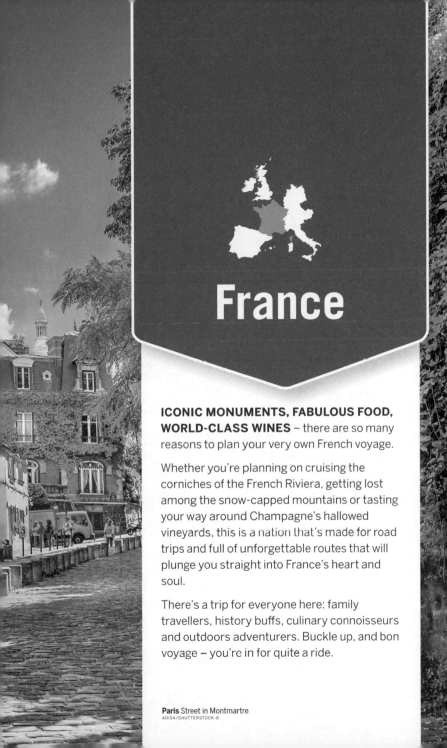

France

ICONIC MONUMENTS, FABULOUS FOOD, WORLD-CLASS WINES – there are so many reasons to plan your very own French voyage.

Whether you're planning on cruising the corniches of the French Riviera, getting lost among the snow-capped mountains or tasting your way around Champagne's hallowed vineyards, this is a nation that's made for road trips and full of unforgettable routes that will plunge you straight into France's heart and soul.

There's a trip for everyone here: family travellers, history buffs, culinary connoisseurs and outdoors adventurers. Buckle up, and bon voyage – you're in for quite a ride.

France

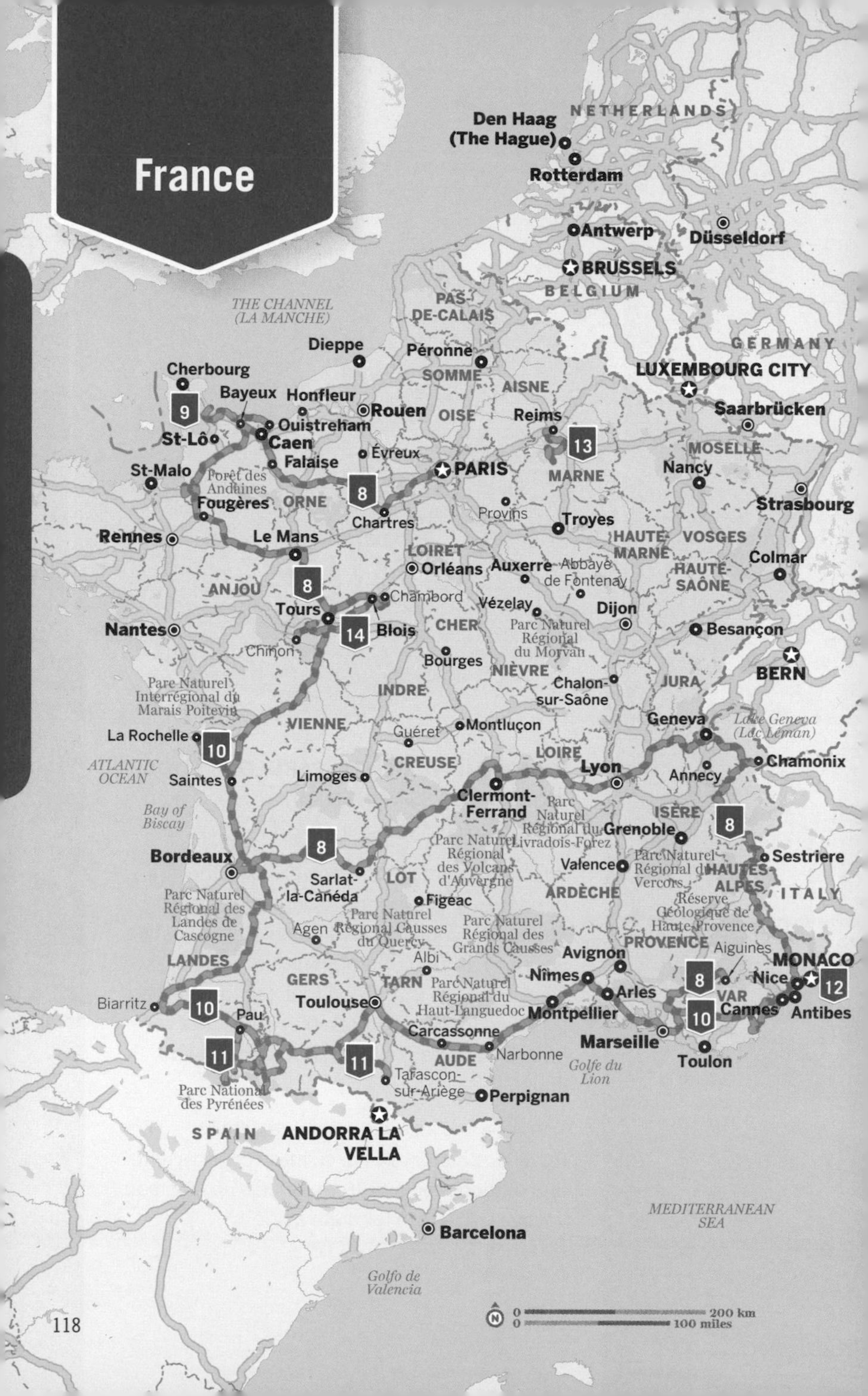

NETHERLANDS
Den Haag (The Hague)
Rotterdam
Antwerp
Düsseldorf
BRUSSELS
BELGIUM
THE CHANNEL (LA MANCHE)
PAS-DE-CALAIS
GERMANY
Dieppe
Péronne
SOMME
LUXEMBOURG CITY
Cherbourg
AISNE
Bayeux
Honfleur
Rouen
OISE
Reims
Saarbrücken
9
Ouistreham
13
St-Lô
Caen
Évreux
MOSELLE
St-Malo
Falaise
PARIS
Nancy
Forêt des Andaines
MARNE
8
Strasbourg
Fougères
ORNE
Provins
Chartres
Troyes
Rennes
Le Mans
HAUTE-MARNE
VOSGES
LOIRET
Colmar
Orléans
Auxerre
Abbaye de Fontenay
HAUTE-SAÔNE
ANJOU
8
Chambord
Vézelay
Dijon
Tours
Nantes
14
Blois
CHER
Parc Naturel Régional du Morvan
Besançon
Chinon
Bourges
BERN
NIÈVRE
Chalon-sur-Saône
JURA
Parc Naturel Interrégional du Marais Poitevin
INDRE
VIENNE
Geneva
Lake Geneva (Lac Léman)
La Rochelle
Guéret
Montluçon
10
LOIRE
Chamonix
ATLANTIC OCEAN
CREUSE
Lyon
Annecy
Saintes
Limoges
Clermont-Ferrand
Parc Naturel Régional du Livradois-Forez
ISÈRE
Bay of Biscay
8
Grenoble
8
Parc Naturel Régional des Volcans d'Auvergne
Bordeaux
Valence
Parc Naturel Régional du Vercors
Sestriere
HAUTES-ALPES
Sarlat-la-Canéda
LOT
Parc Naturel Régional des Landes de Gascogne
ARDÈCHE
ITALY
Figeac
Réserve Géologique de Haute-Provence
Parc Naturel Régional Causses du Quercy
Parc Naturel Régional des Grands Causses
Agen
PROVENCE
Aiguines
Albi
Avignon
MONACO
LANDES
GERS
TARN
Parc Naturel Régional du Haut-Languedoc
Nîmes
8
Nice
12
Arles
VAR
Biarritz
10
Toulouse
Montpellier
Cannes
Antibes
Pau
10
Carcassonne
Marseille
11
11
Narbonne
Toulon
AUDE
Golfe du Lion
Tarascon-sur-Ariège
Parc National des Pyrénées
Perpignan
SPAIN
ANDORRA LA VELLA
MEDITERRANEAN SEA
Barcelona
Golfo de Valencia
0 200 km
0 100 miles

8 **Essential France 21 Days**
This grand tour visits some of France's most unmissable sights.

9 **D-Day's Beaches 3 Days**
Follow the course of the WWII invasion on Normandy's beaches.

10 **Atlantic to Med 10 Days**
The ultimate south-of-France trip, linking two very different seas.

11 **The Pyrenees 7 Days**
Explore the majestic mountain landscape, easily the equal of the Alps.

12 **Riviera Crossing 4 Days**
The best beaches, cities, villages and nature along the Mediterranean coast.

13 **Champage Taster 3 Days**
Taste your way around the cellars of Champagne on this fizz-fuelled trip.

14 **Châteaux of the Loire 5 Days**
France's greatest châteaux, from medieval towers to royal palaces.

 DON'T MISS

Longues-sur-Mer

See where parts of the famous D-Day film, The Longest Day (1962), were filmed on Trip **9**

Chateau de Chambord

The Loire's star expression of Renaissance architecture, capped by its world-famous double-helix staircase. Discover it on Trip **14**

Fenocchio

Enjoy some original flavours at this iconic ice-cream parlour on Trip **12**

Lac de Gaube

One of the Pyrenees' finest trails leads to the glittering Lac de Gaube. Catch the cable car to the trail on Trip **11**

Essential France

City to city, coast to coast, this grand tour visits some of France's most unmissable sights. There's some epic driving involved, but this is one trip you won't forget in a hurry.

8

TRIP HIGHLIGHTS

335 km

Bayeux
Check out the world's longest comic strip

START
⭐ PARIS

Caen

4

2100 km

Chamonix
Savour sky-high views
of Mont Blanc

10

Poitiers

Clermont-
Ferrand

8

FINISH

13

Cannes

1445 km

Sarlat-la-Canéda
Explore the medieval
heart of this gorgeous
Dordogne town

Gorges du Verdon
Experience France's
answer to the
Grand Canyon

3060 km

**3 WEEKS
3060KM / 1902
MILES**

GREAT FOR...

BEST TIME TO GO
April to June for
sunny weather, longer
days and flowers.

 **ESSENTIAL
PHOTO**
Overlooking the
Parisian panorama
from the Basilique du
Sacré-Coeur.

✅ **BEST FOR
FAMILIES**
Braving the space-age
rides and roller-coaster
thrills of Futuroscope.

Essential France

This is the big one – an epic trek that travels all the way from the chilly waters of the English Channel to the gleaming blue Mediterranean. Along the way, you'll stop off at some of France's most iconic sights: the château of Versailles, the abbey of Mont St-Michel, the summit of Mont Blanc and the beaches of the French Riviera. *Allez-y!*

Bayeux
9
4
St-Lô
St-
Brieuc   Mont
St-Michel   5
Falais
A84
Fougères
Rennes   A81
Angers
Nantes
A83
Parc Naturel
Interrégional du
Marais Poitevin
La Rochelle
A10
ATLANTIC
OCEAN
Saint
Bordeaux   7
Parc
Naturel
Régional des
Landes de
Cascogne
Bay of
Biscay
A70
A65
San
Sebastián
Pau

❶ Paris

For that essentially Parisian experience, it's hard to beat Montmartre – the neighbourhood of cobbled lanes and cafe-lined squares beloved by writers and painters since the 19th century. This was once a notoriously ramshackle part of Paris, full of bordellos, brothels, dance halls and bars, as well as the city's first can-can clubs. Though its hedonistic heyday has long since passed, Montmartre still retains a villagey charm, despite the throngs of tourists.

The centre of Montmartre is **place du Tertre**, once the village's main square, now packed with buskers and portrait artists. You can get a sense of how the area would once have looked at the **Musée de Montmartre** (☎01 49 25 89 39; www.museedemontmartre.fr; 12 rue Cortot, 18e; adult/child €13/7, garden only €5; ⊙11am-6pm Wed-Fri, to 7pm Sat & Sun Apr-Sep, to 6pm Wed-Sun Oct-Mar; Ⓜ Lamarck–Caulaincourt), which details the area's bohemian past. It's inside Montmartre's oldest building, a 17th-century manor house once occupied by Renoir and Utrillo.

Nearby, Montmartre's finest view unfolds from the dome of the **Basilique du Sacré-Coeur** (☎01 53 41 89 00; www.sacre-coeur-montmartre.com; Parvis du Sacré-Cœur, 18e; basilica

free, dome adult/child €6/4;
🕑 basilica 6am-10.30pm,
dome 10.30am-8.30pm;
Ⓜ Anvers, Abbesses). On a
clear day, you can see for
up to 30km.

🍴🛏 p130

The Drive » From the centre
of Paris, follow the A13 west
from Porte d'Auteuil and take
the exit marked 'Versailles

**LINK
YOUR
TRIP**

9 **D-Day's Beaches**
Take a side trip
from Caen to follow
the course of the WWII
invasion on Normandy's
beaches.

12 **Riviera Crossing**
Combine this
journey with our jaunt
down the French Riviera,
which begins in Cannes.

Château'. Versailles is 28km southwest of the city.

---

❷ Versailles

Louis XIV transformed his father's hunting lodge into the **Château de Versailles** (☎01 30 83 78 00; www.chateauversailles.fr; place d'Armes; adult/child passport ticket incl estate-wide access €20/free, with musical events €27/free, palace €18/free except during musical events; ⏰9am-6.30pm Tue-Sun Apr-Oct, to 5.30pm Tue-Sun Nov-Mar; Ⓜ RER Versailles-Château–Rive Gauche) in the mid-17th century, and it remains France's most majestic palace. The royal court was based here from 1682 until 1789, when revolutionaries massacred the palace guard and dragged Louis XVI and Marie Antoinette back to Paris, where they were ingloriously guillotined.

The architecture is truly eye-popping. Highlights include the **Grands Appartements du Roi et de la Reine** (State Apartments) and the famous **Galerie des Glaces** (Hall of Mirrors), a 75m-long ballroom filled with chandeliers and floor-to-ceiling mirrors. Outside, the vast park incorporates terraces, flower beds, paths and fountains, as well as the **Grand and Petit Canals**.

Northwest of the main palace is the **Domaine de Trianon** (Trianon Estate; www.chateauversailles.fr; Château de Versailles; adult/child €12/free, with passport ticket free; ⏰noon-6.30pm Tue-Sun Apr-Oct, to 5.30pm Tue-Sat Nov-Mar), where the royal family would have taken refuge from the intrigue and etiquette of court life.

The Drive » The N10 runs southwest from Versailles

VISITING VERSAILLES

Versailles is one of the country's most popular destinations, so planning ahead will make your visit more enjoyable. Avoid the busiest days of Tuesday and Sunday, and remember that the château is closed on Monday. Save time by pre-purchasing tickets on the château's website, or arrive early if you're buying at the door – by noon queues spiral out of control.

You can also access off-limits areas (such as the Private Apartments of Louis XV and Louis XVI, the Opera House and the Royal Chapel) by taking a 90-minute **guided tour** (☎01 30 83 77 88; www.chateauversailles.fr; Château de Versailles; tours €10, plus palace entry).

---

through pleasant countryside and forest to Rambouillet. You'll join the D906 to Chartres. All told, it's a journey of 76km.

---

❸ Chartres

You'll know you're nearing Chartres long before you reach it thanks to the twin spires of the **Cathédrale Notre Dame** (www.cathedrale-chartres.org; place de la Cathédrale; ⏰8.30am-7.30pm daily year-round, also to 10pm Tue, Fri & Sun Jul & Aug), considered to be one of the most important structures in Christendom.

The present cathedral was built during the late 12th century after the original was destroyed by fire. It's survived wars and revolutions remarkably intact, and the brilliant-blue stained-glass windows have even inspired their own shade of paint (Chartres blue). The cathedral also houses the Sainte Voile (Holy Veil), supposedly worn by the Virgin Mary while giving birth to Jesus.

The best views are from the 112m-high **Clocher Neuf** (North Tower; Cathédrale Notre Dame; adult/child €6/free; ⏰10am-12.30pm & 2-6pm Mon-Sat, 2-6pm Sun May-Aug, shorter hours Sep-Apr).

✕ 🛏 p130

The Drive » Follow the D939 northwest for 58km to Verneuil-sur-Avre, then take the D926 west for 78km to Argentan –

both great roads through typical Norman countryside. Just west of Argentan, the D158/N158 heads north to Caen, then turns northwest on the N13 to Bayeux, 94km further.

TRIP HIGHLIGHT

④ Bayeux

The **Bayeux Tapestry** (La Tapisserie de Bayeux; ☎02 31 51 25 50; www.bayeuxmuseum. com; 15bis rue de Nesmond; adult/child €9.50/7.50; ☻9.30am-12.30pm & 2-6pm, closed Jan) is without doubt the world's most celebrated (and ambitious) piece of embroidery. Over 58 panels, the tapestry recounts the invasion of England in 1066 by William I, or William the Conqueror, as he's now known.

Commissioned in 1077 by Bishop Odo of Bayeux, William's half-brother, the tapestry retells the battle in fascinating detail: look out for Norman horses getting stuck in the quicksands around Mont St-Michel, and the famous appearance of Halley's Comet in scene 32. The final showdown at the Battle of Hastings is particularly graphic, complete with severed limbs, decapitated heads, and the English King Harold getting an arrow in the eye.

The Drive » Mont St-Michel is 125km southwest of Bayeux; the fastest route is along the D6 and then the A84 motorway.

----

⑤ Mont St-Michel

You've already seen it on a million postcards, but nothing prepares you for the real **Mont St-Michel** (☎02 33 89 80 00; www. abbaye-mont-saint-michel.fr/ en; adult/child incl guided tour €11/free; ☻9am-7pm May-Aug, 9.30am-6pm Sep-Apr, last entry 1hr before closing). It's one of France's architectural marvels, an 11th-century island abbey marooned in the middle of a vast bay.

When you arrive, you'll be steered into one of the Mont's huge car parks. You then walk along the causeway (or catch a free shuttle bus) to the island itself. Guided tours are included, or you can explore solo with an audioguide.

The **Église Abbatiale** (Abbey Church) is reached via a steep climb along the **Grande Rue**. Around the church, the cluster of buildings known as **La Merveille** (The Marvel) includes the cloister, refectory, guest hall, ambulatory and various chapels.

For a different perspective, take a guided walk across the sands with **Découverte de la Baie du Mont-Saint-Michel** (☎02 33 70 83 49; www.decou vertebaie.com; 1 rue Montoise, Genêts; adult/child from €10/5.50; ☻9am-12.30pm & 1.30-6pm daily Apr-Oct, Mon-Fri Nov-Mar) or **Chemins de la Baie** (☎02 33 89 80 88; www.cheminsdelabaie.com;

34 rue de l'Ortillon, Genêts; adult/child from €9/5), both based in Genêts. Don't be tempted to do it on your own – the bay's tides are notoriously treacherous.

🛏 p130

The Drive » Take the A84, N12 and A81 for 190km to Le Mans and the A28 for 102km to Tours, where you can follow a tour through the Loire Valley if you wish. Chambord is about 75km from Tours via the D952.

----

⑥ Chambord

If you only have time to visit one château in the Loire, you might as well make it the grandest – and **Chambord** (☎info 02 54 50 40 00, tour & show reservations 02 54 50 50 40; www.chambord. org; adult/child €14.50/free, parking distant/near €4/6; ☻9am-6pm Apr-Oct, to 5pm Nov-Mar; 👫) is the most lavish of them all. It's a showpiece of Renaissance architecture, from the double-helix staircase up to the turret-covered rooftop. With 426 rooms, the sheer scale of the place is mindboggling – and in the Loire, that's really saying something. If you have time, detour to the richly furnished and very elegant **Château de Chenonceau** (☎02 47 23 90 07; www.chenonceau. com; adult/child €15/12, with audio guide €19/15.50; ☻9am or 10am-5pm or 6.30pm).

The Drive » It's 425km to Bordeaux via Blois and the A10 motorway. You could

WHY THIS IS A GREAT TRIP
OLIVER BERRY, WRITER

It's epic in every sense: in scale, views, time and geography. This once-in-a-lifetime journey covers France from every possible angle: top to bottom, east to west, city and village, old-fashioned and modern, coast and countryside. It links together many of the country's truly unmissable highlights, and by the end you'll genuinely be able to say you've seen the heart and soul of France.

Above: Mont St-Michel
Left: Gorges du Verdon
Right: Stained glass window, Cathédrale Notre Dame, Chartres

consider breaking the journey with stop-offs at Futuroscope and Poitiers, roughly halfway between the two.

- - - - - - - - - - - - - - - - -

⑦ Bordeaux

When Unesco decided to protect Bordeaux's medieval architecture in 2007, it simply listed half the city in one fell swoop. Covering 18 sq km, this is the world's largest urban World Heritage Site, with grand buildings and architectural treasures galore.

Top of the heap is the **Cathédrale St-André** (📞05 56 44 6/ 29; www.cathedrale-bordeaux.fr; place Pey Berland; treasury adult/child €2/free, ⏰2-7pm Mon, 10am-noon & 2-6pm Tue-Sat, 9.30am-noon & 2-6pm Sun, treasury 2.30-5.30pm Wed, Sat & Sun), known for its stone carvings and generously gargoyled belfry, the **Tour Pey Berland** (📞05 56 81 26 25; www.pey-berland.fr; place Pey Berland; adult/child €6/free; ⏰10am-6pm Jun-Sep, 10am-12.30pm & 2-5.30pm Oct-May). But the whole old city rewards wandering, especially around the **Jardin Public** (cours de Verdun; ⏰7am-8pm Jul & Aug, shorter hours rest of year), the pretty squares of **esplanade des Quinconces** and **place Gambetta**, and the city's 4km-long **riverfront esplanade**, with its playgrounds, paths and paddling pools. There's also the superb **La Cité du Vin** (📞05 56 16 20 20; www.laciteduvin.com; 134

quai de Bacalan; adult/child €20/9, priority access €25/14; ⏱10am-7pm May–Aug, shorter hours rest of year), a must see for wine-lovers.

✕ 🛏 p130

The Drive » It's a 194km drive to Sarlat-la-Canéda via the A89 motorway, or you can take a longer but more enjoyable route via the D936.

TRIP HIGHLIGHT

⑧ Sarlat-la-Canéda

If you're looking for France's heart and soul, you'll find it among the forests and fields of the Dordogne. It's the stuff of French fantasies: river-bank châteaux, medieval villages, wooden-hulled *gabarres* (flat-bottomed barges) and market stalls groaning with truffles, walnuts and wines. The town of Sarlat-la-Canéda makes the perfect base, with a beautiful medieval centre and lots of lively markets.

It's also ideally placed for exploring the Vézère Valley, about 20km to the northwest, home to France's finest cave paintings. Most famous of all are the ones at the **Grotte de Lascaux**, although to prevent damage to the paintings, you now visit a replica of the cave's main sections in a nearby **grotto** (International Centre for Cave Art; 📞05 53 50 99 10; www.lascaux. fr; Montignac; adult/child €20/12.90; ⏱8.30am-6pm Jul & Aug, 9am-5pm Apr–Jun, Sep & Oct, 10am-4pm Nov–Mar, closed Jan).

The Drive » The drive east to Lyon is a long one, covering well over 400km and travelling across the spine of the Massif Central. A good route is to follow the A89 all the way to exit 6, then turn off onto the N89/D89 to Lyon. This route should cover between 420km and 430km.

⑨ Lyon

Fired up by French food? Then you'll love Lyon, with its *bouchons* (small bistros), bustling markets and fascinating food culture. Start in **Vieux Lyon** and the picturesque quarter of **Presqu'île**, then catch the funicular to the top of **Fourvière** to explore the city's Roman ruins and enjoy cross-town views.

Film buffs will also want to make time for the **Musée Lumière** (📞04 78 78 18 95; www.institut-lumiere.org; 25 rue du Premier Film, 8e; adult/child €8.50/free; ⏱10am-6.30pm Tue–Sun; Ⓜ Monplaisir-Lumière), where the Lumière Brothers (Auguste and Louis) shot the first reels of the world's first motion picture, *La Sortie des Usines Lumières,* on 19 March 1895.

✕ 🛏 p131

The Drive » Take the A42 towards Lake Geneva, then the A40 towards St-Gervais-les-Bains. The motorway becomes the N205 as it nears Chamonix. It's a drive of at least 225km.

TRIP HIGHLIGHT

⑩ Chamonix

Snuggling among snow-clad mountains – including Europe's highest summit, Mont Blanc – adrenaline-fuelled Chamonix is an ideal springboard for the French Alps. In winter, it's a mecca for skiers and snowboarders, and in

FUTUROSCOPE

Halfway between Chambord and Bordeaux on the A10, 10km north of Poitiers, **Futuroscope** (📞05 49 49 11 12; www.futuroscope.com; av René Monory, Chasseneuil-du-Poitou; day/evening ticket valid from 5pm €46/20; ⏱10am-11.15pm Jun–mid-Jul, 9.30am-11pm mid-Jul–early Aug, 8.30am-10.45pm Aug, shorter hours rest of year, closed Jan–mid-Feb; 🅿🛗) is one of France's top theme parks. It's a futuristic experience that takes you whizzing through space, diving into the ocean depths, racing around city streets and on a close encounter with creatures of the future. Note that many rides have a minimum height of 120cm.

You'll need at least five hours to check out the major attractions, or two days to see everything. The park is in the suburb of Jaunay-Clan; take exit 28 off the A10.

summer, once the snows thaw, the high-level trails become a trekkers' paradise.

There are two really essential Chamonix experiences. First, catch the dizzying cable car to the top of the **Aiguille du Midi** to snap a shot of Mont Blanc.

Then take the combination mountain train and cable car from the **Gare du Montenvers** ([📞]04 50 53 22 75; www. montblancnaturalresort.com; 35 place de la Mer de Glace; adult/child return €34/28.90; [🕙]10am–4pm late Dec–mid-Mar, to 5pm mid-Mar–Apr) to the **Mer de Glace** (Sea of Ice), France's largest glacier. Wrap up warmly if you want to visit the glacier's sculptures and ice caves.

The Drive » The drive to the Riviera is full of scenic thrills. An attractive route is via the D1212 to Albertville, and then via the A43, which travels over the Italian border and through the Tunnel de Fréjus. From here, the N94 runs through Briançon, and a combination of the A51, N85 and D6085 carries you south to Nice. You'll cover at least 430km.

⓫ French Riviera

If there's one coast road in France you simply have to drive, it's the French Riviera, with its rocky cliffs, maquis-

scented air and dazzling Mediterranean views. Sun-seekers have been flocking here since the 19th century, and its scenery still never fails to seduce.

Lively **Nice** and cinematic **Cannes** make natural starts, but for the Riviera's loveliest scenery, you'll want to drive down the gorgeous **Corniche de l'Estérel** to **St-Tropez**, still a watchword for seaside glamour. Crowds can make summer hellish, but come in spring or autumn and you'll have its winding lanes and fragrant hills practically to yourself. For maximum views, stick to the coast roads: the D6098 to Antibes and Cannes, the D559 around the Corniche de l'Estérel, and the D98A to St-Tropez. It's about 120km via this route.

The Drive » From St-Tropez, take the fast A8 for about 125km west to Aix-en-Provence.

⓬ Aix-en-Provence

Sleepy Provence sums up the essence of *la douce vie* (the sweet life). Cloaked in lavender and spotted with hilltop villages, it's a region that sums up everything that's good about France.

Cruising the back roads and browsing the

markets are the best ways to get acquainted with the region. Artistic Aix-en-Provence encapsulates the classic Provençal vibe, with its pastel buildings and Cézanne connections, while **Mont Ste-Victoire**, to the east, makes for a superb outing.

[✕][🏠] p131

The Drive » The gorges are 140km northeast of Aix-en-Provence, via the A51 and D952.

TRIP HIGHLIGHT

⓭ Gorges du Verdon

Complete your cross-France adventure with an unforgettable expedition to the Gorges du Verdon – sometimes known as the Grand Canyon of Europe. This deep ravine slashes 25km through the plateaux of Haute-Provence; in places, its walls rise to a dizzying 700m, twice the height of the Eiffel Tower (321m).

The two main jumping-off points are the villages of **Moustiers Ste-Marie**, in the west, and **Castellane**, in the east. Drivers and bikers can take in the canyon panorama from two vertigo-inducing cliffside roads, but the base of the gorge is only accessible on foot or by raft.

Eating & Sleeping

Paris ❶

✖ Holybelly — International €

(www.holybellycafe.com; 5 & 19 rue Lucien Sampaix, 10e; dishes €6-16.50; ⏰9am-5pm; 🛜📶; Ⓜ Jacques Bonsergent) Friendly vibes, sassy breakfast 'n' lunch dishes and specialist coffee define this duo. Holybelly at No 5 cooks all-day pancakes and eggs, while the Holybelly original at No 19 serves more creative, seasonal dishes to share. Last orders 4pm. No reservations.

🛏 Hôtel Amour — Design Hotel €€

(📞01 48 78 31 80; www.hotelamourparis.fr; 8 rue de Navarin, 9e; d from €165; 🛜; Ⓜ St-Georges, Pigalle) The inimitable black-clad Amour ('Love') in south Pigalle plays on its long-ago incarnation as a brothel, featuring a soft pink facade and nude artwork (some more explicit than others) in each of its 24 rooms. (No TVs, but that's not the point here.) The beloved ground-floor bistro–bar – open until 2am – has a leafy summer patio garden.

Chartres ❸

✖ Le Tripot — Bistro €€

(📞02 37 36 60 11; www.letripot.wixsite.com/chartres; 11 place Jean Moulin; 2-/3-course lunch menus €16/19, dinner menus €28-38, mains €22; ⏰noon-1.45pm & 7.30-9.15pm Wed-Sat, noon-1.45pm Sun) Tucked off the tourist trail and easy to miss even if you do chance down its narrow street, this atmospheric space with low-beamed ceilings is a treat for authentic and adventurous French fare like saddle of rabbit stuffed with snails or grilled turbot in truffled hollandaise sauce. Locals are on to it, so booking ahead is advised.

🛏 Le Grand Monarque — Hotel €€

(📞02 37 18 15 15; www.bw-grand-monarque.com; 22 place des Épars; d from €120; ❇🛜) With teal-blue shutters gracing its 1779 façade, a lovely stained-glass ceiling and a treasure trove of period furnishings, old B&W photos and knick-knacks, the epicentral Grand Monarque is a historical gem. Some rooms have

air-conditioning; staff are charming. A host of hydrotherapy treatments are available at its spa. Its elegant restaurant, **Georges** (📞02 37 18 15 15; www.bw-grand-monarque.com; 22 place des Épars; menus €59-103; ⏰noon-1pm & 7.30-9.30pm Tue-Sat), has a Michelin star. Family rooms have sofa beds; cots and babysitting services are available.

Mont St-Michel ❺

🛏 Vent des Grèves — B&B €

(📞Estelle 02 33 48 28 89; www.ventdesgreves.com; 27 rte de la Côte, Ardevon; s/d from €50/60; 🛜) Offering outstanding value, this friendly, family-run B&B has five modern, simply furnished rooms with magical views of the Mont. It's located an easily walkable 1km east of the shuttle stop in La Caserne. Breakfast is included in rates.

Bordeaux ❼

✖ Au Bistrot — French €€

(📞06 63 54 21 14; www.facebook.com/aubistrotbordeaux; 61 place des Capucins; mains €16-26; ⏰noon-2.30pm & 7-11pm Wed-Sun) There's nothing flashy or fancy about this hardcore French bistro, an ode to traditional market cuisine with charismatic François front of house and talented French-Thai chef Jacques In'On in the kitchen. Marinated herrings, lentil salad topped with a poached egg, half a roast pigeon or a feisty *andouillette* (tripe sausage) roasted in the oven are some of the dishes on offer – 80% of produce is local or from the surrounding Aquitaine region.

🛏 Mama Shelter — Design Hotel €€

(📞05 57 30 45 45; www.mamashelter.com/en/bordeaux; 19 rue Poquelin Molière; d €89-199; ❇@🛜) With personalised iMacs, video booths and free movies in every room, Mama Shelter is up-to-the-minute. White rooms are small, medium or large; XL doubles have a sofa bed. The joyous ground-floor restaurant sports the same signature rubber rings strung above the bar as other Philippe Starck–designed hotels. Summertime drinks and dinner are served on the sensational rooftop terrace. Weekends usher concerts, gigs and other cultural happenings onto the small stage. Should you be wondering why on earth the strange tower is protruding from the hotel building, know that Mama Shelter squats inside the city's landmark Gas Tower building, designed by Modernist architects in 1927.

Lyon ❾

✖ Le Poêlon d'Or   Bouchon €

(☏04 78 37 65 60; www.lepoelondor-restaurant. fr; 29 rue des Remparts d'Ainay, 2e; menus €18-35; ⏱noon-2pm & 7-9.30pm Mon-Fri; Ⓜ Ampère-Victor Hugo) This upmarket *bouchon*, around the corner from the Musée des Tissus, is well known among local foodies, who recommend its superb *andouillette* (sausages made from pigs' intestines) and pike dumplings. Save room for the delicious chocolate mousse.

🛏 Mob Hotel   Boutique Hotel €€

(☏04 58 55 55 88; www.mobhotel.com; 55 quai Rambaud, 2e; d from €75; Ⓟ 🛜; 🚋T1) The Mob Hotel is a magnet for designers and the creative set. Metal lacework encases the avant-garde building overlooking the Saône, while the inside is a playful mixture of polished concrete, pale blond woods, artful lighting and subtle pastels. Book a Master Mob room for a balcony and ample space.

The 1st-floor terrace is the place to be on warm days, and the restaurant serves excellent pizzas made from organic, locally sourced ingredients. Regular events include yoga and Pilates classes, as well as DJ-fuelled parties on weekends.

Aix-en-Provence

✖ Le Petit Verdot   Provencal €€

(☏04 42 27 30 12; www.lepetitverdot.fr; 7 rue d'Entrecasteaux; mains €20-25; ⏱7pm-midnight Mon-Sat) It's all about hearty, honest dining here, with tabletops made out of old wine crates, and a lively chef-patron who runs the place with huge enthusiasm, happily showing how good Provençal food and wine can be. Expect dishes such as *onglet* (skirt steak) in green-pepper sauce or Pata Negra pork with mustard and honey, accompanied by great wines and seasonal veggies.

🛏 Villa Gallici   Historic Hotel €€€

(☏04 42 23 29 23; www.villagallici.com; 18 av de la Violette; r from €315, Ⓟ ❄ 🛜 🏊) Baroque and beautiful, this fabulous villa was built as a private residence in the 18th century and still feels marvellously opulent. Rooms are more like museum pieces, stuffed with gilded mirrors, toile de Jouy wallpaper and filigreed furniture. It has a lovely lavender-filled garden to breakfast in, plus a pool, a superb restaurant and a wine cellar.

D-Day's Beaches

9

Explore the events of D-Day, when Allied troops stormed ashore to liberate Europe from Nazi occupation. From war museums to landing beaches, it's a fascinating and sobering experience.

88 km

Omaha Beach
Pay your respects at the American Cemetery & Memorial

Utah Beach
FINISH

8

7

Carentan

Isigny-sur-Mer

Sully

1

START

Pointe du Hoc
Wander amongst shell craters that haven't changed since D-Day

98 km

Caen
Visit an award-winning multimedia D-Day museum

0 km

**3 DAYS
142KM / 88 MILES**

GREAT FOR...

BEST TIME TO GO
April to July, to avoid summer-holiday traffic around the beaches.

ESSENTIAL PHOTO
The forest of white marble crosses at the Normandy American Cemetery & Memorial.

BEST FOR HISTORY
The Caen-Normandie Mémorial provides you with a comprehensive D-Day overview.

9 D-Day's Beaches

The beaches and bluffs are quiet today, but on 6 June 1944 the Normandy shoreline witnessed the arrival of the largest armada the world has ever seen. This patch of the French coast will forever be synonymous with D-Day (known to the French as Jour-J), and the coastline is strewn with memorials, museums and cemeteries – reminders that though victory was won on the Longest Day, it came at a high price.

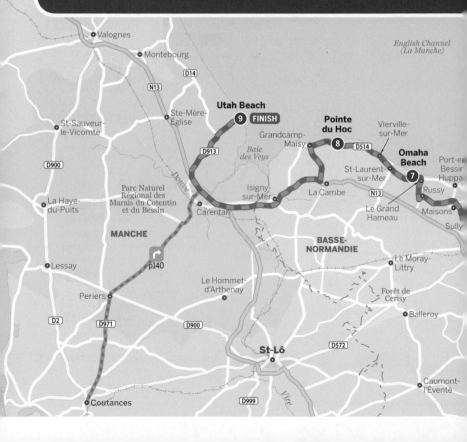

❶ Caen

Situated 3km north-west of Caen, the award-winning **Caen-Normandie Mémorial** (☎02 31 06 06 44; www.memorial-caen.fr; esplanade Général Eisenhower; adult/child pass €14.50/free; ☉9am-7pm daily Apr-Sep, 9.30am-6pm daily Oct, 9.30am-5pm Sat & Sun Nov-Mar) is a brilliant place to begin with some background on the historic events of D-Day and the wider context of WWII. Housed in a purpose-designed building covering 14,000 sq metres, the memorial offers an immersive experience, using sound, lighting, film, animation and audio testimony to evoke the grim realities of war, the trials of occupation and the joy of liberation.

The visit begins with a whistle-stop overview of Europe's descent into total war, tracing events from the end of WWI through to the rise of fascism in Europe, the German occupation of France and the Battle of Normandy. A second section focuses on the Cold War. There's also the well-preserved original bunker used by German command in 1944.

On your way around, look out for a Hawker Typhoon fighter plane and a full-size Sherman tank.

✕ 🛏 p141

The Drive » From the museum, head northeast along Esplanade Brillaud de Laujardière, and follow signs to Ouistreham. You'll join the E46 ring road; follow it to exit 3a (Porte d'Angleterre), and merge onto the D515 and D84 to Ouistreham. Park on the seafront on bd Aristide Briand. In all it's a trip of 18km.

❷ Ouistreham

On D-Day, the sandy seafront around Ouistreham was code-named **Sword Beach** and was the focus of attack for the British 3rd Infantry Division.

S LINK YOUR TRIP

8 Essential France
The island abbey of Mont St-Michel is about 140km from the Normandy coastline, about two hours' drive via the A84 motorway.

13 Champagne Taster
For a change in focus head east, about four hours from Caen, to the cellars of Épernay for a fizz-fuelled tour.

135

There are precious few reminders of the battle now, but on D-Day the scene was very different: most of the surrounding buildings had been levelled by artillery fire, and German bunkers and artillery positions were strung out along the seafront. Sword Beach was the site of some of the most famous images of D-Day – including the infamous ones of British troops landing with bicycles, and bagpiper Bill Millin piping troops ashore while under heavy fire.

The Drive » Follow the seafront west onto rue de Lion, following signs for 'Overlord –

L'Assaut' onto the D514 towards Courseulles-sur-Mer, 18km west. Drive through town onto rue de Ver, and follow signs to 'Centre Juno Beach'.

----

❸ Juno & Gold Beaches

On D-Day, Courseulles-sur-Mer was known as Juno Beach, and was stormed mainly by Canadian troops. It was here that the exiled French General Charles de Gaulle came ashore after the landings – the first 'official' French soldier to set foot in mainland Europe since 1940. He was followed by Winston Churchill on 12 June and King George VI on 16 June. A Cross of Lorraine marks the historic spot.

The area's only Canadian museum, the **Juno Beach Centre** (☎02 31 37 32 17; www.junobeach. org; voie des Français Libres, Courseulles-sur-Mer; museum adult/child €7/6, incl park €12/10; ☉9.30am-7pm Jul & Aug, 10am-6pm Apr-Jun, Sep & Oct, 10am-5pm Nov, Dec, Feb & Mar, closed Jan) has exhibits on Canada's role in the war effort and the landings, and offers guided tours of Juno Beach, including the bunker there, from April to October.

A short way west is Gold Beach, attacked by the British 50th Infantry on D-Day.

The Drive » Drive west along the D514 for 14km to Arromanches. You'll pass a car park and viewpoint marked with a statue of the Virgin Mary, which overlooks Port Winston and Gold Beach. Follow the road into town and signs to Musée du Débarquement.

----

❹ Arromanches

This seaside town was the site of one of the great logistical achievements of D-Day. In order to unload the vast quantities of cargo needed by the invasion forces without capturing one of the heavily defended Channel ports, the Allies set up prefabricated marinas off two landing beaches, code named **Mulberry Harbour**. These consisted of 146 massive

D-DAY IN FIGURES

Code named 'Operation Overlord', the D-Day landings were the largest military operation in history. On the morning of 6 June 1944, swarms of landing craft – part of an armada of over 6000 ships and 13,000 aeroplanes – hit the northern Normandy beaches, and tens of thousands of soldiers from the USA, the UK, Canada and elsewhere began pouring onto French soil. The initial landing force involved some 45,000 troops; 15 more divisions were to follow once successful beachheads had been established.

The majority of the 135,000 Allied troops stormed ashore along 80km of beaches north of Bayeux code named (from west to east) Utah, Omaha, Gold, Juno and Sword. The landings were followed by the 76-day Battle of Normandy, during which the Allies suffered 210,000 casualties, including 37,000 troops killed. German casualties are believed to have been around 200,000; another 200,000 German soldiers were taken prisoner. About 14,000 French civilians also died.

For more background and statistics, see www. normandie44lamemoire.com, www.dday.org and www.6juin1944.com.

cement caissons towed over from England and sunk to form a semi-circular breakwater in which floating bridge spans were moored. In the three months after D-Day, the Mulberries facilitated the unloading of a mind-boggling 2.5 million men, four million tonnes of equipment and 500,000 vehicles.

At low tide, the stanchions of one of these artificial quays, **Port Winston** (named after Winston Churchill), can still be seen on the sands at Arromanches.

Beside the beach, the **Musée du Débarquement** (Landing Museum; 📞02 31 22 34 31; www.musee-arromanches.fr; place du 6 Juin; adult/child €8/6; ⊙9am-7pm Jul & Aug, 10am-12.30pm & 1.30-5pm Sep-Nov & Feb-Jun) explains the logistics and importance of Port Winston; the museum was expanded and renovated for the 75th anniversary of D-Day in 2019.

The Drive ≫ Continue west along the D514 for 6km to the village of Longues-sur-Mer. You'll see the sign for the Batterie de Longues on your right.

---

⑤ Longues-sur-Mer

At Longues-sur-Mer you can get a glimpse of the awesome firepower available to the German defenders in the shape of a row of 150mm artillery guns, still housed in their concrete casements. On

D-DAY DRIVING ROUTES

There are several signposted driving routes around the main battle sites – look for signs for 'D-Day-Le Choc' in the American sectors and 'Overlord – L'Assaut' in the British and Canadian sectors. A free booklet called *The D-Day Landings and the Battle of Normandy,* available from tourist offices, has details on the main routes.

Maps of the D-Day beaches are widely available in the region.

D-Day they were capable of hitting targets over 20km away – including Gold Beach (to the east) and Omaha Beach (to the west). Parts of the classic D-Day film *The Longest Day* (1962) were filmed here.

The Drive ≫ Backtrack to the crossroads and head straight over onto the D104, signed to Vaux-sur-Aure/Bayeux, for 8km. When you reach town, turn right onto the D613, and follow signs to the 'Musée de la Bataille de Normandie'.

---

⑥ Bayeux

Though best known for its medieval tapestry, Bayeux has another claim to fame: it was the first town to be liberated after D-Day (on the morning of 7 June 1944).

It's also home to the largest of Normandy's 18 Commonwealth military cemeteries – the **Bayeux War Cemetery** (www.cwgc.org; 1945 bd Fabien Ware; ⊙24hr), situated on bd Fabien Ware. It contains 4848 graves of soldiers from the UK and 10 other

countries – including Germany. Across the road is a memorial for 1807 Commonwealth soldiers whose remains were never found. The Latin inscription reads: 'We, whom William once conquered, have now set free the conqueror's native land'.

Nearby, the **Musée Mémorial de la Bataille de Normandie** (Battle of Normandy Memorial Museum; 📞02 31 51 46 90; www.bayeuxmuseum.com; bd Fabien Ware; adult/child €7.50/5; ⊙9.30am-12.30pm & 2-6pm, closed Jan) explores the battle through photos, personal accounts, dioramas and film.

🍴 🛏 p141

The Drive ≫ After overnighting in Bayeux, head northwest of town on the D6 towards Port-en-Bessin-Huppain. You'll reach a supermarket after about 10km. Go round the roundabout and turn onto the D514 for another 8km. You'll see signs to the 'Cimetière Americain' near the hamlet of Le Bray. Omaha Beach is another 4km further on, near Vierville-sur-Mer.

JACKTHEFLIPPER/GETTY IMAGES ©

FRANCK LEGROS/SHUTTERSTOCK ©

ICI LE 6 JUIN 1944
L'HEROISME DES
FORCES ALLIÉES
LIBERA L'EUROPE

HERE, ON THE 6* JUNE 1944
EUROPE WAS LIBERATED
BY THE HEROISM
OF THE ALLIED FORCES

WHY THIS IS A GREAT TRIP
OLIVER BERRY, WRITER

You'll have heard the D-Day story many times before, but there's nothing quite like standing on the beaches where this epic struggle played out. D-Day marked the turning point of WWII and heralded the end for Nazism in Europe. Paying your respects to the soldiers who laid down their lives in the name of freedom is an experience that will stay with you forever.

Above: Utah Beach
Left: Juno Beach
Right: Pointe du Hoc

LIONEL LOURDEL/GETTY IMAGES ©

TRIP HIGHLIGHT

➐ Omaha Beach

If anywhere symbolises the courage and sacrifice of D-Day, it's Omaha – still known as 'Bloody Omaha' to US veterans. It was here, on the 7km stretch of coastline between Vierville-sur-Mer, St-Laurent-sur-Mer and Colleville-sur-Mer, that the most brutal fighting on D-Day took place. US troops had to fight their way across the beach towards the heavily defended cliffs, exposed to underwater obstacles, hidden minefields and withering crossfire. The toll was heavy: of the 2500 casualties at Omaha on D-Day, more than 1000 were killed, most within the first hour of the landings.

High on the bluffs above Omaha, the **Normandy American Cemetery & Memorial** (☏02 31 51 62 00; www.abmc.gov; Colleville-sur-Mer; ⏱9am-6pm Apr-Sep, to 5pm Oct-Mar) provides a sobering reminder of the human cost of the battle. Featured in the opening scenes of *Saving Private Ryan*, this is the largest American cemetery in Europe, containing the graves of 9387 American soldiers, and a memorial to 1557 comrades 'known only unto God'.

Start off in the very thoughtfully designed visitor centre, which

139

has moving portrayals of some of the soldiers buried here. Afterwards, take in the expanse of white marble crosses and Stars of David that stretch off in seemingly endless rows, surrounded by an immaculately tended expanse of lawn.

The Drive » From the Vierville-sur-Mer seafront, follow the rural D514 through quiet countryside towards Grandcamp-Maisy. After about 10km you'll see signs to 'Pointe du Hoc'.

TRIP HIGHLIGHT

8 Pointe du Hoc

West of Omaha, this craggy promontory was the site of D-Day's most audacious military exploit. At 7.10am, 225 US Army Rangers commanded by Lt Col James Earl Rudder scaled the sheer 30m cliffs, where the Germans had stationed a battery of artillery guns trained onto the beaches of Utah and Omaha. Unfortunately, the guns had already been moved inland, and Rudder and his men spent the next two days repelling counterattacks. By the time they were finally relieved on 8 June, 81 of the rangers had been killed and 58 more had been wounded.

Today the **Pointe du Hoc Ranger Memorial**

DETOUR: COUTANCES

Start: 9 Utah Beach

The lovely old Norman town of Coutances makes a good detour when travelling between the D-Day beaches and Mont St-Michel. At the town's heart is its Gothic **Cathédrale Notre-Dame de Coutances** (📞02 33 45 00 41; http://cathedralecoutances.free.fr; parvis Notre-Dame; 🕐8am-7pm Nov-Mar, to 6pm Apr-Oct). Interior highlights include several 13th-century windows, a 14th-century fresco of St Michael skewering the dragon, and an organ and high altar from the mid-1700s. You can climb the lantern tower on a tour (adult/child €8/4).

Coutances is 50km south of Utah Beach by the most direct route via the D913 and D971.

(📞02 31 51 62 00; www.abmc. gov; 🕐9am-6pm Apr-Sep, to 5pm Oct-Mar), which France turned over to the US government in 1979, looks much as it did on D-Day, complete with shell craters and crumbling gun emplacements.

The Drive » Stay on the D514 to Grandcamp-Maisy, then continue south onto the D13. Stay on the road till you reach the turn-off for the D913, signed to St-Marie-du-Mont/Utah Beach. It's a drive of 44km.

9 Utah Beach

The D-Day tour ends at Ste-Marie-du-Mont, aka Utah Beach, assaulted by soldiers of the US 4th and 8th Infantry Divisions.

The beach was relatively lightly defended, and by midday the landing force had linked with the paratroopers from the 101st Airborne. By nightfall, some 20,000 men and 1700 vehicles had arrived on French soil, and the road to European liberation had begun.

Today the site is marked by military memorials and the **Musée du Débarquement** (Utah Beach Landing Museum; 📞02 33 71 53 35; www.utah-beach. com; Plage de la Madeleine, Ste-Marie-du-Mont; adult/child €8/5; 🕐9.30am-7pm Jun-Sep, 10am-6pm Oct-May, closed Jan), a modern and impressive museum just inland from the beach.

Eating & Sleeping

Caen ①

✖ À Contre Sens   French €€

(☎02 31 97 44 48; www.acontresens.fr; 8-10 rue des Croisiers; mains €21-44, menus from €44; ☺7.30-9.15pm Tue, noon-1.15pm & 7.30-9.15pm Wed-Sat) À Contre Sens' stylish interior and serene atmosphere belie the hotbed of creativity to be found in the kitchen. Under the direction of chef Anthony Caillot, meals are thoughtfully crafted and superbly presented. Expect dishes such as seaweed risotto with apple and coriander or veal rubbed with herbs, endive and ham.

✖ Café Mancel   French €€

(☎02 31 86 63 64; www.cafemancel.com; Château de Caen; menus €18-25; ☺9am-9.30pm Tue-Sat, to 2pm Sun) In the same building as the **Musée des Beaux-Arts** within the Château de Caen, this stylish place serves up delicious, traditional French cuisine – everything from pan-fried Norman-style beefsteak to hearty Caen style *tripes*, delivered by attentive staff. There's a lovely sun terrace, which also makes a fine spot for a drink outside of busy meal times. After your meal, enjoy a walk along the ramparts of the castle.

🛏 Hôtel des Quatrans   Hotel €

(☎02 31 86 25 57; www.hotel-des-quatrans.com; 17 rue Gémare; r from €80; ☻) This typically modern hotel has an excellent central location, with 47 comfy, unfussy rooms in white and chocolate. The breakfast buffet can be enjoyed in the brightly coloured cafe or you can retreat to your room.

Bayeux ⑥

✖ L'Alchimie   French €€

(☎02 14 08 03 97; 49 rue St-Jean; menus €13-25; ☺noon-1.30pm & 7-9pm Mon-Wed, Fri & Sat) On a street lined with restaurants, L'Alchimie

has a simple but elegant design, with beautifully presented dishes. Choose from the day's specials listed on a chalkboard menu, which might include hits such as *brandade de morue* (baked codfish pie) or *pastilla de poulet au gingembre et cumin* (chicken pastilla with ginger and cumin). Book ahead.

✖ Au Ptit Bistrot   French €€

(☎02 31 92 30 08; www.facebook.com/auptitbistrot; 31 rue Larcher; lunch menus €18-21, dinner menus €32-36, mains €19-28; ☺noon-1.30pm & 7-9pm Tue-Sat) Near the cathedral, this friendly, welcoming eatery whips up creative dishes that highlight the Norman bounty without pretension. Recent popular dishes include braised beef cheek with red wine, polenta, grapefruit tapenade and vegetables, or roast pigeon with mushrooms and mashed parsnip. The kids' menu is €12. Reservations essential.

🛏 Logis Les Remparts   B&B €

(☎02 31 92 50 40; www.lecornu.fr; 4 rue Bourbesneur; r from €75; ☻) The three rooms of this delightful and well-managed *maison de famille* ooze old-fashioned cosiness. Our favourite, the Bajocasse, has parquet flooring, a canopy bed and Toile de Jouy wallpaper. The largest room is the Bourbesneur suite at 430 sq ft. The large shop downstairs is the perfect place to stock up on top-quality, homemade cider and *calvados* (apple brandy).

🛏 Villa Lara   Boutique Hotel €€€

(☎02 31 92 00 55; www.hotel-villalara.com; 6 place du Québec; r from €200; P ❋ ☻) This modern and luxurious 28-room hotel combines an appealing blend of minimalist colour schemes, top-quality fabrics and decor juxtaposing 18th- and 21st-century tastes. Amenities include a bar, a gym and a comfortable library-lounge with a fireplace. Most rooms have cathedral views and are well equipped and tastefully decorated, with attractive bathrooms.

Atlantic to Med

10

Atlantic ports, pristine mountain vistas, the bouquet of fine wine, reminders of Rome and Hollywood glam: this sea-to-sea trip takes you through the best of southern France.

TRIP HIGHLIGHTS

0 km

La Rochelle
Made for waterfront mooching, lunching and sunset drinks

1 START

175 km

St-Émilion
Wine tasting and shopping for some of the world's finest drops

2 St-Émilion

FINISH
Nice

Montpellier

Bayonne

6

8

Narbonne

Carcassonne
Walk the ramparts of France's most magnificent fortress city

863 km

Marseille
Visit MuCEM, icon of modern Marseille, with stunning views to boot

1158 km

**10 DAYS
1498KM / 931
MILES**

GREAT FOR...

BEST TIME TO GO

Spring or autumn, for warm weather sans the crowds.

 ESSENTIAL PHOTO

Pose like a film star on the steps of Cannes's Palais des Festivals et des Congrès.

 BEST FOR FAMILIES

La Rochelle, with child-friendly attractions and boats.

10 | Atlantic to Med

In May the film starlets of the world pour into Cannes to celebrate a year of movie-making. Let them have their moment of glam – by the time you've finished scaling Pyrenean highs, chewing Basque tapas, acting like a medieval knight in a turreted castle and riding to the moon in a spaceship, you too will have the makings of a prize-winning film.

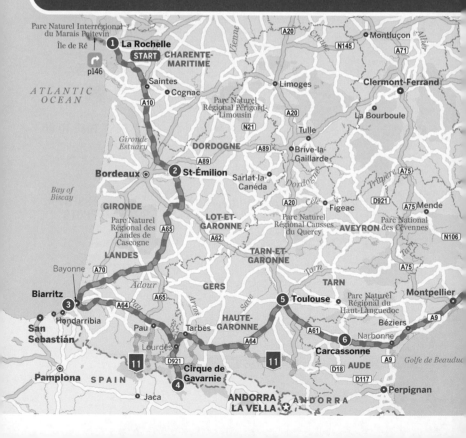

TRIP HIGHLIGHT

❶ La Rochelle

Known as La Ville Blanche (the White City), La Rochelle is home to luminous limestone façades, arcaded walkways, half-timbered houses and gargoyles glowing in the coastal sunlight. A prominent French seaport from the 14th to the 17th centuries, it remains one of France's most attractive seafaring cities.

There are several defensive towers around the **Vieux Port** (Old Port), including the lacy **Tour de la Lanterne** (www.tours -la-rochelle.fr; rue sur les Murs; 3 towers adult/child €9.50/ free; ◷10am-6.30pm Jul & Aug, 10am-1pm & 2.15-6.30pm Apr, Jun & Sep, 10am-1pm & 2.15-5.30pm Oct-Mar), that once served to protect the town at night in times of war. Scale their sturdy stone heights for fabulous city and coastal views.

La Rochelle's number-one tourist attraction is its state-of-the-art **aquarium** (☎05 46 34 00 00; www.aquarium-larochelle.com; quai Louis Prunier; adult/child €16.50/12, online €14.50/10; ◷9am-11pm Jul & Aug, to 8pm Apr-Jun & Sep, 10am-8pm Oct-Mar). Equally fun for families is the **Musée Maritime** (Maritime Museum; ☎05 46 28 03 00; www.mu seemaritimelarochelle.fr; place Bernard Moitessier; adult/child €9/6.50; ◷10am-6.30pm Apr-Oct, 2-5.30pm Mon-Fri, 10am-5.30pm Sat & Sun Nov-Mar), with its fleet of boats to explore; and a trip out to sea with **Croisières Inter-Îles** (☎08 25 13 55 00; www.inter-iles.com; cours des Dames) to admire the unusual iceberg of an island fortress, Fort Boyard.

🛏 p151

The Drive » Using the main A10 toll road it's 187km (about 2½ hours) to St-Émilion. Turn off the A10 at exit 39a, signed for Libourne. Skirt this industrial town and follow the D243 into St-Émilion.

LINK YOUR TRIP

11 **The Pyrenees**
Take a side trip east or west from the A64 to further explore this majestic mountain landscape.

12 **Riviera Crossing**
Starting in Nice, this drive takes you through the glitzy, glam French Riviera.

❷ St-Émilion

Built of soft honey-coloured rock, medieval St-Émilion produces some of the world's finest red wines. Visiting this pretty town, and partaking in some of the tours and activities on offer, is the easiest way to get under the (grape) skin of Bordeaux wine production. The **Maison du Vin de St-Émilion** (☎05 57 55 50 55; www.maisonduvinsaint emilion.com; place Pierre Meyrat; ⏱9.30am-6.30pm May-Oct, 9.30am-12.30pm & 2-6pm Nov-Apr) runs wine-tasting classes and has a superb exhibition covering wine essentials.

Guided tours of the town (adult/child from €9/free) and surrounding châteaux are run by the **tourist office** (☎05 57 55 28 28; www.saint-emilion-tour isme.com; place des Créneaux; ⏱9.30am-7.30pm Jul & Aug, shorter hours rest of year); reserve ahead in season. Several tours include tastings and vineyard visits.

✖ p151

The Drive » Leave St-Émilion on the D243 to Libourne, cross the town, then pick up the D1089 signposted 'Agen, Bergerac, Bordeaux'. Continue on the N89 towards Bordeaux until you see signs for the A630 toll road – at which point sit back and hit cruise control for the remaining 226km to Biarritz. Count 240km and about 2½ hours in all.

❸ Biarritz

This coastal town is as ritzy as its name makes out. Biarritz boomed as a resort in the mid-19th century due to the regular visits by Napoléon III and his Spanish-born wife, Eugénie. Along its rocky coastline are architectural hallmarks of this golden age, and the Belle-Époque and art-deco eras that followed.

Biarritz is all about its fashionable beaches, especially the central **Grande Plage** and **Plage**

DETOUR: ILE DE RE

Start: ❶ La Rochelle

Bathed in the southern sun, drenched in a languid atmosphere and scattered with villages of green-shuttered, whitewashed buildings with red Spanish-tile roofs, Île de Ré is one of the most delightful places on the west coast of France. The island spans just 30km from its most easterly and westerly points, and just 5km at its widest section. But take note: the secret's out and in high season it can be almost impossible to move around and even harder to find a place to stay.

On the northern coast, about 12km from the toll bridge that links the island to La Rochelle, is the quaint fishing port of **St-Martin-de-Ré**, the island's main town. Surrounded by 17th-century fortifications (you can stroll along most of the ramparts) constructed by Vauban, the port town is a mesh of streets filled with craft shops, art galleries and sea-spray ocean views.

The island's best beaches are along the southern edge – including unofficial naturist beaches at **Rivedoux Plage** and **La Couarde-sur-Mer** – and around the western tip (northeast and southeast of Phare-des-Baleines). Many beaches are bordered by dunes that have been fenced off to protect the vegetation.

From La Rochelle it's 24km and a half-hour drive to St-Martin-de-Ré via the toll bridge **Pont de l'Île de Ré** (www.pont-ile-de-re.com; return ticket €16 mid-June to mid-September, €8 rest of the year).

Miramar. In the heat of summer you'll find them packed end to end with sun-loving bathers.

The Drive » It's 208km (2¾ hours) to the village of Gavarnie. Take the A63 and A64 toll roads to exit 11, then the D940 to Lourdes (worth a look for its religious Disneyland feel). Continue south along the D913 and D921.

- - - - - - - - - - - - - - - -

❹ Cirque de Gavarnie

The Pyrenees doesn't lack impressive scenery, but your first sight of the Cirque de Gavarnie is guaranteed to raise a gasp. This breathtaking mountain amphitheatre is one of the region's most famous sights, sliced by thunderous waterfalls and ringed by sawtooth peaks, many of which top out at over 3000m.

There are a couple of large car parks in the village of Gavarnie, from where it's about a two-hour walk to the amphitheatre. Wear proper shoes, as snow lingers along the trail into early summer.

The Drive » Retrace your steps to Lourdes, then take the N21 towards Tarbes and veer onto the A64 to reach Toulouse. It takes nearly three hours to cover the 228km.

- - - - - - - - - - - - - - - -

❺ Toulouse

The vibrant southern city of Toulouse is dubbed 'La Ville Rose',

a reference to the distinctive blushing-pink brickwork of its classic architecture. Its city centre is tough to navigate by car, but there's a paying car park right beneath Toulouse's magnificent central square, **place du Capitole**, the city's literal and metaphorical heart. South of the square, walk the tangle of lanes in the historic **Vieux Quartier** (Old Town). Then, of course, there are the soothing twists and turns of the nearby Garonne River and mighty Canal du Midi – laced with footpaths to stretch your legs.

Having a car is handy for visiting two out-of-town sights celebrating modern Toulouse's role as an aerospace hub: the gigantic museum of Airbus, **Aeroscopia** (📞05 34 39 42 00; www.musee-aeroscopia.fr; allée André Turcat; adult/child €14/11; ⊘9.30am-6pm, closed early Jan; P; 🚋T1 to Beauzelle), just north of the airport; and, across town, **Cite de l'Espace** (📞05 67 22 23 24; www.cite-espace.com; av Jean Gonord; adult €21-26, child €16-19.50; ⊘10am-7pm daily Jul & Aug, to 5pm or 6pm rest of year, closed Mon in Feb, Mar & Sep-Dec, closed Jan; P 🚻), which brings this interstellar industry vividly to life through a shuttle simulator, a planetarium, a 3D cinema, a simulated observatory and so on. Both have free parking.

✕ 🍴 p151

The Drive » It's an easy 95km (one hour) down the fast A61 to Carcassonne. Notice how the vegetation becomes suddenly much more Mediterranean about 15 minutes out of Toulouse.

- - - - - - - - - - - - - - - -

TRIP HIGHLIGHT

❻ Carcassonne

Perched on a rocky hilltop and bristling with zigzagging battlements, stout walls and spiky turrets, from afar the fortified city of Carcassonne is most people's perfect idea of a medieval castle. Four million tourists a year stream through its city gates to explore La Cité, visit its **keep** (www.remparts-carcassonne.fr; 1 rue Viollet le Duc, Cité Médiévale; adult/child €9.50/free; ⊘10am-6.30pm Apr-Sep, 9.30am-5pm Oct-Mar) and ogle at stunning views along the city's ancient ramparts.

The Drive » Continue down the A61 to the Catalan-flavoured town of Narbonne, where you join the A9 (very busy in summer) and head east to Nîmes. From there the A54 will take you into Arles. Allow just over two hours to cover the 223km and expect lots of toll booths.

- - - - - - - - - - - - - - - -

❼ Arles

Arles' poster boy is the celebrated impressionist painter Vincent van Gogh. If you're familiar with his work, you'll be familiar with Arles:

WHY THIS IS A GREAT TRIP
NICOLA WILLIAMS, WRITER

I simply cannot resist the big blue or fine wine, so this tasty seafaring trip is right up my alley. Feasting on fresh oysters on the seashore aside, I strongly advise a long lazy lunch at La Terrasse Rouge (p151) near St-Émilion. This spectacular vineyard restaurant was borne out of Jean Nouvel's designer revamp of Château La Dominique's wine cellars: dining on its uber-chic terrace overlooking a field of dark-red glass pebbles is the ultimate French road-trip reward.

Above: Les Arènes, Arles
Left: Cirque de Gavarnie
Right: Wine, St-Émilion

the light, the colours, the landmarks and the atmosphere, all faithfully captured. But long before Van Gogh rendered this grand Rhône River locale on canvas, the Romans valued its worth. Today it's the reminders of Rome that are probably the town's most memorable attractions. At **Les Arènes** (Amphithéâtre; ☎08 91 70 03 70; www.arenes-arles. com; Rond-Point des Arènes; adult/child incl Théâtre Antique €9/free; ⊙9am-8pm Jul & Aug, to 7pm May, Jun & Sep, shorter hours Oct-Apr) slaves, criminals and wild animals (including giraffes) met their dramatic demise before a jubilant 20,000-strong crowd during Roman gladiatorial displays.

🛏 p151

The Drive » From Arles take the scenic N568 and A55 route into Marseille. It's 88km (an hour's drive) away.

- - - - - - - - - - - - - -

TRIP HIGHLIGHT

⑧ Marseille

With its history, fusion of cultures, *souq*-like markets, millennia-old port and *corniches* (coastal roads) along rocky inlets and sun-baked beaches, Marseille is a captivating and exotic city. Ships have docked for more than 26 centuries at the colourful **Vieux Port** (Old Port) and it remains a thriving harbour. Guarding the harbour are **Bas Fort St-Nicolas** and

DETOUR: AIX-EN-PROVENCE

Start: 7 Arles

Aix-en-Provence is to Provence what the Left Bank is to Paris: an enclave of bourgeois-bohemian chic. Art, culture and architecture abound here. A stroller's paradise, the highlight is the mostly pedestrian old city, **Vieil Aix**. South of cours Mirabeau, **Quartier Mazarin** was laid out in the 17th century, and is home to some of Aix's finest buildings. Central Place des Quatre Dauphins, with its fish-spouting fountain (1667), is particularly enchanting. Further south locals play *pétanque* beneath plane trees in peaceful **Parc Jourdan** (av Anatole France; ☉9am-sunset). From Arles it's a 77km (one-hour) drive down the A54 toll road to Aix-en-Provence. To rejoin the main route take the A51 and A7 for 32km (30 minutes) to Marseille.

Fort St-Jean, founded in the 13th century by the Knights Hospitaller of St John of Jerusalem. A vertigo-inducing footbridge links the latter with the stunning **Musée des Civilisations de l'Europe et de la Méditerranée** (MuCEM, Museum of European & Mediterranean Civilisations; ☎04 84 35 13 13; www.mucem.org; 7 promenade Robert Laffont; adult/child incl exhibitions €11/free; ☉11am-6pm Nov-Apr, to 7pm May, Jun & Oct, 10am-8pm Jul-Sep, closed Tue year-round; ⚅; Ⓜ Vieux Port, Joliette), the icon of modern Marseille.

From the Vieux Port, hike up to the fantastic history-woven quarter of **Le Panier**, a mishmash of steep lanes hiding *ateliers* (workshops) and terraced houses strung with drying washing.

The Drive » To get from Marseille to Cannes, take the northbound A52 and join the A8 toll road just east of Aix-en-Provence. It's 181km and takes just under two hours.

----

9 Cannes

The eponymous film festival only lasts for two weeks in May, but thanks to regular visits from celebrities the buzz and glitz are in Cannes year-round. The imposing Palais des Festivals et des Congrès (p165) is the centre of the glamour. Climb the red carpet, walk down the auditorium, tread the stage and learn about cinema's most prestigious event on a 1½-hour guided tour run by the **tourist office** (☎info 08 26 50 05 00, tour booking 04 91 13 89 16; www.marseille-tourisme.com; 11 La Canebière; ☉10am-5pm; Ⓜ Vieux Port).

The Drive » Leave the motorways behind and weave along the D6007 to Nice, taking in cliffs framing turquoise Mediterranean waters and the yachties' town of Antibes. It's 31km and, on a good day, takes 45 minutes.

----

10 Nice

You don't need to be a painter or an artist to appreciate the extraordinary light in Nice. Matisse, Chagall et al spent years lapping up the city's startling luminosity, and for most visitors to Nice, it is this magical light that seduces. The city has several world-class sights, but the star attraction is the seafront **Promenade des Anglais**. Stroll and watch the world go by.

🍴 🛏 p151, p172

Eating & Sleeping

La Rochelle ❶

🛏 La Fabrique   Design Hotel €€

(📞05 46 41 45 00; www.hotellafabrique.com; 7-11 rue de la Fabrique; d €58-160; 🏵@🛜) At home in a former rope factory, design-driven La Fabrique sports 58 rooms arranged in a quad, above a vast open-plan lounge with Chesterfield sofas and an aerial art installation. Serene, almost-all-white rooms enjoy walk-in Italian showers, and summertime breakfasts (€12) are served on a peaceful patio.

St-Émilion ❷

✖ La Terrasse Rouge   French €€

(📞05 57 24 47 05; www.laterrasserouge.com; 1 Château La Dominique; 3-course menu €39, mains €21-32; ⏱noon-2.30pm Sun & Mon, noon-2.30pm & 7.30-9.30pm Thu-Sat; 🅿🛜♿) Foodies in the know adore this spectacular vineyard restaurant, born out of Jean Nouvel's designer revamp of Château La Dominique's wine cellars, 5km north of St-Émilion. Chefs work with small local producers to source the seasonal produce used in their creative cuisine. Oysters are fresh from Cap Ferret, caviar comes from Neuvic in the Dordogne, and the wine list is naturally extraordinary.

Toulouse ❺

✖ Une Table à Deux   French €€

(📞06 50 06 00 34; www.unetableadeux.fr; 10 rue de la Pléau; lunch/dinner menus from €17/35; ⏱noon-1.30pm & 7.30-9.30pm Mon-Fri, closed lunch Wed) It takes some searching to find this exciting little gem, whose talented, well-travelled chefs turn super-fresh locally sourced produce into short but wonderfully inspired, regularly changing menus. Veggie option usually available.

🛏 Villa du Taur   Boutique Hotel €€

(📞05 34 25 28 82; www.villadutaur.com; 62 rue du Taur; d €89-159; 🅿🏵🛜) This hip yet super-friendly hotel has stylishly comfortable guest rooms that double as mini galleries, with the artworks available for sale – even the Banksy vinyls. Showers are fashioned like luxury cages and you get an in-room Illy coffee maker.

Arles ❼

🛏 Le Cloître   Design Hotel €€

(📞04 88 09 10 00; www.hotelducloitre.com; 18 rue du Cloître; r €185; 🏵@🛜) The traditional Mediterranean courtyard that greets you on arrival at 'The Cloister' is charming enough, but doesn't betray the inventiveness of the warm, colourful design within. Le Cloître's 19 rooms are all distinct, with Italian showers and unusual furniture that sacrifices no comfort. There's a panoramic rooftop terrace and excellent meals are available from the neighbouring Épicerie du Cloître.

Nice ❿

✖ Bar des Oiseaux   French €€

(📞04 93 80 27 33; 5 rue St-Vincent; 3-course lunch menu €20, dinner menus from €30; ⏱10am-10pm Tue-Sat) Hidden down a narrow backstreet, this old-town classic has been in business since 1961, serving as a popular nightclub before reincarnating itself as a restaurant (some of its original saucy murals have survived the transition). Nowadays it's a lively bistro serving superb traditional French cuisine spiced up with modern twists. The weekday lunch special offers phenomenal value. Book ahead.

🛏 Hôtel Villa Rivoli   Boutique Hotel €€

(📞04 93 88 80 25; www.villa-rivoli.com; 10 rue de Rivoli; d €89-215; 🏵🛜; 🚌7, 9, 22, 27, 59, 70 to Rivoli) This charming but strangely shaped villa dates back to 1890, and it's packed with period detail – gilded mirrors, fireplaces, cast-iron balconies and old-world wallpapers, as well as little conifer trees on the balconies and a sweeping marble staircase. Rooms are on the small side, with the least expensive on the ground floor, and service is excellent. There's a small garden and a car park beside the hotel.

The Pyrenees

Traversing hair-raising roads, sky-top passes and snow-dusted peaks, this roller coaster of a trip ventures deep into the sublime beauty of the Pyrenees mountains.

11

TRIP HIGHLIGHTS

277 km

Cauterets
Hit the trails at this chic and historic ski resort

522 km

Tarascon-sur-Ariège
See prehistoric art in a Pyrenean cavern

START
Oloron Ste-Marie ● Pau

6 **7**

2

St-Girons ● Foix

9

FINISH

Vallée d'Aspe
Escape the outside world in this wonderfully rural valley

80 km

Col du Tourmalet
Marvel at the mountain panorama from the Pic du Midi

322 km

**7 DAYS
522KM / 324 MILES**

GREAT FOR...

BEST TIME TO GO
June to September, when roads are snow-free. October for fiery autumn colours.

ESSENTIAL PHOTO
Posing in the imposing Cirque de Gavarnie.

BEST FOR OUTDOORS
Hiking to the Lac de Gaube or Refuge Wallon near Cauterets.

Cauterets Lac de Gaube

11 The Pyrenees

They might not have the altitude of the Alps, but what the Pyrenees do have is an unsurpassed beauty. The mountains are laced through with deep, green valleys punctuated by pretty stone villages. The lower slopes glow red and orange in autumn, thanks to vast beech forests, and higher up lies a wilderness of snow-dusted peaks and glittering lakes. With every valley and massif offering something new it's a thrilling region to travel through and even the most hardened driver will feel the urge to get out of the car and take to a hiking trail.

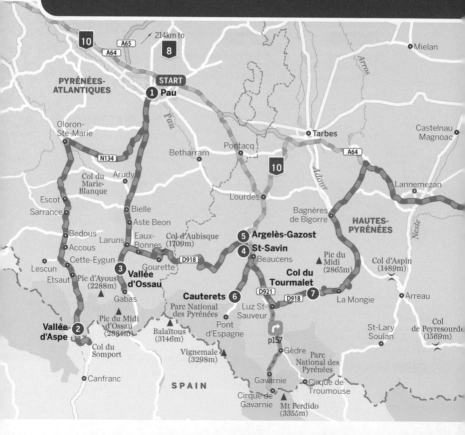

❶ Pau

Palm trees might seem out of place in this mountainous region, but Pau (rhymes with 'so') has long been famed for its mild climate. In the 19th century this elegant town was a favourite wintering spot for the wealthy, and their legacy is visible in the town's grand villas and smart promenades.

Its main sight is the **Château de Pau** (📞05 59 82 38 00; www.chateau-pau.fr; 2 rue du Château; adult/child €7/free; ⏰9.30am-12.15pm & 1.30-5.45pm, gardens open longer hours), built by the monarchs of Navarre and transformed into a Renaissance château in the 16th century. It's home to a fine collection of Gobelins tapestries and Sèvres porcelain.

Pau's tiny old centre extends for around 500m around the château, and boasts many attractive medieval and Renaissance buildings.

Central street parking in Pau is mostly *payant*

🔗 LINK YOUR TRIP

8 Atlantic to Med
From Foix, head just over an hour northeast to Carcassone and then east for the balmy Med or west for the slower paced Atlantic coast.

10 Essential France
From Foix, it's four hours' drive east to Aix-en-Provence, where you can commence the grand tour of France in reverse.

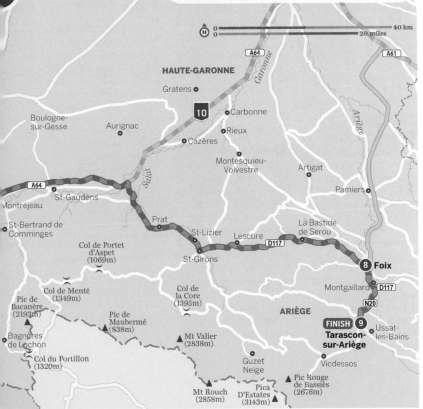

THE TRANSHUMANCE

If you're travelling through the Pyrenees between late May and early June and find yourself stuck behind a cattle-shaped traffic jam, there's a good chance you may have just got caught up in the Transhumance, in which shepherds move their flocks from their winter pastures up to the high, grassy uplands.

This ancient custom has been a fixture on the Pyrenean calendar for centuries, and several valleys host festivals to mark the occasion. The spectacle is repeated in October, when the flocks are brought back down before the winter snows set in.

(chargeable), though there's limited free parking at the central Stadium de la Gare.

✗ 🛏 p161

The Drive ≫ To reach the Vallée d'Aspe from Pau, take the N193 to Oloron-Ste-Marie. The first 30km are uneventful, but over the next 40km south of Oloron the mountain scenery unfolds in dramatic fashion, with towering peaks stacking up on either side of the road.

TRIP HIGHLIGHT

❷ Vallée d'Aspe

The westernmost of the Pyrenean valleys makes a great day trip from Pau. Framed by mountains and bisected by the Aspe River, it's awash with classic Pyrenean scenery. Allow yourself plenty of time for photo stops, especially around pretty villages such as **Sarrance**, **Borcé** and **Etsaut**.

Near the quiet village of **Bedous**, it's worth detouring up the narrow road to **Lescun**, a

tiny hamlet perched 5.5km above the valley, overlooking the peak of **Pic d'Anie** (2504m) and the **Cirque de Lescun**, a jagged ridge of mountain peaks that close out the head of the valley.

The return drive to Pau is just over 80km.

The Drive ≫ To reach the Vallée d'Ossau from Pau, take the N134 south of town, veering south onto the D934 towards Arudy/Laruns. From Pau to Laruns, it's about 42km.

----

❸ Vallée d'Ossau

More scenic splendour awaits in the Vallée d'Ossau, which tracks the course of its namesake river for a spectacular 60km. The first part of the valley as far as Laruns is broad, green and pastoral, but as you travel south the mountains really start to pile up, before broadening out again near Gabas.

Halfway between Arudy and Laruns, you can spy on some of the

mightiest birds of the western Pyrenees, griffon vultures, at the **Falaise aux Vautours** (Cliff of the Vultures; 📞05 59 82 65 49; www.falaise-aux-vautours. com; Aste-Béon; adult/child €6/4; ⏱10.30am-12.30pm & 2-6.30pm daily Jul & Aug, 1.30-5.30pm Mon-Fri Apr-Jun & Sep). Live CCTV images are beamed from their nests to the visitors centre in Aste-Béon. Griffon vultures are common throughout the western part of the Pyrenees. Much rarer cousins include the Egyptian vulture and the massive lammergeier.

The ski resort of **Artouste-Fabrèges**, 6km east of Gabas, is linked by cable car to the **Petit Train d'Artouste** (📞05 59 05 36 99; https://artouste.fr; adult/child/family €25/18/80; ⏱mid-May–mid-Oct), a miniature mountain railway built for dam workers in the 1920s. The train is only open between June and September; reserve ahead and allow four hours for a visit.

The Drive ≫ The D918 between Laruns and Argelès-Gazost is one of the Pyrenees' most breathtaking roads, switchbacking over the lofty Col d'Aubisque. The road feels exposed, but it's a wonderfully scenic drive. You'll cover about 52km, but allow yourself at least 1½ hours. Once you reach Argelès-Gazost, head further south for 4km along the D101 to St-Savin.

④ St-Savin

After the hair-raising drive over the Col d'Aubisque, St-Savin makes a welcome refuge. It's a classic Pyrenean village, with cobbled lanes, quiet cafes and timbered houses set around a fountain-filled main square.

It's also home to one of the Pyrenees' most respected hotel-restaurants, **Le Viscos** (📞05 62 97 02 28; www.hotel-leviscos.com; 1 rue Lamarque, St-Savin; menus €32-75; ⏱12.30-1.30pm Tue-Sun, 7.30-8.30pm Tue-Sat; 🅿❄🛜), run by celeb chef Jean-Pierre St-Martin, known for his blend of Basque, Breton and Pyrenean flavours (as well as his passion for foie gras). After dinner, retire to one of the cosy country-style rooms and watch the sun set over the snowy mountains.

🛏 p161

The Drive » From St-Savin, travel back along the D101 to Argelès-Gazost. You'll see signs to the Parc Animalier des Pyrénées as you approach town.

⑤ Argelès-Gazost

The Pyrenees has a diverse collection of wildlife, but spotting it in the wild isn't always simple. Thankfully then, the **Parc Animalier des Pyrénées** (📞05 62 97 91 07; www.parc-animalier-pyrenees. com; 60bis av des Pyrénées, Argelès-Gazost; adult/child €20/14.50; ⏱9.30am-6pm or 7pm Apr-Oct) does all the hard work for you. It's home to a menagerie of endangered Pyrenean animals including wolves, marmots, lynxes, ravens, vultures, beavers and even a few brown bears (whose limited presence in the Pyrenees is highly controversial).

The Drive » Take the D921 south of Argelès-Gazost for 6km to Pierrefitte-Nestalas. Here, the road forks; the southwest branch (the D920) climbs up a lush, forested valley for another 11km to Cauterets.

TRIP HIGHLIGHT

⑥ Cauterets

For alpine scenery, the century-old ski and spa resort of Cauterets is perhaps the signature spot in the Pyrenees. Hemmed in by mountains and forests, it has clung on to much of its fin de siècle character, with a stately spa and grand 19th-century residences.

To see the scenery at its best, drive through town along the D920 (signed to the 'Pont d'Espagne'). The road is known locally as the **Chemins des Cascades** after the waterfalls that crash down the mountainside; it's 6.5km of nonstop hairpins, so take it steady.

At the top, you'll reach the giant car park at **Pont d'Espagne** (cable cars adult/child €15/12). From here, a combination *télécabine* and *télésiege* ratchets up the mountainside allowing access to the area's trails, including the popular hike to the sapphire-tinted **Lac de Gaube** and the even more beautiful, but longer walks to the **Refuge Wallon** (4 hours return) and **Refuge Oulette de Gaube** (5 to 6 hours return).

🍴🛏 p161

↱ DETOUR: CIRQUE DE GAVARNIE

Start: ⑥ **Cauterets**

For truly mind-blowing mountain scenery, it's well worth taking a side trip to see the Cirque de Gavarnie, a dramatic glacially formed amphitheatre of mountains 20km south of Luz-St-Sauveur. It's a return walk of about two hours from the village, and you'll need to bring sturdy footwear. There's another spectacular – and quieter – circle of mountains 6.5km to the east, the **Cirque de Troumouse**. It's reached via a hair-raising 8km toll road (€5 per vehicle; open April to October). There are no barriers and the drops are really dizzying, so drive carefully.

WHY THIS IS A GREAT TRIP
STUART BUTLER, WRITER

The craggy peaks of the Pyrenees are home to some of France's rarest wildlife and most unspoilt landscapes, and every twist and turn in the road seems to reveal another knockout view. I've spent the past two decades living at the western foot of these mountains and still never tire of exploring them. For me, there is simply no more beautiful mountain range on earth. This west-to-east drive through the mountains showcases some of its finest, and most easily accessible, sights, views and experiences.

Above: Cauterets
Left: Grotte de Niaux, Tarascon-sur-Ariège
Right: Griffon vulture, Pyrenees

STEPHANIE AUGRAS/SHUTTERSTOCK ©

FRANCE 11 THE PYRENEES

The Drive » After staying overnight in Cauterets, backtrack to Pierrefitte-Nestalas and turn southeast onto the D921 for 12km to Luz-St-Sauveur. The next stretch on the D918 is another mountain stunner, climbing up through Barèges to the breathtaking Col du Tourmalet.

TRIP HIGHLIGHT

❼ Col du Tourmalet

At 2115m, Col du Tourmalet is the highest road pass in the Pyrenees, and it usually only opens between June and October. It's often used as a punishing mountain stage in the Tour de France, and you'll feel uncomfortably akin to a motorised ant as you crawl up towards the pass.

From the ski resort of La Mongie (1800m), a cable car climbs to the top of **Pic du Midi** (www.picdu midi.com; rue Pierre Lamy de la Chapelle; adult/child €45/27; ⊙9.30am-7pm Jun-Sep, 10am-5.30pm Oct-Apr). This high-altitude observatory commands otherworldly views – but it's often blanketed in cloud, so make sure you check the forecast before you go.

The Drive » The next stage to Foix is a long one. Follow the D918 and D935 to Bagnères de Bigorre, then the D938 and D20 to Tournay, a drive of 40km. Just before Tournay, head west onto the A64 for 82km. Exit onto the D117, signed to St-Girons. It's another 72km to Foix, but with twisting roads all the way and lots of 30km/h zones this last part takes at least 1½ hours.

ROAD PASSES IN THE PYRENEES

The high passes between the Vallée d'Ossau, the Vallée d'Aspe and the Vallée de Gaves are often closed during winter. Signs are posted along the approach roads indicating whether they're *ouvert* (open) or *fermé* (closed). The dates given below are approximate and depend on seasonal snowfall.

Col d'Aubisque (1709m, open May-Oct) The D918 links Laruns in the Vallée d'Ossau with Argèles-Gazost in the Vallée de Gaves. An alternative that's open year-round is the D35 between Louvie-Juzon and Nay.

Col de Marie-Blanque (1035m, open most of year) The shortest link between the Aspe and Ossau valleys is the D294, which corkscrews for 21km between Escot and Bielle.

Col du Pourtalet (1795m, open most of year) The main crossing into Spain generally stays open year-round except during exceptional snowfall.

Col du Tourmalet (2115m, open Jun-Oct) Between Barèges and La Mongie, this is the highest road pass in the Pyrenees. If you're travelling east to the Pic du Midi (for example from Cauterets), the only alternative is a long detour north via Lourdes and Bagnères de Bigorre.

⑧ Foix

Looming above Foix is the triple-towered **Château de Foix** (☎05 61 05 10 10; rue du Rocher; adult/child €11.50/8; ⏰9am-6pm summer, shorter hours rest of year), constructed in the 10th century as a stronghold for the counts of the town. The view from the battlements is wonderful and a refurbishment has spruced up the displays on medieval life. There's usually at least one daily tour in English in summer.

Afterwards, head 4.5km south to **Les Forges de Pyrène** (☎05 34 09 30 60; www.forges-de-pyrene. com; rte de Paris, Montgailhard; adult/child €10.20/6.80; ⏰10am-6pm Tue-Sat Jul-Oct; 🚼), a fascinating 'living museum' that explores Ariège folk traditions. Spread over 5 hectares, it illustrates traditional trades such as glass blowing, tanning, thatching and nail making, and even has its own blacksmith, baker and cobbler.

🛏 p161

The Drive » Spend the night in Foix, then head for Tarascon-sur-Ariège, 17km south of Foix on the N20. Look out for brown signs to the Parc de la Préhistoire.

TRIP HIGHLIGHT

⑨ Tarascon-sur-Ariège

Thousands of years ago, the Pyrenees were home to thriving communities of hunter-gatherers, who used the area's caves as shelters and left behind many stunning examples of prehistoric art.

Near Tarascon-sur-Ariège, the **Parc de la Préhistoire** (☎05 61 05 10 10; Tarascon-sur-Ariège; adult/child €11.50/8; ⏰10am-7pm Jul & Aug, to 6pm Sep, Oct & Apr-Jun) provides a handy primer on the area's ancient past. It explores everything from prehistoric carving to the arts of animal-skin tent making and ancient spear-throwing.

About 6.5km further south, the **Grotte de Niaux** (☎05 61 05 10 10; www.sites-touristiques-ariege. fr; adult/child €14/10; ⏰tours hourly 10.15am-4.15pm, extra tours in summer) is home to the Pyrenees' most precious cave paintings. The centrepiece is the **Salon Noir**, reached after an 800m walk through the darkness and decorated with bison, horses and ibex. The cave can only be visited with a guide. From April to September there's usually one daily tour in English at 1.30pm. Bookings are advisable.

Eating & Sleeping

Pau ❶

✖ Les Papilles Insolites   French €€

(☎05 59 71 43 79; www.lespapillesinsolites.
blogspot.co.uk; 5 rue Alexander Taylor; tapas
€8-12; ☺3-10pm Wed, 11am-1.30pm & 7-10pm
Thu-Sat) Run by a former Parisian sommelier,
this cosy wine bar serves beautifully prepared
small plates like Galician-style octopus, scallops
with leeks or lamb with cumin. Complete the
experience with the owner's choice of one of
the 350-odd wines stacked around the shop.
Gorgeously Gallic.

⌂ Hôtel Bristol   Hotel €€

(☎05 59 27 72 98; www.hotelbristol pau.
com; 3 rue Gambetta; s €80-100, d €90-110, f
€120-130; P🛜) A classic old French hotel but
with up-to-date rooms, all wrapped in a grand
19th-century building. Each room is uniquely
designed, with stylish decor, bold artwork and
elegant furniture, while big windows fill the
rooms with light. Ask for a mountain-view room
with balcony. Breakfast is pricey at €12.

St-Savin ❹

⌂ Hôtel des Rochers   Hotel €

(☎05 62 97 09 52; www.lesrochershotel.com;
1 place du Castillou, St-Savin; d €68-76, f €110;
P🛜) In the idyllic village of St-Savin, 16km
south of Lourdes, this handsomely landscaped
hotel makes a perfect mountain retreat. It's
run by an expat English couple, John and
Jane, who have renovated the rooms in clean,
contemporary fashion – try for one with a
mountain view. Half-board is available and the
hotel can provide picnic lunches that will satisfy
the hungriest hiker.

Cauterets ❻

✖ La Grande Fache   French €€

(☎06 06 44 99 55; 5 rue Richelieu; fondue per
person €19-24; ☺noon-2.30pm & 7-10pm)
You're in the mountains, so really you should be
eating artery-clogging, cheese-heavy dishes
such as *tartiflette* (potatoes, cheese and bacon
baked in a casserole), *raclette* and fondue.
This family-run restaurant will oblige, served
in a dining-room crammed with mountain
memorabilia.

⌂ Hôtel du Lion d'Or   Hotel €€

(☎05 62 92 52 87; www.liondor.eu; 12 rue
Richelieu; d €84-168, 🛜) This country-cottage-
style hotel oozes mountain character from
every nook and cranny. In business since 1913,
it is deliciously eccentric, with charming old
rooms in polka-dot pinks, sunny yellows and
duck-egg blues, and mountain-themed knick-
knacks dotted throughout, from antique sleds
to snowshoes. Breakfast includes homemade
honey and jams, and the restaurant serves
hearty Pyrenean cuisine.

Foix ❽

⌂ La Ciboulette   B&B €

(☎05 61 01 10 88; www.laciboulette.net; rte
St Pierre-de-Rivière, Lieu-Dit La Rochelle; s
€49-69, d €64-89, f €109) In a peaceful setting
some 3km west of Foix, this small family-run
guesthouse has several attractive rooms
decorated with artwork and elegant furnishings.
Views over the mountains add to the charm.
Don't miss a meal of creatively prepared local
dishes in the excellent restaurant on-site (open
Thursdays to Mondays, mains €14.50-18.50).

Riviera Crossing

French road trips just don't get more glamorous than this: cinematic views, searing sunshine, art history aplenty and the Med around every turn.

12

TRIP HIGHLIGHTS

110 km
Èze
End with a sundowner in a dreamy hilltop village

62 km
La Grande Corniche
Cruise the Côte d'Azur's most famous road

FINISH
Menton

Roquebrune-Cap-Martin
Monaco

Nice
Delve into busy markets and an atmospheric old town
48 km

3

St-Paul de Vence
Paint your own pictures in this hilltop artists' hideaway
28 km

Antibes
Juan-les-Pins
START
1

Cannes
Cinematic heritage and cinematic views to match
0 km

4 DAYS
110KM / 68 MILES

GREAT FOR...

BEST TIME TO GO
Anytime, but avoid July and August's crowds.

  ESSENTIAL PHOTO
Standing by Augustus' monumental Trophée des Alpes, with Monaco and the Mediterranean far below.

  BEST FOR GLAMOUR
Strolling La Croisette in Cannes and fulfilling your film-star fantasies.

12 Riviera Crossing

Cruising the Côte d'Azur is as dazzling and chic as road trips get. From film town Cannes to sassy Nice via the corkscrew turns of the Corniches and into millionaire's Monaco, it's a drive you'll remember forever. Filmmakers, writers, celebs and artists have all had their hearts stolen by this glittering stretch of coastline: by the end of this trip, you'll understand why.

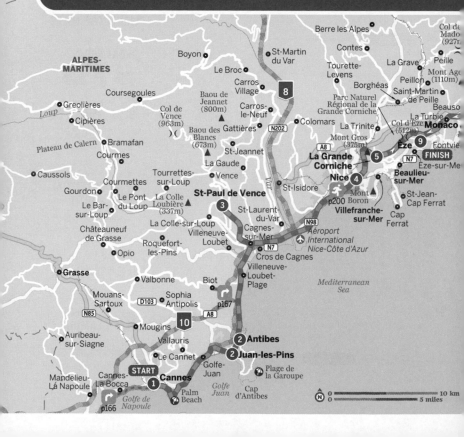

TRIP HIGHLIGHT

1 Cannes

What glitzier opening could there be to this Côte d'Azur cruise than Cannes, as cinematic as its reputation suggests. Come July during the film festival, the world's stars descend on **boulevard de la Croisette** (aka La Croisette) to stroll beneath the palms, plug their latest opus and hobnob with the media and movie moguls. Getting your picture snapped outside the

Palais des Festivals (Festival & Congress Palace; www. palaisdesfestivals.com; 1 bd de la Croisette; guided tour adult/ child €6/free) is a must-do, as is a night-time stroll along the boulevard, illuminated by coloured lights.

Outside festival time, Cannes still feels irresistibly ritzy. Private beaches and grand hotels line the seafront; further west lies old Cannes. Follow rue St-Antoine and snake your way up **Le Suquet**, Cannes' atmospheric original village. Pick up the region's best produce at **Marché Forville** (www. marcheforville.com; 11 rue du Marché Forville; 7.30am-1pm Tue-Fri, to 2pm Sat & Sun), a couple of blocks back from the port.

Need nature? Then head to the **Îles de Lérins**, two islands located a 20-minute boat ride away. Tiny and traffic-free, they're perfect for walks or a picnic. Boats for the islands leave from quai des Îles, on the western side of the harbour.

The Drive » The most scenic route to Antibes is via the coastal D6007. Bear right onto av Frères Roustan before Golfe Juan. With luck and no traffic jams, you should hit Juan-les-Pins in 30 minutes or so.

2 Antibes & Juan-les-Pins

A century or so ago, Antibes and Juan-les-Pins were a refuge for artists, writers, aristocrats and hedonistic expats looking to escape the horrors of post-WWI Europe. They came in their droves – F Scott Fitzgerald wrote several books here, and Picasso rented a miniature castle (it's now a museum dedicated to him).

First stop is the beach resort of **Juan-les-Pins**. It's a long way from the fashionable resort of Fitzgerald's day, but the beaches are still good for sun-lounging (even if you do have to pay).

Then it's on around the peninsula of **Cap d'Antibes**, where many

Castellar LIGURIA Rovering
Agnès Ventimiglia
io Garavan Mortola
ebrune 7 **Menton**
Carnolès
6 **Roquebrune-**
Cap **Cap-Martin**
Martin
d'Azur

LINK YOUR TRIP

8 **Essential France**
This trip makes a natural extension of our grand tour of France's unmissable sights.

10 **Atlantic to Med**
Cover the whole south of France by combining these coastal trips which intersect at Cannes and Nice.

DETOUR: CORNICHE DE L'ESTEREL

Start: ❶ Cannes

West of Cannes, the winding coast road known as the **Corniche de l'Estérel** (sometimes known as the Corniche d'Or, the Golden Road) is well worth a side trip if you can spare the time. Opened in 1903 by the Touring Club de France, this twisting coast road is as much about driving pleasure as getting from A to B; it runs for 30 unforgettable coastal kilometres all the way to St-Raphael. En route you'll pass seaside villages, secluded coves (sandy, pebbled, nudist, you name it) and the rocky red hills of the Massif de l'Estérel, dotted with gnarly oaks, juniper and wild thyme. Wherever you go, the blue Mediterranean shimmers alongside, tempting you to stop for just one more swim. It's too much to resist.

of the greats had their holiday villas: the Hotel Cap du Eden Roc was one of their favourite fashionable haunts. Round the peninsula is pretty **Antibes**, with a harbour full of pleasure boats and an old town ringed by medieval ramparts. Aim to arrive before lunchtime, when the atmospheric **Marché Provençal** (cours Masséna; ⊙7.30am-1pm Tue-Sun Sep-Jun, daily Jul & Aug) will still be in full swing, and then browse the nearby **Musée Picasso** (☎04 92 90 54 26; www.antibes-juanlespins. com/culture/musee-picasso; Château Grimaldi, 4 rue des Cordiers; adult/concession €8/6; ⊙10am-6pm Tue-Sun mid-Jun–mid-Sep, 10am-1pm & 2-6pm Tue-Sun rest of year) to see a few of the artist's Antibes-themed works.

🛏 p172

The Drive » Brave the traffic on the D6007 and avoid signs to turn onto the A8 motorway: it's the D2 you want, so follow signs for Villeneuve-Loubet. When you reach the town, cross the river. You'll pass through a tunnel into the outskirts of Cagnes-sur-Mer; now start following signs to St-Paul de Vence.

- - - - - - - - - - - - - - - -

TRIP HIGHLIGHT

❸ St-Paul de Vence

Once upon a time, hilltop St-Paul de Vence was just another village like countless others in Provence. But then the artists moved in: painters such as Marc Chagall and Pablo Picasso sought solitude here, painted the local scenery and traded canvases for room and board. This is how the hotel **La Colombe d'Or** (☎04 93 32 80 02; www.

la-colombe-dor.com; place de Gaulle; d €225-480; ❋ 🛜 🛋) came by its stellar art collection.

It's now one of the Riviera's most exclusive locations, a haven for artists, film stars and celebrities, not to mention hordes of sightseers, many of whom are here to marvel at the incredible art collection at the **Fondation Maeght** (☎04 93 32 81 63; www.fondation -maeght.com; 623 chemin des Gardettes; adult/child €16/11; ⊙10am-7pm Jul-Sep, to 6pm Oct-Jun). Created in 1964 by collectors Aimé and Merguerite Maeght, it boasts works by all the big 20th-century names – including Miró sculptures, Chagall mosaics, Braque windows and canvases by Picasso, Matisse and others.

While you're here, it's worth taking a detour northwards to Vence, where the marvellous **Chapelle du Rosaire** (Rosary Chapel; ☎04 93 58 03 26; http://chapellematisse.fr; 466 av Henri Matisse; adult/child €7/4; ⊙10am-noon & 2-6pm Tue, Thu & Fri, 2-6pm Wed & Sat Apr-Oct, to 5pm Nov-Mar) was designed by an ailing Henri Matisse. He had a hand in everything here, from the stained-glass windows to the altar and candlesticks.

The Drive » Return the way you came, only this time follow the blue signs onto the A8 motorway to Nice. Take exit 50 for Promenade des Anglais, which will take you all 18km along the Baie des Anges. The views are great, but you'll hit nightmare traffic at rush hour.

- - - - - - - - - - - - - - - - - -

TRIP HIGHLIGHT

④ Nice

With its mix of real-city grit, old-world opulence and year-round sunshine, Nice is the undisputed capital of the Côte d'Azur. Sure, the traffic is horrendous and the beach is made entirely of pebbles (not a patch of sand in sight!), but that doesn't detract from its charms. It's a great base, with loads of hotels and restaurants, and character in every nook and cranny.

Start with a morning stroll through the huge food and flower markets on **cours Saleya** (cours Saleya; ⊙6am-5.30pm Tue-Sat, 6.30am-1.30pm Sun), then delve into the winding alleyways of the old town, **Vieux Nice**, where there are many backstreet restaurants at which you can try local specialities such as *pissaladière* (onion tart topped with olives and anchovies) and *socca* (chickpea-flour pancake). Stop for an ice cream at famous Fenocchio (p172) – flavours include tomato, lavender, olive and fig – then spend the afternoon sunbathing on the beaches along the seafront **Promenade des Anglais** (🚌8, 52, 62) before catching an epic sunset.

If you have the time, the city has some great museums too – you'll need at least an afternoon to explore all of the modern masterpieces at the **Musée d'Art Moderne et d'Art Contemporain** (MAMAC; 🕿04 97 13 42 01; www.mamac-nice.org; place Yves Klein; museum pass 24hr/7 days €10/20; ⊙10am-6pm Tue-Sun late Jun–mid-Oct, from 11am rest of year; 🚌1 to Garibaldi).

✕ ⌂ p172, p151

The Drive » Exit the city through Riquier on the D2564. You don't want the motorway – you want bd Bischoffsheim, which becomes bd de l'Observatoire as it climbs to the summit of Mont Gros. The next 12km are thrilling, twisting past the Parc Naturel Régional de la Grande Corniche. Stop for a picnic or a hilly hike, then continue towards La Turbie.

- - - - - - - - - - - - - - - - - -

TRIP HIGHLIGHT

⑤ La Grande Corniche

Remember that sexy scene from Hitchcock's *To Catch a Thief,* when Grace Kelly and Cary Grant cruised the hills in a convertible, enjoying sparkling banter and searing blue Mediterranean views? Well you're about to tackle the very same drive – so don your shades, roll down the windows and hit the asphalt.

It's a roller coaster of a road, veering through hairpins and switchbacks

DETOUR: BIOT

Start: ② Antibes & Juan-les-Pins

About an 8km drive from Antibes along the coast road and the D4, this 15th-century hilltop village was once an important pottery-manufacturing centre. The advent of metal containers brought an end to this, but Biot is still active in handicraft production, especially glassmaking. At the foot of the village, the **Verrerie de Biot** (🕿04 93 65 03 00; www.verreriebiot.com; chemin des Combes; guided tour adult/child €6/3, museum adult/child €3/1.50; ⊙10am-8pm Mon-Sat, 10.30am-1.30pm & 2.30-7.30pm Sun May-Sep, to 6pm Oct-Apr) produces bubbled glass by rolling molten glass into baking soda; bubbles from the chemical reaction are then trapped by a second layer of glass. You can watch skilled glass-blowers at work and browse the adjacent art galleries and shop. There are also guided tours (€6), during which you get the chance to try your hand at a spot of glass-blowing – and learn why it's probably best left to the professionals.

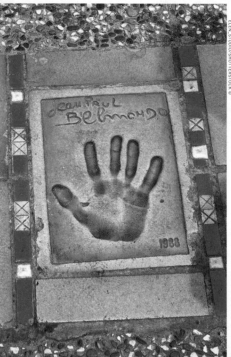

WHY THIS IS A GREAT TRIP
CELESTE BRASH, WRITER

With light that inspired Picasso and Matisse, history you can feel in your soul and a view over the Mediterranean at every hairpin turn, this drive takes in every dreamy hue of the Côte d'Azur. Each kilometre is special, from the glamour of Cannes and perfumeries of Grasse to the brassiness of Nice, audaciousness of Monaco and all the hilltop villages between.

Above: Menton
Left: Boulevard de la Croisette, Cannes
Right: Èze

as it heads into the hills above Nice. There are countless picnic spots and photo opportunities along the way, including the **Col d'Èze**, the road's highest point at 512m. Further on you'll pass the monumental Roman landmark known as the **Trophée des Alpes** (☏04 93 41 20 84; www. trophee-auguste.fr; 18 av Albert 1er; adult/child €6/free; ⏱9.30am-1pm & 2.30-6.30pm Tue-Sun mid-May–mid-Sep, 10am-1.30pm & 2.30-5pm rest of year), a magnificent triumphal arch built to commemorate Augustus' victory over the last remaining Celtic-Ligurian tribes who had resisted conquest. The views from here are jaw-dropping, stretching all the way to Monaco and Italy beyond.

The Drive » Monte Carlo may sparkle and beckon below, but keep your eyes on the road; the principality will keep for another day. Stay on the D2564 to skirt Monaco for another amazing 10km, then turn right into the D52 to Roquebrune.

- - - - - - - - - - - - - - - - -

❻ Roquebrune-Cap-Martin

This village of two halves feels a world away from the glitz of nearby Monaco: the coastline around **Cap Martin** remains relatively unspoilt, as if Roquebrune had left its clock on medieval time. The historic half of the town, Roquebrune itself, sits 300m high on

PERFUME IN GRASSE

Up in the hills to the north of Cannes, the town of Grasse has been synonymous with perfumery since the 16th century, and the town is still home to around 30 makers – several of whom offer guided tours of their factories, and the chance to hone your olfactory skills.

It can take up to 10 years to train a *perfumier*, but since you probably don't have that much time to spare, you'll have to make do with a crash course. Renowned maker **Molinard** (☎04 92 42 33 21; www.molinard.com; 60 bd Victor Hugo; 20min/1hr/2hr workshops €30/69/199; ⏱9.30am-6.30pm) runs workshops where sessions range from 30 minutes to two hours, during which you get to create your own custom perfume (sandalwood, vanilla, hyacinth, lily of the valley, civet, hare and rose petals are just a few of the potential notes you could include). At the end of the workshop, you'll receive a bottle of *eau de parfum* to take home. **Galimard** (☎04 93 09 20 00; www.galimard.com; 73 rte de Cannes; workshops from €55; ⏱9am-12.30pm & 2-6pm) and **Fragonard's Usine Historique** (☎04 93 36 44 65; www.fragonard.com/fr/usines/musee-du-parfum; 20 bd Fragonard; ⏱9am-6pm) offer similar workshops.

For background, make time to visit the excellent **Musée International de la Parfumerie** (MIP; ☎04 97 05 58 11; www.museesdegrasse.com; 2 bd du Jeu de Ballon; adult/child €4/free, combo ticket incl Les Jardins du MIP €6/free; ⏱10am-7pm May-Sep, to 5.30pm Oct-Apr; 👪) and its nearby **gardens** (☎04 92 98 62 69; www.museesdegrasse.com; 979 chemin des Gourettes, Mouans-Sartoux; adult/child €4/free, combo ticket incl MIP €6/free; ⏱10am-7pm May-Aug, to 5.30pm Apr & Sep-Nov, closed Dec-Mar), where you can see some of the many plants and flowers used in scent-making. Needless to say, the bouquet is overpowering.

a pudding-shaped lump. It towers over the Cap, but they are, in fact, linked by innumerable, very steep steps.

The village is delightful and free of tack, and there are sensational views of the coast from the main village square, **place des Deux Frères**. Of all Roquebrune's steep streets, **rue Moncollet** – with its arcaded passages and stairways carved out of rock – is the most impressive. Scurry upwards to find architect Le Corbusier's grave at the cemetery at the top of the village (in section J, and yes, he did design his own tombstone).

The Drive » Continue along the D52 towards the coast, following promenade du Cap-Martin all the way along the seafront to Menton. You'll be there in 10 minutes, traffic permitting.

- - - - - - - - - - - - - - - -

❼ Menton

Last stop on the coast before Italy, the beautiful seaside town of Menton offers a glimpse of what the Riviera once looked like, before the high-rises, casinos and property developers moved in. It's ripe for wandering, with peaceful gardens and Belle Époque mansions galore, as well as an attractive yacht-filled harbour. Meander the historic quarter all the way to the **Cimetière du Vieux Château** (montée du Souvenir; ⏱7am-8pm Apr-Oct, 8am-5pm Nov-Mar) for the best views in town.

Menton's miniature microclimate enables exotic plants to flourish here, many of which you can see at the **Jardin Botanique Exotique du Val Rahmeh** (☎04 93 35 86 72; www.mnhn.fr/fr/visitez/lieux/jardin-botanique-exotique-menton; av St-Jacques; adult/child €7/5; ⏱9.30am-12.30pm & 2-6pm Wed-Mon Apr-Sep, 10am-12.30pm & 2-5pm Wed-Mon Oct-Mar), where terraces overflow with fruit trees, and the beautiful, once-abandoned **Jardin de la Serre de la Madone** (☏04 93 57 73 90; www.serredelamadone.com; 74 rte de Gorbio; adult/child €8/4; ⏰10am-6pm Tue-Sun Apr-Oct, to 5pm Jan-Mar, closed Nov & Dec), overgrown with rare plants. Spend your second night in town.

 p173

The Drive » Leave Menton on the D6007, the Moyenne Corniche, skirting the upper perimeter of Monaco. When you're ready, turn off into Monaco. All the car parks charge the same rate. Good options include the Chemin des Pêcheurs and Stade Louis II for old Monaco, or the huge underground Casino car park by allées des Boulingrins for central Monte Carlo.

❽ Monaco

This pint-sized principality (covering barely 200 hectares) is ridiculous, absurd, ostentatious and fabulous all at once. A playground of the super-rich, with super-egos to match, it's the epitome of Riviera excess – especially at the famous **Casino de Monte Carlo** (☏98 06 21 21; www.casinomontecarlo. com; place du Casino; morning visit incl audio guide adult/child Oct-Apr €17/8, May-Sep €17/12, salons ordinaires gaming €17; ⏰ visits 9am-1pm, gaming 2pm-late), where cards turn, roulette wheels spin and eye-watering sums are won and lost.

For all its glam, Monaco is not all show. Up in the hilltop quarter of **Le Rocher**, shady streets surround the **Palais Princier de Monaco** (☏93 25 18 31; www.palais.mc; place du Palais; adult/child €10/5, incl Collection de Voitures Anciennes car museum €8/4, incl Musée Océanographique €16/10; ⏰10am-6pm Apr-Jun & Sep–mid-Oct, to 7pm Jul & Aug), the wedding-cake castle of Monaco's royal family (time your visit for the pomptastic changing of the guard at 11.55am).

Nearby is the impressive **Musée Océanographique de Monaco** (☏93 15 36 00; www.oceano.mc; av St-Martin; adult/child high season €16/10; ⏰9.30am-8pm Jul & Aug, 10am-7pm Apr-Jun & Sep, to 6pm Oct-Mar), stocked with all kinds of deep-sea denizens. It even has a 6m-deep lagoon complete with circling sharks.

Round things off with a stroll around the cliffside **Jardin Exotique** (☏93 15 29 80; www.jardin-exotique.mc; 62 bd du Jardin Exotique; adult/child €8/4; ⏰9am-7pm mid-May–mid-Sep, to 6pm rest of year) and the obligatory photo of Monaco's harbour, bristling with over-the-top yachts.

The Drive » Pick up where you left off on the Moyenne Corniche (D6007), and follow its circuitous route back up into the hills all the way to Èze.

TRIP HIGHLIGHT

❾ Èze

This rocky little village perched on an impossible peak is outrageously romantic. The main attraction is technically the medieval village, with small higgledy-piggledy stone houses and winding lanes (and, yes, galleries and shops). It's undoubtedly delightful, but it's the ever-present views of the coast that are truly mesmerising. They just get more spectacular from the **Jardin Exotique d'Èze** (☏04 93 41 10 30; www.jardinexotique-eze.fr; rue du Château; adult/child €6/3.50; ⏰9am-7.30pm Jul-Sep, to 6.30pm Apr-Jun & Oct, to 4.30pm Nov-Mar), a surreal cactus garden at the top of the village, so steep and rocky it may have been purpose-built for mountain goats. It's also where you'll find the old castle ruins; take time to sit, draw a deep breath and gaze, as few places on earth offer such a panorama.

Èze gets very crowded between 10am and 5pm; if you prefer a quiet wander, plan to be here early in the morning or before dinner. Or even better, treat yourself to a night and supper at the swish Château Eza (p173), a fitting finish to this most memorable of road trips.

 p173

FRANCE **12** RIVIERA CROSSING

Eating & Sleeping

Cannes ❶

✖ Bobo Bistro   Mediterranean €€€

(📞04 93 99 97 33; www.facebook.com/
BoboBistroCannes; 21 rue du Commandant
André; pizzas €15-18, mains €18-32; ⏰noon-
3pm & 7-11pm Mon-Sat) Predictably, it's a
'bobo' (bourgeois bohemian) crowd that
gathers at this achingly cool bistro in Cannes'
fashionable Carré d'Or. Decor is stylishly retro,
with attention-grabbing objets d'art including a
tableau of dozens of spindles of coloured yarn.
Cuisine is local, seasonal and invariably organic:
including artichoke salad, dorado ceviche with
avocado, or rotisserie chicken with mash *fait
masion* (homemade).

🛏 Hôtel Le Mistral   Boutique Hotel €€

(📞04 93 39 91 46; www.mistral-hotel.com; 13 rue
des Belges; d €118-168; ❄ 📶) For super-pricey
Cannes, this little three-star offers amazing
value. The 10 rooms are small but decked out in
flattering red and plum tones – Privilege rooms
have quite a bit more space, plus a fold-out sofa
bed. There are sea views from two rooms on
the 4th floor, and the hotel is just 50m from La
Croisette. There's no lift, though.

🛏 Villa Garbo   Boutique Hotel €€€

(📞04 93 46 66 00; www.villagarbo-cannes.
com; 62 bd d'Alsace; d €220-800; ❄ @ 📶) For
a taste of Cannes' celeb lifestyle, this indulgent
stunner is hard to beat. Rooms are more like
apartments, offering copious space, plus
kitchenettes, king-size beds, sofas and more.
The style is designer chic – acid tones of puce,
orange and lime contrasted with blacks and
greys, supplemented by quirky sculptures and
objets d'art. Unusually, rates include breakfast.

Antibes ❷

🛏 Hôtel La Jabotte   B&B €€

(📞04 93 61 45 89; www.jabotte.com; 13 av Max
Maurey; d €87-130, ste €254; ❄ @ 📶) Just
150m inland from Plage de la Salis and 2km
south of the old town towards Cap d'Antibes,
this pretty little hideaway makes a cosy base.
Hot pinks, sunny yellows and soothing mauves

dominate the homey, feminine decor, and
there's a sweet patio where breakfast is served
on sunny days. There's a minimum stay of three
nights in summer.

Nice ❹

✖ Fenocchio   Ice Cream €

(📞04 93 80 72 52; www.fenocchio.fr; 2 place
Rossetti; 1/2 scoops €3/5; ⏰9am-midnight
Mar-Nov) There's no shortage of ice-cream
sellers in the old town, but this *maître glacier*
(master ice-cream maker) has been king of
the scoops since 1966. The array of flavours is
mind-boggling – cactus, cinnamon, fig, lavender
and rosé to name a few. Dither too long over the
98-plus flavours and you'll never make it to the
front of the queue.

✖ Le Bistrot d'Antoine   French €€

(📞04 93 85 29 57; 27 rue de la Préfecture; mains
€17-32; ⏰9am-1.45pm & 7-10pm Tue-Sat) A
quintessential French bistro, right down to
the checked tablecloths, streetside tables
and impeccable service – not to mention the
handwritten blackboard, loaded with classic
dishes such as rabbit pâté, pot-cooked pork,
blood sausage and duck breast. If you've never
eaten classic French food, this is definitely the
place to start; no matter what, you're in for a
treat.

🛏 Hôtel Le G   Hotel €€

(📞04 93 56 84 79; www.le-g-chineurs.
com; 1 rue Cassini; r €121-297; ❄ 📶; 🚌1 to
Garibaldi) Location, location, location! Nice's
best nightlife is right outside your door at this
renovated corner hotel off place Garibaldi, bang
in the heart of the lively Petit Marais district.
Bedrooms look sleek in cool greys, crimsons
and charcoals; bathrooms are modern and
well-appointed. Breakfast is served in the
ground-floor cafe, brimful of vintage bric-a-brac
and mismatched furniture.

🛏 Hôtel Windsor   Boutique Hotel €€

(📞04 93 88 59 35; www.hotelwindsornice.
com; 11 rue Dalpozzo; d €137-225; ❄ @ 📶 🏊;
🚌7, 9, 22, 27, 59, 70 to Grimaldi or Rivoli) Don't
be fooled by the staid stone exterior: inside,

owner Odile Redolfi has enlisted the collective creativity of several well-known artists to make each of the 57 rooms uniquely appealing. Some are frescoed and others are adorned with experimental chandeliers or photographic murals. The garden and pool out the back are delightful, as are the small bar and attached restaurant.

Menton ⑦

✕ Au Baiser du Mitron   Bakery €

(The Baker's Kiss; ☎04 93 57 67 82; www. aubaiserdumitron.com; 8 rue Piéta; items from €1; ⌚7.30am-1pm Wed-Sun) This one-of-a-kind *boulangerie* showcases breads from the Côte d'Azur, inland Provence and other favourite spots from baker-owner Kevin Le Meur's world travels. Everything is baked in a traditional *four à bois* (wood bread oven) from 1906, using 100% natural ingredients and no preservatives. The *tarte au citron de Menton* (Menton lemon tart) is the best there is.

🛏 Hôtel Napoléon   Boutique Hotel €€

(☎04 93 35 89 50; www.napoleon-menton. com; 29 porte de France; d €170-340, junior ste €298-462; ❄ @ 🛜 🌊) Standing tall on the seafront, the Napoléon is Menton's most stylish sleeping option. Everything from the pool to the restaurant-bar and the back garden (a haven of freshness in summer) has been beautifully designed. Rooms are decked out in white and blue, with Cocteau drawings on headboards. Sea-facing rooms have balconies but are a little noisier because of the traffic.

Èze ⑨

🛏 Château Eza   Luxury Hotel €€€

(☎04 93 41 12 24; www.chateaueza.com; rue de la Pise; d €215-580; ❄ 🛜) If you're looking for a place to propose, well, there can be few more memorable settings than this wonderful clifftop hotel, perched dramatically above the glittering blue Mediterranean. There are only 14 rooms, so it feels intimate, but the service is impeccable, and the regal decor (gilded mirrors, sumptuous fabrics, antiques) explains the sky-high price tag.

Champagne Taster

From musty cellars to vine-striped hillsides, this Champagne adventure whisks you through the heart of this Unesco World Heritage region and explores the world's favourite celebratory tipple.

13

TRIP HIGHLIGHTS

0 km

Reims
Descend into the cellars of Mumm and Taittinger

● Vrigny

① START

25 km

Verzenay
Climb to the top of a lighthouse for Champagne views

Rilly-la-
Montagne ●

②

Mailly-
Champagne ●

Cumières ● Dizy

65 km

⑤

Épernay
Tick off the prestigious names along the av de Champagne

85 km

⑦

FINISH

Le Mesnil-sur-Oger
View vintage Champagne-making equipment at the village museum

3 DAYS
85KM / 53 MILES

GREAT FOR...

BEST TIME TO GO

April to June for spring sunshine or September and October to see the harvest in Champagne.

ESESSENTIAL PHOTO

Overlooking glossy vineyards from the Phare de Verzenay.

BEST FOR CULTURE

Sip Champagne in the cellars of Moët & Chandon.

Biscuits roses (pink biscuits) and Champagne

175

13 | Champagne Taster

'My only regret in life is that I didn't drink enough Champagne,' wrote the economist John Maynard Keynes, but by the end of this tour, you'll have drunk enough bubbly to last several lifetimes. Starting at the prestigious Champagne centre of Reims, passing through Épernay and ending in Le Mesnil-sur-Oger, this fizz-fuelled trip includes stops at some of the world's most famous producers – with ample time for tasting en route.

TRIP HIGHLIGHT

❶ Reims

There's nowhere better to start your Champagne tour than the regal city of **Reims**. Several big names have their *caves* (wine cellars) nearby. **Mumm** (☎03 26 49 59 70; www.mumm.com; 34 rue du Champ de Mars; tours incl tasting €23-42), pronounced 'moom', is the only *maison* in central Reims. Founded in 1827, it's the world's third- or fourth-largest Champagne producer, depending on the year.

One-hour tours explore its enormous cellars, filled with 25 million bottles of bubbly, and include tastings of several vintages.

North of town, **Taittinger** (☎03 26 85 45 35; https://cellars-booking. taittinger.fr; 9 place St-Niçaise; tours €25-77; ☺tours 9.30am-5.30pm) provides an informative overview of how Champagne is actually made – you'll leave with a good understanding of the production process, from grape to bottle. Parts of the cellars occupy Roman stone

quarries dug in the 4th century.

Before you leave town, don't forget to drop by **Waïda** (5 place Drouet d'Erlon; 🕒7.30am-7.30pm Tue-Fri, 8am-8pm Sat, 8am-2pm & 3.30-7.30pm Sun), an old-fashioned confectioner which sells Reims' famous *biscuits roses* (pink biscuits), a sweet treat traditionally nibbled with a glass of Champagne.

✕ 🛏 p183

The Drive » The countryside between Reims and Épernay is carpeted with vineyards, fields and back roads that are a dream to drive through. From Reims, head south along the D951 for 13km. Near Mont Chenot, turn onto the D26, signposted to Rilly and the 'Route Touristique du Champagne'. The next 12km takes you through the pretty villages of Rilly-la-Montagne and Mailly-Champagne en route to Verzenay.

LINK YOUR TRIP

8 **Essential France**
Lying 150km west of Épernay, Paris marks the beginning of our epic journey around France's most essential sights.

9 **D-Day's Beaches**
From Épernay head west, skirting Paris, to Caen (four hours' drive) to follow the course of the Normandy invasion of WWII.

2 Verzenay

Reims marks the start of the 70km **Montagne de Reims Champagne Route**, the prettiest (and most prestigious) of the three signposted road routes which wind their way through the Champagne vineyards. Of the 17 *grand cru* villages in Champagne, nine lie on and around the Montagne, a hilly area whose sheltered slopes and chalky soils provide the perfect environment for viticulture (grape growing).

Most of the area's vineyards are devoted to the pinot noir grape. You'll pass plenty of produc-ers offering *dégustation* (tasting) en route. It's up to you how many you visit – but whatever you do, don't miss the pano-rama of the vineyards of Verzenay from the top of the **Phare de Verzenay** (Verzenay Lighthouse; www.lepharedeverzenay.com; D26; lighthouse adult/child €3/2, museum €8/4, combined ticket €9/5; ☺10.30am-

CHAMPAGNE KNOW-HOW

Types of Champagne

Blanc de Blancs Champagne made using only chardonnay grapes. Fresh and elegant, with very small bubbles and a bouquet reminiscent of 'yellow fruits' such as pear and plum.

Blanc de Noirs A full-bodied, deep golden Champagne made solely with black grapes (despite the colour). Often rich and refined, with great complexity and a long finish.

Rosé Pink Champagne (mostly served as an aperitif) with a fresh character and summer-fruit flavours. Made by adding a small percentage of red pinot noir to white Champagne.

Prestige Cuvée The crème de la crème of Champagne. Usually made with grapes from *grand cru* vineyards and priced and bottled accordingly.

Millésimé Vintage Champagne produced from a single crop during an exceptional year. Most Champagne is nonvintage.

Sweetness

Brut Dry; most common style; pairs well with food.

Extra Sec Fairly dry but sweeter than Brut; nice as an aperitif.

Demi Sec Medium sweet; goes well with fruit and dessert.

Doux Very sweet; a dessert Champagne.

Serving & Tasting

Chilling Chill Champagne in a bucket of ice for 30 minutes before serving. The ideal serving temperature is 7°C to 9°C.

Opening Grip the bottle securely and tilt it at a 45-degree angle facing away from you. Rotate the bottle slowly to ease out the cork – it should sigh, not pop.

Pouring Hold the flute by the stem at an angle and let the Champagne trickle gently into the glass – less foam, more bubbles.

Tasting Admire the colour and bubbles. Swirl your glass to release the aroma and inhale slowly before tasting the Champagne.

5pm Tue-Sun, closed Jan), a lighthouse constructed as a publicity gimmick in 1909.

**The Drive ›› ** Continue south along the D26 for 3km.

----

❸ Verzy

This village is home to several small vineyards that provide an interesting contrast to the big producers. **Étienne and Anne-Laure Lefevre** (☎03 26 97 96 99; www.champagne-etienne-lefevre.com; 30 rue de Villers; ⊗10am-noon & 2-6pm Mon-Fri, to 5pm Sat) run group tours of their family-owned vineyards and cellars – if you're on your own, ring ahead to see if you can join a pre-arranged tour. There are no flashy videos or multimedia shows – the emphasis is firmly on the nitty-gritty of Champagne production.

For a glass of fizz high above the treetops, seek out the sleek **Perching Bar** (www.facebook.com/perchingbar; Forêt de Brise-Charrette, Verzy; ⊗noon-8pm Wed-Sun mid-Apr–mid-Dec) deep in the forest.

**The Drive ›› ** Stay on the D26 south of Verzy, and enjoy wide-open countryside views as you spin south to Ambonnay. Detour west onto the D19, signed to Bouzy, and bear right onto the D1 along the northern bank of the Marne River. When you reach the village of Dizy, follow signs onto the D386 to Hautvillers. It's a total drive of 32km or 45 minutes.

Reims Champagne *cave* (cellar)

----

❹ Hautvillers

Next stop is the hilltop village of Hautvillers, a hallowed name among Champagne aficionados: it's where a Benedictine monk by the name of Dom Pierre Pérignon is popularly believed to have created Champagne in the late 16th century. The great man's tomb lies in front of the altar of the **Église Abbatiale** (rue de l'Abbaye; ⊗9am-6.30pm Mon-Fri, from 10am Sat & Sun).

The village itself is well worth a stroll, with a jumble of lanes, timbered houses and stone-walled vineyards. On place de la République, the **tourist office** (☎03 26 57 06 35; www.tourisme-hautvillers.com; place de la République; ⊗9.30am-1pm & 1.30-5.30pm Mon-Sat, 10am-4pm Sun, shorter hours Nov–mid-Apr) hands out free maps detailing local vineyard

walks; one-hour guided tours cost €7 (€9 with a tasting).

Steps away is **Au 36** (www.au36.net; 36 rue Dom Pérignon; ⊗10.30am-6pm Apr-Oct, to 4pm Fri-Tue Nov-Dec & Mar), a wine boutique with a 'wall' of Champagne quirkily arranged by aroma. There's a tasting room upstairs; a two-/three-glass session costs €13/17.

**The Drive ›› ** From the centre of the village, take the rte de Cumières for grand views across the vine-cloaked slopes. Follow the road all the way to the D1, turn left and follow signs to Épernay's centre-ville, 6km to the south.

TRIP HIGHLIGHT

❺ Épernay

The prosperous town of Épernay is the self-proclaimed *capitale du Champagne* and is home to many of the most

WHY THIS IS A GREAT TRIP
KERRY CHRISTIANI,
WRITER

You can sip Champagne anywhere, but a road trip really slips under the skin of these Unesco-listed vineyards. Begin with an eye-opening, palate-awakening tour and tasting at *grande maison* cellars in Épernay and Reims. I love the far-reaching view from Phare de Verzenay and touring the back roads in search of small producers, especially when the aroma of new wine hangs in the air and the vines are golden in autumn.

Above: Phare de Verzenay, Verzenay
Left: Champagne tasting
Right: Chardonnay grapes, Le Mesnil-sur-Oger

EDOVAG/SHUTTERSTOCK ©

illustrious Champagne houses. Beneath the streets are an astonishing 110km of subterranean cellars, containing an estimated 200 million bottles of vintage bubbly.

Most of the big names are arranged along the grand av de Champagne. **Moët & Chandon** (☎03 26 51 20 20; www.moet.com; 20 av de Champagne; 1½hr tour with tasting €25-47, 10-17yr €10; ⏰ tours 9.30-11.30am & 2-4.30pm) offers frequent and fascinating one-hour tours of its prestigious cellars, while at nearby **Mercier** (☎03 26 51 22 22; www.champagnemercier.fr; 68-70 av de Champagne; adult incl 1/2/3 glasses €18/25/28, 10-17yr €8; ⏰ tours 9.30-11.30am & 2-4.30pm, closed mid-Dec–mid-Feb) tours take place aboard a laser-guided underground train.

Finish with a climb up the 237-step tower at **De Castellane** (☎03 26 51 19 19; www.castellane.com; 57 rue de Verdun; adult incl 1 glass €14, under 12yr free; ⏰ tours 10-noon & 2-6pm Wed-Sun, closed Christmas–mid-Mar), which offers knockout views over the town's rooftops and vine-clad hills.

✕ 🛏 p183

The Drive » Head south of town along av Maréchal Foch or av du 8 Mai 1945, following 'Autres Directions' signs across the roundabouts until you see signs for Cramant. The village is 10km southeast of Épernay via the D10.

THE SCIENCE OF CHAMPAGNE

Champagne is made from the red pinot noir (38%), the black pinot meunier (35%) or the white chardonnay (27%) grape. Each vine is vigorously pruned and trained to produce a small quantity of high-quality grapes. Indeed, to maintain exclusivity (and price), the designated areas where grapes used for Champagne can be grown and the amount of wine produced each year are limited.

Making Champagne according to the *méthode champenoise* (traditional method) is a complex procedure. There are two fermentation processes, the first in casks and the second after the wine has been bottled and had sugar and yeast added. Bottles are then aged in cellars for two to five years, depending on the *cuvée* (vintage).

For two months in early spring the bottles are aged in cellars kept at 12°C and the wine turns effervescent. The sediment that forms in the bottle is removed by *remuage*, a painstakingly slow process in which each bottle, stored horizontally, is rotated slightly every day for weeks until the sludge works its way to the cork. Next comes *dégorgement:* the neck of the bottle is frozen, creating a blob of solidified Champagne and sediment, which is then removed.

6 Cramant

You'll find it hard to miss this quaint village, as the northern entrance is heralded by a two-storey-high Champagne bottle. From the ridge above the village, views stretch out in all directions across the Champagne countryside, taking in a patchwork of fields, farmhouses and rows upon rows of endless vines. Pack a picnic and your own bottle of bubbly for the perfect Champagne country lunch.

The Drive » Continue southeast along the D10 for 7km, and follow signs to Le-Mesnil-sur-Oger.

TRIP HIGHLIGHT

7 Le Mesnil-sur-Oger

Finish with a visit to the excellent **Musée de la Vigne et du Vin** (☎03 26 57 50 15; www.champagne-lau nois.fr; 2 av Eugène Guil laume, cnr D10; adult incl 3 flutes €15; ☺ tours 10am & 2.30pm Mon-Fri, 10.30am Sat & Sun), where a local wine-growing family has assembled a collection of century-old Champagne-making equipment. Among the highlights is a massive 16-tonne oak-beam grape press from 1630. Reservations must be made by phone or online; ask about the availability of English tours when you book.

Round off your trip with lunch at **La Gare** (☎03 26 51 59 55; www. lagarelemesnil.com; 3 place de la Gare; menus €18-26; ☺ noon-1.30pm Mon-Wed, noon-1.30pm & 7-9pm Thu-Sat; ♠), which prides itself on serving bistro-style grub prepared with seasonal produce, simple as pork tenderloin with cider and potatoes. There's a €9 menu for *les petits*.

Eating & Sleeping

Reims ❶

✕ Brasserie Le Boulingrin
Brasserie €€

(📞03 26 40 96 22; www.boulingrin.fr; 29-31 rue de Mars; menus €25-45; ⊙noon-2.30pm daily & 7-11pm Mon-Sat) A genuine, old-time brasserie – the decor and zinc bar date back to 1925 – whose ambience and cuisine make it an enduring favourite. From September to June, the culinary focus is on *fruits de mer* (seafood) such as Breton oysters.

✕ L'Assiette Champenoise
Gastronomy €€€

(📞03 26 84 64 64; www.assiettechampenoise. com; 40 av Paul-Vaillant-Couturier, Tinqueux; menus €125-325; ⊙noon-2pm & 7.30-10pm Thu-Mon) Heralded far and wide as one of Champagne's finest tables and crowned with the holy grail of three Michelin stars, L'Assiette Champenoise is headed up by chef Arnaud Lallemen. Listed by ingredients, his intricate, creative dishes rely on outstanding produce and play up integral flavours – be they Breton scallops or milk-fed lamb with preserved vegetables. One for special occasions.

▥ Les Telliers
B&B €€

(📞09 53 79 80 74; https://telliers.fr; 18 rue des Telliers; s €68-85, d €80-121, tr €117-142, q €133-163; 🅿🛜) Enticingly positioned down a quiet alley near the cathedral, this bijou B&B extends one of Reims' warmest *bienvenues* (welcomes). The high-ceilinged rooms are big on art-deco character, and handsomely decorated with ornamental fireplaces, polished oak floors and the odd antique. Breakfast costs an extra €9 and is a generous spread of pastries, fruit, fresh-pressed juice and coffee.

Épernay ❺

✕ La Cave à Champagne
French €€

(📞03 26 55 50 70; https://cave-champagne. fr; 16 rue Gambetta; menus €25-40; ⊙noon-2pm & 7-10pm Thu-Mon; 👪) 'The Champagne Cellar' is well regarded by locals for its humble *champenoise* cuisine (snail-and-pig's-trotter casserole, fillet of beef in pinot noir), served in a warm, traditional, bourgeois atmosphere. Pair these dishes with inexpensive regional Champagnes and wines.

✕ La Grillade Gourmande
French €€

(📞03 26 55 44 22; www.lagrilladegourmande. com; 16 rue de Reims; lunch menus €22, dinner menus €33-59; ⊙noon-1.45pm & 7.30-9.30pm Tue-Sat) This chic, art-slung bistro is an inviting spot to try chargrilled meats and dishes rich in texture and flavour, such as crayfish pan-tried in Champagne, and lamb cooked in rosemary and honey until meltingly tender. Diners spill out onto the covered terrace in the warm months. Both the presentation and service are flawless.

▥ La Villa Eugène
Boutique Hotel €€€

(📞03 26 32 44 76; www.villa-eugene.com; 84 av de Champagne; d €175-315, ste from €354; 🅿❄🛜🏊) Sitting handsomely astride the **Avenue de Champagne**, with an outdoor pool, La Villa Eugène is a class act. It's in a beautiful 19th-century town mansion that once belonged to the Mercier family. The roomy doubles exude understated elegance, with soft, muted hues and the odd antique. Splash out more for a private terrace or four-poster bed.

Châteaux of the Loire

France's longest river has been the backdrop for royal intrigue and extravagant castles for centuries. This trip weaves together nine of the Loire Valley's most spectacular châteaux.

14

TRIP HIGHLIGHTS

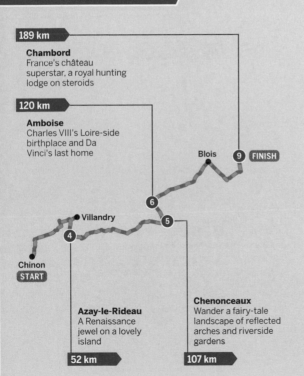

189 km

Chambord
France's château superstar, a royal hunting lodge on steroids

120 km

Amboise
Charles VIII's Loire-side birthplace and Da Vinci's last home

Blois **9** FINISH

6

Villandry **5**

4

Chinon
START

Azay-le-Rideau
A Renaissance jewel on a lovely island

52 km

Chenonceaux
Wander a fairy-tale landscape of reflected arches and riverside gardens

107 km

5 DAYS
189KM / 118 MILES

GREAT FOR...

BEST TIME TO GO
May and June for good cycling weather; July for gardens and special events.

ESSENTIAL PHOTO
Château de Chenonceau's graceful arches reflected in the Cher River.

BEST TWO DAYS
The stretch between Chenonceau and Chambord takes in the true classics.

Chenonceaux Château de Chenonceau

14 | Châteaux of the Loire

From warring medieval warlords to the kings and queens of Renaissance France, a parade of powerful men and women have left their mark on the Loire Valley. The result is France's most magnificent collection of castles. This itinerary visits nine of the Loire's most evocative châteaux, ranging from austere medieval fortresses to ostentatious royal pleasure palaces. Midway through, a side trip leads off the beaten track to four lesser-known châteaux.

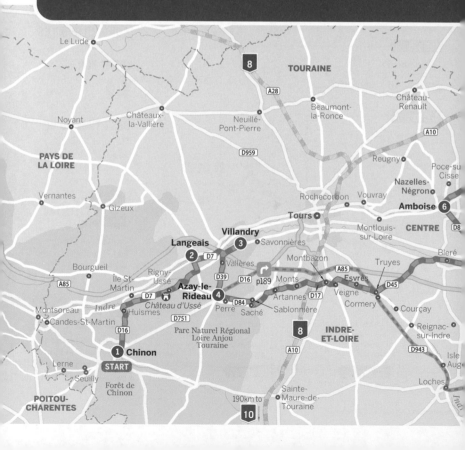

1 Chinon

Tucked between the medieval **Forteresse Royale de Chinon** (☎02 47 93 13 45; www.forteressechinon.fr; adult/child €10.50/8.50; ⊙9.30am-7pm May-Aug, to 5pm or 6pm Sep-Apr) – a magnificent hilltop castle – and the Vienne River, Chinon is known to French schoolchildren as the venue of Joan of Arc's first meeting with Charles VII, future king of France, in 1429. Highlights include superb panoramas from the castle's ramparts and, down in the medieval part of town (along rue Voltaire), several fine buildings dating from the 15th to 17th centuries.

✕ ⊨ p193

The Drive » Follow the D16 north of Chinon for 10km, then head 15km east on the riverside D7 past the fairy-tale Château d'Ussé (the inspiration for the fairy tale Sleeping Beauty) to Lignières, where you catch the D57 3km north into Langeais.

- - - - - - - - - - - - - - - - - -

2 Langeais

The most medieval of the Loire châteaux, the **Château de Langeais** (☎02 47 96 72 60; www.

chateau-de-langeais.com; adult/child €10.50/5.20; ⊙9.30am-6.30pm or 7pm daily Apr–mid-Nov, 10am-5pm or 5.30pm mid-Nov–Mar) – built in the 1460s – is superbly preserved inside and out, looking much as it did at the tail end of the Middle Ages, with crenellated ramparts and massive towers dominating the surrounding village. Original 15th-century furniture and Flemish tapestries fill its flagstoned chambers. In one room, a life-size wax-figure tableau portrays the marriage of Charles VIII and Anne of Brittany, held here on 6 December 1491, which brought about the historic union of France and Brittany.

Langeais presents two faces to the world. From the town you see a fortified castle, nearly windowless, with machicolated

§ **LINK YOUR TRIP**

8 **Essential France**
From Chambord either head north for Versailles and Paris, or south for a longer trip taking in wineries, the Alps and the Mediterranean.

10 **Atlantic to Med**
Head south-east to La Rochelle (a little over 200km) to begin a leisurely meander from coast to coast.

walls rising forbiddingly from the drawbridge. But the newer sections facing the courtyard have large windows, ornate dormers and decorative stonework designed for more refined living.

Behind the château stands a ruined stone **keep** constructed in 994 by the warlord Foulques Nerra, France's first great château builder. It is the oldest such structure in France.

The Drive ⟫ Backtrack south across the Loire River on the D57, then follow the riverbank east 10km on the D16 to Villandry.

❸ Villandry

The six glorious land-scaped gardens at the **Château de Villandry** (📞02 47 50 02 09; www.chateauvillandry.com; 3 rue Principale; chateau & gardens adult/child €12/7.50, gardens only €7.50/5, cheaper Dec-Feb, audio guide €4; ⏱9am-5pm or 6.30pm year-round, château interior closed mid-Nov–early Dec & early Jan-early Feb) are among the finest in France, with over 6 hectares of cascading flowers, ornamental vines, mani-cured lime trees, razor-sharp box hedges and tinkling fountains. Try to visit when the gardens are blooming, between April and October; midsummer is most spectacular.

Wandering the pebbled walkways, you'll see the classical **Jardin d'Eau** (Water Garden), the **Laby-rinthe** (Maze) and the

Jardin d'Ornement (Or-namental Garden), which depicts various kinds of love (fickle, passionate, tender and tragic). But the highlight is the 16th-century-style **Potager Décoratif** (Decorative Kitchen Garden), where cabbages, leeks and car-rots are laid out to create nine geometrical, colour-coordinated squares.

For bird's-eye views across the gardens and the nearby Loire and Cher Rivers, climb to the top of the **donjon** (keep), the only medieval remnant in this otherwise Renaissance-style château.

The Drive ⟫ Go southwest 4km on the D7, then turn south 7km on the D39 into Azay-le-Rideau.

‒ ‒ ‒ ‒ ‒ ‒ ‒ ‒ ‒ ‒ ‒ ‒ ‒ ‒ ‒ ‒ ‒

TRIP HIGHLIGHT

❹ Azay-le-Rideau

Romantic, moat-ringed **Azay-le-Rideau** (📞02 47 45 42 04; www.azay-le-rideau.fr; adult/child €11.50/free, audioguide €3; ⏱9.30am-7pm Jul & Aug, to 6pm Apr-Jun & Sep, 10am-5.15pm Oct-Mar), built in the early 1500s on a natural island in the middle of the Indre River, is wonderfully adorned with elegant turrets, Renaissance-style dormer windows, delicate stonework and steep slate roofs. Its most famous feature is an Italian-style **loggia staircase** overlook-ing the central courtyard, decorated with the royal salamanders and ermines of François I and Queen Claude. The interior

furnishings are mostly 19th century. Outside, the lovely English-style gardens are great for a stroll. A sound-and-light spectacular, **Les Nuits Fantastiques**, is usually projected on the chateau's walls in July and August.

The Drive ⟫ Follow the D84 east 6km through the tranquil Indre valley, then cross the river south into Saché, home to an attractive château and Balzac museum. From Saché continue 26km east on the D17, 11km northeast on the D45 and 9km east on the D976. Cross north over the Cher River and follow the D40 east 1.5km to Chenonceaux village and the Château de Chenonceau.

‒ ‒ ‒ ‒ ‒ ‒ ‒ ‒ ‒ ‒ ‒ ‒ ‒ ‒ ‒ ‒ ‒

TRIP HIGHLIGHT

❺ Chenonceaux

Spanning the languid Cher River atop a su-premely graceful arched bridge, the **Château de Chenonceau** (📞02 47 23 90 07; www.chenonceau.com; adult/child €15/12, with audio guide €19/15.50; ⏱9am or 10am-5pm or 6.30pm) is one of France's most elegant castles. It's hard not to be moved and exhilarated by the glorious setting, the formal gardens, the magic of the architecture and the château's fascinating history. The interior is decorated with rare fur-nishings and a fabulous art collection.

This extraordinary complex is largely the work of several remark-able women (hence its nickname, Le Château des Dames). The distinctive

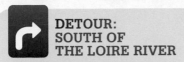

DETOUR: SOUTH OF THE LOIRE RIVER

Start: ④ Azay-le-Rideau

Escape the crowds by detouring to four less-visited châteaux between Azay-le-Rideau and Chenonceaux. First stop: **Loches**, where Joan of Arc, fresh from her victory at Orléans in 1429, famously persuaded Charles VII to march to Reims and claim the French crown. The undisputed highlight here is the walled **Cité Royale** (📞02 47 19 18 08; www.citeroyaleloches.fr; 🕑24hr), a vast citadel that spans 500 years of French château architecture in a single site, from Foulques Nerra's early 11th-century **donjon** to the Flamboyant Gothic and Renaissance styles of the **Logis Royal**. To get here from Azay-le-Rideau, head 55km east and then southeast along the D751, A85 and D943.

Next comes the quirky **Château de Montrésor** (📞02 47 92 60 04; www.chateaude montresor.fr; D760, Montrésor; adult/child €9/5; 🕑10am-6pm or 7pm Mar–mid-Nov), 19km east of Loches on the D760, still furnished much as it was 160 years ago, when it belonged to Polish-born count, financier and railroad magnate Xavier Branicki. The eclectic Second Empire decor includes a Cuban mahogany spiral staircase, a piano once played by Chopin and a sumptuous library. Next, head 20km north on the D10 and D764 to the turreted **Château de Montpoupon** (📞02 47 94 21 15; www.montpoupon. com; D764; adult/child €10/5; 🕑10am-6pm or 7pm Jul-Oct, shorter hours May & Jun, also open Sat, Sun & school holidays early Feb-Mar), idyllically situated in rolling countryside. Furnished in the late 19th and early 20th centuries by the family that still resides there, it has an intimate, lived-in feel. Continue 12km north on the D764 to the ruins of the hilltop **Château de Montrichard**, another massive fortress constructed in the 11th century by Foulques Nerra. You can picnic in the park by the Cher River or taste sparkling wines at **Caves Monmousseau** (📞02 54 32 35 15; www.monmousseau.com; 71 rue de Vierzon, Montrichard; €5; 🕑10am-noon & 2-5.30pm Mon-Sat Nov-Mar, 10am-12.30pm & 1.30-6pm Apr-Jun & Sep-Oct, 10am-6pm Jul & Aug). From Montrichard, head 10km west on the D176 and D40 to rejoin the main route at Chenonceaux.

arches and the eastern formal garden were added by Diane de Poitiers, mistress of King Henri II. Following Henri's death, Catherine de Médicis, the king's scheming widow, forced Diane (her 2nd cousin) to exchange Chenonceau for the rather less grand Château de Chaumont. Catherine completed the château's construction and added the yew-tree maze and the western rose garden. Chenonceau had an 18th-century heyday under the aristocratic Madame

Dupin, who made it a centre of fashionable society; guests included Voltaire and Rousseau.

The château's pièce de résistance is the 60m-long, chequerboard-floored **Grande Gallerie** over the Cher. From 1940 to 1942 it served as an escape route for Jews and other refugees fleeing from German-occupied France (north of the Cher) to the Vichy-controlled south.

The Drive » Follow the D81 north 13km into Amboise; 2km south of town, you'll pass the

Mini-Châteaux theme park (www.parcminichateaux.com), whose intricate scale models of 41 Loire Valley châteaux are great fun for kids!

- - - - - - - - - - - - - - - - - -

> **TRIP HIGHLIGHT**

⑥ Amboise

Towering above town, the **Château Royal d'Amboise** (📞02 47 57 00 98; www. chateau-amboise.com; place Michel Debré; adult/child €13.10/9; 🕑9am-12.30pm & 1.30pm-5.30pm mid-Nov–Feb, 9am-6.15pm or 7.45pm Mar–mid-Nov) was a favoured retreat for all of France's

WHY THIS IS A GREAT TRIP
DANIEL ROBINSON, WRITER

Travel doesn't get more splendidly French – or elegantly sumptuous – than this tour of the most famous Loire Valley châteaux, which bring together so many of the things I love most about France: supremely refined architecture, dramatic history, exquisite cuisine and delectable wines. My kids especially enjoy the forbidding medieval fortresses of Langeais and Loches, which conjure up a long-lost world of knights, counts and court intrigue.

Above: Château de Chambord, Chambord
Left: Château Royal de Blois, Blois
Right: Château de Villandry, Villandry

Valois and Bourbon kings. The ramparts afford thrilling views of the town and river, and you can visit the furnished **Logis** (Lodge) and the Flamboyant Gothic **Chapelle St-Hubert** (1493), where Leonardo da Vinci's presumed remains have been buried since 1863.

Amboise's other main sight is **Le Clos Lucé** ([☎]02 47 57 00 73; www.vinci-closluce.com; 2 rue du Clos Lucé; adult/child €17/12, mid-Nov–Mar €14/11; [☉]9am-7pm or 8pm Feb-Oct, 9am or 10am-6pm Nov-Jan; [♿]), the grand manor house where Leonardo da Vinci (1452–1519) took up residence in 1516 and spent the final years of his life at the invitation of François I.

The most exciting Loire château to open to visitors in years, the **Château Gaillard** ([☎]02 47 30 33 29; www.chateau-gaillard-amboise.fr; 99 av Léonard de Vinci & 29 allée du Pont Moulin; adult/child €13/11; [☉]11am-7pm, shorter hours Jan-early Feb) is the earliest expression of the Italian Renaissance in France.

[✕][🛏] p193

The Drive » Follow the D952 northeast along the Loire's northern bank, enjoying 35km of beautiful river views en route to Blois. The Château de Chaumont-sur-Loire, renowned for its world-class contemporary art and magnificent international garden festival (April to early November), makes a wonderful stop.

❼ Blois

Seven French kings lived in the **Château Royal de Blois** (📞02 54 90 33 33; www.chateaudeblois.fr; place du Château; adult/child €12/6.50, audioguide €3; 🕙9am-6.30pm or 7pm Apr-early Nov, 10am-5pm early Nov-Mar), whose four grand wings were built during four distinct periods in French architecture: Gothic (13th century), Flamboyant Gothic (1498–1501), early Renaissance (1515–20) and classical (1630s). You can easily spend a half-day immersing yourself in the château's dramatic and bloody history and its extraordinary architecture.

In the Renaissance wing, the most remarkable feature is the spiral **loggia staircase**, decorated with fierce salamanders and curly Fs, heraldic symbols of François I. The **King's Chamber** was the setting for one of the bloodiest episodes in the château's history. In 1588 Henri III had his archrival, Duke Henri I de Guise, murdered by royal bodyguards. Dramatic and very graphic oil paintings illustrate these gruesome events next door in the **Council Chamber**.

🍴 📠 p193

The Drive » Cross the Loire and continue 16km southeast into Cheverny via the D765 and, for the final 1km, the D102.

❽ Cheverny

Perhaps the Loire's most elegantly proportioned château, **Cheverny** (📞02 54 79 96 29; www.chateau-cheverny.fr; av du Château, Cheverny; château & gardens adult/child €12.50/9; 🕙9.15am-6.30pm Apr-Sep, 10am-5pm Oct-Mar) represents the zenith of French classical architecture: the perfect blend of symmetry, geometry and aesthetic order. Inside are some of the most elegantly furnished rooms anywhere in the Loire Valley. Highlights include the formal **dining room**, with panels depicting the story of Don Quixote; the **king's bedchamber**, with ceiling murals and tapestries illustrating stories from Greek mythology; and a children's **playroom** complete with toys from the time of Napoléon III.

Cheverny's **kennels** house about 100 pedigreed hunting dogs. Feeding time, known as the **Soupe des Chiens**, takes place on Monday, Wednesday, Thursday and Friday at 11.30am (daily from April to mid-September). Behind the château, the 18th-century **orangerie**, which sheltered priceless artworks – including (apparently) the *Mona Lisa* – during WWII, is now a tearoom (open April to mid-November).

Fans of Tintin may recognise the château's façade as the model for Captain Haddock's ancestral home, Marlinspike Hall. **Les Secrets de**

Moulinsart (Château de Cheverny; adult/child €4.50/4; 🎟) has interactive exhibits about the comics hero and his adventures.

📠 p193

The Drive » Take the D102 10km northeast into Bracieux, then turn north on the D112 for the final 8km run through the forested Domaine National de Chambord, the largest walled park in Europe. Catch your first dramatic glimpse of France's most famous château on the right as you arrive in Chambord.

TRIP HIGHLIGHT

❾ Chambord

One of the crowning achievements of French Renaissance architecture, the **Château de Chambord** (📞info 02 54 50 40 00, tour & show reservations 02 54 50 50 40; www.chambord.org; adult/child €14.50/free, parking distant/near €4/6; 🕙9am-6pm Apr-Oct, to 5pm Nov-Mar; 🎟) – with 426 rooms, 282 fireplaces and 77 staircases – is by far the largest, grandest and most visited château in the Loire Valley.

Rising through the centre of the structure, the world-famous **double-helix staircase** – very possibly designed by the king's chum Leonardo da Vinci – ascends to the great **lantern tower** and the rooftop, where you can marvel at a veritable skyline of cupolas, domes, turrets, chimneys and lightning rods and gaze out across the vast grounds.

Eating & Sleeping

Chinon ❶

🛏 Hôtel Diderot   Historic Hotel €

(📞02 47 93 18 87; www.hoteldiderot.com; 4
rue de Buffon; d €70-110, q €160; P 🛜) This
gorgeous town house is tucked amid luscious
rose-filled gardens and crammed with polished
antiques. The owners – Jean-Pierre, who's
French, and Jamie, who hails from Florida –
impart the sort of charm you'd expect for
twice the price. The 26 cheerful rooms are all
individually styled, some with 18th-century-
style *jouy* wallpaper. No lift. Situated 250m
north of place Jeanne d'Arc. Rates drop 30%
from November to April.

Amboise ❻

🍴 Sunday Food Market   Market €

(quai du Général de Gaulle; 🕑7.30am-1.30pm
Sun, small market 7.30am-1pm Fri) Voted
France's *marché préféré* (favourite market) a
few years back, this riverfront extravaganza,
400m southwest of the château, hosts 200 to
300 open-air stalls selling everything you need
for a scrumptious picnic. So delicious it's worth
timing your visit around.

🛏 Le Clos d'Amboise   Historic Hotel €€€

(📞02 47 30 10 20; www.leclosamboise.com; 27
rue Rabelais; d €89-229, 6-person ste €209-369;
P ❄ @ 🛜 ⛱) Overlooking a lovely garden
with a 200-year-old cedar and a heated pool,
this posh pad – most of it built in the 17th
century – offers exquisite country living in the
heart of town. Stylish features abound, from
luxurious fabrics to antique furnishings. Half of
the 20 rooms still have their original, now non-
functioning, marble fireplaces. The restaurant
serves traditional French cuisine.

Blois ❼

🍴 L'Orangerie du Château   Gastronomy €€€

(📞02 54 78 05 36; www.orangerie-du-chateau.
fr; 1 av du Dr Jean Laigret; menus €40-88;
🕑noon-1.45pm & 7-9.15pm Tue-Sat; P) Serves
cuisine gastronomique inventive inspired by
French tradition and seasonal local products,
including Sologne-raised caviar and black
truffles. For dessert try the house speciality,
soufflé, in versions that change with the
seasons.

🛏 Hôtel Anne de Bretagne   Hotel €

(📞02 54 78 05 38; www.hotelannedebretagne.
com; 31 av du Dr Jean Laigret; d €54-89,
q €79-119; 🕑 reception 7am-11pm; P 🛜) This
ivy-covered hotel, in a great location midway
between the train station and the château, has
friendly staff, a cosy piano-equipped *salon* and
29 rooms with snow-white quilts. A three-
course packed picnic lunch costs €11.50. Rents
out bicycles (€16) and has free enclosed bike
parking.

Cheverny ❽

🛏 La Levraudière   B&B €

(📞02 54 79 81 99; www.lalevraudiere.fr; 1
chemin de la Levraudière, Cheverny; d with
breakfast €85-95, 4-person ste €150; 🛜 ⛱) In
a peaceful 1892 farmhouse, amid 3.5 hectares
of grassland, La Levraudière's four spacious
rooms are comfortable and homey, with colorful
pillows and furry bedspreads. Sonia Maurice, the
friendly owner, speaks English and is happy to
arrange bike rental. Situated 1.5km south of the
Château de Cheverny (p192), just west of the
D102. The 10m heated swimming pool is open
from April or May to September. A homemade,
Sologne-style dinner that includes four courses,
an aperitif, wine and coffee costs €30.

NEED ᵀᴼ KNOW

CURRENCY
Euro (€)

LANGUAGE
French

VISAS
Visas are not required for stays of up to 90 days for travellers from 62 non-EU countries.

FUEL
Petrol stations are common around main towns. Unleaded costs around €1.40 per litre; *gazole* (diesel) is usually at least €0.15 cheaper.

RENTAL CARS
Avis (www.avis.com)

Auto Europe (www.autoeurope.com)

Europcar (www.europcar.com)

Hertz (www.hertz.com)

IMPORTANT NUMBERS
Ambulance (SAMU) ☏ 15

Police ☏ 17

Fire ☏ 18

Europe-wide emergency ☏ 112

Climate

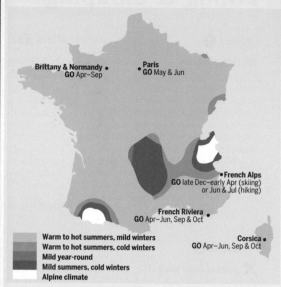

Brittany & Normandy •
GO Apr–Sep

Paris
• GO May & Jun

• French Alps
GO late Dec–early Apr (skiing) or Jun & Jul (hiking)

French Riviera •
GO Apr–Jun, Sep & Oct

Corsica •
GO Apr–Jun, Sep & Oct

■ Warm to hot summers, mild winters
■ Warm to hot summers, cold winters
■ Mild year-round
■ Mild summers, cold winters
□ Alpine climate

When to Go

High Season (Jul & Aug)
» Queues at big sights and on roads.

» Christmas, New Year and Easter equally busy.

» Late December to March is high season in Alpine ski resorts.

» Book accommodation and restaurants in advance.

Shoulder (Apr–Jun & Sep)
» Accommodation rates drop in southern France and other hot spots.

» Spring brings warm weather, flowers and local produce.

» The *vendange* (grape harvest) is reason to visit in autumn.

Low Season (Oct–Mar)
» Prices up to 50% lower than high season.

» Sights, attractions and restaurants open fewer days and shorter hours.

» Hotels and restaurants in rural regions (like the Dordogne) close.

Your Daily Budget

Budget: Less than €130

» Dorm bed: €18–30

» Double room in a budget hotel: €60–90

» Admission to many attractions first Sunday of month: free

» Lunch *menus* (set meals): less than €20

Midrange: €130–220

» Double room in a midrange hotel: €90–190

» Lunch *menus* in gourmet restaurants: €20–40

Top end: More than €220

» Double room in a top-end hotel: €190–350

» Top restaurant dinner: *menu* €65, à la carte €100–150

Eating

Restaurants and bistros Range from unchanged for a century to contemporary minimalist.

Brasseries Open from dawn until late, these casual eateries are great for dining in between standard meal times.

Cafes Ideal for breakfast and light lunch; many morph into bars after dark.

Price ranges refer to the average cost of a two-course meal:

€	less than €20
€€	€20–40
€€€	more than €40

Sleeping

B&Bs Enchanting properties with maximum five rooms.

Hostels New-wave hostels are design-driven, lifestyle spaces with single/double rooms as well as dorms.

Hotels Hotels embrace every budget and taste. Refuges and *gîtes d'étape* (walkers' lodges) for hikers on trails.

Price ranges refer to a double room in high season, with private bathroom, excluding breakfast unless otherwise noted:

€	less than €90
€€	€90–190
€€€	more than €190

Arriving in France

Aéroport de Charles de Gaulle (Paris)

Trains, buses and RER suburban trains run to the city centre every 15 to 30 minutes between 5am and 11pm, after which night buses kick in (12.30am to 5.30am). Fares are €10.30 by RER and €2 to €13.70 by bus. Flat fare of €53/58 for 30-minute taxi journey to right-/left-bank central Paris (15% higher between 5pm and 10am, and Sundays).

Aéroport d'Orly (Paris)

Linked to central Paris by Orlyval rail then RER (€12.10) or bus (€2 to €9.50) every 15 minutes between 5am and 11pm. Or T7 tram to Villejuif-Louis Aragon then metro to the centre (€3.80). The 25-minute journey by taxi costs €32/37 to right-/left-bank central Paris (15% higher between 5pm and 10am, and Sundays).

Mobile Phones

European and Australian phones work, but only American cells with 900 and 1800 MHz networks are compatible. Use a French SIM card with a French number to make cheaper calls.

Internet Access

Wi-fi is available at major airports, in most hotels, and at many cafes, restaurants, museums and tourist offices.

Money

ATMs at every airport, most train stations and on every second street corner in towns and cities. Visa, MasterCard and Amex widely accepted.

Tipping

By law, restaurant and bar prices are *service compris* (include a 15% service charge), so there is no need to leave a *pourboire* (tip).

Useful Websites

French Government Tourist Office (www.france.fr) Sights, activities, transport and special-interest holidays.

Lonely Planet (www.lonelyplanet.com/france)

Mappy (www.mappy.fr) Mapping and journey planning.

Opening Hours

Banks 9am–noon and 2–5pm Monday to Friday or Tuesday to Saturday

Restaurants noon–2.30pm and 7–11pm six days a week

Cafes 7am–11pm

Bars 7pm–1am

Shops 10am–noon and 2–7pm Monday to Saturday

Language

The sounds used in spoken French can almost all be found in English. There are a couple of exceptions: nasal vowels (represented in our pronunciation guides by o or u followed by an almost inaudible nasal consonant sound m, n or ng), the 'funny' *u* (ew in our guides) and the deep-in-the-throat *r*. Bearing these few points in mind and reading our pronunciation guides below as if they were English, you'll be understood just fine.

BASICS

Hello.	*Bonjour.*	bon·zhoor
Goodbye.	*Au revoir.*	o·rer·vwa
Yes./No.	*Oui./Non.*	wee/non
Excuse me.	*Excusez-moi.*	ek·skew·zay·mwa
Sorry.	*Pardon.*	par·don
Please.	*S'il vous plaît.*	seel voo play
Thank you.	*Merci.*	mair·see

You're welcome.
De rien. der ree·en

Do you speak English?
Parlez-vous anglais? par·lay·voo ong·glay

I don't understand.
Je ne comprends pas. zher ner kom·pron pa

How much is this?
C'est combien? say kom·byun

ACCOMMODATION

Do you have any rooms available?
Est-ce que vous avez es·ker voo za·vay
des chambres libres? day shom·brer lee·brer

How much is it per night/person?
Quel est le prix kel ay ler pree
par nuit/personne? par nwee/per·son

DIRECTIONS

Can you show me (on the map)?
Pouvez-vous m'indiquer poo·vay·voo mun·dee·kay
(sur la carte)? (sewr la kart)

Where's ...?
Où est ...? oo ay ...

EATING & DRINKING

What would you recommend?
Qu'est-ce que vous kes·ker voo
conseillez? kon·say·yay

I'd like ..., please.
Je voudrais ..., zher voo·dray ...
s'il vous plaît. seel voo play

I'm a vegetarian.
Je suis végétarien/ zher swee vay·zhay·ta·ryun/
végétarienne. (m/f) vay·zhay·ta·ryen

Please bring the bill.
Apportez-moi a·por·tay·mwa
l'addition, la·dee·syon
s'il vous plaît. seel voo play

EMERGENCIES

Help!
Au secours! o skoor

I'm lost.
Je suis zhe swee·
perdu/perdue. (m/f) pair·dew

Want More

For in-depth language information and handy phrases, check out Lonely Planet's *French Phrasebook*. You'll find it at **shop.lonelyplanet.com**.

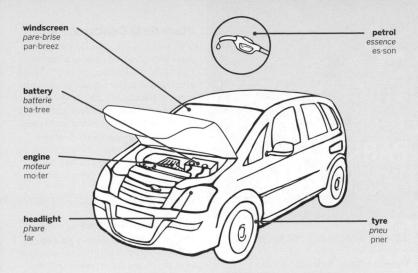

windscreen
pare-brise
par·breez

petrol
essence
es·son

battery
batterie
ba·tree

engine
moteur
mo·ter

headlight
phare
far

tyre
pneu
pner

Signs

Cédez la Priorité	Give Way
Sens Interdit	No Entry
Entrée	Entrance
Péage	Toll
Sens Unique	One Way
Sortie	Exit

I'm ill.
Je suis malade. zher swee ma·lad

Call the police!
Appelez la police! a·play la po·lees

Call a doctor!
Appelez un médecin! a·play un mayd·sun

ON THE ROAD

I'd like to hire a/an ...	*Je voudrais louer ...*	zher voo·dray loo·way ...
4WD	*un quatre-quatre*	un kat·kat
automatic/ manual	*une auto- matique/ manuel*	ewn o·to· ma·teek/ ma·nwel
motorbike	*une moto*	ewn mo·to

How much is it daily/weekly?
Quel est le tarif par jour/semaine? kel ay ler ta·reef par zhoor/ser·men

Does that include insurance?
Est-ce que l'assurance est comprise? es·ker la·sew·rons ay kom·preez

Does that include mileage?
Est-ce que le kilométrage est compris? es·ker ler kee·lo·may·trazh ay kom·pree

What's the speed limit?
Quelle est la vitesse maximale permise? kel ay la vee·tes mak·see·mal per·meez

Is this the road to ...?
C'est la route pour ...? say la root poor ...

Can I park here?
Est-ce que je peux stationner ici? es·ker zher per sta·syo·nay ee·see

Where's a service station?
Où est-ce qu'il y a une station-service? oo es·keel ya ewn sta·syon·ser·vees

Please fill it up.
Le plein, s'il vous plaît. ler plun seel voo play

I'd like (20) litres.
Je voudrais (vingt) litres. zher voo·dray (vung) lee·trer

Please check the oil/water.
Contrôlez l'huile/l'eau, s'il vous plaît. kon·tro·lay lweel/lo seel voo play

I need a mechanic.
J'ai besoin d'un mécanicien. zhay ber·zwun dun may·ka·nee·syun

The car/motorbike has broken down.
La voiture/moto est tombée en panne. la vwa·tewr/mo·to ay tom·bay on pan

I had an accident.
J'ai eu un accident. zhay ew un ak·see·don

197

STRETCH YOUR LEGS
PARIS

Start Place de la Concorde

Finish Place du Panthéon

Distance 4.5km

Duration Three hours

Paris is one of the world's most strollable cities, whether that means window-shopping on the boulevards or getting lost among the lanes of Montmartre. This walk starts by the Seine, crosses to the Île de la Cité and finishes in the Latin Quarter, with monuments and museums aplenty en route.

Take this walk on Trip

Place de la Concorde

If it's Parisian vistas you're after, the place de la Concorde makes a fine start. From here you can see the Arc de Triomphe, the Assemblée Nationale (the lower house of parliament), the Jardin des Tuileries and the Seine. Laid out in 1755, the square was where many aristocrats lost their heads during the Revolution, including Louis XVI and Marie Antoinette. The obelisk in the centre originally stood in the Temple of Ramses at Thebes (now Luxor).

The Walk » Walk east through Jardin des Tuileries.

Jardin des Tuileries

This 28-hectare landscaped **garden** (rue de Rivoli, 1er; ⏰7am-11pm Jun-Aug, 7am-9pm Apr, May & Sep, 7.30am-7.30pm Oct-Mar; Ⓜ Tuileries, Concorde) was laid out in 1664 by André Le Nôtre, who also created Versailles' gardens. Filled with fountains, ponds and sculptures, the gardens are part of the Banks of the Seine World Heritage Site.

The Walk » Walk across place du Carrousel onto the Cour Napoléon.

Musée du Louvre

Overlooking the Cour Napoléon is the mighty **Louvre**, with its controversial 21m-high glass **Grande Pyramide**, designed by IM Pei in 1989. Nearby is the **Pyramide Inversée** (Upside-Down Pyramid), which acts as a skylight for the underground Carrousel du Louvre shopping centre.

The Walk » Continue southeast along riverside Quai du Louvre to Pont Neuf metro station.

Pont Neuf

As you cross the Seine, you'll walk over Paris' oldest bridge – ironically known as the 'New Bridge', or Pont Neuf. Henri IV inaugurated the bridge in 1607 by crossing it on a white stallion.

The Walk » Cross the Pont Neuf onto the Île de la Cité. Walk southeast along Quai des Horloges, and then turn right onto bd du Palais.

Conciergerie

On bd du Palais, the elegant **Conciergerie** (☎01 53 40 60 80; www.paris-conciergerie.

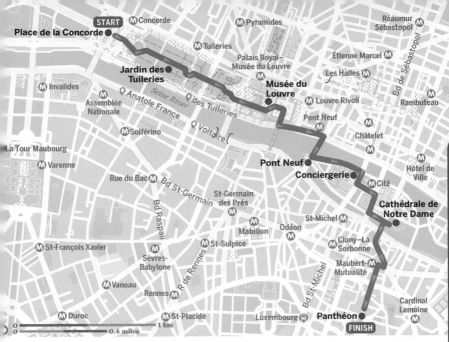

fr; 2 bd du Palais, 1er; adult/child €9.50/free, combined ticket with Sainte-Chapelle €17/ free; ⏱10.30am-6.30pm; M Cité) is a royal palace that became a prison and torture chamber for enemies of the Revolution. The 14th-century Salle des Gens d'Armes (Cavalrymen's Hall) is Europe's largest surviving medieval hall. The nearby church of **Sainte-Chapelle** (joint ticket with Conciergerie €17) has stunning stained glass.

The Walk » Continue east along rue de Lutèce, then cross place du Parvis Notre Dame and walk towards the cathedral.

Cathédrale de Notre Dame

Built on a site occupied by earlier churches and, a millennium prior, a Gallo-Roman temple, **Notre Dame** (www. notredamedeparis.fr; 6 Parvis Notre Dame – place Jean-Paul-II, 4e) was begun in 1163 and largely completed by the early 14th century. While its interior is closed following the devastating fire of April 2019, this French Gothic masterpiece remains the city's geographic and spiritual heart. Its grand exterior, with its two enduring towers and flying buttresses, is a definitive Parisian landmark and symbol of hope during its restoration to its former glory.

The Walk » Cross the river on Pont au Double and follow rue Lagrange to bd St-Germain. Then take rue des Carmes and rue Valette south to the place du Panthéon.

Panthéon

Once you reach the left bank you'll be in the Latin Quarter, the centre of Parisian higher education since the Middle Ages, and still home to the city's top university, the Sorbonne. It's also where you'll find the **Panthéon** (☎01 44 32 18 00; www. paris-pantheon.fr; place du Panthéon, 5e; adult/ child €11.50/free; ⏱10am-6.30pm Apr-Sep, to 6pm Oct-Mar; M Maubert-Mutualité or RER Luxembourg), the neoclassical mausoleum where some of France's greatest thinkers are entombed, including Voltaire, Rousseau and Marie Curie.

The Walk » It's a long walk back, so catch the metro. Walk east to place Monge, take line 7 to Palais Royal Musée du Louvre, then line 1 west to Concorde.

STRETCH YOUR LEGS
NICE

Start Hotel Negresco, Promenade des Anglais

Finish Promenade des Anglais

Distance 5.8km

Duration 2 hours

Get to know Nice's bustling heart with this walk that begins with a seaside stroll, then takes you into the tangled alleys of the old town, and finally up and over the city's soaring headland to the port. Along the way shop, eat and drink in Niçois style.

Take this walk on Trips

Promenade des Anglais

Nice personified, the Prom seductively blends hedonism with history, pumping beach clubs with quiet seaside gazing. Why 'Anglais'? English expats paid out-of-work citrus farmers to build the Prom in 1822. Don't miss the palatial façades of Belle Époque **Hôtel Negresco** and art deco **Palais de la Méditerranée**.

The Walk » Turn up av de Verdun to place Masséna. Take in the elegant architecture, then head down the steps. Take rue de l'Opéra to our next stop.

Rue St-François de Paule

Window-shop or gift shop on this elegant street just back from the seaside. First stop: **Moulin à Huile d'Olive Alziari** (☎04 93 62 94 03; www.alziari.com.fr; 14 rue St-François de Paule; ⊗9am-7pm Mon-Sat, from 10am Sun) for superb local olive oil. Head west to the florid **Opera House**; then shop for soap and sweets along the charming pedestrianised street.

The Walk » Continue on past soap sellers into the open square. This eventually becomes cours Saleya.

Cours Saleya

A top tourist destination that remains Niçois to the core, this bustling market square is the place to greet the day with espresso and banter with flower sellers, lunch with locals or getting rowdy after dark with the town's cool kids.

The Walk » Any of the streets running away from the beach take you to rue de la Préfecture.

Vieux Nice

Soak in the labyrinthine streets of Nice's old town, stumbling upon Baroque gems like **Cathédrale Ste-Réparate** (☎04 93 92 01 35; https://cathedrale-nice.fr; place Rossetti; ⊗2-6pm Mon, 9am-noon & 2-6pm Tue-Sun). Stop to eat – book **Le Bistrot d'Antoine** (☎04 93 85 29 57; 27 rue de la Préfecture; mains €17-32; ⊗9am-1.45pm & 7-10pm Tue-Sat), or grab an aperitif at **Les Distilleries Idéales**

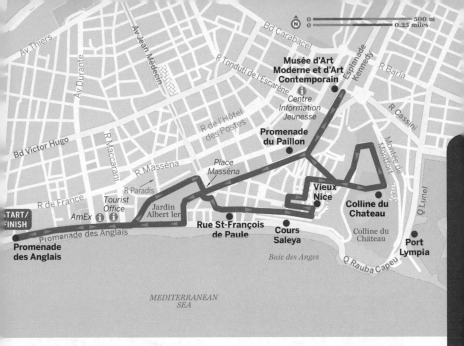

(📞 04 93 62 10 66; www.facebook.com/ldinice; 24 rue de la Préfecture; ⏰ 9am-12.30am). Snacks, ice cream, gift shopping and more are ubiquitous.

The Walk » Take the stairs at rue Rossetti (or if you can't face the climb, the lift at rue des Ponchettes).

Colline du Château

On a rocky outcrop towering over Vieux Nice, the **Parc de la Colline du Château** (Castle Hill; ⏰ 8.30am-8pm Apr-Sep, to 6pm Oct-Mar; 🚌 1 to Garibaldi/Le Château) offers a panorama of the whole city – Baie des Anges on one side, the port on the other. Fabulous for picnics (there's a waterfall) or to let kids loose in the playground.

The Walk » Head towards the cemetery, then follow Allée Font aux Oiseaux and the Montée du Château back into the old town. Take backstreets to bd Jean Jaurès and cross to Promenade du Paillon.

Promenade du Paillon

The grounds of this lovely park unfold from the Théâtre National to place Masséna with a succession of green spaces, play areas and water features. It's a favourite among Niçois for evening strolls.

The Walk » Follow the park as it heads northeast and exit onto av St-Sébastien.

Musée d'Art Moderne et d'Art Contemporain

Nice's modern art **museum** (MAMAC; 📞 04 97 13 42 01; www.mamac-nice.org; place Yves Klein; museum pass 24hr/7 days €10/20; ⏰ 10am-6pm Tue-Sun late Jun–mid-Oct, from 11am rest of year; 🚌 1 to Garibaldi) focuses on the European and American avant-garde from the 1950s to the present, with works by artists such as Yves Klein and César. The building's rooftop works as an exhibition space (with knockout panoramas of the city). Then it's back to the Promenade des Anglais for a post-walk *pastis* (aniseed-flavoured aperitif).

Great Britain

GREAT BRITAIN OVERFLOWS WITH UNFORGETTABLE EXPERIENCES AND SPECTACULAR SIGHTS. There's the grandeur of Scotland's mountains, England's quaint villages and country lanes, and the haunting beauty of the Welsh coast. You'll also find wild northern moors, the exquisite university colleges of Oxford and Cambridge, and a string of vibrant cities boasting everything from Georgian architecture to 21st-century art.

From the world-famous to the well-hidden, our trips will help you discover all the elements that make Britain truly great. History, cities, food, scenery, the arts – we've unearthed the best experiences and crafted them into superb drives.

Dartmoor National Park Rolling hills in a vast national park
MERC67/GETTY IMAGES ©

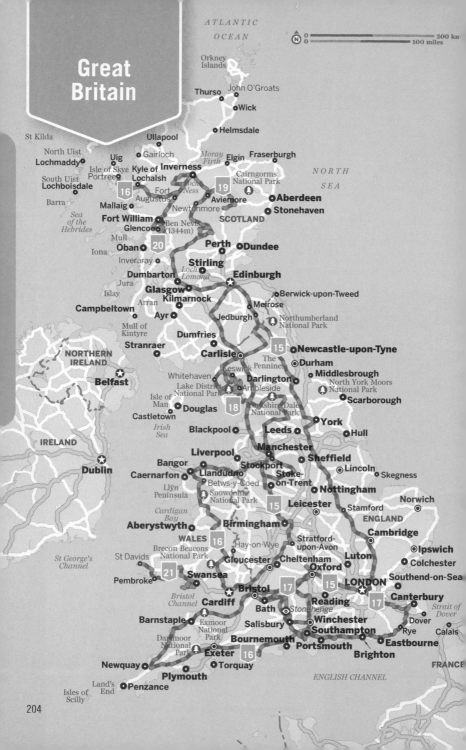

Great Britain

ATLANTIC OCEAN

NORTH SEA

Orkney Islands

St Kilda

North Uist
Lochmaddy
South Uist
Lochboisdale
Barra

Thurso
John O'Groats
Wick
Helmsdale

Ullapool
Gairloch
Uig
Isle of Skye
Portree
Kyle of Lochalsh
Mallaig
Fort Augustus
Newtonmore

Moray Firth
Elgin
Fraserburgh
Inverness
Loch Ness
Cairngorms National Park
16
19
Aviemore
Aberdeen
Stonehaven

SCOTLAND

Sea of the Hebrides
Mull
Iona
Fort William
Glencoe
Ben Nevis (1344m)
Oban
20
Inveraray

Perth
Dundee
Stirling
Loch Lomond
Edinburgh
Dumbarton
Glasgow
Kilmarnock
Campbeltown
Arran
Ayr
Mull of Kintyre
Islay
Jura

Berwick-upon-Tweed
Melrose
Jedburgh
Northumberland National Park

Dumfries
Stranraer
Carlisle
Keswick
The Pennines
15
Newcastle-upon-Tyne
Durham
Middlesbrough
North York Moors National Park
Scarborough

NORTHERN IRELAND
Belfast

IRELAND
Dublin

Isle of Man
Castletown
Douglas
Irish Sea

Whitehaven
Lake District National Park
Ambleside
18
Yorkshire Dales National Park
Darlington

Blackpool
Leeds
York
Hull

Liverpool
Manchester
Bangor
Caernarfon
Llandudno
Betws-y-Coed
Snowdonia National Park
Stockport
Sheffield
Lincoln
Skegness
Stoke-on-Trent
Nottingham
Stamford
Norwich

Llŷn Peninsula
Cardigan Bay
15
Leicester
ENGLAND
Aberystwyth
Birmingham
WALES
16
Hay-on-Wye
Stratford-upon-Avon
Cambridge
Ipswich
St Davids
Brecon Beacons National Park
Gloucester
Cheltenham
Oxford
Luton
Colchester
21
Swansea
17
15
LONDON
Southend-on-Sea
Pembroke
Cardiff
Bristol
17
Canterbury
Bristol Channel
Bath
Stonehenge
Reading
17
Dover
Strait of Dover
Barnstaple
Exmoor National Park
Salisbury
Winchester
Southampton
Rye
Calais
Dartmoor National Park
Bournemouth
Portsmouth
Eastbourne
Brighton
Newquay
16
Exeter
Torquay
Plymouth
Penzance
Land's End
ENGLISH CHANNEL
FRANCE
Isles of Scilly

St George's Channel

15 **The Best of Britain 21 Days**
Three countries and several millennia of history.

16 **Britain's Wild Side 21 Days**
A fresh-air fuelled tour of Britain's best wilderness spots, including eight gloriously diverse national parks.

17 **The Historic South 9–11 Days**
Three of England's most spectacular cathedrals, plus London and Bath's Georgian city-scape.

18 **Classic Lakes 5 Days**
Literary links a-plenty, England's highest hill and utterly unforgettable views.

19 **Royal Highlands & Cairngorms 4–5 Days**
Where roads swerve between majestic mountains and the Royals come to relax.

20 **Great Glen 2–3 Days**
Bewitching lakes and mountains – plus some monster spotting at Loch Ness.

21 **West Wales: Swansea to St Davids 4 Days**
A glorious blast west beside sweeping beaches and vast sand dunes.

 DON'T MISS

Hardknott Pass & Wrynose Pass
Drive England's two steepest road routes where gradients reach 30% on Trip **18**

Kinlochleven
Tackling the ladders and bridges of the 500m via ferrata climbing route which weaves through the crags of Grey Mare's Tail on Trip **2**

Kidwelly Castle
The battlements of lesser-known Kidwelly prove particularly satisfying to clamber around on Trip **21**

The Best of Britain

Journey through three countries and several millennia of history as you take in a greatest-hits parade of Britain's chart-topping sights.

15

TRIP HIGHLIGHTS

716 miles

13

Edinburgh
Delve into the tangle of alleyways around the Scottish capital's Royal Mile

Carlisle

York

0 miles

Manchester

London
This electrifying metropolis is one of the world's great cities

Cambridge

284 miles

Oxford

Cardiff
Visit the Welsh capital's castle, museums and lively streetlife

9

Bath

1

Salisbury

START/ FINISH

Winchester

**21 DAYS
1128 MILES /
1815KM**

GREAT FOR...

BEST TIME TO GO
Myriad festivals take place between May and September.

 ESSENTIAL PHOTO

Britain's biggest city spread below the London Eye.

 BEST FOR HISTORY

Follow atmospheric footpaths through the world's largest stone circle at Avebury.

---

15 The Best of Britain

London's bright lights, blockbuster attractions and stirring history bookend this epic expedition around the British mainland. In between, you'll explore ancient ruins and historic architecture, follow trails that lead from King Arthur to Shakespeare, and discover masterpiece-filled museums and galleries, all connected by quaint villages, patchworked farmland and glorious rolling green open countryside. Rest from life on the road with the best of British drinking, dining and nightlife.

TRIP HIGHLIGHT

❶ London

Prepare for your trip with at least a couple of days in Britain's most exhilarating city. Traversed by the serpentine River Thames, London is awash with instantly recognisable landmarks and open spaces, from **Trafalgar Square** (Ⓤ Charing Cross or Embankment) to the **London Eye** (www.londoneye.com; near County Hall, SE1; adult/child from £24.50/22; ⏱10am-8.30pm, reduced hours in low season; Ⓤ Waterloo or Westminster). Other unmissable sights include the **Houses of Parliament** (📞 tours 020-7219 4114; www.parliament.uk; Parliament Sq, SW1; Ⓤ Westminster), topped by clock tower **Big Ben** (www.parliament.uk/visiting/visiting-and-tours/tours-of-parliament/bigben; Bridge St; Ⓤ Westminster); **Westminster Abbey** (📞 020-7222 5152; www.westminster-abbey.org; 20 Dean's Yard, SW1; adult/child £24/10, half price Wed 4.30pm; ⏱9.30am-3.30pm Mon, Tue, Thu & Fri, to 6pm Wed, to 3pm Sat May-Aug, to 1pm Sat Sep-Apr; Ⓤ Westminster); **St James's Park** (www.

royalparks.org.uk/parks/
st-jamess-park; The Mall, SW1;
⊙5am–midnight; ⓤSt James's
Park or Green Park) and
Palace (www.royal.uk/royal
-residences-st-jamess-palace;
Cleveland Row, SW1; ⓤGreen
Park); **Buckingham Palace**
(☏0303 123 7300; www.rct.
uk/visit/the-state-rooms-buck
ingham-palace; Buckingham
Palace Rd, SW1; ⊙9am–6pm
mid-Jul–end Sep; ⓤGreen Park
or St James's Park); **Hyde
Park** (www.royalparks.org.uk/
parks/hyde-park; ⊙5am–
midnight; ⓤMarble Arch, Hyde
Park Corner, Knightsbridge or
Queensway); **Kensington
Gardens** (☏0300 061
2000; www.royalparks.org.
uk/parks/kensington-gardens;
⊙6am–dusk; ⓤQueensway or
Lancaster Gate) and **Palace**
(www.hrp.org.uk/kensington-
palace; Kensington Gardens,
W8; adult/child £21.50/10.70,
cheaper weekdays after 2pm;

LINK YOUR TRIP

19 Royal Highlands & Cairngorms

Take a detour mid-trip to
explore classic Scottish
countryside: from
Edinburgh head two hours
north through Perthshire to
the lovely village of Braemar.

18 Classic Lakes

Break up the long
drive between Manchester
and Edinburgh by turning
west off the M6 onto the
A590 to tour the charming
Lake District.

⊙10am-6pm, to 4pm Nov-Feb; Ⓤ High St Kensington); and **Tower Bridge** (🕿020-7403 3761; www.towerbridge.org. uk; Tower Bridge, SE1; Ⓤ Tower Hill). World-leading, often-free museums and art galleries include the **Tate Modern** (🕿020-7887 8888; www.tate.org.uk; Bankside, SE1; ⊙10am-6pm Sun-Thu, to 10pm Fri & Sat; Ⓤ Southwark) and the **British Museum** (🕿020-7323 8000; www. britishmuseum.org; Great Russell St, WC1; ⊙10am-5pm, last entry 3.30pm; Ⓤ Tottenham Court Rd or Russell Sq).

London's drinking, dining and nightlife options are limitless (Soho and Shoreditch make great starting points), as are its entertainment venues, not least grand theatre stages such as **Shakespeare's Globe** (🕿020-7401 9919; www. shakespearesglobe.com; 21 New Globe Walk, SE1; ⊙ box office 10am-6pm; Ⓤ Blackfriars or London Bridge).

🛏 p219

TOP TIP: LONDON'S CONGESTION CHARGE

Central London levies a congestion charge from 7am to 10pm daily. Entering the 'C'-marked zone costs £15. You can pay online, at petrol stations or some shops.

In addition, if your car is not a new, cleaner, greener model, the Ultra Low Emission Zone (ULEZ) charge (£12.50) needs to be paid in the same zone 24/7.

You can pay online or over the phone. For full details, see the TFL website (www.tfl.gov.uk).

The Drive ≫ Take the M40 northwest through High Wycombe and the Chilterns Area of Outstanding Natural Beauty (AONB) to Oxford (59 miles in total).

- - - - - - - - - - - - - - - - - -

❷ Oxford

The elegant honey-toned buildings of the university's colleges, scattered throughout the city, wrap around tranquil courtyards and along narrow cobbled lanes. The oldest colleges date back to the 13th century and little has changed inside since, although there's a busy, lively world beyond the college walls. **Christ Church** (🕿01865-276492; www.chch. ox.ac.uk; St Aldate's; adult/child £15/14; pre-booking essential; ⊙10am-5pm Mon-Sat, from 2pm Sun) is the largest of all of Oxford's colleges, with the grandest quad. From the quad, you access 12th-century **Christ Church Cathedral** (🕿01865-276150; www.chch. ox.ac.uk/cathedral; St Aldate's;

⊙10am-5pm Mon-Sat, from 2pm Sun), originally the abbey church and then the college chapel, before it was declared a cathedral by Henry VIII.

Other highlights include Oxford's **Bodleian Library** (🕿01865-287400; www.bodleian.ox.ac.uk/bodley; Catte St; ⊙9am-5pm Mon-Sat, from 11am Sun), one of the oldest public libraries in the world; and Britain's oldest public museum, the 1683-established **Ashmolean Museum** (🕿01865-278000; www. ashmolean.org; Beaumont St; ⊙10am-5pm Tue-Sun, to 8pm last Fri of month; ♿), second in repute only to London's British Museum.

The Drive ≫ Head southwest on the A420 to Pusey and continue southwest on the B4508. You'll reach the car park for the White Horse 2.3 miles southwest of Uffington off the B4507, a 24-mile journey altogether.

- - - - - - - - - - - - - - - - - -

❸ Uffington White Horse

Just below Oxfordshire's highest point, the highly stylised **Uffington White Horse** (NT; www.national trust.org.uk; White Horse Hill; ⊙dawn-dusk) image is the oldest chalk figure in Britain, dating from the Bronze Age. It was created around 3000 years ago by cutting trenches out of the hill and filling them with blocks of chalk; local inhabitants have maintained the figure for centuries. Perhaps it was planned for the gods: it's best seen from the air above. It's a half-mile walk east through fields from the hillside car park.

The Drive >> It's a 49-mile trip to Winchester: return to the B4507 and drive southeast to Ashbury and take the B4000 southeast to join the southbound A34.

④ Winchester

Set in a river valley, this ancient cathedral city was the capital of Saxon kings and a power base of bishops. It also evokes two of England's mightiest myth-makers: famous son Alfred the Great (commemorated by a **statue**) and King Arthur – a 700-year-old copy of the round table resides in Winchester's cavernous **Great Hall** (☎01962-846476; www.hants. gov.uk/greathall; Castle Ave; adult/child £3/free; ◷10am-5pm), the only part of 11th-century Winchester Castle that Oliver Cromwell spared from destruction.

Winchester's architecture is exquisite, from the handsome Elizabethan and Regency buildings in the narrow streets to the wondrous **Winchester Cathedral** (☎01962-857200; www.winchester-cathedral. org.uk; The Close; adult/child £10/free; ◷10am-4pm) at its core. One of southern England's most awe-inspiring buildings, the 11th-century cathedral has a fine Gothic facade and one of the longest medieval naves in Europe (164m). Other highlights include intricately carved medieval choir stalls, Jane Austen's grave (near the entrance, in the northern aisle) and one of the UK's finest illuminated manuscripts, the dazzling, four-volume Winchester Bible dating from the 12th century. Book ahead for excellent tours of the ground floor, crypt and tower.

🛏 p219, p245, p289

The Drive >> From Winchester, hop on the B3049 then the A30 for the 26-mile drive west to Salisbury.

⑤ Salisbury

Salisbury has been an important provincial city for more than a thousand years, and its streets form an architectural timeline ranging from medieval walls and half-timbered Tudor town houses to Georgian mansions and Victorian villas. Its centrepiece is the majestic 13th-century **Salisbury Cathedral** (☎01722-555150; www. salisburycathedral.org.uk; The Close; requested donation adult/child £7.50/3; ◷9am-4pm Mon-Sat). This early-English Gothic–style structure has an elaborate exterior decorated with pointed arches and flying buttresses, and is topped by Britain's tallest spire at 123m, which was added in the mid-14th century. Beyond the cathedral's highly decorative West Front, a small passageway leads into the 70m-long nave. In the north aisle look out for a fascinating medieval clock dating from 1386, probably the oldest working timepiece in the world. Don't miss the cathedral's original, 13th-century copy of the Magna Carta in the chapter house, or, if they've resumed, a 90-minute tower tour, which sees you climbing 332 vertigo-inducing steps to the base of the spire for jaw-dropping views across the city and the surrounding countryside.

The Drive >> It's just 9.6 miles northwest from Salisbury via the A360 to other-worldly Stonehenge.

⑥ Stonehenge

Stonehenge (EH; ☎0370 333 1181; www.english-heri tage.org.uk; near Amesbury; adult/child £21/13; ◷9.30am-5pm, hours may vary; P) is one of Britain's most enduring archaeological mysteries: despite countless theories about the site's purpose, ranging from a sacrificial centre to a celestial timepiece, no one knows for sure what drove prehistoric Britons to expend so much time and effort on its construction. The first phase of building started around 3000 BCE, when

WHY THIS IS A GREAT TRIP
ANTHONY HAM, WRITER

Anything labelled Best of Britain has a lot to live up to, which this trip certainly does. The classy contemporary cities you'll visit here provide a nice counterpoint to so many sites where history is writ large upon the land. Throw in castles, cathedrals and Shakespeare's home town and you really will enjoy Britain's finest.

Above: Stonehenge
Left: Cardiff Castle, Cardiff
Right: Christ Church Cathedral, Oxford

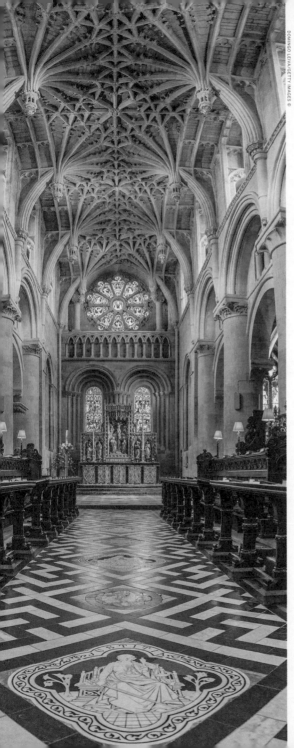

DOMINGO LEIVA/GETTY IMAGES ©

the outer circular bank
and ditch were erected.
A thousand years later,
an inner circle of granite
stones, known as blue-
stones, was added.

An ultramodern
makeover has brought an
impressive visitor centre
and the closure of an in-
trusive road (now restored
to grassland). The result
is a far stronger sense of
historical context; dignity
and mystery returned to
an archaeological gem. A
pathway frames the ring
of massive stones. Al-
though you can't walk in
the circle, unless on a recommended **Stone Circle
Access Visit** (📞0370 333
0605; www.english-heritage.org.
uk; adult/child £47/28), you
can get close-up views.
Admission is through
timed tickets – secure a
place well in advance.

The Drive » Drive east to
Durrington and take the A345
north, climbing over the grassy
Pewsey Downs National Nature
Reserve (home to another chalk
figure, the Alton Barnes White
Horse, dating from 1812), to
reach Avebury (24 miles in total).

❼ Avebury

With a diameter of 348m,
Avebury (NT; 📞01672-
539250; www.nationaltrust.
org.uk; parking per day £7;
🕐 dawn-dusk; 🅿) is the
largest stone circle in the
world. It is also one of the
oldest, dating from 2500
to 2200 BCE. Though
it lacks the dramatic
trilithons of its sister site,
Stonehenge, the massive

stone circle is just as rewarding to visit. Today, more than 30 stones are in place (pillars show where missing stones would have been) and a large section of the village is actually inside the stones – footpaths wind around them, allowing you to really soak up the extraordinary atmosphere. Check whether the National Trust–run guided walks of the site (£3), which were suspended in 2020, have resumed.

The Drive » It's a 27-mile drive along the A4 past patchwork fields, country pubs and a smattering of villages to the Georgian streetscapes of Bath.

❽ Bath

World Heritage–listed Bath was founded on top of natural hot springs and has been a tourist draw for some 2000 years. Its 18th-century heyday saw the construction of magnificent Georgian architecture from the 18th century. The best way to explore the city's Roman Baths complex and beautiful neoclassical buildings is on foot (p294).

Bath is known to many as a location in Jane Austen's novels, including *Persuasion* and *Northanger Abbey*. Although Austen lived in Bath for only five years, from 1801 to 1806, she remained a regular visitor and a

keen student of the city's social scene. At the **Jane Austen Centre** (📞01225-443000; www.janeausten.co.uk; 40 Gay St; adult/child £12/6.20; ⏰9.45am-5.30pm Apr-Oct, 10am-4pm Sun-Fri, 9.45am-5.30pm Sat Nov-Mar), guides in Regency costumes regale you with Austenesque tales as you tour memorabilia relating to the writer's life in Bath.

🛏 p219, p245

The Drive » It's 56.5 miles from Bath to the Welsh capital. Take the A46 north and join the westbound M4 over the Severn Estuary on the six-lane, cable-stayed Second Severn Crossing bridge.

TRIP HIGHLIGHT

❾ Cardiff

Between an ancient fort and ultramodern waterfront, Cardiff has been the capital of Wales since only 1955, but has embraced the role with vigour and is now one of Britain's leading urban centres, as you can see on a stroll through its compact streets.

Cardiff Castle (📞029-2087 8100; www.cardiffcastle.com; Castle St; adult/child £14.50/10, incl guided tour £19.50/14; ⏰9am-6pm Mar-Oct, to 5pm Nov-Feb) has a medieval keep at its heart, but it's the later additions that really capture the imagination. Explore, and you may wind up concurring with the fortress's claim to

be the most fascinating castle in Wales. Devoted mainly to art and natural history, the **National Museum Cardiff** (📞0300 111 2333; www.museum.wales/cardiff; Gorsedd Gardens, CF10 3NP; ⏰10am-5pm Tue, Thu, Sat & Sun; P 🚻) fills a grand neoclassical building. It's both a part of the Welsh National Museum and one of Britain's best museums.

If you time it right, you can catch a fired-up rugby test at Cardiff's **Principality Stadium** (Millennium Stadium; 📞tickets & tours 029-2082 2432; www.principalitystadium.wales; Westgate St; tours adult/child £13.75/9.90; ⏰tours 10am-5pm Mon-Sat, 10.15am-4pm Sun).

🛏 p219

The Drive » Take the A48 northeast for 32 miles, bypassing Newport, to riverside Chepstow.

----

❿ Chepstow

Nestled in an S-bend in the River Wye, Chepstow (Welsh: Cas-gwent) was first developed as a base for the Norman conquest of southeast Wales, later prospering as a port for the timber and wine trades. As river-borne commerce gave way to the railways, Chepstow's importance diminished to reflect its name, which means 'marketplace' in Old English.

One of Britain's oldest castles, imposing **Chepstow Castle** (Cadw;

01291-624065; www.cadw. gov.wales; Bridge St; adult/child £6.50/3.90; ◔10am-1pm & 2-5pm Wed-Sun Mar-Oct, to 4pm Nov-Feb; 🐕) perches atop a limestone cliff overhanging the river, guarding the main river crossing from England into South Wales. Building commenced in 1067, less than a year after William the Conqueror invaded England, and it was extended over the centuries. Today there are plenty of towers, battlements and wall walks to explore. A cave in the cliff below the castle is one of many places where legend says King Arthur and his knights are napping until the day they're needed to save Britain.

The Drive » Farmland makes up most of this 68-mile drive. Head northeast on the A48 along the River Severn to Gloucester then continue northeast on the A46 to Stratford-upon-Avon.

---

⑪ Stratford-upon-Avon

Experiences linked to the life of Stratford's fêted son William Shakespeare range from the touristy (medieval recreations and Bard-themed tearooms) to the humbling – Shakespeare's modest grave in **Holy Trinity Church** (01789-266316; www.stratford-upon-avon. org; Old Town; Shakespeare's grave adult/child £3/2; ◔noon-2pm Mon-Thu, to 4pm

Fri, 11am-4pm Sat) – and the sublime: a play by the **Royal Shakespeare Company** (RSC; box office 01789-331111; www.rsc.org.uk; Waterside). One of the best ways to get a feel for the town's Tudor streets and willow-lined riverbanks is on foot.

Combination tickets are available for the three houses associated with Shakespeare in town – Shakespeare's Birthplace (01789-204016; www.shakespeare.org.uk; Henley St; adult/child £15/11; ◔10am-4pm Mon-Fri, to 5pm Sat & Sun), Shakespeare's New Place

(01789-338536; www. shakespeare.org.uk; cnr Chapel St & Chapel Lane; adult/child £12.50/8; ◔10am-5pm Apr-Aug, to 4.30pm Sep & Oct, to 3.30pm Nov-Feb) and Hall's Croft. If you also plan to visit the childhood home of Shakespeare's wife, **Anne Hathaway's Cottage** (01789-338532; www.shakespeare.org.uk; Cottage Lane, Shottery; adult/child £12.50/8; ◔9am-5pm Apr-Aug, to 4.30pm Sep & Oct, 10am-3.30pm Nov-Mar), and his mother's farm, **Mary Arden's Farm** (01789-338535; www.shakespeare. org.uk; Station Rd, Wilmcote;

BRITAIN'S BEST FESTIVALS

Expect the following festivals to resume with gusto post-pandemic.

In London, see stunning blooms at the Royal Horticultural Society's **Chelsea Flower Show** (020-3176 5800; www.rhs.org.uk/chelsea; Royal Hospital Chelsea, Royal Hospital Rd, SW3; tickets £39.75-92.75; ◔May; Ⓤ Sloane Sq); military bands and bear-skinned grenadiers during the martial pageant **Trooping the Colour** (www.householddivision.org.uk/trooping-the-colour; Horse Guards Parade, SW1; ◔Jun; Ⓤ Westminster or Charing Cross); or steel drums, dancers and outrageous costumes at the famous multicultural Caribbean-style street festival **Notting Hill Carnival** (www. nhcarnival.org; ◔Aug).

Wales' **National Eisteddfod** (Eisteddfod Genedlaethol Cymru; 08454-090900; www.eisteddfod.cymru; ◔Aug) is descended from ancient Bardic tournaments. It's conducted in Welsh, but welcomes all entrants and visitors. It moves about each year, attracting some 150,000 visitors.

Edinburgh's most famous happenings are the **International Festival** (0131-473 2000; www.eif. co.uk; ◔Aug-Sep) and **Fringe** (0131-226 0026; www. edfringe.com; ◔Aug), but the city also has events throughout the year. Check the full list at www. edinburghfestivals.co.uk.

adult/child £15/10; 🕙10am-5pm Apr-Aug, to 4.30pm Sep & Oct; [♿]), you can buy a combination ticket covering all five properties.

Don't miss a pint with the locals at Stratford's oldest and most atmospheric pub, the 1470-built **Old Thatch Tavern** (www.oldthatchtavernstratford.co.uk; Greenhill St; 🕙11.30am-11pm Mon-Sat, from noon Sun; 🛜).

The Drive » The fastest route from Stratford-upon-Avon to Manchester is to head northwest on Birmingham Rd and pick up the northbound M42, which becomes the M6. You'll see the hilly Peak District National Park to your east. It's a 116-mile journey; this stretch incurs road tolls that vary according to the time of day.

---

⑫ Manchester

A rich blend of history and culture is on show in this northern powerhouse's museums, galleries and innovative, multigenre art centres, such as **HOME** (📞0161-200 1500; www.homemcr.org; 2 Tony Wilson Pl, First St; tickets £5-25; 🕙 box office noon-8pm, bar 10am-11pm Mon-Thu, to midnight Fri & Sat, 11am-10.30pm Sun; 🖥️all city centre).

The **Manchester Art Gallery** (📞0161-235 8888; www.manchesterartgallery.org; Mosley St, M2 3JL; 🕙11am-4pm Thu-Sun; 🚇St Peter's Square) has a superb collection of British art and a hefty number of European masters. The older wing has an impressive selection that includes

37 Turner watercolours, as well as the country's best assemblage of Pre-Raphaelite art, while the newer gallery is home to 20th-century British art starring Lucien Freud, Francis Bacon, Stanley Spencer, Henry Moore and David Hockney. A wonderful collection of British watercolours are also displayed at Manchester's **Whitworth Art Gallery** (📞0161-275 7450; www.whitworth.manchester.ac.uk; University of Manchester, Oxford Rd, M15 6ER; 🕙10am-5pm Fri-Wed, to 9pm Thu; 🚌15, 41, 42, 43, 140, 143 or 147 from Piccadilly Gardens), which has an exceptional collection of historic textiles.

Manchester is famed for its rival football teams **Manchester United** (www.manutd.com) and **Manchester City** (www.mancity.com), and its **National Football Museum** (📞0161-605 8200; www.nationalfootballmuseum.com; Urbis Building, Cathedral Gardens, Corporation St, M4 3BG; adult/child £11/6, Manchester residents free; 🕙10am-4pm Thu-Sun; 🚇Victoria Station or Exchange Square) charts British football's evolution from its earliest days to the multibillion-pound phenomenon it is today.

The city is also world renowned for its live-music scene, with gigs in all genres most nights of the week.

✕ 🛏️ p219

KAMIRA/SHUTTERSTOCK ©

The Drive » This trip's longest drive, at 216 miles, takes you northwest via the M61 and M6, passing between the Yorkshire Dales National Park to your east and the Lake District National Park to your west. Once you cross into Scotland the road becomes the A74 and climbs into the Southern Uplands, then becomes the A702 as it leads into Edinburgh.

Edinburgh The view from Caton Hill

13 Edinburgh

The Scottish capital is entwined with its landscape, with buildings and monuments perched atop crags and overshadowed by cliffs. From the Old Town's picturesque jumble of medieval tenements along the Royal Mile, its turreted skyline strung between the black, bull-nosed Castle Rock and the russet palisade of Salisbury Crags, to the New Town's neat neoclassical grid, the city offers a constantly changing perspective.

Along with a walk through the Old Town, unmissable experiences here include visiting **Edinburgh Castle** (✆0131-225 9846; www. edinburghcastle.scot; Castle Esplanade, EH1 2NG; adult/child £17.50/10.50, audio guide £3.50/1.50; ⏰9.30am-6pm Apr-Sep, to 5pm Oct-Mar, last entry 1hr before closing; 🚌23, 27, 41, 42), which has played a pivotal role in Scottish history, both as a royal residence – King Malcolm Canmore (r 1058–93) and Queen Margaret first made their home here in the

217

LOCAL KNOWLEDGE: SCOTLAND'S CRAFT GIN

Scotland is famed around the world for its whisky, but Scottish craft gin (www.thescottishginsociety.com) is also hugely popular. Over 70% of gin consumed in the UK is produced in Scotland – there are more than 90 gin distilleries in the country, and nearly a dozen in the Edinburgh area. Bars all over the capital are offering cocktails based on brands such as Pickering's, 56 North, Edinburgh Gin and Holyrood.

11th century – and as a military stronghold; and climbing to the hilltop **Arthur's Seat** (Holyrood Park; 🚌35) for city panoramas.

Edinburgh has 700-plus pubs, more per square mile than any other UK city. Sample a dram of Scottish whisky at icons like **Malt Shovel** (📞0131-225 6843; www.maltshovelinn-edinburgh.co.uk; 11-15 Cockburn St, EH1 1BP; ⏰11am-11pm Mon-Wed, to midnight Thu & Sun, to 1am Fri & Sat; 🛜👤; 🚌6), with over 100 single malts behind the bar.

🛏️ p219

The Drive ≫ Drive southeast on the A68, passing through the Scottish Borders, and enter Northumberland National Park at the English border. Join the southbound A1 at Darlington, then take the eastbound A59 to York (191 miles altogether).

- - - - - - - - - - - - - - - - -

🄴 York

A magnificent ring of 13th-century walls

encloses York's medieval spider's web of streets. At its heart lies the immense, awe-inspiring **York Minster** (📞01904-557200; www.yorkminster.org; Deangate; adult/child £11.50/free; ⏰11am-4.30pm Mon-Thu, from 10am Fri & Sat, 12.30-2.30pm Sun). Constructed mainly between 1220 and 1480, it encompasses all the major stages of Gothic architecture. The transepts (1220–55) were built in Early English style; the octagonal chapter house (1260–90) and nave (1291–1340) in the Decorated style; and the west towers, west front and central (or lantern) tower (1470–72) in Perpendicular style.

Don't miss a walk on York's City Walls, which follow the line of the original Roman walls and give a whole new perspective on the city. Cover just the highlights or allow 1½ to two hours for the full circuit of 4.5 miles.

🛏️ p219

The Drive ≫ From York, it's 156 miles to Cambridge. Take the A64 southwest to join onto the A1 heading southeast.

- - - - - - - - - - - - - - - - -

🄵 Cambridge

Surrounded by meadows, Cambridge is a university town extraordinaire, with a tightly packed core of ancient colleges and picturesque riverside 'Backs' (college gardens), which you can stroll around.

The colossal neoclassical pile containing the **Fitzwilliam Museum** (www.fitzmuseum.cam.ac.uk; Trumpington St; by donation; ⏰10am-5pm Tue-Sat, from noon Sun), locally dubbed 'the Fitz', was built to house the treasures that the seventh Viscount Fitzwilliam bequeathed to his old university. Standout exhibits include Roman and Egyptian grave goods, artworks by many of the great masters and some quirkier collections such as banknotes, literary autographs, watches and armour.

For the full Cambridge experience, rent a river boat from operators such as **Scudamore's Punting** (📞01223-359750; www.scudamores.com; Mill Lane; chauffeured punt trips per bench/boat from £70/120, 6-person punt hire from £51; ⏰10am-7pm Mon-Fri, to 8pm Sat & Sun).

The Drive ≫ Hop on the M11 for the 55-mile zip south to London.

Sleeping

London ❶

🛏 Hoxton Shoreditch   Hotel ££

(📞020-7550 1000; www.thehoxton.com/
london/shoreditch/hotels; 81 Great Eastern St,
EC2; r £109-260; ❄ 🛜; ⓤOld St) In the heart
of hip Shoreditch, this hotel takes the low-cost
airline approach – book long enough ahead and
you might pay just £109. The 210 renovated
rooms are small but stylish, with TVs, desks,
fridges with complimentary bottled water and
milk, and breakfast (orange juice, granola,
yoghurt and banana) delivered to your door.

Winchester ❹

🛏 16a   B&B £££

(📞07730 510663; www.16a-winchester.co.uk; 16a
Parchment St; r £145-185; 🛜) The word 'boutique'
gets bandied around freely, but here it fits. The
sumptuous conversion of this old dance hall
sees an antique piano and honesty bar frame a
wood-burning stove. Gorgeous bedrooms feature
exposed brick, lofty ceilings, vast beds and baths
on the mezzanines with views of the stars.

Bath ❽

🛏 Grays Bath   B&B £££

(📞01225-403020; www.graysbath.co.uk; 9
Upper Oldfield Park; r £125-185; Ⓟ 🛜) Boutique
treat Grays is a beautiful blend of modern,
pared-down design and family treasures, many
picked up from the owners' travels. All the rooms
are individual: choose from floral, polka dot or
maritime stripes. Perhaps the pick is the curving,
six-sided room in the attic, with partial city views.

Cardiff ❾

🛏 Hotel Indigo   Boutique Hotel ££

(📞0871 942 9104; www.ihg.com; Dominions
Arcade, Queen St; r/ste from £62/103; 🛜) The
Indigo Hotel Group (IHG) has over a dozen
hotels UK-wide, but only this one in Wales. Like
other IHG offerings, it tailors itself uniquely
to Cardiff and Welsh culture. Spacious rooms

cleverly include aspects such as traditional
Welsh fabrics above bed headboards, pictures
of old industrial scenes and sheep decorating
crockery. Insanely good value.

Manchester ⓬

🛏 King Street
Townhouse   Boutique Hotel £££

(📞0161-667 0707; www.eclectichotels.co.uk;
10 Booth St; r/ste from £180/280; ❄ @ 🛜 ☒;
🖵 all city centre) This beautiful 1872 Italian
Renaissance-style former bank is now an
exquisite boutique hotel with 40 bedrooms
ranging from snug to suite. Furnishings are the
perfect combination of period elegance and
contemporary style. On the top floor is a small
spa with an infinity pool overlooking the town
hall; downstairs is a nice bar and restaurant.
Online rates are cheaper.

Edinburgh ⓭

🛏 Southside Guest House   B&B £££

(📞0131-466 6573; www.southsideguesthouse.
co.uk; 8 Newington Rd, EH9 1QS; s/d from
£145/180; 🛜; 🖵 all Newington buses) Though
set in a typical Victorian terrace, the Southside
transcends the guesthouse category and feels
more like a boutique hotel. Its seven stylish
rooms, featuring the clever use of colours and
modern furniture, ooze interior design. Breakfast
is an event, with Buck's Fizz (cava mixed with
orange juice) on offer to ease the hangover.

York ⓮

🛏 Lawrance   Apartment ££

(📞01904-239988; www.thelawrance.com/
york; 74 Micklegate; 1-/2-bed apt from £90/190;
❄ 🛜) Set back from the road in a huddle
of old red-brick buildings that once formed
a factory, the Lawrance is an excellent find:
super-swish serviced apartments with all mod
cons on the inside and heritage character on the
outside. Some apartments are split-level and
all are comfy and spacious, with leather sofas,
flatscreen TV and luxurious fixtures and fittings.

Britain's Wild Side

Immerse yourself in wild Britain on this tri-country trip through glorious national parks and protected Areas of Outstanding Natural Beauty. There's barely a city in sight.

16

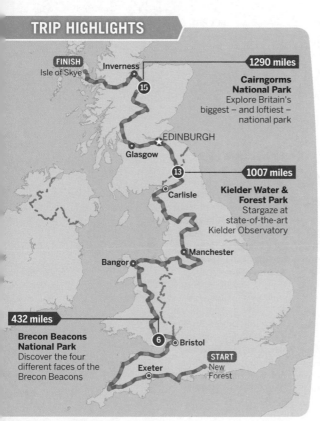

FINISH
Isle of Skye

1290 miles

Cairngorms National Park
Explore Britain's biggest – and loftiest – national park

Inverness

15

EDINBURGH

Glasgow

13

1007 miles

Kielder Water & Forest Park
Stargaze at state-of-the-art Kielder Observatory

Carlisle

Manchester

Bangor

432 miles

Brecon Beacons National Park
Discover the four different faces of the Brecon Beacons

6

Bristol

START
New Forest

Exeter

21 DAYS
1435 MILES / 2310KM

GREAT FOR...

BEST TIME TO GO

June to September offers the best conditions for outdoor activities.

 ESSENTIAL PHOTO

Cornwall's Carnewas at Bedruthan at sunset.

 BEST FOR WILDLIFE

Spot wild red deer, especially in autumn, at Exmoor National Park.

16 Britain's Wild Side

Leave the city lights behind on this adventure into Britain's wild natural heartland. On this intrepid trip you'll get up close to soaring mountain peaks, desolate moorland, sea-sprayed beaches, scalloped bays, lush hills, green dales, high, barren fells, and glassy lakes, some of which teem with wildlife. Along the way, get out and explore the breathtaking countryside on foot, bicycle, horseback and kayak.

1 New Forest

With typical, accidental, English irony the New Forest is anything but new – it was first proclaimed a royal hunting preserve in 1079. It's also not much of a forest, being mostly heathland ('forest' is from the Old French for 'hunting ground'). For an overview of New Forest, which was designated a national park in 2005, stop by the **New Forest Museum** (☎02380-283444; www.new forestcentre.org.uk; main car park, Lyndhurst; ☺10.30am-4.30pm). Wild ponies mooch around pretty scrubland, deer flicker in the distance and rare birds flit among the foliage. Genteel villages dot the landscape, connected by a web of walking and cycling trails. **Lyndhurst tourist office** (☎01425-880020; www.thenewforest.co.uk; main car park, Lyndhurst; ☺10.30am-4.30pm) stocks maps and guides; they're also available from its website. New Forest is also a popular spot for horse riding; **Burley Villa** (Western Riding; ☎01425-610278; www.burleyvilla.co.uk;

Bashley Common Rd, near New Milton) **organises rides using traditional English and also Western saddle styles (per 90 minutes £54).**

📖 p233

The Drive ≫ Take the A31 then the A35 southwest to Weymouth and Chesil Beach. Follow the Jurassic Coast northwest along the B3157 to Lyme Regis (81 miles in total).

❷ Lyme Regis

Fossils regularly emerge from the unstable cliffs surrounding Lyme Regis, exposed by the landslides of a retreating shoreline, making this a key stop along the Unesco-listed Jurassic Coast.

For an overview, **Dinosaurland** (📞0129/-443541; www.dinosaurland.co.uk;

§ **LINK YOUR TRIP**

17 The Historic South

Soak up some of England's rich heritage before starting your wild trip – it's an hour and a half south on the A34 from Oxford to the New Forest.

20 Great Glen

Do this lake-and-mountain themed ramble through the Scottish Highlands in reverse from Inverness.

Coombe St; adult/child £5/4; ☺10am-5pm mid-Feb–mid-Oct, winter hours vary;) overflows with fossilised remains; look out for belemnites, a plesiosaurus and an impressive locally found ichthyosaur. Kids love the lifelike dinosaur models, rock-hard tyrannosaur eggs and 73kg dinosaur dung.

Three miles east of Lyme, the **Charmouth Heritage Coast Centre** (☏01297-560772; www.charmouth.org; Lower Sea Lane, Charmouth; ☺11am-4pm daily Easter-Oct, Fri-Mon Nov-Easter) runs one to seven fossil-hunting trips a week (adult/child £8/4). In Lyme itself, **Lyme Regis Museum** (☏01297-443370; www.lymeregismuseum.co.uk; Bridge St; up to 2 people £12, family £15; ☺10am-4pm Wed-Sat) organises three to seven walks a week (up to six people £125). Book walks ahead.

The Drive ≫ Drive west on the A3052 through the dazzling East Devon AONB to Exeter and take the B3212 up into Postbridge, a small village in the middle of Dartmoor National Park (52 miles all up).

- - - - - - - - - - - - - - -

❸ Dartmoor National Park

Covering 368 sq miles, this vast **national park** (☏01822-890414; www.visitdartmoor.co.uk) feels like it's tumbled straight out of a Tolkien tome, with its honey-coloured heaths, moss-covered boulders, meandering streams and eerie granite tors (hills). It's one of Britain's most wildly beautiful corners.

On sunny days Dartmoor is idyllic: ponies wander and sheep graze beside the road, as seen in Steven Spielberg's WWI epic *War Horse*. But Dartmoor is also the setting for Sir Arthur Conan Doyle's *The Hound of the Baskervilles,* and in sleeting rain and swirling mists the moor morphs into a bleak wilderness where tales of a phantom hound can seem very real. Be aware too that the military uses live ammunition in its training ranges.

Dartmoor is a haven for outdoor activities, including hiking, cycling, riding, climbing and white-water kayaking; the **Dartmoor National Park Authority** (DNPA; www.dartmoor.gov.uk) has detailed information. And there are plenty of rustic pubs to cosy up in when the fog rolls in.

🛏 p233

The Drive ≫ Head west through Tavistock to pass through the Tamar Valley, another AONB, on the A390. At Dobwalls, pick up the A38 and drive west along the forested River Fowey to join the southwest-bound A30. Take the Victoria turn-off and travel northwest past Newquay Cornwall Airport to Carnewas at Bedruthan (62 miles altogether).

- - - - - - - - - - - - - - -

❹ Carnewas at Bedruthan

On Cornwall's surf-pounded coast loom the stately rock stacks of **Bedruthan** (Bedruthan Steps; NT; www.nationaltrust.org.uk). These mighty granite pillars have been carved out by thousands of years of wind and waves, and the area is now owned by the National Trust (NT). The beach itself is accessed via a steep staircase and is submerged at high tide – these were closed at the time of research due to restrictions associated with the coronavirus pandemic. Towards the

---

✓ **TOP TIP: WARNING: DARTMOOR MILITARY RANGES**

Live ammunition is used on Dartmoor's training ranges. Check locations with the **Firing Information Service** (☏0800 458 4868; www.mod.uk/access) or tourist offices. Red flags fly at the edges of in-use ranges by day; red flares burn at night. Beware unidentified metal objects lying in the grass. Don't touch anything; report finds to the **Dartmoor Training Safety Officer** (☏01837-657210).

north end is a rocky shelf known as Diggory's Island, which separates the main beach from another little-known cove.

The Drive » Drive east to join the northeast-bound A39, which runs parallel to the Cornish coast, to the town of Lynmouth in Exmoor National Park (94 miles in total).

➎ Exmoor National Park

In the middle of Exmoor National Park is the higher moor, an empty, expansive, other-worldly landscape of tawny grasses and huge skies.

Exmoor supports one of England's largest wild red deer populations, best experienced in autumn when the annual 'rutting' season sees stags bellowing, charging at each other and clashing horns in an attempt to impress prospective mates. The Exmoor National Park Authority (ENPA; www.exmoor-nationalpark.gov.uk) runs regular wildlife-themed guided walks (free), which include evening deer-spotting hikes. Or head out on an organised jeep safari.

The open moors and a profusion of marked bridleways offer excellent hiking. Cycling is also popular; **Exmoor Adventures** (📱07976 208279; www.exmooradventures.co.uk; Old Bus Garage,

HIKING EXMOOR

The open moors and a profusion of marked bridleways make Exmoor an excellent area for hiking. The best-known routes are the **Somerset & North Devon Coast Path**, which is part of the **South West Coast Path** (www.southwestcoastpath.org.uk), and the Exmoor section of the **Two Moors Way** (www.twomoorsway.org), which starts in Lynmouth and travels 102 miles south over Dartmoor to Ivybridge. From there a 15-mile extension leads to the south Devon coast at Wembury.

Another superb route is the **Coleridge Way** (www.coleridgeway.co.uk), which winds for 51 miles from Lynmouth to Nether Stowey, crossing Exmoor, the Brendon Hills and the Quantocks. Part of the 180-mile **Tarka Trail** (www.tarkatrail.org.uk) cuts through the park. The coastal section sweeps from Lynton to Bideford, before heading down into north Devon.

Check to see if walks run by the Exmoor National Park Authority (www.exmoor-nationalpark.gov.uk) are running. Past events include deer safaris, nightjar birdwatching walks and dark-sky strolls.

ENPA tourist offices also sell a great range of day-walk leaflets (£1).

Porlock Weir; **P**) runs a mountain-biking skills course (from £30) and also rents out bikes (per day £25).

The Drive » From Lynmouth to Libanus in the Brecon Beacons National Park it's 143 miles. Take the A39 east along the coast to join the M5 at Bridgwater. Take the Second Severn Crossing bridge and head west towards Cardiff to join the northwest-bound A470.

TRIP HIGHLIGHT

➏ Brecon Beacons National Park

Brecon Beacons National Park (Parc Cenedlaethol Bannau Brycheiniog) ripples for 45 miles from the English border to near Llandeilo in the west. High mountain plateaus of grass and heather, their northern rims scalloped with glacier-scoured hollows, rise above wooded, waterfall-splashed valleys and green, rural landscapes.

Within the park there are four distinct regions: the wild, lonely **Black Mountain** (Mynydd Du) in the west, with its high moors and glacial lakes; **Great Forest** (Fforest Fawr), whose rushing streams and spectacular waterfalls form the headwaters of the Rivers Tawe and Neath; the **Brecon Beacons** (Bannau

WHY THIS IS A GREAT TRIP
ANTHONY HAM,
WRITER

This classic journey through wild Britain will leave you wondering how such diversity can possibly be within reach on one relatively short trip. Forests and cliffs, mountains and moors – Great Britain is one beautiful place, and this stirring exploration of lakes and national parks showcases the best that Britain's natural world has to offer.

Above: Exmoor National Park
Left: Osprey, Cairngorms National Park
Right: Snowdonia National Park

JUSTIN FOULKES/LONELY PLANET ©

Brycheiniog) proper, a group of very distinctive, flat-topped hills that includes Pen-y-Fan (886m), the park's highest peak; and the rolling heathland ridges of the **Black Mountains** (Y Mynyddoedd Duon) – not to be confused with the Black Mountain (singular) in the west. The park's main **visitor centre** (☎01874-624437; www.breconbeacons.org; Libanus; ☺10am-4pm) has details of walks, hiking and biking trails, outdoor activities, wildlife and geology (call first to check it's open).

🛏 p233

The Drive ≫ Drive north along the A470 to reach the southern boundary of Snowdonia National Park at Mallwyd (79 miles altogether).

❼ Snowdonia National Park

Wales' best-known and most-visited slice of nature, Snowdonia National Park (Parc Cenedlaethol Eryri) became the country's first national park in 1951. Every year more than 350,000 people walk, climb or take the rack-and-pinion **railway** (☎01286-870223; www.snowdonrailway.co.uk; A4086; adult/child return diesel £29/20, steam £37/27; ☺9am-5pm mid-Mar–Oct) to the 1085m summit of Snowdon. The park's 823 sq miles embrace stunning coastline, forests, valleys, rivers, bird-filled estuaries and

Wales' biggest natural lake. The **Snowdonia National Park Information Centre** (📞01690-710426; www.eryri-npa.gov.uk; Royal Oak Stables; 🕐9.30am-12.30pm & 1.30-4.30pm) is an invaluable source of information about walking trails, mountain conditions and more.

The Drive » Continue north on the A470 and take the A5 northwest to Bangor. Cross Robert Stephenson's 1850-built Britannia Bridge over the Menai Strait and take the A545 northwest to Beaumaris (a 72-mile trip).

- - - - - - - - - - - - - - - - - - -

❽ Isle of Anglesey

The 276-sq-mile Isle of Anglesey (Ynys Môn) offers miles of inspiring coastline, hidden beaches and the country's greatest concentration of ancient sites.

Almost all of the Anglesey coast has been designated as an AONB (Area of Outstanding Natural Beauty). Beyond the handsome Georgian town of Beaumaris (Biwmares), there are hidden gems scattered all over the island. It's very much a living centre of Welsh culture, too, as you can see for yourself at **Oriel Ynys Môn** (📞01248-724444; www.orielmon.org; B5111, Rhosmeirch, Llangefni; 🕐10am-4pm Wed-Sun; P). A great, introductory day walk from Beaumaris takes in the ancient monastic site of **Penmon Priory** (Cadw; www.cadw.gov.wales; B5109, Penmon; parking £3; 🕐10am-4pm; P), Penmon Point with views across to Puffin Island, and Blue Flag beach Llanddona.

 p233

The Drive » Return to the mainland and take the A55 northeast, crossing the border into England where the road becomes the M56. Continue northeast towards Manchester before turning off on the southeast-bound M6. At Sandbach turn east on the A534 and follow the signs to Leek, then take the A53 northeast before turning east towards Longnor and then Bakewell (138 miles all up).

- - - - - - - - - - - - - - - - - - -

❾ Peak District National Park

Founded in 1951, the Peak District was England's first national park and is Europe's busiest. But even at peak times, there are 555 sq miles of open countryside in which to soak up the scenery. Caving and climbing, cycling and, above all, walking (including numerous short walks) are the most popular activities. The **Peak District National Park Authority** (📞01629-816200; www.peakdistrict.gov.uk) has reams of information about the park and also operates several cycle-hire centres. The charming town of Bakewell also has a helpful **tourist office** (📞01629-816558; www.visitpeakdistrict.com; Bridge St; 🕐10.30am-4pm).

🛏 p233

The Drive » From Bakewell take the A623 northwest towards Manchester and pick up the northbound M66, then at Burnley take the northeast-bound M65 to Skipton. Enter the Yorkshire Dales National Park on the B6265 to Grassington and

SEEING STARS IN THE BRECON BEACONS

The Brecon Beacons is just one of a handful of places in the world to be awarded 'Dark-Sky Reserve' status. With almost zero light pollution, this is one of the UK's finest places for stargazing. Meteor showers, nebulae, strings of constellations and the Milky Way twinkle brightly in the night sky when the weather is clear. Among the 10 best spots are **Carreg Cennen** (Cadw; 📞01558-822291; www.cadw.gov.wales; Trapp; adult/child £5.50/3.50; 🕐9.30am-5pm), **Sugar Loaf** (Mynydd Pen-y-Fâl) and **Llanthony Priory** (Cadw; www.cadw.gov.wales; 🕐10am-4pm; P♿).

Visitor centres throughout the park can give you information about stargazing events, or check out www.breconbeacons.org/stargazing.

head northwest on the B6265 to Aysgarth. Then take the A684 along the River Ure to Hawes (a total of 118 miles).

---

⑩ Yorkshire Dales National Park

Protected as a national park since the 1950s, the glacial valleys of the Yorkshire Dales (named from the old Norse word *dalr,* meaning 'valleys') are characterised by a distinctive landscape of high heather moorland, stepped skylines and flat-topped hills above valleys patchworked with drystone dykes and little barns. Hawes is home to the **Wensleydale Creamery** (www.wensley dale.co.uk; Gayle Lane; adult/child £1.95/free; ⊙10am-4pm; ⓟ ⓦ), producing famous Wensleydale cheese. In the limestone country of the southern Dales you'll encounter extraordinary examples of karst scenery (created by rainwater dissolving the underlying limestone bedrock).

The Drive ⟫ Head southwest on the B6255 to Ingleton. Take the A65 northwest to Sizergh then the A590 southwest to the Lake District's southern reaches at Newby Bridge. Drive north along Lake Windermere before veering northwest to Hawkshead (53 miles all up).

---

⑪ Lake District National Park

The Lake District (or Lakeland, as it's com-

TOP TIP: WALKING SAFETY TIPS

The British countryside can appear gentle, and often is, but conditions can deteriorate quickly. Year-round on the hills or open moors carry warm waterproof clothing, a map and compass, and high-energy food (eg chocolate) and drinks. If you're really going off the beaten track, leave your route details with someone.

monly known round these parts) is by far the UK's most popular national park. Ever since the Romantic poets arrived in the 19th century, its postcard panorama of craggy hilltops, mountain tarns and glittering lakes has stirred visitors' imaginations. It's awash with outdoor opportunities, from lake cruises to mountain walks.

Many people visit for the region's literary connections: among the many writers who found inspiration here are William Wordsworth, Samuel Taylor Coleridge, Arthur Ransome and, of course, Beatrix Potter, a lifelong lover of the Lakes, whose delightful former farmhouse, **Hill Top** (NT; ☏01539-436269; www.nationaltrust.org.uk/hill-top; garden adult/child £5/2.50; ⊙10am-5.30pm Jun-Aug, to 4.30pm Sat-Thu Apr, May, Sep & Oct, weekends only Nov-Mar), inspired many of her tales, including *Peter Rabbit*.

🛏 p233

The Drive ⟫ Drive northwest on the A591 to join the A595 to Carlisle. Then take the A689 and A69 northeast to Walltown along Hadrian's Wall (72 miles altogether).

---

⑫ Hadrian's Wall

Hadrian's Wall is one of Britain's most revealing and dramatic Roman ruins, its 2000-year-old procession of abandoned forts, garrisons, towers and milecastles marching across the wild and lonely landscape of northern England. The wall was about defence and control, but this edge-of-empire barrier also symbolised the boundary of civilised order – to the north lay the unruly land of the marauding Celts, while to the south was the Roman world of orderly taxpaying, underfloor heating and bathrooms. There's an excellent visitor centre at **Walltown** (Northumberland National Park Visitor Centre; ☏01434-344396; www. northumberlandnation alpark.org.uk; Greenhead; ⊙10am-6pm daily Apr-Sep, to

5pm daily Oct, 10am-4pm Sat & Sun Nov-Mar). The finest sections of the wall run along the southern edge of remote **Northumberland National Park** (☑01434-605555; www.northumberlandnationalpark.org.uk), one of Britain's finest wilderness areas.

The Drive » Follow the B6318 northeast along Hadrian's Wall. Turn north on the B6320 to Bellingham. Continue northwest alongside the North Tyne river and Kielder Water lake to the village of Kielder (a 43-mile journey).

TRIP HIGHLIGHT

⑬ Kielder Water & Forest Park

Adjacent to Northumberland National Park, the Kielder Water & Forest Park is home to the vast artificial lake Kielder Water, holding 200 billion litres. Surrounding its 27-mile-long shoreline is England's largest plantation forest, with 150 million spruce and pine trees. Kielder Water is a water-sports playground (and midge magnet; bring insect repellent), and also has walking and cycling as well as great birdwatching. Comprehensive information is available at www.visitkielder.com.

The lack of population here helped see the area awarded dark-sky status by the International Dark Skies Association in 2013 (the largest

such designation in Europe), with controls to prevent light pollution. For the best views of the Northumberland International Dark Sky Park, attend a stargazing session at state-of-the-art, 2008-built **Kielder Observatory** (☑0191-265 5510; www.kielderobservatory.org; Black Fell, off Shilling Pot; adult/child from £20/15; ☺by reservation). Book ahead and dress warmly as it's seriously chilly here at night.

The Drive » It's a 139-mile drive from Kielder to Balloch on the southern shore of Loch Lomond. Head north into Scotland and join the A68 towards Edinburgh. Take the M8 to Glasgow and then the A82 northwest to Balloch.

---

⑭ Loch Lomond

Loch Lomond is mainland Britain's largest lake and, after Loch Ness, the most famous of Scotland's lochs. It's part of **Loch Lomond & the Trossachs National Park** (☑01389-722600; www.lochlomond-trossachs.org), which extends over a sizeable area, from Balloch north to Tyndrum and Killin, and from Callander west to the forests of Cowal.

From Balloch, **Sweeney's Cruises** (☑01389-752376; www.sweeneyscruiseco.com; Balloch Rd, Balloch) offers, among other trips, a popular one-hour return

cruise to the island of Inchmurrin (adult/child £12.50/8, nine times daily April to September, twice daily October to March). The quay is directly opposite Balloch train station. With departures from Tarbet and Luss on the loch's western shore, **Cruise Loch Lomond** (☑01301-702356; www.cruiselochlomond.co.uk;

Loch Lomond & the Trossachs National Park Red deer

Tarbet; cruises adult/child from £12/7.50; ☉8.30am-5.30pm late Mar-early Nov) runs short cruises and two-hour trips to Arklet Falls and Rob Roy's Cave (adult/child £15/9.50). There are also several options that involve drop-offs and pick-ups with a hike in between.

The Drive ⟫ Follow the A82 along Loch Lomond's western shoreline and pick up the northeast-bound A85 at Crianlarich, then the A827. Then take the northwest-bound A9 to Aviemore (a total of 141 miles).

- - - - - - - - - - - - - - - -

`TRIP HIGHLIGHT`

⑮ Cairngorms National Park

The vast Cairngorms National Park (www. cairngorms.co.uk) stretches from Aviemore in the north – which has a handy **tourist office** (☎01479-810930; www. visitaviemore.com; The Mall, Grampian Rd; ☉10am-4pm Sep-Jun, longer hours Jul & Aug) – to the Angus Glens in the south, and from Dalwhinnie in the west to Ballater and Royal Deeside in the east.

The park encompasses the highest landmass

OUTER HEBRIDES

If you're not ready to return to the mainland after visiting the Isle of Skye, consider a trip to the Outer Hebrides (aka the Western Isles; Na h-Eileanan an Iar in Gaelic) – a 130-mile-long string of islands west of Skye. More than a third of Scotland's registered crofts are here, and no less than 60% of the population are Gaelic speakers. With limited time, head straight for the west coast of Lewis with its prehistoric sites, preserved black houses, beautiful beaches, and arts and crafts studios – the **Stornoway Tourist Office** (☎01851-703088; www.visitouterhebrides.co.uk; 26 Cromwell St, HS1 2DD; ⊙10am-4pm daily Apr-Oct, closed Sun Nov-Mar) can provide a list. Ferries (car £31.65, driver and passenger £6.50 each) run once or twice daily from Uig on Skye to Lochmaddy (1¾ hours) and Tarbert (1½ hours).

in Britain – a broad mountain plateau, riven only by the deep valleys of the Lairig Ghru and Loch Avon, with an average altitude of over 1000m and including five of the six highest summits in the UK. This wild mountain landscape of granite and heather has a sub-Arctic climate and supports rare alpine tundra vegetation and high-altitude bird species, such as snow bunting, ptarmigan and dotterel. Lower down, scenic glens are softened by beautiful open forests of native Scots pine, home to rare animals and birds such as pine martens, Scottish wildcats, red squirrels, ospreys, capercaillies and crossbills.

🛏 p233

The Drive » Take the A9 northwest to Inverness, then the southwest-bound A82 along Loch Ness. At Invermoriston join the westbound A887, which becomes the A87, and continue to Kyle of Lochalsh where you'll cross the Skye Bridge to the Isle of Skye. Continue along the A87 to reach Portree (145 miles all up).

- - - - - - - - - - - - - - - - - -

🔟 Isle of Skye

The Isle of Skye (an t-Eilean Sgiathanach in Gaelic) takes its name from the old Norse *sky-a,* meaning 'cloud island', a Viking reference to the often-mist-enshrouded Cuillin Hills. It's a 50-mile-long patchwork of velvet moors, jagged mountains, sparkling lochs and towering sea cliffs. Lively Portree (Port Righ) has the island's only **tourist office** (☎01478-612992; www.visitscotland.com/destinations-maps/isle-skye; Bayfield Rd, IV51 9EL; ⊙10am-4pm Mon-Sat year-round, longer hours Jun-Aug; 🔋).

Skye offers some of the finest walking in Scotland, including short, low-level routes. The sheltered coves and sea lochs around the coast of Skye provide magnificent sea-kayaking. **Whitewave Outdoor Centre** (☎01470-542414; www.white-wave.co.uk; 19 Linicro, Kilmuir, IV51 9YN; half-day kayak session per person £40-50; ⊙Mar-Oct) runs expeditions and courses for beginners and experienced paddlers to otherwise inaccessible places.

Skye's stunning scenery is the main attraction, but there are castles, crofting museums and cosy pubs and restaurants, along with dozens of art galleries and craft studios.

Eating & Sleeping

New Forest ❶

🍴 The Pig — Boutique Hotel ££££

(📞01590-622354; www.thepighotel.com/brockenhurst; Beaulieu Rd, Brockenhurst; r £189-350; P 📶) One of the New Forest's classiest hotels remains an utter delight: log baskets, croquet mallets and ranks of guest gumboots give things a country-house air; espresso machines and mini-larders lend bedrooms a luxury touch. The effortless elegance makes it feel like you've just dropped by a friend's (very stylish) rural retreat.

Dartmoor National Park ❸

🍴 Tor Royal Farm — B&B ££

(📞01822-890189; www.torroyal.co.uk; Tor Royal Lane, near Princetown; s £70, d £85-115, tr £130; P 📶) An easy-going, country-cottage-styled farmhouse packed with lived-in charm. Heritage-style rooms feature cream-and-white furniture, puffy bedspreads and easy chairs. They'll even rustle up an evening meal, probably featuring the farm's own reared beef or lamb.

Brecon Beacons National Park ❻

🍴 Coach House — B&B ££

(📞01874-620043; www.coachhousebrecon.com; 12 Orchard St; d £89-150; 📶) This appealing 19th-century coaching inn is well attuned to the needs of walkers, with a drying room for hiking gear, generous breakfasts (including good vegetarian options), and packed lunches should you so wish. The six stylish, modern rooms, decorated in soothing taupes and creams, have ultra-comfy beds and great showers.

Isle of Anglesey ❽

🍴 Tredici Italian Kitchen — Italian ££

(📞01248-811230; www.facebook.com/tredicikitchen; 13 Castle St; mains £14-16; ⏰6-9pm Mon-Wed, noon-9pm Thu, noon-3pm & 6-9pm Fri & Sat) Occupying an intimate 1st-floor dining room above a quality butcher and grocer, Tredici has brought a touch of the Mediterranean to Anglesey. While local produce is used where possible (Halen Môn sea salt perks up the fries, and the mussels are from the Menai Strait), the figs, mozzarella and other pizza toppings and calzone fillings are imported from sunnier climes.

Peak District National Park ❾

🍴 Rutland Arms Hotel — Hotel £££

(📞01629-812812; www.rutlandarmsbakewell.co.uk; The Square; d incl breakfast from £168; P 📶🐾) Jane Austen is said to have stayed in room 2 of this aristocratic, 1804-built stone coaching inn while working on *Pride and Prejudice*. Its 33 rooms are in the main house and adjacent courtyard building; higher-priced rooms have lots of Victorian flourishes. Upmarket British classics (£14 to £23) such as pheasant and parsnip pie are served at its restaurant.

Lake District National Park ⓫

🍴 Yewfield — B&B ££

(📞01539-436765; www.yewfield.co.uk; Hawkshead Hill; s £90-115, d £100-145; P 📶) This rambling Victorian mansion is one of the best options around Hawkshead, in a tranquil rural spot near **Tarn Hows** (NT; www.nationaltrust.org.uk/coniston-and-tarn-hows). It's veggie-only and ecofriendly (all heating and hot water comes from a biomass boiler supplied from the hotel's own woodland), and the handsome rooms are stocked with antiques. The spacious landscaped grounds are a highlight.

Cairngorms National Park ⓯

🍴 Cairngorm Hotel — Hotel ££

(📞01479-810233; www.cairngorm.com; Grampian Rd; s/d £75/110; P 📶🚶) Better known as 'the Cairn', this long-established hotel is set in the fine old granite building with the pointy turret opposite the train station. It's a welcoming place with comfortable rooms and a determinedly Scottish atmosphere, with tartan carpets and stags' antlers. There's live music on weekends, so it can get a bit noisy – not for early-to-bedders.

The Historic South

17

England's rich heritage runs like a glittering seam through this remarkable road trip across the south. You'll discover sights nautical, archaeological and architectural as you clock up the miles.

TRIP HIGHLIGHTS

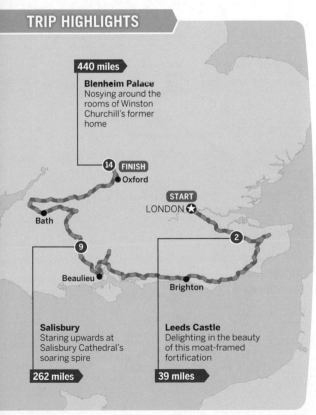

440 miles

Blenheim Palace
Nosying around the rooms of Winston Churchill's former home

14 **FINISH**
● Oxford

START
LONDON ✪

Bath

9

2

Beaulieu

Brighton

Salisbury
Staring upwards at Salisbury Cathedral's soaring spire

262 miles

Leeds Castle
Delighting in the beauty of this moat-framed fortification

39 miles

9–11 DAYS
450 MILES / 720KM

GREAT FOR...

BEST TIME TO GO

Spring and autumn. Plus summer if you don't mind more crowds.

📷 ESSENTIAL PHOTO

Lounging in a punt with a backdrop of Oxford's divine buildings.

☑ BEST FOR SURPRISES

The world's biggest stone circle: Avebury (not Stonehenge).

Leeds Castle Library room

17 The Historic South

Stand by to tour some of the world's most beautiful castles and most memorable archaeological sites. Take in three of England's most impressive cathedrals, Georgian cityscapes, Churchill's palace and Oxford's spires. Discover art and this country's fine tradition of seaside kitsch. Motor to a car museum, explore unspoiled villages and encounter 14th-century fellow travellers' tales. And in doing so, take a road trip through the very best of Britain's past.

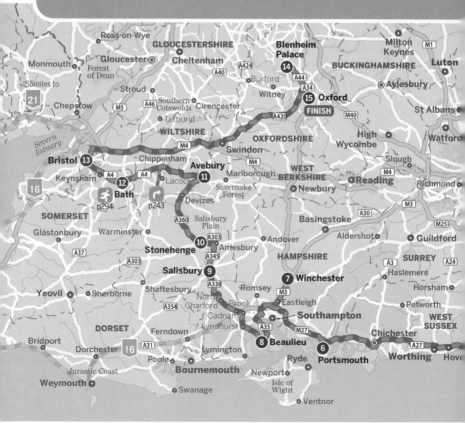

① London

Vibrant London is so packed with historic sights, it can be difficult to know where to start. Try the cathedral that is the capital's touchstone: **St Paul's** (☏020-7246 8357; www.stpauls.co.uk; St Paul's Churchyard, EC4; adult/child £17/7.20; ☺8.30am-4.30pm Mon-Sat; Ⓤst Paul's). Designed by Sir Christopher Wren in 1675 after the Great Fire, its vast dome is famed for avoiding Luftwaffe raids during the Blitz. Head inside and up 257 steps

to the walkway called the Whispering Gallery, then to the Golden Gallery at the top for unforgettable London views. Next walk north to the **Museum of London** (☏020-7001 9844; www.museumoflondon.org.uk; 150 London Wall, EC2; ☺10am-6pm; ⓊBarbican), where the capital's rich past is explored in riveting style. Then head east to elegant Tower Bridge to learn in its **exhibition** (☏020-7403 3761; www.towerbridge.org.uk; Tower Bridge, SE1; adult/child £10.60/5.30, incl Monument £12/5.50; ☺9.30am-5pm; ⓊTower Hill) just how they

raise the arms – and the road – to let ships through.

The Drive » London's streets and suburbs meet bursts of the Kent countryside; you're heading for the A20 towards Sidcup, then the M20 towards Dover. Shortly after Maidstone leave the motorway behind, picking up A20 signs for Lenham and then Leeds Castle, some 40 miles from the capital.

TRIP HIGHLIGHT

② Leeds Castle

Immense and moat-ringed, for many **Leeds Castle** (www.leeds-castle.com; adult/child £27/18.50; ☺10am-6pm Apr-Sep, to 5pm Oct-Mar; ♿) is one of the world's most romantic. The formidable, intricate structure balancing on two islands is known as something of a 'ladies

LINK YOUR TRIP

21 West Wales: Swansea to St Davids

From Oxford, head west on the M4 to Swansea for the sweeping beaches and vast sand dunes of the Welsh coast.

16 Britain's Wild Side

It's an hour and a half south from Oxford to the New Forest to pick up this exploration of Britain's glorious national parks.

237

castle'. This stems from the fact that in its more than 1000 years of history, it has been home to a who's who of medieval queens, most famously Henry VIII's first wife, Catherine of Aragon.

The Drive » Next up is a 25-mile cruise, high up over the vast chalk ridge of the North Downs. Behind you stretch the villages and fields of the Weald of Kent. But you're headed northeast, largely along the A252/A28 – the Canterbury Rd which echoes the old pilgrim footpath to the cathedral city.

---

❸ Canterbury

Canterbury tops the charts for English cathedral cities – and no wonder. Here medieval alleyways frame exquisite architecture, with **Canterbury Cathedral** (www.canterbury-cathedral. org; adult/child £12.50/8.50, tours adult/child £5/4, audio guide £4/3; ⏰10am-4.30pm Mon-Sat, 12.30-4.30pm Sun) the centrepiece.

This towering Gothic masterpiece features fine stonework, a cavernous crypt and the site of English history's most famous murder: Archbishop Thomas Becket was killed here in 1170 after 'hints' from King Henry II, and has drawn pilgrims for more than 800 years since. Knowledgeable guides double up as energetic oarsmen at **Canterbury Historic River Tours** (📞07790 534744; www. canterburyrivertours.co.uk; King's Bridge; adult/child £12.50/7; ⏰10am-5pm Mar-Oct) for fascinating, multi-award-winning River Stour minicruises. For a taste of even older Canterbury, head to the mosaics of the **Roman Museum** (www.canterbury museums.co.uk; Butchery Lane; adult/child £9/free; ⏰10am-5pm).

🛏 p245

The Drive » Now for a 35-mile drive. Head back up and over those creamy North Downs on the A28 towards Ashford. Then plunge down to roll along the A2070, through the verdant valley of the Weald of Kent, then take the A259. Soon you're edging the flatlands of Romney Marsh and arriving at Rye.

---

❹ Rye

Welcome to one of England's prettiest seaside towns. Here cobbled lanes, wonky Tudor buildings and tales of smugglers abound. The best place to start stretching your legs is **Mermaid Street**. It bristles with 15th-century timber-framed houses with quirky names such as 'The House with Two Front Doors' and 'The House Opposite'. The **Rye Heritage Centre** (📞01797-226696; www. ryeheritage.co.uk; Strand Quay; ⏰10am-5pm Apr-Oct, shorter hours Nov-Mar) offers themed walking tours.

The Drive » The next 50-mile leg sees you taking a string of A roads west. They lead past the woods and farms of the High Weald AONB and up another chalk ridge, this time the amphitheatre of hills known as the South Downs. Eventually, it's time to descend to Brighton on the shore.

---

❺ Brighton

Famously hedonistic, exuberant and home to the UK's biggest gay scene, Brighton rocks the south. The bright and

---

THE CANTERBURY TALES

The Canterbury Tales is the best-known work of English literature's father figure: Geoffrey Chaucer (1342–1400). Chaucer was the first English writer to introduce characters – rather than 'types' – into fiction. They feature strongly in *The Canterbury Tales*, an unfinished series of 24 vivid stories told by a party of pilgrims travelling between London and Canterbury. The text remains a pillar of the literary canon. But more than that, it's a collection of rollicking good yarns of adultery, debauchery, crime and edgy romance, and is filled with Chaucer's witty observations about human nature.

breezy seafront boasts the grand, century-old **Brighton Pier** (www. brightonpier.co.uk; Madeira Dr; ◷11am-9pm Mon-Fri, 10am-10pm Sat, 10am-9pm Sun), complete with fairground rides, amusement arcades and candy-floss stalls. Stroll inland to the magnificent **Royal Pavilion** (☎0300-290 9000; http://brightonmuseums. org.uk/royalpavilion; Royal Pavilion Gardens; adult/child £15.50/9.50; ◷9.30am-5 45pm Apr-Sep, 10am-5.15pm Oct-Mar), the glittering palace of Prince George (later King George IV). It's one of the most opulent buildings in England, and Europe's finest example of early-19th-century chinoiserie. Take in the Salvador Dalí sofa modelled on Mae West's lips at the **Brighton Museum & Art Gallery** (www.brightonmuseums.org. uk; Royal Pavilion Gardens; adult/child £6.20/3.60; ◷10am-5pm Tue-Sun), then gear up for a lively night out by shopping amid the boutiques of the tightly packed **Brighton Lanes**.

✕ ⨼ p245

The Drive ≫ Next is a 50-mile blast due west, largely along A roads, to the historic port of Portsmouth. As the 170m-high Spinnaker Tower gets closer on the horizon, pick up signs for the Historic Dockyard Car Park.

----

❻ Portsmouth

For a world-class collection of maritime heritage,

DETOUR: BEACHY HEAD

Start: ❹ Rye

An 8-mile detour off your route leads to a truly remarkable view. Around 25 miles west of Rye, peel off the A27 onto the A22 to Eastbourne. Head to the seafront to take the signed route that climbs to Beachy Head. Pick from several parking spots and follow the footpaths to the cliffs themselves. These 162m-tall sheer chalk faces are the highest point of cliffs that slice across the rugged coastline at the southern end of the South Downs. Far below sits a squat red-and-white-striped lighthouse. Appealing walks include the 1.5-mile hike west to the beach at Birling Gap.

head to **Portsmouth Historic Dockyard** (☎023-9283 9766; www.historic-dockyard.co.uk; Victory Gate; all-attraction Explorer ticket adult/child/family £44/34/95, 1 attraction adult/child from £24/19, 3 attractions adult/child from £34/24; ◷10am-5.30pm Apr-Oct, to 5pm Nov-Mar). The blockbuster draw is Henry VIII's favourite flagship, the **Mary Rose**. A £35-million, boat-shaped museum has now been built around her, giving uninterrupted views of the preserved timbers of her massive hull. Equally impressive is **HMS Victory**. Other nautical sights include the Victorian **HMS Warrior** and a wealth of imaginative museums. Round it all off by strolling around the defences in the historic **Point district**.

The Drive ≫ Time to head inland; a 30-mile motorway cruise (the M27 then the M3) takes you to Winchester.

----

❼ Winchester

Calm, collegiate Winchester is a mellow must-see. One of southern England's most awe-inspiring buildings, 11th-century **Winchester Cathedral** (☎01962-857200; www. winchester-cathedral.org.uk; The Close; adult/child £10/free; ◷10am-4pm) adorns its core. It boasts a fine Gothic facade, one of the longest medieval naves in Europe (164m) and intricately carved medieval choir stalls, sporting everything from mythical beasts to a mischievous green man. Jane Austen's grave is near the entrance, in the northern aisle. The fantastical crumbling remains of **Wolvesey Castle** (EH; ☎0370 333 1181; www.english-heritage. org.uk; College St; ◷10am-5pm Apr-Oct, to 4pm Sat & Sun Nov-Mar) sit nearby,

as does one of England's most prestigious private schools: **Winchester College** (☎01962-621209; www.winchestercollege.org; College St), which you can visit on a tour.

🛏 p219, p245

The Drive » Leave Winchester's ancient streets to take the motorways towards Southampton (initially the M3). After 14 miles turn off onto the A35 towards Lyndhurst. From here it's a 9-mile drive to Beaulieu through the New Forest's increasingly wooded roads.

⑧ Beaulieu

The vintage car museum and stately home at **Beaulieu** (☎01590-612345; www.beaulieu.co.uk; adult/child £25/10; ⊙10am-5pm) is centred on a 13th-century Cistercian monastery that passed to the ancestors of the current proprietors, the Montague family, after Henry VIII's 1536 monastic land-grab. Today its **motor museum** includes F1 cars and jet-powered land-speed record-breakers, as well as wheels driven by James Bond and Mr Bean. The **palace** began life as a 14th-century Gothic abbey gatehouse, and received a 19th-century Scottish baronial makeover from Baron Montague in the 1860s.

The Drive » The SatNav wants to start this 28-mile leg by routing you onto the A326. Resist! Opt for the A and B roads that wind through the villages of Lyndhurst, Cadnam, Brook and North Charford, revealing the New Forest's blend of woods and open heath. Eventually join the A338 to Salisbury. Soon an immense cathedral spire rises over the town.

TRIP HIGHLIGHT

⑨ Salisbury

Salisbury's skyline is dominated by the tallest spire in England, which soars from its central, majestic 13th-century cathedral (☎01722-555150; www.salisburycathedral.org.uk; The Close; requested donation adult/child £7.50/3; ⊙9am-4pm Mon-Sat). This early-English Gothic–style structure's elaborate exterior is decorated with pointed arches and flying buttresses, while its statuary and tombs are outstanding. Don't miss the daily tower tours and the cathedral's original, 13th-century copy of the Magna Carta. The

GREAT BRITAIN **17** THE HISTORIC SOUTH

WHY THIS IS A GREAT TRIP
ANTHONY HAM, WRITER

It doesn't get more classically British than this journey through the south. Quintessentially British seaside towns, at once quaint and kitsch, vie for attention with the cathedrals of Canterbury, Salisbury and Winchester. There's everyone's favourite archaeological ruin, and two towns – Bath and Bristol – that get that whole history-meets-modern-Britain cachet down perfectly.

KRZYCH-34/GETTY IMAGES ©

Left: Ashmolean, Oxford
Right: Avebury

241

surrounding **Cathedral Close** has a hushed, other-worldly feel. Nearby, the hugely important finds at **Salisbury Museum** (☎01722-332151; www.salisburymuseum.org. uk; 65 The Close; adult/child £8/4; ⊙11am-4pm Thu-Sun) include Iron Age gold coins, a Bronze Age gold necklace and the **Stonehenge Archer**, the bones of a man found in the ditch surrounding the stone circle.

📖 p245

The Drive » Next: a 10-mile drive taking you back 5000 years. The A345 heads north. Soon after joining the A303, detail a passenger to watch the right windows – the world's most famous stone circle will soon pop into view. The entry to the site is just beyond.

- - - - - - - - - - - - - - - - - -

❿ Stonehenge

Welcome to Britain's best-known archaeological site: Stonehenge

(EH; ☎0370 333 1181; www. english-heritage.org.uk; near Amesbury; adult/child £21/13; ⊙9.30am-5pm, hours may vary; **P**), a compelling ring of monolithic stones that dates, in parts, back to 3000 BCE. Head into the **Visitor Centre** to see 300 finds from the site and experience an impressive 360-degree projection of the stone circle through the ages and seasons. Next hop on a trolley bus (or walk; it's 1.5 miles) to the monument. There, as you stroll around it, play 'spot-the-stone': look out for the **bluestone horseshoe** (an inner semicircle), the **trilithon horseshoe** (sets of two vertical stones topped by a horizontal one) and the **Slaughter Stone** and **Heel Stone** (set apart, on the northeast side). Then try to work out what on earth it all means. Note that entrance is by timed

ticket; secure yours well in advance.

The Drive » Now for a 24-mile, A-road meander through rural England. After dodging through Devizes, it's not long before signs point left to Avebury's main car park.

- - - - - - - - - - - - - - - - - -

⓫ Avebury

A two-minute stroll from the car park (£7 per day) leads to a ring of stones that's so big an entire village sits inside. Fringed by a massive bank and ditch and with a diameter of 348m, Avebury (NT; ☎01672-539250; www. nationaltrust.org.uk; parking per day £7; ⊙dawn-dusk; **P**) is the largest stone circle in the world. Dating from 2500 to 2200 BCE, more than 30 stones are still in place and you can wander between them and clusters of other stones at will. Houses, the **Henge Shop** (☎01672-539229; www.henge shop.com; High St; ⊙9.30am-5pm) and a pub, the **Red Lion** (☎01672-539266; www. oldenglishinns.co.uk; High St; ⊙11am-10pm Sun-Thu, to 11pm Fri & Sat), also nestle inside the circle.

The Drive » Next a cruise due west; as the A4 winds for 30 miles past fields and through villages to the city of Bath.

- - - - - - - - - - - - - - - - - -

⓬ Bath

Sophisticated, stately and ever-so-slightly snooty, Bath is graced with some of the finest Georgian architecture anywhere

STONEHENGE'S RITUAL LANDSCAPE

As you drive the roads around Stonehenge it's worth registering that the site forms part of a huge complex of ancient monuments. North of Stonehenge and running roughly east–west is the **Cursus**, an elongated embanked oval; the smaller **Lesser Cursus** is nearby. Two clusters of burial mounds, the **Old Barrow** and the **New Kings Barrow**, sit beside the ceremonial pathway **The Avenue**. This routeway cuts northeast of Stonehenge's **Heel Stone** and originally linked the site with the River Avon, 2 miles away. Theories abound as to what these sites were used for, ranging from ancient sporting arenas to processional avenues for the dead.

in Britain. Wandering around the streets (p294) here is a real joy. For an insight into how the city came to look like it does, head to the **Museum of Bath Architecture** (📞01225-333895; www. museumofbatharchitecture. org.uk; The Countess of Huntingdon's Chapel, off the Paragon; adult/child £7/3.50; ⏱1-5pm Mon-Fri, 10am-5pm Sat & Sun mid-Feb–Nov). The **Bath Assembly Rooms** (NT; 📞01225-477789; www. nationaltrust.org.uk; 19 Bennett St; ⏱10.30am-6pm Mar-Oct, to 5pm Nov-Feb), where socialites once gathered, gives an insight into the Georgian world. To discover the city's culinary heritage head for **Sally Lunn's** (📞01225-461634; www.sallylunns.co.uk; 4 North Pde Passage; mains £7-13, afternoon tea £8-40; ⏱10am-8pm), which bakes the famous Bath Bunn (a brioche-meets-bread treat). For a free glass of the spring water that made the city rich, stop by the **Pump Room** (📞01225-477785; www.romanbaths.co.uk; Stall St; ⏱9.30am-5pm). Then perhaps soak yourself at **Thermae Bath Spa** (📞01225-331234; www. thermaebathspa.com; Hot Bath St; spa £37-42, treatments from £72; ⏱9am-9.30pm, last entry 7pm), with its steam rooms, waterfall showers and a choice of swimming pools (including a gorgeous rooftop one).

🛏 p219, p245

DETOUR: LACOCK

Start: ⑪ **Avebury**

Around 16 miles into your Avebury-to-Bath cruise, consider a detour south. Because a drive of just 4 extra miles leads to a real rarity: a medieval village that's been preserved in time. In Lacock, the sweet streets framed by stone cottages, higgledy-piggledy rooftops and mullioned windows are a delight to stroll around. Unsurprisingly, it's a popular movie location – it's popped up in the Harry Potter films, *The Other Boleyn Girl* and a BBC adaptation of *Pride and Prejudice*. The 13th-century former Augustinian nunnery of **Lacock Abbey** (NT; 📞01249-730459, www.nationaltrust.org.uk; Hither Way; adult/child £10/5; ⏱10.30am-5pm Mar-Oct, 11am-4pm Nov-Feb) is a must-see: its deeply atmospheric rooms and stunning Gothic entrance hall are lined with bizarre terracotta figures – spot the scapegoat with a lump of sugar on its nose. The **Fox Talbot Museum** (NT; 📞01249-730459; www.nationaltrust.org.uk; Hither Way; incl in Lacock Abbey admission; ⏱10.30am-5.30pm Mar-Oct, 11am-4pm Nov-Feb) features an intriguing display on early photography, while the **Sign of the Angel** (📞01249-730230; www.signoftheangel.co.uk; 6 Church St; s £85-115, d £115-145; P 🛜 🐾) is a gorgeous, 15th-century restaurant-with-rooms.

The Drive » It's a 13-mile blast from Bath to Bristol along the A36/A4.

⑬ Bristol

In Bristol a fascinating seafaring heritage meets an edgy, contemporary vibe. The mighty **SS Great Britain** (📞0117-926 0680; www.ssgreatbritain. org; Great Western Dock, Gas Ferry Rd; adult/child/family £18/10/48; ⏱10am-6pm Apr-Oct, to 4.30pm Nov-Mar) sits on the city's waterfront. Designed in 1843 by engineering genius Isambard Kingdom Brunel, its interior has been impeccably refurbished, including the galley, the surgeon's quarters and a working model of the original steam engine. The whole vessel is contained in an airtight dry dock, dubbed a 'glass sea'. At the **Bristol Museum & Art Gallery** (📞0117-922 3571; www.bristol museums.org.uk; Queen's Rd; ⏱10am-5pm Tue-Sun) take in the *Paint-Pot Angel* by world-famous street artist Banksy. In the suburb of **Clifton** explore Georgian architecture, especially in Cornwallis and Royal York Crescents. The **Clifton Observatory** ([☎]0117-974 1242; www.cliftonobservatory.com; Litfield Rd, Clifton Down; adult/child £2.50/1.50; [⏱]10am-5pm Mar-Oct, to 4pm Oct-Feb), meanwhile, features a rare camera obscura which offers incredible views of the deep fissure that is the Avon Gorge.

[✗] p245

The Drive » Travelling partly on the M4 and partly on A roads, the next 80-mile leg sees you skirting Oxford (for now) and arriving at the tree-lined avenue that leads to one of Britain's finest stately homes.

⑭ Blenheim Palace

Blenheim Palace

([☎]01993-810530; www.blenheimpalace.com; Woodstock; adult/child £28.50/16.50, park & gardens only £18.50/8.60; [⏱]palace 10.30am-4.30pm, park & gardens 9.30am-6.30pm or dusk; [P]), a monumental baroque fantasy designed by Sir John Vanbrugh and Nicholas Hawksmoor, was built between 1705 and 1722. The house is filled with statues, tapestries, ostentatious furniture, priceless china and giant oil paintings. Highlights include the **Great Hall**, a soaring space topped by a 20m-high ceiling adorned with images of the first duke. Britain's legendary WWII prime minister, Sir Winston Churchill, was born here in 1874 – the **Churchill Exhibition** is dedicated to his life, work, paintings and writings. The house is encircled by vast, lavish **gardens** and **parklands**, parts of which were landscaped by the great Lancelot 'Capability' Brown. A minitrain (£1) whisks you to the **Pleasure Gardens**, which feature a yew **maze**, adventure playground, lavender garden and butterfly house.

The Drive » From Blenheim's grandeur, it's a 10-mile trip down the A44/A34/A4144 to Oxford's dreaming spires.

⑮ Oxford

One of the world's most famous university towns, the centre of Oxford is rich in history and studded with august buildings. The city has 38 colleges – Christ Church ([☎]01865-276492; www.chch.ox.ac.uk; St Aldate's; adult/child £15/14, pre-booking essential; [⏱]10am-5pm Mon-Sat, from 2pm Sun) is the largest, with 650 students, and has the grandest quad. Christ Church was founded in 1524 by Cardinal Thomas Wolsey, and alumni include Albert Einstein and 13 British prime ministers. It's also famous as a location for the Harry Potter films. At the **Ashmolean** ([☎]01865-278000; www.ashmolean.org; Beaumont St; [⏱]10am-5pm Tue-Sun, to 8pm last Fri of month; [♿]), Britain's oldest public museum has had a modern makeover; interactive displays and glass walls revealing multilevel galleries help showcase treasures that include Egyptian mummies, Indian textiles and Islamic art. Beautiful **Magdalen College** ([☎]01865-276000; www.magd.ox.ac.uk; High St; adult/child £7/6, pre-booking required; [⏱]10am-7pm late Jun-late Sep, 1pm-dusk rest of year) is worth a visit for its medieval chapel, 15th-century cloisters and 40-hectare grounds. Nearby, head to **Magdalen Bridge Boathouse** ([☎]01865-202643; www.oxfordpunting.co.uk; High St; chauffeured 4-person punts per 30min £30, punt rental per hr £22; [⏱]9.30am-dusk Feb-Nov) for a ride on a chauffeured punt.

[✗][🛏] p245

Eating & Sleeping

Canterbury ❸

🛏 **ABode Canterbury** Boutique Hotel ££
(☎01227-766266; www.abodecanterbury.co.uk; 30-33 High St; r from £74; 🛜) The 72 rooms at this super-central hotel, the only boutique hotel in town, are graded from 'comfortable' to 'fabulous' (via 'enviable'), and for the most part live up to their names. They come with features such as handmade beds, chesterfield sofas, tweed cushions and beautiful modern bathrooms. There's a splendid champagne bar, restaurant and tavern, too.

Brighton ❺

🛏 **Artist Residence** Boutique Hotel £££
(☎01273-324302; www.artistresidencebrighton. co.uk; 34 Regency Sq; d £120-290; 🛜) Eclectic doesn't quite describe the rooms at this wonderful 24-room town-house hotel, set amid the splendour of Regency Sq. As befits the name, every bedroom is a hip blend of bold wall murals, bespoke and vintage furniture, rough wood cladding and in-room roll-top baths. The Set Restaurant downstairs enjoys a glowing reputation.

Winchester ❼

🛏 **Wykeham Arms** Inn £££
(☎01962-853834; www.wykehamarmswinches ter.co.uk; 75 Kingsgate St; s £84, d £144-194; 🅿🛜) At 250-odd years of age, the Wykeham bursts with history – it used to be a brothel and also put Nelson up for a night (some say the events coincided). Creaking stairs lead to plush bedrooms that manage to be both deeply established and on-trend – sleigh beds meet jazzy fabrics, oak dressers sport stylish lights. Simply smashing.

Salisbury ❾

🛏 **Chapter House** Inn £££
(☎01722-341277; www.thechapterhouseuk.com; 9 St Johns St; s £95-145, d £115-155; 🛜) In this 800-year-old boutique beauty, wood panels and wildly wonky stairs sit beside duck-your-head beams. The cheaper bedrooms are swish but the posher ones are stunning, starring slipper baths and the odd heraldic crest. The pick is room 6, where King Charles is reputed to have stayed. Lucky him.

Bath ⓬

🛏 **Queensberry** Hotel £££
(☎01225-985086; www.thequeensberry.co.uk; 4 Russell St; r £235-323, ste £460-510; 🅿🛜) Stylish but unstuffy Queensberry is Bath's best luxury spoil. In these Georgian town houses heritage roots meet snazzy gingham checks, bright upholstery, original fireplaces and free-standing tubs. It's witty (see The Rules on the website), independent (and proud of it), and service is first-rate.

Bristol ⓭

🍴 **Riverstation** British ££
(☎0117-914 4434; www.riverstation.co.uk; The Grove; bar/restaurant mains £14/17; ⏱10am-10pm Mon-Sat, to 6pm Sun) Riverstation's waterfront views are hard to beat, but it's the food that truly shines. Rich, classical flavours define dishes served up in the restaurant and less formal bar. Expect truffle-fragranced wild mushrooms for breakfast, seasonal risotto for lunch, and stone bass and samphire for dinner.

Oxford ⓯

🛏 **Head of the River** Hotel £££
(☎01865-721600; www.headoftheriveroxford. co.uk; Folly Bridge, St Aldate's; r incl breakfast £189; 🛜) One of the more central Oxford hotels, this large and characterful place at Folly Bridge, immediately south of Christ Church, was originally a Thames-side warehouse. Each of its 20 good-sized rooms is individually decorated with contemporary flair, featuring exposed brickwork and/or tongue-and-groove panelling plus modern fittings. Rates include breakfast cooked to order in the (excellent) **pub** (⏱8am-10.30pm Sun-Thu, to 11.30pm Fri & Sat) downstairs.

Classic Lakes

Beloved of poets and painters, this road trip takes in the scenic wonders of the UK's largest and loveliest national park.

18

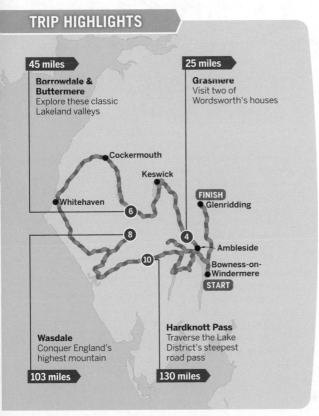

TRIP HIGHLIGHTS

45 miles

Borrowdale & Buttermere
Explore these classic Lakeland valleys

25 miles

Grasmere
Visit two of Wordsworth's houses

Cockermouth

Keswick

FINISH
Glenridding

Whitehaven

6

8

4

10

Ambleside

Bowness-on-Windermere

START

Wasdale
Conquer England's highest mountain

103 miles

Hardknott Pass
Traverse the Lake District's steepest road pass

130 miles

---

5 DAYS
162 MILES / 260KM

GREAT FOR...

BEST TIME TO GO
Summer and Easter can be hectic in the Lakes; spring and autumn are best.

ESSENTIAL PHOTO
Striking a pose in Wasdale, surrounded by England's highest hills.

BEST FOR FAMILIES
Bike trails, sculptures and zip lines at Grizedale Forest.

18 | Classic Lakes

William Wordsworth, Samuel Taylor Coleridge and Beatrix Potter are just a few of the literary luminaries who have fallen in love with the Lake District. It's been a national park since 1951, and is studded by England's highest hills (fells), including the highest of all, Scafell Pike. This drive takes in lakes, forests, hills and valleys, with country houses, hill walks and cosy pubs thrown in for good measure.

Solway Firth
A596
Workington
A66
Parton
Whitehaven
Rowra
Frizington
Cleator Moor
Parks
p255
St Bees
Egremont
A595
Sellafield Nuclear Plant
River Ehen
Seascale
Irish Sea

❶ Bowness-on-Windermere

At 10.5 miles long, Windermere is the largest body of water in England: more a loch than a lake. It's also one of the most popular places in the Lake District, and has been a tourist centre since the late 19th century, especially for lake cruises.

Windermere gets its name from the old Norse, 'Vinandr mere' (Vinandr's lake; so 'Lake Windermere' is actually tautologous). Encompassing 5.7 sq miles between Ambleside and Newby Bridge, the lake is a mile wide at its broadest point, with a maximum depth of about 220m. There are 18 islands on Windermere: the largest is Belle Isle, encompassing 16 hectares and an 18th-century Italianate mansion, while the smallest is Maiden Holme, little more than a patch of soil and a solitary tree.

The wonderful **Windermere Jetty Museum** (📞01539-637940; www.lakelandarts.org.uk/windermere-jetty-museum; Rayrigg Rd; adult/child £9/4.50; ⏱10am-5pm Mar-Oct, 10.30am-4.30pm Nov-Feb), finally opened after years of development, explores the history of cruising with a glorious collection of vintage boats, punts and steam yachts – including the *Esperance*, which provided the inspiration for Captain Flint's

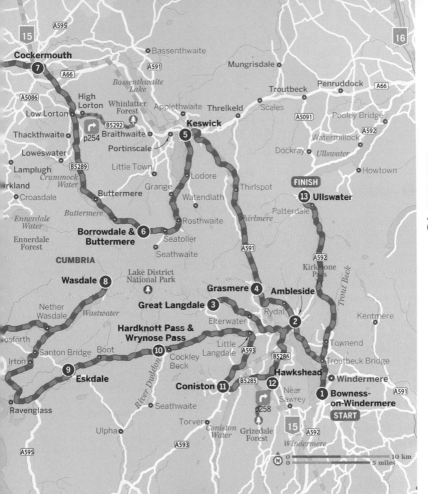

houseboat in Arthur Ransome's *Swallows and Amazons*. Best of all, you can take your own trip aboard the 1902 *Osprey* or the 1930 *Penelope II*. There's simply no more stylish way to see Windermere.

Alternatively, **Windermere Lake Cruises**

LINK YOUR TRIP

15 The Best of Britain
Start this circuit of Britain's greatest hits by picking up the M6 at Penrith between Manchester and Edinburgh.

16 Britain's Wild Side
Head north or south along the A591 to visit more of the Britain's glorious natural beauty spots.

(☎01539-443360; www.
windermere-lakecruises.co.uk;
cruises from £9.50) offers
sightseeing trips depart-
ing from Bowness Pier.

🛏 p259

The Drive » From Bowness,
follow Rayrigg Rd north until it
joins the A591, which rolls all the
way to Ambleside, 6 miles north.

----

❷ Ambleside

At the northern end of
Windermere lies the old
mill town of Ambleside.
It's a pretty place, well
stocked with outdoors
shops and some excellent
restaurants: don't miss a
meal at the fabulous Lake
Road Kitchen (p259),
run by an imaginative
chef who trained at
the legendary Noma in
Copenhagen.

Afterwards, work
off some calories with
a half-hour walk up to
the waterfall of **Stock
Ghyll Force**, a clattering
18m-high waterfall on
the edge of town. The

trail is signposted behind
the old Market Hall at
the bottom of Stock
Ghyll Lane. If you feel
energetic, you can follow
the trail beyond the falls
up Wansfell Pike (482m),
a reasonably steep walk
of about two hours.

✗ p259

The Drive » Take the A593
west towards Skelwith Bridge,
and follow signs to Elterwater
and Great Langdale. It's a
wonderful 8-mile drive that gets
wilder and wilder the deeper
you head into the valley. There's
a large car park beside the Old
Dungeon Ghyll Hotel, but it gets
busy in summer; there's usually
overflow parking available in a
nearby field.

----

❸ Great Langdale

The Lake District has
some truly stunning val-
leys, but Great Langdale
definitely ranks near the
top. As you pass through
the pretty village of
Elterwater and its village
green, the scenery gets
really wild and empty.

Fells stack up like domi-
noes along the horizon,
looming over a patch-
work of barns and fields.

If you're up for a
hike, then you might
consider tackling the
multipeak circuit around
the **Langdale Pikes** – a
tough, full-day hike
into the wild fells above
Langdale, which allows
you to pick off between
three and five sum-
mits depending on your
route, including the
four main 'Pikes' of Pike
O' Stickle (709m), Loft
Crag (682m), Harrison
Stickle (736m) and Pavey
Ark (700m). You'll need
proper boots, hiking
gear and an Ordnance
Survey map.

Alternatively, the
more sedentary option
is to just admire the
views over a pint of
locally brewed ale from
the cosy bar of the **Old
Dungeon Ghyll** (☎01539-
437272; www.odg.co.uk; Great
Langdale; s £62.50, d £116-135;
P🛜🐾), a classic hikers'
haunt.

The Drive » Retrace the road
to Ambleside and head north
to Grasmere on the A591 for
5 miles.

TRIP HIGHLIGHT

❹ Grasmere

The lovely little village of
Grasmere is inextricably
linked with the poet
William Wordsworth,
who made it his home in
the late 18th century and
never left unless he really
had to. Two of his houses

✓ **TOP TIP:
NATIONAL TRUST
MEMBERSHIP**

Being a member of the **National Trust** (NT; www.
nationaltrust.org.uk) comes in very handy in the Lake
District. The Trust owns several key attractions,
including Hill Top and the Beatrix Potter Gallery near
Hawkshead, Wordsworth House in Cockermouth and
Fell Foot and Wray Castle near Windermere. Best of
all, you get to park for free at all the NT's car parks –
handy in celebrated beauty spots like Buttermere,
Borrowdale, Wasdale, Gowbarrow Park and Tarn
Hows.

are now open to the public. The most famous is **Dove Cottage** (☎01539-435544; www.wordsworth.org.uk; adult/child £9.50/4.50; ⏰9.30am-5.30pm Mar-Oct, 10am-4.30pm Nov, Dec & Feb), a tiny house where he lived with his sister Dorothy, wife Mary and three children between 1798 and 1808. Guided tours explore the house, and next door the Jerwood Museum has lots of memorabilia and original manuscripts relating to the Romantic poets.

A little way south of Grasmere is the house where Wordsworth spent most of his adult life, **Rydal Mount** (☎01539-433002; www.rydalmount.co.uk; adult/child £7.50/4, grounds only £5; ⏰9.30am-5pm Apr-Oct, 11am-4pm Wed-Sun Nov, Dec, Feb & Mar). It's still owned by the poet's descendants, and is a much grander affair than Dove Cottage: you can have a look around the library, visit the poet's attic study and wander around the gardens he designed. Below the house, **Dora's Field** is filled with daffodils in springtime; it was planted in memory of Wordsworth's daughter, who died of tuberculosis.

If you have a sweet tooth, you'll also want to pick up a souvenir at **Sarah Nelson's Gingerbread Shop** (☎01539-435428; www.grasmeregingerbread.co.uk; Church Cottage; ⏰9.15am-5.30pm Mon-Sat,

12.30-5pm Sun), which still makes its gingerbread to a recipe formulated in 1854.

🛏 p259

The Drive » From Grasmere, continue north on the A591. You'll pass through the dramatic pass known as Dunmail Raise, where a great battle is said to have taken place between the Saxons and the Celtic king Dunmail, who was slain near the pass. Stay on the road past the lake of Thirlmere all the way to Keswick (13 miles).

---

❺ Keswick

Another of the Lake District's classic market towns, Keswick is a place that revolves around the great outdoors. Several big fells lie on its doorstep, including the imposing lump of **Skiddaw** and the dramatic ridge of **Blencathra**, but it's the lake of **Derwentwater** that really draws the eye: it was said to be Beatrix Potter's favourite, and she supposedly got the idea for Squirrel Nutkin while watching red squirrels frolicking on its shores.

The **Keswick Launch** (☎01768-772263; www.keswick-launch.co.uk; round-the-lake pass adult/child/family £11/5.70/27.50) travels out around the lake year-round: you could combine it with an easy hike up to the top of **Catbells** (451m), a favourite first-time fell for many walkers. The views of the lake and the

distant hills are absolutely breathtaking.

Back in town, don't miss a visit to **George Fisher** (☎01768-772178; www.georgefisher.co.uk; 2 Borrowdale Rd; ⏰9am-5.30pm Mon-Sat, 10am-4pm Sun), the most famous outdoors shop in the Lake District: if you need a new pair of hiking boots, this is definitely the place to come.

🍴 🛏 p259

The Drive » The drive into Borrowdale on the B5289 is a beauty, passing several pretty villages as it travels through the valley. You can't get lost en route to Honister Pass (10 miles from Keswick) – there's only one road to take; Buttermere lies on the other side of the pass. You'll want to stop for numerous photos on the way.

TRIP HIGHLIGHT

❻ Borrowdale & Buttermere

South of Keswick, the B5289 tracks along the eastern side of Derwentwater and enters the bucolic valley of Borrowdale, a classic Lakeland canvas of fields, fells, streams and endless drystone walls. It's worth stopping off to see the geological oddity of the **Bowder Stone**, a huge boulder deposited by a glacier, and for a quick hike up to the top of **Castle Crag**, which has the best views of the valley.

Then it's up and over the perilously steep **Honister Pass**, where the Lake District's last

WHY THIS IS A GREAT TRIP
OLIVER BERRY, WRITER

For classic English scenery, nowhere quite compares to the Lake District. With its fells and waterfalls, valleys and villages, lakes and meadows, it's like a postcard that's come to life. It's visited by some 13 million people every year, but it's still easy to find peace and serenity – whether it's rowing across a lake, cycling through the countryside or standing atop a fell. Pack spare memory cards – you'll need them.

Above: Hiking up Scafell Pike
Left: Drunken Duck, Hawkshead
Right: Coniston Water, Coniston

BRIBAR/GETTY IMAGES ©

working **slate mine**
(📞01768-777230; www.
honister.com; mine tour adult/
child £17.50/9.50, all-day
pass incl mine tour & classic/
extreme via ferrata £55/47;
⊙10am-5pm) is still doing
a thriving trade. You can
take a guided tour down
into the mine or brave
the heights along the
stomach-upsetting via
ferrata, and pick up slate
souvenirs in the shop.

Nearby Buttermere
has a sparkling twinset
of lakes, **Buttermere**
and **Crummock Water**,
and is backed by a string
of impressive fells. The
summit of **Haystacks** is a
popular route: it was the
favourite fell of Alfred
Wainwright, who penned
the definitive seven-
volume set of guidebooks
of the Lake District's fells
between the 1950s and
'70s. It's a two- to three-
hour return walk from
Buttermere.

The Drive >> From Buttermere
village, bear left on the B5289
signed towards Loweswater
and Crummock Water, which
continues into the Lorton Valley.
At Low Lorton, stay on the
B5289, which continues 4 miles
to Cockermouth. (Total distance:
11 miles.)

- - - - - - - - - - - - - - - - -

❼ Cockermouth

Grasmere might be
Wordsworth central, but
completists will want to
visit the poet's **childhood
home** (NT; 📞01900-824805;
www.nationaltrust.org.uk/
wordsworth-house; Main
St; adult/child £8.80/4.40;

⏱11am-5pm Sat-Thu Mar-Oct) in Cockermouth. Now owned by the National Trust, it's been redecorated in period style according to details published in Wordsworth's own father's accounts: you can wander round the drawing room, kitchen, pantry and garden, and see the rooms where little Willie and his brother John slept. Costumed guides wander around the house for added period authenticity. Outside is the walled kitchen garden mentioned in Wordsworth's autobiographical epic *The Prelude*.

The Drive » Head west on the A66 and detour onto the A595, which tracks the coast all the way to Whitehaven. To reach Wasdale (35 miles all up), turn off at Gosforth, and then follow signs to Nether Wasdale and Wasdale Head. It's quite easy to miss the

turning, so keep your eyes peeled; satnavs can be very unreliable here.

TRIP HIGHLIGHT

⑧ Wasdale

Wild Wasdale is arguably the most dramatic valley in the national park. Carving its way for 5 miles from the coast, it was gouged out by a long-extinct glacier during the last Ice Age; if you look closely you can still see glacial marks on the scree-strewn slopes above Wastwater. It's a truly dramatic drive that feels rather like heading into the depths of a remote Scottish glen: in terms of mountain scenery, it's probably the most impressive stretch of road this side of the Highlands.

Most people come for the chance to reach the summit of **Scafell Pike**,

England's highest point (978m); it's a tough six- to seven-hour slog, but the views from the top are quite literally as good as they get (assuming the weather plays ball, of course).

Afterwards, reward yourself with a meal at the **Wasdale Head Inn** (☎01946-726229; www.wasdale.com; s/d/tr £60/120/180; 🅿🛜), a gloriously olde-worlde hostelry with lashings of mountain heritage: it was here that the sport of rock climbing was pioneered in the mid-19th century.

The Drive » Retrace your route to Gosforth, and take the coast road (A595) south to Ravenglass and follow signs to Eskdale (22 miles). Alternatively, there's a shortcut into Eskdale via Nether Wasdale and Santon Bridge, but it's easy to get lost, especially if you're relying on satnav; a good road map is really handy here.

----

⑨ Eskdale

The valley of Eskdale was once a centre for mineral mining, and a miniature steam train was built to carry ore down from the hillsides to the coast. Now known as the **Ravenglass & Eskdale Railway** (☎01229-717171; www.ravenglass-railway.co.uk; adult/child return £18/12; 🚂) (or La'al Ratty to locals), its miniature choo-choos are a beloved Lakeland attraction. They chuff for 7 miles along the valley from the station at

DETOUR: WHINLATTER FOREST PARK

Start: ⑥ Buttermere

Encompassing 4.6 sq miles of pine, larch and spruce, **Whinlatter** (www.forestry.gov.uk/whinlatter) is England's only true mountain forest, rising sharply to 790m about 5 miles from Keswick. The forest is a designated red squirrel reserve; you can check out live video feeds from squirrel cams at the visitor centre. It's also home to two exciting mountain-bike trails and a treetop assault course. You can hire bikes next to the visitor centre.

To get to Whinlatter Forest Park from Buttermere, look out for the right turn onto the B5292 at Low Lorton, which climbs up to Whinlatter Pass.

Ravenglass to the final terminus at Dalegarth, stopping at several stations in between. Nearby, the **Boot Inn** (☎019467-23224; www.thebooteskdale.co.uk; Boot; mains £10-18) makes a pleasant stop for lunch.

The Drive » Since you're driving, the most sensible idea is to park near Dalegarth Station, ride the train to Ravenglass and back, and then set off for Hardknott Pass. There's only one road east. Take it and get ready for a hair-raising, white-knuckle drive. It's 6 (very steep!) miles from Eskdale to Hardknott Pass.

TRIP HIGHLIGHT

❿ Hardknott Pass & Wrynose Pass

At the eastern end of Eskdale lie England's two steepest road passes, Hardknott and Wrynose. Reaching 30% gradient in some places, and with precious few passing places on the narrow, single-file road, they're absolutely not for the faint-hearted or for nervous drivers – but the views are amazing, and they're doable if you take things slow (although it's probably best to leave the caravan or motor home in the garage). Make sure your car has plenty of oil and water, as you'll do much of the road in 1st gear, and the strain on the engine can be taxing. Take it slow, and take breaks – you need

to keep your focus on the road ahead.

From Eskdale, the road ascends via a series of very sharp, steep switchbacks to the remains of **Hardknott Fort**, a Roman outpost where you can still see the remains of some of the walls. Soon after you reach **Hardknott Pass** at 393m (1289ft). The vistas here are magnificent: you'll be able to see all the way to the coast on a clear day. Next you'll drop down into Cockley Beck before continuing the climb up to **Wrynose Pass** (393m/1289ft). Near the summit is a small car park containing the **Three Shire Stone**, where the counties of Cumberland, Westmorland and Lancashire historically met. Then it's a slow descent down through hairpins and

corners to the packhorse Slaters Bridge and on into the valley of **Little Langdale**. Phew! You made it.

The Drive » Once you reach Little Langdale, follow the road east until you reach the A593, the main road between Skelwith Bridge and Coniston. Turn right and follow it for 5 miles.

⓫ Coniston

South of Ambleside, the old mining village of Coniston is dominated by its hulking fell, the **Old Man of Coniston**, an ever-popular objective for hikers, but it's perhaps best known for the world speed record attempts made here by father and son Malcolm and Donald Campbell between the 1930s and 1960s. Though they jointly broke many records, in 1967 Donald was tragically killed

DETOUR: ST BEES HEAD

Start: ❼ Cockermouth

Cumbria's coastline might not have the white sandy beaches of Wales or the epic grandeur of the Scottish coast, but it has a bleak beauty all of its own – not to mention a renowned seabird reserve at **St Bees Head** (RSPB; stbees.head@rspb.org.uk), where you can spot species including fulmars, herring gulls, kittiwakes and razorbills – as well as England's only nesting black guillemots at nearby Fleswick Bay. Just try and forget the fact that one of the UK's largest nuclear reactors, Sellafield, is round the corner.

The village of St Bees lies 5 miles south of Whitehaven, and the headland is signposted from there.

during an attempt in his jetboat *Bluebird;* the little **Ruskin Museum** (📞01539-441164; www.ruskin museum.com; adult/child £6.50/3.25; ⏰10am-4.30pm mid-Mar–mid-Nov) has the full story.

Coniston Water is also said to have been the inspiration for Arthur Ransome's classic children's tale, *Swallows and Amazons*. The best way to explore is aboard the **Steam Yacht Gondola** (NT; 📞01539-0432733; www.nationaltrust. org.uk/steam-yacht-gondola; Coniston Jetty; cruises adult/ child/family £17/8.50/38), a beautifully restored steam yacht built in 1859. It travels over the lake to the stately home

of **Brantwood** (📞01539-441396; www.brantwood.org. uk; gardens only adult/child £6.20/free; ⏰10.30am-5pm), owned by the Victorian polymath, critic, painter and inveterate collector John Ruskin. The house is packed with furniture and crafts, and the gardens are glorious.

🛏 p259

The Drive » Heading north from Coniston, turn right onto the B5285 up Hawkshead Hill. You'll pass Tarn Hows and the Drunken Duck en route to Hawkshead, about 4 miles east.

⑫ Hawkshead

If you're searching for the perfect chocolate-box lakeland village, look no further – you've found

it in Hawkshead, an improbably pretty confection of whitewashed cottages, winding lanes and slate roofs. It's car-free, so you can wander at will: don't miss the **Beatrix Potter Gallery**, which has a collection of the artist's original watercolours and botanical paintings (she had a particular fascination with fungi).

Nearby, it's worth making a detour to have a stroll around the lake of **Tarn Hows** (NT; www.nationaltrust.org.uk/ coniston-and-tarn-hows) – a bucolic place, but one that's artificially created (it was made by joining three neighbouring tarns in the 19th century).

After your walk, pop in for lunch at the Lake District's finest dining pub, the wonderfully named Drunken Duck.

✗ p259

The Drive » Head back to Ambleside and then follow the A591 back towards Windermere. Just before you reach it, take the turn-off onto the A592 to Troutbeck Bridge, which climbs up to the lofty Kirkstone Pass – at 454m this is the highest mountain pass in Cumbria that's open to road traffic. It's steep, but it's a main A road so it's well maintained.

⑬ Ullswater

From the windlashed heights of Kirkstone Pass, the A592 loops down towards the last

HILL TOP

Two miles from Hawkshead in the tiny village of Near Sawrey, the idyllic cottage at **Hill Top** (NT; 📞01539-436269; www.nationaltrust.org.uk/hill-top; garden adult/child £5/2.50; ⏰10am-5.30pm Jun-Aug, to 4.30pm Sat-Thu Apr, May, Sep & Oct, weekends only Nov-Mar) is the most famous house in the whole of the Lake District. It belonged to Beatrix Potter, and was used as inspiration for many of her tales: the house features directly in *Samuel Whiskers, Tom Kitten, Pigling Bland* and *Jemima Puddle-Duck,* and you will doubtless recognise the kitchen garden from *Peter Rabbit*.

Following her death in 1943, Beatrix bequeathed Hill Top (along with more than 1600 hectares of land) to the National Trust, with the proviso that the house be left with her belongings and decor untouched. The house formed the centrepiece for celebrations to mark the author's 150th birthday in 2016.

It's probably the Lake District's most popular attraction, however, so don't expect to have it all to yourself...

Eskdale Hardknott Pass

257

stop on this jaunt around the Lake District: stately Ullswater, the national park's second-largest lake (after Windermere). It's an impressive sight, with its silvery surface framed by jagged fells and plied by the puttering **Ullswater 'Steamers'** (☎01768-482229; www. ullswater-steamers.co.uk; cruise 'all piers' pass adult/child £16.80/10.10); you can also hire your own vessels from the Glenridding Sailing Centre.

As you skirt up the lake's western edge, it's worth stopping for a walk around **Gowbarrow Park** (NT; www.nationaltrust. org.uk), where there's a clattering waterfall to admire called **Aira Force**, and impressive displays of daffodils in springtime (Wordsworth dreamt up his most

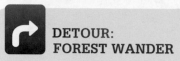

DETOUR: FOREST WANDER

Start: ⓬ **Hawkshead**

Stretching for more than 2400 hectares across the hilltops between Coniston Water and Esthwaite Water, **Grizedale Forest** (www.forestry.gov.uk/grizedale) is a wonderful place for a wander. It's criss-crossed by cycling trails, and is also home to more than 40 outdoor sculptures created by artists since 1977, including a xylophone and a man of the forest. There's an online guide at www.grizedalesculpture.org. As you leave the Hawkshead car park, you'll immediately see a brown sign for Grizedale, heading right onto North Lonsdale Rd. Just follow the brown signs from here – it's 3 miles' drive from the village.

famous poem while walking nearby).

For an epic end to the trip, strap on your hiking boots and tackle the famous ridge climb via Striding Edge to the summit of **Helvellyn**, the Lake District's third-highest mountain at 950m. You'll need a head for heights, but you'll feel a real sense of achievement: you've just conquered perhaps the finest hill walk in all of England.

Eating & Sleeping

Bowness-on-Windermere ❶

🛏 Rum Doodle   B&B ££

(☎01539-445967; www.rumdoodlewindermere.
com; Sunny Bank Rd, Windermere Town; d £79-
139; [P] [📶]) Named after a classic travel novel
about a fictional mountain in the Himalaya,
this B&B zings with imagination. Its rooms are
themed after places and characters in the book,
with details such as book-effect wallpaper,
vintage maps and old suitcases. Top of the
heap is the Summit, snug under the eaves with
a separate sitting room. Two-night minimum in
summer.

Ambleside ❷

✕ Lake Road Kitchen   Bistro £££

(☎01539-422012; www.lakeroadkitchen.
co.uk; Lake Rd; 5-/8-course tasting menu
£65/90; ⊙6-9.30pm Wed-Sun) Quite simply
one of the hottest places to dine in the Lakes.
Its Noma-trained head chef, James Cross,
explores 'cold climate' cooking (think Scandi-
inspired, impeccably presented and laced
with experimental ingredients aplenty). From
shore-sourced seaweed to pickled vegetables
and forest-picked mushrooms, the flavours are
constantly surprising – and the stripped-back
styling feels very appropriate.

Grasmere ❹

🛏 Forest Side   Boutique Hotel £££

(☎01539-435250; www.theforestside.com;
Keswick Rd; r £189-369; [P] [📶]) This boutique
beauty – a former hunting lodge – is hard to
top for luxury. Renovated at huge expense by
hotelier Andrew Wildsmith, it's a design temple:
crushed-velvet sofas, Zoffany fabrics, stag
heads and 20 country-chic rooms from 'Cosy'
to 'Master'. Its restaurant is Michelin-starred,
and the grounds (including a working kitchen
garden) are gorgeous.

Keswick ❺

✕ Cottage in the Wood   Hotel £££

(☎01768-778409; www.thecottageinthewood.
co.uk; Braithwaite; lunch/dinner menu £40/55;
⊙lunch 12.30-1.30pm, dinner 6.30-9.30pm;
[P] [📶]) Under chef Ben Wilkinson, this Michelin-
starred coaching inn en route to Whinlatter
Pass has become Keswick's premier dining
destination. The food is seasonal, flavoursome
and delicately presented – the Taste Cumbria
menu (themed around Stream, Woodland,
Coasts and Fells) is an inventive delight. If you
fancy making a night of it, sleek rooms survey
woods and countryside.

Coniston ⓫

🛏 Bank Ground Farm   B&B ££

(☎01539-441264; www.bankground.com; East
of the Lake Rd; d from £110; [P]) This lakeside
farmhouse has literary cachet: Arthur Ransome
used it as the model for Holly Howe Farm in
Swallows and Amazons. Parts of the house date
back to the 15th century, so the rooms are snug.
Some have sleigh beds, others exposed beams.
The tearoom is a beauty, and there are cottages
for longer stays. Two-night minimum.

Hawkshead ⓬

✕ Drunken Duck   Pub Food £££

(☎01539-436347; www.drunkenduckinn.
co.uk; Barngates; mains £24; ⊙noon-2.30pm &
6-8.45pm; [P] [📶]) Long one of the Lakes' premier
dining destinations, the Drunken Duck is a blend
of historic pub and fine-dining restaurant. On
a wooded crossroads on the top of Hawkshead
Hill, it's renowned for its luxurious food and
home-brewed ales, and the flagstones and
sporting prints conjure a convincing country
atmosphere. Book well ahead.

If you fancy staying, you'll find the rooms (£125
to £250) are as fancy as the food. The pub's tricky
to find: drive along the B5286 from Hawkshead
towards Ambleside and look for the brown signs.

Royal Highlands & Cairngorms

19

The heart of the Scottish Highlands features a feast of castles and mountains, wild roller-coaster roads, ancient Caledonian pine forest, and the chance to see Highland wildlife up close and personal.

TRIP HIGHLIGHTS

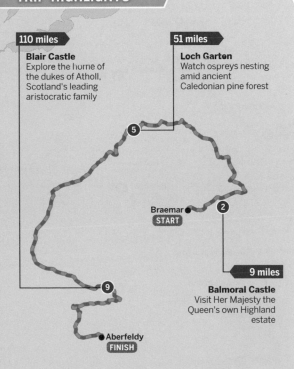

110 miles

Blair Castle
Explore the home of the dukes of Atholl, Scotland's leading aristocratic family

51 miles

Loch Garten
Watch ospreys nesting amid ancient Caledonian pine forest

5

Braemar
START

2

9 miles

Balmoral Castle
Visit Her Majesty the Queen's own Highland estate

9

Aberfeldy
FINISH

4–5 DAYS
149 MILES / 238KM

GREAT FOR...

BEST TIME TO GO

July and August mean good weather and all attractions are open.

 ESSENTIAL PHOTO

The gorgeous view of Schiehallion mountain from Queen's View on Loch Tummel.

 BEST FOR WILDLIFE

Watching the nesting ospreys at Loch Garten.

Balmoral Castle One of the royal family's residences

19 Royal Highlands & Cairngorms

You'll tick off the highlights of Royal Deeside and the central Highlands as you make this circuit around Cairngorms National Park. Queen Victoria kick-started the Scottish tourism industry when she purchased Balmoral Castle in the middle of the 19th century, and her descendants still holiday here. Later, heed the call of the great outdoors with a visit to an osprey nesting site.

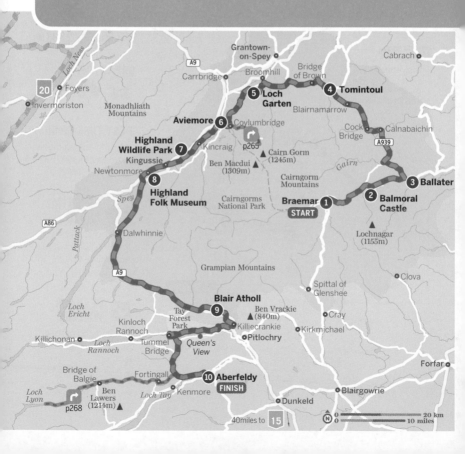

Loch Ness

20 Foyers

Invermoriston

Monadhliath Mountains

A9

Grantown-on-Spey

Carrbridge

Broomhill

Bridge of Brown

Cabrach

5 Loch Garten

4 Tomintoul

Blairnamarrow

Aviemore 6

Coylumbridge

Cock Bridge

Calnabaichin

A939

Highland Wildlife Park 7

Kincraig

p265

Cairn Gorm (1245m)

Kingussie

Ben Macdui (1309m)

Gairn

Newtonmore

8

Cairngorm Mountains

3 Ballater

Spey

Highland Folk Museum

Cairngorms National Park

Braemar 1

2 Balmoral Castle

START

A86

Pattack

Dalwhinnie

Lochnagar (1155m)

A9

Grampian Mountains

Clova

Spittal of Glenshee

Loch Ericht

Blair Atholl

9

Ben Vrackie (840m)

Cray

Kirkmichael

Tay Forest Park

Killiecrankie

Killichonan

Kinloch Rannoch

Loch Rannoch

Tummel Bridge

Pitlochry

Queen's View

Forfar

Bridge of Balgie

Fortingall

10 Aberfeldy

FINISH

Loch Lyon

Ben Lawers (1214m)

Loch Tay

Kenmore

Dunkeld

Blairgowrie

p268

40miles to 15

N 0   20 km
  0   10 miles

❶ Braemar

Braemar is a pretty little village with a grand location on a broad plain ringed by mountains where the Dee valley and Glen Clunie meet. In winter this is one of the coldest places in the country – temperatures as low as -29°C have been recorded.

Just north of the village, turreted **Braemar Castle** (www.braemarcastle. co.uk; adult/child £10/4; ⊙10am-5pm daily Jul & Aug, Wed-Sun Apr-Jun, Sep & Oct; P) dates from 1628 and served as a government garrison after the 1745 Jacobite rebellion. It was taken over by the local community in 2007, and now offers guided tours of the historic castle apartments.

LINK YOUR TRIP

20 **Great Glen**
The stirring wilderness of the northwest Highlands awaits – it's an hour and three-quarters west to Glen Coe.

15 **The Best of Britain**
Head an hour and a half south to Edinburgh to begin our epic loop of Britain's greatest hits at its midpoint.

There are Highland games in many towns and villages throughout the summer, but the best known is the **Braemar Gathering** (www.brae margathering.org), which takes place on the first Saturday in September.

🛏 p269

The Drive » The upper valley of the River Dee stretches east from Braemar to Aboyne. Made famous by its long association with the monarchy, the region is often called Royal Deeside. Head east from Braemar on the A93 for 9 miles to the car park at the entrance to Balmoral Castle.

TRIP HIGHLIGHT

❷ Balmoral Castle

Built for Queen Victoria in 1855 as a private residence for the royal family, **Balmoral Castle** (☎01339-742534; www. balmoralcastle.com; Crathie; guided tour adult/child £15/6; ⊙10am-5pm Apr-Jul, limited dates Oct-Dec; P) kicked off the revival of the Scottish Baronial style of architecture that characterises so many of Scotland's 19th-century country houses. Admission is by guided tour (book ahead); the tour is interesting and well-thought-out but very much an outdoor one through garden and grounds.

As for the castle itself, only the ballroom, which displays a collection of Landseer paintings and royal silver, is open to the public. Don't expect to

see the Queen's private quarters! The main attraction is learning about Highland estate management, rather than royal revelations.

You can buy a booklet that details several waymarked walks within Balmoral Estate; the best is the climb to **Prince Albert's Cairn**.

The Drive » Continue east on the A93 for another 8 miles to Ballater.

❸ Ballater

The attractive village of Ballater owes its 18th-century origins to the curative waters of nearby Pannanich Springs (now bottled commercially as Deeside Natural Mineral Water), and its prosperity to nearby Balmoral Castle.

After the original station was destroyed by fire in 2015, the **Old Royal Station** (☎01339-755306; Station Sq; ⊙tourist office 10am-3pm) building – newly restored to exactly replicate the one built in 1866 to receive Queen Victoria when she visited Balmoral by train – reopened in 2018. It houses a tourist office, a tearoom and a cafe-bistro. Behind the tourist office is a replica of Queen Victoria's carriage.

There are many pleasant walks in the surrounding area. The steep woodland walk up **Craigendarroch** (400m) takes just over one hour; ask at the tourist office for more info. You can hire bikes from **CycleHighlands** (📞01339-755864; www.cyclehighlands.com; The Pavilion, Victoria Rd; Santa Cruz mountain-bike hire per day £80; 🕐9am-5pm Mon-Thu & Sat, to 4pm Fri & Sun) and **Bike Station** (📞01339-754004; www.bikestationballater.co.uk; Station Sq; bicycle hire per day adult/child £20/10; 🕐9am-6pm), which also offer guided bike rides and advice on local trails.

🛏 p269

The Drive » The A939 strikes north through the mountains from Ballater to Tomintoul (25 miles). The section beyond Cock Bridge is a magnificent roller-coaster of a road, much loved by motorcyclists, summiting at the Lecht pass (637m) where there's a small skiing area (it's usually the first road in Scotland to be blocked by snow when winter closes in).

---

❹ Tomintoul

Tomintoul (tom-in-towel) is a pretty, stone-built village with a grassy, tree-lined main square. It was built by the Duke of Gordon in 1775 on the old military road that leads over the Lecht pass from Corgarff, a route now followed by the A939. The **Tomintoul & Glenlivet Discovery Centre** (📞01807-580760; discovery@tgdt.org.uk; The Square; 🕐10am-5pm Apr-Oct) celebrates local history, with reconstructions of

a crofter's kitchen and a blacksmith's forge.

There's excellent mountain biking at the **BikeGlenlivet** (www.glen livetestate.co.uk; trails free, parking £3) trail centre, 4.5 miles north of Tomintoul, off the B9136 road.

🍴 🛏 p269

The Drive » Continue northwest from Tomintoul on the A939 for 8.5 miles before turning left on a minor road to the village of Nethy Bridge. In the village, turn left towards Aviemore on the B970 then, after 600m, turn left again on a minor road to Loch Garten (total 17 miles).

TRIP HIGHLIGHT

❺ Loch Garten

A car park on the shores of Loch Garten, amid beautiful open forest of Scots pine, gives access to the **RSPB Loch Garten Osprey Centre** (📞01479-831694; www.rspb.org.uk/lochgarten; Tulloch; osprey hide adult/child £5/2.50; 🕐osprey hide 10am-6pm Apr-Aug). Ospreys nest in a tall pine tree on the reserve – you can watch from a hide as the birds feed their young, and see live CCTV feeds from the nest. These rare and beautiful birds – the only bird of prey in the world that eats only fish – migrate here each spring from Africa, arriving in April and leaving in August (check the website to see if they're in residence).

The Drive » The minor road leads back to the B970, where you turn left along the banks of the River Spey to Coylumbridge; turn right here to reach Aviemore (11 miles).

---

❻ Aviemore

The gateway to the Cairngorms, Aviemore may not be the prettiest town in Scotland – the main attractions are in the surrounding area – but when bad weather puts the hills off limits, Aviemore fills up with hikers, cyclists and climbers (plus skiers and snowboarders in winter) cruising the outdoor-equipment shops or recounting their latest adventures in the cafes and bars.

Strathspey Steam Railway (📞01479-810725; www.strathspeyrailway.co.uk; Station Sq; adult/child return £16.25/8.10) runs steam trains on a section of restored line between Aviemore and Broomhill, 10 miles to the north-east, via Boat of Garten. There are four or five trains daily from June to August, and a more limited service in April, May, September, October and December, with the option of eating afternoon tea, Sunday lunch or a three-course dinner on board.

🛏 p269

The Drive » From Aviemore, drive south on the B9152, which follows the valley of the River Spey; after 8.5 miles, soon after passing through the village of

Kincraig, you'll see a sign on the right for the Highland Wildlife Park.

❼ Highland Wildlife Park

The **Highland Wildlife Park** (☎01540-651270; www.highlandwildlifepark. org; Kincraig; adult/child £18.50/12.50; ☺10am-6pm Jul & Aug, to 5pm Apr-Jun, Sep & Oct, to 4pm Nov-Mar; P) features a drive-through safari park and animal enclosures that offer the chance to view rarely seen native wildlife, such as Scottish wildcats, capercaillies, pine martens and red squirrels. It is also home to species that once roamed the Scottish hills but have long since disappeared, including wolves, lynx, wild boars, beavers and European bison. Last entry is two hours before closing.

The Drive » Continue southwest on the B9152 through Kingussie to the Highland Folk Museum (6.5 miles).

❽ Highland Folk Museum

The old Speyside towns of Kingussie (kin-yew-see) and Newtonmore sit at the foot of the great heather-clad humps known as the Monadhliath Mountains. Newtonmore is best known as the home of the excellent **Highland Folk Museum** (☎01540-673551; www.highlandfolk.com; Kingussie Rd; ☺10.30am-4pm Wed-Sun; P), an open-air collection of historical buildings and artefacts revealing many aspects of Highland culture and lifestyle. Laid out like a farming township, it has a community of traditional thatch-roofed cottages, a sawmill, a schoolhouse, a shepherd's bothy (hut) and a rural post office.

The Drive » Join the main A9 Inverness to Perth road and follow it south for 35 miles to Blair Atholl, passing through bleak mountain scenery and

DETOUR: CAIRNGORM MOUNTAIN

Start: ❻ Aviemore

Cairngorm Mountain (1245m), 10 miles southeast of Aviemore, is the sixth-highest summit in the UK and home to Scotland's biggest ski area. From Aviemore, it's a 10-mile drive to Coire Cas car park at the end of Ski Rd; from here the climb to the summit is 2 miles and takes about two hours to the top (a challenging climb that requires a map and compass; beware of changeable weather conditions). The old funicular railway here closed in 2018.

From Aviemore, the road to Cairngorm Mountain passes through the **Rothiemurchus Estate**, famous for having one of Scotland's largest remnants of Caledonian forest, the ancient forest of Scots pine that once covered most of the country. The **Rothiemurchus Centre** (☎01479-812345; www.rothiemurchus.net; Ski Rd, Inverdruie; ☺9.30am-5.30pm; P) has maps detailing more than 50 miles of footpaths and cycling trails, including the 4-mile trail around **Loch an Eilein**, with its ruined castle and peaceful pine woods.

Six miles east of Aviemore, the road passes **Loch Morlich**, surrounded by some 8 sq miles of pine and spruce forest that make up the Glenmore Forest Park. Its attractions include a sandy beach (at the east end) and a water-sports centre.

Nearby, the **Cairngorm Reindeer Centre** (☎01479-861228; www.cairngormreindeer. co.uk; Glenmore; adult/child £17.50/12.50; 🚶) runs guided walks to see and feed Britain's only herd of reindeer, which are free-ranging but very tame. Walks take place at 11am daily (weather-dependent), plus another at 2.30pm from May to September. Book tickets in advance by phone.

WHY THIS IS A GREAT TRIP
ISABEL ALBISTON, WRITER

The wild and romantic landscape of the Cairngorms is ever changing: tempestuous skies flit from ominous grey to dazzling sunshine, whipping winds give way to moments of serene calm, snow melts and the mountains turn purple with heather that carpets the forest floors in summer. This trip reveals the area's haunting beauty, packing in wildlife encounters, castles and even a whisky distillery.

Above: Glen Lyon
Left: Blair Castle, Blair Atholl
Right: Braemar Gathering, Braemar

JEFF J MITCHELL/GETTY IMAGES ©

climbing to a high point of 460m
at the Pass of Drumochter.

TRIP HIGHLIGHT

9 Blair Atholl

The picturesque vllage
of Blair Atholl dates only
from the early 19th cen-
tury, built by the Duke of
Atholl, head of the Mur-
ray clan, whose seat –
magnificent **Blair Castle**
(☏01796-481207; www.blair-
castle.co.uk; house & gardens
adult/child £14/8.50, gardens
only £7.70/3.50; ⊙10am-
5.30pm Easter-Oct, to 4pm Sat
& Sun Nov-Easter; P ♿) – is
one of the most popular
tourist attractions in
Scotland.

Thirty rooms are open
to the public and they present a wonderful picture
of upper-class Highland
life from the 16th century
on. The original tower
was built in 1269, but the
castle underwent signifi-
cant remodelling in the
18th and 19th centuries.
Highlights include the
2nd-floor **Drawing Room**
with its ornate Georgian
plasterwork and Zoffany
portrait of the 4th duke's
family, complete with a
pet lemur called Tommy;
and the **Tapestry Room**
draped with 17th-century
wall hangings created
for Charles I. The **dining
room** is sumptuous –
check out the 9-pint wine
glasses.

There are more than
50 miles of cycling trails
through the estate; hire
a bike from **Blair Atholl**

DETOUR:
GLEN LYON

Start: 🔟 Aberfeldy

The 'longest, loneliest and loveliest glen in Scotland', according to Sir Walter Scott, stretches for 32 unforgettable miles of rickety stone bridges, native woodland and heather-clad hills, becoming wilder and more uninhabited as it snakes its way west. The ancients believed it to be a gateway to Faerieland, and even the most sceptical of visitors will be entranced by the valley's magic.

There are no villages in the glen – the majestic scenery is the main reason to be here – just a cluster of houses at Bridge of Balgie, where the **Glenlyon Tearoom** (📞01887-866221; Bridge of Balgie; snacks £3-4; ⏱10am-5pm Apr-Oct; 🅿🛜), with a suntrap of a terrace overlooking the river, serves as a hub for walkers, cyclists and motorists. The owner is a fount of knowledge about the glen, and her pistachio and almond cake is legendary.

There are several waymarked woodland walks beginning from a car park a short distance beyond Bridge of Balgie, and more challenging hill walks into the surrounding mountains (see www.walkhighlands.co.uk/perthshire).

From Aberfeldy, the B846 leads to the pretty village Fortingall, famous for its ancient yew tree, where a narrow minor road strikes west up the glen; another steep and spectacular route from Loch Tay crosses the hills to meet it at Bridge of Balgie. The road continues west as far as the dam on Loch Lyon, passing a memorial to Robert Campbell (1808–94), a Canadian explorer and fur trader who was born in the glen.

Bike Hire (📞0845-548 2270; www.segway-ecosse.com/bike-hire; Blair Castle Caravan Park; per day adult/child £28/20; ⏱9am-6pm).

🍴 p269

The Drive » Follow the B8079 southeast out of Blair Atholl for a few miles, past the historic battle site of Killiecrankie, and turn right on the B8019 Strathtummel road. This gloriously scenic road leads along Loch Tummel (stop for photographs at Queen's View) to Tummel Bridge; turn left here on the B846 over the hills to Aberfeldy (29 miles).

🔟 Aberfeldy

Aberfeldy is the gateway to Breadalbane (the historic region surrounding Loch Tay), and a good base: adventure sports, angling, art and castles all feature on the menu here. It's a peaceful, pretty place on the banks of the Tay, but if it's moody lochs and glens that steal your heart, you may want to push further west into **Glen Lyon**.

You arrive in the town by crossing the River Tay via the elegant **Wade's Bridge**, built in 1733 as part of the network of military roads designed to tame the Highlands. At the eastern end of town is **Aberfeldy Distillery** (www.dewarsaberfeldydistillery.com; tours adult/child from £9/free; ⏱10am-6pm Mon-Sat, noon-4pm Sun Apr-Oct, 10am-4pm Mon-Sat Nov-Mar; 🅿), home of the famous Dewar's whisky; entertaining tours of the whisky-making process are followed by a tasting of venerable Aberfeldy single malts and others.

🛏 p269

Eating & Sleeping

Braemar ❶

🛏 Craiglea   B&B $$

(📞01339-741641; www.craigleabraemar.com; Hillside Rd; d/tr £90/115; 🅿 📶) Craiglea is a homely B&B set in a pretty stone cottage with double, twin and family rooms, all en suite. Packed lunches are available for a day in the hills and the owners can give advice on local walks. Minimum stay of two nights.

🛏 Braemar Lodge Hotel   Hotel $$$

(📞01339-741627; www.braemarlodge.co.uk; Glenshee Rd; dm/s/d from £25/85/140, 3-bed cabin per week from £770; 🅿 📶) This Victorian shooting lodge on the southern outskirts of Bracmar has bags of character, not least in the wood-panelled Malt Room bar, which is as well stocked with mounted deer heads as it is with single malt whiskies. There's a good restaurant with views of the hills (mains £11 to £35), plus a 12-bed hikers' bunkhouse (book in advance).

Ballater ❸

🛏 Auld Kirk   B&B $$$

(📞01339-755762; www.theauldkirk.com; Braemar Rd; s/d from £130/140; 🅿 📶🍽) Here's something a little out of the ordinary – a seven-bedroom B&B and coffee lounge housed in a converted 19th-century church. The interior blends original features with sleek modern decor – the pulpit now serves as the reception desk, while the lounge is bathed in light from leaded Gothic windows.

Tomintoul ❹

✖ Clockhouse Restaurant   Scottish $$

(📞01807-580378; www.clockhouserestaurant. com; The Square; mains £13-24; ⏲11am-9pm Apr-Oct) Serves light lunches and bistro dinners made with fresh Highland lamb, beef, venison and salmon.

🛏 Argyle Guest House   B&B $$

(📞01807-580766; www.argyletomintoul.co.uk; 7 Main St; s/d/f £45/72/99; 📶🍽) Well-run B&B offering six comfortable rooms of varying sizes (two rooms share a bathroom) and the best porridge in the Cairngorms.

Aviemore ❻

🛏 Cairngorm Hotel   Hotel $$

(📞01479-810233; www.cairngorm.com; Grampian Rd; s/d £75/110; 🅿 📶) Better known as 'the Cairn', this long-established hotel is set in the fine old granite building with the pointy turret opposite the train station. It's a welcoming place with comfortable rooms and a determinedly Scottish atmosphere, with tartan carpets and stags' antlers. There's live music on weekends, so it can get a bit noisy – not for early-to-bedders.

The restaurant serves traditional Highland comfort food such as fish pie, fillet of venison and haggis, neeps and tatties (£10 to £23).

Blair Atholl ❾

✖ Blair Atholl Watermill   Cafe $

(📞01796-481321; www.blairathollwatermill. com; Ford Rd; mains £4-7; ⏲9.30am-4pm Apr-Oct; 🅿 📶♿) This working watermill grinds its own flour and bakes its own bread, and serves it up in this atmospheric cafe as deliciously fresh sandwiches. You can watch the mill at work, and even sign up for bakery courses.

Aberfeldy ❿

🛏 Tigh'n Eilean Guest House   B&B $$

(📞01887-820109; www.tighneilean.co.uk; Taybridge Dr; s/d from £48/80; 🅿 📶🍽) Everything about this property screams comfort. It's a gorgeous place overlooking the Tay, with individually designed rooms – one has a Jacuzzi, while another is set on its own in a cheery yellow summer house in the garden, giving you a bit of privacy. The garden itself is fabulous and the riverbank setting is delightful.

Great Glen

20

This lake-and-mountain-themed trip leads you through some of the Highlands' scenic hotspots, and along the shores of world-famous Loch Ness – here be monsters!

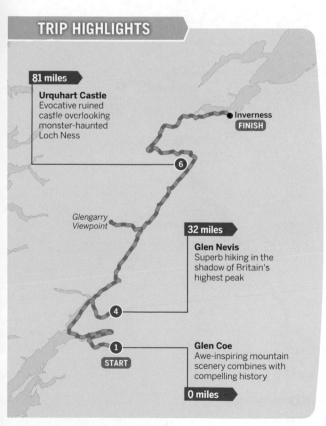

81 miles

Urquhart Castle
Evocative ruined castle overlooking monster-haunted Loch Ness

Inverness
FINISH

6

Glengarry Viewpoint

32 miles

Glen Nevis
Superb hiking in the shadow of Britain's highest peak

4

1
START

Glen Coe
Awe-inspiring mountain scenery combines with compelling history

0 miles

2–3 DAYS
147 MILES / 235KM

GREAT FOR...

BEST TIME TO GO
April to see snow on the mountains, October for autumn colours in the forests.

ESSENTIAL PHOTO
Failing a shot of the Loch Ness monster, crossing the wire bridge at Steall Falls.

 BEST FOR FAMILIES
Taking a Nessie-hunting cruise from Fort Augustus.

Glen Coe One of Scotland's most famous glens

271

20 Great Glen

The Great Glen is a geological fault running in an arrow-straight line across Scotland, filled by a series of lochs including Loch Ness. This trip follows the A82 road along the glen (completed in 1933 – a date that coincides with the first sightings of the Loch Ness monster!) and links two areas of outstanding natural beauty – Glen Coe to the south, and Glen Affric to the north.

TRIP HIGHLIGHT

❶ Glen Coe

Scotland's most famous glen is also one of its grandest. The A82 road leads over the **Pass of Glencoe** and into the narrow upper glen. The southern side is dominated by three massive, brooding spurs, known as the **Three Sisters**, while the northern side is enclosed by the continuous steep wall of the knife-edged **Aonach Eagach** ridge, a

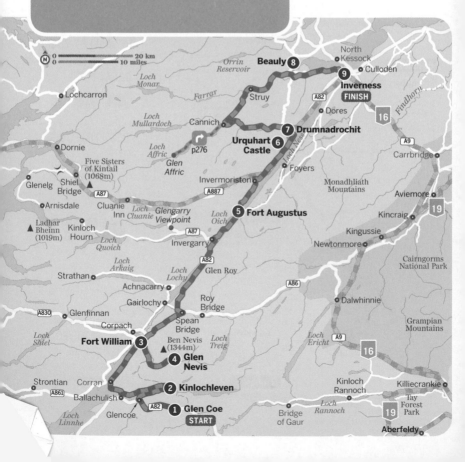

classic mountaineering challenge.

Glencoe Visitor Centre (NTS; ☎01855-811307; www.nts.org.uk; parking £4; ⏰9.30am-4pm; 🅿) provides comprehensive information on the geological, environmental and cultural history of Glencoe, charts the development of mountaineering in the glen, and tells the story of the Glencoe Massacre in all its gory detail.

 p277

The Drive ➤➤ From Glencoe village at the foot of the glen, head east on the B863 for 7 miles along the southern shore of Loch Leven to Kinlochleven.

─────────────

❷ Kinlochleven

Kinlochleven is hemmed in by high mountains at the head of beautiful Loch

LINK YOUR TRIP

19 **Royal Highlands & Cairngorms**

Get your fill of Scottish splendour by beginning with this tour of castles and mountains before heading west to Glen Coe.

16 **Britain's Wild Side**

Explore more of Britain's natural beauty spots by taking this trip in reverse from Inverness.

Leven, where the West Highland Way brings a steady stream of hikers through the village. It is also the starting point for walks up the glen of the River Leven, through pleasant woods to the **Grey Mare's Tail** waterfall, and harder mountain hikes into the Mamores.

Scotland's first **Via Ferrata** (☎01397-747111; www.verticaldescents.com; Unit 3, Kinlochleven Business Park; per person/family £65/240) – a 500m climbing route equipped with steel ladders, cables and bridges – snakes through the crags around the Grey Mare's Tail, allowing non-climbers to experience the thrill of climbing (you'll need a head for heights, though!).

 p277

The Drive ➤➤ Return west along the north side of Loch Leven, perhaps stopping for lunch at the excellent Lochleven Seafood Cafe, then head north on the A82 to Fort William (22 miles).

─────────────

❸ Fort William

Basking on the shores of Loch Linnhe amid magnificent mountain scenery, Fort William has one of the most enviable settings in the whole of Scotland. If it wasn't for the busy dual carriageway crammed between the less-than-attractive town centre and the loch, and one of the highest rainfall records in the

country, it would be almost idyllic. Even so, the Fort has carved out a reputation as Outdoor Capital of the UK (www.outdoorcapital.co.uk).

The small but fascinating **West Highland Museum** (☎01397-702169; www.westhighlandmuseum.org.uk; Cameron Sq; ⏰10am-2pm Tue-Fri) is packed with all manner of Highland memorabilia. Look out for the secret portrait of Bonnie Prince Charlie – after the Jacobite rebellions, all things Highland were banned, including pictures of the exiled leader, and this tiny painting looks like nothing more than a smear of paint until viewed in a cylindrical mirror.

 p277

The Drive ➤➤ At the roundabout on the northern edge of Fort William, take the minor road that runs into Glen Nevis; it leads to a car park at the far end of the glen, 6.5 miles away.

─────────────

TRIP HIGHLIGHT

❹ Glen Nevis

Scenic Glen Nevis – used as a filming location for *Braveheart* and the Harry Potter movies – wraps around the base of Ben Nevis, Britain's highest mountain. The **Glen Nevis Visitor Centre** (☎01349-781401; parking £4; ⏰8.30am-4pm, longer hours Jul & Aug) is situated 1.5 miles up the glen, and provides information on hiking, weather forecasts, and specific advice on climbing **Ben Nevis**.

From the car park at the end of the road, 5 miles beyond the visitor centre, there is an excellent 1.5-mile walk through the spectacular, verdant **Nevis Gorge** valley to **Steall Falls**, a 100m-high bridal-veil waterfall. You can reach the foot of the falls by crossing the river on a wobbly, three-cable wire bridge – one cable for your feet and one for each hand – a real test of balance!

The Drive >> Return down Glen Nevis and head north on the A82. At Invergarry, turn left onto the A87 which climbs high above Loch Garry; stop at the famous Glengarry Viewpoint (layby on left). By a quirk of perspective, the lochs to the west appear to form the map outline of Scotland. Return to the A87 and continue to Fort Augustus (44 miles).

- - - - - - - - - - - - - - - - - -

⑤ Fort Augustus

Fort Augustus, at the junction of four old military roads, was originally a government garrison and the headquarters of General George Wade's road-building operations in the early 18th century. Today, it's a neat and picturesque little place bisected by the Caledonian Canal.

Boats using the canal are raised and lowered 13m by a 'ladder' of five consecutive locks. It's fun to watch, and the neatly landscaped canal banks are a great place to soak up the sun. The **Caledonian Canal Centre** (Ardchattan House, Canalside; ⏰10am-4pm Wed-Sun), beside the lowest lock, has information on the history of the canal.

Cruise Loch Ness (☎01320-366277; www.cruiselochness.com; adult/child £15/9; ⏰10am, noon, 2pm & 4pm daily Apr-Nov, fewer sailings Dec-Mar), at the jetty beside the canal bridge, operates one-hour cruises on Loch Ness accompanied by the latest high-tech sonar equipment so you can keep an underwater eye open for the Loch Ness monster.

The Drive >> It's a straightforward but scenic 17-mile drive along the shores of Loch Ness to Urquhart Castle.

- - - - - - - - - - - - - - - - - -

`TRIP HIGHLIGHT`

⑥ Urquhart Castle

Commanding a superb location with outstanding views over Loch Ness, **Urquhart Castle** (HES; ☎01456-450551; www.historicenvironment.scot; adult/child £9.60/5.80; ⏰9.30am-6pm Apr-Oct, to 4.30pm Nov-Mar; P) is a popular Nessie-hunting hotspot. The castle was repeatedly sacked and rebuilt (and sacked and rebuilt) over the centuries; in 1692 it was blown up to prevent the Jacobites from using it. The

five-storey tower house at the northern point is the most impressive remaining fragment and offers wonderful views across the water.

The visitor centre includes displays of medieval items discovered in the castle and a video theatre: the film, with a dramatic 'reveal' of the castle at the end, can be downloaded onto

Urquhart Castle Overlooking Loch Ness

your phone using a QR code if the visitor centre is closed.

The Drive » A short hop of 2 miles leads to Drumnadrochit.

7 Drumnadrochit

Deep, dark and narrow, Loch Ness stretches for 23 miles between Inverness and Fort Augustus. Its bitterly cold waters have been extensively explored in search of Nessie, the elusive Loch Ness monster, but most visitors see her only in the form of a cardboard cutout at Drumnadrochit's monster exhibitions.

The **Loch Ness Centre** (☎01456-450573; www. lochness.com; adult/child £8.45/4.95; ☺9.30am-6pm Jul & Aug, to 5pm Easter-Jun, Sep & Oct, 10am-4pm Nov- Easter; P ♦) adopts a scientific approach that allows you to weigh the evidence for yourself. Exhibits include the original equipment – sonar survey vessels, miniature submarines, cameras and sediment coring tools – used in various monster hunts, as well as original photographs and film footage of sightings. You'll find

DETOUR: GLEN AFFRIC

Start: 7 Drumnadrochit

Glen Affric, one of the most beautiful glens in Scotland, extends deep into the hills beyond Cannich, halfway between Drumnadrochit and Beauly. The upper reaches of the glen, now designated as **Glen Affric Nature Reserve**, are a scenic wonderland of shimmering lochs, rugged mountains and native Scots pine forest, home to pine martens, wildcats, otters, red squirrels and golden eagles.

A narrow, dead-end road leads southwest from Cannich; about 4 miles along is **Dog Falls**, a scenic spot where the River Affric squeezes through a narrow, rocky gorge. A circular walking trail (red waymarks) leads from Dog Falls car park to a footbridge below the falls and back on the far side of the river (2 miles, allow one hour).

The road continues beyond Dog Falls to a parking area and picnic site at the eastern end of **Loch Affric**, where there are several short walks along the river and the loch shore. The circuit of Loch Affric (10 miles, allow five hours walking, two hours by mountain bike) follows good paths right around the loch and takes you deep into the heart of some very wild scenery.

out about hoaxes and optical illusions, as well as learning a lot about the ecology of Loch Ness – is there enough food in the loch to support even one 'monster', let alone a breeding population?

The Drive >> Head west on the A831 which leads to the village of Cannich – jumping-off point for the Glen Affric detour – before turning north along lovely Strathglass to reach Beauly (30 miles).

8 Beauly

Mary, Queen of Scots is said to have given this village its name in 1564 when she visited, exclaiming in French: 'Quel beau lieu!' (What a beautiful place!). Founded in 1230, the red-sandstone **Beauly Priory** is now an impressive ruin, haunted by the cries of rooks nesting in a magnificent centuries-old sycamore tree.

Corner on the Square makes a good place to break your journey; it's well worth the stop.

 p277

The Drive >> Drive east on the A862 for 12 miles to Inverness.

9 Inverness

Inverness has a great location astride the River Ness at the northern end of the Great Glen. In summer it overflows with visitors intent on monster hunting at nearby Loch Ness, but it's worth a visit in its own right for a stroll along the picturesque River Ness, a cruise on Loch Ness, and a meal in one of the city's excellent restaurants.

The main attraction in Inverness is a leisurely stroll along the river to the **Ness Islands**. Planted with mature Scots pine, fir, beech and sycamore, and linked to the riverbanks and each other by elegant Victorian footbridges, the islands make an appealing picnic spot. They're a 20-minute walk south of the castle – head upstream on either side of the river (the start of the Great Glen Way), and return on the opposite bank.

🛏 p277

Eating & Sleeping

Glen Coe ❶

✕ Glencoe Café Cafe $

(📞01855-811168; www.glencoecafe.co.uk; Lorn Dr, Glencoe village; mains £4.50-10; ⏰11am-5pm Fri-Wed May-Oct, to 4pm Nov-Apr; P🤖) This friendly cafe is the social hub of Glencoe village, serving breakfast fry-ups (including vegetarian versions) till 11.30am, light lunches based on local produce and the best cappuccino in the glen.

🛏 Clachaig Inn Hotel $$$

(📞01855-811252; www.clachaig.com; s/d £78/155; P🤖👣) The Clachaig, 2 miles southeast of Glencoe village, has long been a favourite haunt of hill walkers and climbers. As well as comfortable accommodation (opt for a room with a Glen Coe view), there's a lounge bar with snug booths and high refectory tables serving good food (mains £11 to £20) from noon to 9pm.

Kinlochleven ❷

✕ Lochleven Seafood Cafe Seafood $$

(📞01855-821048; www.lochlevenseafoodcafe.co.uk; mains £11-40, whole lobster £40; ⏰meals noon-3pm & 6-9pm, coffee & cake 10am-noon & 3-5pm mid-Mar–Oct; P👣) This place serves superb shellfish freshly plucked from live tanks – oysters, razor clams, scallops, lobster and crab – plus a daily fish special and some non-seafood dishes. For warm days, there's an outdoor terrace with a view across the loch to the Pap of Glencoe. The cafe is 5 miles west of Kinlochleven, on the north shore of the loch.

Fort William ❸

✕ Lime Tree Scottish $$

(📞01397-701806; www.limetreefortwilliam.co.uk; Achintore Rd; mains £19-22.50, set menu £30; ⏰6.30-9.30pm; P🤖) The restaurant at this small **hotel** (d £155-175) and art gallery has put the UK's Outdoor Capital on the gastronomic map. The chef turns out delicious dishes built around fresh Scottish produce, such as Loch Fyne oysters, Loch Awe trout and Ardnamurchan venison.

🛏 Grange B&B $$$

(📞01397-705516; www.grangefortwilliam.com; Grange Rd; d £195-225; ⏰closed Sun; P🤖) An exceptional 19th-century villa set in its own landscaped grounds, the Grange is crammed with antiques and warmed by log fires. It has two luxury suites fitted with leather sofas, handcrafted furniture and roll-top baths, one situated in a charming self-contained cottage in the sprawling gardens, all with a view over Loch Linnhe. No children.

Beauly ❽

✕ Corner on the Square Cafe $

(📞01463-783000; www.corneronthesquare.co.uk; 1 High St; dishes £2.50-8.50; ⏰8.30am-5pm Mon-Fri, to 8pm Sat, 9am-5pm Sun) Beauly's best lunch spot is this superb little delicatessen and cafe that serves breakfast (till 11.30am), daily lunch specials (11.30am to 4.30pm) and excellent coffee.

Inverness ❾

🛏 Heathmount Hotel Boutique Hotel $$$

(📞01463-235877; www.heathmounthotel.com; Kingsmills Rd; d from £170; P🤖) Small and friendly, the Heathmount combines a popular local bar and restaurant with eight designer hotel rooms, each one different, ranging from a boldly coloured family room in purple and gold to a slinky black velvet four-poster double. Five minutes' walk east of the city centre.

West Wales: Swansea to St Davids

21

This route links two distinctly Welsh cities – Wales' second largest and the UK's tiniest – by way of Wales' two most famously beautiful tracts of coast.

TRIP HIGHLIGHTS

125 miles

St Davids
Historic micro-city set in an ancient landscape

10
St Davids
FINISH

● Haverfordwest

● Carmarthen

Pembroke ●

7 ● Tenby

Llanelli ●

START
Swansea

Rhossili **4**

86 miles

Tenby
Postcard-perfect beach town with a medieval core

Rhossili
Miles of golden sand backed by steep-sloped downs

20 miles

---

4 DAYS
129 MILES / 207KM

GREAT FOR...

BEST TIME TO GO
June, July and August offer the best beach weather; in April, May or September the jaw-dropping sandy beaches have fewer crowds.

ESSENTIAL PHOTO

The view of Three Cliffs Bay from Pennard Castle.

BEST FOR FAMILIES

Splashing about on the beach at Tenby.

---

21 | West Wales: Swansea to St Davids

The broad sandy arc of Swansea Bay is only a teaser for what is to come. Escape the city sprawl, and the majesty of the Welsh coast immediately begins to assert itself. Waves crash against sheer cliffs painted from a rapidly changing palate of grey, purple and inky black. In between are some of Britain's very best beaches: glorious sandy stretches and remote coves alike.

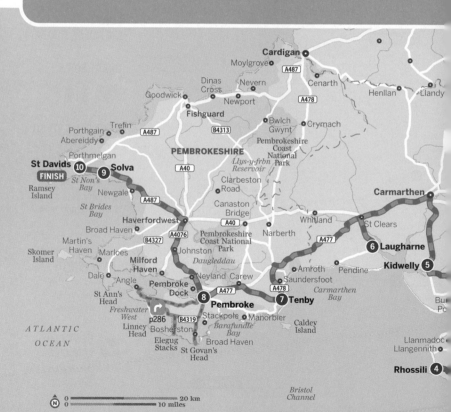

❶ Swansea

Wales' second city has its own workaday charm and an enviable setting on 5-mile-long, sandy Swansea Bay. An active bar scene is enthusiastically supported by a large student population, while a new brace of affordable ethnic eateries and swimmingly good seafood restaurants have improved the city's once drab dining options no end. Literature lovers will relish the handsome Uplands area where the country's best-known writer Dylan Thomas was born, bred, inspired and inebriated.

Fuel up on everything from wondrous Welsh cakes to tantalising Thai food at one of the nation's best markets, **Swansea Market** (www.swanseaindoormarket.co.uk; Oxford St; ⏱8.30am-4.30pm Mon-Sat), then dive into the whizz-bang **National Waterfront Museum** (☎0300 111 2333; www.museum.wales/swansea; South Dock Marina, Oystermouth Rd; ⏱11am-4pm Thu, Sat & Sun). Dylan Thomas fans can tour the district surrounding his **birthplace** (☎01/92-472555; www.dylanthomasbirthplace.com; 5 Cwmdonkin Dr, Uplands, SA2 0RA; adult/child £8/6; ⏱10.30am-4.30pm), explore his legacy at the **Dylan Thomas Centre** (☎01792-463980; www.dylanthomas.com; Somerset Pl; ⏱10am-4.30pm) and visit some of the (many!) pubs he famously frequented.

🛏 p288

The Drive ❯❯ Broad Oystermouth Rd traces the edge of Swansea Bay, changing its name to Mumbles Rd halfway along. It's only 4 miles from central Swansea to the heart of The Mumbles strip.

❷ Mumbles

Swansea's swanky seaside suburb sprawls along the western curve of Swansea Bay and terminates in the pair of rounded hills which may have gifted the area its unusual name (from the French *Les Mamelles* – 'the breasts'). The Norman fortress of **Oystermouth Castle** (☎01792-635478; www.swansea.gov.uk/oystermouthcastle; Castle Ave) stands guard over the fashionable Newton Rd and seafronting Mumbles Rd with their spread of tempting restaurants and bars.

Pick up an ice cream at **Joe's** (☎01792-368212; www.joes-icecream.com; 526 Mumbles Rd; ⏱10.30am-5.30pm Mon, from 10am Tue-Fri, to 6.30pm Sat & Sun),

- Lampeter
- Llanybydder
- Llangadog
- Llandeilo
- Ammanford
- Pontarddulais
- 30miles to **15**
- 70miles to **17**
- Llanelli
- **START** Swansea ❶
- A4118 ❸ Parkmill
- ❷ Mumbles

❾ LINK YOUR TRIP

17 **The Historic South**
Sample some heritage and culture before hitting the wild coast: from Oxford, it's 2½ hours west on the M4 to Swansea.

15 **The Best of Britain**
The Welsh coast tour is an obvious side trip from our grand tour of the best sights of Britain – it's an hour's drive between Swansea and Cardiff.

a Swansea institution founded by an Italian immigrant in 1922, and take a stroll along the waterside promenade to the Victorian **pier** (☎01792-365200; www.mumbles-pier.co.uk; Mumbles Rd; ☺noon-10pm Mon-Fri, 10am-10pm Sat & Sun). There's a pretty little sandy beach tucked just beneath it. If you're peckish, there are some good cafes and restaurants spread along the waterfront, some serving the region's highly regarded seafood, and plenty of pubs and bars too.

 p288

The Drive ≫ From the Mumbles it's 6 miles to Parkmill on the Gower Peninsula. Head uphill on Newton Rd, following the Gower signs. Eventually the houses give way to fields and, at the village of Murton, a sharp right-hand turn leads to the B4436 and on to the A4118, the main Gower road.

3 Parkmill

The spectacular coastal landscape of the Gower Peninsula was recognised by officialdom when it was declared the UK's first Area of Outstanding Natural Beauty in 1956.

In the gateway village of Parkmill, historic mill buildings have been converted into the **Gower Heritage Centre** (☎01792-371206; www.gowerheritagecentre.co.uk; adult/child £6.75/5.75; ☺10am-5.30pm; ♿). Despite its worthy-

sounding name, it's a great place to take kids, incorporating a petting zoo and a puppet theatre. Nearby **Parc-le-Breos** contains the remains of a 5500-year-old burial chamber.

However, the real reason to stop in Parkmill is to take a stroll to **Three Cliffs Bay**. Recognised as one of Britain's most beautiful sandy beaches, Three Cliffs has a memorable setting, with a ruined 13th-century castle above and a triple-pointed rock formation framing a natural arch at its eastern end.

The Drive ≫ From Parkmill, head west along the A4118, following the signs to Rhossili. Eventually the road turns left towards the village of Scurlage and the Rhossili turn-off. All up, it's a distance of 10 miles along good roads, but it's quite likely you'll be sporadically stuck behind a slow-moving campervan or tractor.

TRIP HIGHLIGHT

4 Rhossili

The 3 miles of surf-battered golden sands of **Rhossili Bay** make it the Gower Peninsula's most spectacular strand. Rhossili village at the southern end of the beach makes the best casual stop. There's a National Trust **visitor centre** (☎01792-390707; www.nationaltrust.org.uk/rhosili-and-south-gower-coast; Coastguard Cottages; ☺11am-5pm daily Mar-Sep,

Fri-Sun Oct) here, and the excellent Bay Bistro & Coffee House (p288). Beware of swimming here: tides can make it dangerous.

This end of the beach is abutted by **Worms Head**, a dragon-shaped promontory which turns into an island at high tide and is home to seals and many seabirds. It's safe to explore on foot for 2½ hours either side of low tide. Don't get cut off by incoming tides!

Surfers tend to prefer Llangennith, near the north end of the beach, as a base.

 p288

The Drive ≫ It's only 31 miles from Rhossili to Kidwelly, but allow an hour as the first part of the journey zigzags along tiny byways on the Gower Peninsula's northern edge. Before and after navigating the scraggly outskirts of Llanelli, it's a pleasantly rural drive.

5 Kidwelly

Castles are a dime a dozen in this part of Wales – a legacy of a time when Norman 'Marcher' lords were given authority and a large degree of autonomy to subjugate the Welsh in the south and along the English border. The cute little Carmarthenshire town of Kidwelly has a particularly well-preserved example.

Originally erected in 1106, only 40 years after

the Norman invasion of England, **Kidwelly Castle** (Cadw; ☎01554-890104; www.cadw.gov.wales; Castle Rd; adult/child £5.10/3.10; ⊙10am-1pm & 2-5pm Wed-Sun) got its current configuration of imposing stone walls in the 13th century. Wander around and explore its remaining towers and battlements, or just stop by to take a photo of the grey walls looming above the peaceful river far below.

Extensive **Pembrey Country Park** (☎01554-742435; www.pembreycountrypark.wales; parking 2hr/all day £3/5.50; ⊙6am-10pm; ♿) is 5 miles south of Kidwelly. With 200 hectares of trail-crossed woods abutting one of Wales' longest sandy beaches, you could spend hours mooching about here.

The Drive » From Kidwelly, motor north along the A484 through the green fields of Carmarthenshire. At Carmarthen, a pleasant but unremarkable county town, switch to the A40 dual carriageway to St Clears, and then follow the A4066 south to the becalmed estuary town of Laugharne: 21 miles in total.

- - - - - - - - - - - - - - - - -

❻ Laugharne

While shooting down the highway between Carmarthen and Tenby, it's worth considering taking a left at St Clears to visit the town of Laugharne (pronounced *'larn'*) on the Taf estuary.

Perched picturesquely above the reed-lined shore, **Laugharne Castle** (Cadw; ☎01994-427906; www.cadw.gov.wales; cnr King & Wogan Sts; adult/child £3.80/2.20; ⊙10am-1pm & 2-5pm Thu-Mon) is a hefty 13th-century fortress, converted into a mansion in the 16th century.

Swansea may have been Dylan Thomas' birthplace, but Laugharne is where he lived out his final years, getting inspiration for his classic play for voices *Under Milk Wood*. Many fans make the pilgrimage here to visit the **boathouse** (☎01994-427420; www.dylanthomasboathouse.com; Dylan's Walk; adult/child £4.75/3.75; ⊙2-5pm Fri-Mon) where he lived, the shed where he wrote and his final resting place in the graveyard of St Martin's Church. Also worth a visit is cosy **Brown's**

Hotel (King St), one of his favourite watering holes. Then there is the **Dylan Thomas Birthday Walk** (www.laugharnetownship-wcc.gov.uk), taking you on a trail around the town and nearby estuary to spots associated with the poet.

Laugharne is situated 4 miles off the highway: allocate a few hours to explore it properly. Although you can continue southwest from here on narrow roads, you're better off backtracking to the A477 to get to Tenby.

The Drive » Twenty miles of verdant farmland separate Laugharne from Tenby via the A477 and then, once you hit Kilgetty, the A478.

- - - - - - - - - - - - - - - - -

TRIP HIGHLIGHT

❼ Tenby

Sandy, family-friendly beaches spread out in either direction from

LOCAL KNOWLEDGE: ST DAVID'S DAY

St David's Day is to the Welsh what St Patrick's Day is to the Irish – a day to celebrate one's essential Welshness, albeit somewhat more soberly than Ireland does. If you're in Wales on 1 March, there's no better place to be than the saint's own city, St Davids. Around the cathedral, a host of golden daffodils flower seemingly right on cue; people pin leek, daffodil or red dragon badges to their lapels; streets are strung with flags bearing the black-and-gold St David's cross; and *cawl* (a traditional soupy stew) is consumed in industrial qualities. You should also visit the cathedral, where the saint's remains lie (year-round) in a recently restored shrine.

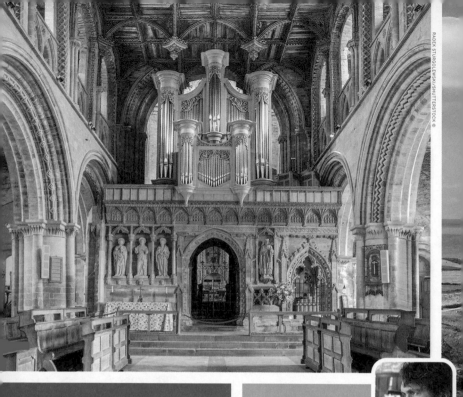

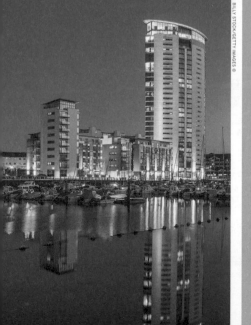

WHY THIS IS A GREAT TRIP
LUKE WATERSON, WRITER

Traversing two of Wales' most acclaimed beauty spots (the Gower Peninsula and the Pembrokeshire Coast), this journey also offers up a couple of urban extremes in the form of a large post-industrial city (Swansea) and its near antithesis, an ancient settlement that is Britain's smallest and most westerly city (St Davids). Meander there via time-lost fishing villages, thickset fortresses and serendipitous sandy beaches.

Above: St David's Cathedral, St Davids
Left: Swansea
Right: Worms Head, Rhossili

this pretty pastel-hued resort town tumbling over the headland above. Pembrokeshire's (if not Wales') premier seaside resort it is, but Tenby's eclectic blend of architecture and steep twisty streets, still part-wrapped by Norman walls, almost evoking Greek island towns at times, impress most.

The beaches are the major attraction here, plus the variety of eateries stashed away amid the sinuous cobbled streets. The other big draws – the sea-bashed crag of **St Catherine's Island** (www. saintcatherinesisland.co.uk; adult/child £5/2.50; ☉ late Mar-Dec) **topped by its bombastic fort, along with the Tenby Boat Trips** (☎07980-864509; www. tenbyboattrips.co.uk; Tenby Harbour; ☉Apr-Oct; 🚗) **out to Caldey Island, home to seals, seabirds, beaches and a community of Cistercian monks – are lovely additional strings to Tenby's bow.**

🍴 🛏 p288

The Drive ≫ From Tenby, it's a short, sweet 10-mile hop to Pembroke. From the town centre, head west on Greenhill Rd, go under the railway bridge and turn right at the roundabout. Follow Hayward Lane (the B4318) through a patchwork of fields until you reach the Sageston roundabout. Turn left onto the A477, and then veer left on the A4075 (or plump for the equally distanced but quieter A4139 via Jameston, where enticing lanes shoot off

285

to the likes of Manorbier and Freshwater East beaches).

⑧ Pembroke

Pembroke is dominated by hulking **Pembroke Castle** (📞01646-681510; www.pembroke-castle.co.uk; Main St; adult/child £7/6; 🕙10am-5pm; 🅿️), which looms over the end of the town's main street. The fortress is best viewed from the Mill Pond, a pretty lake which forms a moat on three sides of the headland from which the castle rises. Pembroke played a leading role in British history as the birthplace of the first Tudor king, Henry VII. The castle is in extremely good condition, with lots of well-preserved towers, dungeons and wall walks to explore.

A strip of mainly Georgian and Victorian buildings leads down from the castle, including some good pubs and the excellent **Food at Williams** (📞01646-689990; 18 Main St; light bites £3.50-8, mains £8.50-16; 🕙9am-3pm Mon-Sat, from 10am Sun; 🛜) cafe.

🛏️ p289

The Drive » The 24-mile journey to Solva heads through the port town of Pembroke Dock, crosses the Daugleddau estuary and then traverses Pembrokeshire's nondescript county town Haverfordwest. Exit Haverfordwest on the A487, trundling through farmland before reaching the coast at Newgale, a vast sandy surf beach backed by a high bank of pebbles. From here the road more or less shadows the coast.

⑨ Solva

Clustered around a long, hook-shaped harbour, Solva is the classic Welsh fishing village straight out of central casting.

DETOUR: WEST OF PEMBROKE

Start: ⑧ Pembroke

The remote peninsula that forms the bottom lip of the long, deep-sea harbour of Milford Haven has some of the Pembrokeshire Coast's most dramatic geological features and blissful little beaches. An especially lovely area includes the golden sands of **Barafundle Bay** and **Broad Haven South**, and a network of walking tracks around **Bosherston Lily Ponds**.

The B4319 winds south from Pembroke to Bosherston. Continue past Bosherston to the coast and a short, steep path leads to the photogenic shell of **St Govan's Chapel** (📞01646-662367), wedged into a slot in the cliffs just above the pounding waves. Sadly, the coast here and just west is part of a military firing range: when red flags are flying there's no public access to some of the Pembrokeshire Coast's most arresting natural sights – neither the chapel, nor **Elegug Stacks**, nor the gigantic arch known as the Green Bridge of Wales.

After sidestepping the firing range, the road continues on to **Freshwater West** – a moody, wave-battered stretch of coast that has provided a brooding backdrop for movies such as *Harry Potter and the Deathly Hallows* and Ridley Scott's *Robin Hood*. It's widely held to be Wales' best surf beach, but also one of the most dangerous for swimmers.

From Pembroke, it's just over 6 miles to Barafundle Bay (heading southeast) or 8 miles to Freshwater West (heading west). For all these sights, you could easily make a day of it. Best is to take the B4319 heading south from Pembroke; Bosherston and the Elegug Stack Rocks are reached from narrow country lanes branching off it. The B4319 continues past Freshwater West and terminates at the B4320, where you can turn right to return to Pembroke.

Pastel-hued cottages line the gurgling stream running through its lower reaches, while Georgian town houses cling to the cliffs above. When the tide's out, the water disappears completely from the harbour, leaving the sailing fleet striking angular poses on the sand.

Lower Solva is the part of interest to travellers. Amble about antique shops and galleries, settle in somewhere cosy for a meal or walk a section of the Pembrokeshire Coast Path, which approaches its most exquisite around Solva. Our favourite eatery for its sheer novelty is MamGu Welsh cakes (p289), a lively cafe specialising in wacky takes on the typical Welsh sweet snack of Welsh cakes.

If you need to shed some calories afterwards, a 1-mile walk will take you upstream to the **Solva Woollen Mill** (☎01437-721112; www. solvawoollenmill.co.uk; Middle Mill; ☻10am-5.30pm Mon, to 4pm Tue-Fri), the oldest working mill of its kind in Pembrokeshire.

 p289

The Drive ≫ You really can't go wrong on the 3-mile drive to St Davids. Just continue west.

TRIP HIGHLIGHT

❿ St Davids

A city only by dint of its prestigious cathedral, pretty St Davids feels more like an oversized village. Yet this little settlement looms large in the Welsh consciousness as the hometown of its patron saint and has a very special vibe as a result.

Mesmeric **St David's Cathedral** (www. stdavidscathedral.org.uk; The Pebbles; ☻10am-3pm Mon-Sat, 1-4pm Sun) stands on the site of the saint's own 6th-century religious settlement. Wonderful stone and wooden carvings decorate the interior, and there's a treasury and historic library hidden within.

St David was born at **St Non's Bay**, a ruggedly attractive section of coast with a holy well and a cute little chapel, a short walk from the centre of town. If it's a swim or surf you covet, head to broad, beautiful **Whitesands Bay** (Porth Mawr), although there are other, quieter beaches dotted between the headlands hereabouts.

Also not to be missed are the city's distinguished bunch of cafes and restaurants, which are ever-ready to sate weary travellers' bellies.

But do not just dally in St Davids now that you have come this far west. Get out and roam the emerald-green, undulating landscape around as it bows to sandy and stony bays where you will truly feel the significance of the Welsh word *'Penfro'* which explains how Pembrokeshire gets its name. The meaning? 'Land's end.'

 p289

Tenby Fishing boats

Eating & Sleeping

Swansea ❶

🛏 Dylan Thomas Birthplace
Guesthouse $$$

(☎01792-472555; www.dylanthomasbirthplace. com; 5 Cwmdonkin Dr, Uplands, SA2 0RA; r from £179) Dylan Thomas fans now have the unique opportunity to stay in the house where the poet was born and spent his first 23 years. The house has been diligently maintained in period style, and you'll have the choice of staying in the bedrooms once occupied by Nancy (his sister), DJ and Florrie (his parents), and of course Dylan himself.

Booking a room entails exclusive use of the house, so solo travellers will get it all to themselves! At the time of research there was a two-night minimum stay, although the price given was for one/two people for one night.

Mumbles ❷

✕ Môr
Seafood $$

(☎07932 385217; www.mor-mumbles.co.uk; 620 Mumbles Rd; mains £12-20; ⏱5.30-9pm Tue, 12.30-3.30pm & 5.30-9pm Wed-Sat, 12.30-8pm Sun) Some of the area's scrummiest seafood is proffered at this slick restaurant, such as succulent sea bass with bacon and dashi, although there is also turf beside the surf on the menu. Book in advance. 'Môr' in Welsh simply means sea.

🛏 Tides Reach Guest House
B&B $$

(☎01792-404877; www.tidesreachguesthouse. com; 388 Mumbles Rd; s/d from £65/80; P 🛜) Tides Reach has maintained the same friendly service and delicious breakfasts across the years. Some rooms have sea views; we dig sea-facing Room 6. Two-night minimum stays can apply in peak periods.

Rhossili ❹

✕ Bay Bistro & Coffee House
Bistro $

(☎01792-390519; www.thebaybistro.co.uk; mains £7-15; ⏱10am-4pm Mon-Fri, 9am-5pm Sat & Sun; 🍴) This buzzy beach cafe has a sunny terrace, good surfy vibrations and the kind of drop-your-panini views that would make anything taste good – although the roster of burgers, sandwiches, salads, cakes and coffee stands up well regardless. On summer evenings it opens for alfresco meals.

Tenby ❼

✕ Plantagenet House
Modern British $$$

(☎01834-842350; www.plantagenettenby. co.uk; Quay Hill; mains lunch £10-12, dinner £25-28; ⏱noon-2.30pm & 6-9pm, reduced hours in winter; 🍴 ♿) Atmosphere-wise, this place sure has the wow factor, ramping up the romance with cheek-by-jowl tables and candlelight. Tucked down an alley in Tenby's oldest house, parts of which date to the 10th century, it's dominated by an immense 12th-century Flemish chimney hearth. Tenby-caught fish, seafood and local organic beef are seasoned with freshly picked herbs, and the wine list is second to none.

🛏 Penally Abbey
Hotel $$$

(☎01834-843033; www.penally-abbey. com; Penally; r from £165; P 🛜📺) One of Pembrokeshire's most alluring escapes, this ivy-wreathed fantasy of a Strawberry Gothic country house sits on a hillside amid expanses of gardens and woodland, with soul-stirring views across Carmarthen Bay. Rooms blend calm colours and contemporary style with period charm, arched windows, embroidered white bedspreads and espresso machines. Built on the site of an ancient abbey in the village of Penally, it is 2 miles southwest of Tenby along the A4139.

For romance, top billing goes to the superior double with four-poster bed and dreamy views across the bay to Caldey Island. The country house's restaurant, **Rhosyn** (mains £25-31; ⏱2-4.30pm & 6.30-9pm Wed-Sat), is one for special occasions, too.

Pembroke 8

🛏 Woodbine   B&B $$

(📞01646-686338; www.pembrokebed
andbreakfast.co.uk; 84 Main St; s/d £65/85;
🛜) This well-kept, forest-green Georgian town
house presents a smart face to Pembroke's
main drag. The three pretty guest rooms are
tastefully furnished, with original fireplaces,
sash windows and bold colour schemes. A
17th-century Welsh slate floor and inglenook
fireplace grace the breakfast room.

Solva 9

✖ MamGu Welshcakes   Cafe $

(📞01437-454369; www.mamguwelshcakes.
com; 20 Main St; lunch mains £5.50-7, box 6
Welsh cakes £4; 🕓9.30am-5pm Mon-Sat,
10am-4pm Sun) You'll see the humble Welsh
cake in a whole new light after a visit to MamGu.
Friends Becky and Thea travelled the world
before landing in the fishing village of Solva
and working their magic with a griddle. At this
rustic-cool coastal cafe, Welsh cakes traverse
the entire taste spectrum, with flavours from
leek and cheese to ginger and chilli-chocolate.
All are delicious.

🛏 Haroldston House   B&B $$

(📞01437-721404; www.haroldstonhouse.co.uk;
29 High St; 3-night stay from £264; P🛜)
Occupying a Georgian merchant's house, this
eco-aware B&B has a dash of contemporary
boutique style. The tasteful self-catering
apartments feature art by owner Ian McDonald
as well as other Wales-based artists. Quarters
are big on charm, whether you opt for the
deep-blue Blue Room, with original floorboards,
shutters and log burner, or the Stable Studio in
a stylishly converted 18th-century stable pigsty.

St Davids 10

✖ Really Wild Emporium   Cafe $

(📞01437-721755; www.thereallywildemporium.
co.uk; 24 High St; cakes £2.50-3, mains £8.50;
🕓10am-4pm) Foragers Julia and John from
Wild About Pembrokeshire (📞01437-
721035; www.wildaboutpembrokeshire.co.uk;
foraging per person from £12; 🕓Apr-Oct; 🚶)
have had fun converting a high-ceilinged art
deco building into this fabulous emporium in
central St Davids. Exposed brick, reclaimed
wood and corrugated iron set an industro-
cool scene for dishes peppered with foraged
ingredients – from pad thai with wild garlic
seeds to insanely delicious seaweed brownies.

🛏 Twr y Felin   Hotel $$$

(📞01437-725555; www.twryfelinhotel.com;
Caerfai Rd; d £250-290, ste £320-420; P🛜)
Pembrokeshire-born architect Keith Griffiths
put his stamp on Twr y Felin, using a 19th-
century windmill as the impetus for this slickly
modern hotel in private landscaped grounds.
A collection of specially commissioned,
large-scale contemporary art (including works
by Welsh street artist Pure Evil) enlivens the
monochrome, distinctly minimalist interiors.
All rooms are luxurious, but top billing goes to
the spectacular three-level circular suite in the
tower itself.

Enjoy an aperitif in the subtly lit, gallery-style
lounge bar before dinner at **Blas** (📞01437-
725555; www.blasrestaurant.com; Caerfai Rd;
mains £22-34, 7-course tasting menu £69),
hands down one of the top tables in town.

NEED ᵀᴼ KNOW

CURRENCY
Pound sterling (£)

LANGUAGE
English; also Welsh and Scottish Gaelic

VISAS
Generally not needed for stays of up to six months. Britain is not a member of the Schengen Zone, so you will need to show your passport when arriving and leaving from the UK border.

FUEL
Urban petrol (gas) stations are plentiful; service stations are regularly spaced on motorways. Fill up before heading into rural areas, though, where they're scarcer. Expect to pay around £1.25 per litre.

RENTAL CARS
Avis (www.avis.co.uk)

Budget (www.budget.co.uk)

Europcar (www.europcar. co.uk)

Thrifty (www.thrifty.co.uk)

IMPORTANT NUMBERS
Emergency (☏112 or ☏999) Police, fire, ambulance, mountain rescue, coastguard

AA (☏0800 88 77 66) Roadside assistance

RAC (☏0330 159 0740) Roadside assistance

Climate

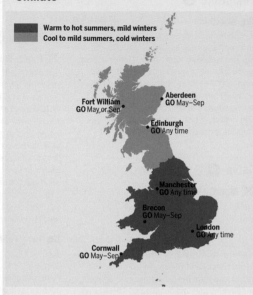

■ Warm to hot summers, mild winters
■ Cool to mild summers, cold winters

Fort William
GO May or Sep

Aberdeen
GO May–Sep

Edinburgh
GO Any time

Manchester
GO Any time

Brecon
GO May–Sep

London
GO Any time

Cornwall
GO May–Sep

When to Go

High Season (Jun–Aug)
» Weather at its best. Accommodation rates peak – especially for August school holidays.

» Roads are busy, especially in seaside areas, national parks and popular cities such as Oxford, Bath, Edinburgh and York.

Shoulder (Mar–May, Sep & Oct)
» Crowds reduce. Prices drop.

» Weather often good. March to May has both sunny spells and sudden showers; September to October can feature balmy Indian summers.

» For outdoor activities in much of Scotland, May and September are the best months.

Low Season (Nov–Feb)
» Wet and cold. Snow falls in mountain areas, especially up north.

» Opening hours reduced October to Easter; some places shut for winter. Big-city sights (particularly London's) operate all year.

Your Daily Budget

Budget: Less than £60

» Dorm beds: £15–30

» Budget hotel double: under £65 (London under £100)

» Cheap cafe and pub meals: £7–11

Midrange: £60–120

» Double hotel or B&B room: £65–130 (London £100–200)

» Restaurant main meal: £12–22

Top End: More than £120

» Four-star hotel room: from £130 (London from £200)

» Three-course meal in a good restaurant: around £40

» Car rental per day: from £35

Eating

Restaurants From cheap and cheerful to Michelin-starred, covering all cuisines.

Pubs Serve reasonably priced meals, some are top-notch.

Cafes Good daytime option for casual breakfasts, lunch or afternoon tea.

Vegetarian Find meat-free restaurants in towns and cities. But rural menus may contain just one 'choice'.

Sleeping

Hotels Anything from small, budget town houses to grand, boutique mansions.

B&Bs Range from a room in someone's house (with shared bathroom) to luxury spoils.

Inns Rooms above rural pubs; can be a cosy choice.

Hostels Bare-bones, often dorm-style accommodation.

Arriving in Great Britain

Heathrow airport Trains, London Underground (tube) and buses to central London from 5am to around midnight (night buses run later) £5.10 to £25. Taxis to central London cost £50 to £100.

Gatwick airport Trains to central London from 4.30am to 1.35am £10 to £20; 24-hour buses (hourly) to central London from £10. Taxis to central London £100.

Mobile Phones

The UK uses the GSM 900/1800 network, which covers Europe, Australia and New Zealand, but isn't compatible with the North American GSM 1900, although most modern mobiles can function on both networks.

Internet Access

» Mobile broadband coverage is good in urban centres, but limited in rural areas – using a local SIM card helps keep data costs down.

» Most accommodation providers and many eateries have wi-fi access.

» Internet cafes (from £1 per hour) are rare away from tourist spots.

Money

ATMs ('cash machines') are common in cities and towns. Visa and MasterCard are widely accepted although some B&Bs take cash only.

Tipping

Restaurants Around 10% to 15% in eateries with table service.

Pubs & Bars If you order and pay at the bar, tips are not expected. If you order at the table, your meal is brought to you, and you pay afterwards, then 10% is usual.

Taxis Roughly 10%.

Useful Websites

BBC (www.bbc.co.uk) National broadcaster.

Lonely Planet (www.lonelyplanet.com/great-britain) Travel tips, accommodation, recommendations and more.

Visit Britain (www.visitbritain.com) Comprehensive tourist information.

Opening Hours

In rural areas opening hours may be shorter between October and April; some places close completely.

Banks 9.30am to 4pm or 5pm Monday to Friday; some open 9.30am to 1pm Saturday.

Pubs & Bars Noon to 11pm Monday to Thursday, until 1am Friday and Saturday, 12.30pm to 11pm Sunday.

Shops 9am to 5.30pm or 6pm Monday to Saturday, and often 11am to 5pm Sunday. Cities have 24/7 convenience stores.

Restaurants Lunch is noon to 3pm, dinner 6pm to 9pm or 10pm (later in cities).

STRETCH YOUR LEGS
CAMBRIDGE

Start/Finish: Grand Arcade

Distance: 2.5 miles

Duration: 3 hours

Historic Cambridge is best explored on foot. This tour takes in prestigious colleges, magnificent chapels and a punt on the River Cam; check the latest college opening times and prices before you set off.

Take this walk on Trip

Grand Arcade

You won't find much history in Cambridge's glitzy Grand Arcade, but it's one of the few places you can park centrally.

The Walk >> Head for the Downing St exit, and turn right towards Pembroke St then left on Trumpington St.

Fitzwilliam Museum

This colossal neoclassical treasure house (p218) was one of the first public art museums in Britain. There are obvious parallels to the British Museum, and highlights include Roman, Egyptian and Cypriot grave goods, artworks by great masters and one of the country's finest collections of ancient, medieval and modern pottery.

The Walk >> About-turn and go north on Trumpington St to the corner with Pembroke St for a sweet, sticky rest stop.

Fitzbillies

Cambridge's oldest bakery, **Fitzbillies** (www.fitzbillies.com; 52 Trumpington St; mains £5-15; ⊗8.30am-5pm Mon-Fri, 9am-5.30pm Sat & Sun) has a soft, doughy place in the hearts of generations of students. Its stock-in-trade is sticky Chelsea buns and cream teas, served packed to go or in the attached cafe.

The Walk >> Continue north on Trumpington St and dip left onto Silver St for a glimpse of the rickety-looking wooden Mathematical Bridge, then continue north to reach King's Pde.

King's College Chapel

The grandiose 16th-century **King's College Chapel** (☎01223-331100; www.kings.cam.ac.uk; King's Pde; adult/child £10/8; ⊗9.30am-3.15pm Mon-Sat, 1.15-2.30pm Sun term time, 9.30am-4.30pm rest of year) is one of England's most extraordinary Gothic monuments. During services, the sound of the choir rises to an almost impossibly intricate fan-vaulted ceiling – think of it as a firework display, expressed as architecture.

The Walk » You'll see your next stop just north along King's Pde, rising proudly above the surrounding buildings.

Great St Mary's Church

The grand facade of **Great St Mary's** ([☎]01223-747273; www.gsm.cam.ac.uk; Senate House Hill; tower per person/family £6/16; [◷]11am-5pm Tue-Sun) was largely the result of a major expansion from 1478 to 1519, but the best thing about this imposing Gothic church is the **tower**, which offers awe-inspiring views over Cambridge's dreaming spires.

The Walk » Cross King's Pde and duck down Senate House Passage to marvel at the occult-looking Porta Honoris, side gate to Gonville & Caius College, then continue on Trinity St.

Trinity College

The largest of Cambridge's colleges, elegant **Trinity College** ([☎]01223-338400; www.trin.cam.ac.uk; Trinity St) is reached through an epic Tudor gateway, topped by a stern-looking statue of Henry VIII. Beyond lies the sweeping Great Court, the biggest of its kind, and (if it's open) the renowned **Wren Library**, containing 55,000 books dated before 1820.

The Walk » Continue north past St John's College, then turn left onto Bridge St to reach the river. Rent a punt from Quayside to see another side of the Cambridge colleges.

The Backs

The rear ends of the grand colleges along King's Pde spill onto the river-banks in a long sweep of parks, gardens and even grazing pastures for livestock. Known as **The Backs**, the parklands can be explored on foot when the colleges are open, but are best viewed from a punt on the river, passing under a succession of elegant bridges, including the famous **Bridge of Sighs**.

The Walk » Returning your punt to the depot, retrace your steps to reach Sidney St, then duck right onto Pety Cury to reach the north entrance to the Grand Arcade.

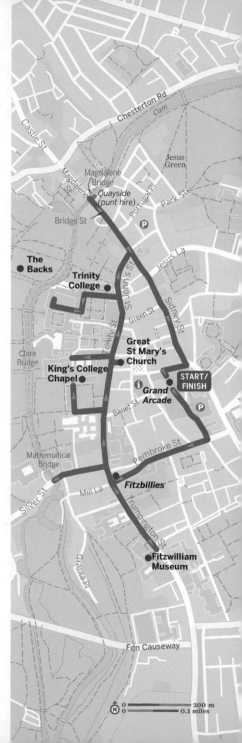

STRETCH YOUR LEGS
BATH

Start/Finish: SouthGate

Distance: 2.5 miles

Duration: Three hours

Bath's cityscape is simply sumptuous. So stunning, it has World Heritage status. On this walk you'll encounter architecture ranging from Roman baths to a medieval cathedral to exquisite Georgian designs.

Take this walk on Trips

SouthGate
Head into Bath, following signs to SouthGate car park.

The Walk >> Exit into St Lawrence St, heading north to join Stall St. Then cut right down Abbeygate St towards the Roman Baths.

Roman Baths
The Romans built this **bathhouse** (☎01225-477785; www.romanbaths.co.uk; Abbey Church Yard; adult £16-23, child £8.50-15.50; ⏲9.30am-5pm Nov-Feb, 9am-5pm Mar–mid-Jun, Sep & Oct, 9am-9pm mid-Jun–Aug) above three natural hot springs. They emerge at a toasty 46°C (115°F), forming one of the best-preserved ancient Roman spas in the world. A tour reveals the steaming **Great Bath**, bathing pools and changing rooms.

The Walk >> It's a few steps east to Bath Abbey.

Bath Abbey
The building of **Bath Abbey** (☎01225-422462; www.bathabbey.org; Abbey Church Yard; suggested donation adult/child £5/2.50; ⏲9.30am-5.30pm Mon, 9am-5.30pm Tue-Fri, to 6pm Sat, 12.15-1.45pm & 4-6.30pm Sun) started after 1499, making it England's last great medieval church. On the striking **west facade** angels climb up and down stone ladders; find out more on **tower tours** (☎01225-422462; www.bathabbey.org; adult/child £8/4; ⏲10am-4pm Mon-Sat).

The Walk >> Cross the square south of Bath Abbey, then wind onto Parade Gardens, passing the rushing weir to gracious Pultney Bridge (1773). Then make your way to Green St.

Old Green Tree
Duck into the tiny, traditional **Old Green Tree** (☎01225-448259; 12 Green St; ⏲11am-11pm Mon-Sat, noon-6.30pm Sun) pub for real ales and soups and casseroles (noon to 3pm Tuesday to Sunday).

The Walk >> Turn right into elegant Milsom St. Then head, via George St, into trendy Bartlett St.

Assembly Rooms
When they opened in 1771, Bath's **Assembly Rooms** (NT; ☎01225-477789; www.

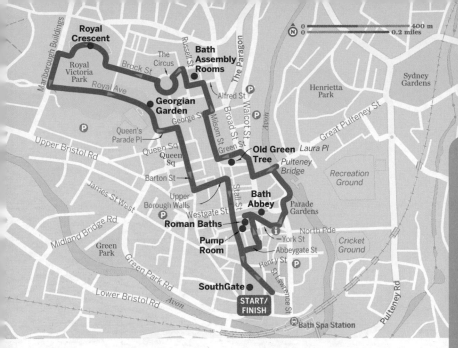

nationaltrust.org.uk; 19 Bennett St; ⏰10.30am-6pm Mar-Oct, to 5pm Nov-Feb) were where fashionable socialites gathered to waltz, play cards and listen to chamber music. Tour the card room, tearoom and ballroom, lit by the original 18th-century chandeliers.

The Walk » Next, the Circus (1768), a ring of 33 honey-coloured, semicircular terraces. From there, gracious Brock St gradually reveals Bath's exquisite Royal Crescent.

Royal Crescent

The imposing Royal Crescent curls around private lawns. Designed by John Wood the Younger and built between 1767 and 1775, the houses appear perfectly symmetrical from the outside, but the owners were allowed to tweak the interiors, so no two are quite the same.

The Walk » From the Crescent's far end, stroll back along Royal Ave. Just before the Royal Pavilion Cafe, cut left, up a short flight of steps, to the gate in the wall leading into the Georgian Garden.

Georgian Garden

The period plants and gravel walkways of the tiny, walled **Georgian Garden** (📞01225-394041; off Royal Ave; ⏰9am-7pm) provide intriguing insights into what would have lain behind the Circus' grand facades.

The Walk » Skirt Georgian Queen Sq. Just before the elaborate Theatre Royal (1805), turn left into Upper Borough Walls. It marks medieval Bath's northern edge. From here it's a short stroll to the Pump Room.

Pump Room

The grand **Pump Room** (📞01225-477785; www.romanbaths.co.uk; Stall St; ⏰9.30am-5pm) features an ornate spa from which Bath's famous hot springs flow. Ask staff for a glass (50p); it's minerally and startlingly warm – an impressive 38°C (100°F).

The Walk » Cut down Stall St, back into St Lawrence St and back to your car.

Ireland

YOUR MAIN REASON FOR VISITING? MOST LIKELY TO EXPERIENCE IRELAND OF THE POSTCARD – captivating peninsulas and dramatic wildness and undulating hills. Scenery, history, culture, bustling cosmopolitanism and the stillness of village life – you'll visit blockbuster attractions and replicate famous photo ops. But there are plenty of surprises too – and they're all within easy reach of each other. Whether you want to drive through the wildest terrain or sample great food while hopping between spa treatments, we've got something for you.

Skellig Michael Home to Unesco World Heritage–listed monastery ruins

Ireland

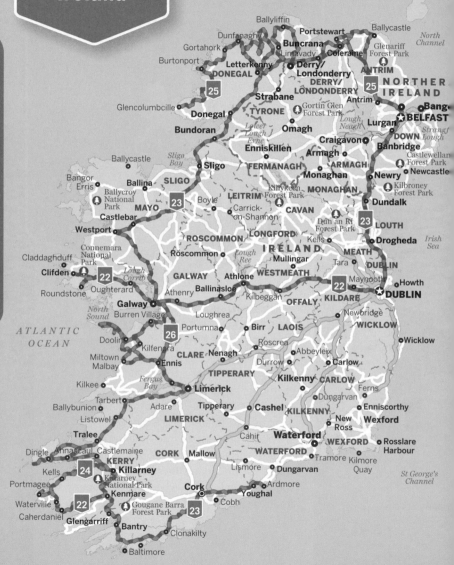

Iconic Ireland 7 Days
22 The best of Ireland's five-star cultural and natural attractions.

The Long Way Round 14 Days
23 Ireland's crenellated coastlines, vibrant port cities and island treasures.

Ring of Kerry 4 Days
24 Weave your way past jaw-dropping scenery as you circumnavigate the Iveragh Peninsula.

The North in a Nutshell 10 Days
25 Big cities, big-name sights, hidden beaches, tiny islands – an epic drive.

Musical Landscapes 5 Days
26 A ride round County Clare's hottest trad music spots.

✓ DON'T MISS

Killarney Jaunting Cars
Clip-clop in a traditional horse-drawn jaunting car on Trip **24**

Belfast
When previously warring communities have the courage to strive for peace, it's inspiring. Witness that transformation on Trip **25**

Arranmore Island
Ancient pubs, turf fires and late-night music sessions make overnighting special. Do a Robinson Crusoe on Trip **25**

Ennistimon
This authentic market town in County Clare gives a genuine taste of country living. Savour its fine bars on Trip **26**

Galway
You may find it hard to leave the City of Tribes. Go for its culture, conviviality and craic on Trip **22**

Iconic Ireland

22

This trip gives you a glimpse of the very best Ireland has to offer, including the country's most famous attractions, spectacular countryside, and most popular towns and villages.

TRIP HIGHLIGHTS

0 km

Dublin
World-class museums, superb restaurants and terrific nightlife

Roundstone

1 START

5

Ennis

460 km

Cliffs of Moher
Majestic sea cliffs rising over 200m from a churning sea

7

Killorglin **Killarney**
FINISH
Kenmare

670 km

Dingle
Traditional pubs, enticing craft studios and music, music everywhere

7 DAYS
959KM / 596 MILES

GREAT FOR...

BEST TIME TO GO
April to September for the long days and best weather.

ESSENTIAL PHOTO
The Lakes of Killarney from Ladies' View on the Ring of Kerry.

BEST TWO DAYS
The Connemara peninsula and the Ring of Kerry.

22 | Iconic Ireland

Every time-worn truth about Ireland will be found on this trip: the breathtaking scenery of stone-walled fields and wave-dashed cliffs; the picture-postcard villages and bustling towns; the ancient ruins that have stood since before history was written. The trip begins in Ireland's storied, fascinating capital and transports you to the wild west of Galway and Connemara before taking you south to the even wilder folds of County Kerry.

TRIP HIGHLIGHT

1 Dublin

World-class museums, superb restaurants and the best collection of entertainment in the country – there are plenty of good reasons why the capital is the ideal place to start your trip. Get some sightseeing in on a walking tour (p366) before 'exploring' at least one of the city's storied – if not historic – pubs.

Your top stop should be the grounds of Trin-ity College (☎01-896 1000; www.tcd.ie; College Green; ⊙8am-10pm; 🚌 all city centre, 🚆Westmoreland or Trinity), home to the gloriously illuminated **Book of Kells**. It's kept in the stunning 65m Long Room of the **Old Library** (www.tcd.ie; Library Sq; adult/ student/family €16/14/32, online €14/12/28; ⊙8.30am-5pm Mon-Sat, 9.30am-5pm Sun May-Sep, 9.30am-5pm Mon-Sat, noon-4.30pm Sun Oct-Apr; 🚌 all city centre, 🚆Westmoreland or Trinity).

✕ 🛏 p310, p326

The Drive » It's a 208km trip to Galway city across the country along the M6 motorway, which has little in terms of visual highlights beyond green fields, which get greener and a little more wild the further west you go. Twenty-two kilometres south of Athlone (about halfway) is a worthwhile detour to Clonmacnoise.

② Galway City

The best way to appreciate Galway is to amble – around Eyre Sq and down Shop St towards the Spanish Arch and the River Corrib, stopping off for a little liquid sustenance in one of the city's classic old pubs. Top of our list is **Tig**

LINK YOUR TRIP

23 **The Long Way Round**

For comprehensive coverage of the best of the south and north, combine these two trips making a loop from Galway.

26 **Musical Landscapes**

Take a detour from Galway through County Clare's hottest trad music spots, picking up the trail again in Lisdoonvarna.

Cóilí (☎091-561 294; www.facebook.com/tig.choili; Mainguard St; ☺10.30am-11.30pm Mon-Thu, to 12.30am Fri & Sat, 12.30-11pm Sun), a fire-engine-red pub that draws them in with its two live *céilidh* (traditional music and dancing sessions) each day. A close second is **Tigh Neachtain** (www.tighneachtain.com; 17 Upper Cross St; ☺10.30am-11.30pm Mon-Thu, to 12.30am Fri & Sat, 11am-11.30pm Sun), known simply as Neachtain's (*nock*-tans) or Naughtons – stop and join the locals for a pint.

✕ 🏠 p310, p361

The Drive ≫ The most direct route to Roundstone is to cut through Connemara along the N59, turning left on the Clifden Rd – a total of 76km. Alternatively, the 103km coastal route, via the R336 and R340, winds its way around small bays, coves and lovely seaside hamlets.

❸ Roundstone

Huddled on a boat-filled harbour, Roundstone (Cloch na Rón) is one of Connemara's gems. Colourful terrace houses and inviting pubs overlook the dark recess of Bertraghboy Bay, which is home to lobster trawlers and traditional *currachs* (rowing boats) with tarred canvas bottoms stretched over wicker frames.

Just south of the village, in the remains of an old Franciscan monastery, is Malachy Kearns' **Roundstone Musical Instruments** (☎095-35808; www.bodhran.com; Monastery Rd; ☺11am-6pm Apr-Nov, 11.30am-5pm Mon-Sat Dec-Mar). Kearns is Ireland's only full-time maker of traditional bodhráns (hand-held goatskin drums). Watch him work and buy a tin whistle, harp or booklet filled with Irish ballads; there's also a small free folk museum and a cafe.

The Drive ≫ The 22km inland route from Roundstone to Clifden is a little longer, but the road is better (especially the N59) and the brown, barren beauty of Connemara is yours

DETOUR: THE SKY ROAD

Start: ❹ Clifden

From the N59 heading north out of Clifden, signs point towards the Sky Road, a 12km route tracing a spectacular loop out to the township of Kingston and back to Clifden, taking in some rugged, stunningly beautiful coastal scenery en route. It's a cinch to drive, but you can also easily walk or cycle it.

to behold. The 18km coastal route along the R341 brings you through more speckled landscape; to the south you'll have glimpses of the ocean.

❹ Clifden

Connemara's 'capital', Clifden (An Clochán) is an appealing Victorian-era country town with an amoeba-shaped oval of streets offering evocative strolls. It presides over the head of the narrow bay where the River Owenglin tumbles into the sea. The surrounding countryside beckons you to walk through woods and above the shoreline.

✕ 🏠 p310

The Drive ≫ It's 154km to the Cliffs of Moher; you'll have to backtrack through Galway city (take the N59) before turning south along the N67. This will take you through the unique striated landscape of the Burren, a moody, rocky and at times fearsome space accented with ancient burial chambers and medieval ruins.

TRIP HIGHLIGHT

❺ Cliffs of Moher

Star of a million tourist brochures, the Cliffs of Moher (Aillte an Mothair, or Ailltreacha Mothair) are one of the most popular sights in Ireland.

The entirely vertical cliffs rise to a height of 214m, their edge falling away abruptly into the constantly churning sea. A series of heads, the dark limestone seems to march in a rigid formation that amazes, no matter how many times you look.

Such appeal comes at a price: crowds. This is check-off tourism big time and bus loads come and go constantly in summer. A vast **visitor centre** (☎065-708 6141; www.cliffsofmoher.ie; R478; adult/child incl parking €8/ free; � 8am-9pm May-Aug, to 7pm Mar, Apr, Sep & Oct, 9am-5pm Nov-Feb) handles the hordes.

Like so many over-popular natural wonders, there's relief and joy if you're willing to walk for 10 minutes. Past the end of the 'Moher Wall', a 5km trail leads south along the cliffs to Hag's Head – few venture this far.

The Drive » The 39km drive to Ennis goes inland at Lahinch (famous for its world-class golf links); it's then 24km to your destination, through flat south Clare. Dotted with stone walls and fields, it's the classic Irish landscape.

6 Ennis

As the capital of a renowned music county, Ennis (Inis) is filled with pubs featuring trad music. In fact, this is the best reason to stay here. Where's best changes often; stroll the streets pub-hopping to find what's on any given night.

If you want to buy an authentic (and well-made) Irish instrument,

LOCAL KNOWLEDGE: ENNIS' BEST TRAD SESSION PUBS

Cíaran's Bar (☎065-684 0180; Francis St; � noon-11.30pm Mon-Sat, to 11pm Sun) Slip into this small place by day and you can be just another geezer pondering a pint. At night there's usually trad music. Bet you wish you had a copy of the Guinness mural out front!

Brogan's (☎065-684 4365; www.brogansbarandrestaurant.com; 24 O'Connell St; � noon-midnight) On the corner of Cooke's Lane, Brogan's sees a fine bunch of musicians rattling even the stone floors from about 9pm Monday to Thursday, plus even more nights in summer.

Cruise's Pub (☎065-682 8963; www.queenshotelennis.com; Abbey St; � 5.30pm-1am; ☎) There are trad-music sessions most nights from 9.30pm.

Poet's Corner Bar (☎065-682 8127; www.oldgroundhotelennis.com/poets-corner-bar.html; Old Ground Hotel, O'Connell St; ☎ 11am-11pm Mon-Thu, to 12.30am Fri & Sat, noon-11pm Sun; ☎) This old pub often has massive trad sessions on Fridays.

pop into **Custy's Music Shop** (☎065-682 1727; www.custysmusic.com; Cook's Lane; ☎ 9am-6pm Mon-Sat), which sells fiddles and other musical items as well as giving general info about the local scene.

🛏 p310

The Drive » It's 186km to Dingle if you go via Limerick city, but only 142km if you go via the N68 to Killimer for the ferry across the Shannon estuary to Tarbert. The views are fabulous beyond Tralee, especially if you take the 456m Connor Pass, Ireland's highest.

TRIP HIGHLIGHT

7 Dingle Town

In summer, Dingle's hilly streets can be clogged

with visitors, there's no way around it; in other seasons, its authentic charms are yours to savour. Many pubs double as shops, so you can enjoy Guinness and a singalong among screws and nails, wellies and horseshoes.

🍴🛏 p310, p327

The Drive » It's only 17km to Slea Head along the R559. The views – of the mountains to the north and the wild ocean to the south and west – are a big chunk of the reason you came to Ireland in the first place.

8 Slea Head

Overlooking the mouth of Dingle Bay, Mt Eagle and the Blasket Islands, Slea

WHY THIS IS A GREAT TRIP
FIONN DAVENPORT, WRITER

The loop from Dublin west to Galway and then south through Kerry into Cork explores all of Ireland's scenic heavy hitters. It's the kind of trip I'd make if I was introducing visiting friends to Ireland at its very best, a taster trip that would entice them to come back and explore the country in greater depth.

Above: Killarney National Park, Killarney
Left: Puffin, Skellig Michael
Right: Cliffs of Moher

Head has fine beaches, good walks and superbly preserved structures from Dingle's ancient past, including **beehive huts**, forts, inscribed stones and church sites. Dunmore Head is the westernmost point on the Irish mainland and the site of the wreckage in 1588 of two Spanish Armada ships.

The Iron Age **Dunbeg Fort** is a dramatic example of a promontory fortification, perched atop a sheer sea cliff about 7km southwest of Ventry on the road to Slea Head. The fort has four outer walls of stone. Inside are the remains of a house and a beehive hut, as well as an underground passage.

The Drive ›› The 88km to Killarney will take you through Annascaul (home to a pub once owned by Antarctic explorer Tom Crean) and Inch (whose beach is seen in *Ryan's Daughter*). At Castlemaine, turn south towards Miltown then take the R563 to Killarney.

- - - - - - - - - - - - - - - -

❾ Killarney

Beyond its proximity to lakes, waterfalls, woodland and moors dwarfed by 1000m-plus peaks, Killarney has many charms of its own as well as being the gateway to the Ring of Kerry, perhaps *the* outstanding highlight of many a visit to Ireland.

Besides the breathtaking views of the

mountains and glacial lakes, highlights of the 102-sq-km Killarney National Park include Ireland's only wild herd of native red deer, the country's largest area of ancient oak woods and 19th-century Muckross House.

✗ ⊨ p311, p339

The Drive » It's 27km along the narrow and winding N71 to Kenmare, much of it through magnificent scenery, especially at Ladies' View (much loved by Queen Victoria's ladies-in-waiting) and, 5km further on, Moll's Gap, a popular stop for photos and food.

- - - - - - - - - - - - - - - - -

⑩ Kenmare

Picturesque Kenmare carries its romantic reputation more stylishly than does Killarney, and there is an elegance about its handsome central square and attractive buildings. It still gets very busy in summer, all the same. The town stands where the delightfully named Finnihy, Roughty and Sheen Rivers empty into Kenmare River. Kenmare makes a pleasant alternative to Killarney as a base for visiting the Ring of Kerry and the Beara Peninsula.

✗ ⊨ p311, p327, p339

The Drive » The 47km to Caherdaniel along the southern stretch of the Ring of Kerry duck in and out of view of Kenmare River, with the marvellous Beara Peninsula to the south. Just before you reach Caherdaniel, a 4km detour north takes you to the rarely visited Staigue Fort, which dates from the 3rd or 4th century.

- - - - - - - - - - - - - - - - -

⑪ Caherdaniel

The big attraction here is **Derrynane National Historic Park** (☎066-947 5113; www.derrynanehouse. ie; Derrynane; adult/child €5/3; ⊙10.30am-6pm mid-Mar–Sep, 10am-5pm Oct, to 4pm Sat & Sun Nov–early Dec; P), the family home of Daniel O'Connell, the campaigner for Catholic emancipation. His ancestors bought the house and surrounding parkland, having grown rich on smuggling with France and Spain. It's largely furnished with O'Connell memorabilia, including the restored triumphal chariot in which he lapped Dublin after his release from prison in 1844.

The Drive » Follow the N70 for about 18km and then turn left onto the Skellig Ring (roads R567 and R566), cutting through some of the wildest and most beautiful scenery on the peninsula, with the ragged outline of Skellig Michael never far from view. The whole drive is 35km long.

- - - - - - - - - - - - - - - - -

⑫ Portmagee & Valentia Island

Portmagee's single street is a rainbow of colourful houses, and is much photographed. On summer mornings, the small pier comes to life with boats embarking on the choppy crossing to the Skellig Islands.

A bridge links Portmagee to 11km-long **Valentia Island** (Oileán Dairbhre), an altogether homier isle than the brooding Skelligs to the southwest. Like the Skellig Ring it leads to, Valentia is an essential, coach-free detour from the Ring of Kerry. Some lonely ruins are worth exploring.

Valentia was chosen as the site for the first transatlantic telegraph cable. When the connection was made in 1858, it put Caherciveen in direct contact with New York. The link worked for 27 days before failing, but went back into action years later.

The island makes an ideal driving loop. From April to October, there's a frequent, quick ferry trip at one end, as well as the bridge to Portmagee on the mainland at the other end.

The Drive » The 55km between Portmagee and Killorglin keep the mountains to your right (south) and the sea – when you're near it – to your left (north). Twenty-four kilometres along is the unusual Glenbeigh Strand, a tendril of sand protruding into Dingle Bay with views of Inch Point and the Dingle Peninsula.

- - - - - - - - - - - - - - - - -

⑬ Killorglin

Killorglin (Cill Orglan) is a quiet enough town,

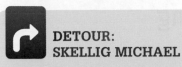

DETOUR:
SKELLIG MICHAEL

Start: ⑫ Portmagee & Valentia Island

The jagged, 217m-high rock of **Skellig Michael** (www.heritageireland.ie; ⊙mid-May–Sep) – Archangel Michael's Rock; like St Michael's Mount in Cornwall and Mont Saint Michel in Normandy – is the larger of the two Skellig Islands and a Unesco World Heritage Site. Early Christian monks survived here from the 6th until the 12th or 13th century; their determined quest for ultimate solitude led them to this remote, wind-blown edge of Europe.

Skellig Michael featured as Luke Skywalker's secret retreat in the Star Wars movies *The Force Awakens* (2015) and *The Last Jedi* (2017), attracting a whole new audience to the island's dramatic beauty.

It's a tough place to get to, and requires care to visit, but it's worth every effort. The 12km sea crossing can be rough, and there are no toilets or shelter, so bring something to eat and drink, and wear stout shoes and weatherproof clothing. Due to the steep (and often slippery) terrain and sudden wind gusts, it's unsuitable for young children or people with limited mobility.

Note that the island's fragility requires limits on the number of daily visitors. The 15 boats are licensed to carry no more than 12 passengers each, for a maximum of 180 people at any one time. It's wise to book ahead in July and August, bearing in mind that if the weather's bad the boats may not sail (about two days out of seven). Trips usually run from Easter until September, depending, again, on weather.

Boats (about €100 per person) leave Portmagee, Ballinskelligs and Derrynane at around 10am, returning at 3pm. Boat owners generally restrict you to two hours on the island, which is the bare minimum to see the monastery, look at the birds and have a picnic. The crossing takes about 1½ hours from Portmagee, 35 minutes to one hour from Ballinskelligs and 1¾ hours from Derrynane.

but that all changes in mid-August, when it erupts in celebration for **Puck Fair**, Ireland's best-known extant pagan festival. First recorded in 1603, with hazy origins, this lively (read: boozy) festival is based around the custom of installing a billy goat (a poc, or puck), the symbol of mountainous Kerry, on a pedestal in the town, its horns festooned with ribbons. Other entertainment ranges from a horse fair and bonny baby competition to street theatre, concerts and fireworks; the pubs stay open until 3am.

Author Blake Morrison documents his mother's childhood here in *Things My Mother Never Told Me* (2002).

Eating & Sleeping

Dublin ❶

✖ Clanbrassil House   Irish €€

(📞01-453 9786; www.clanbrassilhouse.com; 6 Upper Clanbrassil St; mains €19-29; ⊙5-10pm Tue-Fri, 11.30am-2.30pm & 5-10pm Sat; 🚌9, 16, 49, 54A from city centre) With an emphasis on family-style sharing plates, this intimate restaurant consistently turns out exquisite dishes, cooked on a charcoal grill. Think rib-eye with bone marrow and anchovy, or ray wing with capers and brown shrimp butter. The hash brown chips are a thing of glory, too.

✖ Greenhouse   Scandinavian €€€

(📞01-676 7015; www.thegreenhouserestaurant. ie; Dawson St; 3-course lunch menu €65, 4-/6-course dinner menu €129/149; ⊙noon-2pm & 6-9.30pm Tue-Sat; 🚌all city centre, 🚇St Stephen's Green) Chef Mickael Viljanen might just be one of the most exciting chefs working in Ireland today thanks to his Scandi-influenced tasting menus, which have made this arguably Dublin's best restaurant. The lunchtime set menu (€65) is good value for a Michelin-starred meal. Reservations necessary.

Galway City ❷

✖ Oscar's   Seafood €€

(📞091-582 180; www.facebook.com/oscars. bistro; Upper Dominick St; mains €18-30; ⊙5.30-9.30pm Mon-Sat) The menu changes daily at this outstanding seafood restaurant but it might include monkfish poached in saffron and white wine and served with cockles, seaweed-steamed Galway Bay lobster with garlic-lemon butter, or lemon sole with samphire. The intensely flavoured fish soup is a delight.

⮕ House Hotel   Boutique Hotel €€

(📞091-538 900; www.thehousehotel.ie; Spanish Pde; d €185-265; 🛜) Inside a former warehouse in the liveliest part of the city, Galway's hippest hotel has a stunning lobby with retro-styled furnishings and modern art. The 40 soundproofed rooms are small but plush, with vivid colour schemes and quality

fabrics. Bathrooms come with toiletries by Irish designer Orla Kiely.

Clifden ❹

✖ Mitchell's   Seafood €€

(📞095-21867; www.mitchellsrestaurantclifden. com; Market St; mains lunch €8-16, dinner €18-29; ⊙noon-9pm Mar-Oct) Seafood from the surrounding waters takes centre stage at this elegant spot, from velvety chowder and open crab sandwiches at lunchtime to intricate dinner mains. The highlight is a standout seafood platter (€27.50). Book ahead.

⮕ Blue Quay Rooms   B&B €€

(📞087 621 7616; www.bluequayrooms.com; Beach Rd; d €70-100; 🅿🛜) Painted a vivid shade of blue, this boutique property is even more stunning inside. Adorned with a brass ship's wheel, the nautical-themed lounge has black-and-white chequerboard floor tiles, designer fabrics and fresh flowers. Rooms also blend vintage and contemporary furnishings; all but one have harbour views.

Ennis ❻

⮕ Old Ground Hotel   Hotel €€€

(📞065-682 8127; www.oldgroundhotelennis. com; O'Connell St; s €130, d €180-200, ste €230-275; 🛜) Entered through a lobby of polished floorboards, cornice-work, antiques and open fires, this prestigious landmark dates back to the 1800s. The 83 rooms vary greatly in size and decor, which ranges from historic to cutting-edge. The ground-floor Poet's Corner Bar (⊙11am-11pm Mon-Thu, to 12.30am Fri & Sat, noon-11pm Sun; 🛜) is one of Ennis' best pubs.

Dingle ❼

✖ Reel Dingle Fish Co   Fish & Chips €

(📞066-915 1713; Bridge St; mains €5-15; ⊙1-10pm) Locals queue along the street to get hold of the freshly cooked local haddock (or cod, or monkfish, or hake, or mackerel...) and chips at this tiny outlet. Reckoned to be one of the best chippies in Kerry, if not in Ireland.

✖ Out of the Blue   Seafood €€€
(☎066-915 0811; www.outoftheblue.ie; The Wood; mains €21-39; ⏱5-9.30pm Mon-Sat, 12.30-3pm & 5-9.30pm Sun) Occupying a waterfront fishing shack, this rustic spot is one of Dingle's top restaurants, with an intense devotion to fresh local seafood (and only seafood). Highlights might include Dingle Bay prawn bisque with lobster. If staff don't like the catch, they don't open, and they resolutely don't serve chips.

🛏 Pax House   B&B €€€
(☎066-915 1518; www.pax-house.com; Upper John St; d €140-260; ⏱Mar-Dec; P⏺) From its highly individual decor (including contemporary paintings) to the outstanding views over the estuary from the glass-framed terrace and balconies opening from some rooms, Pax House is a treat. Breakfast incorporates produce grown in its own garden. It's 1km southeast of the town centre.

Killarney ⑨

✖ Celtic Whiskey Bar & Larder   Gastropub €€
(☎064-663 5700; www.celticwhiskeybar.com; 93 New St; mains €16-30; ⏱kitchen noon-9.45pm; ⏺) This buzzing gastropub serves some of the tastiest food in town, with menu highlights ranging from cheese and charcuterie platters and aged fillet steaks to steamed Glenbeigh mussels. The bar stocks hundreds of Irish whiskeys and a dozen craft beers.

🛏 Crystal Springs   B&B €€
(☎064-663 3272; www.crystalspringsbandb.com; Ballycasheen Cross, Woodlawn Rd; s/d from €95/130; P⏺) The timber deck of this wonderfully relaxing B&B overhangs the River Flesk. Rooms are richly furnished with patterned wallpapers and walnut timber; private bathrooms (most with spa bath) are huge. The glass-enclosed breakfast room also overlooks the rushing river. It's about a 15-minute stroll into town.

Kenmare ⑩

✖ Boathouse Bistro   Bistro €€
(☎064-664 2889; www.dromquinnamanor.com; Dromquinna Manor, Sneem Rd; mains €17-35; ⏱12.30-9pm daily mid-Mar–Sep, Fri-Sun only Oct- mid Mar; P) At the water's edge, this blue-and-white 1870s boathouse 4.5km west of Kenmare has been stunningly converted to a beach-house-style bistro specialising in local seafood delivered daily to its own wharf. Expertly cooked dishes might include Kenmare Bay crab claws in chilli and garlic butter.

🛏 Brook Lane Hotel   Boutique Hotel €€€
(☎064-664 2077; www.brooklanehotel.com; Sneem Rd; s/d/f from €135/195/305; P⏺) Chic rooms warmed by underfloor heating are individually decorated with bespoke furniture and luxurious fabrics at this contemporary olive-green property on the northwestern edge of town. Public areas mix vintage and designer pieces. Its adjoining stone-and-brick gastropub, Casey's, is first-rate. It's a 750m stroll from the centre.

The Long Way Round

Why go in a straight line when you can perambulate at leisure? This trip explores Ireland's jagged, scenic and spectacular edges; a captivating loop that takes in the whole island.

23

TRIP HIGHLIGHTS

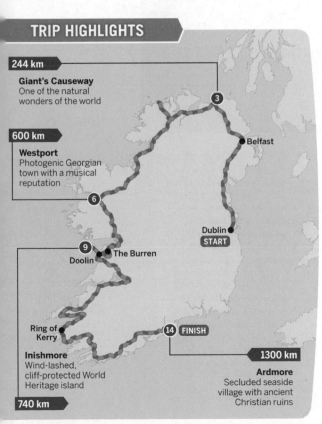

244 km

Giant's Causeway
One of the natural wonders of the world

❸

● Belfast

600 km

Westport
Photogenic Georgian town with a musical reputation

❻

Dublin ●
START

❾ ● The Burren
Doolin ●

Ring of Kerry

Inishmore
Wind-lashed, cliff-protected World Heritage island

740 km

⑭ FINISH

1300 km

Ardmore
Secluded seaside village with ancient Christian ruins

14 DAYS
1300KM / 807 MILES

GREAT FOR...

BEST TIME TO GO
You'll have the best weather (and the crowds) in June and August, but September is ideal.

 ESSENTIAL PHOTO

Killahoey Beach from the top of Horn Head.

 BEST TWO DAYS

Stops 7 to 9 allow you to experience the very best of the wild west, including a day trip to the Aran Islands.

Ring of Kerry Caherdaniel

ATLANTIC
OCEAN

23 The Long Way Round

There's a strong case to be made that the very best Ireland has to offer is closest to its jagged, dramatic coastlines: the splendid scenery, the best mountain ranges (geographically, Ireland is akin to a bowl, with raised edges) and most of its major towns and cities – Dublin, Belfast, Galway, Sligo and Cork. The western edge – between Donegal and Cork – corresponds to the Wild Atlantic Way driving route.

❶ Dublin

From its music, art and literature to the legendary nightlife that has inspired those same musicians, artists and writers, Dublin (p366) has always known how to have fun and does it with deadly seriousness.

Should you tire of the city's more highbrow offerings, the **Guinness Storehouse** (www.guinness -storehouse.com; St James's Gate, S Market St; adult/child €25/16, Connoisseur Experience €60; ⏰9.30am-7pm Sep-Jun, to 9pm Jul & Aug;

🚌13, 21A, 40, 51B, 78, 78A, 123 from Fleet St, 🚋James's) is the most popular place to visit in town. It's a beer-lover's Disneyland and multimedia bells-and-whistles homage to the country's most famous export and the city's most enduring symbol. The old grain storehouse is a suitable cathedral in which to worship the black gold; shaped like a giant pint of Guinness, it rises seven impressive storeys high around a stunning central atrium.

🍴🛏 p310, p326

SCOTLAND

Campbeltown

Giant's
Causeway

③

Ballycastle

*North
Channel*

Dunfanaghy

Buncrana

④

Coleraine

p318

*Rosses
Bay*

p319
Letterkenny

N56

N13

A2

A37

A26

Derry

Larne

Strabane

Ballymena

A2

A5

Antrim

*Donegal
Bay*

Donegal

Omagh

Belfast ②

Lisburn

N15

Bundoran

Enniskillen

A4

Armagh

Dromore

Banbridge

A1

Sligo ⑤

Ballysadare

Monaghan

Newry

N17

Dundalk

*Dundalk
Bay*

Charlestown

N4

Longford

N3

Droghedá

*Irish
Sea*

Roscommon

N55

Mullingar

M1

Tuam

Athlone

M6

Swords

Ballinasloe

22

Dublin ① START

M6

N65

Tullamore

M7

Naas

Bray

26

Birr

p366

Greystones

Portlaoise

Wicklow

Nenagh

M7

Carlow

Arklow

Thurles

Kilkenny

M11

Limerick

Cashel

M9

Enniscorthy

Tipperary

Clonmel

New Ross

Wexford

M8

Waterford

Rosslare
Harbour

Ballyduff

N25

Mallow

Dungarvan

*St George's
Channel*

Youghal

Cork ⑬

N25

⑭ Ardmore

Cobh

FINISH

*ATLANTIC
OCEAN*

Ⓝ 0 ————————————— 100 km
   0 ————————————— 50 miles

The Drive ≫ It's 165km of dual carriageway to Belfast – M1 in the Republic, A1 in Northern Ireland – but remember that the speed limit changes from kilometres to miles as you cross into the North.

 Belfast

Belfast is in many ways a brand-new city. Once lumped with Beirut, Baghdad and Bosnia as one of the four 'Bs' for travellers to avoid, it has pulled off a remarkable transformation from bombs-and-bullets pariah to a hip-hotels-and-hedonism party town.

The old shipyards on the Lagan continue to give way to the luxury apartments of the Titanic Quarter, whose centrepiece, the stunning, star-shaped edifice housing the **Titanic Belfast**

IRELAND **23** THE LONG WAY ROUND

§ **LINK YOUR TRIP**

22 **Iconic Ireland**
For comprehensive coverage of the best of north and south, combine these two trips making a loop from Galway.

26 **Musical Landscapes**
Take a detour from Galway through County Clare's hottest trad music spots, picking up the trail again in Ennis.

Giant's Causeway A natural arrangement of hexagonal stone columns

centre (www.titanicbelfast.com; Queen's Rd; adult/child £19/8.50; ☺9am-7pm Jun & Jul, to 8pm Aug, to 8pm Apr, May & Sep, 10am-5pm Oct-Mar; 🚇G2), covering the ill-fated liner's construction here, has become the city's number-one tourist draw.

New venues keep popping up – historic **Crumlin Road Gaol** (☎028-9074 1500; www.crumlinroadgaol.com; 53-55 Crumlin Rd; tour adult/child £12/7.50; ☺10am-5.30pm, last tour 4.30pm; 🚇12B, 57) and **SS Nomadic** are now open to the public, and WWI warship **HMS Caroline** is a floating museum. They all add to a list of attractions that includes beautifully restored Victorian architecture, a glittering waterfront lined with modern art,

a fantastic foodie scene and music-filled pubs.

🍴 🛏 p326

The Drive ≫ The fastest way to the causeway is to take the A26 north, through Ballymena, before turning off at Ballymoney – a total of 100km – but the longer (by 16km), more scenic route is to take the A8 to Larne and follow the coast through handsome Cushendall and popular Ballycastle.

- - - - - - - - - - - - - - - -

TRIP HIGHLIGHT

❸ Giant's Causeway

When you first see it you'll understand why the ancients believed the causeway was not a natural feature. The vast expanse of regular, closely packed, hexagonal stone columns dipping gently beneath the waves looks for all the world like the handiwork of giants.

This spectacular rock formation – a national nature reserve and Northern Ireland's only Unesco World Heritage Site – is one of Ireland's most impressive and atmospheric landscape features, but it can get very crowded. If you can, try to visit midweek or out of season to experience it at its most evocative. Sunset in spring and autumn is the best time for photographs.

Visiting the Giant's Causeway itself is free of charge but you pay to use the car park on a combined ticket with the **Giant's Causeway Visitor Experience** (☎028-2073 1855; www.nationaltrust.org.uk; 60 Causeway Rd; adult/child £13.50/6.75; ☺9am-7pm Jun-Sep, to 6pm Mar-May & Oct, to 5pm Nov-Feb);

DETOUR: GIANT'S CAUSEWAY TO BALLYCASTLE

Start: ❸ Giant's Causeway

Between the Giant's Causeway and Ballycastle lies the most scenic stretch of the Causeway Coast, with sea cliffs of contrasting black basalt and white chalk, rocky islands, picturesque little harbours and broad sweeps of sandy beach. It's best enjoyed on foot, following the 16.5km of waymarked **Causeway Coast Way** (www.walkni.com) between the Carrick-a-Rede car park and the Giant's Causeway, although the main attractions can also be reached by car or bus.

About 8km east of the Giant's Causeway is the meagre ruin of 16th-century **Dunseverick Castle**, spectacularly sited on a grassy bluff. Another 1.5km on is the tiny seaside hamlet of **Portbradden**, with half a dozen harbourside houses. Visible from Portbradden and accessible via the next junction off the A2 is the spectacular **White Park Bay**, with its wide, sweeping sandy beach.

The main attraction on this stretch of coast is the famous – or notorious, depending on your head for heights – **Carrick-a-Rede Rope Bridge** (p344). The 20m-long, 1m-wide bridge of wire rope spans the chasm between the sea cliffs and the little island of Carrick-a-Rede, swaying gently 30m above the rock-strewn water.

parking-only tickets
aren't available.

 p326

The Drive » Follow the A29
and A37 as far as Derry, then
cross the invisible border into
the Republic and take the N13
to Letterkenny before turning
northwest along the N56 to
Dunfanaghy. It's a total of
136km.

- - - - - - - - - - - - - -

➍ Dunfanaghy

Huddled around the
waterfront beneath the
headland of Horn Head,
Dunfanaghy's small, at-
tractive town centre has
a surprisingly wide range
of accommodation and
some of the finest dining
options in the county's
northwest. Glisten-
ing beaches, dramatic
coastal cliffs, mountain
trails and forests are all
within a few kilometres.

 p326

The Drive » The 145km
south to Sligo town will take you
back through Letterkenny (this
stretch is the most scenic), after
which you'll follow the N13 as
far as Ballyshannon and then, as
you cross into County Sligo, the
N15 to Sligo town.

- - - - - - - - - - - - - -

➎ Sligo Town

Sligo is in no hurry
to shed its cultural
traditions but it doesn't
sell them out either.
Pedestrian streets lined
with inviting shopfronts,
stone bridges spanning
the River Garavogue and
céilidh sessions spilling
from pubs contrast with

DETOUR:
HORN HEAD

Start: ➍ Dunfanaghy

Horn Head has some of Donegal's most spectacular
coastal scenery and plenty of birdlife. Its dramatic
quartzite cliffs, covered with bog and heather, rear
over 180m high, and the view from their tops is heart-
pounding.

The road circles the headland; the best approach
by car is in a clockwise direction from the Falcarragh
end of Dunfanaghy. On a fine day, you'll encounter
tremendous views of Tory, Inishbofin, Inishdooey
and tiny Inishbeg islands to the west; Sheep Haven
Bay and the Rosguill Peninsula to the east; Malin
Head to the northeast; and the coast of Scotland
beyond. Take care in bad weather as the route can be
perilous.

genre-bending contempo-
rary art and glass towers
rising from prominent
corners of the compact
town.

 p326

The Drive » It's 100km to
Westport, as you follow the N17
(and the N5 once you leave
Charlestown); the landscape is
flat, the road flanked by fields,
hedge rows and clusters of
farmhouses. Castlebar, 15km
before Westport, is a busy
county town.

- - - - - - - - - - - - - -

TRIP HIGHLIGHT

➏ Westport

There's a lot to be said
for town planning,
especially if 18th-century
architect James Wyatt
was the brain behind the
job. Westport (Cathair na
Mairt), positioned on the
River Carrowbeg and the
shores of Clew Bay, is easily Mayo's most beautiful

town and a major tourist
destination for visitors to
this part of the country.

It's a Georgian classic,
its octagonal square and
tidy streets lined with
trees and handsome
buildings, most of which
date from the late 18th
century.

The Drive » Follow the N5
then the N84 as far as the
outskirts of Galway city – a
trip of about 100km. Take the
N67 south into County Clare.
Ballyvaughan provides a good
base to explore the heart of the
Burren.

- - - - - - - - - - - - - -

➐ The Burren

The karst landscape
of the Burren is not
the green Ireland of
postcards. But there are
wildflowers in spring,
giving the 560-sq-km
Burren brilliant, if
ephemeral, colour amid

WHY THIS IS A GREAT TRIP
FIONN DAVENPORT, WRITER

Not only are you covering the spectacular landscapes of mountains and jagged coastlines of the Wild Atlantic Way, but you can explore the modern incarnation of the country's earliest settlements, taking you from prehistoric monuments to bustling cities.

Above: Dingle
Left: Donkey, Inishmore
Right: Guinness Storehouse, Dublin

GUINNESS
STOREHOUSE

its austere beauty. Soil may be scarce, but the small amount that gathers in the cracks and faults is well drained and nutrient-rich. This, together with the mild Atlantic climate, supports an extraordinary mix of Mediterranean, Arctic and alpine plants. Of Ireland's native wildflowers, 75% are found here, including 24 species of beautiful orchids, the creamy-white burnet rose, the little starry flowers of mossy saxifrage and the magenta-coloured bloody cranesbill.

It's some 40km to Doolin, heading south first via the N67 then onto the R480, which corkscrews over the lunar, limestone landscape of the Burren's exposed hills. Next curve west onto the R476 to meander towards Doolin via more familiar Irish landscapes of green fields, and the villages of Kilfenora and Lisdoonvarna – great for pit stops and trad-music sessions.

----

8 Doolin

Doolin is renowned as a centre of Irish traditional music, but it's also known for its setting – 6km north of the Cliffs of Moher – and down near the ever-unsettled sea, the land is windblown, with huge rocks exposed by the long-vanished topsoil.

Many musicians live in the area, and they have a symbiotic relationship with the tourists: each desires the other and each year things grow a little larger. But given the heavy concentration of visitors, it's inevitable that standards don't always hold up to those in some of the less-trampled villages in Clare.

🛏 p361

The Drive ≫ Ferries from Doolin to Inishmore take about 1½ hours to make the crossing.

- - - - - - - - - - - - - - -

TRIP HIGHLIGHT

❾ Inishmore

A step (and boat or plane ride) beyond the desolate beauty of the Burren are the Aran Islands. Most visitors are satisfied to explore only Inishmore (Inis Mór) and its main

attraction, **Dun Aengus** (Dún Aonghasa; ☎099-61008; www.heritageireland.ie; adult/child €5/3; ☺9.30am-6pm Apr-Oct, to 4pm Nov-Mar), the stunning stone fort perched perilously on the island's towering cliffs. Powerful swells pound the 87m-high cliff face. A complete lack of rails or other modern additions that would spoil this amazing ancient site means that you can not only go right up to the cliff's edge but also potentially fall to your doom below quite easily. When it's uncrowded, you can't help but feel the extraordinary energy that must have been harnessed to build this vast site.

The arid landscape west of Kilronan (Cill Rónáin), Inishmór's main settlement, is dominated

by stone walls, boulders, scattered buildings and the odd patch of deep-green grass and potato plants.

🛏 p327, p361

The Drive ≫ Once you're back on terra firma at Doolin, it's 223km to Dingle via the N85 to Ennis then the M18 to Limerick city. The N69 will take you into County Kerry as far as Tralee, beyond which it's 50km on the N86 to Dingle.

- - - - - - - - - - - - - - -

❿ Dingle

Unlike the Ring of Kerry, where the cliffs tend to dominate the ocean, it's the ocean that dominates the smaller Dingle Peninsula. The opal-blue waters surrounding the promontory's multihued landscape of green hills and golden sands give rise to aquatic adventures and to fishing fleets that haul in fresh seafood that appears on the menus of some of the county's finest restaurants.

Centred on charming Dingle town, there's an alternative way of life here, lived by artisans and idiosyncratic characters and found at trad sessions and folkloric festivals across Dingle's tiny settlements.

The classic loop drive around Slea Head from Dingle town is 47km, but allow a day to take it all in – longer if you have time to stay overnight in Dingle town.

✗ p310, p327

LOCAL KNOWLEDGE: DOOLIN'S MUSIC PUBS

Doolin's three main music pubs (others are recent interlopers) are, in order of importance to the music scene:

McGann's (p360) Trad sessions take place most nights year-round, with crowds often spilling onto the street. Inside you'll find locals playing darts in its warren of small rooms, some with peat fires.

Gus O'Connor's (p360) Music plays from 9.30pm nightly from late February to November and at weekends year-round. On some summer nights you won't squeeze inside.

McDermott's (p360) Renowned music sessions kick off at 9pm nightly from Easter to October, and several nights a week the rest of the year.

IRELAND **23** THE LONG WAY ROUND

The Drive ❯❯ Take the N86 as far as Annascaul and then the coastal R561 as far as Castlemaine. Then head southwest on the N70 to Killorglin and the Ring of Kerry. From Dingle, it's 53km.

- - - - - - - - - - - - - - - - - -

⑪ Ring of Kerry

The Ring of Kerry is the longest and the most diverse of Ireland's big circle drives, combining jaw-dropping coastal scenery with emerald pastures and villages.

The 179km circuit usually begins in Killarney and winds past pristine beaches, the island-dotted Atlantic, medieval ruins, mountains and loughs (lakes). The coastline is at its most rugged between Waterville and Caherdaniel in the southwest of the peninsula. It can get crowded in summer, but even then, the remote Skellig Ring can be uncrowded and serene – and starkly beautiful.

The Ring of Kerry can easily be done as a day trip, but if you want to stretch it out, places to stay are scattered along the route. Killorglin and Kenmare have the best dining options, with some excellent restaurants; elsewhere, basic (sometimes very basic) pub fare is the norm. The Ring's most popular diversion is the Gap of Dunloe, an awe-inspiring mountain pass at the western edge of

AN ANCIENT FORT

For a look at a well-preserved *caher* (walled fort) of the late Iron Age to early Christian period, stop at **Caherconnell Fort** (☎065-708 9999; www.caherconnell. com; R480; adult/child €6/4, sheepdog demonstration €6/3, combination ticket €10/5.60; ⏰10am-6pm Jul & Aug, to 5.30pm May, Jun & Sep, 10.30am-5pm Mar, Apr & Oct), a privately run heritage attraction that's more serious than sideshow. Exhibits detail how the evolution of these defensive settlements may have reflected territorialism and competition for land among a growing, settling population. The drystone walling of the fort is in excellent condition. The top-notch visitor centre also has information on many other monuments in the area. It's about 1km south of Poulnabrone Dolmen on the R480.

Killarney National Park. It's signposted off the N72 between Killarney to Killorglin. The incredibly popular 19th-century Kate Kearney's Cottage is a pub where most visitors park their cars before walking up to the gap.

- - - - - - - - - - - - - - - - - -

⑫ Kenmare

If you've done the Ring in an anticlockwise fashion (or cut through the Gap of Dunloe), you'll end up in handsome Kenmare, a largely 18th-century town and the ideal alternative to Killarney as a place to stay overnight.

🍴 🛏 p311, p327, p339

The Drive ❯❯ Picturesque villages, a fine stone circle and calming coastal scenery mark the less-taken 143km route from Kenmare to Cork city. When you get to Leap, turn right

onto the R597 and go as far as Rosscarbery; or, even better, take twice as long (even though it's only 24km more) and make your way along narrow roads near the water the entire way.

- - - - - - - - - - - - - - - - - -

⑬ Cork City

Ireland's second city is first in every important respect, at least according to the locals, who cheerfully refer to it as the 'real capital of Ireland'. The compact city centre is surrounded by interesting waterways and is chock-full of great restaurants fed by arguably the best foodie scene in the country.

🍴 🛏 p327

The Drive ❯❯ It's only 60km to Ardmore, but stop off in Midleton, 24km east of Cork along the N25, and visit the whiskey museum. Just beyond Youghal, turn right onto the R673 for Ardmore.

MNSTUDIO/SHUTTERSTOCK ©

 LOCAL KNOWLEDGE: THE HEALY PASS

Instead of going directly into County Cork along the N71 from Kenmare, veer west onto the R571 and drive for 16km along the northern edge of the Beara Peninsula. At Lauragh, turn onto the R574 and take the breathtaking **Healy Pass Road**, which cuts through the peninsula and brings you from County Kerry into County Cork. At Adrigole, turn left onto the R572 and rejoin the N71 at Glengarriff, 17km east.

TRIP HIGHLIGHT

⑭ Ardmore

Due to its location off the main drag, Ardmore is a sleepy seaside village and one of the southeast's loveliest spots – the ideal destination for those looking for a little waterside R&R.

St Declan reputedly set up shop here sometime between 350 and 420 CE, which would make Ardmore the first Christian bastion in Ireland – long before St Patrick landed. The village's 12th-century round tower, one of the best examples of these structures in Ireland, is the town's most distinctive architectural feature, but you should also check out the ruins of St Declan's church and holy well, 1km east on a bluff on Ardmore's signposted 5km cliff walk.

The Burren Wildflowers dot this karst landscape

Eating & Sleeping

Dublin ❶

✗ Pi Pizza
Pizza €€

(www.pipizzas.ie; 73-83 S Great George's St; pizzas €9-16; ⊙ noon-10pm Sun-Wed, to 10.30pm Thu-Sat; 🔲 all city centre) This fabulous restaurant opened in 2018, and it's already a contender for best pizzeria in town. The smallish menu has just eight pizzas, each an inspired interpretation of a Neapolitan classic. Highly recommended are the *funghi* (mushroom) or *broccolini*, 'white' pizzas made without the tomato layer.

🛏 Westbury Hotel
Hotel €€€

(☎01-679 1122; www.doylecollection.com; Grafton St; r/ste from €430/580; 🅿 @ 🛜; 🔲 all city centre, 🚇 St Stephen's Green) Tucked away just off Grafton St is one of the most elegant hotels in town. The upstairs lobby is a great spot for afternoon tea or a drink, and the two restaurants on-site – Balfes and Wilde – are both exceptional.

Belfast ❷

✗ Eipic
Modern Irish £££

(☎028-9033 1134; www.deaneseipic.com; 34-40 Howard St; set menu £45-70; ⊙ 5.30-8pm Wed-Sat; 🅿; 🔲 G1, G2) The finest, seasonal local ingredients are given a creative twist at the flagship restaurant in Michael Deane's portfolio, the Michelin-starred Eipic. Head chef Alex Greene is originally from Dundrum in County Down; his tasting menus are full of theatrical surprises.

🛏 Merchant Hotel
Hotel £££

(☎028-9023 4888; www.themerchanthotel. com; 16 Skipper St; d/ste from £200/380; 🅿 @ 🛜; 🔲 3A, 4D, 5A, 6A) Belfast's most flamboyant hotel occupies the palatial former Ulster Bank head office. Rooms are individually decorated with a fabulous fusion of contemporary styling and old-fashioned elegance; those in the original Victorian building have opulent floor-length silk curtains while newer rooms have an art deco–inspired theme.

Facilities include a luxurious spa and an eight-person rooftop hot tub.

Giant's Causeway ❸

✗ Causeway Hotel
Irish ££

(www.thecausewayhotel.com; 40 Causeway Rd; mains £10-21; ⊙ noon-8.30pm) The restaurant at the Causeway Hotel serves an all-day menu of hearty dishes like chowder with wheaten bread, fish and chips, burgers and pasta. The dinner menu is more refined and features the likes of oven-baked salmon and cod, crispy duck breast and sirloin steak. Diners can park at the hotel for free.

Dunfanaghy ❹

✗ Cove
Modern Irish €€

(☎074-913 6300; www.facebook.com/ coverestaurantdonegal; off N56, Rockhill, Port-na-Blagh; mains €20-30; ⊙ 6.30-9.30pm Tue-Sun) Owners Siobhan Sweeney and Peter Byrne are perfectionists who tend to every detail in Cove's art-filled dining room as well as on your plate. The cuisine is fresh and inventive. Seafood specials are deceptively simple with subtle Asian influences, and after dinner you can enjoy the elegant lounge upstairs. There's an excellent wine list too. Book ahead.

Sligo Town ❺

✗ Lyons Cafe
Irish €

(☎071-914 2969; www.lyonscafe.com; Quay St; mains €8-16; ⊙ 8.30am-6pm Mon-Sat) The cafe in Sligo's flagship department store, Lyons, first opened in 1926, but the food served in the airy, 1st-floor eatery is bang up to date. Acclaimed chef and cookbook author Gary Stafford offers a fresh and seasonal menu that's inventive yet casual. The gourmet sandwiches feature superb artisan bread baked by the in-store bakery on the ground floor.

🛏 Glass House   Hotel €€

(📞071-919 4300; www.theglasshouse.ie; Swan Point; s €123, d €132-149, ste €158-175; 📶) You can't miss this cool and contemporary four-star hotel in the centre of town, its sharp glass facade jutting skyward. Inside, the food areas have good river views, there are two bars and the 116 well-equipped rooms come in a choice of zesty colours.

Inishmore ⑨

🛏 Kilmurvey House   B&B €€

(📞099-61218, Kilmurvey, s/d from €60/95; ☺Apr–mid-Oct; 📶) There's a dash of grandeur about Kilmurvey House, where 12 spacious rooms sit in an imposing, 18th-century stone mansion. Breakfasts are convivial affairs, with homemade granola, porridge with whiskey and own-baked scones. It's a 500m stroll east to swim at pretty Kilmurvey Beach.

Dingle Town ⑩

✖ Doyle's   Seafood €€€

(📞066-915 2674; www.doylesrestaurantdingle.ie; 4 John St; mains €22-34; ☺5-9.30pm Mon-Sat, to 7.30pm Sun) Cherry-red-painted Doyle's serves some of the best seafood in the area (which in these parts is really saying something). Starters such as Dingle Bay crab claws or oysters *au naturel* team up with mains like fennel-scented Spanish fish stew, seafood linguine and roast monkfish cassoulet.

Kenmare ⑫

✖ Tom Crean Base Camp   Irish €€

(📞064-664 1589; www.tomcrean.ie; Main St; mains €17-31; ☺noon-7pm Thu-Mon, daily Jul &

Aug; 📶) Named for Kerry's pioneering Antarctic explorer, and run by his granddaughter, Tom Crean Base Camp has a restaurant serving seafood, pizzas and burgers that go perfectly with a pint of Expedition Red Ale or Scurvy Dog IPA from the on-site brewery. Twice-daily brewery tours (€15) cover the brewing process and the history of Tom Crean. Upstairs, the 19th-century townhouse has boutique rooms with king-size beds (doubles from €85).

Cork City ⑬

✖ Market Lane   Irish €€

(📞021-427 4710; www.marketlane.ie; 5 Oliver Plunkett St; mains lunch €8-19, dinner €16-29; ☺noon-9.30pm Mon-Wed, to 10pm Thu, to 10.30pm Fri & Sat, 1-9.30pm Sun; 📶🚻) It's always hopping at this bright corner bistro. The menu is broad and hearty, changing to reflect what's fresh at the English Market: perhaps roast hake with wild garlic velouté, or beetroot, walnut and feta cakes? No reservations for fewer than six diners; sip a drink at the bar till a table is free. Lots of wines by the glass.

🛏 Montenotte Hotel   Boutique Hotel €€€

(📞021-453 0050; www.themontenottehotel.com; Middle Glanmire Rd; d/f from €189/229; 🅿📶🛗) Built as a private residence for a wealthy merchant in the 1820s, the Montenotte has been reimagined as a boutique hotel that skilfully blends its 19th-century legacy with bold designer colour schemes. The hilltop location commands superb views, especially from the roof-terrace bar and restaurant, and guests can enjoy the hotel's sunken Victorian garden, private cinema and luxurious spa.

Ring of Kerry

24

Circumnavigating the Iveragh Peninsula, the Ring of Kerry is the longest and most diverse of Ireland's prized peninsula drives, combining coastal scenery with soaring mountains.

TRIP HIGHLIGHTS

189 km

Muckross Estate
Magnificent garden-set mansion, deer parks, waterfall and abbey

START/FINISH
● Killarney

● Rossbeigh Strand

⑩ ⑪

● Kenmare

⑦

Caherdaniel
Aquatic activities galore and horse rides along the beach

90 km

158 km

Gap of Dunloe
Rocky bridges cross crystal-clear streams and lakes

4 DAYS
202KM / 125 MILES

GREAT FOR...

BEST TIME TO GO

May and September for temperate weather free of summer crowds.

ESSENTIAL PHOTO

Ross Castle as you row a boat to Inisfallen.

BEST FOR WILDLIFE

Killarney National Park, home to Ireland's only wild herd of native red deer.

Killarney National Park Lough Leane

24 Ring of Kerry

You can drive the Ring of Kerry in a day, but the longer you spend here, the more you'll enjoy it. The circuit winds past pristine beaches, medieval ruins, mountains, loughs and the island-dotted Atlantic, with the coastline at its most rugged between Waterville and Caherdaniel in the peninsula's southwest. You'll also find plenty of opportunities for serene, starkly beautiful detours, such as the Skellig Ring and the Cromane Peninsula.

① Killarney

A town that's been in the business of welcoming visitors for more than 250 years, Killarney is a well-oiled tourism machine fuelled by the sublime scenery of its namesake national park, and competition keeps standards high. Killarney nights are lively and most pubs put on live music.

Killarney and its surrounds have likely been inhabited since the Neolithic period, but it wasn't until the 17th century that Viscount Kenmare developed the region as an Irish version of England's Lake District; among its notable 19th-century tourists were Queen Victoria and Romantic poet Percy Bysshe Shelley. The town itself lacks major attractions, but the landscaped grounds of nearby Killarney House and Muckross House frame photoworthy panoramas of lake and mountain, while former carriage drives around these aristocratic estates now serve as scenic hiking and biking trails open to all.

The town can easily be explored on foot in an hour or two, or you can get around by horse-drawn jaunting car.

✗ ⊨ p311, p339

The Drive » From Killarney, head 22km west to Killorglin along the N72, with views south to Ireland's highest mountain range, Macgillycuddy's Reeks. The mountains' elegant forms were

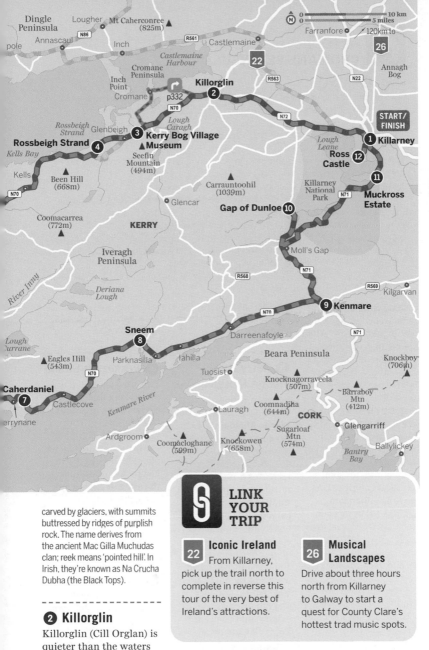

LINK YOUR TRIP

22 Iconic Ireland
From Killarney, pick up the trail north to complete in reverse this tour of the very best of Ireland's attractions.

26 Musical Landscapes
Drive about three hours north from Killarney to Galway to start a quest for County Clare's hottest trad music spots.

carved by glaciers, with summits buttressed by ridges of purplish rock. The name derives from the ancient Mac Gilla Muchudas clan; reek means 'pointed hill'. In Irish, they're known as Na Crucha Dubha (the Black Tops).

- - - - - - - - - - - - - - - - - -

② Killorglin

Killorglin (Cill Orglan) is quieter than the waters of the River Laune that

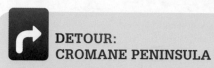

DETOUR:
CROMANE PENINSULA

Start: ❷ **Killorglin**

Open fields give way to spectacular water vistas and multihued sunsets on the Cromane Peninsula, with its tiny namesake village sitting at the base of a narrow shingle spit.

Cromane's exceptional eating place, **Jacks' Coastguard Restaurant** (☏066-976 9102; www.jackscromane.com; mains €19-36; ☺6-9pm Thu-Sun, 1-3pm Sun, hours can vary; P♿), is a local secret and justifies the trip. Entering this 1866-built coastguard station feels like arriving at a low-key village pub, but a narrow doorway at the back of the bar leads to a striking, whitewashed contemporary space with lights glittering from midnight-blue ceiling panels, stained glass and metallic fish sculptures, and huge picture windows looking out across the water. Seafood is the standout, but there's also steak, roast lamb and a veggie dish of the day.

Cromane is 9km from Killorglin. Heading southwest from Killorglin along the N70, take the second right and continue straight ahead until you get to the crossroads. Turn right; Jack's Coastguard Restaurant is on your left.

---

lap against its 1885-built eight-arched bridge – except in mid-August, when there's an explosion of time-honoured ceremonies at the famous **Puck Fair** (Aonach an Phuic; www.puckfair.ie; ☺mid-Aug), a pagan festival first recorded in 1603. A statue of King Puck (a goat) peers out from the Killarney end of the bridge.

Killorglin has some of the finest eateries along the Ring – **Bianconi** (☏066-976 1146; www.bianconi.ie; Lower Bridge St; mains €10-28; ☺10.30am-11.30pm Mon-Thu, to 12.30am Fri & Sat; ☎) and **Jack's Bakery** (Lower Bridge St; dishes €2.50-8; ☺8am-6.45pm Mon-Fri, to 6pm Sat, 9am-2pm Sun) are both good spots for a late breakfast or early lunch.

The Drive » Killorglin sits at the junction of the N72 and the N70; continue 13km along the N70 to the Kerry Bog Village Museum.

---

❸ Kerry Bog Village Museum

Between Killorglin and Glenbeigh, the **Kerry Bog Village Museum** (www.kerrybogvillage.ie; Ballincleave, Glenbeigh; adult/child €6.50/4.50; ☺9am-6pm; P) recreates a 19th-century settlement typical of the small communities that carved out a precarious living in the harsh environment of Ireland's ubiquitous peat bogs. You'll see the thatched homes of the turf cutter, blacksmith, thatcher and labourer, as well as a dairy, and meet rare Kerry Bog ponies.

The Drive » It's less than 1km from the museum to the village

of Glenbeigh; turn off here and drive 2km west to unique Rossbeigh Strand.

---

❹ Rossbeigh Strand

This unusual beach is a 3km-long finger of shingle and sand protruding into Dingle Bay, with views of Inch Point and the Dingle Peninsula. On one side, the sea is ruffled by Atlantic winds; on the other, it's sheltered and calm.

The Drive » Rejoin the N70 and continue 25km southwest to Cahersiveen.

---

❺ Cahersiveen

Cahersiveen's population – over 30,000 in 1841 – was decimated by the Great Famine and emigration to the New World. A sleepy outpost remains, overshadowed by the 688m peak of **Knocknadobar**. It looks rather dour compared with the peninsula's other settlements, but the atmospheric remains of 16th-century **Ballycarbery Castle**, 2.4km along the road to White Strand Beach from the town centre, are worth a look.

Along the same road are two stone ring forts. The larger, **Cahergall**, dates from the 10th century and has stairways on the inside walls, a *clochán* (circular stone building shaped like an old-fashioned beehive) and the remains of a house. The smaller, 9th-century **Leacanabuile** has an entrance to an underground passage. Their inner walls and chambers give a strong sense of what life was like in a ring fort. Leave your car in the parking area next to a stone wall and walk up the footpaths.

The Drive » From Cahersiveen you can continue 17km along the classic Ring of Kerry on the N70 to Waterville, or take the ultrascenic route via Valentia Island and the Skellig Ring, and rejoin the N70 at Waterville.

- - - - - - - - - - - - - - - - - - -

⑥ Waterville

A line of colourful houses on the N70 between Lough Currane and Ballinskelligs Bay, Waterville is charm-challenged in the way of many mass-consumption beach resorts. A statue of its most famous guest, Charlie

DETOUR: VALENTIA ISLAND & THE SKELLIG RING

Start: ⑤ **Cahersiveen**

Crowned by Geokaun Mountain, 11km-long **Valentia Island** (Oileán Dairbhre) makes an ideal driving loop, with some lonely ruins that are worth exploring. Knightstown, the only town, has pubs, food and walks.

The **Skellig Experience** (☑066-947 6306; www.skelligexperience.com; adult/child €5/3, incl cruise €40/25; ☺10am-7pm Jul & Aug, to 6pm May, Jun & Sep, to 5pm Fri-Wed Mar, Apr, Oct & Nov; [P]) heritage centre, in a distinctive building with turf-covered barrel roofs, has informative exhibits on the Skellig Islands offshore. From April to October, it also runs two-hour cruises around the Skelligs (no landing; adult/child €40/25, including museum entry).

If you're here between April and October, and you're detouring via Valentia Island and the Skellig Ring, a ferry service from Reenard Point, 5km southwest of Cahersiveen, provides a handy shortcut to Valentia Island. The five-minute crossing departs every 10 minutes. Alternatively, there's a bridge between Portmagee and the far end of the island.

Immediately across the bridge on the mainland, Portmagee's single street is a rainbow of colourful houses. On summer mornings the small pier comes to life with boats embarking on the choppy crossing to the Skellig Islands.

Portmagee holds **set-dancing workshops** (www.moorings.ie) over the May bank holiday weekend, with plenty of stomping practice sessions in the town's **Bridge Bar** (☑066-947 7108; www.moorings.ie; mains €13-27; ☺9am-11.30pm Mon-Sat, to 11pm Sun, kitchen to 9pm; [♦]), a friendly local gathering point that's also good for impromptu music year-round and more formal sessions in summer.

The wild and beautiful, 18km-long **Skellig Ring** road links Portmagee and Waterville via a Gaeltacht (Irish-speaking) area centred on Ballinskelligs (Baile an Sceilg), with the ragged outline of Skellig Michael never far from view.

WHY THIS IS A GREAT TRIP
NEIL WILSON, WRITER

In a land criss-crossed with classic drives, the Ring of Kerry is perhaps the most classic of all. Now a key stretch of the Wild Atlantic Way, this trip showcases Ireland's most spectacular coastal scenery, its ancient and recent history, traditional pubs with crackling turf fires and spontaneous, high-spirited trad music sessions, and the Emerald Isle's most engaging asset: its welcoming, warm-hearted locals.

Above: Gap of Dunloe
Left: Muckross Abbey, Muckross Estate
Right: Torc Waterfall, Muckross Estate

Chaplin, beams from the seafront. The **Charlie Chaplin Comedy Film Festival** (www.chaplin filmfestival.com) is held in August.

Waterville is home to a world-renowned **links golf course**. At the north end of Lough Currane, **Church Island** has the ruins of a medieval church and beehive cell reputedly founded as a monastic settlement by St Finian in the 6th century.

🛏 p339

The Drive » Squiggle your way for 14km along the Ring's most tortuous stretch, past plunging cliffs, craggy hills and stunning views, to Caherdaniel.

TRIP HIGHLIGHT

❼ Caherdaniel

The scattered hamlet of Caherdaniel counts two of the Ring of Kerry's highlights: Derrynane National Historic Park, the childhood home of the 19th-century hero of Catholic emancipation, Daniel O'Connell; and what is plausibly claimed as 'Ireland's finest view' over rugged cliffs and islands, as you crest the hill at Beenarourke (there's a large car park here).

Most activity here centres on the Blue Flag beach. **Derrynane Sea Sports** (☎087 908 1208; www.derrynaneseasports.com; Derrynane Beach) organises sailing, canoeing, surfing, windsurfing and

TOP TIP: AROUND & ACROSS THE RING

Tour buses travel anticlockwise around the Ring, and authorities generally encourage visitors to drive in the same direction to avoid traffic congestion and accidents. If you travel clockwise, watch out on blind corners, especially on the section between Moll's Gap and Killarney. There's little traffic on the Ballaghbeama Gap, which cuts across the peninsula's central highlands, with some spectacular views.

waterskiing (from €40 per person), as well as equipment hire (around €20 per hour).

The Drive » Wind your way east along the N70 for 21km to Sneem.

⑧ Sneem

Sneem's Irish name, An tSnaidhm, translates as 'the knot', which is thought to refer to the River Sneem that twists and turns, knot-like, into nearby Kenmare Bay. Take a gander at the town's two cute squares, then pop into the **Blue Bull** (📞064-664 5382; South Sq; mains €10-15, dinner €14-29; ⏰ kitchen noon-9pm, bar 11.30am-midnight), a perfect little old stone pub, for a pint.

🛏 p339

The Drive » Along the 27km drive to Kenmare, the N70 drifts away from the water to take in views towards the Kerry mountains.

⑨ Kenmare

The copper-covered limestone spire of Holy Cross Church, drawing the eye to the wooded hills above town, may make you forget for a split second that Kenmare is a seaside town. With rivers named Finnihy, Roughty and Sheen emptying into Kenmare Bay, you couldn't be anywhere other than southwest Ireland.

In the 18th century Kenmare was laid out on an X-shaped plan, with a triangular market square in the centre. Today the inverted V to the south is the focus. Kenmare River (actually an inlet of the sea) stretches out to the southwest, and there are glorious mountain views.

Signposted southwest of the square is an early Bronze Age **stone circle**, one of the biggest in southwest Ireland. Fifteen stones ring a boulder dolmen, a burial monument rarely found

outside this part of the country.

🍴🛏 p311, p327, p339

The Drive » The coastal scenery might be finished but, if anything, the next 23km are even more stunning as you head north from Kenmare to the Gap of Dunloe on the narrow, vista-crazy N71, winding between crag and lake, with plenty of lay-bys to stop and admire the views (and recover from the switchback bends).

TRIP HIGHLIGHT

⑩ Gap of Dunloe

Just west of Killarney National Park, the Gap of Dunloe is ruggedly beautiful. In the winter it's an awe-inspiring mountain pass, squeezed between Purple Mountain and Macgillycuddy's Reeks.

In high summer it's a magnet for the tourist trade, with buses ferrying countless visitors here for horse-and-trap rides through the Gap.

On the southern side, surrounded by lush, green pastures, is **Lord Brandon's Cottage**, accessed by turning left at Moll's Gap on the R568, then taking the first right, another right at the bottom of the hill, then right again at the crossroads (about 13km from the N71 all up).

A simple 19th-century hunting lodge, it has an open-air cafe and a dock for boats from Ross Castle near Killarney. From here a (very) narrow road weaves up the hill to the Gap – theoretically you can drive this 8km route to the 19th-century pub **Kate Kearney's Cottage** (📞064-664 4146; mains €10-24; 🕐kitchen noon-9pm, bar to 11.30pm Mon-Thu, to 12.30am Fri & Sat, to 11pm Sun; 🅿🐕) and back but *only* outside summer.

Even then walkers and cyclists have right of way and the precipitous hairpin bends are nerve-testing. It's worth walking or taking a jaunting car (or, if you're carrying two wheels, cycling) through the Gap: the scenery is a fantasy of rocky bridges over clear mountain streams and lakes. Alternatively, there are various options for exploring the Gap from Killarney.

The Drive » Continue on the N71 north through Killarney National Park to Muckross Estate (32km).

TRIP HIGHLIGHT

⓫ Muckross Estate

The core of Killarney National Park is Muckross Estate, donated to the state by Arthur Bourn Vincent in 1932. **Muckross House** (📞064-667 0144; www.muckross-house. ie; adult/child €9.25/6.25, incl Muckross Traditional Farms €15.50/10.50; 🕐9am-7pm Jul & Aug, to 6pm Apr-Jun, Sep & Oct, to 5pm Nov-Mar; 🅿) is a 19th-century mansion, restored to its former glory and packed with period fittings. Entrance is by guided tour.

The beautiful **gardens** slope down, and a building behind the house contains a restaurant, craft shop and studios where you can see potters, weavers and bookbinders at work.

Jaunting cars wait to run you through deer parks and woodland to **Torc Waterfall** and **Muckross Abbey** (about €20 each, return; haggling can reap discounts). The visitor centre has an excellent cafe.

Adjacent to Muckross House are the **Muckross Traditional Farms**

KILLARNEY NATIONAL PARK

Designated a Unesco Biosphere Reserve in 1982, **Killarney National Park** (www. killarneynationalpark.ie) is among the finest of Ireland's national parks. And while its proximity to one of the southwest's largest and liveliest urban centres (including pedestrian entrances right in Killarney's town centre) encourages high visitor numbers, it's an important conservation area for many rare species. Within its 102 sq km is Ireland's only wild herd of native red deer, which has lived here continuously for 12,000 years, as well as the country's largest area of ancient oak woods and views of most of its major mountains.

Glacier-gouged Lough Leane (the Lower Lake or 'Lake of Learning'), Muckross Lake and the Upper Lake make up about a quarter of the park. Their crystal waters are as rich in wildlife as the surrounding land: great crested grebes and tufted ducks cruise the lake margins, deer swim out to graze on islands, and salmon, trout and perch prosper in a pike-free environment.

With a bit of luck, you might see white-tailed sea eagles, with their 2.5m wingspan, soaring overhead. The eagles were reintroduced here in 2007 after an absence of more than 100 years. There are now more than 50 in the park and they're starting to settle in Ireland's rivers, lakes and coastal regions. And like Killarney itself, the park is also home to plenty of summer visitors, including migratory cuckoos, swallows and swifts.

Keep your eyes peeled, too, for the park's smallest residents – its insects, including the northern emerald dragonfly, which isn't normally found this far south in Europe and is believed to have been marooned here after the last ice age.

(☎064-663 0804; www.
muckross-house.ie; adult/
child €9.25/6.25, incl Muckross
House €15.50/10.50; ⏰10am-
6pm Jun-Aug, from 1pm Apr,
May & Sep, from 1pm Sat & Sun
Mar & Oct).

These reproductions
of 1930s Kerry farms,
complete with chickens,
pigs, cattle and horses,
recreate farming and
living conditions when
people had to live off the
land.

The Drive » Continuing a
further 2km north through the
national park brings you to
historic Ross Castle.

⑫ Ross Castle

Restored **Ross Castle**
(☎064-663 5851; www.herit
ageireland.ie; Ross Rd; adult/
child €5/3; ⏰9.30am-5.45pm
Mar-Oct; ℗) dates back to
the 15th century, when
it was a residence of the
O'Donoghues. It was the
last place in Munster to
succumb to Cromwell's
forces, thanks partly to
its cunning spiral stair-
case, every step of which
is a different height in
order to break an at-
tacker's stride. Access is
by guided tour only.

You can take a motor-
boat trip (around €10 per
person) from Ross Castle
to **Inisfallen**, the largest
of Killarney National

Park's 26 islands. The
first monastery on Inis-
fallen is said to have been
founded by St Finian the
Leper in the 7th century.
The island's fame dates
from the early 13th
century when the Annals
of Inisfallen were written
here. Now in the Bodleian
Library at Oxford, they
remain a vital source
of information on early
Munster history. Inisfall-
en shelters the ruins of a
12th-century oratory with
a carved Romanesque
doorway and a monastery
on the site of St Finian's
original.

The Drive » It's just 3km
north from Ross Castle back to
Killarney.

Eating & Sleeping

Killarney ①

✗ Murphy Brownes   International €€
(☎064-667 1446; www.murphybrownes.com; 8 High St; mains €16-29; ⏰5-9.30pm Mar-early Jan) Elegant and candlelit, but pleasantly informal, this place is ideal for a relaxing dinner. Service is smiling and attentive without being overbearing, and the crowd-pleasing menu is a mix of Irish and international favourites, with local mussels, Kerry lamb shank and fish and chips sitting alongside beef lasagne, chicken curry and Caesar salad.

🛏 Cahernane House Hotel   Heritage Hotel €€€
(☎064-663 1895; www.cahernane.com; Muckross Rd, Muckross; d/ste from €260/340, 4-course dinner menu €60; P 🛜) A tree-lined driveway leads to this magnificent manor 2km south of town, dating from 1877. A dozen of its 38 antique-furnished rooms (some with claw-foot bath or Jacuzzi) are in the original house; garden-wing rooms have balcony or patio. Fishing is possible in the River Flesk, which flows through the grounds. Its restaurant (nonguests by reservation) is sublime.

Waterville ⑥

🛏 Butler Arms Hotel   Historic Hotel €€
(☎066-947 4156; www.butlerarms.com; New Line Rd; s/d from €132/145; P 🛜) The castellated towers of the Butler Arms have dominated the northern end of the village since 1884, and the hotel has provided accommodation for many famous guests through the years – Walt Disney in the 1940s, Charlie Chaplin in the 1960s.

Sneem ⑧

🛏 Parknasilla Resort & Spa   Hotel €€€
(☎064-667 5600; www.parknasillaresort. com; Parknasilla; d/f/ste from €265/285/415; P @ 🛜 ♒) On the tree-fringed shores of the Kenmare River with views to the Beara Peninsula, this hotel has been wowing guests (including George Bernard Shaw) since 1895. From the modern, luxuriously appointed bedrooms to the top-grade spa and elegant restaurant, everything here is done just right.

Kenmare ⑨

✗ No 35   Irish €€
(☎064-664 1559; www.no35kenmare.com; 35 Main St; mains €20-29; ⏰5.30-9.30pm Fri-Tue) Hand-cut limestone walls, exposed timber beams, stained-glass windows and an open fire set the stage for some of Kenmare's most creative cuisine. All-Irish produce features in dishes like slow-cooked rare saddleback pork (from the owners' own farm) with caraway-spiced swede. Great Irish craft beers and ciders too.

✗ Mulcahy's   Bistro €€€
(☎064-664 2383; www.mulcahyskenmare. ie; 8 Main St; mains €20-32; ⏰5-10pm) At Kenmare's best-known restaurant, chef Bruce Mulcahy weaves his culinary magic with Asian- or Mediterranean-inspired twists on local seafood, sitting alongside more traditionally Irish dishes.

🛏 Dromquinna Manor   Tented Camp €€
(☎064-664 2888; www.dromquinnamanor.com; Sneem Rd; d/f €165/190; ⏰May-Aug; P) This country estate on the shores of Kenmare River, 4.5km west of Kenmare, has 14 sturdy safari-style tents, luxuriously outfitted with plush double beds and antique furniture (but shared showers and toilets), on a gorgeous landscaped site sloping down to the sea. A picnic-hamper breakfast is delivered each morning.

The North in a Nutshell

25

The North's must-do trip takes in unmissable cities and big-name sights. It also heads off the tourist trail, revealing secret beaches, quaint harbours, waterfalls and music-filled pubs.

TRIP HIGHLIGHTS

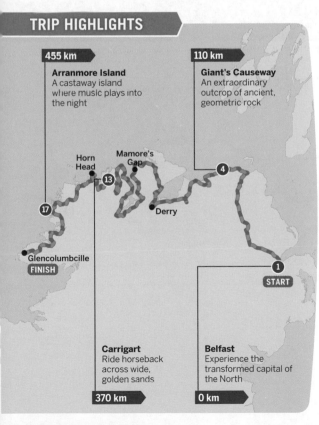

455 km

Arranmore Island
A castaway island where music plays into the night

110 km

Giant's Causeway
An extraordinary outcrop of ancient, geometric rock

Horn Head

Mamore's Gap

13

17

4

Derry

1

START

Glencolumbcille
FINISH

Carrigart
Ride horseback across wide, golden sands

Belfast
Experience the transformed capital of the North

370 km

0 km

---

10 DAYS
470KM / 292 MILES

GREAT FOR...

BEST TIME TO GO
March to June and September mean good weather but fewer crowds.

ESSENTIAL PHOTO
Crossing the Carrick-a-Rede Rope Bridge as it swings above the waves.

✓ **BEST FOR SCENERY**
Stops 16 to 20 head into the heart of wild, wind-whipped Donegal.

Carrick-a-Rede Rope Bridge A crossing 30m above the waves

341

The North in a Nutshell

On this road-trip-to-remember you'll drive routes that cling to cliffs, cross borders and head high onto mountain passes. You'll witness Ireland's turbulent past and its inspiring path to peace. And you'll also explore rich faith, folk and music traditions, ride a horse across a sandy beach, cross a swaying rope bridge and spend a night on a castaway island. Not bad for a 10-day drive.

❶ Belfast

In bustling, big-city Belfast the past is palpably present – walk the city's former sectarian battlegrounds for a profound way to start exploring the North's story. Next, cross the River Lagan and head to the Titanic Quarter. Dominated by the towering yellow Harland and Wolff (H&W) cranes, it's where RMS *Titanic* was built. **Titanic Belfast** (www. titanicbelfast.com; Queen's Rd; adult/child £19/8.50; ☺9am-7pm Jun & Jul, to 8pm Aug, to 6pm Apr, May & Sep, 10am-5pm Oct-Mar; 🚐G2) is a stunning multisensory experience: see bustling shipyards, join crowds at *Titanic's* launch, feel temperatures drop as it strikes that iceberg, and look through a glass floor at watery footage of the vessel today. Slightly to the west, don't miss the **Thompson Graving Dock** (www.titanicsdock. com; Queen's Rd; adult/child £6.50/2.50; ☺10am-5pm Apr-Oct, 10.30am-4pm Nov & Dec, 10.30am-5pm Jan & Feb; 🚐G2), where you descend into the immense dry dock where the liner was fitted out.

The Drive ❯❯ As you drive the M3/M2 north, the now-familiar H&W cranes recede. Take the A26 through Ballymena; soon the Antrim Mountains loom large to the right. Skirt them, following the A26 then the A44 into Ballycastle, 96km from Belfast.

❷ Ballycastle

Head beyond the sandy beach to the harbour at the appealing resort of Ballycastle. From here, daily **ferries** (📞028-2076 9299; www.rathlinballycastle ferry.com; return trip adult/ child/bicycle £12/6/3.30) depart for Rathlin Island, where you'll see sea stacks and thousands of guillemots, kittiwakes, razorbills and puffins.

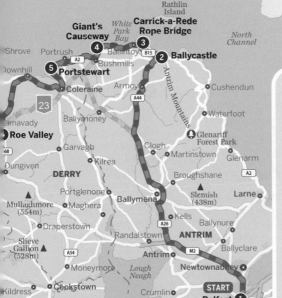

LINK YOUR TRIP

22 Iconic Ireland
Trip down to Dublin (four hours via the N3) to add the best of the south's attractions to your northern jaunt.

23 The Long Way Round
From Glencolumbcille head 53km west to Donegal to complete the west and south legs of this coastal tour of vibrant port cities and island treasures.

🛏 p351

The Drive » Pick up the B15 towards Ballintoy, which meanders up to a gorse-dotted coastal plateau where hills part to reveal bursts of the sea. As the road plunges downwards, take the right turn to the Carrick-a-Rede Rope Bridge (10km).

----

❸ Carrick-a-Rede Rope Bridge

The **Carrick-a-Rede Rope Bridge** (📞028-2073 3335; www.nationaltrust.org.uk/carrick-a-rede; 119 Whitepark Rd, Ballintoy; adult/child £10/5; ⊗9.30am-6pm Apr-Oct, to 3.30pm Nov-Mar) loops across a surging sea to a tiny island 20m offshore. This walkway of planks and wire rope sways some 30m above the waves, testing your nerve and head for heights. The bridge was originally put up each year by salmon fishers to help them set their nets, and signs along the 1km clifftop hike to the bridge detail the fascinating process.

Declining stocks have put an end to fishing, however. If you want to cross the bridge, it's best to book a ticket online in advance as numbers are limited.

The Drive » The B15 then the A2 snake west along clifftops and past views of White Park Bay's sandy expanse. Swing right onto the B146, passing Dunseverick Castle's fairy-tale tumblings, en route to the Giant's Causeway (11km).

TRIP HIGHLIGHT

❹ Giant's Causeway

Stretching elegantly out from a rugged shore, the **Giant's Causeway** (www.nationaltrust.org.uk; ⊗dawn-dusk) is one of the world's true geological wonders. Clambering around this jetty of fused geometric rock chunks, it's hard to believe it's not human-made. Legend says Irish giant Finn McCool built the Causeway to cross the sea to fight Scottish giant Benandonner. More prosaically, scientists tell

us the 60-million-year-old rocks were formed when a flow of molten basaltic lava cooled and hardened from the top and bottom inwards. It contracted and the hexagonal cracks spread as the rock solidified.

Entry to the Causeway site is free, but to use the National Trust car park you'll need to buy a ticket that includes the **Giant's Causeway Visitor Experience** (📞028-2073 1855; www.nationaltrust.org.uk; 60 Causeway Rd; adult/child £13.50/6.75; ⊗9am-7pm Jun-Sep, to 6pm Mar-May & Oct, to 5pm Nov-Feb).

The Drive » Continue west, through Bushmills, with its famous distillery, picking up the A2 Coastal Causeway route, signed to Portrush. You'll pass wind-pruned trees, crumbling Dunluce Castle and Portrush's long sandy beaches before arriving at Portstewart (16km).

----

❺ Portstewart

Time for some unique parking. Head through resort-town Portstewart, following signs for the **Strand** (beach). Ever-sandier roads descend to an immense shoreline that doubles as a car park for 1000 vehicles. It's a decidedly weird experience to drive and park (£7) on an apparently endless expanse of hard-packed sand. It's also at your own risk, which doesn't deter the locals (but do stick

CAUSEWAY COAST WALKS

The official **Causeway Coast Way** (www.walkni.com) stretches for 53km from Ballycastle to Portstewart, but individual chunks can be walked whenever you feel like stretching your legs. Day hikes include the supremely scenic 16.5km section between Carrick-a-Rede and the Giant's Causeway – one of the finest coastal walks in Ireland. Shorter options also abound, including a 2km ramble around Portrush, a 1.5km stroll on sandy White Park Bay and a 300m scramble around ruined Dunluce Castle.

to central, compacted areas). Nearby, a 1km **walking trail** meanders up a sand ladder, through huge dunes and past marram grass and occasional orchids.

🛏 p351

The Drive » Take the A2 west, through Coleraine towards Downhill. About 1km after the Mussenden Temple's dome appears, take Bishop's Rd left up steep hills with spectacular Lough Foyle views. Descend, go through Limavady and onto the B68 (signed Dungiven). Soon a brown Country Park sign points to Roe Valley (42km).

---

⑥ Roe Valley

This beguiling **country park** (Dogleap Rd; ⊘9am-dusk) is packed with rich reminders of a key Irish industry: linen production. The damp valley was ideal for growing the flax that made the cloth; the fast-flowing water powered the machinery. The **Green Lane Museum** (📞028-7776 0650; ⊘1-4.45pm Sat-Thu Jun-Aug, 1-4.45pm Sat & Sun Apr, May & Sep), near the car park, features sowing fiddles, flax breakers and spinning wheels. Look out for nearby watchtowers, built to guard linen spread out to bleach in the fields, and Scutch Mills, where the flax was pounded.

The Drive » Head back into Limavady to take the A2 west to Derry (28km). Green fields give way to suburbs then city streets.

TOP TIP: THE BORDER

Driving 20 minutes north out of Derry will see you entering another country: the Republic of Ireland. On road signs, be aware speed limits will suddenly change from mph to km/h, while wording switches from English to Irish and English. Stock up on euros in Derry or visit the first post-border ATM.

---

⑦ Derry

Northern Ireland's second city offers another powerful insight into the North's troubled past and the remarkable steps towards peace. It's best experienced on foot by walking the old city walls. Partway round, drop into the **Tower Museum** (www.derrystrabane.com/towermuseum; Union Hall Pl; adult/child £4/2; ⊘10am-5.30pm, last entry 4pm). Its imaginative Story of Derry exhibit leads you through the city's history, from the 6th-century monastery of St Colmcille (Columba) to the 1960s Battle of the Bogside.

🛏 p351

The Drive » The A2 heads north towards Moville. Soon speed-limit signs switch from mph to km/h: welcome to the Republic of Ireland. Shortly after Muff take the small left turn, signed Iskaheen, up the hill. Park beside Iskaheen church (11km).

---

⑧ Iskaheen

It's completely off the tourist trail, but Iskaheen church's tiny **graveyard** offers evidence of two of Ireland's most significant historical themes: the poverty that led to mass migration and the consequences of sectarian violence. One gravestone among many is to the McKinney family, recording a string of children dying young: at 13 years, 11 months, nine months and six weeks. It also bears the name of 34-year-old James Gerard McKinney, one of 13 unarmed civilians shot dead when British troops opened fire on demonstrators on Bloody Sunday, 1972.

The Drive » Rejoin the R238 north, turning onto the R240 to Carndonagh, climbing steeply into rounded summits. After quaint Ballyliffin and Clonmany, pick up the Inis Eoghain Scenic Route signs towards Mamore's Gap, and park at the Glenevin Waterfall car park.

---

⑨ Glenevin Waterfall

Welcome to Butler's Bridge – from here a 1km trail winds beside a

WHY THIS IS A GREAT TRIP
ISABEL ALBISTON, WRITER

Starting in Belfast, a city whose turbulent history seems finally to come second to its flourishing future, this trip gives a sense of the north's past and present while showcasing a stunning natural landscape so old – the striking hexagonal rocks of the Giant's Causeway date back 60 million years – it makes the region's troubles seem like a blip on the timeline.

Above: Derry
Left: Glenevin Waterfall
Right: Titanic Belfast, Belfast

APEXPHOTOS/GETTY IMAGES © ARCHITECT: ERIC KUHNE

stream through a wooded glen to Glenevin Waterfall, which cascades 10m down the rock face. It's an utterly picturesque, gentle, waymarked route – the perfect leg stretch.

🛏 p351

The Drive » The Inis Eoghain snakes south up to Mamore's Gap, a high-altitude, white-knuckle mountain pass that climbs 260m on single-lane, twisting roads, past shrines to the saints. After a supremely steep descent (and glorious views) go south through Buncrana, and on to Fahan (37km), parking beside the village church.

⑩ Fahan

St Colmcille founded a monastery in Fahan in the 6th century. Its creeper-clad ruins sit beside the church. Among them, hunt out the beautifully carved **St Mura Cross**. Each face of this 7th-century stone slab is decorated with a cross in intricate Celtic weave. The barely discernible Greek inscription is the only one known in Ireland from this early Christian period and is thought to be part of a prayer dating from 633.

The Drive » Take the N13 to Letterkenny, before picking up the R245 to Ramelton (aka Rathmelton), a 10km sweep north through the River Swilly valley. Turn off for the village, heading downhill to park beside the water in front of you (50km).

NORTH WEST 200 ROAD RACE

Driving this delightful coast can have its challenges, so imagine doing it at high speed. Each May the world's best motorcyclists do just that, going as fast as 300km/h in the **North West 200** (www.northwest200.org), which is run on a road circuit taking in Portrush, Portstewart and Coleraine. This classic race is Ireland's biggest outdoor sporting event and one of the last to take place on closed public roads anywhere in Europe. It attracts up to 150,000 spectators; if you're not one of them, it's best to avoid the area on the race weekend.

⑪ Rathmelton

In this picture-perfect town, rows of Georgian houses and rough-walled stone warehouses curve along the River Lennon. Strolling right takes you to a string of three-storey, three-bay Victorian warehouses; walking back and left up Church Rd leads to the ruined **Tullyaughnish Church** with its Romanesque carvings in the eastern wall. Walking left beside the river leads past Victorian shops to the three-arched, late-18th-century Ramelton Bridge.

🛏 p351

The Drive » Cross the town bridge, turning right (north) for Rathmullan. The hills of the Inishowen Peninsula rise ahead and Lough Swilly swings into view – soon you're driving right beside the shore. At Rathmullan (11km), make for the harbour car park.

⑫ Rathmullan

Refined, tranquil Rathmullan was the setting for an event that shaped modern Ireland. In 1607 a band of nobles boarded a ship here, leaving with the intention of raising an army to fight the occupying English. But they never returned. Known as the Flight of the Earls, it marked the end of the Irish (Catholic) chieftains' power. Their estates were confiscated, paving the way for the Plantation of Ulster with British (Protestant) settlers. Beside the sandy beach, look for the striking modern **sculpture**, depicting the earls' departure, waving to their distressed people as they left.

The Drive » Head straight on from the harbour, picking up Fanad/Atlantic Dr, a rollercoaster road that surges up Lough Swilly's shore, round huge Knockalla, past the exquisite beach at Ballymastocker Bay and around Fanad Head.

It then hugs the (ironically) narrow Broad Water en route to Carrigart (74km), with its village-centre horse-riding centre.

TRIP HIGHLIGHT

⑬ Carrigart

Most visitors scoot straight through laid-back Carrigart, heading for the swimming beach at Downings. But they miss a real treat: a horse ride on a vast beach. The **Carrigart Riding Centre** (☏074-915 3583, 087 227 6926; per hr adult/child €20/15; ☺10am-6pm) is just across the main street from sandy, hill-ringed Mulroy Bay, meaning you can head straight onto the beach for an hour-long ride amid the shallows and the dunes. Trips go on the hour, but it's best to book.

🛏 p351

The Drive » Head south for Creeslough. An inlet with a creamy, single-towered castle soon pops into view. The turn-off comes on the plain, where brown signs point through narrow lanes and past farms to Doe Castle (12km) itself.

⑭ Doe Castle

The best way to appreciate the charm of early-16th-century **Doe Castle** (☏086 843 7533; www.heritageireland.ie; Sheephaven Bay; tour €3; ☺grounds 9am-6pm, castle tours Jul & Aug only) is to wander the peaceful grounds, admiring its slender tower and crenellated battlements. The castle was the stronghold of the Scottish Mac-Sweeney family until it fell into English hands in the 17th century. It's a deeply picturesque spot: a low, water-fringed promontory with a moat hewn out of the rock.

The Drive » Near Creeslough, the bulk of Muckish Mountain rears up before the N56 to Dunfanaghy undulates past homesteads, loughs and sandy bays. Once in Dunfanaghy, with its gently kooky vibe, welcoming pubs and great places to sleep, look out for the signpost pointing right to Horn Head (25km).

- - - - - - - - - - - - - - - - -

⑮ Horn Head

This headland provides one of Donegal's best clifftop drives: along sheer, heather-clad quartzite cliffs with views of an island-dotted sea. A circular road bears left to the coastguard station – park to take the 20-minute walk due north to the signal tower. Hop back in the car, continuing east – around 1km later a viewpoint tops cliffs 180m high. There's another superb vantage point 1km further round – on a fine day you'll see Ireland's most northerly point, Malin Head.

The Drive » The N56 continues west. Settlements thin out, the road climbs and the pointed peak of Mt Errigal fills more and more of your windscreen before the road

swings away. At tiny Crolly follow the R259 towards the airport then turn right, picking up signs for Leo's Tavern (35km) in Meenaleck.

- - - - - - - - - - - - - - - - -

⑯ Meenaleck

You never know who'll drop by for one of the legendary singalongs at **Leo's Tavern** (☎074-954 8143; www.leostavern.com; off R259, Crolly; mains €10.50-14.50; ⊙kitchen 5-8.45pm Mon-Fri, from 1pm Sat & Sun, bar 4pm-midnight Mon-Fri, from noon Sat & Sun; 🛜) in Meenaleck. It's owned by Bartley Brennan, brother of Enya and her siblings Máire, Ciaran and Pól (aka the group Clannad). The pub glitters with gold, silver and platinum discs and is packed with musical mementos – there's live music nightly in summer.

The Drive » Continue west on the R259 as it bobbles

and twists besides scattered communities and an at-first-boggy then sandy shore. Head on to the pocket-sized port of Burtonport, following ferry signs right, to embark for Arranmore Island (25km).

- - - - - - - - - - - - - - - - -

TRIP HIGHLIGHT

⑰ Arranmore Island

Arranmore (Árainn Mhór) offers a true taste of Ireland. Framed by dramatic cliff faces, cavernous sea caves and clear sandy beaches, this 9km-by-5km island sits 5km offshore. Here you'll discover a prehistoric triangular fort and an offshore bird sanctuary fluttering with corncrakes, snipes and seabirds. Irish is the main language spoken, pubs put on turf fires and traditional-music sessions run late into the night. The **Arranmore Island Ferry** (☎074-954 2233, 074-952 0532;

DETOUR: FINTOWN RAILWAY

Start: ⑰ Arranmore Island

You've been driving for days now – time to let the train take the strain. The charming **Fintown Railway** (☎074-954 6280; www.antraen.com; off R250, Fintown; adult/child €8/5; ⊙11am-4pm Mon-Sat, 1-5pm Sun Jul & Aug, Thu-Sun only Jun & Sep) runs along a rebuilt 5km section of the former County Donegal Railway track beside picturesque Lough Finn. It's been lovingly restored to its original condition and a return trip in the red-and-white, 1940s diesel railcar takes around 40 minutes. From Burtonport head south on the R259 to Dungloe, then east on the N56 and R252 to reach the railway. Then settle back to enjoy the ride.

www.arranmoreferry.com; Burtonport; return adult/child €15/7, car & driver €30; ⊙4-8 daily sailings year-round) takes 20 minutes and runs up to eight times a day.

🛏 p351

The Drive » The R259 bounces down to Dungloe, where you take the N56 south into a rock-strewn landscape that's backed by the Blue Stack Mountains. After a stretch of rally-circuit-esque road, the sweep of Gweebarra Bay emerges. Take the sharp right towards peaceful Narin (R261), following signs to the beach (trá), 45km from Burtonport.

----

⑱ Narin

You've now entered the beautiful Loughrea Peninsula, which glistens with tiny lakes cupped by undulating hills. Narin boasts a spectacular 4km-long, wishbone-shaped Blue Flag beach, the sandy tip of which points towards **Iniskeel Island**. You can walk to the island at low tide along a 500m sandy causeway. Your reward? An intimate island studded with early Christian remains: St Connell, a

cousin of St Colmcille, founded a monastery here in the 6th century.

🛏 p351

The Drive » Continue south on the R261 through tweed-producing Ardara. Shortly after leaving town, take the second turning (the first turning after the John Malloy factory outlet), marked by a hand-painted sign to 'Maghera', following a road wedged between craggy hills and an increasingly sandy shore. In time the Assarancagh Waterfall (14km) comes into view.

----

⑲ Assarancagh Waterfall

Stepping out of the car reveals just what an enchanting spot this is. As the waterfall streams down the sheer hillside, walk along the road (really a lane) towards the sea. This 1.5km route leads past time-warp farms – sheep bleat and the tang of peat smoke scents the air. At tiny Maghera head through the car park, down a track, over a boardwalk and onto a truly stunning expanse of pure-white sand. This exquisite place belies a bloody past.

Some 100 villagers hid from Cromwell's forces in nearby caves – all except one were discovered and massacred.

The Drive » Drive west through Maghera on a dramatic route that makes straight for the gap in the towering hills. At the fork, turn right, heading deeper into the remote headland, making for Glencolumbcille (20km).

----

⑳ Glencolumbcille

The welcome in the scattered, pub-dotted, bayside village of Glencolumbcille (Gleann Cholm Cille) is warm. This remote settlement also offers a glimpse of a disappearing way of life. **Father McDyer's Folk Village** (www.glenfolkvillage.com; Doonalt; adult/child €6/5; ⊙10am-6pm Mon-Sat, from noon Sun Easter-Sep, 11am-4.30pm Oct) took traditional life of the 1960s and froze it in time. Its thatched cottages recreate daily life with genuine period fittings, while the Craft Shop sells local crafts, marmalade and whiskey truffles – a few treats at your journey's end.

Sleeping

Ballycastle ➋

🛏 An Caislean Guesthouse
Guesthouse ££

(📞028-2076 2845; 42 Quay Rd; s £40, d £70-80, f £90-120; P 📶) An Caislean has a large guest lounge and a warm and welcoming family atmosphere, just a few minutes' walk from the beach. Some rooms share bathrooms.

Portstewart ➎

🛏 Saltwater House
B&B £££

(📞028-7083 3872; www.saltwaterhouse.co.uk; 63 Strand Rd; d £120-150) More like a boutique hotel than a B&B, Saltwater House has four beautiful wooden-shuttered rooms, bike rental and an ocean-facing terrace. It also serves scrumptious breakfasts. Minimum two-night stay.

Derry ➐

🛏 Merchant's House
B&B ££

(📞028-7126 9691; www.thesaddlershouse.com; 16 Queen St; d from £85; @ 📶) This historic, Georgian-style townhouse is a gem of a B&B. It has an elegant lounge and dining room with marble fireplaces and antique furniture, TV, coffee-making facilities, homemade marmalade at breakfast and bathrobes in the bedrooms (some rooms have shared bathroom). Call at **Saddler's House** (36 Great James St; d from £75; 📶) first to pick up a key.

Glenevin Waterfall ➒

🛏 Glen House
Guesthouse €€

(📞074-937 6745; www.glenhouse.ie; Straid, Clonmany; s/d from €95/150; P 📶) Despite the grand surroundings and luxurious rooms, you'll find neither pretension nor high prices at Glen House, where rooms are a lesson in restrained sophistication and the setting is totally tranquil. Rooms at the front have gorgeous views of the lough, and the walking trail to Glenevin Waterfall and the Urris Hills is right next door.

Rathmelton ⓫

🛏 Frewin House
B&B €€

(📞074-915 1246; www.frewinhouse.com; Rectory Rd; s/d €125/170; 🕑Mar-Oct; P 📶) This fine Victorian rectory combines antique furniture and open fires with contemporary style. There's also a self-catering cottage available.

Carrigart ⓭

🛏 Beach
Hotel €€

(Óstán na Trá; 📞074 915 5303; www.beachhotel.ie; R248, Downings; d €110-150; P 📶) The bright, modern rooms at this large family-run hotel come in calming neutral tones and many have ocean views. You can refuel in its restaurant (mains €12 to €23). It's in Downings, 4km north of Carrigart.

Dunfanaghy ⓮

🛏 Corcreggan Mill
Guesthouse €

(📞074-913 6409; www.corcreggan.com; Castlebane, off N56; campsites €18, r €95, glamping from €90; @ 📶) As well as spotless double and family rooms in the lovingly restored former mill-house, Corcreggan has sites for camping and a number of quirky glamping cabins. The mill is 2.5km southwest of town.

Arranmore Island ⓱

🛏 Claire's B&B
B&B €

(📞074-952 0042; www.clairesbandb.wordpress.com; Leabgarrow; d €70; 📶) This modern house with simple rooms is right by the ferry port.

Narin ⓲

🛏 Carnaween House
B&B €€

(📞074-954 5122; www.carnaweenhouse.com; s/d from €60/110, cottage from €175; 📶) Carnaween House glows with brilliant white bedrooms in a luxury beach-house style – indeed, the sands on the adjoining beach are *almost* as white.

Musical Landscapes

From the busker-packed streets of Galway city, this rip-roaring ride guides you around County Clare and the Aran Islands to delight in fine festivals and traditional-music pubs.

26

TRIP HIGHLIGHTS

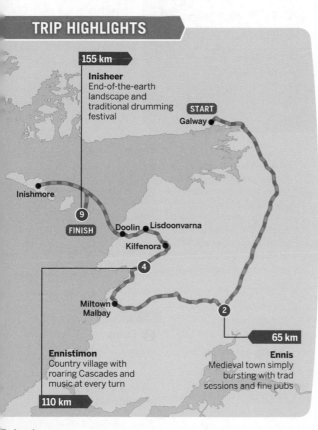

155 km

Inisheer
End-of-the-earth landscape and traditional drumming festival

START
Galway

Inishmore

9
FINISH

Doolin Lisdoonvarna
Kilfenora

4

Miltown Malbay

Ennistimon
Country village with roaring Cascades and music at every turn

110 km

2

Ennis
Medieval town simply bursting with trad sessions and fine pubs

65 km

5–6 DAYS
155KM / 96 MILES

GREAT FOR...

BEST TIME TO GO
The summer months for outdoor *céilidh* and music festivals.

ESSENTIAL PHOTO
Set-dancing at the crossroads, in Vaughan's of Kilfenora.

BEST FOR TUNES
Ennis, on summer nights, where local musicians showcase their skills.

26 Musical Landscapes

Prepare for an embarrassment of musical riches. Join the big bawdy get-togethers of Galway's always-on music scene and Ennis' rollicking urban boozers. Then take a seat at the atmospheric small pub sessions in crossroad villages like Kilfenora and Kilronan on the Aran Islands, where pretty much everyone joins in. Whatever way you like it, this region is undeniably one of Ireland's hottest for toe-tapping tunes.

Greatman's Bay

Gorumna Island Carraro
Lettermullen

Lettermullen Island

North Sound

Inishmore
⑧ Kilronan 23

Aran Islands *Inishma*

ATLANTIC OCEAN

0 ————— 10 km
0 ————— 5 miles

❶ Galway City

Galway (Gaillimh) has a young student population and a largely creative community that give a palpable energy to the place. Walk its colourful medieval streets, packed with heritage shops, street-side cafes and pubs, all ensuring there's never a dull moment. Galway's pub selection is second to none and some swing to tunes every night of the week. **Crane Bar** (☎091-587 419; www.thecranebar.com; 2 Sea Rd; ⊙10.30am-11.30pm Mon-Thu,

to 1am Fri, 12.30pm-1am Sat, to 11.30pm Sun), an atmospheric old pub west of the River Corrib, is the best spot in Galway to catch an informal *céilidh* most nights. Or for something more contemporary, **Róisín Dubh** (☎091-586 540; www.roisindubh.net; 9 Upper Dominick St; ⊙6pm-2am Sun-Thu, to 2.30am Fri & Sat) is *the* place to hear emerging international and local singer-songwriters.

✕ 🛏 p310, p361

The Drive » From Galway city centre, follow the coast road (R338) east out of town as

far as the M18 and then cruise south to Ennis (65km), where your great musical tour of Clare begins.

TRIP HIGHLIGHT

❷ Ennis

Ennis (Inis), a medieval town in origin, is packed with pubs featuring trad music. **Brogan's** (☎065-684 4365; www.brogansbarand

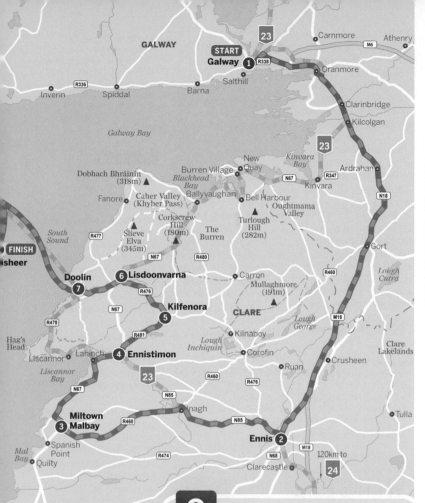

restaurant.com; 24 O'Connell St; ☺noon-midnight), on the corner of Cook's Lane, sees a fine bunch of musicians rattling even the stone floors almost every night in summer, while the wood-panelled **Poet's Corner Bar** (☎065-682 8127; www.oldgroundhotelennis. com/poets-corner-bar.html; Old Ground Hotel, O'Connell St; ☺11am-11pm Mon-Thu, to

🔗 LINK YOUR TRIP

23 The Long Way Round

From Galway, pick up this trip north or south for crenellated coastlines, vibrant port cities and island treasures.

24 Ring of Kerry

Head south to Killarney via Limerick to encounter jaw-dropping scenery around the Iveragh Peninsula.

12.30am Fri & Sat, noon-11pm Sun; 🎵) is a hideout for local musicians serious about their trad sessions. The tourist office collates weekly live music listings for the town's pubs. **Cois na hAbhna** (📞065-682 4276; www.coisnahabhna. ie; Gort Rd; ⏰opening hours vary), a pilgrimage point for traditional music and culture, has frequent performances and a full range of classes in dance and music; it's also an archive and library of Irish traditional music, song, dance and folklore. Traditional music aficionados might like to time a visit with **Fleadh Nua** (www.fleadhnua.com; ⏰May), a lively festival held in late May.

The Drive » From the N85, which runs south of the Burren, you'll arrive at the blink-and-you'll-miss-it village of Inagh. Swing right on to the smaller R460 for the run into Miltown Malbay – some 32km in all.

❸ Miltown Malbay

Miltown Malbay was a resort favoured by well-to-do Victorians, though the beach itself is 2km southwest at **Spanish Point**. To the north of the Point there are beautiful walks amid the low cliffs, coves and isolated beaches. A classically friendly place in the chatty Irish way, Miltown Malbay hosts the annual Willie Clancy Summer School, one of Ireland's great trad music events. In town, one of a couple of genuine old-style places with occasional trad sessions is **Friel's Bar** (Lynch's; 📞065-708 5883; Mullagh Rd; ⏰6pm-midnight Mon-Thu, to 1am Fri & Sat, 2pm-midnight Sun) – don't be confused by the much bigger sign on the front proclaiming 'Lynch's'. Another top music pub is the dapper **Hillery's** (📞065-708 4188; Main St; ⏰3pm-1am).

The Drive » Hugging the coast, continue north on the N67 until you come to the small seaside resort of Lahinch. Just a few streets backing a wide beach, it's renowned for surfing. From here, it's only 4km up the road to the lovely heritage town of Ennistimon.

TRIP HIGHLIGHT

❹ Ennistimon

Ennistimon (Inis Díomáin) is one of those charming market towns where people go about their business barely noticing the characterful buildings lining Main St. Behind this bustling facade there's a surprise: the roaring **Cascades**, the stepped falls of the River Inagh. After heavy rain they surge, beer-brown and foaming, and you risk getting drenched on windy days in the flying drizzle. Not to be missed, **Cooley's House** (📞065-707 1712; Main St; ⏰11am-11.30pm Mon-Thu, to 12.30am Fri & Sat, noon-11pm Sun) is a great trad pub, with music most nights in summer and several evenings a week in winter.

✕ 🛏 p361

The Drive » Heading north through a patchwork of green fields and stony walls on the R481, you'll land at the tiny village of Kilfenora, some 9km later. Despite its diminutive size, the pulse of Clare's music scene beats strongly in this area.

THE PIED PIPER

Half the population of Miltown Malbay seems to be part of the annual **Willie Clancy Summer School** (www.scoilsamhraidhwillieclancy.com; ⏰Jul), a tribute to a native son and one of Ireland's greatest pipers. The eight-day festival, now in its fourth decade, begins on the first Saturday in July, when impromptu sessions occur day and night, the pubs are packed and Guinness is consumed by the barrel – up to 10,000 enthusiasts from around the globe turn up for the event. Specialist workshops and classes underpin the event; don't be surprised to attend a recital with 40 noted fiddlers.

Galway City Boats at the city's docks

5 Kilfenora

Underappreciated Kilfenora (Cill Fhionnúrach) lies on the southern fringe of the Burren. It's a small place, with a diminutive 12th-century **cathedral** (off Main St; ☺9.30am-5.30pm Jun-Aug, 10am-5pm Mar-May, Sep & Oct) which is best known for its high crosses. The town has a strong music tradition that rivals that of Doolin, but without the crowds. The celebrated **Kilfenora Céili Band** (www.kilfenoraceiliband. com) has been playing for more than a century. Its traditional music features fiddles, banjos, squeeze boxes and more, and can be enjoyed most Wednesday evenings at **Linnane's Pub** (☎065-708 8157; Main St; ☺10.30am-11.30pm, hours can vary).

A short stroll away, **Vaughan's** (☎065-708 8004; www.vaughanspub.ie; Main St; ☺10.30am-11.30pm, hours can vary) has music in the bar every night during the summer and terrific set-dancing sessions in the neighbouring barn on Sunday nights.

The Drive » From Kilfenora the R476 meanders northwest 8km to Lisdoonvarna, home of

357

WHY THIS IS A GREAT TRIP
BELINDA DIXON, WRITER

To witness a proper traditional session in one of the music houses of Clare or the fine old pubs of Galway can be a transcendent experience, especially if it's appropriately lubricated with a pint (or few) of stout. Sure, there'll be plenty of tourists about, but this is authentic, traditional Ireland at its most evocative.

Above: Inishmore
Left: Guinness stout
Right: Buskers, Galway City

the international matchmaking festival. Posh during Victorian times, the town is a little less classy today, but friendly, good-looking and far less overrun than Doolin.

----

❻ Lisdoonvarna

Lisdoonvarna (Lios Dún Bhearna), often just called 'Lisdoon', is well known for its mineral springs. For centuries people have been visiting the local spa to swallow its waters. Down by the river at **Roadside Tavern** (☎065-707 4084; www. roadsidetavern.ie; Kincora Rd; ☺noon-11.30pm Mon-Thu, to 12.30am Fri & Sat, to 11pm Sun Mar-Oct, shorter hours Nov-Feb), third-generation owner Peter Curtin knows every story worth telling. There are trad sessions nightly in summer and on Friday and Saturday evenings in winter. Look for a trail beside the pub that runs 400m down to two **wells** by the river. A few paces from the tavern, the **Burren Smokehouse** (☎065-707 4432; www. burrensmokehouse.ie; Kincora Rd; ☺9am-6pm May-Aug, 10am-4pm Sep-Apr) is where you can learn about the ancient Irish art of oak-smoking salmon.

The Drive ❯❯ Just under 10 minutes' drive west, via the R478/479, you'll reach the epicentre of Clare's trad music scene, Doolin. Also known for its setting – 6km north of the Cliffs of Moher – Doolin is really three small neighbouring villages. First comes Roadford, then 1km west, sits Doolin itself, then another 1km west comes pretty Fisherstreet, nearest the water.

- - - - - - - - - - - - - - - -

❼ Doolin

Doolin gets plenty of press as a centre of Irish traditional music, owing to a trio of pubs that have sessions through the year. **McGann's** (☎065-707 4133; www.mcgannspubdoolin. com; Roadford; ⏰10am-11.30pm Mon-Wed, to 12.30am Thu-Sat, to 11pm Sun; 📶) has all the classic touches of a full-on Irish music pub; the action often spills out onto the street. Right on the water, **Gus O'Connor's** (☎065-707 4168; www.gusoconnors doolin.com; Fisherstreet; ⏰9.30am-midnight Mon-Thu, to 2am Fri-Sun), a sprawling favourite, has a rollicking atmosphere. It easily gets the most crowded and has the highest tourist quotient. **McDermott's** (MacDiarmada's; ☎065-707 4328; www.mcdermottspub. com; Roadford; ⏰10am-11.30pm Mon-Wed, to 12.30am Thu-Sat, to 11pm Sun) is a simple and sometimes rowdy old pub popular with locals. When the fiddles get going, it can seem like a scene out of a John Ford movie.

🛏 p361

The Drive » This 'drive' is really a sail – you'll need to leave your car at one of Doolin's many car parks to board the ferry (www.doolin2aranferries.com or www.doolinferry.com) to the Aran Islands.

- - - - - - - - - - - - - - - -

❽ Inishmore

The Aran Islands sing their own siren song to thousands of travellers each year, who find their desolate beauty beguiling. The largest and most accessible Aran, Inishmore (Inis Mór), is home to ancient fort Dun Aengus (p322), one of the oldest archaeological remains in Ireland, as well as some lively pubs and restaurants in the only town, **Kilronan**. Irish remains the local tongue, but most locals speak English with visitors. Tí Joe Watty's Bar (p361) is the best pub in Kilronan, with traditional sessions most summer nights. Turf fires warm the air on the 50 weeks a year when this is needed. Informal music sessions, glowing fires and a broad terrace with harbour views make **Tí Joe Mac's** (⏰11am-11pm Mon-Thu, 11am-12.30am Fri & Sat, noon-10pm Sun) another local favourite, as is **The Bar** (☎099-61130; www. inismorbar.com; ⏰noon-11pm Sun-Thu, 11.30am-midnight Fri & Sat), which has nightly live music from May to mid-October, and weekends the rest of the year.

✕ 🛏 p327, p361

The Drive » In the summer passenger ferries run regularly between the Aran Islands. They cost €10 to €15; schedules can be a little complex – book in advance.

- - - - - - - - - - - - - - - -

❾ Inisheer

On Inisheer (Inis Oírr), the smallest of the Aran Islands, the breathtakingly beautiful end-of-the-earth landscape adds to the island's distinctly mystical aura. Steeped in mythology, traditional rituals are very much respected here. Locals still carry out a pilgrimage with potential healing powers, known as the *Turas*, to the Well of Enda, an ever-burbling spring in the southwest. For a week in late June the island reverberates to the thunder of traditional drums during **Craiceann** (www. craiceann.com; ⏰late Jun). Bodhrán masterclasses, workshops and pub sessions are held, as well as Irish dancing. Rory Conneely's atmospheric inn **Tigh Ruairí** (Rory's; ☎099-75002; d €55-94; 📶) hosts live music sessions and, here since 1897, **Tigh Ned** (☎099-75004; www.tighned.com; dishes €7-15; ⏰kitchen noon-4pm Apr-Oct, bar 10am-11.30pm Apr-Oct) is a welcoming, unpretentious place, with harbour views and lively traditional music.

🛏 p361

Eating & Sleeping

Galway City ❶

🍴 Loam   Gastronomy €€€
(📞091-569 727; www.loamgalway.com; Fairgreen Rd; 2/3/7/9 courses €45/55/119/159; ⏱6-10pm Tue-Sat) Enda McEvoy is one of the most groundbreaking chefs in Ireland today (with a Michelin star to prove it), producing inspired flavour combinations from home-grown, locally sourced or foraged ingredients such as dried hay, fresh moss, edible flowers and hand-cut peat.

🛏 Glenlo Abbey Hotel   Historic Hotel €€€
(📞091-519 600; www.glenloabbeyhotel.ie; Kentfield Bushy Park, off N59; d €357-448, ste €538-984; 🛜) Set on the shores of Lough Corrib, 4km northwest of Galway, this 1740-built stone manor is the ancestral home of the Ffrench family, one of Galway's 14 tribes. Exceptionally preserved period architecture is combined with antique furnishings, sumptuous marble bathrooms, duck-down duvets and king-sized pillows.

Ennistimon ❹

🛏 Falls Hotel   Hotel €€
(📞065-707 1004; www.fallshotel.ie; off N67; s/d/f/tr €110/180/220/270; P🛜🏊) Built on the ruins of an O'Brien castle on the western edge of town, the vast, Georgian Falls Hotel was once the family home of Caitlín MacNamara, who married Dylan Thomas. Today it houses a large indoor pool, a spa and 142 modern rooms overlooking the rushing River Inagh and 20 hectares of wooded grounds.

Doolin ❼

🛏 Cullinan's Guesthouse   Inn €€
(📞065-707 4111; www.hoteldoolin.ie/cullinans -guesthouse.html; s €100, d €120-140; ⏱Mar-

Nov; P🛜) This mustard-coloured inn on the River Aille has eight spotless, comfortable, pine-furnished rooms. A couple of rooms are slightly smaller than the others, but have river views. There's also a lovely back terrace for enjoying the views.

Inishmore ❽

🍺 Tí Joe Watty's Bar   Pub €€
(📞086 049 4509; www.joewattys.ie; Kilronan; ⏱noon-midnight Sun-Thu, 11.30am-12.30am Fri & Sat Apr-Oct, 4pm-midnight Mon-Fri, noon-midnight Sat & Sun Nov-Mar) Warmed by peat fires, the island's oldest and most popular pub has trad sessions every night in summer from 9pm or 10pm, and weekends the rest of the year. Wednesday's darts night is a local fixture.

🛏 Pier House Guest House   Inn €€
(📞099-61417; www.pierhousearan.com; Kilronan; d from €100; 🛜) You won't have time to lose your sea legs on the 50m walk from the ferry to this two-storey inn set on a small rise. The 12 rooms are decorated in rich shades of red, and come with tea- and coffee-making facilities. The sun terrace at the front is the perfect spot to watch harbour life go by.

Inisheer ❾

🛏 South Aran
House & Restaurant   B&B €€
(📞099-75073; www.southaran.com; s/d €65/84; ⏱Apr-Oct; 🛜) There's an idyllic feel to this rustic B&B; lavender grows outside windows framing broad Atlantic views, and the four bedrooms have underfloor heating and wrought-iron beds. Breakfasts feature apple fritters with potato cakes and the evening restaurant (mains €17 to €25) showcases local seafood and organic produce; booking required.

NEED ᵀᴼ KNOW

CURRENCY
Republic of Ireland: euro (€)

Northern Ireland: pound sterling (£)

LANGUAGE
English, Irish

VISAS
Not required by most citizens of Europe, Australia, New Zealand, USA and Canada.

FUEL
Petrol (gas) stations are everywhere, but are limited on motorways. Expect to pay €1.40 per litre of unleaded (€1.30 for diesel) in the Republic, £1.25 for unleaded and diesel in Northern Ireland.

RENTAL CARS
Avis (www.avis.ie)

Europcar (www.europcar.ie)

Hertz (www.hertz.ie)

Thrifty (www.thrifty.ie)

IMPORTANT NUMBERS
Country code (☏ 353 Republic, ☏ 44 Northern Ireland)

Emergencies (☏ 999)

Roadside Assistance (☏ 1800 667 788, ☏ 0800 887 766 in Northern Ireland)

Climate

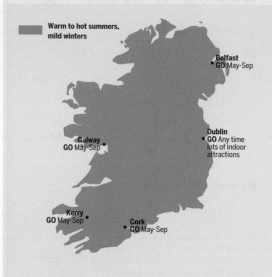

Warm to hot summers, mild winters

Belfast
GO May-Sep

Dublin
GO Any time lots of indoor attractions

Galway
GO May-Sep

Kerry
GO May-Sep

Cork
GO May-Sep

When to Go

High Season (Jun–mid-Sep)
》 Weather at its best.

》 Accommodation rates at their highest (especially in August).

》 Tourist peak in Dublin, Kerry and southern and western coasts.

Shoulder (Easter–May, mid-Sep–Oct)
》 Weather often good: sun and rain in May, often-warm 'Indian summers' in September.

》 Summer crowds and accommodation rates drop off.

Low Season (Nov–Easter)
》 Reduced opening hours from October to Easter; some destinations close.

》 Cold and wet weather throughout the country; fog can reduce visibility.

》 Big city attractions operate as normal.

Daily Costs

Budget: Less than €60
» Dorm bed: €12–20

» Cheap meal in cafe or pub: €6–12

» Pint: €4.50–5 (more expensive in cities)

Midrange: €60–120
» Double room in hotel or B&B: €80–180 (more expensive in Dublin)

» Main course in midrange restaurant: €12–25

» Car rental (per day): from €25–45

Top End: More than €120
» Four-star hotel stay: from €150

» Three-course meal in good restaurant: around €50

» Top round of golf (midweek): from €90

Eating

Restaurants From cheap cafes to Michelin-starred feasts, covering every imaginable cuisine.

Cafes Good for all-day breakfasts, sandwiches and basic dishes.

Pubs Pub grub ranges from toasted sandwiches to carefully crafted dishes.

Hotels All hotel restaurants take non-guests; a popular option in the countryside.

Price categories indicate the cost of a main dish:

Republic/Northern Ireland	
€/£	<€12/£12
€€/££	€12–25/£12–20
€€€/£££	>€25/£20

Sleeping

Hotels From chain hotels with comfortable digs to Norman castles with rainfall shower rooms – with prices to match.

B&Bs The ubiquitous B&B is the bedrock of Irish accommodation.

Hostels Feature clean dorms and wi-fi. Some have laundry and kitchen facilities.

Price categories indicate the cost of a double room in high season:

Republic/ Northern Ireland	
€/£	<€80/£50
€€/££	€80–180/£50–120
€€€/£££	>€180/£120

Arriving in Ireland

Dublin Airport
Rental cars The main rental agencies have offices at the airport.

Taxi €25–30; 30 to 45 minutes to the centre.

Bus €8; private coaches run every 10 to 15 minutes to the city centre.

Cork Airport
Rental cars There are car-hire desks for all the main companies.

Taxis A taxi to/from town costs €22 to €26.

Bus €2.80; every half hour between 6am and 10pm to the train station and bus station.

Dun Laoghaire Ferry Port
Train DART (suburban rail) takes about 25 minutes to the centre of Dublin.

Bus Public bus takes around 45 minutes to the centre of Dublin.

Mobile Phones

All European and Australasian phones work in Ireland, as do North American phones not locked to a local network. Check with your provider. Prepaid SIM cards cost from €10/£10.

Internet Access

Free wi-fi is available in most hotels, hostels and B&Bs, and in many bars and cafes.

Money

ATMs are widely available. Credit and debit cards can be used in most places, but check first. Chip-and-PIN is the norm for card transactions.

Tipping

Not obligatory, but 10% to 15% for good service in restaurants; €1/£1 per bag for hotel porters.

Useful Websites

Lonely Planet (lonelyplanet.com/ireland, lonelyplanet.com/ireland/northern-ireland) Travel tips, accommodation, recommendations and more.

Entertainment Ireland (www.entertainment.ie) Countrywide listings.

Failte Ireland (www.discoverireland.ie) Official tourist-board website for the Republic.

Northern Ireland Tourist Board (www.nitb.com) Official tourist-board website.

Language

Irish (Gaeilge) is the country's official language. In 2003 the government introduced the Official Languages Act, whereby all official documents and street signs must be either in Irish or in both Irish and English. Despite its official status, Irish is really only spoken in pockets of rural Ireland known as the Gaeltacht, the main ones being Cork (Corcaigh), Donegal (Dún na nGall), Galway (Gaillimh), Kerry (Ciarraí) and Mayo (Maigh Eo).

Ask people outside the Gaeltacht if they can speak Irish and nine out of 10 of them will probably reply, 'ah, cupla focal' (a couple of words), and they generally mean it – but many adults also regret not having a greater grasp of it. Irish is a compulsory subject in schools for those aged six to 15. In recent times, a new Irish curriculum has been introduced, cutting the hours devoted to the subject, but making the lessons more fun, practical and celebratory.

Irish divides vowels into long (those with an accent) and short (those without), and also distinguishes between broad (a, á, o, ó, u) and slender (e, é, i and í), which can affect the pronunciation of preceding consonants. Other than a few clusters, such as mh and bhf (both pronounced as w), consonants are generally pronounced the same as in English.

Irish has three main dialects: Connaught Irish (in Galway and northern Mayo), Munster Irish (in Cork, Kerry and Waterford) and Ulster Irish (in Donegal). Our pronunciation guides are an anglicised version of modern standard Irish, which is essentially an amalgam of the three – if you read them as if they were English, you'll be able to get your point across in Gaeilge without even having to think about the specifics of Irish pronunciation or spelling.

BASICS

Hello.
Dia duit.   deea gwit

Hello. (reply)
Dia is Muire duit.   deeas moyra gwit

Good morning.
Maidin mhaith.   mawjin wah

Good night.
Oíche mhaith.   eekheh wah

Goodbye. (when leaving)
Slán leat.   slawn lyat

Goodbye. (when staying)
Slán agat.   slawn agut

Yes.
Tá.   taw

No.
Níl.   neel

It is.
Sea.   sheh

It isn't.
Ní hea.   nee heh

Thank you (very) much.
Go raibh (míle)   goh rev (meela)
maith agat.   mah agut

Excuse me.
Gabh mo leithscéal.   gamoh lesh scale

I'm sorry.
Tá brón orm.   taw brohn oruhm

Do you speak (Irish)?
An bhfuil (Gaeilge) agat?   on wil (gaylge) oguht

I don't understand.
Ní thuigim.   nee higgim

What is this?
Cad é seo?   kod ay shoh

Want More

For in-depth language information and handy phrases, check out Lonely Planet's *Irish Language & Culture*. You'll find it at **shop.lonelyplanet.com**.

Signs

Dúnta	Closed
Gardaí	Police
Leithreas	Toilet
Ná Caitear Tobac	No Smoking
Oifig An Phoist	Post Office
Oifig Eolais	Tourist Information
Oscailte	Open
Páirceáil	Parking
Fir	Men
Mná	Women

What is that?
Cad é sin? — kod ay shin

I'd like to go to ...
Ba mhaith liom — baw wah lohm
dul go dtí ... — dull go dee ...

I'd like to buy ...
Ba mhaith liom ... — bah wah lohm ...
a cheannach. — a kyanukh

another/one more
ceann eile — kyawn ella

nice
go deas — goh dyass

MAKING CONVERSATION

Welcome.
Ceád míle fáilte. — kade meela fawlcha
(lit: 100,000 welcomes)

Bon voyage!
Go n-éirí an bóthar leat! — go nairee on bohhar lat

How are you?
Conas a tá tú? — kunas aw taw too

I'm fine.
Táim go maith. — thawm go mah

... please.
... más é do thoil é. — ... maws ay do hall ay

Cheers!
Slainte! — slawncha

What's your name?
Cad is ainm duit? — kod is anim dwit

My name is (Sean Frayne).
(Sean Frayne) is ainm dom. — (shawn frain) is anim dohm

Impossible!
Ní féidir é! — nee faydir ay

Nonsense!
Ráiméis! — rawmaysh

That's terrible!
Go huafásach! — guh hoofawsokh

Take it easy.
Tóg é gobogé . — tohg ay gobogay

DAYS OF THE WEEK

Monday	*Dé Luaín*	day loon
Tuesday	*Dé Máirt*	day maart
Wednesday	*Dé Ceádaoin*	day kaydeen
Thursday	*Déardaoin*	daredeen
Friday	*Dé hAoine*	day heeneh
Saturday	*Dé Sathairn*	day sahern
Sunday	*Dé Domhnaigh*	day downick

NUMBERS

1	*haon*	hayin
2	*dó*	doe
3	*trí*	tree
4	*ceathaír*	kahirr
5	*cúig*	kooig
6	*sé*	shay
7	*seacht*	shocked
8	*hocht*	hukt
9	*naoi*	nay
10	*deich*	jeh
11	*haon déag*	hayin jague
12	*dó dhéag*	doe yague
20	*fiche*	feekhe
21	*fiche haon*	feekhe hayin

STRETCH YOUR LEGS
DUBLIN

Start/Finish: Trinity College

Distance: 4.9km

Duration: 3 hours

Dublin's most important attractions are concentrated on the south side of the Liffey, split between the older medieval town dominated by the castle and the two cathedrals, and the handsome 18th-century city that is a showcase of exquisite Georgian aesthetic.

Take this walk on Trips

Trinity College

Ireland's most prestigious **university** (📞01-896 1000; www.tcd.ie; College Green; ⏰8am-10pm; 🚌all city centre, 🚊Westmoreland or Trinity) is a masterpiece of architecture and landscaping, and Dublin's most attractive bit of historical real estate, beautifully preserved in Georgian aspic.

The Walk » From Trinity College, walk west along Dame St and turn into Dublin Castle.

Chester Beatty Library

The world-famous **library** (📞01-407 0750; www.chesterbeatty.ie; Dublin Castle; ⏰9.45am-5.30pm Thu-Tue, to 8pm Wed, closed Mon Nov-Feb; 🚌all city centre), in the grounds of Dublin Castle, houses the collection of mining engineer Sir Alfred Chester Beatty (1875–1968). Spread over two floors, the breathtaking collection includes more than 20,000 manuscripts, rare books, miniature paintings, clay tablets, costumes and other objects of historical and aesthetic importance.

The Walk » Exit the castle and walk west; you'll see Christ Church directly in front of you.

Christ Church Cathedral

Its hilltop location and eye-catching flying buttresses make this the most photogenic by far of Dublin's three **cathedrals** (Church of the Holy Trinity; www.christchurchcathedral.ie; Christ Church Pl; adult/student/child €8/6.50/3.50; ⏰9.30am-7pm Mon-Sat, 12.30-3pm & 4.30-7pm Sun Apr-Sep, shorter hours Oct-Mar; 🚌50, 50A, 56A from Aston Quay, 54, 54A from Burgh Quay) as well as one of the capital's most recognisable symbols. It was founded in 1030 on what was then the southern edge of Dublin's Viking settlement. The Normans rebuilt the lot in stone from 1172.

The Walk » Go south along Nicholas St (which becomes New St); St Patrick's is 400m along.

St Patrick's Cathedral

It was at this **cathedral** (📞01-453 9472; www.stpatrickscathedral.ie; St Patrick's Close;

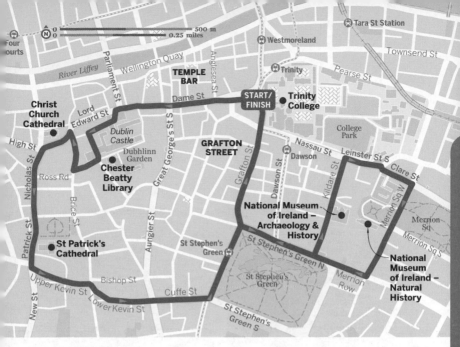

adult/student €8/7; ⏰9.30am-5pm Mon-Fri, 9am-6pm Sat, 9-10.30am, 12.30 2.30pm & 4.30-6pm Sun Mar-Oct, shorter hours Nov-Feb; 🚌50, 50A, 56A from Aston Quay, 54, 54A from Burgh Quay), reputedly, that St Paddy himself dunked the Irish heathens into the waters of a well. Although there's been a church here since the 5th century, the present building dates from 1190 or 1225 (opinions differ).

The Walk » Just south of St Patrick's, turn left onto Kevin St and keep going until you reach St Stephen's Green; turn onto Kildare St.

National Museum of Ireland – Archaeology & History

The star attraction of this branch of the **National Museum of Ireland** (www.museum.ie; Kildare St; ⏰10am-5pm Tue-Sat, 1-5pm Sun & Mon; 🚌all city centre) is the Treasury, home to the finest collection of Bronze Age and Iron Age gold artefacts in the world, and the world's most complete collection of medieval Celtic metalwork.

The Walk » Walk north on Kildare St and turn right on Nassau St, then stay right on Clare St.

National Museum of Ireland – Natural History

Dusty, weird and utterly compelling, and a window into Victorian times, this **museum** (www.museum.ie; Upper Merrion St; ⏰10am-5pm Tue-Sat, 1-5pm Sun & Mon; 🚌7, 44 from city centre) has barely changed since Scottish explorer Dr David Livingstone opened it in 1857 – before disappearing into the African jungle for a meeting with Henry Stanley.

The Walk » Turn right onto Merrion Row, skirt St Stephen's Green and go right into Grafton St to head back to Trinity College.

Spain

SPECTACULAR BEACHES, MOUNTAINTOP CASTLES, MEDIEVAL VILLAGES, STUNNING ARCHITECTURE and some of the most celebrated restaurants on the planet – Spain has an allure that few destinations can match. There's much to see and do amid the enchanting landscapes that inspired Picasso and Velàzquez. You can spend your days feasting on seafood in coastal Galician towns, feel the heartbeat of Spain at soul-stirring flamenco shows or hike across the flower-strewn meadows of the mountains. The journeys in this region offer something for everyone: beach lovers, outdoor adventurers, family travellers, music fiends, foodies and those simply wanting to delve into Spain's rich art and history.

Alicante View over the city's waterfront
WILLIAM87/GETTY IMAGES ©

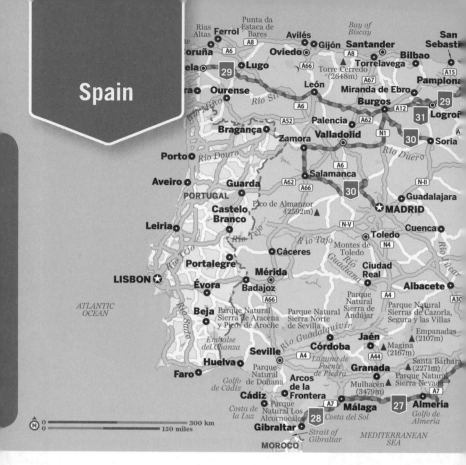

Spain

27 **Mediterranean Meander 7 Days**
Over 1000km of coastline celebrating the ever-changing Mediterranean.

28 **Costa del Sol**
Beyond the Beaches 3–4 Days
More than touristy resorts on the misunderstood southern coast.

29 **Northern Spain**
Pilgrimage 5–7 Days
Roads that crisscross the Camino de Santiago pilgrim route.

30 **Historic Castilla y León 7 Days**
Madrid to Soria via some of inland Spain's captivating towns and villages.

31 **Roving La Rioja**
Wine Region 2–3 Days
Discover the wealth of the grape on this peaceful countryside drive.

 DON'T
MISS

Cabo de Gata

A slice of arid coastline that the developers forgot to dig up. Fortunately, it's now protected in a natural park and sports abundant flora and birdlife. Explore it on Trip 27

Orchidarium

Meander through Europe's largest orchid collection, in the Costa del Sol beach town of Estepona, on Trip 28

Meeting God

From rock-cut churches to the Camino de Santiago, Islamic monuments to the pagan hills of Fisterra, there's always somewhere to commune with your God along Trip 29

Covarrubias

Step behind the walls of this stunning riverside village and into another world on Trip 30

Wine Tasting

La Rioja is home to the best red wines in Spain – bodegas, tours, tastings and museums will inform as you consume on Trip 31

Mediterranean Meander

From Málaga to Barcelona, discover the treasures of Spain's Mediterranean seaboard – Roman ruins, dramatic castles, artistic masterpieces and fabulous festivals.

27

TRIP HIGHLIGHTS

1107 km

Barcelona
Stretch your legs on La Rambla, Barcelona's celebrated boulevard

Tarragona
12
FINISH

756 km

Valencia
See the future at the cutting edge Ciudad de las Artes y las Ciencias

9
Xàtiva

Cartagena

START
1
Mojácar
4

Málaga
Admire works by Picasso in his hometown

1 km

Cabo de Gata
Precious enclave of pure unblemished Mediterranean coastline

249km

**7 DAYS
1107KM / 688 MILES**

GREAT FOR...

BEST TIME TO GO

March to June is sunny, but not too hot, and there are plenty of festivals, including Las Fallas.

ESSENTIAL PHOTO

The chameleonic Sagrada Familia changes every time you visit.

BEST FOR OUTDOORS

Parque Natural de Cabo de Gata-Nijar.

---

27 Mediterranean Meander

From the Costa Daurada to the Costa del Sol, from Catalan pride to Andalucian passion, from Roman ruins in Tarragona to Barcelona's flamboyant Modernisme buildings: this drive provides technicolour proof that not all southern Spain is a beach bucket of cheesy tourist clichés. The full 1107km trajectory passes through four regions, two languages, Spain's second, third and sixth largest cities, and beaches too numerous to count.

TRIP HIGHLIGHT

1 Málaga

The Costa del Sol can seem a pretty soulless place until you hit Málaga, the Andalucian city everyone is talking about. For decades the city was overlooked by the millions of tourists who crowded the Costa's seaside resorts but in recent years it has transformed itself into a hip, stylish metropolis brimming with youthful vigour. It boasts 30-odd museums and an edgy urban art scene as well as contemporary restaurants, boutique hotels and stylish shopping.

Art-lovers are spoiled for choice at museums such as the **Museo Ruso de Málaga** (📞951 92 61 50; www.coleccionmuseo ruso.es; Avenida de Sor Teresa Prat 15; €6, incl temporary exhibitions €8, free 4-8pm Sun; ⏱9.30am-8pm Tue-Sun; P) and **Centre Pompidou Málaga** (📞951 92 62 00; www.centrepompidou.es; Pasaje Doctor Carrillo Casaux, Muelle Uno; €7, incl temporary exhibition €9; ⏱9.30am-8pm Wed-Mon), while the **Museo de Málaga** (📞951 91 19 04; www.museosdeandalucia. es/museodemalaga; Plaza de la Aduana; EU member/non-member free/€1.50; ⏱9am-9pm Tue-Sat, to 3pm Sun) houses an extensive archaeology collection. The city's premier museum is the unmissable **Museo Picasso Málaga** (📞952 12 76 00; www.museopicassoma laga.org; Calle San Agustín 8; €9, incl temporary exhibition €12, free last 2hr before closing Sun; ⏱10am-8pm Jul & Aug, to 7pm Mar-Jun, Sep & Oct, to 6pm Nov-Feb), dedicated to the Málaga-born artist.

For an edgier, urban scene head to the **Soho**

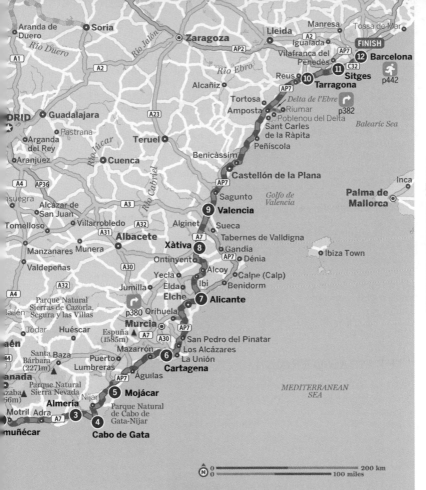

neighbourhood near the port where you'll find giant murals, arty cafes, ethnic restaurants and street markets.

 p386

The Drive » Head east out of Málaga on the A7. This is southern Spain's main coastal road (also known as the E15) and will be your companion for much of this trip. The coast

LINK YOUR TRIP

28 Costa del Sol Beyond the Beaches

Can't get enough of the Mediterranean? Jump on this trip in Málaga and hug the coast all the way to Gibraltar.

30 Historic Castilla y León

From Barcelona it's nearly six hours west to Madrid, but you'll encounter some of Spain's most captivating historic towns and villages.

375

gets ever more precipitous as you move east into Granada province. After 68km turn south on the N340 and follow for 8km into Almuñécar.

----

2 Almuñécar

There's a hint of Italy's Amalfi Coast about the Costa Tropical, Granada province's 80km coastline. Named for its subtropical microclimate, it's often dramatically beautiful, with dun-brown mountains and whitewashed villages huddled into coves and bays. The area's main resort is the popular summer destination of Almuñécar.

Summer action is focused on Almuñécar's long seafront whose two beaches are divided by a rocky outcrop, the **Peñón del Santo** (⊙7am-midnight May-Sep, 8am-10pm Oct-Apr). To the west of this stretches the pebbly **Playa de San Cristóbal**, while to the east the grey-sanded **Playa Puerta del Mar** fronts the old town.

Up in the *casco antiguo*, the small **Museo Arqueológico Cueva de Siete Palacios** (☑958 83 86 23; Calle San Joaquín; combined ticket Castillo de San Miguel adult/child €2.35/1.60; ⊙10am-1.30pm & 6.30-9pm Tue-Sat, 10am-1pm Sun Jul–

mid-Sep, shorter hours mid-Sep–Jun) displays ancient finds in a series of underground stone cellars. Tickets also include entry to the hilltop **Castillo de San Miguel** (☑650 027584; Explanada del Castillo; combined ticket Museo Arqueológico adult/child €2.35/1.60, free 10am-1pm Fri; ⊙10am-1.30pm & 6.30-9pm Tue-Sat, 10am-1pm Sun Jul-mid-Sep, shorter hours mid-Sep–Jun).

The Drive » Continue eastwards on the A7, skirting around Motril and passing increasing numbers of unsightly plastic greenhouses as the landscape becomes ever more arid. Almería beckons. All told, it's about 130km to Almería.

----

3 Almería

Don't overlook Almería, an energetic waterfront city with an illustrious past. Once the main port for the 10th-century Córdoba caliphate, the sun-baked city has a handsome centre, punctuated by palm-fringed plazas and old churches, as well as several museums and plenty of fantastic tapas bars. Its main draw is its spectacular **Alcazaba** (☑950 80 10 08; Calle Almanzor; ⊙9am-3pm & 7-10pm Tue-Sat mid-Jun–mid-Sep, 9am-8pm Tue-Sat Apr–mid-Jun, 9am-6pm Tue-Sat mid-Sep–Mar, 9am-3pm Sun year-round), once one of the most powerful Moorish fortresses in Spain.

At the foot of the hilltop fort sprawls the maze-like **Almedina**, the

THE PICASSO TRAIL

Málaga and Barcelona are linked by more than Mediterranean beaches – both cities have a strong connection with Pablo Ruiz Picasso (1881-1973). The great painter was born in Málaga and spent the first 10 years of his life there. In 1891 he and his family moved to A Coruña and then, in 1895, he transferred to Barcelona where he lived on and off during the early 1900s.

In Málaga you can get an intimate insight into the painter's childhood at the **Casa Natal de Picasso** (www.fundacionpicasso.malaga.eu; Plaza de la Merced 15; €3, incl Sala de Exposiciones €4; ⊙9.30am-8pm, closed Tue Nov-Mar), the house where he was born in 1881. Nearby, the **Museo Picasso Málaga** (p374) displays more than 200 of his works. The collection at the **Museu Picasso** (p385) in Barcelona is even larger, comprising around 3500 works, many from his formative early years.

On a more modest scale, Alicante's **Museo de Arte Contemporáneo** (p380) displays his *Portrait d'Arthur Rimbaud* (1960), while the **Museu Cau Ferrat** (p384) is housed in the Sitges home of his friend, the late artist Santiago Rusiñol.

old Moorish quarter. Continue through this to the city's six-towered **cathedral** (🕿605 396483; www.catedralalmeria.com; Plaza de la Catedral 8, entrance Calle Velázquez; €5; ⏱10am-7pm Mon-Fri, 10am-2.30pm & 3.30-7pm Sat, 1.30-7pm Sun Apr-Sep, to 6:30pm Oct-Mar), another formidable structure with an impressive Gothic interior. Nearby, the **Museo de la Guitarra** (🕿950 27 43 58; Ronda del Beato Diego Ventaja; adult/reduced €3/2; ⏱10.30am-1.30pm Tue-Sun year-round, plus 6-9pm Tue-Sat Jun-Sep, 5-8pm Tue-Sat Oct-May) charts Almería's role in the development of the iconic instrument.

Round off your sightseeing with a soak at the **Hammam Aire de Almería** (🕿950 28 20 95; www.beaire.com; Plaza de la Constitución 5; 1½hr session €29 Mon-Thu, €35 Fri-Sun; ⏱9am-10.30pm), a modern-day version of an Arabic bathhouse.

🍴 p386

The Drive » Head east out of Almería on the N340a to join up with the AL12 airport road and its continuation the N344. Continue on this, following signs to San José through a series of small roundabouts near Retamar. Eventually you should emerge onto the AL3108 which runs through low hills to Cabo de Gata (total distance 40km).

- - - - - - - - - - - - - - - - -

TRIP HIGHLIGHT

④ Cabo de Gata

Covering Spain's southeastern tip, the **Parque Natural de Cabo de Gata-Níjar** boasts some of Andalucía's most flawless and least crowded beaches. These glorious *playas* lie strung along the area's dramatic cliffbound coastline while inland remote white villages dot the stark, semi-desert hinterland.

On the park's east coast, the low-key resort of **San José** makes an ideal base. It's well set up with hotels and restaurants and the surrounding coastline hides several sublime beaches. The most beautiful, including **Playa de los Genoveses** (🅿) and **Playa de Mónsul** (🅿), are accessible by a dirt road signposted 'Playas' and/or 'Genoveses/Mónsul.'

For more active pursuits, you can walk the park's coastal paths or organise diving, kayaking, bike hire and guided tours at agencies across town – try **Medialun-**Aventura** (🕿667 224861; www.medialunaventura.com; Calle del Puerto 7; rental per hour/day kayak €12/40, double kayak €18/60, SUP €12/45, bike hire per half-day/day €15/20; ⏱9am-2pm & 5-8pm, to 10pm summer).

The Drive » Follow the AL3108 inland from San José until you hit the A7 just shy of Níjar. Head northeast towards Valencia for 43km to exit 520. Come off here and follow signs to Mojácar along the A370 and AL6111.

- - - - - - - - - - - - - - - - -

⑤ Mojácar

Tucked away in an isolated corner of Almería province, Mojácar is both a seaside resort and a charming hill town. Mojácar Pueblo, a picturesque jumble of white-cube houses, sits atop a hillside 3km inland from Mojácar Playa, a modern low-rise resort fronting 7km of sandy beach.

Exploring Mojácar Pueblo is mainly a matter

TOP TIP: TOLL ROADS

The AP7 (also known as E15), is a toll-charging *autopista* (motorway) that parallels much of Spain's southern and eastern coastlines. You will have to stop periodically to pay a toll at manned booths. However, as of 1 January 2020, tolls were scrapped on the AP7 between Tarragona and Alicante.

The confusingly named A7 follows a similar route to the AP7, but is entirely toll-free. The N340 is a third road paralleling Spain's southern coast, although much of it has merged with the A7. Some of the N340 follows the route of the Roman Vía Augustus.

WHY THIS IS A GREAT TRIP
DUNCAN GARWOOD, WRITER

What makes this epic coastal drive so special is the sheer variety it provides. There's history and culture galore with Roman ruins in Tarragona, Picasso paintings in Málaga and modern architecture in Barcelona and Valencia. Boisterous beach resorts offer hedonism and hard partying while peace-lovers will enjoy the unsullied coastal beauty of Cabo de Gata, one of Andalucía's great natural highlights.

Above: Playa de Mónsul, Cabo de Gata
Left: Centre Pompidou Málaga, Málaga
Right: Museo del Teatro Romano, Cartagena

of wandering its maze-like streets, stopping off at craft shops, galleries and boutiques. You can see how life in the town once was at the **Casa La Canana** (📞950 16 44 20; Calle Esteve 6, Mojácar Pueblo; adult/child €2.50/1; 🕐10.30am-2.30pm daily, plus 5-8pm Tue, Wed, Fri & Sat), and admire sweeping views from the lofty **Mirador del Castillo** (Plaza Mirador del Castillo, Mojácar Pueblo).

Down at Mojácar Playa, you'll find the best sands at the southern end of town, which also has a pleasant seafront promenade.

🛏 p386

The Drive » Retrace your steps from Mojácar back onto the northbound A7. After 10km merge onto the toll-charging AP7 near Vera and continue to the exit for Cartagena Oeste. Take this and follow the signposted route along the N332 into the city. Mojácar to Cartagena is 134km.

- - - - - - - - - - - - - - - - - -

❻ Cartagena

Cartagena's fabulous natural harbour has been used for thousands of years. Stand on the battlements of the castle that overlooks the city and you can literally see layer upon layer of history spread below you, from the wharf where Phoenician traders docked their ships to the streets where Roman legionaries once marched,

DETOUR: ORIHUELA

Start: ⑥ Cartagena

Beside the Río Segura and flush with the base of a barren mountain of rock, Orihuela harbours some superb Gothic, Renaissance and baroque buildings. Its old town, once the second city of the kingdom of Valencia, is strung out between the river and the castle-capped mountain.

Standout sights include the 14th-century Catalan Gothic **Catedral de San Salvador** (📞965 30 48 28; Calle Doctor Sarget; adult/child €2/free; ⏱10.30am-2pm & 4-6.30pm Mon-Fri, 10.30am-2pm Sat), which features three finely carved portals and an exquisite two-level cloister. Nearby, the **Museo Diocesano de Arte Sacro** (📞673 425 681; Calle Mayor de Ramón y Cajal; adult/child €4/free; ⏱10am-2pm & 4-7pm Mon-Sat, 10am-2pm Sun) has a fine display of religious art, culminating in Velázquez' *Temptation of St Thomas*. Also worth searching out is the **Colegio de Santo Domingo** (📞965 30 02 40; http://colegio.cdsantodomingo.com; Calle Adolfo Clavarana; adult/child €2/1; ⏱9.30am-1.30pm or 2pm & 4-7pm or 5-8pm Tue-Fri, from 10am Sat, 10am-2pm Sun), a 16th-century convent with two fine Renaissance cloisters.

To reach Orihuela, branch west off the AP7 around 60km north of Cartagena and continue on the CV945 and CV95.

towards Alicante. After 75km the autopista rejoins the A7. Follow this for 32km before taking exit 17A signposted for Alicante.

- - - - - - - - - - - - - - - - - -

⑦ Alicante

Of all mainland Spain's provincial capitals, Alicante is the most tourist-driven. Nevertheless, it's a dynamic, attractive city with a castle, old quarter and long waterfront. The eating scene is exciting and the nightlife is legendary.

There are sweeping views over the city from the large 16th-century **Castillo de Santa Bárbara** (📞965 15 29 69; www.castillodesantabarbara.com; Calle Vázquez de Mella; ⏱10am-10pm Apr-Sep, to 8pm Oct-Mar), which also houses a museum recounting the history of Alicante. Further historical artefacts await in the **Museo Arqueológico de Alicante** (MARQ; 📞965 14 90 00; www.marqalicante.com; Plaza Dr Gómez Ulla; adult/child €3/1.50; ⏱10am-7pm Tue-Fri, 10am-8.30pm Sat, 10am-2pm Sun mid-Sep–mid-Jun, 10am-2pm & 6-10pm Tue-Sat, 10am-2pm Sun mid-Jun–mid-Sep) which has a strong collection of ceramics and Iberian art. For a more contemporary outlook, the free **Museo de Arte Contemporáneo de Alicante** (MACA; 📞965 21 31 56; www.maca-alicante.es; Plaza Santa María 3; ⏱10am-8pm Tue-Sat, from 11am summer, 10am-2pm Sun) impresses with its

from the factories of the industrial age to the contemporary warships of what is still an important naval base.

As archaeologists continue to unearth the city's ancient roots, it is finally starting to get the recognition it deserves. Highlights include the **Museo Nacional de Arqueología Subacuática** (ARQUA; 📞968 12 11 66; http://museoarqua.mcu.es; Paseo de Alfonso XII 22; adult/child €3/free, Sat afternoon & Sun free; ⏱10am-8pm or 9pm

Tue-Sat, 10am-3pm Sun), an excellent museum dedicated to underwater archaeology and maritime history, and the **Museo del Teatro Romano** (www.teatroromanocartagena.org; Plaza del Ayuntamiento 9; adult/child €6/5; ⏱10am-8pm Tue-Sat, 10am-2pm Sun May-Sep, 10am-6pm Tue-Sat, 10am-2pm Sun Oct-Apr), centred on a 1st-century BCE Roman theatre.

✗ p386

The Drive » Double back to the AP7 and head north

displays of works by the likes of Dalí, Miró, Picasso and others.

🍴 p386

The Drive » Leave Alicante on the A77 signposted Valencia and continue on to the A7. The autovia proceeds north, passing through a couple of tunnels and heading progressively downhill as it forges inland towards Valencia. After almost 90km, exit on the CV645 signposted Xàtiva. From here it's about 5km to the town.

----

❽ Xàtiva

Xàtiva (Spanish: Játiva) is often visited on a day trip from Valencia or, as in this case, as a stop on the way north from Alicante. It has an intriguing historic quarter and a mighty castle strung along the crest of the Serra Vernissa, with the town snuggled at its base.

The Muslims established Europe's first paper manufacturing plant in Xàtiva, which is also famous as the birthplace of the Borgia Popes Calixtus III and Alexander VI. The town's glory days ended in 1707 when Felipe V's troops torched most of the town.

Xàtiva's **castle** (📞962 274 274; www.xativaturismo.com; adult/child €2.40/1.20; 🕙10am-6pm Tue-Sun Nov-Mar, to 7pm Apr-Oct), which clasps the summit of a double-peaked hill overlooking the old town, is one of the most evocative in the Valencia region.

Behind its crumbling battlements you'll find flower gardens (bring a picnic), tumbledown turrets, towers and other buildings. The walk up to the castle is a long one (2km), but the views are sensational.

The Drive » Use the N340 to rejoin the A7 and head north to Valencia. Just outside the city, where the A7 merges with the AP7, take the V31, Valencia's main southern access road for the final push into the city centre. All told, the 63km journey should take around 50 minutes.

TRIP HIGHLIGHT

❾ Valencia

Valencia, Spain's third-largest city, exudes confidence. Content for Madrid and Barcelona to grab the headlines, it quietly gets on with being a wonderfully liveable spot, hosting thriving cultural, eating and nightlife scenes. Its star attraction is the strikingly futuristic **Ciudad de las Artes y las Ciencias** (City of Arts & Sciences; 📞961 97 46 86; www.cac.es; Avenida del Professor

⬤ LOCAL KNOWLEDGE: FESTIVALS

If you're undertaking this trip in February, March or August, look out for the following festivals.

Feria de Malaga (www.feria.malaga.eu; 🕙mid-Aug) Málaga's nine-day *feria* (fair), launched by a huge fireworks display, is the most ebullient of Andalucía's summer *ferias*. Head for the city centre to be in the thick of it. At night, festivities switch to large fairgrounds and nightly rock and flamenco shows at Cortijo de Torres, 3km southwest of the city centre.

Las Fallas de San José (www.fallas.com; 🕙Mar) The exuberant, anarchic swirl of Las Fallas de San José – fireworks, music, festive bonfires and all-night partying – is a must if you're visiting Valencia in mid-March. The *fallas* themselves are huge papier mâché sculptures satirising celebrities, current affairs and local customs. After midnight on the final day, each *falla* goes up in flames.

Sitges Carnaval (www.visitsitges.com; 🕙Feb/Mar) Carnaval in Sitges is a sparkly week-long booze-soaked riot, complete with masked balls and capped by extravagant gay parades on the Sunday and Tuesday, featuring flamboyantly dressed drag queens, giant sound systems and a wild all-night party.

López Piñero;) on the old Turia riverbed. Counting an opera house, science museum, 3D cinema and aquarium, the complex was largely the work of local-born starchitect Santiago Calatrava.

Other brilliant contemporary buildings grace the city, which also has a fistful of fabulous Modernista buildings, great museums, a long stretch of beach and a large, characterful old quarter. Look out for **La Lonja** (📞962 08 41 53; www.valencia.es; Calle de la Lonja; adult/child €2/1, Sun free; 🕙10am-7pm Mon-Sat, to 2pm Sun), Valencia's late 15th-century silk and commodity exchange, and the **Mercado Central** (📞963 82 91 00; www.mercadocentralvalencia.es; Plaza del Mercado; 🕙7.30am-3pm Mon-Sat), the vast Modernista market.

The city also enjoys premiership foodie credentials, as the home of paella but its buzzing dining scene offers plenty more besides.

 p386

The Drive › Leave Valencia on the V21 signposted Puçol. After 23km or so you'll rejoin your old friend, the AP7, which will whisk you 200km up the coast into Catalonia. Come off at exit 38 and continue on the A7 for the final 35km into Tarragona. Reckon on 257km for the entire leg.

---

⑩ Tarragona

In the effervescent port city of Tarragona, Roman history collides with beaches, bars and a food scene that perfumes the air with freshly grilled seafood. The main drawcard is the city's collection of ancient ruins, including those housed in a mosaic-packed museum and a seaside amphitheatre where gladiators once faced each other (or wild animals) in mortal combat. The Unesco-listed Roman sites are scattered around town but you can get a combined ticket at the **Museu d'Historia de Tarragona** (MHT; www.tarragona.cat/patrimoni/museu-historia; adult per site/4 sites/all sites €3.30/7.40/11.05, children free).

A roll-call of fantastic places to eat and drink is a good reason to linger in the attractive medieval centre. This maze of cobbled lanes is encircled by steep walls and crowned by a towering **cathedral** (www.catedraldetarragona.com; Plaça de la Seu; adult/child €5/3; 🕙10am-8pm Mon-Sat mid-Jun–mid-Sep, to 7pm Mon-Sat mid-Mar–mid-Jun & mid-Sep–Oct, to 5pm Mon-Fri, to 7pm Sat Nov–mid-Mar) with Romanesque and Gothic flourishes.

 p387

↱ **DETOUR: DELTA DE L'EBRE**

Start: ⑨ Valencia

Near Catalonia's southern border, the Delta de l'Ebre is a remote, exposed place of reed-fringed lagoons, dune-backed beaches and mirror-smooth marshes. Some 78 sq km are protected in the **Parc Natural del Delta de l'Ebre**, northern Spain's most important waterbird habitat. Migration season (October and November) sees bird populations peak, but birds are also numerous in winter and spring. Even if you're not a twitcher, the park is worth a visit. The landscape, with its whitewashed farmhouses and electric-green rice paddies, is hauntingly beautiful and the flat waterside trails are ideal for cyclists and ramblers.

Scruffy **Deltebre** sits at the centre of the delta but smaller villages like **Riumar** or **Poblenou del Delta** are more appealing.

To reach Deltebre, branch off the AP7 at exit 41, 180km north of Valencia. Take the N340 to connect with the TV3454 which leads to the town some 13km to the east.

Valencia Traditional Valencian paella

The Drive » From Tarragona use the N240 to get back on the AP7 and head east towards Barcelona. After about 11km take exit 31 onto the C32. Follow this for just over 30km, crossing one viaduct and burrowing through two tunnels, to Sitges.

⓫ Sitges

Just 40km shy of Barcelona, Sitges has been a favourite beach resort since the 19th century. The former fishing village, which was a key location for the Modernisme art movement and is now one of Spain's premier gay destinations, is renowned for its party beach life, riotous carnival celebrations and hedonistic nightlife – at its most bacchanalian in July and August. Despite this, it remains a classy destination with a good array of galleries and museums and plenty of restaurants in its boutique-laden historic centre.

Sunseekers will enjoy its long sandy beach which is flanked by the seafront **Passeig Maritim**. The cultural highlight is the **Museu del Cau Ferrat** (www. museusdesitges.cat; Carrer de Fonollar; incl Museu de Maricel adult/child €10/free; ☉10am-8pm Tue-Sun Jul-Sep, to 7pm Mar-Jun & Oct, to 5pm Nov-Feb), built in the 1890s as a house-studio by artist Santiago Rusiñol – a pioneer of the Modernisme movement. The whitewashed mansion is full of his own art and that of his contemporaries, including his friend Picasso.

The Drive » It's only 40km to Barcelona. Get back onto the toll-charging C32 and fly through a multitude of tunnels. After about 30km, exit at junction 16B and follow signs for Barcelona, Gran Via and Centre Ciutat.

TRIP HIGHLIGHT

⓬ Barcelona

Barcelona is a guidebook in itself and a cultural colossus to rival Paris or Rome. The city's ever-evolving symbol is Gaudí's **Sagrada Familia** (☎93 208 04 14; www. sagradafamilia.org; Carrer de la Marina; adult/child €20/free; ☉9am-8pm Apr-Sep, to 7pm Mar & Oct, to 6pm Nov-Feb; Ⓜ Sagrada Família), which rises like an unfinished symphony over L'Eixample district. The surrounding neighbourhood is renowned for its Modernisme architecture, which appears in buildings such as **La Pedrera** (Casa Milà; ☎93

LEGACY OF THE ROMANS

What did the Romans ever do for us? Well, quite a lot actually, as you'll discover as you drive up Spain's Mediterranean coast.

The Roman colonies in Hispania (their name for the Iberian peninsula) lasted from around 400 BCE to 200 BCE, and reminders of their existence lie dotted along the coast, from Andalucía to Catalonia.

In **Málaga** you can admire an **amphitheatre** (Roman Theatre; ☎951 50 11 15; Calle Alcazabilla 8; ☉10am-6pm Tue-Sat, to 4pm Sun), dating from the 1st century CE when the settlement was called Malaca. An adjacent interpretive centre outlines its history and displays a few artefacts unearthed on the site.

Cartagena (Carthago Nova to the Romans) boasts several Roman sites, including the **Museo del Teatro Romano** (p380), centred on a 1st-century BCE Roman theatre.

Further north, **Tarragona** (Tarraco) was once capital of Rome's Spanish provinces and has ruins to prove it, including an **amphitheatre** (Parc de l'Amfiteatre; adult/child €3.30/free; ☉9am-9pm Tue-Sat Easter-Sep, to 7pm Tue-Sat Oct-Easter, to 3pm Sun year round), a forum, street foundations and the two-tiered **Aqüeducte de les Ferreres** (Pont del Diable; ☉24hr; Ⓟ). Ocean-themed mosaics can be seen in the nearby **Museu Nacional Arqueològic de Tarragona** (www.mnat.cat; Plaça del Rei 5).

Sitges A popular beach-resort town

214 25 76; www.lapedrera.com; Passeig de Gràcia 92; adult/child 7-12 yrs from €25/14; ⏲9am-8.30pm & 9-11pm Mar-Oct, 9am-6.30pm & 7-9pm Nov-Feb; Ⓜ Diagonal), a madcap Unesco-listed masterpiece with a rippling grey-stone facade and chimney pots resembling medieval knights. For more conventional, historical sights head to the Barri Gótic, home to the city's vast Gothic **cathedral** (📞93 342 82 62; www.catedralbcn.org; Plaça de la Seu; €7, roof or choir €3, chapter house €2; ⏲worship 8.30am-12.30pm & 5.45-7.30pm Mon-Fri, 8.30am-12.30pm & 5.15-8pm Sat, 8.30am-1.45pm & 5.15-8pm Sun, tourist visits 12.30-7.45pm Mon-Fri, 12.30-5.30pm Sat, 2-5.30pm Sun; Ⓜ Jaume I), and the medieval La Ribera quarter where you'll find the excellent **Museu Picasso** (📞93 256 30 00; www.museupicasso. bcn.cat; Carrer de Montcada 15-23; adult/concession/under 18yr permanent collection & temporary exhibit €14/7.50/free, 6-9.30pm Thu & 1st Sun of month free; ⏲10am-5pm Mon, 9am-8.30pm Tue, Wed & Fri-Sun, to 9.30pm Thu; Ⓜ Jaume I).

A good orientation point in this complex city is **La Rambla** (Ⓜ Catalunya, Liceu, Drassanes) whose tree-lined pedestrian promenade was made with the evening *paseo* (stroll) in mind. La Rambla divides the Barri Gòtic and La Ribera from the bohemian, multi-cultural El Raval neighbourhood. To the northeast lies the Modernisme-inspired L'Eixample quarter; to the south are the steep parks and gardens of Montjuic, site of the 1992 Olympics.

✕ ⏢ p387

Eating & Sleeping

Málaga ❶

✗ El Mesón de Cervantes
Tapas €€

(📞952 21 62 74; www.elmesondecervantes.
com; Calle Álamos 11; medias raciones €4-10,
raciones €8-18; ⊙7pm-midnight Wed-Mon)
Cervantes started as a humble tapas bar run
by expat Argentine Gabriel Spatz, but has now
expanded into four bar-restaurants (each with a
slightly different bent), all within a block of each
other. This one is the HQ, where pretty much
everything on the menu is a show-stopper –
lamb stew with couscous; pumpkin and
mushroom risotto; and, boy, the grilled octopus!

⨮ Molina Lario
Hotel €€€

(📞952 06 20 02; www.hotelmolinalario.com;
Calle Molina Lario 20; d €198-325; ❄🌐🏊)
Situated within confessional distance of the
cathedral, this four-star hotel has gracious
service and a sophisticated, contemporary
feel. The spacious, remodelled rooms are
decorated in subdued tones of beige and
white, with natural wood, crisp white linens and
marshmallow-soft pillows. Topping it all off is a
fabulous rooftop terrace and pool with views to
the sea and the cathedral.

Almería ❸

✗ Casa Puga
Tapas €€

(📞950 23 15 30; www.barcasapuga.es; Calle
Jovellanos 7; tapas from €1.70, raciones €7-18;
⊙noon-4pm & 8pm-midnight Mon-Sat) For an
authentic tapas experience, make a beeline for
this long-standing favourite, on the go since
1870. Shelves of ancient wine bottles and walls
plastered with lottery tickets and ancient maps
set the scene while well-practised waiters work
the bar, dishing out classical tapas prepared at
the tiny cooking station. Arrive early or expect
crowds.

Mojácar ❺

⨮ Hostal El Olivar
Hostal €

(📞950 47 20 02; www.hostalelolivar.es; Calle
Estación Nueva 11, Mojácar Pueblo; d incl

breakfast €53-70; ❄🌐) Friendly owners
Alberto and Michaela have completely
revamped this stylish boutiquey hostal, with
new paint, curtains, bedspreads, mini-fridges,
handmade furniture and a massage room.
Three rooms have balconies, and there's a
delightful sun terrace for lounging or lingering
over breakfast. An olive theme runs throughout,
with olive oil soaps and a tree whose 'leaves' are
handwritten notes from past guests.

Cartagena ❻

✗ La Marquesita
Spanish €€

(📞968 50 77 47; www.lamarquesita.net; Plaza
Alcolea 6; mains €13-24; ⊙1-4.30pm Tue, Wed
& Sun, 1-4.30pm & 8-11.30pm Thu-Sat; 🌐) On a
tucked-away plaza just off the pedestrian main
drag, this place is easily spotted by its riot of pot
plants. Sit in or out to enjoy quality fish dishes in
particular, with other traditional plates on offer.
The €22.50 weekday set lunch is excellent – you
might get a whole sea bass as a main.

Alicante ❼

✗ Cervecería Sento
Tapas €

(www.somossento.es; Calle Teniente Coronel
Chápuli 1; tapas €2-10; ⊙9am-midnight Sun-
Thu, to 1am Fri & Sat) Top-notch *montaditos*
(little rolls) and inventive grilled tapas (try the
turrón and pork 'Chupa Chups') are the reason
to squeeze into this brilliant little bar. Watching
the cheeky, nonstop staff in action is quite an
experience too: they make every visit intriguing.
It has bigger branches nearby, but this one has
the atmosphere.

Valencia ❾

✗ Delicat
Tapas €€

(📞963 92 33 57; Calle Conde Almodóvar 4;
dishes €8-18; ⊙1.45-3.30pm & 8.45-11.30pm
Tue-Sat, 1.45-3.30pm Sun; 🌐) At this
particularly friendly, intimate option, the open
kitchen offers an unbeatable-value set menu of
samplers for lunch (€14.50) and delicious tapas

choices for dinner. The decor isn't lavish but the food is memorable, with a range of influences at play. It's best to book ahead as the small space fills fast.

🛏 Caro Hotel · · · · · · · · · · · · · · · · Hotel €€€

(📞963 05 90 00; www.carohotel.com; Calle Almirante 14; d €170-350; 🅿 ❄ 🛜) Housed in a sumptuous 19th-century mansion, this hotel sits atop two millennia of Valencian history, with restoration revealing a hefty hunk of the Arab wall, Roman column bases and Gothic arches. Each room is furnished in soothing dark shades, with a great king-size bed and varnished concrete floors. Bathrooms are tops. For special occasions, reserve the Marqués suite, once the ballroom.

Tarragona ⑩

✕ Mercat Central · · · · · · · · · · · · · · Market €

(Plaza Corsini; ⌚8.30am-9pm Mon-Sat) In a striking Modernista building, this historic 1915 market is looking better than ever thanks to a €47-million renovation completed in 2017. Temptations abound, from delectable fruits to cheeses and bakery items, plus food counters doling out seafood, charcuterie, sushi and Catalan wines. There's also a supermarket hidden downstairs.

🛏 Hotel Plaça de la Font · · · · · · Hotel €€

(📞977 24 61 34; www.hotelpdelafont.com; Plaça de la Font 26; s/d/tr €63/80/100; ❄ 🛜) Comfortable modern rooms, individually decorated with photos of local monuments, make this cheerful, convenient hotel one of

Tarragona's most attractive options. Rooms at the front have tiny balconies and are well soundproofed from the sociable murmur on bustling Plaça de la Font below. With tables right on the square, the hotel cafe is perfect for light breakfasts (€6).

Barcelona ⑫

✕ Tapas 24 · · · · · · · · · · · · · · · · · · · Tapas €

(📞93 488 09 77; www.carlesabellan.com; Carrer de la Diputació 269; tapas €4-12; ⌚9am-midnight; 🛜; Ⓜ Passeig de Gràcia) Hotshot chef Carles Abellán runs this basement tapas haven known for its gourmet renditions of old faves, including the *bikini* (toasted ham-and-cheese sandwich, here with truffle and cured ham), freshly cooked tortilla and zesty lemon-infused *boquerones* (anchovies). You can't book, but it's worth the wait. For dessert, try the creamy *payoyo* cheese. Before 1pm, pop in for superb *entrepans* (filled rolls) and omelettes.

🛏 Praktik Rambla · · · · · · Boutique Hotel €€

(📞93 343 66 90; www.hotelpraktikrambla. com; Rambla de Catalunya 27; s/d/tr from €122/135/169; ❄ 🛜; Ⓜ Passeig de Gràcia) On a leafy boulevard, this early-19th-century gem of a mansion hides a gorgeous little boutique number designed by beloved local interior designer Lázaro Rosa-Violán. While high ceilings, patterned walls and original tiles have been maintained, the 43 rooms have bold ceramics, spot lighting and contemporary art. The relaxed library and back terrace are perfect for enjoying the complimentary coffee and croissants.

Costa del Sol Beyond the Beaches

28

Discover the Costa's most celebrated resorts, as well as some little known gems and the culturally vibrant city of Málaga on this sunny coastal jaunt.

TRIP HIGHLIGHTS

76 km

Torremolinos
Dine on fresh seafood in a former fishing barrio

58 km

Málaga
Get high on culture at Málaga's superb museums

 START

● Nerja

② ③

Mijas●

Fuengirola●

⑥

Estepona●

● **Gibraltar**
FINISH

Marbella
Explore Marbella's picturesque historic centre

135km

3–4 DAYS
208 KM/ 129 MILES

GREAT FOR...

BEST TIME TO GO
March to June or September to November when temperatures are cooler and traffic less.

 ESSENTIAL PHOTO
The old town in Marbella when the bougainvillea is in bloom.

 BEST FOR FAMILIES
Beaches, theme parks, and the Andalucian love for kids.

Costa del Sol Beyond the Beaches

This drive from Nerja in the east to Gibraltar in the west leads through a constantly shifting landscape, taking you from orchards of subtropical fruit trees to shimmering white resorts, from a culture-loving metropolis to the cobbled backstreets of a former fishing village. Be prepared for a trip that challenges any preconceived ideas you may have about this, Spain's most famous, tourist-driven coastline.

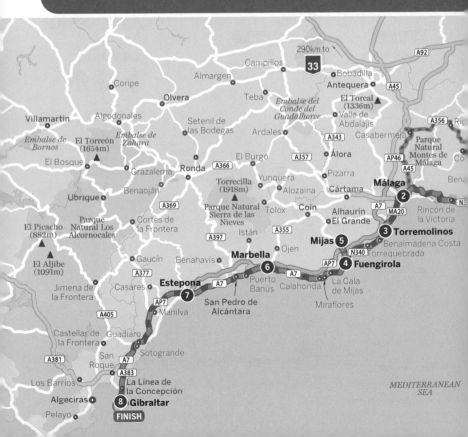

❶ Nerja

Sitting in a charmed spot at the base of the Sierra Almijara mountains, this former fishing village has retained its low-rise village charm, despite the proliferation of souvenir shops and the large number of visitors it sees. At its heart is the **Balcón de Europa**, a seafront balcony built over the site of a Moorish castle. Grab a coffee at one of the terraced cafes before heading north of town to the extraordinary **Cueva de Nerja** (www.cuevadenerja.es; adult/child €14/12; ☉10am-

4.30pm Sep-Jun, to 7pm Jul & Aug). This 4km-long cave complex, which dates back a cool five million years, is a wonderland of extraordinary rock formations, subtle shifting colours, stalactites and stalagmites.

The Drive » The quickest route to Málaga is via the main A7 (E15). More scenic, if slower, is the N340 which meanders along the coast, traversing pretty agricultural land and bypassing centuries-old watchtowers. At Rincón de la Victoria join the A7 for the last few kilometres into Málaga. It's a total drive of 58km (1¼ hours).

- - - - - - - - - - - - - - - -

TRIP HIGHLIGHT

❷ Málaga

Book a night or two to get the best out of Málaga. The city positively crackles with energy, hosting a buzzing bar life and vibrant restaurant scene. It also boasts genuine cultural credentials and its art museums are seriously impressive – check out the **Museo Carmen**

Thyssen (www.carmenthys senmalaga.org; Calle Compañía 10; €10, afternoons 2.30-4pm €6; ☉10am-8pm Tue-Sun), the Museo Ruso (p374) and the unmissable Museo Picasso (p374), dedicated to the city's most famous son. A short walk away, the 16th-century **Catedral de Málaga** (☎952 22 03 45; www.malagacatedral.com; Calle Molina Lario; cathedral & Ars Málaga €6, incl roof €10; ☉10am-6pm Sat, 2-6pm Sun year-round, 10am-8pm Mon-Fri Apr-Jun & Oct, to 9pm Jun-Sep, to 6.30pm Nov-Mar) offers fabulous rooftop views and an interior bedecked with gorgeous retables (a raised shelf above an altar) and 18th-century religious art. Travel further back in time at the Roman Amphitheatre (p384) and adjacent **Alcazaba** (☎952 22 72 30; http://alcaza-baygibralfaro.malaga.eu; Calle Alcazabilla 2; €3.50, incl Castillo de Gibralfaro €5.50; ☉9am-8pm Apr-Oct, to 6pm Nov-Mar), a fascinating 11th-century Moorish palace-fortress.

LINK YOUR TRIP

27 **Mediterranean Meander**

Málaga is the start of this east-coast adventure that takes in several of Spain's most stunning cities, including its final destination: Barcelona.

32 **Alentejo & Algarve Beaches**

For more stunning coast, head west via Seville to the Portuguese border then on to Cacela Velha to do the Algarve trip in reverse. (349km).

DETOUR: FRIGILIANA

Start: ❶ Nerja

After the cavernous gloom of the Cueva de Nerja, consider heading inland to Frigiliana, a *pueblo blanco* once voted Andalucía's prettiest by the Spanish tourism authority. It's an enchanting place with a tangible Moroccan feel and a steeply-banked old town of pretty, whitewashed houses. Wander its quaint streets and pick up some of its famous sweet wine and honey in the small village shops.

It's a straightforward 7km drive from Nerja: take the M5105 inland, passing groves of mango and avocado trees, and follow signs to the *casco historico* (old town) and car park.

✗ 🛏 p397

The Drive » Leaving Málaga, take the A7 in the direction of Algecíras, Torremolinos and Cádiz, then follow the MA20 signposted to Torremolinos. This is a busy stretch of autovía that passes the airport. It's a drive of about 18km or 25 minutes.

TRIP HIGHLIGHT

❸ Torremolinos

Torremolinos, once the poster child of industrial-scale package tourism, now attracts a wide cross-section of people, including trendy clubbers, beach-loving families, gay visitors and, yes, even some Spanish tourists. The centre of town revolves around the pedestrian shopping street **Calle San Miguel**, from where steps lead down to the main beach at **Playamar** (Torremolinos). To the southwest, round a small rocky outcrop (La Punta), **La Carihuela** (Torremolinos) is a former fishing *barrio* which is now, fittingly, home to some hugely popular seafood restaurants such as **Casa Juan** (📞952 37 35 12; www.losmellizos.net; Calle San Ginés 20, La Carihuela; mains €14-22; ⏲1-4.30pm & 8pm-midnight Tue-Sat, 1-4.30pm Sun). The beachfront *paseo* continues to Benalmádena, Torre's western twin, where you'll find a large marina designed as a kind of homage to Gaudí and a giant **Buddhist stupa** (www.stupabenalmade na.org; Benalmádena Pueblo; ⏲10am-2pm & 4-6.30pm Tue-Sun; 🅿).

✗ p397

The Drive » It's a straightforward 17km drive to Fuengirola on the N340, which hugs the coast and passes through the busy coastal resort of Benalmádena Costa. Note that there's a 50km speed limit on this scenic stretch.

---

❹ Fuengirola

Fuengirola's appeal, apart from its 7km of beaches, lies in the fact that it is a genuine Spanish working town, as well as a popular resort. It has a large population of foreign residents, many of whom arrived in the '60s and stayed long after their ponytails had gone grey. Stop by **Plaza de la Constitucíon**, a pretty square overlooked by the baroque-style facade of Fuengirola's main church, then explore the surrounding streets lined with idiosyncratic shops and tapas bars. A five-minute walk away, the **Bioparc** (📞952 66 63 01; www.bioparcfuengirola.es; Avenida Camilo José Cela; adult/child €22/17; ⏲10am-sunset; 🅿) is the Costa's best zoo with spacious enclosures and conservation and breeding programmes.

The Drive » From Fuengirola, take Avenida Alcalde Clemente Díaz Ruiz then the Carretera de Mijas to join the A387. This crosses the A7 and continues up to Mijas about 9km (20 minutes) away. In Mijas follow signs to the underground car park (€1 for 24 hours).

---

❺ Mijas

The *pueblo blanco* (white village) of Mijas has retained its sugar-cube cuteness despite being on the coach-tour circuit. Art buffs should check out the **Centro de Arte Contemporáneo de Mijas**

(CAC; www.cacmijas.info; Calle Málaga 28; adult/child €3/ free; ☺10am-6pm Mon-Sat), a contemporary art museum that houses the world's second-largest collection of Picasso ceramics. Otherwise the village is all about strolling the narrow cobbled streets, dipping into tapas bars and shopping for souvenirs. Be sure to walk up to the **Plaza de Toros**, an unusual square-shaped bullring at the top of the village, surrounded by lush ornamental gardens with spectacular coastal views. For more exercise, there are numerous trails leading out from the village, including a tough, well-marked route up to **Pico Mijas** (1151m) – allow about five hours to get there and back.

The Drive » Return to the A7 autovia. This dual carriageway traverses the most densely built-up stretch of the Costa, passing through resorts like Calahonda and Miraflores that were developed during the Costa's 1980s boom period. Continue west along the A7 until you reach the exit for Marbella; a total drive of 33km or 25 minutes.

- - - - - - - - - - - - - - -

TRIP HIGHLIGHT

❻ Marbella

Marbella is the Costa del Sol's most high-profile resort town and a good choice for an overnight stop. Well known for its star-studded clubs, shiny restaurants and expensive

hotels, it also has other, less ostentatious charms: a magnificent natural setting, sheltered by the beautiful Sierra Blanca mountains, and a gorgeous old town replete with pristine white houses, narrow traffic-free lanes and well-tended flower boxes. At its heart is picturesque **Plaza de los Naranjos**, dating back to 1485 with tropical plants, palms and orange trees. From here you can walk down to the seafront via the lush **Parque de la Alameda** gardens. Follow along the so-called **Golden Mile** (actually, it's about 6km) and you'll eventually reach the

luxurious marina of **Puerto Banús**. En route, take time to check out the **Museo Ralli** (www. museoralli.es; Urbanización Coral Beach; ☺10am-3pm Tue-Sat), a wonderful private museum displaying works by primarily Latin American and European artists in bright, well-lit galleries.

✕ ⌂ p397

The Drive » Continue west on the A7 autovia, following signs to Algeciras and Cádiz. This stretch of highway is less built up and passes by San Pedro de Alcántara, as well as five golf courses (they don't nickname this the Costa del Golf for nothing!). It's a snappy 20

DETOUR: COMARES

Start: ❷ Málaga

Heading northeast from Málaga brings you to La Axarquía, an area of rugged hiking country stippled with pretty, unspoiled *pueblos* (villages). A highlight, quite literally, is Comares which sits like a snowdrift on a lofty mountain (739m), commanding spectacular views over the surrounding mountains. Stroll its steep winding lanes and don't miss the remarkable summit cemetery. There are also several walking trails that start here, as well as a 436m-long zip line, the **Tirolina de Comares** (1/2 rides €15/20), which provides a 50-second ride over to the opposite slopes. This is generally open on an appointment-only basis so it's best to book a ride through an activity company like **Vive Aventura** (☎697 218289; www.viveaventura.es). To get to Comares from Málaga, take the A45 towards Granada, Córdoba and Seville, then exit for Casabermeja and continue onto Comares via the A356 (through Riogordo) and MA3107. The journey is about 60km and should take about 70 minutes.

WHY THIS IS A GREAT TRIP
DUNCAN GARWOOD, WRITER

Loud, brash and always fun, Spain's most famous Costa makes for a wonderfully entertaining trip. Our route reveals the sunshine coast in all its gaudy glory, taking in Malaga's cultural hits, a giant Buddhist stupa in party-loving Torremolinos, and Marbella's star-studded seafront. Providing the grand finale is Gibraltar, the legendary Rock that guards the gateway to the Mediterranean.

Above: Málaga
Left: Sardines, Torremolinos
Right: St Michael's Cave, Gibraltar

LEONID ANDRONOV/SHUTTERSTOCK ©

minutes or just 24km to your
next stop: Estepona.

- - - - - - - - - - - - - - - - - -

❼ Estepona

Estepona was one of the
first resorts to attract
tourists almost 50 years
ago and, despite the sur-
rounding development,
it retains a charming
historic centre of narrow
cobbled streets, simple
pueblo houses and well-
tended pots of gerani-
ums. Make a beeline for
Plaza de las Flores with
its fountain centrepoint,
orange trees and handy
tourist office (☎952 80 80
81; www.estepona.es; Plaza
de las Flores; ⏱9am-3pm
Mon-Fri, 10am-2pm Sat). A
10-minute walk from
here, Estepona's fabulous
Orchidarium (☎951 51 70
74, www.orchidariumestepona.
com; Calle Terraza 86; adult/
child €3/1; ⏱9am-2pm &
3-6pm Tue-Fri, 10am-2pm &
3-6pm Sat, 10am-2pm Sun)
houses 1500 species
of orchid – the largest
collection in Europe – as
well as 5000 subtropical
plants, flowers and trees,
and a 17m-high artificial
waterfall. To the south-
west of the town centre,
Puerto Deportivo is the
focal point of the town's
nightlife, especially at
weekends, and is also
excellent for water sports.

✗ p397

The Drive ⟫ For the final leg
consider taking the AP7 toll road
for the first 20km (€3.35 in peak
summer months) as the N340
here is very slow, with numerous

**TOP TIP:
TOLL ROAD AP SEVEN**

If you're travelling in July and August, consider taking the AP7 toll road, at least between Fuengirola and Marbella, as the A7 can become horribly congested. This particular A7 stretch (formerly part of the N340) used to be notorious for accidents, however the situation has improved since the introduction of a 80km/h speed limit in former trouble spots.

roundabouts. At Guadiaro the AP7 merges with the A7 for the rest of the 49km journey. Consider a refreshment stop at swanky Sotogrande harbour, home to Spain's leading golf course, the Real Club Valderrama.

- - - - - - - - - - - - - - - - - -

⑧ Gibraltar

Red pillar boxes, fish-and-chip shops and creaky 1970s seaside hotels – there's no getting away from Gibraltar's Britishness. Poised strategically at the jaws of Europe and Africa, Gibraltar, with its Palladian architecture and camera-hogging Barbary apes, makes an interesting finale to

your trip. The Rock is one of the most dramatic landforms in southern Europe and most of its upper sections (but not the main lookouts) fall within the **Upper Rock Nature Reserve** (incl attractions adult/child £13/8, excl attractions pedestrian £5, combined ticket incl cable car adult/child £22/14; ⊙9.30am-6.45pm Apr-Sep, 9am-5.45pm Oct-Mar). Entry to this includes admission to **St Michael's Cave** (St Michael's Rd; incl Upper Rock Nature Reserve & attractions adult/child £13/8; ⊙9.30am-6.45pm Apr-Sep, 9am-5.45pm Oct-Mar), the **Apes' Den**, the **Great Siege Tunnels** (incl Upper Rock Nature Reserve & attractions adult/

child £13/8; ⊙9.30am-6.45pm Apr-Sep, 9am-5.45pm Oct-Mar), the **Military Heritage Centre** (cnr Willis' & Queen's Rds; incl Upper Rock Nature Reserve adult/child £13/8; ⊙9.30am-6.45pm Apr-Sep, 9am-5.45pm Oct-Mar) and **Nelson's Anchorage** (100-Tonne Gun; Rosia Rd; incl Upper Rock Nature Reserve adult/child £13/8; ⊙9.30am-6.15pm Apr-Sep, 9am-5.45pm Oct-Mar). The Rock's most famous residents are the 160 or so tailless Barbary macaques that hang around the top cable-car station and Apes' Den. Most Gibraltar visits start in Grand Casemates Sq, once the sight of public executions but now a jolly square surrounded by bars and restaurants. Learn more about the Rock's history at the fine **Gibraltar Museum** (⊡200 74289; www.gibmuseum.gi; 18-20 Bomb House Lane; adult/child £5/2.50; ⊙10am-6pm Mon-Fri, to 2pm Sat) which displays exhibits ranging from prehistoric and Phoenician Gibraltar to the infamous Great Siege (1779–83).

Eating & Sleeping

Málaga ❷

✗ Uvedoble Taberna   Tapas €

(www.uvedobletaberna.com; Calle Císter 15; tapas €2.40-3.90; ⏱12.30-4pm & 8pm-midnight Mon-Sat; 📶) A newish tapas bar that draws on old traditions, this boisterous, crowded place evokes the tiled taverns of yore – though you'll likelier see modern art than dog-eared bullfighting posters on its walls. Similarly, the tapas put a modern spin on classic Málaga ingredients: try the smoked sardines on rosemary-tomato focaccia, or tuna tataki with *porra antequerana* (Antequera's lusciously garlicky soup).

🛏 Dulces Dreams   Guesthouse €

(📞951 35 78 69; www.dulcesdreamshostel.com; Plaza de los Mártires 6; d with shared/private bathroom from €60/74; ❄📶) Managed by an enthusiastic young team and delightfully situated in a pedestrianised plaza overlooking a red-brick church, Dulces (sweet) Dreams is a great budget option. The bright, high ceilinged and whimsically decorated rooms are, appropriately, named after desserts: Cupcake is one of the best. Note that there's no lift, and street noise can be an issue for light sleepers.

Torremolinos ❸

✗ El Gato Lounge   Fusion €€

(📞676 452504; www.elgatolounge.com; Paseo Marítimo 1K; mains €5-10, tapas box menus €16-22; ⏱noon-late Feb-Oct) Don't expect the default sardines at this trendsetting fusion favourite across from Playamar beach's western end. Asian flavours abound in offerings like Sri Lankan curry, chicken satay, tuna tataki and Thai shrimp cakes – but the real showstopper is El Gato's 'tapas experience', featuring a flamboyant assortment of 12 Mediterranean-Asian tapas finished off with apple pie and cinnamon ice cream.

Marbella ❻

✗ Garum   International €€

(📞952 85 88 58; www.garummarbella.com; Paseo Marítimo; mains €12-23; ⏱noon-11.30pm; 📶) Finnish-owned and set in a dreamy location right on the 'Golden Mile' across from the beach, Garum has a menu that will please those seeking a little gourmet variety. Expect dishes ranging from smoked-cheese soup to Moroccan chicken samosas and red-lentil falafel.

🛏 Hotel San Cristóbal   Hotel €€

(📞952 77 12 50; www.hotelsancristobal.com; Avenida Ramón y Cajal 3; s €67-79, d €82-96 incl breakfast; 📶) Not the most 'Marbella' (ie flashy) of Marbella's hotels, the well-located San Cristóbal dates back to the 1960s. However, regular revamps have kept the place looking solidly contemporary: rooms sport tasteful pale-grey and cream decor and smart navy fabrics. Most rooms have balconies.

Estepona ❼

✗ La Escollera   Seafood €

(📞952 80 63 54; Puerto Pesquero; mains €8-14; ⏱1-4.30pm & 8-11.30pm Tue-Sat, 1-4.30pm Sun) Locals in the know – from dock workers swigging beers to families celebrating a first communion – flock to this port-side eatery to dine on arguably the freshest and best seafood in town. The atmosphere is agreeably bustling and no-frills basic, with plastic tables and paper cloths. But when the fish tastes this good and the beer is this cold, who cares?

Northern Spain Pilgrimage

Travel in the footprints of millions of pilgrims past and present as you journey along the highroads and backroads of the legendary Camino de Santiago pilgrimage trail.

29

TRIP HIGHLIGHTS

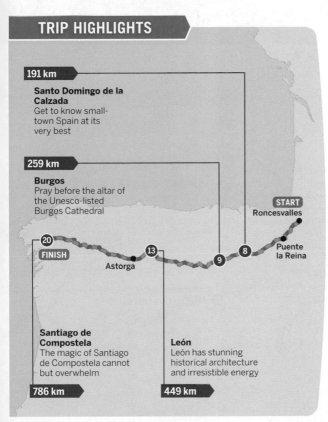

191 km

Santo Domingo de la Calzada
Get to know small-town Spain at its very best

259 km

Burgos
Pray before the altar of the Unesco-listed Burgos Cathedral

20
FINISH
Astorga

13

9

8

START
Roncesvalles

Puente la Reina

Santiago de Compostela
The magic of Santiago de Compostela cannot but overwhelm

786 km

León
León has stunning historical architecture and irresistible energy

449 km

5–7 DAYS
786KM / 488 MILES

GREAT FOR...

BEST TIME TO GO
April to June for fields of poppies, September and October for golden leaves.

ESSENTIAL PHOTO
Standing outside the cathedral of Santiago de Compostela.

BEST FOR A SENSE OF ACHIEVEMENT
Reaching Santiago de Compostela

29 Northern Spain Pilgrimage

For over a thousand years pilgrims have marched across the top of Spain on the Camino de Santiago (Way of St James) to the tomb of St James the Apostle in Santiago de Compostela. Real pilgrims walk, but by driving you'll enjoy religious treasures, grand cathedrals, big skies and wide open landscapes – and no blisters.

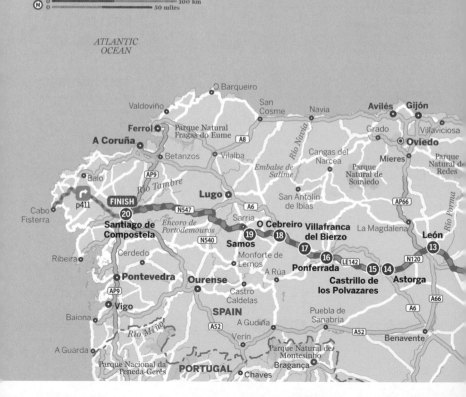

❶ Roncesvalles

History hangs thick in the air of the **Roncesvalles monastery complex** (☎948 79 04 80; www.roncesvalles.es; Carretera de Francia; guided tours adult/child €5.20/2.50; ⏰10am-2pm & 3.30-7pm Apr-Oct, 10am-2pm & 3-6pm Mar & Nov, 10.30am-2.30pm Thu-Tue Feb & Dec), where pilgrims give thanks for a successful crossing of the Pyrenees. The monastery contains a number of different buildings of interest, including the 13th-century Gothic **Real**

Colegiata de Santa María (☎948 79 04 80; www.roncesvalles.es; Carretera de Francia; ⏰9am-8.30pm) which houses a much-revered, silver-covered statue of the Virgin beneath a modernist-looking cano-

py. Also of interest is the cloister, containing the tomb of King Sancho VII (El Fuerte) of Navarra, leader of one of the victorious Christian armies in the battle of Las Navas de

LINK YOUR TRIP

30 Historic Castilla y León

From Burgos you can head south to discover the rich heritage of the cities of the Spanish plain.

31 Roving La Rioja Wine Region

With the Camino de Santiago ticked off, carry on to Fisterra and a spectacular trip along Galicia's awe-inspiring coast.

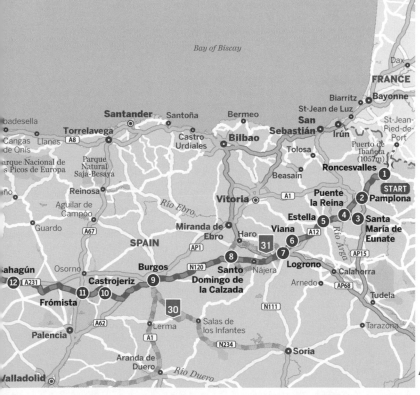

WHAT IS THE CAMINO DE SANTIAGO

The Camino de Santiago (Way of St James) originated as a medieval pilgrimage. For more than a millennium people have taken up the challenge of the Camino and walked to Santiago de Compostela. It all began in the 9th century when a remarkable event occurred in the poor Iberian hinterlands: following a shining star, a religious hermit named Pelayo unearthed the tomb of St James the Apostle (Santiago in Spanish). The news was confirmed by the local bishop, the Asturian king and later the pope.

Compostela became the most important destination for Christians after Rome and Jerusalem. Its popularity increased with an 11th-century papal decree granting it Holy Year status: pilgrims could receive a plenary indulgence (a full remission of your life's sins) during a Holy Year. These occur when Santiago's feast day (25 July) falls on a Sunday: 2021 is such a year and the next is 2027 – but driving there doesn't count...

The 11th and 12th centuries marked the heyday of the pilgrimage. The Reformation was devastating for Catholic pilgrimages and by the 19th century the Camino had nearly died out. In its startling late-20th-century reanimation, which continues today, it's equally popular as a personal and spiritual journey of discovery as for primarily religious motives. These days over 350,000 people a year arrive in Santiago on foot, or sometimes bicycle and occasionally horseback, having completed one of the many Camino routes that lead to the city from all points of the Iberian Peninsula and beyond. The most popular route has always been the Camino Francés, which in its full extent crosses some 770km of northern Spain from the Pyrenees, and attracts walkers of all backgrounds and ages from across the world. For pilgrims, it's equal to visiting Jerusalem, and by finishing it you can expect a healthy chunk of time off purgatory.

Tolosa, fought against the Muslims in 1212.

The Drive » It's 49km (one hour) basically downhill to Pamplona – a pretty drive along the N135 through mountainscapes, forests and gentle farmland. Innumerable hamlets and villages are painted in the red and white Basque colours and centred on old stone churches, many of them crammed with religious treasures.

- - - - - - - - - - - - - - - - - -

❷ Pamplona

Renowned across the world for the Sanfermines festival (6 to 14 July), when bulls tear through the streets at 8am causing chaos as they go (and alcohol-fuelled revellers cause chaos for the remainder of the day – and night), Pamplona (Iruña in Basque) is a quiet, low-key city at any other time of the year. Animal welfare groups condemn the bull-running as a cruel tradition. Pamplona's history stretches back to Roman times, and is best traced in the fantastic **Museo de Navarra** (🕿848 42 64 93; www.navarra.es; Calle Cuesta de Santo Domingo 47; adult/child €2/ free, free Sat afternoon & Sun; 🕙9.30am-2pm & 5-7pm Tue-Sat, 11am-2pm Sun), whose highlights include huge Roman mosaics. Another Pamplona highlight is the tour of the **Catedral** (www.catedraldepamplona. com; Calle Dormitalería; adult/child €5/3; 🕙10.30am-7pm Mon-Sat Apr-Oct, to 5pm Nov-Mar, tower climb 11.15am), a late-medieval Gothic gem with a neoclassical facade. The tour takes you into the cloisters and a museum displaying the remains of a Roman-era house and the tiny skeleton of a seven-month-old baby found there. The 11.15am tour also goes up the bell tower to see (and possibly hear) the second-largest church bell in Spain.

 p412

The Drive » Take the A12 southwestward. After about 10 minutes take exit 9 onto the driver-friendly NA1110. Drive through Astraín and continue along this peaceful country road for 15 minutes to Legarda and Muruzábal, then it's 2km southeast to Santa María de Eunate. Total 22km; about 40 minutes.

❸ Santa María de Eunate

Surrounded by cornfields and brushed by wildflowers, the near-perfect octagonal Romanesque chapel of **Santa María de Eunate** (www.santamariadeeunate.es; Carretera de Campanas; adult/child €1.50/1; ⏰10.30am-1.30pm Tue-Fri, 11am-1.30pm & 4.30-6.30pm Sat & Sun Apr-Jun, Sep & Oct, 10.30am-1.30pm & 5-6.30pm Wed-Mon Jul & Aug) is one of the most picturesque churches along the Camino. It dates from around the 12th century but its origins – and the reason why it's located in the middle of nowhere – are a mystery.

The Drive » From the chapel it's just a 5km drive along the NA6064 and NA1110 to gorgeous Puente la Reina.

❹ Puente la Reina

The chief calling card of Puente la Reina (Basque: Gares) is the spectacular six-arched **medieval bridge** dominating the western end of town, but Puente la Reina rewards on many other levels. A key stop on the Camino de Santiago, the town's pretty streets throng with the ghosts of a multitude of pilgrims. Pilgrims' first stop here is the late-Romanesque **Iglesia del Crucifijo**. Erected by the Knights Templar, it contains one of the finest Gothic crucifixes in existence.

The Drive » The fastest way between Puente la Reina and Estella is on the A12 (20km, 20 minutes), but the more enjoyable drive is along the slower, more rural, NA1110, taking about half an hour. You'll probably spy a few Camino pilgrims striding along.

❺ Estella

Estella (Basque: Lizarra) was known as 'La Bella' in medieval times because of the splendour of its monuments and buildings, and though the old dear has lost some of its beauty to modern suburbs, it still has charm. During the 11th century Estella became a main reception point for the growing flood of pilgrims along the Camino. Today most visitors are continuing that same tradition. The attractive old quarter has a couple of notable churches, including the 12th-century **Iglesia de San Pedro de la Rúa**, whose cloisters are a fine example of Romanesque sculptural work. Across the river and overlooking the town is the **Iglesia de San Miguel**, with a fine Romanesque north portal. The countryside around Estella is littered with monasteries. Two of the most impressive are **Monasterio de Iratxe** (off Carretera NA1110, Ayegui; ⏰10am-1.15pm & 4-6pm Wed-Sun mid-Jan–mid-Nov), 2.5km southwest near Ayegui, and **Monasterio de Irantzu** (off Carretera NA7135, Abárzuza; €2.50; ⏰10am-2pm & 4-8pm Apr-Sep, to 6pm Oct-Mar), 11km north near Abárzuza.

TOP TIP: FUENTE DEL VINO FOUNTAIN OF WINE

Opposite the Monasterio de Iratxe is the well-known local wine producer, **Bodegas Irache** (☎948 55 19 32; www.irache.com; Monasterio de Irache, off Carretera NA1110, Ayegui; ⏰shop 10am-2pm & 3-7pm Sat & Sun Jul-Sep, to 6pm Sat & Sun Oct-Jun). For the benefit of Camino de Santiago pilgrims the winery has installed two taps providing free liquid. From one flows water; from the other, wine – 100L per day.

WHY THIS IS A GREAT TRIP
JOHN NOBLE,
WRITER

Millions of people following the Camino de Santiago over 1200 years have given rise to an unrivalled heritage of monumental cathedrals, tiny chapels, ancient inns and other landmarks. To follow the pilgrims' path today is to breathe the aura of countless journeys and to sense the excitement of those doing it on foot. You might even be inspired to come back and walk it yourself one day!

Above: Castrojeriz
Left: Scallop shell, Camino de Santiago
Right: Pilgrim passport, Camino de Santiago

JUSTIN FOLKES/LONELY PLANET ©

The Drive » It's a 40km (50 minute) drive to Viana. Take the A12 westward and turn onto the NA1110 at junction 58. Follow the NA1110 through the sleepy villages of Los Arcos, Sansol and Torres del Río. In hillside Torres you'll find a remarkably intact eight-sided Romanesque chapel, the Iglesia del Santo Sepulcro.

❻ Viana

Overlooked by many non-pilgrim tourists, Viana, the last town in Navarra, started life as a garrison town defending the kingdom of Navarra from Castilla. The old part of the town, which sits atop a hill, is still largely walled and is an interesting place to wander about for a couple of hours. Work started on the **Iglesia de Santa María** in the 13th century and it's one of the more impressive religious structures on this eastern part of the Camino. Viana's former **bullring** is now a plaza in the middle of town, where children booting footballs are considerably more common than bulls.

The Drive » It's 10km to Logroño. The first half of the drive is through open, big-sky countryside; the last part through the city suburbs. There's a large car park under Paseo del Espolón on the south edge of Logroño's old town.

❼ Logroño

Logroño, capital of La Rioja – Spain's wine-growing region par excellence – doesn't feel the need to be loud and brash. Instead it's a stately town with a heart of tree-studded squares, narrow streets and a monumentally good selection of *pintxos* (tapas) bars. It's the sort of place where you can't help feeling contented. And it's not just the wine. The superb **Museo de la Rioja** (☎941 29 12 59; www.museodelarioja.es; Plaza San Agustín 23; ☺10am-2pm & 4-9pm Tue-Sat, 10am-2pm Sun) in the centre takes you on a wild romp through Riojan history and culture, from the days when dinner was killed with arrows to recreations of the kitchens that many a Spanish granny grew up using. The other major attraction is the **Catedral de Santa María de la Redonda** (www.laredonda.org; Calle de Portales 14; ☺8.30am-1pm & 6-8.45pm Mon-Sat, 8.30am-2pm Sun); it started life as a Gothic church before maturing into a full-blown cathedral in the 16th century.

✕ ⎙ p412, p435

The Drive ⟫ For the 45km (35-minute) hop to Santo Domingo de la Calzada, the Camino walking trail parallels – mostly at a respectful distance – the fast, and dull, A12. There's not much reason for you to veer off the motorway (none of the quieter roads really follow the Camino).

TRIP HIGHLIGHT

❽ Santo Domingo de la Calzada

Santo Domingo is small-town Spain at its very best. A large number of the inhabitants still live in the partly-walled old quarter, a labyrinth of medieval streets where the past is alive and the sense of community is strong. The **Catedral de Santo Domingo de la Calzada** (☎941 34 00 33; www.catedralsantodomingo.com; Plaza del Santo 4; adult/child €7/2; ☺10am-8pm Mon-Fri, to 7pm Sat, 10am-noon & 2-8pm Sun Apr-Oct, shorter hours Nov-Mar) and its attached museum glitter with the gold that attests to the great wealth the Camino has bestowed on otherwise backwater towns. The cathedral's most eccentric feature is the white rooster and hen that forage in a glass-fronted cage opposite the entrance to the crypt. Their presence celebrates a long-standing legend, the Miracle of the Rooster, which tells of a young man who was unfairly executed only to recover miraculously, while the broiled cock and hen on the plate of his judge suddenly leapt up and chickened off, fully fledged.

The Drive ⟫ It's 68km (one hour) to Burgos. Again you're sort of stuck with using the main road, the N120.

TRIP HIGHLIGHT

❾ Burgos

On the surface, conservative Burgos seems to embody all the stereotypes of a north-central Spanish town, with sombre grey stone architecture, the fortifying cuisine of the high *meseta* (plateau) and a climate of extremes. But Burgos is a city that rewards. The historic centre is austerely elegant, guarded by monumental gates and with the **cathedral** (p422) as its centrepiece – a World Heritage–listed masterpiece that started life as a modest Romanesque church, but over time became one of the most impressive cathedrals in a land of impressive cathedrals. Read more about Burgos in Trip 1: Historic Castilla y León.

✕ ⎙ p412, p425

The Drive ⟫ It's 48km (45 minutes) to castle-topped Castrojeriz. Head southwest on the A62 to junction 32 and turn off northwest along the minor BU400.

❿ Castrojeriz

With its mix of old and new buildings huddled around the base of a hill that's topped with what's left of a crumbling **castle**, Castrojeriz is a typical small *meseta* town. It's worth a climb up to the castle if only for the views. The town's church,

Iglesia de San Juan, is worth a look as well.

The Drive » From Castrojeriz it's 26km (30 minutes) along the BU403 and P432 to Frómista. The scenery is classic meseta and if you're lucky you'll catch a glimpse of such evocative sights as a flock of sheep being led over the alternately burning or freezing plateau by a shepherd.

---

⑪ Frómista

The main (and some would say only) reason for stopping here is the village's exceptional **Iglesia de San Martín** (📞979 81 01 44; Plaza de San Martín, Frómista; adult/child €2/free; 🕓9.30am-2pm & 4.30-8pm Apr-Sep, 10am-2pm & 3.30-6.30pm Oct-Mar). Dating from 1066 and restored in the early 20th century, this harmoniously proportioned church is one of the premier Romanesque churches in rural Spain, adorned with human and animal forms below the eaves. The capitals within are also richly decorated.

The Drive » Take the P980 (the Camino runs alongside it) to Carrión de los Condes, then the more major A231 west to Sahagún (56km; 45 minutes).

---

⑫ Sahagún

Despite appearances, Sahagún was an immensely powerful and wealthy Benedictine centre by the 12th century. The brick Romanesque churches, some with later Mudéjar additions, merit a visit.

The Drive » The 60km (50-minute) stretch from Sahagún to León along the A231 and A60 isn't a memorable drive. Still, you have to feel for those walking the Camino: some pilgrims bus between Burgos and León because so much of the route is next to busy roads.

TRIP HIGHLIGHT

⑬ León

León is a wonderful city, combining stunning historical architecture with an irresistible energy. Its standout attraction is the 13th-century **Catedral** (📞987 87 57 70; www.catedraldeleon.org; Plaza Regla; adult/concession/under 12yr €6/5/free, combined ticket with Claustro & Museo Catedralicio-Diocesano €9/8/free; 🕓9.30am-1.30pm &

4-8pm Mon-Fri, 9.30am-noon & 2-6pm Sat, 9.30-11am & 2-8pm Sun May-Sep, 9.30am-1.30pm & 4-7pm Mon-Sat, 9.30am-2pm Sun Oct-Apr), one of the most beautiful cathedrals in Spain and arguably the country's premier Gothic masterpiece. Whether spotlit at night or bathed in glorious sunshine, it exudes an almost luminous quality. The showstopping facade has a radiant rose window, three richly sculpted doorways and two muscular towers. Inside, an extraordinary gallery of stained-glass windows awaits. The even older **Real Basílica de San Isidoro** (📞987 87 61 61; Plaza de San Isidoro; 🕓7.30am-11pm) provides

WHO WAS ST JAMES THE APOSTLE

St James, or James the Greater, was one of the 12 disciples of Jesus. He may even have been the first disciple. He was also probably the first to be martyred, by King Herod in 44 CE. So, if St James was living in the Holy Lands 2000 years ago, an obvious question persists: what were his remains doing in northwest Spain 800 years later? The legend (and we're not standing by its historical accuracy) suggests that two of St James' own disciples secreted his remains on a stone boat which sailed across the Mediterranean and passed into the Atlantic to moor at present-day Padrón (Galicia). After various trials and tribulations, they buried his body in a forest named Libredón (present-day Santiago de Compostela). All was then forgotten until about 820 CE, when a religious hermit found the remains. Further legends attest that during his lifetime St James preached in various parts of Spain including Galicia, which might explain why his remains were brought here.

a stunning Romanesque counterpoint to the cathedral's Gothic strains. Fernando I and Doña Sancha founded this church in 1063 to house the remains of San Isidoro, and of themselves and 21 other early Leonese and Castilian monarchs. The main basilica is a hotchpotch of styles, but the two main portals on the southern facade are pure Romanesque. The attached **Real Colegiata de San Isidoro** (Panteón Real; ☎987 87 61 61; www.museosanisidor odeleon.com; Plaza de San Isidoro; adult/child €5/free; ⏰10am-2pm & 4-7pm Mon-Sat, 10am-2pm Sun) houses royal sarcophagi, which rest with quiet dignity beneath a canopy of some of the finest Romanesque frescoes in Spain. Motif after colourful motif of biblical scenes drench the vaults and arches of this extraordinary hall.

 p412

The Drive >> Taking the N120 to Astorga will keep you on the route of the Camino, which runs alongside the road for long stretches. It's a 50km (one-hour) drive. The AP71 is much faster, but what's the point in coming all this way to drive on a road like that?

⑭ Astorga

Perched on a hilltop on the frontier between the bleak plains of northern Castilla and the mountains that rise west towards Galicia, Astorga is a fascinating small town with a wealth of attractions way out of proportion to its size. The most eye-catching sight is the **Palacio Episcopal**, a rare flight of fancy in this part of the country, designed by Antoni Gaudí. There's also a smattering of Roman ruins (Astorga was once an important Roman settlement called Astúrica Augusta), a fine Gothic and plateresque **cathedral** (Plaza de la Catedral; incl museum & cloister €5; ⏰10am-8.30pm Mon-Sat, 10-11.15am & 1-8.30pm Sun Apr-Oct, 10.30am-6pm Nov-Mar) and even a **Museo del Chocolate** (☎987 61 62 20; Avenida de la Estación 16; adult/child €2.50/free, incl Museo Romano adult/child €4/free; ⏰10.30am-2pm & 4.30-7pm Tue-Sat, 10.30am-2pm Sun; 🚼), dedicated to the town's long chocolate-making tradition. Less sinfully, the town sees a steady stream of pilgrims passing through along the Camino de Santiago.

The Drive >> It's just 8km (15 minutes) along the rural LE142 to Castrillo de los Polvazares. Non-residents are not allowed to drive into Castrillo, so park in one of the parking areas on the edge of the village.

⑮ Castrillo de los Polvazares

One of the prettiest villages along the Camino – if a little twee – is Castrillo de los Polvazares. It consists of little but one main cobbled street, a small church and an array of well-preserved 18th-century stone houses. If you can be here before the tour buses arrive, or after they have left, then it's an absolute delight of a place and one in which the spirit of the Camino can be strongly felt.

The Drive >> Continue along the LE142 to Ponferrada

Castrillo de los Polvazares The village's main cobbled street

(53km; 1¼ hours). It runs pretty much beside the Camino and you'll pass through attractive stone villages, most of which have churches topped with storks' nests. Rabanal del Camino, with its 18th-century church Ermita del Bendito Cristo de la Vera Cruz, is worth a quick stop.

- - - - - - - - - - - - - - - -

16 Ponferrada

Ponferrada is not the region's most enticing town, but its castle and remnants of the old town centre (around the stone clock tower) make it worth a brief stop. Built by the Knights Templar in the 13th century, the walls of the fortress-monastery **Castillo Templario** rise high over the Río Sil with a lonely and impregnable air, and its square, crenellated towers ooze romance and history.

The Drive » If you're not in a huge hurry, take the NVI to Villafranca del Bierzo (24km, 30 minutes). It's slower but gentler than the A6 motorway.

- - - - - - - - - - - - - - - -

17 Villafranca del Bierzo

Villafranca del Bierzo has a very well-preserved

old core and a number of interesting churches and other religious buildings. Chief among these are **San Nicolás El Real**, a 17th-century convent with a baroque altarpiece, and the 12th-century **Iglesia de Santiago**. The northern doorway of this church is called the 'door of forgiveness'. Pilgrims who were sick, or otherwise unable to continue to Santiago de Compostela, were granted the same godly favours as if they'd made it all the way.

The Drive » It's 32km (45 minutes) uphill to O Cebreiro using the NVI, or a bit quicker via the A6. On the NVI you can admire or pity the pilgrims making the Camino's longest, hardest climb, right beside the road on several stretches. Turn off at Pedrafita do Cebreiro and take the LU633 for the last 4km.

⑱ O Cebreiro

O Cebreiro, 1300m high, is the first village in Galicia on the Camino. It's an atmospheric and picturesque little place, busy with pilgrims happy to have completed the climb from Villafranca. O Cebreiro contains several *pallozas* (circular, thatched dwellings known in Galicia since pre-Roman times). A former village priest here, Elías Valiño (1929-1989), is considered to have been the driving force behind the revival of the Camino de Santiago in the late 20th century.

The Drive » The marvellous 33km drive to Samos winds down the LU633 through refreshingly green countryside with great long-distance views, frequently criss-crossing the Camino.

⑲ Samos

A pretty village in the Río Sarria valley, Samos is built around the very fine Benedictine **Mosteiro de Samos** (☎982 54 60 46; www.abadia desamos.com; tours €5; ⏰tours hourly 9.30am-12.30pm & 4.30-6.30pm Mon-Sat, 12.45pm & hourly 4.30-6.30pm Sun May-Oct, hourly 10am-noon, 4.30pm & 5.30pm Mon & Wed-Sat, 12.45pm, 4.30pm, 5.30pm Sun Nov-Apr; Ⓟ). This monastery has two beautiful big cloisters – one Gothic, with distinctly unmonastic Greek nymphs adorning its fountain, the other neoclassical and filled with roses.

🍴 p412

The Drive » Follow the LU633 and N547 to stay fairly close to the Camino and pass through attractive villages and small

THE PORTICO DE LA GLORIA

Santiago cathedral's artistically unparalleled **Pórtico de la Gloria** features 200 Romanesque sculptures by Maestro Mateo, who was placed in charge of the cathedral-building programme in the late 12th century. These detailed and remarkably lifelike sculptures add up to a comprehensive review of major figures and scenes from the Bible. The Old Testament and its prophets (including a famously smiling Daniel) are on the north side; the New Testament, Apostles and Last Judgement are on the south; and glory and resurrection are depicted in the central archway.

Visits are limited to 25 people at a time. Spanish-language **guided visits** (45 minutes; adult/concession/child €10/8/free) are conducted several times daily, with tickets sold up to 90 days ahead through the cathedral website or on the same day (if available) at the **Pazo de Xelmírez** adjoining the cathedral, where the visit starts. Fifteen-minute **unguided visits** happen from 7pm to 8pm Monday to Saturday; 50 tickets for these (free) are given out between 7pm and 8pm the day before at the Fundación Catedral office in the **Casa do Deán** (Rúa do Vilar 3). For Monday visits go on Saturday. Take your ID document.

towns such as Portomarín. There's no avoiding the A54 motorway to get past Santiago airport. Follow 'Centro Histórico' signs towards the city centre (137km, 2¾ hours from Samos). Private vehicles are barred from the Old Town; underground car parks around its fringes charge around €15 per 24 hours. Cheaper are Aparcadoiro Xoan XXIII (€11) and open-air Aparcadoiro Belvís (€7.50).

TRIP HIGHLIGHT

🔟 Santiago de Compostela

This, then, is it. The end of The Way. And what a spectacular finish. Santiago de Compostela, with its granite buildings and frequent drizzle, is one of the most beautiful and fascinating cities in Spain. With over 350,000 pilgrims arriving here annually, Santiago has a busy, festive atmosphere throughout the warmer half of the year (May to October). The magnificent **Catedral de Santiago de Compostela** (www.catedraldesantiago.es; Praza do Obradoiro; Pórtico de la Gloria guided tour adult/concession/child €10/8/free; 🕘9am-8pm) soars above the city centre in a splendid jumble of spires and statues. Its beauty is a mix of the original

DETOUR: CABO FISTERRA

Start: 🔟 **Santiago de Compostela**

This spectacular, cliff-girt, wave-lashed cape has, in popular imagination, long been considered the western edge of Spain, and in days way before satnav it was believed to be the very end of the world. The name Fisterra (Finisterre in Castilian Spanish) means 'Land's End'. In fact, Spain's real westernmost point is Cabo Touriñán, 20km north, but that doesn't lessen Fisterra's magnetic appeal. The end point of a highly popular extension to the Camino de Santiago, the cape is an 82km, 1½-hour drive west from Santiago. Camino pilgrims ritually burn smelly socks, T-shirts and the like on the rocks just past the lighthouse. Many people come for sunset but it's a magnificent spot at any time (unless shrouded in fog or rain). Fisterra town, 3.5km before the cape, is a fishing port with a picturesque harbour and some beautiful beaches within a few kilometres.

Romanesque structure (built between 1075 and 1211) and later Gothic and baroque flourishes. The tomb of Santiago beneath the main altar is a magnet for all who arrive here. The artistic high point is the **Pórtico de la Gloria** inside the west entrance.

Grand **Praza do Obradoiro**, in front of the cathedral's west facade, is traffic- and cafe-free and has a unique atmosphere. From here you can start exploring Santiago's other fine squares and churches. At the square's northern end, the **Hostal dos Reis Católicos** (📞981 58 22 00; www.parador.es; Praza do Obradoiro; adult/child €3/free, Mon free; 🕘noon-2pm & 4-6pm Sun-Fri) was built in the 16th century as a refuge for exhausted pilgrims. Today it's a *parador* (luxurious state-owned hotel), but its four courtyards are open to visitors.

🍴🛏 p413

Eating & Sleeping

Pamplona ❷

✖ Bar Gaucho   Pintxos €

(☎948 22 50 73; Calle Espoz y Mina 7; pintxos €2-4.50; ⏱8.30am-12.30am) This bustling bar's multi-award-winning *pintxos* are among the finest in the city. Highlights include smoked eel with tomato jelly, filo pastry–calf's tongue, a shot glass of truffled egg, mushroom crème and crispy ham, and sea urchin mousse served in the shell.

Logroño ❼

✖ La Cocina de Ramón   Spanish €€€

(☎941 28 98 08; www.lacocinaderamon.es; Calle de Portales 30; mains €18-27; ⏱1.30-4pm & 8.30-11pm Mon, Tue & Thu-Sat, 1.30-4pm Wed) It looks unassuming from the outside, but Ramón's high-quality, locally grown produce and tried-and-tested family recipes, such as chargrilled lamb cutlets or beef tenderloin cooked with wines from La Rioja, has earned him a lot of fans. The fine cooking is matched by the top service and white tablecloths; Ramón likes to come and explain the dishes to guests.

Burgos ❾

✖ La Favorita   Tapas €€

(☎947 20 59 49; www.lafavoritaburgos.com; Calle de Avellanos 8; tapas from €4; ⏱10am-midnight Mon-Fri, noon-12.30am Sat & Sun) Away from the main Burgos tapas hub but still close to the cathedral, La Favorita has an appealing, barn-like interior of exposed brick and wooden beams. The emphasis is on local cured meats and cheeses (try the cheese platter for €15); wine by the glass starts at €2. The tapas menu includes beef sirloin with foie gras.

🛏 Hotel Norte y Londres   Historic Hotel €€

(☎947 26 41 25; www.hotelnorteylondres.com; Plaza de Alonso Martínez 10; s/d from €40/45; P@🖥) Set in a former 16th-century palace and decorated with understated period charm, this fine, family-run hotel promises spacious rooms with antique furnishings and polished wooden floors. All rooms have pretty balconies and double-glazed windows; those on the 4th floor are more modern. The bathrooms are exceptionally large and the service friendly and efficient.

León ⓭

✖ Restaurante Cocinandos   Modern Spanish €€€

(☎987 07 13 78; www.cocinandos.com; Calle de las Campanillas 1; set menus €50-90; ⏱1.45-3.15pm & 9.30-10.30pm Tue-Sat) The proud owner of León's first Michelin star, Cocinandos brings creative flair to the table with a menu that changes weekly with the seasons and market availability. The atmosphere is slightly formal so dress nicely and book in advance, but the young team puts diners at ease and the food is exceptional (in that zany new-Spanish-cuisine kind of way).

🛏 La Posada Regia   Historic Hotel €€

(☎987 21 31 73; www.regialeon.com; Calle de Regidores 9-11; s €54-70, d €59-130; 🖥) This place has the feel of a *casa rural* (village or farmstead accommodation) despite being in the city centre. The secret is a 14th-century building, magnificently restored (with wooden beams, exposed brick and understated antique furniture), with individually styled rooms and supremely comfortable beds and bathrooms. As with anywhere in the Barrio Húmedo, weekend nights can be noisy.

Samos ⓳

🛏 Casa de Díaz   Heritage Hotel €

(☎982 54 70 70; www.hotelcasadediaz.com; Vilachá; r €42-68, breakfast €4-8; ⏱Apr-Oct; P@🖥🐾) Samos has plenty of inexpensive lodgings, but a good option is to continue 3.5km west to the welcoming Casa de Díaz, an 18th-century farmhouse turned rural hotel at Vilachá. It has 12 comfy rooms in olde-worlde style and (except Sundays) serves three-course dinners

(€18) by reservation. The spacious gardens, pool and games room make it a good place to hang out if you're with children.

Santiago de Compostela ⑳

✕ Mercado de Abastos   Market €

(www.mercadodeabastosdesantiago.com; Rúa das Ameas 5-8; ◷8am-2pm Mon-Sat) Santiago's food market is a fascinating, always lively scene. It's very clean, with masses of fresh produce from the seas and countryside displayed at 300-odd stalls. Saturday is particularly festive, with Galician folk musicians sometimes playing in the surrounding bars. Stock up on *tetilla* cheese, cured meats, sausage, fruit, *empanada* (pastry pie) or the terrific home-made, take-away dishes of **Cocina María** (www.cocinamaria.es; Mercado de Abastos, Nave 1, Posto C61; items €1.50-15; ◷9.30am-3pm Mon-Sat) for a picnic. Bars and restaurants line the street outside, but there are also good options within the market itself, especially **Nave 5 Abastos** (www.facebook.com/nave5abastos; Mercado de Abastos, Nave 5; dishes €4-16; ◷11.30am-4.30pm Mon-Sat), where chefs in Aisle 5 cook up top-class fresh seafood and fish, *filloas* (Galician crêpes), Mexican tacos and more, and you sit at long tables or stools to enjoy it. Drinks too, at equally reasonable prices. Also in Nave 5, popular **Mariscomanía** (Mercado de Abastos, Nave 5, Posto 81; ◷9am-3pm Tue-Sat) will, for €5 per person, cook up seafood or meat that you buy elsewhere in the market (though they don't do octopus or fish). Around the outside of the buildings you'll find stallholders selling the produce of their orchards or veggie gardens.

✕ A Moa   Galician €€

(☎981 07 18 18; www.amoa32.com; Rúa de San Pedro 32; mains €15-18, tapas €3-7, lunch menú Tue-Fri €10-15; ◷1-4pm & 8pm-midnight Tue-Sat, 1-4pm Sun; 🖉) A Moa produces a great mix of traditional Galician and more international fare in its street-level wine bar and stone-walled downstairs restaurant which opens onto a verdant garden area. Starters and tapas range over octopus croquettes, a great lemony ceviche, falafel and vegetarian salads. Main dishes are mostly a little more conventional: roast lamb, BBQ pork ribs, fish of the day. It's all great, and enhanced by service which manages to be efficient, friendly and relaxed all at the same time.

🛏 Altaïr Hotel   Boutique Hotel €€

(☎981 55 47 12; www.altairhotel.net; Rúa dos Loureiros 12; s €50-85, d €60-130; ◷closed Jan; 🏵🛜) The Altaïr combines stone walls and solid oak floors with cosy comfort, attentive staff, soft furnishings and splashes of contemporary design. Breakfast (€8.50) is a gourmet affair, and there are great city views from some rooms.

🛏 San Francisco Hotel Monumento   Historic Hotel €€€

(☎981 58 16 34; www.sanfranciscohm.com; Campillo de San Francisco 3; incl breakfast s €105-138, d €154-334; 🅿🏵@🛜🛎) The three cloister-courtyards and low-lit hallways recall the hotel's former life as a Franciscan monastery. But the rooms are large and all about contemporary comfort, and there's a great indoor pool as well as a huge grassy garden, cafe, and good restaurant.

Historic Castilla y León

30

This journey through Spain's Castilian heartlands takes in some of the country's most engaging historic cities and larger towns, with many time-worn pueblos (villages) en route.

TRIP HIGHLIGHTS

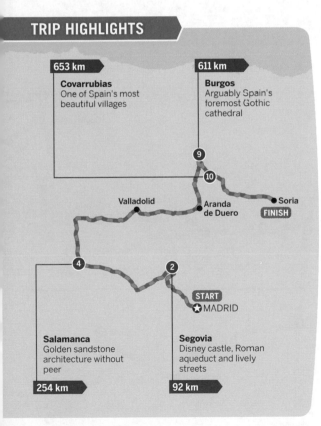

653 km

Covarrubias
One of Spain's most beautiful villages

611 km

Burgos
Arguably Spain's foremost Gothic cathedral

9

10

Valladolid

Aranda de Duero

Soria
FINISH

4

2

START
MADRID

Salamanca
Golden sandstone architecture without peer

254 km

Segovia
Disney castle, Roman aqueduct and lively streets

92 km

7 DAYS
764KM / 475 MILES

GREAT FOR...

BEST TIME TO GO
March to May, and September and October to avoid extremes of heat and cold.

ESSENTIAL PHOTO
Plaza Mayor, Salamanca, floodlit at night.

 BEST FOR CULTURE
Irresistible Salamanca street life against a glorious architectural backdrop.

30 Historic Castilla y León

From Segovia to Soria, the towns of Castilla y León rank among Spain's most appealing historic centres. Architecture may be central to their attraction, but these are no museum pieces. Instead, the relentless energy of life lived Spanish-style courses through the streets, all set against a backdrop of grand cathedrals and animating stately squares. Out in the countryside, postcard-perfect villages complement the clamour of city life.

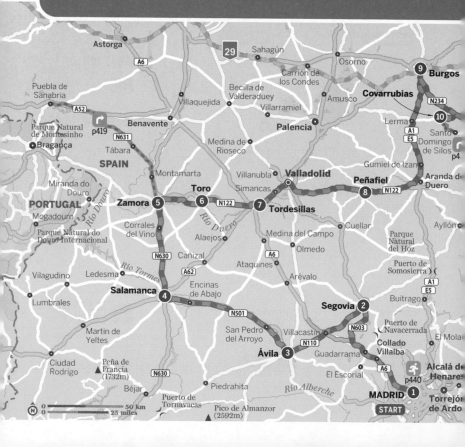

❶ Madrid

Madrid is the most Spanish of all of Spain's cities. Its food culture, drawn from the best the country has to offer, makes it one of Europe's more underrated culinary capitals, while its nightlife and irresistible *alegría* (joy) exist like some Spanish stereotype given form. But there is more to Madrid than just nonstop colour and movement. This is one of the premier art cities on the continent, with three world-class

galleries – the **Museo del Prado** (www.museodelprado. es; Paseo del Prado; adult/ concession/child €15/7.50/ free, 6-8pm Mon-Sat & 5-7pm Sun free, audio guide €3.50, admission plus official guidebook €24; ⏱10am-8pm Mon-Sat, to 7pm Sun; Ⓜ Banco de España), **Museo Thyssen-Bornemisza** (Ⓙ902 760511; www. museothyssen.org; Paseo del Prado 8; adult/child €13/free, Mon free; ⏱10am-7pm Tue-Sun, noon-4pm Mon; Ⓜ Banco de España) and **Centro de Arte Reina Sofía** (Ⓙ91 774 10 00; www.museoreinasofia. es; Calle de Santa Isabel 52; adult/concession €10/free, 1.30-7pm Sun, 7-9pm Mon & Wed-Sat free; ⏱10am-9pm Mon & Wed-Sat, to 7pm Sun; Ⓜ Estación del Arte) – all clustered close to one of the city's main boulevards and a short walk from the Parque del Buen Retiro, one of the loveliest and most expansive monumental parks in Europe. In short, this is a city that rewards those who linger and long to immerse themselves in all things Spanish.

The Drive ≫ Getting out of Madrid can be a challenge, with a complicated system of numbered motorways radiating out from the city. Drive north along the Paseo de la Castellana, turn west along the M50 ring road, then take the A6, direction A Coruña. Of the two main roads to Segovia from the A6, the N603 is the prettier (92km).

TRIP HIGHLIGHT

❷ Segovia

Unesco World Heritage–listed Segovia is a stunning confluence of everything that's good about the beautiful towns of Castilla. There are historic landmarks in abundance, among them the Roman **Acueducto**, the fairy-tale **Alcázar** (Ⓙ921 46 07 59; www. alcazardesegovia.com; Plaza de la Reina Victoria Eugenia; adult/concession/under 6yr €5.50/3.50/free, tower €2.50, audio guide €3; ⏱10am-8pm Apr-Oct, to 6pm Nov-Mar; ♿), which is said to have inspired Walt Disney, and Romanesque gems such as the **Catedral** (Ⓙ921 46 22 05; www.turismodesegovia. com; Plaza Mayor; adult/child

🔗 LINK YOUR TRIP

29 Northern Spain Pilgrimage

Crisscross the Camino de Santiago pilgrim route, two-and-a-half hours' north from Soria.

31 Roving La Rioja Wine Region

Discover the wealth of the grape on this peaceful countryside drive, just an hour-and-a-half-north from Soria.

Map labels: Logroño, Río Ebro, Nájera, 9, 31, Hontoria del Pinar, Navaleno, N234, FINISH, ⓫ Soria, Matañazor, Río Duero, Almazán, maz, Atienza, Imón, Medinaceli, nares, Torija, Cifuentes, Guadalajara, Priego, astrana

LOCAL KNOWLEDGE: FROG-SPOTTING IN SALAMANCA

A compulsory task facing all visitors to Salamanca is to search out the frog sculpted into the facade of the **Universidad Civil** (☎923 29 44 00, ext 1150; www.salamanca.es; Calle de los Libreros; adult/concession €10/5, audio guide €2; �an10am-7pm Mon-Sat, to 2pm Sun mid-Sep–Mar, 10am-8pm Mon-Sat, to 2pm Sun Apr–mid-Sep). Once pointed out, it's easily enough seen, but the uninitiated can spend considerable time searching. Why bother? Well, they say that those who detect it without help can be assured of good luck and even marriage within a year. Some hopeful students see a guaranteed examination's victory in it. If you believe all this, stop reading now. If you need help, look at the busts of the Reyes Católicos (Catholic Monarchs) Fernando and Isabel. From there, turn your gaze to the largest column on the extreme right of the front. Slightly above the level of the busts is a series of skulls, atop the leftmost of which sits our little amphibious friend (or what's left of his eroded self).

€3/free, Sun morning free, tower tour €4; ☺9am-9.30pm Apr-Oct, 9.30am-6.30pm Nov-Mar, tower tours 10.30pm, noon, 1.30pm & 4pm year-round, plus 6pm & 7.30pm Apr-Oct) or the **Iglesia de San Martín** (Plaza de San Martín; ☺10am-6pm Mon-Sat). This is also one of the most dynamic towns in the country, a winning mix of students and international visitors filling the city's bars and public spaces with an agreeable crescendo of noise. To cap it all, the setting is simply superb – a city strung out along a ridge, its warm terracotta and sandstone hues arrayed against a backdrop of Castilla's rolling hills and the often snow-capped

Sierra de Guadarrama. There are many vantage points to take in the full effect, but our favourite can be found anywhere in the gardens near the entrance to the Alcázar.

✕ 🛏 p424

The Drive » It's 66km from Segovia to Ávila along the N110. The road runs southwest, parallel to the Sierra de Guadarrama, with some pretty views en route. Around halfway, you'll cross the A6 motorway.

---

❸ Ávila

Ávila's old city, surrounded by 12th-century *murallas* (walls) with eight monumental gates, 88 watchtowers and over 2500 turrets, is one of the best-preserved

walled cities in Spain. Two sections of the **Murallas** (☎920 35 00 00; www.muralladeavila.com; incl multilingual audio guide adult/ under 12yr €5/3.50, 2-4pm Tue free; ☺10am-8pm Apr-Jun & Sep-Oct, to 9pm Jul & Aug, to 6pm Tue-Sun Nov-Mar; ♿) can be climbed – a 300m stretch accessed from just inside the Puerta del Alcázar, and a longer 1300m stretch that runs along the old city's northern perimeter. The best views are those at night from **Los Cuatro Postes** (Calle de los Cuatro Postes, off N110), a short distance northwest of the city. Ávila is also the home city of Santa Teresa, with the **Convento de Santa Teresa** (☎920 21 10 30; www.teresadejesus.com; Plaza de la Santa; church & relic room free, museum €2; ☺10am-2pm & 4-7pm Tue-Sun) as its centrepiece and plenty of other important religious buildings nearby.

✕ 🛏 p424

The Drive » The N501 runs northwest of Ávila to Salamanca, in the process traversing the pancake-flat high meseta (plateau) of central Spain and covering 109km en route.

TRIP HIGHLIGHT

❹ Salamanca

Whether floodlit by night or bathed in the sunset, there's something magical about Salamanca. This is a city of rare beauty, awash with golden sandstone overlaid with ochre-tinted Latin inscriptions; an extraordinary virtuosity of plateresque and Renaissance styles. The monumental highlights are many, with the exceptional **Plaza Mayor** (illuminated to stunning effect at night) an unforgettable highlight. Built between 1729 and 1755, it is widely considered to be Spain's most beautiful central plaza. But this is also Castilla's liveliest city: home to a massive Spanish and international student population that throngs the streets at night and provides the city with so much youth and vitality.

 p424

The Drive » The N630 runs due north from Salamanca to Zamora (67km), a relatively quiet road by Spanish standards and one that follows the contours of the rolling hill country of Castilla y León's west.

----

❺ Zamora

If you're arriving by road, first appearances can be deceiving and, as in so many Spanish towns, your introduction to provincial Zamora is likely to be nondescript apartment blocks. But persevere as the *casco historico* is hauntingly beautiful, with sumptuous medieval monuments that have earned Zamora the popular sobriquet 'Romanesque Museum'. Much of the old town is closed to motorised

transport and walking is easily the best way to explore this subdued encore to the monumental splendour of Salamanca. Zamora is also one of the best places to be during Semana Santa, with haunting processions of hooded penitents parading through the streets. Whatever time of year you're here, don't miss the **Museo de Semana Santa** (📞980 53 60 72; www.semanasantadezamora. com; Plaza de Santa María La Nueva; adult/child €4/2; ☉10am-2pm & 5-8pm Tue-Sat, 10am-2pm Sun).

 p424

The Drive » The A11 tracks east of Zamora – not far out along the sweeping plains that

---

↱ DETOUR: PUEBLA DE SANABRIA

Start: ❺ Zamora

Northwest of Zamora, close to the Portuguese border, this captivating village is a tangle of medieval alleyways that unfold around a 15th-century castle and trickle down the hill. This is one of Spain's loveliest hamlets and it's well worth the detour, or even stopping overnight: the quiet cobblestone lanes make it feel like you've stepped back centuries. Wandering the village is alone worth the trip here but a few attractions are worth tracking down. Crowning the village's high point and dominating its skyline for kilometres around, the **Castillo** (adult/child under 12yr €3/ free; ☉11am-2pm & 4-8pm; P📶) has some interesting displays on local history, flora and fauna and superb views from the ramparts. Also at the top of the village, the striking **Plaza Mayor** is surrounded by some fine historical buildings. The 17th-century *ayuntamiento* (town hall) has a lovely arched facade and faces across the square to **Iglesia de Nuestra Señora del Azogue** (Plaza Mayor; ☉noon-2pm & 4-6pm Fri, 11am-2pm & 4-7pm Sat & Sun), a pretty village church which was first built in the 12th century. If you're staying the night, the **Posada Real La Cartería** (📞980 62 03 12; www.lacarteria.com; Calle de Rúa 16; r from €90-150; ❄@🖥) captures the essence of Puebla de Sanabria's medieval appeal with rooms and a restaurant.

MILOSK50/SHUTTERSTOCK ©

BPPERRY/SHUTTERSTOCK ©

WHY THIS IS A GREAT TRIP
ANTHONY HAM,
WRITER

The towns north and west of Madrid are windows on the Spanish soul, each with their own distinctive appeal. Segovia, Ávila, Salamanca, Zamora and Burgos are all Spanish classics, dynamic cities with extraordinary architectural backdrops. Throw in some beautiful villages along the way and you've captured the essence of this remarkable country in just a week.

Above: Catedral, Burgos
Left: Convento de Santa Teresa, Ávila
Right: Semana Santa, Zamora

JASPER JUINEN/GETTY IMAGES ©

bake in summer, take the turn-off to Toro. Total distance: 40km.

---

⑥ Toro

With a name that couldn't be more Spanish and a picaresque history that overshadows its present, Toro is your archetypal Castilian town. It was here that Fernando and Isabel cemented their primacy in Christian Spain at the Battle of Toro in 1476. The town sits on a rise high above the north bank of Río Duero and has a charming historic centre with half-timbered houses and Romanesque churches. The high point, literally, is the 12th-century **Colegiata Santa María La Mayor** (Plaza de la Colegiata; church free, sacristy €4; ⊙10.30am-2pm & 5-7.30pm Tue-Sun Apr-Oct, 10am-2pm & 4.30-6.30pm Tue-Sun Nov-Mar), which rises above the town and boasts the magnificent Romanesque-Gothic Pórtico de la Majestad.

The Drive » Return to the east–west N122 road that lies east of Toro and continue to Tordesillas (46km).

---

⑦ Tordesillas

Commanding a rise on the northern flank of Río Duero, this pretty little town has a historical significance that belies its size. Originally a Roman settlement, it later played a major role in world history when, in 1494, Isabel and Fernando sat down with Portugal here to hammer out a treaty determining who got what in Latin America. Portugal got Brazil and much of the rest went to Spain. Explaining it all is the excellent **Museo del Tratado de Tordesillas** (🖉983 77 10 67; Calle de Casas del Tratado; ⊙10am-1.30pm & 5-7.30pm Tue-Sat, 10am-2pm Sun Jun-Sep, 10am-1.30pm & 4-6.30pm Tue-Sat, 10am-2pm Sun Oct-May). Not far away, the heart of town is formed by the delightful porticoed and cobbled **Plaza Mayor**, its mustard-yellow paintwork offset by dark-brown woodwork and black grilles.

The Drive » From Tordesillas, E80 sweeps northeast, skirts the southern fringe of Valladolid and then continues east as the N122, through the vineyards of the Ribera del Duero wine region all the way into Peñafiel (83km).

- - - - - - - - - - - - - - - -

8 Peñafiel

Peñafiel is the gateway to the Ribera del Duero wine region and it's an appealing small town in its own right. **Plaza del Coso** is one of Spain's most picturesque plazas. This rectangular 15th-century 'square' is considered one of the most important forerunners to the *plazas mayores* across Spain. It's still used for bullfights on ceremonial occasions. But no matter where

you are in Peñafiel, your eyes will be drawn to the **Castillo de Peñafiel** (Museo Provincial del Vino; 🖉983 88 11 99; Peñafiel; castle adult/child €3.30/free, incl museum €6.60/free; ⊙10.30am-2pm & 4-8pm Tue-Sun Apr-Sep, 10.30am-2pm & 4-6pm Tue-Sun Oct-Mar), one of Spain's longest and narrowest castles. Within the castle's crenulated walls is the state-of-the-art **Museo Provincial del Vino**, the local wine museum.

✕ 🛏 p425

The Drive » The N122 continues east of Peñafiel. At Aranda del Duero, turn north along the E5 and make for Lerma, an ideal place to stop for lunch. Sated, return to the E5 and take it all the way into Burgos (108km).

- - - - - - - - - - - - - - - -

TRIP HIGHLIGHT

9 Burgos

Dominated by its Unesco World Heritage–listed cathedral but with plenty more to turn the head, Burgos is one of Castilla y León's most captivating towns. The extraordinary Gothic **Catedral** (🖉947 20 47 12; www.catedraldeburgos.es; Plaza del Rey Fernando; adult/child under 14yr incl audio guide €7/2, from 4.30pm Tue free; ⊙9.30am-7.30pm mid-Mar–Oct, 10am-7pm Nov–mid-Mar) is one of Spain's glittering jewels of religious architecture and looms large over the city and skyline. Inside is the last place of El Cid

and there are numerous extravagant chapels, a gilded staircase and a splendid altar. Some of the best cathedral views are from up the hill at the lookout, just below the 9th-century Castillo de Burgos. Elsewhere in town, two monasteries – the **Cartuja de Miraflores** (🖉947 25 25 86; www.cartuja.org; ⊙10.15am-3pm & 4-6pm Mon-Sat, 11am-3pm & 4-6pm Sun) and the **Monasterio de las Huelgas** (🖉947 20 16 30; www.monasteriodelashuelgas.org; Calle de Alfonso XIII; €6, 4-5.30pm Wed & Thu free; ⊙10am-1pm & 4-5.30pm Tue-Sat, 10.30am-2pm Sun) – are worth seeking out, while the city's eating scene is excellent.

✕ 🛏 p412, p425

The Drive » Take the E5 south of Burgos but almost immediately after leaving the city's southern outskirts, take the N234 turnoff and follow the signs over gently undulating hills and through green valleys to the walled village of Covarrubias (42km from Burgos).

- - - - - - - - - - - - - - - -

TRIP HIGHLIGHT

10 Covarrubias

Inhabiting a broad valley in eastern Castilla y León and spread out along the shady banks of Río Arlanza with a gorgeous riverside aspect, Covarrubias is only a short step removed from the Middle Ages. Once you pass beneath the formidable stone archways that mark the village's entrances, Covarrubias takes

DETOUR: SANTO DOMINGO DE SILOS

Start: ⑩ Covarrubias

Nestled in the rolling hills just off the Burgos–Soria (N234) road, this tranquil, pretty village is built around a monastery with an unusual claim to fame: monks from here made the British pop charts in the mid-1990s with recordings of Gregorian chants. Notable for its pleasingly unadorned Romanesque sanctuary dominated by a multidomed ceiling, the **church** (Calle de Santo Domingo; ⏱6am-2pm & 4.30-10pm, vespers 6am, 7.30am, 9am, 1.45pm, 7pm & 9.30pm) is where you can hear the monks chant. The monastery, one of the most famous in central Spain, is known for its stunning **cloister** (📞947 39 00 49; www.abadiadesilos. es; Calle de Santo Domingo 2; adult/child €3.50/free; ⏱10am-1pm & 4.30-6pm Tue-Sat, noon-1pm & 4-6pm Sun), a two-storey treasure chest of some of Spain's most imaginative Romanesque art. Don't miss the unusually twisted column on the cloister's western side. For sweeping views over the town, pass under the Arco de San Juan and climb the grassy hill to the south to the Ermita del Camino y Via Crucis.

visitors within its intimate embrace with tightly huddled and distinctive, arcaded half-timbered houses opening out onto cobblestone squares. Simply wandering around the village is the main pastime, and don't miss the charming riverside pathways or outdoor tables that spill out onto the squares. Otherwise, the main attraction is the **Colegiata de San Cosme y Damián** (€2.50; ⏱ guided tours 11am, noon, 1pm, 4.30pm & 5.30pm Mon & Wed-Sat, 1pm

& 4.30pm Sun), which has the evocative atmosphere of a mini cathedral and Spain's oldest still-functioning church organ. Also note the gloriously ostentatious altar, fronted by several Roman stone tombs, plus that of Fernán González, the 10th-century founder of Castilla. Don't miss the graceful cloisters and the sacristy with its vibrant 15th-century paintings by Van Eyck and tryptic *Adoración de los Magos*.

The Drive » The N234 winds southwest of Covarrubias through increasingly contoured country all the way to Soria (111km). En route there are signs to medieval churches and hermitages marking many minor roads leading off into the trees.

- - - - - - - - - - - - - - -

⑪ Soria

In the heart of the Castilian countryside, Soria is one of Spain's smaller provincial capitals. It's a great place to escape 'tourist Spain', with an appealing and compact old centre and a sprinkling of stunning monuments across the town and down by the Río Duero. The streets of the old town centre are pretty enough, but by the river is the **Monasterio de San Juan de Duero** (📞975 22 13 97; Camino Monte de las Ánimas; €1, Sat & Sun free; ⏱10am-2pm Sun year round, 10am-2pm & 4-8pm Tue-Sat Jul-Sep, 10am-2pm & 4-7pm Tue-Sat Feb-Jun & Oct, 10am-2pm & 4-6pm Tue-Sat Nov-Jan), Soria's most striking sight, and it's a pretty 2.3km walk to the **Ermita de San Saturio** (📞975 18 07 03; Paseo de San Saturio; ⏱10.30am-2pm & 4.30-8.30pm Tue-Sat, 10.30am-2pm Sun Jul & Aug, shorter hours rest of year) hillside chapel. The stroll is especially pretty in autumn.

🍴 🛏 p425

Eating & Sleeping

Segovia ②

✕ Restaurante
El Fogón Sefardí   Jewish €€

(☎921 46 62 50; www.lacasamudejar.com;
Calle de Isabel La Católica 8; tapas from €3.75,
mains €13-22, set menus €20-35; ☺1.30-
4.30pm & 8.30-11.30pm) Located within the
Hospedería La Gran Casa Mudéjar, this is one
of the most original places in town. Sephardic
Jewish cuisine is served either on the intimate
patio or in the splendid dining hall with original
15th-century Mudéjar flourishes. The theme
in the bar is equally diverse. Stop here for a
taste of the award-winning tapas. Reservations
recommended.

🛏 Hotel Palacio
San Facundo   Historic Hotel €€

(☎921 46 30 61; www.hotelpalaciosanfacundo.
com; Plaza de San Facundo 4; r incl breakfast
from €81; ❄ @ ☎) Segovia's hotels are adept
at fusing stylishly appointed modern rooms
with centuries-old architecture. This place is
one of the best, with an attractive columned
courtyard, a warm colour scheme, chic room
decor and a central location. The breakfast
buffet is more generous than most.

Ávila ③

✕ Soul Kitchen   Castilian €€

(☎920 21 34 83; www.soulkitchen.es; Calle de
Caballeros 13; mains €9-19; ☺10am-midnight
Mon-Fri, 11am-2am Sat, to midnight Sun) This
place has the kind of energy that can seem
lacking elsewhere. The eclectic menu changes
regularly and ranges from salads with dressings
like chestnut and fig to hamburgers with cream
of setas (oyster mushrooms). Lighter dishes
include bruschetta with tasty toppings. Live
music, poetry readings (and similar) happen in
summer.

🛏 Hotel El Rastro   Historic Hotel €

(☎920 35 22 25; www.elrastroavila.com; Calle
Cepedas; s €30-45 d €45-90; ❄ ☎) This
atmospheric hotel occupies a former 16th-
century palace with original stone, exposed

brickwork and a natural, earth-toned colour
scheme exuding a calm, understated elegance.
Each room has a different form, but most have
high ceilings and plenty of space. Note that the
owners also run a marginally cheaper hostal
(budget hotel) of the same name around the
corner.

Salamanca ④

✕ La Cocina de Toño   Tapas €€

(☎923 26 39 77; www.lacocinadetoño.es; Calle
Gran Via 20; tapas from €1.60, mains €11-23, set
menus from €17; ☺11am-4.30pm & 8-11.30pm
Tue-Sat, 11am-4.30pm Sun; ☎) This place
owes its loyal following to its creative pinchos
(tapas) and half-servings of dishes such as
escalope of foie gras with roast apple and
passionfruit jelly. The restaurant serves more
traditional fare as befits the decor, but the
bar is one of Salamanca's gastronomic stars.
Slightly removed from the old city, it draws a
predominantly Spanish crowd.

🛏 Microtel
Placentinos   Boutique Hotel €€

(☎923 28 15 31; www.microtelplacentinos.com;
Calle de Placentinos 9; r incl breakfast €38-110;
❄ ☎) One of Salamanca's most charming
boutique hotels, Microtel Placentinos is tucked
away on a quiet street and has rooms with
exposed stone walls and wooden beams. The
service is faultless, and the overall atmosphere
is one of intimacy and discretion. All rooms have
a hydromassage shower or tub and there's an
outside whirlpool spa (summer only).

Zamora ⑤

✕ La Rua   Castilian €€

(☎980 53 40 24; Rúa de los Francos 21; mains
€9-21; ☺1-4pm Sun-Fri, 1-4pm & 8.30-11.30pm
Sat) Devoted to down-home Zamora cooking,
this central place is a good place to try arroz a la
zamorana (rice with pork and ham or chorizo),
although you'll usually need two people ordering
for staff to make it. It is sometimes closed on
Tuesdays in winter.

🛏 NH Palacio del Duero   Hotel €€

(📞980 50 82 62; www.nh-hotels.com; Plaza de la Horta 1; r from €80; P ❄ @ 🛜) In a superb position next to a lovely Romanesque church, the seemingly modern building has cleverly encompassed part of the former convent, as well as – somewhat bizarrely – a 1940s power station (the lofty brick chimney remains). As you'd expect from this excellent chain, the rooms here are stylishly furnished and the service is attentive.

Peñafiel ⑧

🍴 Asados Alonso   Spanish €€

(📞983 88 08 34; www.facebook.com/restaurantcasadosalonso; Calle de Derecha al Coso 14; mains €14-23; ⏱1-4.30pm Sun & Tue-Thu, 1-4.30pm & 8.30-11.30pm Fri & Sat) Staff keep it simple at this long-standing *asador* (restaurant specialising in roasted meats), with roasted spring lamb cooked in a wood-fired oven and served with salad – many a visitor's idea of bliss.

🛏 Hotel Convento
Las Claras   Historic Hotel €€

(📞983 87 81 68; www.hotelconventolasclaras.com; Plaza Adolfo Muñoz Alonso; r/ste from €85/199; P ❄ 🛜 🏊) This cool, classy hotel – a former convent – is an unexpected find in little Peñafiel, with quietly elegant rooms, as well as a full spa with thermal baths and treatments. On-site is an excellent restaurant with, as you'd expect, a carefully chosen wine list. Lighter meals are available in the cafeteria.

Burgos ⑨

🍴 Cervecería Morito   Tapas €

(📞947 26 75 55; Calle de Diego Porcelos 1; tapas/raciones from €4/6; ⏱12.30-3.30pm & 7-11.30pm) Cervecería Morito is the undisputed king of Burgos tapas bars and as such it's always crowded. A typical order is *alpargata* (lashings of cured ham with bread, tomato and olive oil) or the *revueltos Capricho de Burgos* (scrambled eggs served with potatoes, blood sausage, red peppers, baby eels and mushrooms) – the latter is a meal in itself.

Soria ⑪

🍴 Baluarte   Castilian €€€

(📞975 21 36 58; www.baluarte.info; Calle de los Caballeros 14; set menus €57 70; ⏱1.30 4pm & 8.45-10.45pm Tue-Sat, 1.30-4pm Sun) Óscar García Marina is one of Spain's most exciting chefs and this Michelin-starred venture in Soria appropriately showcases his culinary talents. Dishes are based on classic Castilian ingredients but treated with just enough foam and drizzle to ensure that they're both exciting and satisfying without being too pretentious. Reservations essential.

🛏 Apolonia   Boutique Hotel €€

(📞975 23 90 56; www.hotelapoloniasoria.com; Puertas de Pro 5; s/d from €60/68; ❄ @ 🛜) This smart hotel has a contemporary urban feel with its charcoal, brown and cream colour scheme, abundance of glass, abstract artwork and, in four of the rooms, an interesting, if revealing, colour-lighting effect between the main room and the large walk-in shower – possibly best for romancing couples.

Roving La Rioja Wine Region

Learn about the gift of the grape on this quiet road trip through vine-studded countryside. Along the way, visit wineries and wine museums and admire stunning architecture.

31

TRIP HIGHLIGHTS

95 km

Briones
Obtain wine-fuelled knowledge at Vicanco, a space-age museum

125 km

Laguardia
Spin back the wheels of time in this wine-soaked fortress town

Haro

6

8

Santo Domingo
de la Calzada

4

Nájera

1 START/
FINISH

San Millán
de Cogolla

Santo Domingo de la Calzada
The old town buzzes with Camino pilgrims

66 km

Logroño
Delve into the fabulous culinary scene of this understated city

1 km

**2–3 DAYS
145 KM / 90 MILES**

GREAT FOR...

BEST TIME TO GO
September and October when the grapes are being harvested.

 ESSENTIAL PHOTO

Waving at the camera from in front of the Hotel Marqués de Riscal.

 BEST FOR FOOD

Logroño has some of the best tapas bars in Spain.

Logroño La Rioja vineyard

427

31 | Roving La Rioja Wine Region

La Rioja is home to the best wines in Spain and on this short-and-sweet road trip along unhurried back roads you'll enjoy gorgeous vine-striped countryside and asleep-at-noon villages of honey-coloured stone. But the overriding interest is reserved for food and drink: winery tours, cutting-edge museums and some of the best tapas in Spain make this drive an essential for any food-and-wine lover.

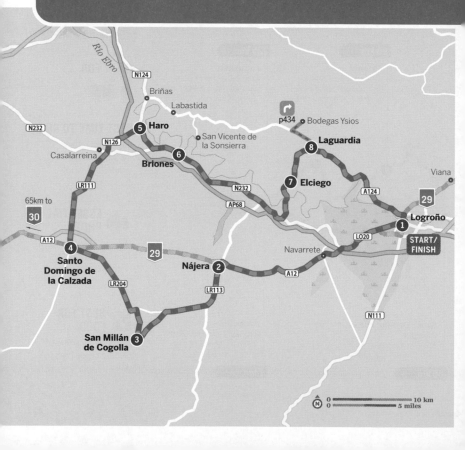

① Logroño

Small, low-key Logroño is the capital of La Rioja. The city doesn't receive all that many tourists and there aren't all that many things to see and do, but the historic centre makes for pleasant strolling and there is a monumentally good selection of *pintxo* (tapas) bars. In fact, Logroño is quickly gaining a culinary reputation to rival anywhere in Spain.

Rioja Trek (☏941 58 73 54; www.riojatrek.com; Calle Francisco de Quevedo 12), based 2.5km southeast of the city centre, offers a wide range of customisable winery tours (which can include visiting a traditional vineyard and bodega and even doing

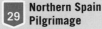

LINK YOUR TRIP

29 Northern Spain Pilgrimage

Follow the path of pilgrims on the road to Santiago de Compostela. You can join The Way in Logroño.

30 Historic Castilla y León

A quick skip south to Soria will let you do this captivating inland tour in reverse.

some wine-making yourself), as well as wine tastings, tapas tours, hikes along some of La Rioja's fabulous mountain trails and activities for families with children.

🛏 p435

The Drive » It's only a short drive of 28km (25 minutes) from Logroño to Nájera, starting along the LO20, which transforms into the A12 motorway around the halfway point.

② Nájera

The main attraction of this otherwise unexciting town, which lies on the Camino de Santiago, is the Gothic **Monasterio de Santa María la Real** and, in particular, its fragile-looking, early-16th-century cloisters. The monastery was built in 1032, but was significantly rebuilt in the 15th century.

The Drive » The dry landscapes around Nájera become greener and more rolling as you head southwest along the LR113 and LR205 for 18km (20 minutes) to San Millán de Cogolla. In the far distance rise the 2000m-plus mountains of the Sierra de la Demanda – snow-capped in winter.

③ San Millán de Cogolla

The hamlet of San Millán de Cogolla is home to two remarkable monasteries, which between them helped give birth to the Castilian (Spanish)

language. On account of their linguistic heritage and artistic beauty, they have been recognised by Unesco as World Heritage sites.

The **Monasterio de Yuso** (☏941 37 30 49; www.monasteriodesanmillan.com/yuso; Calle Convento; adult/child €7/3; ⊙10am-1.30pm & 4-6.30pm Tue-Sun Apr-Sep, also open Mon Aug, to 5.30pm Tue-Sun Oct-Mar) contains numerous treasures in its museum. You can only visit as part of a guided tour (in Spanish, with English and French information sheets available). Tours last 50 minutes and run every half-hour or so.

A short distance away is the **Monasterio de Suso** (☏941 37 30 82; www.monasteriodesanmillan.com/suso; Calle de Suso; €4; ⊙9.30am-1.30pm & 3.30-6.30pm Tue-Sun Apr-Sep, to 5.30pm Oct-Mar). It's believed that in the 13th century a monk named Gonzalo de Berceo wrote some of the first Castilian words here. Again, it can only be visited on a guided tour. Tickets include a short bus ride up to the monastery from the Monasterio de Yuso, whose reception area sells them; you can't arrive independently.

The Drive » It's a 20km (20-minute) drive along the delightfully quiet LR206 and LR204 to Santo Domingo de la Calzada. The scenery is a mix of vast sunburnt fields, red-tinged soils, vineyards and patches of forest.

LOCAL KNOWLEDGE:
TAPAS IN LOGRONO

Make no mistake about it: Logroño is an eater's delight. There are several very good restaurants, and then there are the tapas (which here are often called by their Basque name, *pintxos*). Few cities have such a dense concentration of excellent tapas bars. Most of the action takes place on Calle Laurel and Calle San Juan. *Pintxos* cost around €2 to €4, and most of the bars are open from about 8pm to midnight, Tuesday to Sunday. Here are some of our favourites:

Bar Torrecilla (☏608 344694; Calle Laurel 15; pintxos €2-3.50; ☺1-4pm & 8pm-12.30am Wed-Sun) The best *pintxos* in town? You be the judge. Go for the melt-in-your-mouth foie gras or the mini-burgers, or anything else that takes your fancy, at this modern bar on buzzing Calle Laurel.

Tastavin (www.facebook.com/tastavinbardepinchos; Calle San Juan 25; pintxos €2.50-4; ☺8-11pm Tue, 1-4pm & 8-11pm Wed-Sun; ☎) On *pintxo* bar–lined San Juan, stylish Tastavin whips up some of the tastiest morsels in town, including smoked trout and lemon cream cornets, fried artichokes, tuna tataki and braised oxtail. The wines are outstanding.

Bar Soriano (Travesía de Laurel 2; tapas €1.50; ☺11.45am-3pm & 7-11.45pm Mon, Tue, Thu & Fri, 11am-3pm & 6-11pm Sat, 11am-10pm Sun) This venerable bar has been serving just one tapa, a mushroom stack topped with a prawn, since 1972.

TRIP HIGHLIGHT

❹ Santo Domingo de la Calzada

The small, walled old town of Santo Domingo is the kind of place where you can be certain that the baker knows all his customers by name and that everyone will turn up for María's christening. Santiago-bound pilgrims have long been a part of the fabric of this town, and that tradition continues to this day, with most visitors being foot-weary pilgrims. All this helps to make Santo Domingo one of the most enjoyable places in La Rioja. The biggest attraction in town, aside from the very worthwhile pursuit of just strolling the streets and lounging in the main old-town plaza, is a visit to the monumental **cathedral** (☏941 34 00 33; www.

catedralsantodomingo.com; Plaza del Santo 4; adult/child €7/2; ☺10am-8pm Mon-Fri, to 7pm Sat, 10am-noon & 2-8pm Sun Apr-Oct, shorter hours Nov-Mar).

The Drive ≫ The LR111 (becoming the N126) goes in an almost ruler-straight line across fields of crops and under a big sky to the workaday town of Haro (20km, 20 minutes).

---

❺ Haro

Despite its fame in the wine world, there's not much of a heady bouquet to Haro, La Rioja's premier wine-producing town. But it has a cheerful pace, and the compact old quarter, leading off Plaza de la Paz, has some intriguing alleyways with bars and wine shops aplenty.

There are plenty of wine bodegas in the vicinity of the town, some of which are open to visitors (but almost always with advance reservation). One of the more receptive to visitors is **Bodegas Muga** (☏941 31 18 25; www.bodegasmuga.com; Barrio de la Estación; 1hr winery tour €15, 2.5-hour hot-air balloon tour €170; ☺by reservation Mon-Sat), which is just after the railway bridge on the way out of town to the north. It gives guided tours and tastings, in Spanish and English, daily except Sunday.

The Drive » Briones is almost within walking distance of Haro. It's just 9km away (10 minutes) along the N124 and N232.

- - - - - - - - - - - - - - - - -

TRIP HIGHLIGHT

❻ Briones

One man's dream has put the small, obscenely quaint village of Briones firmly on the Spanish wine and tourism map. The sunset-gold village crawls gently up a hillside and offers commanding views over the surrounding vine-carpeted plains. It's on these plains where you will find the fantastic wine museum **Vivanco** (Museo de la Cultura del Vino; ☎941 32 23 23; www.vivancoculturadevino.es; Carretera Nacional, Km 232; museum only adult/child €16.50/free, guided visit with wine tasting €45-97; ⏰10am-6pm Tue-Fri & Sun, 10am-8pm Sat). Over several floors you will learn all about the history and culture of wine and the various processes that go into its production. All of this is done through interesting displays brought to life with computer technology. The treasures on display include Picasso-designed wine jugs, Roman and Byzantine mosaics, and gold-draped, wine-inspired religious artefacts. Various guided tours take you behind the scenes of the winery and include tastings.

🛏 p435

The Drive » It's 23km (30 minutes) along the N232, LR211 and A3210 to Elciego. The scenery, which is made up of endless vineyards, will delight anyone who enjoys wide open spaces (and vine leaves). In the distance are strange, sheer-faced, table-topped mountains.

- - - - - - - - - - - - - - - - -

❼ Elciego

Rioja wine's most flamboyant flourish lurks in the village of Elciego (Eltziego in Basque) in the showstopping form of the Hotel Marqués de Riscal (p435) – not unlike a rainbow-hued Guggenheim museum (not surprising, perhaps, as both buildings were

THE WEALTH OF THE GRAPE

La Rioja, and the surrounding areas of Navarra and the Basque province of Álava, comprise Spain's best-regarded wine-producing region. The principal grape of Rioja is the tempranillo. The first taste of a tempranillo is of leather and cherries and the wine lingers on the tongue.

The Riojans have had a long love affair with wine. There's evidence that both the Phoenicians and the Celtiberians produced and drank wine here and the earliest written evidence of grape cultivation in La Rioja dates to 873 CE. Today, some 250 million L of wine bursts forth from the grapes of La Rioja annually. Almost all of this (around 85%) is red wine, though some quality whites and rosés are also produced. The Riojan love of wine is so great that in the town of Haro they even have a fiesta devoted to it. It culminates with a messy 'wine battle', in which thousands of litres of wine gets chucked around, turning everyone's clothes red in the process. This takes place on 29 June.

How to find a good bottle? Spanish wine is subject to a complicated system of classification, similar to the ones used in France and Italy. La Rioja is the only wine region in Spain classed as *Denominación de Origen Calificada* (DOC), the highest grade and a guarantee that any wine labelled as such was produced according to strict regional standards. The best wines are often marked with the designations 'Crianza' (aged more than two years, with at least one year in an oak barrel), 'Reserva' (aged for at least three years, at least one of them in an oak barrel) or 'Gran Reserva' (aged for at least two years in an oak barrel and three years in the bottle).

WHY THIS IS A GREAT TRIP
JOHN NOBLE
WRITER

How can anyone not love an area sloshing in wine, and with fine restaurants and plenty of tempting tapas bars too? There's a soothingly slow pace and sense of space that adds an extra dimension to touring La Rioja, Spain's premier wine-producing region, with broad, vine-carpeted plains, big skies, sleepy honey-toned *pueblos* (villages) and plenty of sunshine, even in winter when the distant hills are capped with snow.

Above: Laguardia
Left: Cathedral, Santo Domingo de la Calzada
Right: Wine barrels, Haro

designed by Canadian Frank Gehry). Casual visitors are not welcome at the hotel, but if you want to see it, you have three options. The easiest is to join one of the **Marqués de Riscal winery tours** (Vinos de los Herederos del Marqués de Riscal; ☎945 18 08 88; www.marquesderiscal. com; Hotel Marqués de Riscal, Calle Torrea 1, Elciego; tours €12; ⏱tours 10.30am-1pm & 4-6pm) – there's at least one English-language tour a day, but it's best to book in advance. You won't get inside the building, but you will get to see its exterior from some distance. A much closer look can be obtained by reserving a table at one of the two superb in-house restaurants: the Michelin-starred **Restaurante Marqués de Riscal** (☎945 18 08 80; www.restaurantemarquesder iscal.com; Hotel Marqués de Riscal, Calle Torrea 1; 14-/21-course menu €110/140; ⏱8-10pm Tue, 1.30-3.30pm & 8-10pm Wed-Sun) or the **1860 Tradición** (☎945 18 08 80; www.hotel-marques deriscal.com; Hotel Marqués de Riscal, Calle Torrea 1; mains €22-36; ⏱1.30-3.30pm & 8-10pm). For the most intimate look at the building, you'll need to reserve a hotel room for the night.

🛏 p435

The Drive » It's only 10 minutes (7km) along the A3210 from Elciego to wonderful Laguardia, which rises up off

DETOUR:
BODEGAS YSIOS

Start: **8** Laguardia

Just a couple of kilometres north of Laguardia is **Bodegas Ysios** (945 60 06 40; www.bodegasysios.com; Camino de la Hoya; 90min tour & tasting €25; tours 11am daily), architecturally perhaps the most gobsmacking bodega in Spain. Designed by Santiago Calatrava as a 'temple dedicated to wine', it features a cedar exterior with an aluminium wave for a roof that matches the flow of the rocky mountains behind it – and looks best after dark when pools of light flow out of it. Tours provide an insight into wine production; book ahead.

the otherwise flat, vine-striped countryside.

- - - - - - - - - - - - - - - - - -

TRIP HIGHLIGHT

8 Laguardia

It's easy to spin back the wheels of time in the medieval fortress town of Laguardia, or the 'Guard of Navarra' as it was once appropriately known, sitting proudly on its rocky hilltop. As well as memories of long-lost yesterdays, the town further entices visitors with its wine-producing present. **Bodegas Palacio** (945 60 00 57; www.bodegaspalacio. com; San Lazaro 1; 90min tour & tasting from €25; by appointment), just 800m south of Laguardia, arranges tours and tastings by appointment. Check the website for details of its wine courses (from €35 for one hour). On the southeast edge of town is the **Centro Temático del Vino Villa Lucía** (945 60 00 32; www.villa-lucia.com; Carretera de Logroño; 90min tour €12; 9am-2pm & 4-8pm Tue-Sat, 9am-2pm Sun), a wine museum and shop selling high-quality wine from a variety of small, local producers. Museum visits are by guided tour only and finish with a 4D film and wine tasting.

✗ ▭ p435

The Drive » From Laguardia it's a short 18km (20 minutes) down the A124 back to Logroño where you started this tour.

Eating & Sleeping

Logroño **❶**

🛏 Hotel Calle Mayor   Hotel €€

(📞941 23 23 68; www.hotelcallemayor.com; Calle Marqués de San Nicolás 71; s/d/ste from €95/125/235; [P] [❄] [📶]) Set within a restored 16th-century building, classy Hotel Calle Mayor has a dozen large, comfortable rooms bathed in light, some with wooden beams and balconies, and modern neutral-toned bathrooms.

Santo Domingo de la Calzada **❹**

✕ Los Caballeros   Spanish €€€

(📞941 34 27 89; www.restauranteloscaballeros. com; Calle Mayor 56; mains €18-32; ⊙1-3.30pm & 7.30-10.30pm Tue-Sat, 1-3.30pm Sun) Beside the cathedral in a classy dining room set with exposed brick, wood-beamed ceiling and stained-glass details, Los Caballeros serves suckling pig and lamb, among other classic Navarran fare. Don't miss house speciality cinnamon and vanilla *nuestra tarta del abuelito* ('our grandfather's pudding') for dessert. Advance reservations are a must at busy times.

🛏 Parador de Santo Domingo de la Calzada   Historic Hotel €€

(📞941 34 03 00; www.parador.es; Plaza del Santo 3; d from €100; [P] [📶]) Occupying the town's 12th-century former hospital opposite the cathedral, this palatial hotel has spacious rooms (some with canopied beds and small balconies) and magnificent public areas, including the in-house restaurant (mains €11 to €19).

Briones **❻**

🛏 Los Calaos de Briones   Hotel €€

(📞941 32 21 31; www.loscalaosdebriones.com; San Juan 13; d from €65) At this lovely hotel, some rooms have romantic four-poster beds; those facing east have beautiful views over the countryside. The attached restaurant (mains €11 to €17), in an old wine cellar, specialises in local lamb and seasonal vegetables.

Elciego **❼**

🛏 Hotel Marqués de Riscal   Design Hotel €€€

(📞945 18 08 80; www.hotel-marquesderiscal. com; Calle Torrea 1, Elciego; d from €371; [P] [❄] [📶]) When the owner of Elciego's Bodegas Marqués de Riscal decided he wanted to create something special, he didn't hold back. The result is the spectacular Frank Gehry–designed Hotel Marqués de Riscal, which opened in 2006. Costing around €85 million, the building is a flamboyant wave of multicoloured titanium sheets that stand in utter contrast to the village behind.

Laguardia **❽**

✕ Restaurante Amelibia   Spanish €€

(📞945 62 12 07; www.restauranteamelibia.com; Barbacana 14; mains €15-22; ⊙1-3.30pm Mon & Wed-Sun, 8.30-10.30pm Fri & Sat; [👶]) Gaze out the windows at a view over the scorched plains and distant mountain ridges while dining on sublime traditional cuisine, such as oxtail and wild mushrooms in red wine sauce with seasonal vegetables, or pig's trotters in a sherry reduction. Half-portions are available for kids.

🛏 Posada Mayor de Migueloa   Historic Hotel €€

(📞945 60 01 87; www.mayordemigueloa.com; Calle Mayor 20; s/d incl breakfast from €83/106; [❄] [📶]) This 17th-century mansion-hotel has seven atmospheric rooms that evoke a bygone age with old stone walls, low-beamed ceilings and polished antique furnishings. Be sure to pay a visit to the hotel's wine cellar. The on-site restaurant (mains €18 to €24.50) is also top notch.

NEED TO KNOW

CURRENCY
Euro (€)

LANGUAGE
Spanish (Castilian). Also Catalan, Basque and Galician.

VISAS
Generally not required for stays of up to 90 days (not at all for members of EU or Schengen countries). Some nationalities need a Schengen visa.

FUEL
Petrol stations (usually open 24 hours) can be found along major highways. Expect to pay €1.35 to €1.80 per litre.

RENTAL CARS
Hertz (www.hertz.com)
Holiday Autos (www. holidayautos.com)
Pepecar (www.pepecar.com)

IMPORTANT NUMBERS
Europe-wide emergencies (☎112)
International access code (☎00)
Country code (☎34)

Climate

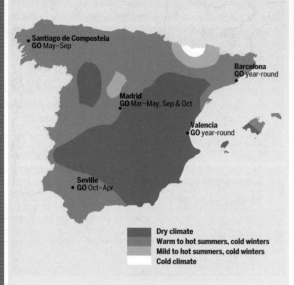

- Dry climate
- Warm to hot summers, cold winters
- Mild to hot summers, cold winters
- Cold climate

Santiago de Compostela
GO May–Sep

Barcelona
GO year-round

Madrid
GO Mar–May, Sep & Oct

Valencia
GO year-round

Seville
GO Oct–Apr

When to Go

High Season (Jun–Aug, public holidays)
» Accommodation books out and prices increase by up to 50%.

» Low season in parts of inland Spain.

» Expect warm, dry and sunny weather; more humid in coastal areas.

Shoulder (Mar–May, Sep & Oct)
» A good time to travel: mild, clear weather and fewer crowds.

» Local festivals can send prices soaring.

» Fewer hikers on trails but weather unpredictable.

Low Season (Nov–Feb)
» Cold in central Spain; rain in the north and northwest.

» Mild temperatures in Andalucía and the Mediterranean coast.

» This is high season in ski resorts.

» Many hotels are closed in beach areas, but elsewhere along the coast prices plummet.

Daily Costs

Budget: Less than €80
» Dorm bed: €20–30

» Double room in *hostal* (budget hotel): €50–65 (€60–75 in Madrid, Barcelona and Balearics)

» Self-catering and lunch *menú del día* (set menu): €20–30

Midrange: €80–175
» Double room in midrange hotel: €65–140 (€75–200 in Madrid, Barcelona and Balearics)

» Lunch and/or dinner in local restaurant: €20–40

» Car rental: per day from €25

Top end: More than €175
» Double room In top-end hotel: €140 and up (over €200 in Madrid, Barcelona and Balearics)

» Fine dining for lunch and dinner: €150–250

» Admission to Madrid's Museo del Prado: €15

Eating

Tapas bar Tapas and drinks; open longer hours than restaurants.

Taberna Rustic place serving tapas and *raciones* (large tapas).

Panadería Bakery; good for pastries and coffee.

Vinoteca Wine bar where you order by the glass.

Cervecería Beerhall; the place to go for snacks and *cerveza* (draft beer).

Price categories indicate the cost of a main course:

€	less than €12
€€	€12–20
€€€	more than €20

Sleeping

Casas rurales Comfy village houses or farmhouses for hire in the countryside.

Hostales Simple guesthouses with ensuite rooms.

Paradores State-funded accommodation often in castles, converted monasteries and old mansions.

Pensión Inexpensive, extremely basic guesthouses, often with shared bathrooms.

Price categories indicate the cost of a double room with private bathroom in high season:

	BARCELONA & MADRID/ ELSEWHERE
€	less than €75/€65
€€	€75–200/€65–140
€€€	more than €200/€140

Arriving in Spain

Barajas Airport (Madrid)
Rental cars Major car-rental agencies are in the arrival terminals.

Metro & buses Around €5; every five to 10 minutes from 6.05am to 1.30am; 30 to 40 minutes to the centre.

Taxis €30; reach the centre in 20 minutes.

El Prat Airport (Barcelona)
Rental cars Car-rental agencies are in the arrival terminals.

Buses €5.90; every five to 10 minutes from 6.10am to 1.05am; 30 to 40 minutes to the centre.

Trains €4.10; every 30 minutes from 5.42am to 11.38pm; 25 to 30 minutes to the centre.

Taxis €25–30; reach the centre in 30 minutes.

Mobile Phones

Local SIM cards are widely available and can be used in European and Australian mobile phones. Not compatible with many North American or Japanese systems.

Internet Access

Wi-fi is available in most lodgings and cafes (and is usually free). Internet cafes are rare.

Money

ATMs widely available. Credit cards accepted in most hotels and restaurants.

Tipping

Menu prices indicate a service charge. Most people leave small change if satisfied: 5% is fine; 10% is considered generous.

Useful Websites

Lonely Planet (lonelyplanet.com/spain) Travel tips, accommodation, recommendations and more.

Tour Spain (www.spain.info) Spanish tourism authority with interactive maps featuring key attractions in every region.

RAC (www.rac.co.uk/drive/travel/driving-abroad) Info for British drivers on driving in Spain and Portugal.

Language

The pronunciation of most Spanish sounds is very similar to that of their English counterparts. If you read our coloured pronunciation guides as if they were English, you'll be understood. Note that kh is a throaty sound (like the 'ch' in the Scottish *loch*), r is strongly rolled, ly is pronounced as the 'lli' in 'million' and ny as the 'ni' in 'onion'. You may also notice that the 'lisped' th sound is pronounced as s in Andalucia. In our pronunciation guides stressed syllables are indicated with italics.

SPANISH BASICS

Hello.	*Hola.*	o·la
Goodbye.	*Adiós.*	a·dyos
How are you?	*¿Qué tal?*	ke tal
Fine, thanks.	*Bien, gracias.*	byen gra·syas
Excuse me.	*Perdón.*	per·*don*
Sorry.	*Lo siento.*	lo syen·to
Yes.	*Sí.*	see
No.	*No.*	no
Please.	*Por favor.*	por fa·*vor*
Thank you.	*Gracias.*	gra·syas
You're welcome.	*De nada.*	de na·da

My name is ...
Me llamo ...   me *lya*·mo ...

What's your name?
¿Cómo se llama Usted?   ko·mo se *lya*·ma oo·*ste* (pol)
¿Cómo te llamas?   ko·mo te *lya*·mas (inf)

Do you speak English?
¿Habla inglés?   a·bla een·*gles* (pol)
¿Hablas inglés?   a·blas een·*gles* (inf)

I don't understand.
No entiendo.   no en·*tyen*·do

DIRECTIONS

Where's ...?
¿Dónde está ...?   don·de es·*ta* ...

What's the address?
¿Cuál es la dirección?   kwal es la dee·rek·*syon*

Can you please write it down?
¿Puede escribirlo, por favor?   pwe·de es·kree·*beer*·lo por fa·*vor*

Can you show me (on the map)?
¿Me lo puede indicar (en el mapa)?   me lo pwe·de een·dee·*kar* (en el ma·pa)

EMERGENCIES

Help!	*¡Socorro!*	so·ko·ro
I'm lost.		
Estoy perdido/a.		es·toy per·dee·do/a (m/f)

ON THE ROAD

I'd like to hire a ...	*Quisiera alquilar ...*	kee·sye·ra al·kee·lar ...
4WD	*un todo-terreno*	oon to·do·te·re·no
bicycle	*una bicicleta*	oo·na bee·see·kle·ta
car	*un coche*	oon ko·che
motorcycle	*una moto*	oo·na mo·to

Want More?

For in-depth language information and handy phrases, check out Lonely Planet's *Spanish Phrasebook*. You'll find it at **shop.lonelyplanet.com**.

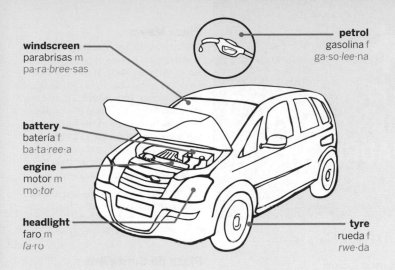

windscreen
parabrisas m
pa·ra·*bree*·sas

petrol
gasolina f
ga·so·*lee*·na

battery
batería f
ba·ta·*ree*·a

engine
motor m
mo·*tor*

headlight
faro m
fa·ro

tyre
rueda f
rwe·da

child seat	asiento de seguridad para niños	a·*syen*·to de se·goo·ree·*da* pa·ra *nee*·nyos
diesel	gasóleo	ga·so·le·o
helmet	casco	*kas*·ko
mechanic	mecánico	me·*ka*·nee·ko
petrol	gasolina	ga·so·*lee*·na
service station	gasolinera	ga·so·lee·*ne*·ra

How much is it per day/hour?
¿Cuánto cuesta por día/hora?
kwan·to *kwes*·ta por dee·a/o·ra

Is this the road to ...?
¿Se va a ... por esta carretera?
se va a ... por *es*·ta ka·re·*te*·ra

(How long) Can I park here?
¿(Por cuánto tiempo) Puedo aparcar aquí?
(por *kwan*·to *tyem*·po) *pwe*·do a·par·*kar* a·*kee*

The car has broken down (at ...).
El coche se ha averiado (en ...).
el ko·che se a a·ve·*rya*·do (en ...)

I have a flat tyre.
Tengo un pinchazo.
ten·go oon peen·*cha*·tho

I've run out of petrol.
Me he quedado sin gasolina.
me e ke·*da*·do seen ga·so·*lee*·na

Where's a petrol station?
¿Dónde hay una gasolinera?
don·de ai *oo*·na ga·so·lee·*ne*·ra

I had an accident.
He tenido un accidente.
e te·*nee*·do oon ak·thee·*den*·te

I need a mechanic.
Necesito un/una mecánico/a. m/f
ne·the·*see*·to oon/*oo*·na me·*ka*·nee·ko/a

Are there cycling paths?
¿Hay carril bicicleta?
ai ka·*reel* bee·thee·*kle*·ta

Is there bicycle parking?
¿Hay aparcamiento de bicicletas?
ai a·par·ka·*myen*·to de bee·thee·*kle*·tas

Signs

Stop	Stop
Ceda el Paso	Give Way
Prohibido	No Entry
Acceso	Entrance
Peaje	Toll
Dirección Única	One Way
Vía Acceso	Freeway Exit
Aparcamiento	Parking
Prohibido Aparcar	No Parking

STRETCH YOUR LEGS
MADRID

Start/Finish Plaza Mayor

Distance 3.8km

Duration Two to three hours

Madrid's compact and historic centre is ideal for exploring on foot. So much of Madrid life occurs on the streets and in its glorious plazas, and it all takes place against a spectacular backdrop of architecture, stately and grand.

Take this walk on Trip

Plaza Mayor

So many Madrid stories begin in its grand central square. Since it was laid out in 1619, the Plaza Mayor has seen everything from bullfights to the trials of the Spanish Inquisition. These days the grandeur of the plaza owes much to the warm colours of the uniformly ochre apartments, with 237 wrought-iron balconies offset by the exquisite frescoes of the 17th-century **Real Casa de la Panadería** (Royal Bakery).

The Walk » Walk down Calle de Postas off the plaza's northeastern corner, cross busy Plaza de la Puerta del Sol, then continue east along Carrera de San Jerónimo. At elegant Plaza de Canalejas, turn right.

Plaza de Santa Ana

There are few more iconic Madrid squares than Plaza de Santa Ana, a local favourite since Joseph Bonaparte carved it out of this crowded inner-city neighbourhood in 1810. Surrounded by classic Madrid architecture of pastel shades, the plaza presides over the Barrio de las Letras. The outdoor tables are among the city's most sought-after.

The Walk » Walking west, cross Plaza del Ángel, walk along Calle de la Bolsa, cross Calle de Toledo and make for Calle de la Cava Baja, a glorious medieval street lined with tapas bars. Keep Iglesia de San Andrés on your right, and stroll down the hill to Plaza de la Paja.

Plaza de la Paja

Delightful 'Straw Sq' slopes down into the tangle of lanes that once made up Madrid's Muslim quarter. In the 12th and 13th centuries the city's main market occupied the square and it retains a palpable medieval air, and at times can feel like a Castilian village square. **Delic** (☎91 364 54 50; www.delic.es; Costanilla de San Andrés 14; ⊗11am-2am Sun & Tue-Thu, to 2.30am Fri & Sat; MLa Latina), with tables on the plaza, is brilliant for a mojito, while **Jardín del Príncipe Anglona** (Plaza de la Paja; ⊗10am-10pm Apr-Oct, to 6.30pm Nov-Mar; MLa Latina), a walled 18th-century garden, is a peaceful oasis

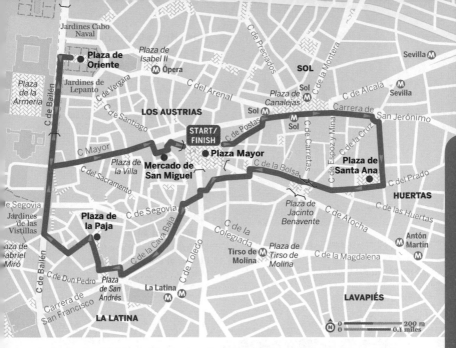

in the heart of this most clamorous of cities.

The Walk » Take any lane heading west through La Morería, the old Muslim quarter, to Calle de Bailén. Turn right, cross the viaduct, pass the cathedral and continue to Plaza de Oriente.

Plaza de Oriente

Cinematic in scope, Plaza de Oriente is grand and graceful. It's watched over by the **Palacio Real** (☎91 454 87 00; www.patrimonionacional.es; Calle de Bailén; adult/concession €10/5, guide/audio guide €4, EU citizens free last 2hr Mon-Thu; ◷10am-8pm Apr-Sep, to 6pm Oct-Mar; Ⓜ Ópera) and Madrid's opera house, **Teatro Real** (☎91 516 06 96; www.teatro-real.com; Plaza de Oriente; guided tour €8-30, audio guide €7; ◷ guided visits 10am-1pm, self-guided visits 10.30am-4.30pm Sep-Jul & 10am-6pm Aug; Ⓜ Ópera), plus sophisticated cafes and apartments that cost the equivalent of a royal salary. At the centre of the plaza is an equestrian statue of Felipe IV designed by Velázquez, and nearby are some 20 marble statues, mostly of ancient monarchs.

Local legend holds that these royals get down off their pedestals at night to stretch their legs.

The Walk » Return south along Calle de Bailén, then turn left (east) up Calle Mayor. After passing the intimate Plaza de la Villa on your right, Mercado de San Miguel appears, also on your right as you climb the hill.

Mercado de San Miguel

One of Madrid's oldest and most beautiful markets, the **Mercado de San Miguel** (☎91 542 49 36; www.mercadode sanmiguel.es; Plaza de San Miguel; tapas from €1; ◷10am-midnight Sun-Thu, to 1am Fri & Sat; Ⓜ Sol) is now an exciting gastronomic space. Within the early-20th-century glass walls, stalls serve up all manner of tapas, from fishy *pintxos* atop mini toasts to *jamón* or other cured meats from Salamanca, plus cheeses, pickled goodies and fine wines.

The Walk » To return to where you started, leave the market, walk down Calle de la Cava de San Miguel, turn left and climb the stairs through the Arco de los Cuchilleros to the Plaza Mayor.

STRETCH YOUR LEGS
BARCELONA

Start Parc de la Ciutadella

Finish Casa Batlló

Distance 3.5km

Duration Three hours

Packed with historic treasures and jaw-dropping architecture, Barcelona is a wanderer's delight. This stroll takes you through atmospheric medieval lanes and along elegant boulevards, leading you past Gothic cathedrals, lively tapas bars and palm-fringed plazas.

Take this walk on Trip

Parc de la Ciutadella

The handsomely landscaped Parc de la Ciutadella is a local favourite for a leisurely promenade. Start in the northeast corner, and descend past the monumental **Cascada** (waterfall), then stroll south across the park, passing a small pond and Catalonia's regional parliament.

The Walk » With your back to the park, cross Passeig de Picasso and walk along restaurant-lined Passeig del Born. According to legend, jousting matches were once held here.

Basílica de Santa Maria del Mar

Nothing prepares you for the singular beauty of **Basílica de Santa Maria del Mar** (☎93 310 23 90; www.santamariadelmar barcelona.org; Plaça de Santa Maria del Mar; guided tour €8.50-10; ☺9am-8.30pm Mon-Sat, 10am-8pm Sun, tours 1-5pm Sat, from 2pm Sun; Ⓜ Jaume I). Barcelona's most stirring Gothic structure, the 14th-century church was built in just 59 years.

The Walk » Take Carrer de l'Argenteria up to Via Laietana. Cross this busy road, continuing along Carrer de la Llibreteria. Turn right onto Carrer de la Freneria. After a few blocks, you'll see the massive cathedral on your left.

La Catedral

For centuries the spiritual heart of Barcelona, **La Catedral** (☎93 342 82 62; www.catedralbcn.org; Plaça de la Seu; €7, roof or choir €3, chapter house €2; ☺worship 8.30am-12.30pm & 5.45-7.30pm Mon-Fri, 8.30am-12.30pm & 5.15-8pm Sat, 8.30am-1.45pm & 5.15-8pm Sun, tourist visits 12.30-7.45pm Mon-Fri, 12.30-5.30pm Sat, 2-5.30pm Sun; Ⓜ Jaume I) is at once lavish and sombre, anchoring the city in its past. Begun in the late 13th century and not completed until six centuries later, the cathedral is Barcelona's history rendered in stone.

The Walk » Turn left down Carrer del Bispe, and take a right onto Plaça Sant Jaume. A few blocks further, turn left onto narrow Carrer del Vidre, which leads to the plaza.

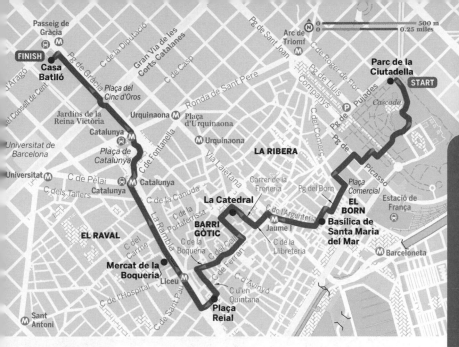

Plaça Reial

One of the most photogenic squares in Barcelona, the Plaça Reial is not to be missed. Numerous eateries, bars and nightspots lie beneath the arcades of 19th-century neoclassical buildings, with a buzz of activity at all hours. The lamp posts by the central fountain are Antoni Gaudí's first known works in the city.

The Walk » Exit the square onto famous La Rambla, a bustling boulevard with a wide pedestrian-filled strip in the middle. Walk north a few blocks until you see the large cast-iron market off to your left.

Mercat de la Boqueria

This temple of temptation is one of Europe's greatest **food markets** (☎93 318 20 17; www.boqueria.barcelona; La Rambla 91; ☺8am-8.30pm Mon-Sat; Ⓜ Liceu). Step inside for a seemingly endless bounty of glistening fruits and vegetables, smoked meats, pungent cheeses and chocolate truffles.

The Walk » Continue north on La Rambla, cross diagonally the Plaça de Catalunya and turn left onto the grand boutique-lined Passeig de Gràcia. A few blocks up, you'll reach Gaudí's architectural masterpiece.

Casa Batlló

Even Gaudí outdid himself with this fantastical **apartment block** (☎93 216 03 06; www.casabatllo.es; Passeig de Gràcia 43; adult/child over 6 yrs €29/26; ☺9am-8pm, last admission 7pm; Ⓜ Passeig de Gràcia), an astonishing confection of rippling balconies, optical illusions and twisted chimney pots along Barcelona's grandest boulevard. The facade, sprinkled with bits of blue, mauve and green tiles and studded with wave-shaped window frames and balconies, rises to an uneven blue-tiled roof with a solitary tower.

The Walk » Since it's a long walk back to the start, hop on the metro and head to Arc de Triomf station, a short stroll from Parc de la Ciutadella.

Portugal

PORTUGAL'S MIX OF THE MEDIEVAL AND THE MARITIME makes it a superb place to visit. A turbulent history involving the Moors, Spain and Napoleon has left the interior scattered with walled medieval towns topped by castles, while the pounding Atlantic has sculpted a coast of glorious sand beaches. The nation's days of exploration and seafaring have created an introspective yet open culture with wide-ranging artistic influences. The eating and drinking scene here is a highlight, with several wine regions, and restaurants that are redolent with aromas of grilling pork or the freshest of fish. Comparatively short distances mean that you get full value for road trips here: less time behind the wheel means you can take more time to absorb the atmosphere of the places you visit.

Algarve A bay near Lagos
KITE_RIN/SHUTTERSTOCK ©

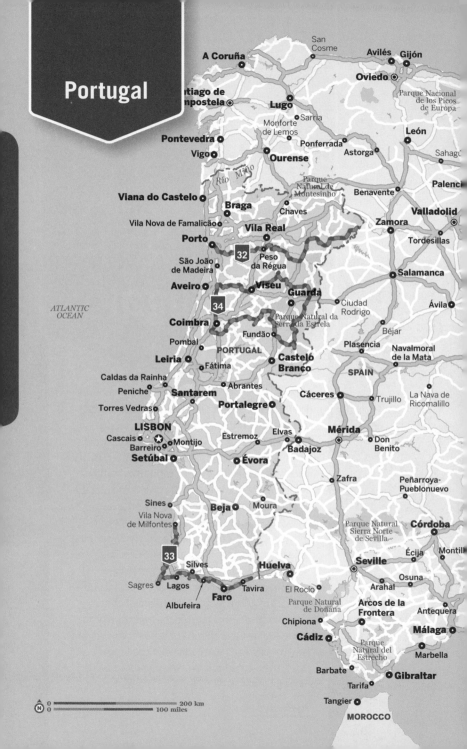

32 **Duoro Valley Vineyard Trails 5–7 Days**
Heart-breakingly beautiful river valley laced with vines producing sensational ports and reds.

33 **Alentejo & Algarve Beaches 4–6 Days**
Some of the world's great beaches and towns with Moorish heritage.

34 **Highlands & History in the Central Interior 5–7 Days**
Student life, evocative villages and spectacular mountain scenery in Portugal's heartland.

 DON'T MISS

Surfing
Portugal is one of Europe's surfing hotspots: despite the Mediterranean vibe, this is the Atlantic, and those are serious waves on Trip **33**

Wine Tasting
Often underrated, Portugal's wines are one of the region's great pleasures. Visit wineries and taste wines and ports on Trip **32**

Hiking
Jump out of the car for some picturesque hill walking on Trips **32** **33**

Castles
Love thy neighbour? Not in Iberia: Portugal is studded with castles staring defiantly towards Spain. See the best of them on Trip **33**

Douro Valley Vineyard Trails

32

The Douro is a little drop of heaven. Uncork this region on Porto's doorstep and you'll soon fall head over heels in love with its terraced vineyards, wine estates and soul-stirring vistas.

TRIP HIGHLIGHTS

5–7 DAYS
381KM / 237 MILES

GREAT FOR...

193 km

Pinhão
Wine tastings and Douro cruises on a gorgeous bend in the river

171 km

Quinta do Crasto
Eyrie-like winery in the Unesco-listed Alto Douro region

FINISH
Miranda do Douro

START
①

Peso da Régua
④ ⑧ ⑦

Vila Nova de Foz Côa

Porto
Medieval core, historic port lodges galore and a whole lotta soul

1 km

Casal de Loivos
Gasp-eliciting views of Douro vines cascading down the hillsides

197 km

BEST TIME TO GO

Spring for wildflowers, early autumn for the grape harvest.

ESSENTIAL PHOTO

The staggering view of the Douro vineyards from Casal de Loivos' miradouro (lookout).

BEST FOR FOODIES

Chef Rui Paula keeps it seasonal and regional at DOC, with sublime vineyard and river views from its terrace.

Porto Traditional houses with *azulejos* (hand-painted tiles)

Douro Valley Vineyard Trails

You're in for a treat. This Unesco World Heritage region is hands-down one of Portugal's most evocative landscapes, with mile after swoon-worthy mile of vineyards spooling along the contours of its namesake river and marching up terraced hillsides. Go for the food, the fabulous wines, the palatial *quintas* (estates), the medieval stone villages and the postcard views around almost every bend.

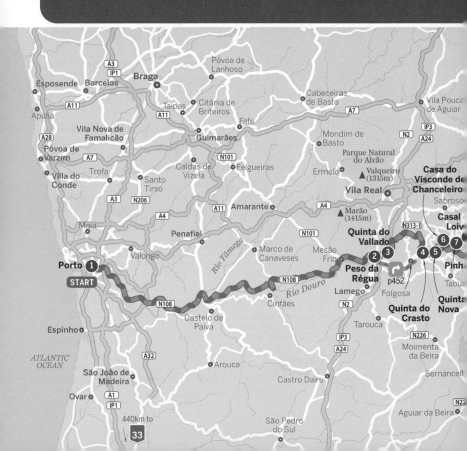

TRIP HIGHLIGHT

❶ Porto

Before kick-starting your road trip, devote a day or two to Porto, snuggled on banks of the Río Douro, where life is played out in the mazy lanes of the medieval Ribeira district. From here, the double-decker bridge **Ponte de Dom Luís I**, built by an apprentice of Gustav Eiffel in 1877, takes the river in its stride. Cross it to reach Vila Nova de Gaia, where grand 17th-century port lodges march up the hillside.

Many open their barrel-lined cellars for guided tours and tastings – usually of three different ports – that will soon help you tell your tawny from your late-bottled vintage. Top billing goes to British-run **Taylor's** (📞223 772 973; www.taylor.pt; Rua do Choupelo 250; tours incl tasting adult/child €15/6; ⏰10am-6pm) with their immense 100,000L barrel, **Graham's** (📞223 776 492, 223 776 490; www.grahams-port.com; Rua do Agro 141; tours incl tasting from €18.50; ⏰9.30am-6.30pm Apr-Oct, to 6pm Nov-Mar) and **Calém** (📞916 113 451; www.calem.pt; Avenida Diogo Leite 344; tours incl tasting from €13; ⏰10am-7pm).

The Drive » There are quicker ways of getting from A to B, but for immersion in Douro wine country, you can't beat the three-hour (137km) drive east on the N108. The serpentine road shadows the Río Douro, with views of hillsides combed with vines, little chapels and woodlands spilling down to the sparkling river.

❷ Peso da Régua

Terraced hills scaled with vines like a dragon's backbone rise around riverside Peso da Régua. The sun-bleached town is the region's largest, abutting the Río Douro at the western end of the demarcated port-wine area. It grew into a major port-wine entrepôt in the 18th century. While not

LINK YOUR TRIP

33 Alentejo & Algarve Beaches

Do one trip in reverse: about four hours south from Porto are great beaches and towns with Moorish heritage.

34 Highlands & History in the Central Interior

Dip south of Porto 120km to Coimbra for a foray into Portugal's history-crammed interior and the inspiring Serra da Estrela mountains.

DETOUR:
DOC

Start: ❷ Peso da Régua

Architect Miguel Saraiva's ode to clean-lined, glass-walled minimalism, **DOC** (📞254 858 123; www. docrestaurante.pt; Estrada Nacional 222, Folgosa; mains €31-35, menu €90-100; ⏱12.30-3.30pm & 7.30-11pm; 🅿) is headed up by Portuguese star chef Rui Paula. Its terrace peering out across the river is a stunning backdrop. Dishes give a pinch of imagination to seasonal, regional flavours, from fish *açordas* (stews) to game and wild mushrooms (plus good vegetarian options) – all of which are paired with carefully selected wines from the cellar. It's in Folgosa, midway between Peso da Régua and Pinhão, on the south side of the river. Take the N2 south of Peso da Régua, then hook onto the N222 heading east.

as charming as its setting, the town is worth visiting for its **Museu do Douro** (www.museudodouro. pt; Rua Marquês de Pombal; adult/concession €6/3; ⏱10am-6pm Mar-Oct, to 5.30pm Nov-Feb). Housed in a beautifully converted riverside warehouse, the museum whisks you through the entire wine spectrum, from impressionist landscapes to the remains of an old flat-bottomed port hauler. Down at the pier, you'll find frequent 50-minute boat trips to Pinhão, offered by **Tomaz do Douro** (📞222 082 286; www.tomazdodouro.pt; Praça da Ribeira 5; cruises from €10), for instance.

✕ 🛏 p457

The Drive » Take the first exit onto the N2 at the roundabout at the end of Rua Dr Manuel de Arriaga, then the third exit at the next roundabout to join the N313. Turn right onto the N313-1 when you see the yellow sign to Quinta do Vallado. It's around a 5km drive.

----

❸ Quinta do Vallado

Ah, what views! The vineyards spread picturesquely before you from **Quinta do Vallado** (📞254 318 081; www.quintadovallado. com; Vilarinho dos Freires; r €200-280; 🅿❄🛜🏊), a glorious 70-hectare winery. It brings together five rooms in an old stone manor and eight swank rooms in an ultra-modern slate building, decked out with chestnut and teak wood, each complete with a balcony. They all share a gorgeous pool. Guests get a free tour of the winery, with a tasting. Have a fine wine-

paired meal and stay the night. The staff can also help arrange activities like cycling, hiking, fishing or canoeing.

The Drive » From Quinta do Vallado, the N313-2, CM1258 and N322-2 take you on a 29km drive east through the curvaceous wine terraces of the Alto Douro, past immaculate rows of vines and chalk-white hamlets, with tantalising glimpses of the river below. After Gouvinhas, the wiggling road takes you south to Quinta do Crasto.

TRIP HIGHLIGHT

❹ Quinta do Crasto

Perched like an eyrie on a promontory above the Río Douro and a spectacular ripple of terraced vineyards, **Quinta do Crasto** (📞254 920 020; www.quintadocrasto.pt; Gouvinhas, Sabrosa; tours incl tasting €25; ⏱by appointment) quite literally takes your breath away. The winery is beautifully set amid the lyrical landscapes of the Alto Douro, a Unesco World Heritage site. Stop by for a tour and tasting or lunch. It produces some of the country's best drops – reds that are complex, spicy and smooth, with wild berry aromas, and whites that are fresh, with a mineral nose and tang of citrus and apples. Designed by Portuguese starchitect Eduardo Souto de Moura, the plunge pool here appears to nosedive directly into the valley below.

The Drive » From Quinta do Crasto it's an easy 4km drive east along the mellow banks of the Río Douro to Quinta Nova via the N322-2 and CM1268.

---

⑤ Quinta Nova

Set on a ridge, surrounded by 120 hectares of ancient vineyards, overlooking the Douro river with mountains layered in the distance, **Quinta Nova** (📞254 730 420; www.quintanova.com; Covas do Douro; r €200-310; 🛜🏊) is simply stunning. Besides plush lodgings in a beautifully restored 19th-century manor, it offers romantic grounds, a pool gazing out across rolling vineyards, a restaurant, wine tours, tastings and some of the region's top walking trails – the longest of which is three hours.

The Drive » It's a 10km drive east from Quinta Nova to Casa do Visconde de Chanceleiros on the CM1268, tracing the contours of the emerald-green vines unfurling around you.

---

⑥ Casa do Visconde de Chanceleiros

Fancy staying the night up in the hills of the sublime Alto Douro? **Casa do Visconde de Chanceleiros** (📞254 730 190; www.chanceleiros.com; r €140-190; 🅿️🛜🏊) is a gorgeous 250-year-old manor house, with spacious rooms featuring classic décor and patios. The expansive views of the valley and lush terraced gardens steal the show, but so does the outdoor pool, tennis court, Jacuzzi, and sauna in a wine barrel. Delicious dinners (€38) are served on request.

The Drive » A gentle 7.5km drive east along the M590, with spirit-lifting views across the terraced vineyards, the deep-green Douro and family-run *quintas*, brings you to Pinhão.

TRIP HIGHLIGHT

⑦ Pinhão

Encircled by terraced hillsides that yield some of the world's best port – and some damn good table wines too – little Pinhão sits on a particularly lovely bend of the Río Douro. Wineries and their competing signs dominate the scene and even the delightful train station has *azulejos* (hand-painted tiles) depicting the grape harvest. The town, though cute, holds little of interest, but makes a fine base for exploring the surrounding vineyards. From here, you can also cruise upriver into the heart of the Alto Douro aboard a traditional flat-bottomed port boat with **Douro-a-Vela** (📞918 793 792; www.douroavela.pt; Estrada Nacional 222, Folgosa; 2hr cruise €60). Catch the boat from the Folgosa do Douro pier. Or enjoy sublime views over two rivers while wine tasting at **Quinta do Tedo** (📞254 789 165; www.quintadotedo.com; N222, Folgosa; tours incl 3-wine tasting €12, other tastings €22-60; ⏰10am-7pm Apr-Oct, 9am-6pm Nov-Mar).

✕ 🛏️ p457

The Drive » Veer slightly west of Pinhão on the N323 and turn right onto the M585, following the sign for Casal de Loivos, 4.5km away. The country road weaving up through the vines, with the river below, later becomes the cobbled Rua da Calçada, passing *socalcos* (stone-walled terrace) vineyards..

TRIP HIGHLIGHT

⑧ Casal de Loivos

It's a tough call, but Casal de Loivos has hands-down one of the most staggeringly beautiful views in the region. From the *miradouro* (viewpoint), the uplifting vista reduces the Douro to postcard format, taking in the full sweep of its stone-walled terraced vineyards, stitched into the hillsides and fringing the sweeping contours of the valley, and the river scything through them. To maximise on these dreamy views, stay the night at **Casa de Casal de Loivros** (📞254 732 149, 927 283 122; www.casadecasaldeloivos.com; Cabo da Rua, Casal de Loivos; r €170-190; @🏊). The elegant house has been in this winemaking family for nearly 350 years. The halls are enlivened by museum-level displays of folkloric dresses, and the

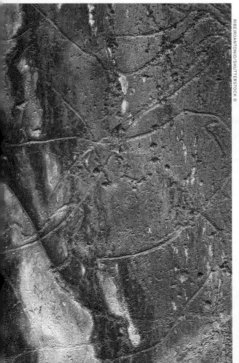

WHY THIS IS A GREAT TRIP
KERRY CHRISTIANI, WRITER

Step down a gear and enjoy the sweet life. Shadowing the bends in the river from Porto to the Spanish border, the Douro plays up romance, with its steeply climbing vines, giddy views and meandering roads leading to chalk-white hamlets, barrel-lined cellars and historic *quintas*. Here, fine meals and Portugal's best wines are served to the backbeat of cicadas.

Above: Casal de Loivos
Left: Paleolithic rock art Parque Arqueológico do Vale do Côa
Right: Taylor's, Porto

perch – high above the Alto Douro – is spectacular. Swim laps in the pool while peering down across the vines spreading in all directions.

The Drive » Backtrack on the N323, then pick up the N222 south of the river for the 64km drive southeast to Vila Nova de Foz Côa. The winding road takes you through some picture-book scenery, with whitewashed hamlets and *quintas* punctuating vines, orchards and olive groves.

----

❾ Vila Nova de Foz Côa

Welcome to the heart of the Douro's *terra quente* (hot land). This once-remote, whitewashed town has been on the map since the 1990s, when researchers, during a proposed project for a dam, stumbled across an astounding stash of Paleolithic art. Thousands of these mysterious rock engravings speckle the Río Côa valley. Come to see its world-famous gallery of rock art at the **Parque Arqueológico do Vale do Côa** (📞279 768 260; www.arte-coa.pt; Rua do Museu; each park site adult/child €15/7.50, museum €6/3; ⏱museum & park 9.30am-6pm Tue-Sun Mar-May, to 7pm Jun-Sep, 9am-5.30pm Oct Feb). The three sites open to the public include Canada do Inferno, with departures at around 9.30am from the park museum in Vila Nova

LOCAL KNOWLEDGE: WINES OF THE DOURO

The Douro has been world-famous for port-wines for centuries, but only recently has the region carved out a reputation for its equally outstanding table wines. The region's steep, terraced slopes, schist soils (allowing good drainage), blisteringly hot summers and cold winters, and old, established vines are a winning combination.

Dozens of grape varieties – nearly all of which are red and uniquely Portuguese – are grown in the region, but the top five grapes are the touriga nacional, tinta barroca, tinto cão, tinta roriz (tempranillo in Spain) and touriga franca. Alone or as a blend, these grapes produce well-structured, tannic and powerful wines, with finesse, length and ripe-fruit flavours. The more expensive ones kept for ageing are usually labelled 'Reserva' or 'Grande Reserva' and these are big, gutsy wines – complex, oaky and full of jammy dark-fruit flavours.

White grapes account for a tiny proportion of wine production, but they have also come on in leaps and bounds. Grapes such as malvasia, viosinho, gouveio and rabigato produce pale whites that are crisp-edged, minerally, fresh and fruity. Those kept for ageing are gold-hued and more complex, with oaky, nutty flavours.

de Foz Côa, which is the ideal place to understand just how close these aeons-old drawings came to disappearing.

The Drive » Wrap up your road trip by driving 120km northeast to Miranda do Douro via the N102, IP2 and IC5. Closer to the Spanish border you'll notice the shift in scenery, with lushness giving way to more arid, rugged terrain, speckled with vineyards and olive groves.

⑩ Miranda do Douro

A fortified frontier town hunkering down on the precipice of the Río Douro canyon, Miranda do Douro was long a bulwark of Portugal's 'wild east'. While its crumbling castle and handsomely severe 16th-century cathedral still lend an air of medieval charm, modern-day Miranda

now receives weekend Spanish tourists, as opposed to Castilian attacks. For an insight on the region's border culture, including ancient rites such as the 'stick dancing' of the *pauliteiros*, visit the **Museu da Terra de Miranda** (Praça de Dom João III 2; €2, Sun morning free; ◷10am-1pm & 2-6pm Wed-Sun, 2-6pm Tue Apr-Oct; 9.30am-1pm & 2-5.30pm Wed-Sun, 2-5.30pm Tue Nov-Mar). If you'd rather get a taste of the rugged nature on Miranda's doorstep, **Europarques** (Crucero Ambiental Arribes del Duero; ☎273 432 396; www.europarques. com; tour €18-22; ◷trips 4pm daily, plus 11am Sat & Sun) runs one- and two-hour river boat trips along a dramatic gorge. Boats leave from beside the dam on the Portuguese side. Stop by the **Parque Natural do Douro Internacional Office** (☎273 431 457; www.natural.pt; Largo do Castelo; ◷8.30am-1pm & 2-4.30pm Mon-Fri) for the inside scoop on hiking among the woods and towering granite cliffs of the 832-sq-km park. It's home to bird species including black storks, Egyptian vultures, peregrine falcons, golden eagles and Bonelli's eagles.

✗ ⌂ p457

Eating & Sleeping

Peso da Régua ❷

✗ Castas e Pratos   Portuguese €€€
(☎254 323 290; www.castasepratos.com;
Avenida José Vasques Osório; mains €22-35;
⏱12.30pm-3.30pm & 7.30-11pm) The coolest
dining room in town is set in a restored wood-
and-stone railyard warehouse with exposed
original timbers. You can order grilled *alheira*
sausage or octopus salad from the tapas bar
downstairs, or opt for green asparagus risotto
or roasted kid goat and potatoes with turnip
sprouts in the mezzanine.

🛏 Casa do Romezal   B&B €€
(☎919 866 186; www.casadoromezal.com;
Calçada do Barreiro, Vilarinho dos Freires; d €110;
⏱Mar-Oct; ❄🏠🏊) Young brother-sister
team Luís and Margarida run this charming
B&B encircled by a small winery, set on a
hillside that's been in their family since the 12th
century. Three colourful, sunlit upstairs rooms
share access to a swimming pool, a shaded
front terrace with dreamy vineyard views, and
a stone-walled library-lounge with wood stove,
foosball table and vinyl record collection.
Guests enjoy free tours of the attached winery,
along with tastings of the wine, olive oil and
jams produced on site.

Pinhão ❼

✗ Veladouro   Portuguese €€€
(☎254 738 166; Rua da Praia 3; mains €16-27;
⏱10am-midnight) Wood-grilled meats and
fish are the speciality at this schist-walled
restaurant by the riverfront. On sunny days, the
vine-shaded front terrace is the place to be, with
views of local fishermen under their umbrellas
on the adjacent dock. From the train station,
follow the main road left for 150m, then turn left
again under a railway bridge to the river.

🛏 Casa Cimeira   Inn €€
(☎254 732 320, 914 550 477; www.casacimeira
-douro.com; Rua do Cimo do Povo, Valença
do Douro; s/d €75/80; P❄🏠🏊) Set in a

200-year-old home at the top of the hilltop town
of Valença – its cobbled streets wrapped with
vineyards and olive tree groves and alive with
old country warmth – this is the domain of the
charming Nogueira family. Rooms are quaint
and spotless, there's a small pool, a sun deck
and family-style dinners featuring their own
house wine.

🛏 Morgadio da
Calçada   Heritage Hotel €€€
(☎915 347 555, 254 732 218; www.morgadio
dacalcada.com; Rua Cabo de Vila 18, Provesende;
r €130-150; P❄🏠🏊) Housed in a 17th-
century manor in the gorgeous hillside village
of Provesende, a 20-minute drive from Pinhão,
this welcoming guesthouse has eight minimalist
rooms inside old stables, with skylights,
pinewood floors and original details. Run by the
19th-generation owner, who also produces wine
and soaps based on an old family recipe, this
special hideaway serves up heritage and stories
aplenty.

Miranda do Douro ❿

✗ São Pedro   Portuguese €€
(☎273 431 321; Rua Mouzinho de Albuquerque
20; mains €9-15; ⏱noon-3pm Sun, noon-3pm &
7-10pm Tue-Sat) Just in from the main old-town
gate, this restaurant serves up a fine *posta
á São Pedro* (grilled veal steak dressed with
garlic and olive oil). The good-value *menu do dia*
(from €13) includes soup or salad, main course,
dessert, wine and water.

🛏 Hotel Parador
Santa Catarina   Hotel €€
(☎273 431 005; www.hotelparadorsanta
catarina.pt; Largo da Pousada; s/d/ste
€60/80/90; P❄🏠) Every guest gets a
private veranda with spectacular views of the
gorge at this luxurious hotel perched on the
canyon's edge. The 12 rooms and suites are a
handsome mix of traditional and contemporary,
with hardwood floors, TVs and large marble
bathrooms. The attached restaurant is the most
upmarket in town.

Alentejo & Algarve Beaches

33

In this sunny coastal drive you'll experience some of Europe's finest beaches and explore the picturesque, formerly Moorish towns of Portugal's south.

TRIP HIGHLIGHTS

70 km

Aljezur
Pretty castle-topped town, gateway to glorious beaches

310 km

Faro
Evocative old town, estuary trips and a bone chapel

Vila Nova de Milfontes
START

Zambujeira do Mar

4

Silves

FINISH
Cacela Velha

9

15

8

Sagres
End-of-the-world cliffs and an impressive fortress

Lagos
Handsome, hedonistic town with great beaches, restaurants and nightlife

145 km

180 km

4–6 DAYS
360KM / 224 MILES

GREAT FOR...

BEST TIME TO GO
Good all year, but crowded in July and August.

 ESSENTIAL PHOTO

The rock formations at Praia da Marinha.

 BEST FOR WILDLIFE

The Sagres area offers great birdwatching and boat trips to view dolphins and perhaps whales.

Carrapateira Bordeira beach

33 Alentejo & Algarve Beaches

Portugal's southern coasts offer a Mediterranean ideal, with fragrances of pine, rosemary, wine and grilling fish drifting over some absolutely stunning beaches. Only this isn't the Mediterranean, it's the Atlantic, so add serious surfable waves, important maritime history and great wildlife-watching opportunities to the mix. This drive takes in some of the finest beaches in the region, and explores the intriguing towns, which conserve their tight-knit Moorish street plans.

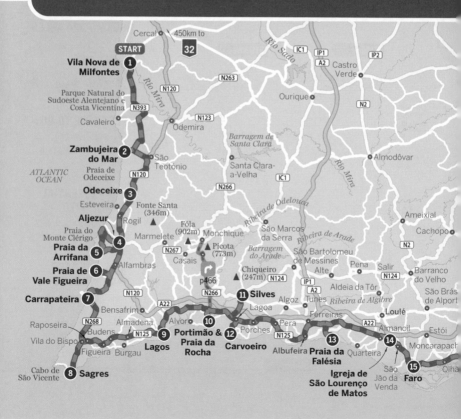

❶ Vila Nova de Milfontes

One of the loveliest towns along this stretch of the coast, Vila Nova de Milfontes has an attractive, whitewashed centre, sparkling beaches nearby and a laid-back population who couldn't imagine living anywhere else. Milfontes remains much more low-key than most resort towns, except in August when it's packed to the hilt with surfers and sunseekers. It's located in the middle of the beautiful Parque Natural do Sudoeste Alentejano e Costa Vicentina and is still a port (Hannibal is said to have sheltered here) alongside a lovely, sand-edged limb of estuary.

Milfonte's narrow lanes, tiny plazas and beach harbour offer varied eating and drinking options. The town beach is sheltered but can get busy; the best strand in the vicinity is fantastic **Praia do Malhão**, backed by rocky dunes and covered in fragrant scrub, around 7km to the north.

The Drive » It's a 26km drive through protected parkland on the N393 south to Zambujeira do Mar.

---

❷ Zambujeira do Mar

Enchantingly wild beaches backed by rugged cliffs form the setting of this sleepy seaside village. The main street terminates at the cliff and paths lead to the attractive sands below. Quieter than Vila Nova, Zambujeira attracts a backpacker, surfy crowd, though in August the town is a party place and hosts the massive music fest, **Festa do Sudoeste**. The high-season crowds obscure Zambujeira's out-of-season charms: fresh fish in family-run restaurants, blustering cliff-top walks and a dramatic, empty coast.

🛏 p469

The Drive » Cutting back to the main road, you then head south on the N120. It's about 25km to Odeceixe through beautiful coastal woodland.

---

❸ Odeceixe

Located just as you cross into the Algarve from the Alentejo, Odeceixe is an endearing whitewashed village cascading down a hill below a picture-perfect windmill on the southern side of the Ribeira de Seixe valley. It's a sleepy town, except in summer, when it fills with people keen

§ LINK YOUR TRIP

32 Douro Valley Vineyard Trails

From the end of this trip it's an easy 192km on the A22 and A49 motorways, skirting Seville, to Carmona, the starting point of this route.

28 Costa del Sol Beyond the Beaches

From the end of this trip, head 75km north to Mértola, the finishing point of this route, and do it in reverse.

on its nearby beach. This tongue of sand is winningly set at a rivermouth and flanked by imposing schist cliffs (try saying that with a mouthful of porridge...). It's a particularly good option for families, as smaller children can paddle on the peaceful river side of the strand while older kids tackle the waves on the ocean side. The beach is 3.5km from Odeceixe itself, along a charming country road. At the beach, a small village has eating and surfing options. The **Rota Vicentina**, a long-distance walking path that leads right to the southwestern tip of Portugal, passes through Odeceixe, and there are great day walks in the vicinity.

The Drive » It's an easy 15km down the N120 to Aljezur, through woodland and open shrubland patched with heather and gorse.

❹ Aljezur

The old part of Aljezur is an attractive village with a Moorish feel. A collection of cottages winds down the hill below a ruined 10th-century hilltop **castle** (Rua dom Paio Pires Correia; ⏱24hr). Aljezur is close to some fantastic beaches, edged by black rocks that reach into the white-tipped, bracing sea – surfing hot spots. The handsomest beach in the Aljezur area, on

the north side of the picturesque rivermouth and backed by wild dunes, is **Praia da Amoreira**. It's 9km by road from Aljezur, signposted off the main road north of town.

The Drive » A couple of kilometres south of Aljezur, the beaches of Monte Clérigo and Arrifana are signposted off to the right. At the top of the hill, head right (towards Monte Clérigo) for the full coastal panorama before winding your way south to Arrifana.

❺ Praia da Arrifana

Arrifana is a seductive fingernail-shaped cove embraced by cliffs. Just to add to the picturesqueness, it also sports an offshore pinnacle and a petite traditional fishing harbour. The beach is wildly popular with surfers of all abilities and there are several surf schools in the area. The beach break is reliable, but there's also a right-hand reef break that can offer some of the Algarve's best surfing when there's a big swell. There's a small, very popular beachside restaurant, and clifftop eateries near the ruined fortress up above, which offers breathtaking vistas. Good diving is also possible here.

The Drive » Praia de Vale Figueira is reached by a rough, partly-paved road that runs some 5km from the main road at a point 10km south of Aljezur.

Before reaching the turnoff, you must turn right off the N120 on to the N268

❻ Praia de Vale Figueira

One of the remoter west coast beaches, this is a long, wide and magnificent stretch of whitish sand with an ethereal beauty, backed by stratified cliffs hazy in the ocean spray. It's reached by a rough, partly paved road and there are no facilities. The beach faces due west and has pretty reliable surf, especially when a southeaster is blowing. It's one of those lonely, romantic beaches that's great to stroll on even when the weather's nasty.

The Drive » Head back to the main road (N268) and turn right onto it. It's about 10km from here to Carrapateira.

❼ Carrapateira

Surf-central Carrapateira is a tranquil, pretty, spread-out village offering two fabulous beaches with spectacular settings and turquoise seas. Bordeira is a mammoth swath of sand merging into dunes 2km from the north side of town. Amado, with even better surf, is at the southern end. The circuit of both from Carrapateira (9km) is a visually stunning hike (or drive), with lookouts over the beaches and rocky coves and cliffs between them. In town, the **Museu do Mar e da Terra da Carrapateira** (☑282 970 000; www.cm-aljezur.pt; Rua do Pescador; adult/child €2.70/1.10; ☺10am-4.30pm Mon-Fri) is an intriguing place to visit, with great views.

The Drive » The N268 barrels on right down to Portugal's tip at Sagres (22km), via the regional centre of Vila do Bispo.

TRIP HIGHLIGHT

❽ Sagres

The small, elongated village of Sagres, with a rich nautical history, has an appealingly out-of-the-way feel. It sits on a remote peninsula amid picturesque seaside scenery with a sculpted coastline and stern **fortress** (☑282 620 142; www.monumentosdoalgarve. pt; adult/child €3/1.50; ☺9.30am-8pm May-Sep, to 5.30pm Oct-Apr) leading to a stunning clifftop walk. It also appeals for its access to fine beaches and water-based activities; it's especially popular with a surfing crowd. Outside town, the striking cliffs of **Cabo de São Vicente** (N258), the southwestern-most point of Europe, make for an enchanting visit, especially at sunset. Make sure you pop into the small **museum** (☑282 624 606; www.faros. pt; N268; adult/child €1.50/1; ☺10am-6pm Apr-Oct, to 5pm Nov-Mar) here, which has interesting background

information on the Algarve's starring role in the Age of Discovery. From Sagres' harbour, worthwhile excursions head out to observe dolphins and seabirds. **Mar Ilimitado** (☑916 832 625; www.marilimitado.com; Porto da Baleeira; tour from €25) is a recommended operator.

✖ ⌂ p469

The Drive » Head back to Vila do Bispo and turn right onto the N125 that will take you to Lagos, a total drive of 34km. Promising beach detours include Zavial and Salema.

TRIP HIGHLIGHT

❾ Lagos

Touristy, likeable Lagos lies on a riverbank, with 16th-century walls enclosing the old town's pretty, cobbled streets and picturesque plazas. A huge range of restaurants and pumping nightlife add to the allure provided by fabulous beaches and numerous watery activities. Aside from the hedonism, there's plenty of history here: start

by visiting the lovably higgledy-piggledy **Museu Municipal** (☑282 762 301; www.cm-lagos.com; Rua General Alberto da Silveira; adult/child €3/1.50; ☺9.30am-12.30pm & 2-5pm Tue-Sun), which incorporates the fabulous baroque church **Igreja de Santo António** (Rua General Alberto da Silveira; adult/child incl museum €3/1.50; ☺9.30am-12.30pm & 2-5pm Tue-Sun). Heading out on to the water is a must, perhaps cetacean-spotting with **Algarve Water World** (☑969 988 027; www.algarvewaterworld. com; Marina de Lagos; 90min tour adult/child €40/25, 75min grotto tour €20/10; ☺Mar-Oct), paddling with **Kayak Adventures** (☑918 888 831; www.kayaktrip.pt; Cais da Solara, Avenida dos Descobrimentos; 2.5-hr kayaking trip €35; ☺Mar-Oct) or learning to surf with **Lagos Surf Center** (☑282 764 734; www.lagossurfcenter.com; Rua da Silva Lopes 31; 1-/3-/5-day courses €60/165/250). East of town stretch the long, golden sands of Meia

TOP TIP: THE SAGRES FOOD SCENE

A closely packed string of surfer-oriented places on Rua Comandante Matoso in Sagres offer a bit of everything, whether it's a coffee or a caipirinha you're after. They are cafes by day, restaurants serving international favourites by night, whatever time hunger drags you away from the beach and lively bars. Further down the same street, near the port, is a cluster of more traditional Portuguese restaurants.

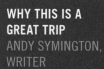

WHY THIS IS A GREAT TRIP

ANDY SYMINGTON, WRITER

I can't think of a more impressive series of beaches than those of Portugal's south; they are simply magical. There's a wild and unspoiled romance to the seasprayed west-coast strands, while a succession of sun-baked golden sands in the south includes intriguing island beaches only reachable by boat. I love wandering the region's tight-knit old towns too, trying to detect which lane that delicious aroma of grilling fish is coming from...

Above: Igreja de Nossa Senhora do Carmo, Faro
Left: Sagres
Right: *Azulejos* (hand-painted tiles), Tavira

Praia, backed by worth-while beach restaurants.

🍴 p469

The Drive » Portimão is really just along the coast from Lagos, but it's a 24km detour inland via the N125 in a car.

- - - - - - - - - - - - - - - - - -

⑩ **Portimão & Praia da Rocha**

The Algarve's second-largest town, Portimão's history dates back to the Phoenicians before it became the region's fishing and canning hub in the 19th century. Though that industry has since declined, it's still an intriguing port with plenty of maritime atmosphere. Learn all about the town's fishing heritage in the excellent **Museu de Portimão** (📞282 405 230; www.museudeportimao.pt; Rua Dom Carlos I; adult/child €3/free; ⏰2.30-6pm Tue, 10am-6pm Wed-Sun Sep-Jul, 7.30-11pm Tue, 3-11pm Wed-Sun Aug), before strolling through the no-frills sardine restaurants of the fishers' quarter of Largo da Barca near the road bridge. At the southern end of Portimão stretches the impressive resort beach of Praia da Rocha, backed by numerous restaurants and nightlife options.

The Drive » The N125 leads east to the junction with the N124-1 that takes you north to Silves. It's a drive of only 20km.

DETOUR: MONCHIQUE

Start: ⑩ Portimão & Praia da Rocha

High above the coast, in cooler mountainous woodlands, the picturesque little town of Monchique makes a lovely detour, with some excellent options for day hikes, including climbing the Algarve's highest hills, Picota and Fóia, for super views over the coast. Monchique and the surrounding area have some excellent eating choices and nearby Caldas de Monchique is a sweet little spa hamlet in a narrow wooded valley.

The N266 heads north from the N124 north of Portimão; it's a 27km drive from Lagos to Monchique, then another 30km on to Silves.

⑪ Silves

Silves is one of the Algarve's prettiest towns and replete with history: it was an important trading city in Moorish times and preserves a tightly woven medieval centre. At the top of the town, its sizeable **castle** (☎282 440 837; www.cm-silves.pt; Rua da Cruz de Portugal; adult/child €2.80/1.40, incl Museu Municipal de Arqueologia €3.90; ⊙9am-7pm Jun, to 10pm Jul & Aug, to 8pm Sep–mid-Oct, to 5.30pm mid-Oct–May) offers great views from the ramparts. Originally occupied in the Visigothic period, what you see today dates mostly from the Moorish era, though the castle was heavily restored in the 20th century. Below this, the atmospheric **cathedral** (Rua da Sé; by donation; ⊙9am-12.30pm & 2-5.30pm Mon-Fri year-round, plus 9am-1pm Sat Jun-Aug) is the region's best-preserved Gothic church. The **Museu Municipal** (☎282 444 838; www.cm-silves.pt; Rua das Portas de Loulé 14; adult/child €2.10/1.05, incl Castelo €3.90; ⊙10am-6pm) gives good background on the city's history and is built around a fascinating Moorish-era well, complete with spiral staircase. The old-town streets are great for strolling.

The Drive » Cruise 14km straight down the N124-1 to the beach at Carvoeiro.

⑫ Carvoeiro

Carvoeiro is a cluster of whitewashed buildings rising up from tawny, gold and green cliffs and backed by hills. This diminutive seaside resort is prettier and more laid-back than many of the bigger resorts. The town beach is pretty but small and crowded – there are lots of other excellent options in the area. The most picturesque of all, with stunning rock formations, is **Praia da Marinha**, 8km east of Carvoeira. On foot, it's best reached by the **Percurso dos Sete Vales Suspensos** clifftop walk, beginning at Praia Vale Centianes, 2.3km east of town.

🛏 p469

The Drive » Head back to Lagoa to join the N125 eastwards. After 25km, turn right and head towards the coast, emerging atop the long beach. It's a 37km total drive.

⑬ Praia da Falésia

This long straight strip of sand offers one of the region's most impressive first glimpses of coast as you arrive from above. It's backed by stunning cliffs in white and several shades of ochre, gouged by weather into intriguing shapes and topped by typical pines. The areas near the car parks get packed in summer (especially as high tides cover much of the beach), but as the strip is over 3km long, it's easy enough to walk and find plenty of breathing room. It's a good beach for strolling, as the cliffscape constantly changes colours and shapes, and there's a surprising range of hardy seaside plants in the cracks and crevices.

Carvoeiro Beach

The Drive >> Head back to the N125 and continue eastwards. Just after bypassing the town of Almancil, there's an exit to 'Almancil, São Lourenço, praias'. The church is signposted from here.

⑭ Igreja de São Lourenço de Matos

It's worth stopping here to visit the marvellous interior of this small **church** (Church of St Lawrence of Rome; www.diocese-algarve.pt; Rua da Igreja, Almancil; €2; ⊗3-6pm Mon, 10am-1pm & 3-6pm Tue-Sat), built over a ruined chapel after local people, while digging a well, had implored the saint for help and then struck water. The resulting baroque masterpiece, built by fraternal master-team Antão and Manuel Borges, is wall-to-wall *azulejos* (hand-painted tiles) inside, with beauti-ful panels depicting the life of the Roman-era saint, and his death by roasting. In the 1755 earthquake, only five tiles fell from the roof.

The Drive >> Back on the N125, head south-eastwards and after 12km you're in Faro.

TRIP HIGHLIGHT

⑮ Faro

The capital of the Algarve has a distinctly Portuguese feel and plenty to see. Its evocative waterside old town is very scenic and has several interesting sights, including the excellent **Museu Municipal** (☑289 870 827; www.cm-faro.pt; Praça Dom Afonso III 14; adult/child €2/free; ⊗10am-6pm Tue-Fri, 10.30am-5pm Sat & Sun), set in a former convent. The area is centred around Faro's **cathedral** (www.paroquiasedefaro.org;

TOP TIP: FAMILY ATTRACTIONS

This central section of the Algarve coast is great for families, with numerous water parks and other attractions in the area. Two of the most popular are **Slide & Splash** (☑282 340 800; www.slidesplash.com; Vale de Deus 125, Estômbar; adult/child €29/21; ⊗10am-6pm Jul–mid-Sep, to 5pm Apr, May & mid-Sep–Oct) and **Aqualand** (☑282 320 230; www.aqualand.pt; N125, Sítio das Areias, Alcantarilha; adult/child €29/21; ⊗10am-6pm Jul-Sep, to 5pm Jun).

LOCAL KNOWLEDGE: MERCADO MUNICIPAL

Faro's impressive modern **market building** (www.mercadomunicipaldefaro.pt; Largo Dr Francisco Sá Carneiro; ⏰stalls 7am-3pm Mon-Sat; 🛜) makes a great place to wander, people-watch, buy fresh produce, sit down on a terrace with a coffee, or lunch at one of the several worthwhile eateries.

Largo da Sé; adult/child €3.50/free; ⏰10am-5.30pm Mon-Fri, to 1pm Sat), built in the 13th century but heavily damaged in the 1755 earthquake. What you see now is a variety of Renaissance, Gothic and Baroque features. Climb the tower for lovely views across the walled town and estuary islands. Part of the Parque Natural da Ria Formosa, these islands can be explored on excellent boat trips run by **Formosamar** (☎918 720 002; www.facebook.com/formosamar; Avenida da República, Faro Marina, Stand 1). The cathedral has a small bone chapel, but much spookier is the one at the **Igreja de Nossa Senhora do Carmo** (http://diocese-algarve.pt; Largo do Carmo; €2; ⏰ church 9am-5pm Mon-Fri, 9am-1pm Sat, chapel 10am-1pm & 3-5.30pm Mon-Fri, 10am-1pm Sat), built from the mortal remains of over a thousand monks.

🍴 p469

The Drive » It's 35km east along the N125 to Tavira. Despite the road's proximity to the coast, you won't see much unless you turn off: Fuzeta is a pleasant waterside village to investigate, with boat connections to island beaches.

----

16 Tavira

Set on either side of the meandering Rio Gilão, Tavira is a charming town. The ruins of a hilltop **castle** (Largo Abu-Otmane; ⏰8am-5pm Mon-Fri, 9am-7pm Sat & Sun Apr-Oct, 8am-5pm Mon-Fri, 9am-5pm Sat & Sun Nov-Mar), now housing a pleasant little botanic garden; the Renaissance **Igreja da Misericórdia** (https://diocese-algarve.pt; Largo da Misericórdia; church incl museum €2.50; ⏰10am-12.30pm & 3-6.30pm Tue-Sat Jul & Aug, 9.30am-12.30pm & 2-5.30pm Tue-Sat Sep-Jun); and the **Núcleo Islâmico** (☎281 320 570; www.cm-tavira.pt; Praça da República 5; adult/child €2/1, incl Palácio da Galeria €3/1.50; ⏰9.15am-12.30pm & 1.30-4.30pm Tue-Sat) museum of Moorish history are among the attractions. It's ideal for wandering; the warren of cobblestone streets hides pretty, historic gardens and shady plazas. Tavira is the launching point for the stunning, unspoilt beaches of the Ilha de Tavira, a sandy island that's another part of the Parque Natural da Ria Formosa.

🛏 p469

The Drive » Cacela Velha is 14km east of Tavira: head along the N125 and you'll see it signposted. It's 1km south of the N125.

----

17 Cacela Velha

Enchanting, small and cobbled, Cacela Velha is a huddle of whitewashed cottages edged with bright borders, and has a pocket-sized fort, orange and olive groves, and gardens blazing with colour. It sits above a gorgeous stretch of sea, with a characterful local bar, plus other restaurants, a church and heart-lifting views. From nearby Fábrica, you can get a boat across to the splendid Cacela Velha beach, which has a low-key LGBTIQ+ scene in summer.

Eating & Sleeping

Zambujeira do Mar ➋

🛏 Herdade do Touril   Inn €€€

(🖉283 950 080; www.herdadedotouril.pt; off CM 1158; r €180-260; @ 🛜 🏊) Four kilometres north of Zambujeira do Mar is this upmarket *quinta* (estate) building with rooms and apartments of the fluffy-pillow variety. Some are within the original building (built in 1826), others are converted farm cottages. The rustic and contemporary design of this tranquil place has an African safari-lodge feel – without the lions, of course.

Sagres ➑

✕ A Tasca   Seafood €€

(🖉282 624 177; Porto da Baleeira; mains €14-30, tapas €4-16, seafood platters €60-120; 🕓12.30-3pm & 6.30-10pm Thu-Tue) Seafood doesn't come fresher than at this converted fish warehouse, with a timber-decked terrace overlooking the marina and Ilhotes do Martinhal limestone islands offshore. Inside, the vaulted interior's walls are inlaid with glass bottles, ceramic plates, shells and pebbles. A live tank sits alongside the bar strung with strands of dried garlic and chillies. Daily-changing platters and *cataplanas* (seafood stews) are specialities.

🛏 Pousada do Infante   Boutique Hotel €€€

(🖉282 620 240; www.pousadas.pt; Rua Patrão António Faustino; d/ste from €170/250; P 🌡 @ 🛜 🏊) On the promontory's clifftop, this modern *pousada* occupies a never-to-be-outbuilt position. All rooms and suites (with king-size beds and whirlpool baths) have balconies, but those at the front face the car park, so it's definitely worth paying extra for one overlooking the fortress and ocean to take in the dazzling sunsets and swimming pool (romantically floodlit at night).

Lagos ➒

✕ A Forja   Portuguese €€

(🖉282 768 588; Rua dos Ferreiros 17; mains €9-24; 🕓noon-3pm & 6.30-10pm Mon-Sat)

Hearty, top-quality traditional food served in a bustling environment at great prices sees this buzzing *adega tipica* (wine bar) pull in the crowds. Daily specials are always reliable, as are simply prepared fish dishes such as grilled sole, turbot and mackerel on stainless steel plates, and two-person *cataplanas*.

Carvoeiro ➓

🛏 O Castelo   Guesthouse €€

(🖉919 729 259; www.ocastelo.net; Rua do Casino 59; d €75-180; 🌡 🛜) Right on the beach, this guesthouse is gleamingly maintained. Most of the 12 rooms with colourful, contemporary striped bed linens have a terrace or balcony with sea (and sunrise) views, and can accommodate an extra bed.

Faro ➊➎

✕ Vila Adentro   Portuguese €€

(🖉933 052 173; www.vilaadentro.pt; Praça Dom Afonso III 17; mains €14-20, cataplanas for two €39-49; 🕓9am-midnight; 🖋 👶) With tables on the square in Faro's old town and a dining room decorated with floor-to-ceiling *azulejos*, this Moorish 15th-century building is a romantic spot for elevated Portuguese cuisine: lobster and mixed seafood *cataplanas* for two, goat's milk cheese puff pastry with figs, and tangerine-stuffed pork tenderloin. Wines hail from around the country.

Tavira ➊➏

🛏 Vila Galé Albacora   Hotel €€€

(🖉281 380 800; www.vilagale.com; Quatro Águas; s/d €135/150; 🕓Mar-Oct; P 🌡 🛜 🏊) Overlooking Ilha de Tavira 4km east of town, this four-star, 161-room property has been converted from, and ingeniously incorporates, an entire former tuna village, complete with the original school and chapel. Along with sleek modern rooms (the former tuna workers' living premises), there are indoor and outdoor pools, a spa, two restaurants and two bars. Kids under 12 stay (and eat) free.

Highlands & History in the Central Interior

This wide-ranging trip takes in many Portuguese historic highlights, from buzzing university town Coimbra to stern borderland fortresses and picturesque villages.

34

TRIP HIGHLIGHTS

620 km

Viseu
Beautiful inland city with strollable historic quarter

200 km

Manteigas
Mountain village at the heart of the Serra da Estrela

Sernancelhe

Trancoso

12

Almeida

START/ FINISH

1

4

Plódão

7

Coimbra
Picturesque and lively university town overlooking a river

1 km

Monsanto
Soaring castle-topped village high above the plains

330 km

5–7 DAYS
770KM / 480 MILES

GREAT FOR...

BEST TIME TO GO
May to October for best temperatures.

 ESSENTIAL PHOTO

The sweeping mountaintop view from Fragão de Covão above Manteigas.

 BEST FOR OUTDOORS

Hiking the Serra da Estrela around Manteigas.

Highlands & History in the Central Interior

History is tangible at every turn in Portugal's interior and this route combines some of the nation's most evocative historic sights, from the venerable university library of Coimbra or Viseu's cathedral, to picture-perfect traditional villages like Piódão or Idanha-a-Velha. Sturdy fortress towns like Almeida and Trancoso shore up the border with Spain, while the Serra da Estrela mountains offer superb vistas and glorious hiking opportunities.

TRIP HIGHLIGHT

1 Coimbra

While Porto and Lisbon take the headlines, the university town of Coimbra, between the two, is one of Portugal's highlights. Its atmospheric historic centre cascades down a hillside above the Rio Mondego: a multi-coloured assemblage of buildings covering a millennium of architectural endeavour.

The spiritual heart of the old town is the **Universidade de Coimbra**

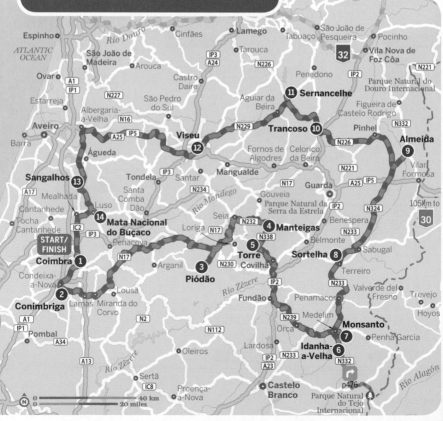

(239 242 744; www.uc.pt/turismo; Pátio das Escolas; adult/child incl Paço das Escolas, Biblioteca Joanina, Capela de São Miguel & Museu da Ciência €12.50/free, without Biblioteca €7/free; 9am-7pm mid-Mar–Oct, 9am-1pm & 2pm-5pm Nov–mid-Mar), whose stunning 16th- to 18th-century buildings surround the Patio des Escolas square. The **Biblioteca Joanina** library is the sumptuous highlight. Within a short stroll are two other Coimbra masterpieces: the **Sé Velha** (Old Cathedral; 239 825 273; www.sevelha-coimbra.org; Largo da Sé Velha, Rua do Norte 4; €2.50; 10am-5.30pm Mon-Sat, 11am-5pm Sun) is one of Portugal's finest Romanesque buildings, while the altogether more modern **Museu Nacional de Machado**

LINK YOUR TRIP

32 Douro Valley Vineyard Trails

Head to Porto, from where you can easily dip into the terraced vineyards and outstanding wineries of the Unesco World Heritage Douro.

30 Historic Casilla y Leon

Visit some of Spain's most appealing cities north and west of Madrid.

COIMBRA FADO

If Lisbon represents the heart of Portuguese fado (traditional Portuguese melancholic song), Coimbra is its head. The 19th-century university was male-only, so the town's womenfolk were of great interest to the student body. Coimbra fado developed partly as a way of communicating with these heavily chaperoned females, usually in the form of serenades sung under the bedroom window. For this reason, fado is traditionally sung only by men, who must be students or ex-students.

The Coimbra style ranges from hauntingly beautiful serenades and lullabies to more boisterous students-out-on-the-piss type of songs. The singer is normally accompanied by a 12-string *guitarra* (Portuguese guitar) and perhaps a Spanish (classical) guitar too. Due to the clandestine nature of these bedroom-window concerts, audience appreciation is traditionally indicated by softly coughing rather than clapping.

There are several excellent venues in Coimbra to hear fado, including **À Capella** (239 833 985; www.acapella.com.pt; Rua do Corpo de Deus; entry with/without drink €10/5; 7pm-2am, shows 9.30pm).

de Castro (239 853 070; www.museumachadocastro.pt; Largo Dr José Rodrigues; adult/child €6/3, cryptoportico only €3; 2pm-6pm Tue, 10am-6pm Wed-Sun) presents an excellent collection of art, as well as taking you down to the city's Roman origins.

🍴 🛏 p480

The Drive » It's a short drive southeast along the IC3/N1 some 16km to Condeixa-a-Nova, on whose outskirts sit the Roman ruins of Conímbriga.

----

② Conímbriga

Hidden amid humble olive orchards in the rolling country southwest of Coimbra, Conímbriga boasts Portugal's most extensive and best-preserved **Roman ruins** (239 941 177; www.conimbriga.pt; Condeixa-a-Velha; ruins & museum adult/child €4.50/free; 10am-7pm Mar-Oct, to 6pm Nov-Feb), and ranks with similarly lauded sites on the entire Iberian Peninsula.

To get your head around the history, begin at the small **museum** near the entrance. Displays present every aspect of Roman life from mosaics to medallions. Then, head out to the **ruins** themselves. A massive defensive wall running right through the site speaks of times of sudden crisis. In contrast, the extraordinary mosaics of the **Casa dos Repuxos** speak of times of peaceful domesticity.

The Drive » It's two hours in the car to the next stop. The most interesting route is to take the N342 east, turning north onto the N236, then taking the N17 and IC6 northeast. The last stretch on the N230 is a spectacular if occasionally nerve-racking drive, following valleys with breathtaking views, sheer drops and tight curves.

----

❸ Piódão

Remote Piódão offers a chance to see rural Portugal at its most pristine. This tiny traditional village clings to a terraced valley in a beautiful, surprisingly remote range of vertiginous ridges, deeply cut valleys, rushing rivers and virgin woodland called the Serra de Açor (Goshawk Mountains).

Until the 1970s you could only reach Piódão on horseback or by foot, and it still feels as though you've slipped into a time warp. The village is a serene, picturesque composition

LOCAL KNOWLEDGE: WALKS FROM MANTEIGAS

The **Trilhos Verdes** (www.manteigastrilhosverdes. com) is an excellent network of marked trails in the Manteigas area. Each route is viewable online and has its own leaflet available at the park information office in town.

The relatively easy ramble (11km one way) through the magnificent, glacier-scoured **Vale do Zêzere**, one of the park's most beautiful and noteworthy natural features, is a highlight. It's quite exposed in summer.

in schist and slate; note the many doorways with crosses over them, said to offer protection against curses and thunderstorms.

Houses descend in terraces to the square, where you'll find the fairy-tale parish church, the **Igreja Nossa Senhora Conceição** (⏰10am-1pm & 2-5pm Wed-Sun), and a low-key touristy scene selling local liqueurs and souvenirs.

🛏 p480

The Drive » It's only 66km to the next stop, but with the winding roads, spectacular scenery and intriguing villages en route, it may take you some time. Retrace your steps, then head northeast on the N338.

The N231 takes you to Seia; from there the N339 then N232 is one of Portugal's great drives, through typical landscapes of the Serra da Estrela and down a vertiginous descent into Manteigas.

TRIP HIGHLIGHT

❹ Manteigas

In the heart of the Serra da Estrela, Portugal's loftiest and most spectacular highland region, this is the most atmospheric of the mountain towns hereabouts. Cradled at the foot of the beautiful Vale do Zêzere, with high peaks and forest-draped slopes dominating the horizon in all directions, Manteigas enjoys a spectacular natural setting. There are lots of good marked walks in the surrounding area, so you may want to set aside a day to explore the *serra* landscapes on foot. Walk through the glacial valley above town and you'll still encounter terraced meadows, stone shepherds' huts and

TOP TIP: VIEWPOINT

At Penhas Douradas, at the top of the hill before the long descent into Manteigas, don't miss the stunning view from a stub of rock called Fragão do Corvo; just follow the signs.

tinkling goat-bells, while in Manteigas itself cobblestone streets and older homes still hold their own against the high-rise development that has taken root on the Serra da Estrela's fringes.

Conímbriga Casa dos Repuxos

🛏 p480

The Drive » The drive from Manteigas to Torre (22km, around 35 minutes) is especially breathtaking, first following the N338 along the Vale do Zêzere. After turning right onto the N339 towards Torre, you pass through the Nave de Santo António – a traditional high-country sheep-grazing meadow – before climbing through a surreal moonscape of crags and gorges. Visible near the turn-off for Torre is Cântaro Magro, a notable rock formation, rising 500m straight from the valley below.

---

❺ Torre

In winter, Torre's road signs are so blasted by freezing winds that horizontal icicles barb their edges. Portugal's highest peak, at 1993m, Torre ('Tower') produces a winter freeze so reliable that it has a small ski resort with mainly beginners' slopes.

Outside the snow season (mid-December to mid-April), Portugal's pinnacle is rather depressing, though a park visitors centre with displays about the region's natural and cultural history is worthwhile.

Even if you give Torre itself a miss, it's worth the drive here to survey the astoundingly dramatic surroundings.

The Drive » Retrace your steps from Torre and continue straight on along the N339 to eventually descend steeply into Covilhã. Take the IP2/A23 motorway south, then the N18 and N239 roughly eastwards, finally reaching the N332 which takes you the last stretch to Idanha-a-Velha. It's a drive of around 90km.

---

❻ Idanha-a-Velha

Extraordinary Idanha-a-Velha is a very traditional small village with a huge history. Nestled in a remote valley of patchwork farms and olive orchards, it was founded as the Roman city of Igaeditânia (Egitana). Roman ramparts still define the town, though it reached its peak under Visigothic rule: they built a **cathedral** (Sé; Rua da Sé; ⏰10am-12.30pm & 2.30-4.30pm Tue-Sun) and made Idanha their regional capital. It's also believed that their legendary King Wamba was born here.

Moors were next on the scene, and the cathedral was turned into a mosque during their tenure. They, in turn, were driven out by the Knights Templar in the 12th century. It's believed that a 15th-century plague virtually wiped out the town's inhabitants. Today a small population of shepherds and farmers live amid the Roman, Visigothic and medieval ruins.

Wandering this picturesque village is an enchanting trip back in time.

The Drive » Head north up the N332 again, then turn right at the N239. The turnoff to Monsanto is clearly marked. It's only a 15km drive. Passengers who want to stretch their legs

DETOUR: PARQUE NATURAL DO TEJO INTERNACIONAL

Start: ❻ **Idanha-a-Velha**

Still one of Portugal's wildest landscapes, this 230-sq-km park shadows the Rio Tejo (Tagus), the border between Portugal and Spain. It shelters some of the country's rarest bird species, including black storks, Bonelli's eagles, royal eagles, Egyptian vultures, black vultures and griffon vultures.

The best-marked hiking trail, the **Rota dos Abutres** (Route of the Vultures), descends from Salvaterra do Extremo (34km southeast of Idanha-a-Velha) into the dramatic canyon of the Rio Erges. It's an 11km circuit that includes a vulture colony viewing point, and great views of a castle over in Spain.

could walk the pretty 7km trail from Idanha to Monsanto.

TRIP HIGHLIGHT

❼ Monsanto

Like an island in the sky, the stunning village of Monsanto towers high above the surrounding plains. A stroll through its steeply cobbled streets, lined with stone houses that seem to merge with the boulder-strewn landscape, is reason enough to come. But to fully appreciate Monsanto's rugged isolation, climb the shepherds' paths above town to the abandoned and crumbling hilltop **castle**. This formidable stone fortress seems almost to have grown out of the boulder-littered hillside that supports it. It's a beautiful site, windswept and populated by lizards and wildflowers.

Immense vistas include Spain to the east and the Barragem da Idanha dam to the southwest. Walkers will also appreciate the network of hiking trails threading through the vast cork-oak-dominated expanses below.

✕ 🛏 p481

The Drive » Sortelha is about 60km north of Monsanto across a variety of hilly landscapes. Head due north from Monsanto, eventually linking up with the N233. Turn off in the village of Terreiro, following the brown signs for Sortelha.

------

❽ Sortelha

Perched on a rocky promontory, Sortelha is the oldest of a string of fortresses guarding the frontier in this region. Its fortified 12th-century castle teeters on the brink of a steep cliff, while immense walls encircle a village of great

charms. Laid out in Moorish times, it remains a winning combination of stout stone cottages, sloping cobblestone streets and diminutive orchards.

'New' Sortelha lines the Santo Amaro–Sabugal road. The medieval hilltop fortress is a short drive, or a 10-minute walk, up one of two lanes signposted '*castelo*'.

The entrance to the fortified old village is a grand, stone Gothic gate. From here, a cobbled lane leads up to the heart of the village, with a *pelourinho* (pillory) in front of the remains of a small castle and the parish church. Higher still is the bell tower – climb it for a view of the entire village. For a more adventurous and scenic climb, tackle the ramparts around the village (beware precarious stairways and big steps).

✕ p481

The Drive » Head east to Sabugal, then turn north, following the N324 north before joining the N340 for the final run northeast to Almeida. It's a drive of around 65km.

------

❾ Almeida

After Portugal regained independence from Spain in the 1640s, the country's border regions were on constant high alert. Almeida's vast, star-shaped fortress is

Monsanto View over hilltop village

the handsomest of the defensive structures built during this period.

The fortified old village is a place of great charm, with enough history and muscular grandeur to set the imagination humming.

Most visitors arrive at the fortress via the **Portas de São Francisco**, two long tunnel-gates separated by an enormous dry moat.

The long arcaded building just inside is the 18th-century **Quartel das Esquadras**, the former infantry barracks.

Not far away, the interesting **Museu Histórico Militar de Almeida** (☏271 571 229; adult/child €3.50/1; ⊙9.15am-noon & 2-5pm Tue-Fri, from 10am Sat & Sun) is built into the *casamatas* (casemates or bunkers), a labyrinth of 20 underground rooms used for storage,

barracks and shelter for troops in times of siege. Piles of cannonballs fill a central courtyard of the museum, with British and Portuguese cannons strewn about nearby.

Make sure you also see the attractive **Picadero d'el Rey**, once the artillery headquarters, and what's left of the **castle**, blown to smithereens during a French siege in 1810.

The Drive » Retrace your steps down the N340, then head northwest on the N324. At Pinhel, turn westwards onto the N221/N226, all the way to Trancoso, around 60km in total.

- - - - - - - - - - - - - - - -

⑩ Trancoso

A warren of cobbled lanes squeezed within Dom Dinis' mighty 13th-century walls makes peaceful Trancoso a delightful retreat from the modern world. The walls run intact for over

1km around the medieval core, which is centred on the main square, Largo Padre Francisco Ferreira. The square, in turn, is anchored by an octagonal *pelourinho* dating from 1510. The Portas d'El Rei (King's Gate), surmounted by the ancient coat of arms, was always the principal entrance, whose guillotine-like door sealed out unwelcome visitors. On a hill in the northeast corner of town is the tranquil **castle** (⊙10am-12.30pm & 2-5.30pm Mon-Fri, 10am-1pm & 3-6pm Sat & Sun), with its crenellated towers and the distinctively slanted walls of the squat, Moorish Torre de Menagem, which you can climb for views.

The Drive » Head 30km northwest along the N226 to reach the next stop, Sernancelhe.

⓫ Sernancelhe

Located 30km northwest of Trancoso, Sernancelhe has a wonderfully preserved centre fashioned out of warm, beige-coloured stone. Sights include a 13th-century church that boasts Portugal's only free-standing Romanesque sculpture, an old Jewish quarter with crosses to mark the homes of the converted and several grand 17th- and 18th-century town houses. The finest manor of all is the **Solar dos Carvalhos** (Praça da República), believed to be the birthplace of the famed 18th-century statesman and strong-armed reformer Marquês de Pombal. Just outside of town are hills that bloom with what are considered to be Portugal's best chestnuts.

The Drive » The N229 leads you 55km southwest through increasingly fertile countryside to Viseu.

TRIP HIGHLIGHT

⓬ Viseu

One of central Portugal's most appealing cities, Viseu has a well-preserved historical centre that offers numerous enticements to pedestrians: cobbled streets, meandering alleys, leafy public gardens and a central square – Praça da República, aka the 'Rossio' – graced with bright flowers and fountains.

Sweeping vistas over the surrounding plains unfold from the town's highest point, the square fronting the 13th-century granite **cathedral** (Sé; Adro da Sé; ⊙9am-noon & 2-6pm), whose gloomy Renaissance facade conceals a splendid 16th-century interior, including an impressive Manueline ceiling.

✕ 🛏 p481

The Drive » It's a drive of 90km to the next stop. The quickest way is to take the A25 motorway west, turning south onto the IC2.

⓭ Sangalhos

In the village of Sangalhos, in the Bairrada wine-producing region between Aveiro and Coimbra, the extraordinary **Aliança Underground Museum** (☎234 732 090; www.bacalhoa. pt; Rua do Comércio 444, Sangalhos; guided tour €3; ⊙tours 10am, 11.30am, 2.30pm, 4pm) is part *adega* (winery), part repository of an eclectic, enormous, and top-quality art and artefact collection. Under the winery, vast vaulted chambers hold sparkling wine, barrels of maturing *aguardente* (distilled spirits; firewater), and a series of galleries displaying a huge range of objects. The highlight is at the beginning: a superb collection of African sculpture, ancient ceramics and masks, but

you'll also be impressed by the spectacular mineral and fossil collection and the beauty of some of the spaces. Other pieces include *azulejos* (tiles), a rather hideous collection of ceramic and faience animals, and an upstairs gallery devoted to India. The only complaint is that there's no information on individual pieces, and you don't have time to linger over a particular item. Phone ahead to book your visit, which can be conducted in English and includes a glass of sparkling wine.

The Drive » It's an easy 20km drive down the N235 to the town of Luso and on up the hill to the Buçaco forest.

⓮ Mata Nacional do Buçaco

This famous, historic **national forest** (☎231 937 000; www.fmb.pt; per car/cyclist/pedestrian €5/free/free; ⊙9am-6pm) is encircled by high stone walls that for centuries have reinforced a sense of mystery. The aromatic forest is criss-crossed with trails, dotted with crumbling chapels and graced with ponds, fountains and exotic trees. In the middle, like in a fairy tale, stands a royal palace. Now a luxury hotel, it was built in 1907 as a royal summer retreat on the site of a 17th-century Carmelite monastery. This wedding cake of a building is over-the-top

Mata Nacional do Buçaco National forest

in every way: outside, its conglomeration of turrets and spires is surrounded by rose gardens and swirling box hedges in geometric patterns; inside (nonguests are more or less prohibited entry) are neo-Manueline carvings, suits of armour on the grand staircases and *azulejos*.

Nearby, **Santa Cruz do Bussaco** (www.fmb.pt; adult/child €2/free, guided tour €3.50; ⏰9am-1pm & 2-6pm) is what remains of a convent where the Duke of Wellington–to-be rested after the Battle of Bussaco in 1810. The atmospheric interior has decaying religious paintings, an unusual passageway right around the chapel, some guns from the battle, and the much-venerated image of *Nossa Senhora do Leite* (Our Lady of Milk), with ex-voto offerings.

Outside the forest walls lies the old-fashioned little spa town of Luso.

✕ ⮡ p481

The Drive » Heading back to Coimbra, ignore your GPS and make sure to take the lovely foresty N235, which later joins the IP3. It's a picturesque drive.

Eating & Sleeping

Coimbra ❶

✗ Sete
Restaurante   Modern Portuguese €€

(📞239 060 065; www.facebook.com/setere
staurante; Rua Dr Martins de Carvalho 10; mains
€12-21; ⏱12.30-3pm & 7-11pm Wed-Mon)
Squeezed into a corner behind the Igreja de
Santa Cruz, this intimate restaurant is one of
the most popular in town. Its casual wine bar
vibe, personable service and modern take on
Portuguese cuisine ensure it's almost always
buzzing. Book ahead to avoid disappointment.

🛏 Casa Pombal   Guesthouse €€

(📞239 835 175; www.casapombal.com; Rua das
Flores 18; r €50-70, with shared bathroom €40-
60; ❄️📶) In a lovely old-town location, this
snug guesthouse squeezes tons of charm into
a small space. Interiors boast dark-wood floors,
ceramic tiles and aquamarine blues, while
rooms are cosy and individually decorated –
two boast magnificent views. Breakfast is good
and the friendly staff can provide multilingual
advice. A small terrace peers out across the
rooftops. Book ahead from Easter to October.

🛏 Quinta das
Lágrimas   Luxury Hotel €€€

(📞239 802 380; www.quintadaslagrimas.pt;
Rua António Augusto Gonçalves; r €175-275;
P❄️📶🏊) Coimbra's sole five-star hotel is
charmingly ensconced in the romantic Jardim
Quinta das Lágrimas on the west bank of the
Mondego. Choose between classic, richly
furnished rooms in the original 18th-century
palace, or go for something more minimalist in
the modern annex. There's a formal fine-dining
restaurant for gourmet dinners, and a fully
equipped spa.

Piodão ❸

🛏 Casa da Padaria   B&B €€

(📞235 732 773; www.casadapadaria.com;
Rua Cónego Manuel Fernandes Nogueira; s/d
€60/65) A picture-perfect rural hideaway, this

handsome B&B has an exceptionally friendly
host, great breakfasts and attractive, rustic
guestrooms. It's in a former bakery on the far
side of the village from where you arrive.

Manteigas ❹

🛏 Casa das Obras   Guesthouse €€

(📞275 981 155; www.casadasobras.pt; Rua Teles
de Vasconcelos; r €60-85; P📶🏊) Live like
nobility at this glorious 18th-century mansion,
the pick of the town-centre accommodation.
The manor house has been in the same family
for centuries and is a picture of old-world charm
with its stone-flagged floors, grand fireplace
and original period furniture. It's no shrine,
though, and you're made to feel very at home.
The antique-filled rooms are stylish, but the
real joy comes from the public areas, including
a wonderful breakfast room where you all eat
around a lord-of-the-manor-style long table, and
a games room with a billiard table. There's also a
pool in a grassy courtyard across the street.

🛏 Casa das
Penhas Douradas   Design Hotel €€€

(📞275 981 045; www.casadaspenhasdouradas.
pt; Penhas Douradas; r €130-190, ste €240-
290; P❄️@📶🏊) Make it up to this
fantastic mountain hideaway and you won't
want to leave. Everything about the place is
just so right, from its panoramic setting to
the minimalist Scandinavian-inspired chalet
design and impeccable service (evening drinks,
afternoon teas). And that's before you've even
plunged into the heated pool or grabbed a
spa treatment (the massages are amazing).
For meals, it's hard to go past the hotel's
gourmet **restaurant** (📞275 981 045; www.
casadaspenhasdouradas.pt; Penhas Douradas;
fixed-price lunch/dinner menu €30/40; ⏱1-3pm
& 8-10pm), which is also open to the public,
yet less fancy snacks are available. When you
eventually decide to hit the outdoors, there are
marked trails and a lake nearby. Rooms vary
from the more modestly priced attic rooms in
the original building to a stylish, airy suite, but
all are immaculate and most offer stirring views.

Monsanto **7**

✗ Adega Típica
O Cruzeiro   Portuguese €€

(📞936 407 676; Rua Fernando Namora 4; mains €11-15; 🕐12.30-3pm & 7-9pm Thu-Mon) Just below the village proper, this likeable place is a rather surprising find, situated as it is in a modern municipal building. The panoramic dining area boasts spectacular views over the plains below, and the superfriendly staff serve tasty dishes from a seasonal menu.

🛏 Monsanto
Geo-Hotel Escola   Design Hotel €€

(📞277 314 061; www.monsantoghe.com; Rua da Capela 1; r €65-130; ❄🛜) This hip hotel brings a dash of contemporary design to Monsanto's granite-grey centre. Occupying a renovated mansion, it has 10 spacious rooms, each a picture of understated cool. Plain white walls are paired with polished wood floors, colourful accents and memorable views. The friendly and welcoming staff are a further plus.

Sortelha **8**

✗ Restaurante
Dom Sancho   Portuguese €€

(📞271 388 267; Largo do Corro; mains €14-20; 🕐 noon-2.30pm & 7-9.30pm Tue-Sat, noon-3pm Sun) The only restaurant in the old village, Dom Sancho sits just inside the main Gothic gate. It's touristy but the traditional food is spot on – mainly game and hearty stews – and its snug, stone-walled dining room is an attractive place to dine. For lighter snacks and drinks, try the bar downstairs (with cosy fireplace in winter).

Viseu **12**

✗ O Cortiço   Portuguese €€

(📞232 416 127; www.facebook.com/cortico. tradicional; Rua Augusto Hilário 45; mains €11-19; 🕐 noon-3pm & 7-10pm Tue-Sat, noon-3pm Sun) With its stone walls and low wood-beamed

ceilings, this cosy eatery specialises in traditional recipes collected from surrounding villages. Generous portions are served in heavy tureens, and the good house wine comes in medieval-style wooden pitchers. Finish your meal with a glass of the local firewater made from olives.

🛏 Palácio dos Melos   Boutique Hotel €€

(📞232 439 290; www.hotelpalaciodosmelos.pt; Rua Chão Mestre 4; s/d €76/100; 🅿❄@🛜) This friendly, central hotel enjoys a remarkable location, in a renovated mansion built into the city walls. Its public areas are elegant with high ceilings and period furniture, while guest rooms come in a range of looks, from modern business-like to refined classical. All are comfortable and spacious, though. Check for money-saving packages online.

Mata Nacional do Buçaco **14**

✗ Pedra de Sal   Portuguese €€

(📞919 701 310; Rua Francisco A Dinis 33, Luso; mains €12-22; 🕐7-10pm Wed, noon-3pm & 7-10pm Thu-Mon) Winningly done out in dark wood, this cosy wine-bar-restaurant is the best in Luso by far. Its menu covers the usual array of meat and fish dishes; however, it's the succulent cuts of Iberian pork and expertly grilled steaks that stand out. The wine list and service are also excellent. Book ahead at weekends.

🛏 Palace Hotel
do Buçaco   Historic Hotel €€€

(📞231 937 970; www.almeidahotels.pt/pt/hotel-coimbra-portugal; Mata Nacional do Buçaco; r €140-275; 🅿) Originally a royal hunting lodge, this Gothic-Manueline palace in the Buçaco forest is a delightfully ostentatious place to stay. Common areas are stunning – particularly the lobby area and grand staircase – though some of the old-fashioned guest rooms feel a little musty. Don't expect mod cons – there's no air-con, and wi-fi is only available in communal areas – but do expect a dreamy setting and memorable meals. Significant discounts are often available online.

NEED ^{TO} KNOW

CURRENCY
Euro (€)

LANGUAGE
Portuguese

VISAS
Generally not required for stays of up to 90 days (not at all for members of EU or Schengen countries). Some nationalities need a Schengen visa.

FUEL
Petrol stations (usually open 24 hours) can be found along major highways. Expect to pay €1.35 to €1.80 per litre.

RENTAL CARS
Hertz (www.hertz.com)

Holiday Autos (www.holidayautos.com)

Pepecar (www.pepecar.com)

IMPORTANT NUMBERS
Europe-wide emergencies (☎112)

International access code (☎00)

Country code (☎351)

Climate

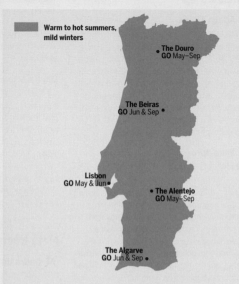

Warm to hot summers, mild winters

The Douro
GO May–Sep

The Beiras
GO Jun & Sep

Lisbon
GO May & Jun

The Alentejo
GO May–Sep

The Algarve
GO Jun & Sep

When to Go

High Season (Jul & Aug)
» Accommodation prices increase 30%.

» Expect big crowds in the Algarve and coastal resort areas.

» Sweltering temperatures are commonplace.

» Warmer ocean temperatures.

Shoulder (Apr–Jun & Sep–Nov)
» Wildflowers and mild days are ideal for hikes and outdoor activities.

» Lively festivals take place in June.

» Crowds and prices are average.

» Colder ocean temperatures.

Low Season (Dec–Mar)
» Shorter, rainier days with freezing temperatures at higher elevations.

» Lower prices, fewer crowds.

» Attractions keep shorter hours, and many beach lodgings close for winter.

» Frigid ocean temperatures, but big waves for surfers.

Daily Costs

Budget: Less than €50

» Dorm bed: €15–22

» Basic hotel room for two: from €35

» Lunch special at a family-run restaurant: €8–10

» Second-class train ticket from Lisbon to Faro: from €23

Midrange: €50–120

» Double room in a midrange hotel: €50–100

» Lunch or dinner in a midrange restaurant: €22–40

» Admission to museums: €3–8

Top end: More than €120

» Boutique hotel room: from €120

» Dinner for two in a top restaurant: from €80

» Three-day surf course: €150

Eating

Tapas Bar Tapas and drinks; open longer hours than restaurants.

Pasteleria Bakery; good for pastries and coffee.

Vinoteca Wine bar where you order by the glass.

Cervejaria Beerhall; the place to go for snacks and *cerveja* (draft beer).

Price categories indicate the cost of a main course:

€	less than €10
€€	€10–20
€€€	more than €20

Sleeping

Casa no Campo Comfy village houses or farmhouses for hire in the countryside.

Pousadas State-funded accommodation often in castles, converted monasteries and old mansions.

Pensão Inexpensive, extremely basic guesthouses, often with shared bathrooms.

Price categories indicate the cost of a double room with bathroom in high season. Unless otherwise stated, breakfast is included in the price.

€	less than €60
€€	€60–120
€€€	more than €120

Arriving in Portugal

Aeroporto de Lisboa (Lisbon)

Rental cars There's a wide choice of car-hire companies at the airport.

Metro €1.90 (including €0.50 Viva Viagem card). Take the red line from Aeroporto station; transfer at Alameda for blue line to Rossioand Baixa-Chiado. It's 20 minutes to the centre; frequent departures from 6.30am to 1am.

AeroBus €3.50; every 20 minutes from 7.45am to 8.15pm.

Taxis €12–16; around 20 minutes to the centre.

Aeroporto de Faro (Faro)

Rental cars Car-rental agencies have desks in the airport.

Buses €1.60; every 30 minutes weekdays, every two hours weekends.

Taxis €10–14; around 20 minutes to the centre.

Mobile Phones

Local SIM cards are widely available and can be used in European and Australian mobile phones. Not compatible with many North American or Japanese systems.

Internet Access

Wi-fi is available in most lodgings and cafes (and is usually free). Internet cafes are rare.

Money

ATMs are widely available, except in the smallest villages. Credit cards are accepted in midrange and high-end establishments.

Tipping

Menu prices indicate a service charge. Most people leave small change if satisfied: 5% is fine; 10% is considered generous.

Useful Websites

Lonely Planet (lonelyplanet. com/portugal) Travel tips, accommodation, recommendations and more.

Portugal Tourism (www. visitportugal.com) Official tourism authority.

RAC (www.rac.co.uk/drive/ travel/driving-abroad) Info for British drivers on driving in Spain and Portugal.

Language

Portuguese pronunciation is not difficult because most sounds are also found in English. The exceptions are the nasal vowels (represented in our pronunciation guides by ng after the vowel), which are pronounced as if you're trying to make the sound through your nose; and the strongly rolled *r* (represented by rr in our pronunciation guides). Also note that the symbol zh sounds like the 's' in 'pleasure'. The stress generally falls on the second-last syllable of a word. In our pronunciation guides stressed syllables are indicated with italics.

PORTUGUESE BASICS

Hello.	*Olá.*	o·*laa*
Goodbye.	*Adeus.*	a·de·*oosh*
How are you?	*Como está?*	*ko*·moo shtaa
Fine, and you?	*Bem, e você?*	beng e vo·*se*
Excuse me.	*Faz favor.*	faash fa·*vor*
Sorry.	*Desculpe.*	desh·*kool*·pe
Yes.	*Sim.*	seeng
No.	*Não.*	nowng
Please.	*Por favor.*	poor fa·*vor*
Thank you.	*Obrigado.* (m)	o·bree·*gaa*·doo
	Obrigada. (f)	o·bree·*gaa*·da

You're welcome. *De nada.* de *naa*·da

What's your name?
Qual é o seu nome? kwaal e oo se·oo *no*·me

My name is ...
O meu nome é ... oo me·oo *no*·me e ...

Do you speak English?
Fala inglês? faa·la eeng·*glesh*

I don't understand.
Não entendo. nowng eng·*teng*·doo

DIRECTIONS

Where's (the station)?
Onde é (a estação)? ong·de e (a shta·*sowng*)

Can you show me (on the map)?
Pode-me mostrar po·de·me moosh·*traar*
(no mapa)? (noo *maa*·pa)

EMERGENCIES

Help!	*Socorro!*	soo·*ko*·rroo
I'm lost.		
Estou perdido. (m)		shtoh per·*dee*·doo
Estou perdida. (f)		shtoh per·*dee*·da

ON THE ROAD

I'd like to hire a ...	*Queria alugar ...*	ke·*ree*·a a·loo·*gaar* ...
bicycle	*uma bicicleta*	*oo*·ma bee·see·*kle*·ta
car	*um carro*	oong *kaa*·rroo
motorcycle	*uma mota*	*oo*·ma *mo*·ta
child seat	*cadeira de criança*	ka·*day*·ra de kree·*ang*·sa
helmet	*capacete*	ka·pa·*se*·te
mechanic	*mecânico*	me·*kaa*·nee·koo
petrol/gas	*gasolina*	ga·zoo·*lee*·na
service station	*posto de gasolina*	*posh*·too de ga·zoo·*lee*·na

---

Want More?

For in-depth language information and handy phrases, check out Lonely Planet's *Portuguese Phrasebook*. You'll find it at **shop.lonelyplanet.com**.

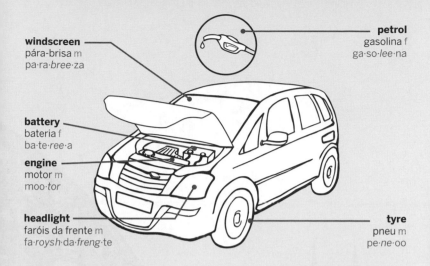

petrol
gasolina f
ga·so·*lee*·na

windscreen
pára-brisa m
pa·ra·*bree*·za

battery
bateria f
ba·te·*ree*·a

engine
motor m
moo·*tor*

headlight
faróis da frente m
fa·*roysh*·da·*freng*·te

tyre
pneu m
pe·*ne*·oo

How much for daily hire?
Quanto custa para alugar por dia? kwang·too koosh·ta pa ra a·loo·gaar poor dee·a

How much for weekly hire?
Quanto custa para alugar por semana? kwang·too koosh·ta pa ra a·loo·gaar poor se·ma·na

Do you have a road map?
Tem um mapa de estradas? teng oong maa·pa de shtraa·dash

Is this the road to ...?
Esta é a estrada para ...? esh·ta e a shtraa·da pa·ra ...

(How long) Can I park here?
(Quanto tempo) Posso estacionar aqui? (kwang·too teng·poo) po·soo shta·see·oo·naar a·kee

What's the speed limit?
Qual é o limite de velocidade? kwaal e oo lee·mee·te de ve·loo·see·daa·de

The car/motorbike has broken down (at ...).
O carro/A mota avariou-se (em ...). oo kaa·rroo/a mo·ta a·va·ree·oh·se (eng ...)

I have a flat tyre.
Tenho um furo no pneu. ta·nyoo oong foo·roo noo pe·ne·oo

I've run out of petrol.
Estou sem gasolina. shtoh seng ga·zoo·lee·na

I need a mechanic.
Preciso de um mecânico. pre·see·zoo de oong me·kaa·nee·koo

Can you fix it (today)?
Pode-se arranjar (hoje)? po·de·se a·rrang·zhaar (o·zhe)

How long will it take?
Quanto tempo vai levar? kwang·too teng·poo vai e·vaar

Signs

Pare	Stop
Dar Prioridade	Give Way
Proibido el Paso	No Entry
Entrada	Entrance
Portagem	Toll
Sentido Unico	One Way
Sair da Autoestrada	Freeway Exit

Germany

Grandiose cities, storybook villages, vine-stitched valleys and bucolic landscapes that beg you to toot your horn, leap out of the car and jump for joy – road-tripping in Germany is a mesmerising kaleidoscope of dramatic landscapes and exciting experiences. The trips in this section take you for a spin from Germany's sophisticated cities to fabled Rhine vineyards and the medieval walled towns of Bavaria. Whether you want to cruise past castles, sip wine or climb into the foothills of the Alps, there's something here for you.

Cologne Hohenzollern Bridge and Cologne Cathedral
WESTEND61/GETTY IMAGES ©

Germany

35 Romantic Rhine 5–7 Days
Fall under the spell of the castle-lined riverscape along the world-famous Rhine.

36 The Romantic Road 10 Days
A ribbon of historical quaintness running through Bavaria's western reaches.

37 German Fairy Tale Road 5 Days
Fantasies and horrors according to those famous Brothers Grimm.

 DON'T MISS

Cologne
The star of the region, Cologne makes its statement from the moment you spot the twin spires of the legendary Dom. See it on Trip 35

Wine Tasting
Learn to love Germany's often excellent white wines. Sample exquisite vintages at source in cosy wineries amid the vineyards on Trip 35

Wurzburg Residenz
See the world's largest fresco within Würzburg's magnificent Unesco-listed palace. Get your ticket as part of Trip 36

Schloss Neuschwanstein
The world's most famous castle inspired Walt Disney's citadel and strikes a fairy-tale pose against Alpine forests. Book your tour on Trip 36

Rothenburg ob der Tauber
Go full circle around this town's medieval walls before celebrating Christmas in July with a tasty snowball! You'll find it on Trip 36

Romantic Rhine

After seeing powerhouse cities Düsseldorf, Cologne and Bonn, epic scenery unfolds as the Rhine valley carves between towering cliffs to delightful Mainz.

35

TRIP HIGHLIGHTS

START
Düsseldorf

Cologne

Koblenz

7

Loreley

13

14 FINISH

198 km

Rüdesheim
Escape the crowds by hiking into the picturesque vineyards

Boppard
One of the Romantic Rhine's prettiest towns

155 km

Mainz
Home to rustic wine taverns and a magnificent cathedral

235 km

Bacharach Medieval old town

491

35 Romantic Rhine

Boats gliding down the Rhine give passengers mesmerising views of the medieval villages, craggy hillsides and castle after castle floating past. But on this trip you'll get up close to its mightiest sights, hike through its high-perched vineyards, and discover hidden treasures and romantic hideaways you'd never see from the water. (Though you'll have plenty of opportunities en route to board a cruise, too.)

❶ Düsseldorf

Survey the mighty Rhine from Düsseldorf's **Medienhafen**. This old harbour area continues to attract red-hot restaurants, bars, hotels and clubs. Crumbling warehouses have transformed into high-tech office buildings, rubbing shoulders with bold new structures designed by celebrated international architects, including Frank Gehry.

Of course, no visit to Düsseldorf is complete without exploring its **Altstadt** (old town), which claims to be the 'longest bar in the world'.

The Drive » It's a 43km drive south via the B1 and the A57 to Cologne. (Fear not: although this section travels through built-up areas and industrial estates, later stages become much more scenic.)

❷ Cologne

A walking tour is the best way to appreciate this engaging city (Germany's fourth largest) on the Rhine. Must-sees include Cologne's world-famous **Dom** (Cologne Cathedral; ☎0221-9258 4720; www.

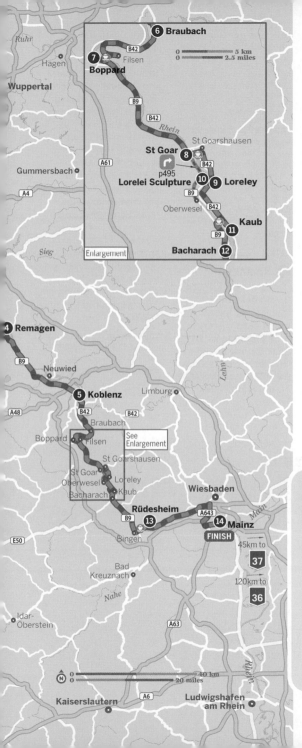

koelner-dom.de; Domkloster 4; tower adult/concession €5/2; ⏰6am-8pm, tower 9am-6pm May-Sep, to 5pm Mar, Apr & Oct, to 4pm Nov-Feb; 🚌5, 16, 18 Dom/Hauptbahnhof), whose twin spires dominate the skyline, as well as superb museums such as the **Römisch-Germanisches Museum** (Roman Germanic Museum; 📞0221-2212 4438; www.roemisch-germanisches-museum.de; Roncalliplatz 4; adult/child €6/3; ⏰10am-5pm Tue-Sun; 🚌5, 16, 18 Dom/Hauptbahnhof); sculptures and ruins displayed outside its entrance are the overture to its symphony of Roman artefacts found along the Rhine.

The Drive » Drive south along the B51 on the Rhine's west bank before joining the A555 (30km all-up).

- - - - - - - - - - - - - - - - - -

❸ Bonn
In a beautiful riverside setting, Ludwig van

LINK YOUR TRIP

37 German Fairy Tale Road

Get on the trail of the Brothers Grimm 65km west of Mainz in Hanau.

36 The Romantic Road
This ribbon of historical quaintness starts at Würzburg, two hours (154km) west from Mainz.

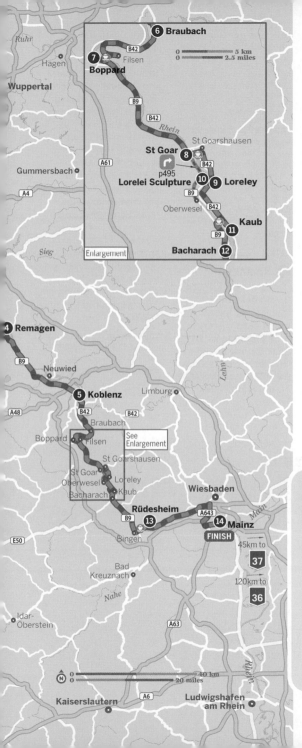

GERMANY **35** ROMANTIC RHINE

Ruhr
Hagen
Wuppertal
B42 🚂 Braubach ❻
❼ Filsen
Boppard
B9
B42
Rhein
St Goarshausen
Gummersbach
A61
St Goar ❽ 🚂
B42
p495
Lorelei Sculpture ❿ ❾ **Loreley**
A4
B9
Oberwesel B42
🚂 **Kaub**
B9 ⓫
Enlargement
Bacharach ⓬
Sieg

❹ **Remagen**
B9
Neuwied
Limburg
Lahn
❺ **Koblenz**
A48
B42 B42
Braubach
Boppard Filsen
See Enlargement
St Goarshausen
St Goar
Oberwesel Loreley
Bacharach Kaub
Wiesbaden
Main
Rüdesheim
B9 ⓭ A643
FINISH ⓮ **Mainz**
E50
Bingen
45km to **37**
Bad Kreuznach
120km to **36**
Nahe
Idar-Oberstein
A63
Rhein
Ⓝ 0 ___ 40 km
0 ___ 20 miles
Kaiserslautern A6 **Ludwigshafen am Rhein**

Beethoven's home town warrants a stop to visit the **Beethoven-Haus Bonn** (Beethoven House; ☎0228-981 7525; www. beethoven-haus-bonn.de; Bonngasse 20; adult/concession €10/7; ⏰10am-6pm), where the great composer was born in 1770. Other landmarks include the soaring **Münster Basilica** (www.bonner -muenster.de; Münsterplatz; ⏰closed for renovation), built on the graves of the two martyred Roman soldiers who later became the city's patron saints.

Bonn's old government quarter dates from its time as West Germany's 'temporary' capital, between 1949 and 1991 (when a reunited German government decided to move to Berlin). For a romp through recent German history from the end of WWII, pop by

the **Haus der Geschichte** (Museum of History; ☎0228-916 5400; www.hdg.de; Willy-Brandt-Allee 14; ⏰9am-7pm Tue-Fri, 10am-6pm Sat & Sun; P; 🚌16, 63, 66 Heussallee/Museumsmeile).

The Drive » Take the B9 southeast for 24km. Once you leave the German state of North Rhine–Westphalia and enter Rhineland–Palatinate, the road returns to the river's west bank; on your right you'll see the hilly wildlife park, Wildpark Rolandseck, as you approach Remagen.

----

❹ Remagen

Remagen was founded by the Romans in 16 CE as Rigomagus, but the town would hardly figure in the history books were it not for one fateful day in early March 1945. As the Allies raced across France and Belgium to rid Germany of Nazism, the Wehrmacht tried

frantically to stave off defeat by destroying all bridges across the Rhine. But the Brücke von Remagen (the steel rail bridge) lasted long enough for Allied troops to cross the river, contributing significantly to the collapse of Hitler's western front. One of the bridge's surviving basalt towers now houses the **Friedensmuseum** (Peace Museum Bridge at Remagen; ☎02642-218 63; www.bruecke-remagen.de; An der Alten Rheinbrücke 11; ⏰museum temporarily closed for renovation; P), with a well-presented exhibit on Remagen's pivotal role in WWII.

The Drive » Take the B9 southeast for 40km. The Rhine winds back and forth away from the road until you reach Koblenz. Stay on the B9 until you've crossed the Moselle to the town centre, or risk getting lost in a maze of concentric flyovers.

CROSSING THE RHINE

No bridges span the Rhine between Koblenz and Mainz; the only way to cross the river along this stretch is by *Autofähre* (car ferry).

Bingen–Rüdesheim (www.bingen-ruedesheimer.de; car & driver €4.80, bicycle & rider €2.70, pedestrian €2.20; ⏰5.30am-9.50pm Sun-Thu, to midnight Fri & Sat May-Oct, 5.30am-9.50pm Nov-Apr)

Boppard–Filsen (www.faehre-boppard.de; car & driver €4.80, bicycle & rider €2.70, pedestrian €2; ⏰6.30am-10pm Jun-Aug, to 9pm Apr, May & Sep, to 8pm Oct-Mar)

Niederheimbach–Lorch (www.mittelrhein-faehre.de; car & driver €4.80, bicycle & rider €2.70, pedestrian €2; ⏰6am-10.50pm Apr-Oct, to 6.50pm Nov-Mar)

Oberwesel–Kaub (www.faehre-kaub.de; car & driver €4.80, bicycle & rider €2.70, pedestrian €2; ⏰6am-8pm Mon-Sat, 8am-8pm Sun Apr-Sep, 6am-7pm Mon-Sat, 8am-7pm Sun Oct-Mar)

St Goar–St Goarshausen (www.faehre-loreley.de; car & driver €4.80, bicycle & rider €2.70, pedestrian €2; ⏰5.30am-10.30pm Mon-Fri, from 6.20am Sat, from 7.20am Sun May-Sep, shorter hours Oct-Apr)

DETOUR: OBERWESEL

Start: **8** St Goar

It's a quick 7.8km south from St Goar along the B9 to the village of Oberwesel. Every April, Oberwesel crowns not a *Weinkönigin* (wine queen), as in most Rhine towns, but a *Weinhexe* (wine witch) – a good witch, of course – who is said to protect the vineyards. Photos of all the *Weinhexen* crowned since 1946 are displayed in the cellar of Oberwesel's **Kulturhaus** (☏06744-714 726; www.kulturhaus -oberwesel.de; Rathausstrasse 23; adult/child €3/1; ☺10am-5pm Tue-Fri, from 2pm Sat & Sun Apr-Oct, 10am-2pm Tue-Fri Nov-Mar), along with 19th-century engravings of the Rhine and models of its riverboats.

Hidden sky-high up a vineyard-striped hillside, the flagstone terrace of **Günderode Haus** (☏06744-714 011; www.guenderodefilmhaus.de; Siebenjungfrauenblick; dishes €5-18; ☺noon-6pm Tue-Sat, 10am-6pm Sun Apr-Oct, shorter hours Nov-Mar; 🛜) is incredible for a glass of wine, beer or brandy, with sweeping views over the Rhine. The adjacent 200-year-old half-timbered house was used as a film set for *Heimat 3* (2004); it now has a cinema room and hosts live music and literary events, as well as wine tastings. From Oberwesel, take the K93 east for 600m, turn right (north) onto the K95; after 1km, the car park's on your right.

5 Koblenz

Koblenz sits at the confluence of the Rhine and Moselle Rivers – marked by the expansive **Deutsches Eck** ('German Corner'), adjoining flower-filled parks and promenades – and the convergence of three low mountain ranges (the Hunsrück, the Eifel and the Westerwald). Its roots go back to the Romans, who founded a military stronghold (Confluentes) here because of the site's supreme strategic value.

On the Rhine's right bank, the 118m-high fortress **Festung Ehren-breitstein** (☏0261-6675 4000; www.tor-zum-welterbe. de; adult/child €7/3.50, incl cable car €14.80/6.60, audioguide €2; ☺10am-6pm Apr-Oct, to 5pm Nov-Mar) proved indestructible to all but Napoleonic troops, who levelled it in 1801. To prove a point, the Prussians rebuilt it as one of Europe's mightiest fortifications. It's accessible by car, on foot and by cable car.

Inside Koblenz' striking glass **Forum Confluentes**, the **Mittelrhein-Museum** (www.mittelrhein-museum. de; Zentralplatz 1; adult/ child €6/free; ☺10am-6pm Tue-Sun) spans 2000 years of the region's history, including 19th-century landscape paintings of the Romantic Rhine by German and British artists.

🛏 p501

The Drive » Take the B49 to the Rhine's east bank and travel south on the B42; it's 13km to Braubach. At this point of the drive, you leave the cityscapes behind and enter an older world of cobblestones, half-timbered villages, densely forested hillsides and ancient vineyards.

6 Braubach

Framed by forest, vineyards and rose gardens, the 1300-year-old town of Braubach centres on its small, half-timbered **Marktplatz**. High above are the dramatic towers, turrets and crenellations of the 700-year-old **Marksburg** (☏02627-206; www.marksburg.de; adult/child €8/6; ☺10am-5pm mid-Mar–Oct, 11am-4pm Nov–mid-Mar), which is unique among the Rhine's fastnesses as it was never destroyed.

WHY THIS IS A GREAT TRIP
CATHERINE LE NEVEZ, WRITER

The romance along this stretch of the Rhine is timeless. Poets and painters, including Lord Byron and William Turner, are among those who have been inspired by this castle-crowned, forest-and-vineyard-cloaked valley. A fabled stop on the original European Grand Tour, the riverscape here is now a designated Unesco World Heritage Site. It doesn't get more classic than that.

Above: Door arch, Cologne Cathedral
Left: Lorelei Sculpture
Right: Boppard

LEONID ANDRONOV/SHUTTERSTOCK ©

The compulsory tour takes in the citadel, the Gothic hall and a grisly torture chamber.

The Drive » Hug the Rhine's east bank for 11km as it curves around to the car-ferry dock at Filsen. It's a five-minute crossing to charming Boppard.

- - - - - - - - - - - - - - - -

TRIP HIGHLIGHT

❼ Boppard

Idyllically located on a horseshoe bend in the river, Boppard (pronounced 'bo-*part*') is one of the Romantic Rhine's prettiest towns, not least because its riverfront and historic centre are both on the same side of the railway tracks.

Boppard's riverfront promenade, the **Rheinallee**, has grassy areas for picnicking and a children's playground.

Many of the town's half-timbered buildings house cosy wine taverns, including its oldest, **Weinhaus Heilig Grab** (www.heiliggrab.de; Zelkesgasse 12; ⏰3pm-midnight Wed-Mon). In summer, sip local Rieslings under the chestnut trees, where live music plays on weekends.

Fantastic hiking trails fan out into the countryside, including the **Hunsrück Trails**, accessed by Germany's steepest scheduled railway route, the **Hunsrückbahn** (www.hunsrueckbahn.de; Hauptbahnhof). Around the **Vierseenblick** (Four-Lakes-View), a panoramic outlook reached by **Sesselbahn**

(Chairlift; ☎06742-2510; http://sesselbahn-boppard.de; Mühltal 12; adult/child one-way €5.50/3.50, return €9/5; ⏰10am-6pm mid-Apr–Sep, shorter hours Oct) creates the illusion that you're looking at four separate lakes rather than a single river.

The Drive » Take the B9 south for 14km, passing Burg Maus across the river near the village of Wellmich. Shortly afterwards, you'll spot Burg Rheinfels on the west bank above St Goar.

⑧ St Goar

Lording over the village of St Goar are the sprawling ruins of **Burg Rheinfels** (☎06741-7753; www. st-goar.de; Schlossberg 47; adult/child €6/3; ⏰9am-6pm Apr-Oct, to 5pm Mar & Nov), once the Rhine's mightiest fortress. Built in 1245 by Count Dieter von Katzenelnbogen as a base for his toll-collecting operations, its size and labyrinthine layout are astonishing. Kids (and

adults) will love exploring the subterranean tunnels and galleries (bring a torch). From St Goar's northern edge, follow the Schlossberg road to the castle.

✕ 🛏 p501

The Drive » Take the five-minute car ferry across to the little village of St Goarshausen. From St Goarshausen's Marktplatz, follow the L338 as it twists steeply uphill through thick forest for 1.2km and turn right onto the K89 for 2.5km to reach Loreley.

⑨ Loreley

The most storied spot along the Romantic Rhine, Loreley is an enormous, almost vertical slab of slate; it owes its fame to a mythical maiden whose siren songs are said to have lured sailors to their death in the river's treacherous currents. Heinrich Heine told the tale in his 1824 poem 'Die Lorelei'.

On the edge of the plateau 4km southeast of

the village of St Goarshausen, the visitor centre **Loreley Besucherzentrum** (☎06771-599 093; www. loreley-besucherzentrum.de; Loreley 7; adult/child €3/2; ⏰10am-5pm Mar-Oct) covers the Loreley myth and local flora, fauna, shipping and winemaking traditions. A 300m gravel path leads to a **viewpoint** at the tip of the Loreley outcrop, 190m above the river.

The Drive » Return to the B42 at the bottom of the hill; on your left, you'll see Burg Katz. Travel south for 2km to the car park by the breakwater for the next stop, the *Lorelei* sculpture.

⑩ Lorelei Sculpture

At the tip of a narrow breakwater jutting into the Rhine, a bronze sculpture of Loreley's famous maiden perches atop a rocky platform. From the car park, you can walk the 600m out to the sculpture, from where there are fantastic views of both riverbanks. Be aware that the rough path is made from jagged slate (wear sturdy shoes!) and the gentler sandy lower path is often underwater.

The Drive » Take the B42 south for 8km to the little village of Kaub; park next to the ferry dock.

⑪ Kaub

Kaub is the gateway to one of the river's iconic sights. As if out of a fairy tale, 1326-built, boat-

CAT & MOUSE

Two rival castles stand either side of the village of St Goarshausen. Burg Peterseck was built by the archbishop of Trier to counter the toll practices of the powerful Katzenelnbogen family. The latter responded by building a much bigger castle high on the other side of town, Burg Neukatzenelnbogen, which was dubbed **Burg Katz**, meaning 'Cat Castle'. Highlighting the obvious imbalance of power between the Katzenelnbogens and the archbishop, Burg Peterseck was soon nicknamed **Burg Maus** ('Mouse Castle'). Both are closed to the public.

shaped toll castle **Pfalzgrafenstein** (☏06774-745; www.burg-pfalzgrafenstein.de; adult/child incl ferry €7/4; ☺10am-6pm Tue-Sun Apr-Oct, 10am-5pm Mar, Sat & Sun Jan, Feb & Nov), with distinctive white-painted walls, red trim and slate turrets, perches on a narrow island in the middle of the Rhine. A once-dangerous rapid here (since modified) forced boats to use the right-hand side of the river, where a chain forced ships to stop and pay a toll. The island makes a fabulously scenic picnic spot.

Alongside Kaub's car-ferry dock you can hop on a little **Fährboot** (www.faehre-kaub.de; adult/child €2/0.80; ☺10am-6pm Tue-Sun Apr-Oct, to 5pm Mar, to 5pm Sat & Sun Nov, Jan & Feb) passenger ferry (it only runs from this side of the river).

The Drive 》 Take the car ferry across to the Rhine's west bank and head south on the B9 for 3km.

---

⑫ Bacharach

Tiny Bacharach conceals its considerable charms behind a **14th-century wall**. Enter one of the thick arched gateways under the train tracks and you'll find yourself in a medieval old town filled with half-timbered mansions. It's possible to walk almost all the way around the centre on top of the walls. The lookout tower on the upper section of the wall provides some panoramic views.

Dating from 1421, **Zum Grünen Baum** (☏06743-1208; www.weingut-bastian-bacharach.de; Oberstrasse 63; ☺noon-10pm, shorter hours Nov-Mar) serves some of Bacharach's best whites in rustic surrounds. Its nearby *vinothèque*, **Weingut Fritz Bastian** (Koblenzer Strasse 1; ☺11am-6pm Sat-Wed Apr-Oct, shorter hours Nov-Mar), by contrast, is state of the art. Owner Friedrich Bastian is a renowned opera singer, so music (and culinary) events take place year-round, including on Bastian's private river-island with its own vineyard.

🛏 p501

The Drive 》 Head south on the B9, passing Burg Reichenstein then Burg Rheinstein on your right. Then, on your left, in the river itself, you'll pass the Mäuseturm, a fortified tower used as a signal station until 1974. Drive through Bingen to the car-ferry dock at its eastern edge, and cross the river to Rüdesheim.

TRIP HIGHLIGHT

⑬ Rüdesheim

Depending on how you look at it, Rüdesheim's town centre – and especially its most famous feature, the tunnel-like medieval alley **Drosselgasse** – is either a touristy nightmare or a lot of kitschy, colourful fun. There's also wonderful walking in the greater area, which is part of the Rheingau wine region, famed for its superior Rieslings.

For a stunning Rhine panorama, head up the wine-producing slopes west of Rüdesheim to the **Niederwald Monument**. Erected between 1877 and 1883, this bombastic monument celebrates the Prussian victory in the Franco-Prussian War and the creation of the German Reich, both in 1871. To save climbing 203 vertical metres, glide above the vineyards aboard the 1400m-long **Seilbahn cable car** (Kabinenbahn; www.seilbahn-ruedesheim.de; Oberstrasse 37; adult/child one-way €6/3, return €9/4.50; ☺9.30am-7pm Jul & Aug, 9.30am-6pm Mon-Fri, to 7pm Sat & Sun Jun & Sep, shorter hours mid-Mar–May & Oct-Dec). A worthwhile network of hiking trails extends from the monument.

🛏 p501

The Drive 》 Head east on the B42 for 23km then turn south on the A643 to cross the bridge over the Rhine. It's then 13km southeast to the centre of Mainz.

TRIP HIGHLIGHT

⑭ Mainz

The Rhine meets the Main at lively Mainz, which has a sizeable university, pretty pedestrian precincts and a *savoir vivre* dating from Napoleon's occupation (1797–1814). Strolling

CRUISING THE RHINE

If you'd like to let someone else drive for a while and get a different perspective of the Rhine, it's easy to park up and hop on a cruise boat.

From around Easter to October (winter services are very limited), passenger ships run by **Köln-Düsseldorfer** (KD; 📞0221-208 8318; www.k-d.com) link Rhine villages on a set timetable. You can travel to the next village or all the way between Mainz and Koblenz (one-way/return €50/55, downstream Mainz to Koblenz/upstream Koblenz to Mainz 5½/8 hours).

Within the segment you've paid for (for example, Boppard–Rüdesheim), you can get on and off as often as you like, but make sure to ask for a free stopover ticket each time you disembark. Return tickets usually cost only slightly more than one-way.

Children up to the age of four travel free, while those up to age 13 are charged a flat fee of €6 regardless of distance. To bring a bicycle, there's a supplement of €3.

A few smaller companies also send passenger boats up and down the river:

Bingen-Rüdesheimer (www.bingen-ruedesheimer.de)

Loreley Linie (www.loreley-linie.com)

Rössler Linie (www.roesslerlinie.de)

along the Rhine and sampling local wines in a half-timbered **Altstadt** tavern are as much a part of any Mainz visit as viewing the sights. Try the 1791 **Weinstube Hottum** (Grebenstrasse 3; ⏰4pm-midnight) for wines purely from the Rheingau and Rheinhessen regions, or vine-draped **Weingut Michel** (Jakobsbergstrasse 8; ⏰4pm-midnight Mon-Sat), Mainz' only *Weingut* (winery) to exclusively serve its own wines.

Highlights you won't want to miss include the fabulous **Mainzer Dom** (📞06131-253 412; www.mainz erdom.bistummainz.de; Markt 10; ⏰9am-6.30pm Mon-Fri, to 4pm Sat, 12.45-6.30pm Sun Mar-Oct, 9am-5pm Mon-Fri, to 3pm Sat, 12.45-3pm & 4-5pm Sun Nov-Feb), the ethereal windows of Chagall in **St-Stephan-Kirche** (www. st-stephan-mainz.bistum-mainz.de; Kleine Weissgasse 12; ⏰10am-5pm Mon-Sat, from noon Sun Mar-Oct, 10am-4.30pm Mon-Sat, from noon Sun Nov-Feb), and the first printed Bible in the **Gutenberg-Museum Mainz** (📞06131-122 503; www.gutenberg-museum. de; Liebfrauenplatz 5; adult/ child €5/2, audioguide €3.50; ⏰9am-5pm Tue-Sat, from 11am Sun). This museum commemorates native son Johannes Gutenberg, who ushered in the information age here in the 15th century by perfecting movable type.

Also well worth a visit is the dungeon-like, brilliantly illuminated Roman archaeological site **Heiligtum der Isis und Mater Magna** (📞06131-600 7493; www.roemisches-mainz.de; Römerpassage 1; ⏰1-6pm Mon-Sat). The easy-to-miss entrance is on the Römer Passage mall's ground floor, just inside the western entrance.

✖ p501

Eating & Sleeping

Koblenz ⑤

🛏 Hotel Stein   Boutique Hotel €€

(📞0261-963 530; www.hotel-stein.de; Mayener Strasse 126; s/d from €89/120; P 🛜) Decorated in soothing beiges, dark timbers and the odd splash of arty colour, Stein's 30 contemporary rooms are all soundproofed for a peaceful night's sleep. The hotel is situated across the Moselle River 2km north of Koblenz' city centre. Michelin-starred restaurant Schiller's is on the ground floor and head chef Mike Schiller also holds cooking courses here.

St Goar ⑧

🍴 Weinhotel Landsknecht   German €€

(📞06741-2011; www.hotel-landsknecht.de; Aussiedlung Landsknecht 4; mains €13.50-23.90; ⏱ noon 2.30pm & 6 9pm Mar–mid-Dec; 🛜) The dining room and terrace at this wonderful spot 1.5km north of St Goar feel like being aboard a cruise boat, with close-up, uninterrupted river views. Delicious home cooking spans pickled salmon with quince mousse, to schnitzel with mushroom and Riesling sauce, and red-wine-marinated plums with rosemary-and-vanilla ice cream. Many of its rooms also have Rhine views.

🛏 Romantik Hotel Schloss Rheinfels   Historic Hotel €€

(📞06741-8020; www.schloss-rheinfels.de; Schlossberg 47; s/d from €95/175; P 🛜🚲) Part of Burg Rheinfels (p498) castle complex is occupied by a romantic hotel boasting 64 rooms and suites that range in size from tiny to palatial. All have antique-style furnishings; pricier rooms come with a river view. The hotel has three restaurants: one rustic, one semiformal and one gourmet. Cots and babysitting services can be arranged. Breakfast costs a whopping €18.

Bacharach ⑫

🛏 Rhein Hotel   Hotel €€€

(📞06743-1243; www.rhein-hotel-bacharach.de; Langstrasse 50; s/d from €130/170; P ✳🛜) Right on the town's medieval ramparts in a half-timbered building, this family-run hotel has 14 well-lit rooms with original artworks that are named for the vineyards they overlook. Rooms facing the river, and therefore the train tracks, have double-glazing. Guests can borrow bikes for free.

Rüdesheim ⑬

🛏 Rüdesheimer Schloss   Boutique Hotel €€

(📞06722-905 00; www.ruedesheimer-schloss. com; Steingasse 10; s/d/ste from €89/129/159; P 🛜) Truly good places to sleep and eat are thin on the ground in central Rüdesheim, but this 18th-century building has 26 surprisingly contemporary rooms designed by local and regional artists. Its restaurant is excellent, serving dishes like cheese-and-Riesling soup, veal liver with truffled mash, and roast duck stuffed with dates and figs. It also has a live pianist and after-dinner dancing.

Mainz ⑭

🍴 Zur Kanzel   European €€

(📞06131-237 137; www.zurkanzel.de; Grebenstrasse 4; mains €10-25; ⏱6pm-1am Tue-Fri, noon-4pm & 6pm-1am Sat) Germany and France intermingle here in seasonally changing dishes like grilled tuna with Riesling-and-sage sauce, garlic-crusted rack of lamb with wilted spinach, schnitzel with Frankfurt-style *Grüne Sosse* (green sauce), and rump steak with herb butter, as well as garlic snails. There's a lovely summer courtyard. Cash only.

The Romantic Road

36

On this trip you'll experience story-book Germany – medieval walled towns, gabled townhouses and crooked streets, all preserved as if time has come to a standstill.

TRIP HIGHLIGHTS

0 km

Würzburg
Bavaria's finest baroque palaces and delicate wines

99 km

Rothenburg ob der Tauber
Wander the streets of this medieval marvel

149 km

Dinkelsbühl
The Romantic Road's quaintest town

350 km

Neuschwanstein & Hohenschwangau Castles
Two of Germany's top castles rise amid Alpine wonder

1 START

4

5

● Nördlingen

Augsburg ●

Schongau ●

14 FINISH

---

10 DAYS
350KM / 217 MILES

GREAT FOR...

BEST TIME TO GO
January and February when the route is blanketed in snow and there are no crowds.

ESSENTIAL PHOTO
The half-timbered buildings of Rothenburg ob der Tauber's Plönlein.

BEST TWO DAYS
The stretch between stops 4 and 6 takes in the most romantic towns of the Romantic Road.

36 | The Romantic Road

From the vineyards of Würzburg to the foot of the Alps, the Romantic Road (Romantische Strasse) is by far the most popular of Germany's touring routes. This well-trodden trail cuts through a cultural and historical cross-section of southern Germany, coming to a crescendo at the gates of King Ludwig II's crazy castles. The route links some of Germany's most picturesque towns, many appearing untouched since medieval times.

TRIP HIGHLIGHT

❶ Würzburg

This lively city in Bavaria's northeastern corner straddles the Main River and is renowned for its art, architecture and delicate wines. A large student population keeps things busy and hip nightlife pulsates through its cobbled streets.

Top billing here goes to the **Würzburg Residenz** (www.residenz-wuerzburg. de; Balthasar-Neumann-Promenade; adult/child €9/ free; ⊙9am-6pm Apr-Oct,

10am-4.30pm Nov-Mar), a vast Unesco-listed palace built by 18th-century architect Balthasar Neumann as the home of the local prince-bishops. It's one of Germany's most important and beautiful baroque palaces. The wonderful zigzagging Treppenhaus (Staircase) is capped by the world's largest fresco, a masterpiece by Giovanni Battista Tiepolo depicting allegories of the four then-known continents (Europe, Africa, America and Asia). The **Dom St Kilian** (☑0931-3866 2900; www. dom-wuerzburg.de; Domstrasse

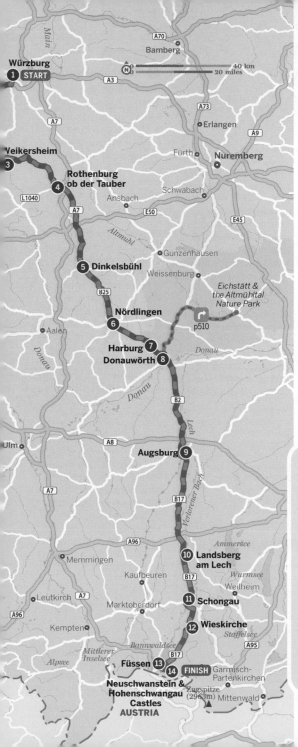

40; ⏰ 8am-7pm Mon-Sat,
to 8pm Sun) is a highly
unusual cathedral with a
Romanesque core and ba-
roque Schönbornkapelle,
also by Neumann.

✕ 🛏 p514

The Drive » Take the B19
south to join the A3 motorway;
follow this to meet the A81,
which goes all the way to
Tauberbischofsheim (37km).

2
Tauberbischofsheim

The main town in the
pretty Tauber Valley,
this small settlement has
a picturesque market-
place dominated by a
neo-Gothic town hall
and lined with typical
half-timbered houses.
Follow the remains of
medieval town walls
to the Kurmainzisches
Schloss, housing the
**Tauberfränkisches
Landschaftsmuseum**

LINK YOUR TRIP

**37 German Fairy
Tale Road**

Do one of the trips in
reverse: the start of the
Grimm Brothers' Fairy Tale
Road is about an hour east
from Würzburg.

35 Romantic Rhine

Würzburg is two
hours (154km) from Mainz,
at the end of this castle-
lined riverside jaunt.

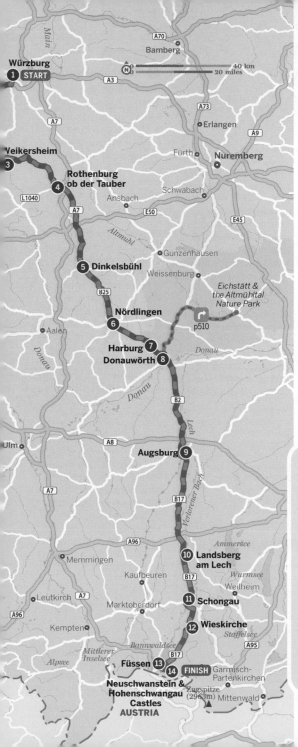

TOP TIP: GUEST CARDS

Overnight anywhere in the Alps and your hotel should issue a free *Gästekarte*, which gives free bus travel plus many other discounts on admission and activities.

(www.tauberfraenkisches-landschaftsmuseum.de; Schlossplatz; adult/child €3/free; ⏰2-4.30pm Tue-Sat, 10am-noon & 2-4.30pm Sun Easter-Oct), where you can learn about Tauberbischofsheim's past.

The Drive >> The 33km dash to Weikersheim along the B290 and L2251 passes through Lauda-Königshofen, a pretty stop in the Tauber Valley.

❸ Weikersheim

Top billing in under-visited Weikersheim is **Schloss Weikersheim** (www.schloss-weikersheim.de; Marktplatz 11; adult/child €6.50/3.30; ⏰9am-6pm Apr-Oct, 10am-5pm Nov-Mar), the Romantic Road's finest palace. Renaissance to the core, it's

surrounded by beautiful formal gardens inspired by Versailles. Highlights include the enormous Knights Hall dating from around 1600 and over 40m long. The rich decor includes a huge painted ceiling, each panel depicting a hunting scene, and the amazingly ornate fireplace. The unforgettable rococo mirror cabinet, with its gilt-and-red decor, is also part of the guided tour, after which you can wander the elegantly laid-out gardens.

The Drive >> The short 28km journey between Weikersheim and Rothenburg ob der Tauber follows minor country roads all the way. You could also detour via Creglingen, a minor stop on the Romantic Road.

❹ Rothenburg ob der Tauber

A meticulously preserved historical town, touristy Rothenburg ob der Tauber is the Romantic Road's most popular stop. Once you're finished with the main sights, there are some less obvious attractions here.

You'll often see the **Plönlein** in brochures and tourist bumf, a gathering of forks in the cobbled road (Obere Schmiedgasse) occupied by possibly the quaintest, most crooked half-timbered house you'll ever see.

Hidden down an alley is the **Alt-Rothenburger Handwerkerhaus** (www.alt-rothenburger-handwerkerhaus.de; Alter Stadtgraben 26; adult/child €3/1.50; ⏰11am-5pm Mon-Fri, from 10am Sat & Sun Easter-Oct, 2-4pm daily Dec), where numerous artisans – coopers, weavers, cobblers and potters – have their workshops, and mostly have had for their house's 700-plus-years' existence. It's half museum, half active workplace; you can easily spend an hour or so watching the artisans at work.

✗ p514

The Drive >> The quickest way to Dinkelsbühl is the A7 motorway (50km). For a slower and longer experience, follow the official Romantic Road route (44km) along country roads via Schillingsfürst, another quaint halt.

ROTHENBURG'S SNOWBALLS

Where can you get your hands on a snowball in July? Why, in Rothenburg ob der Tauber, of course! The town's speciality are *Schneeballen* (snowballs), ribbons of dough shaped into balls, deep-fried then coated in icing sugar, chocolate and other dentist's foes. Some 24 types are made at **Diller's Schneeballen** (www.schneeballen.eu; Obere Schmiedgasse 7; ⏰10am-6pm); a smaller range can be enjoyed all over town.

⑤ Dinkelsbühl

Immaculately preserved Dinkelsbühl is arguably the Romantic Road's most authentically medieval halt. Like Rothenburg, it is ringed by medieval walls, boasting 18 towers and four gates. The joy of Dinkelsbühl is aimless wandering through the crooked lanes, but for a history lowdown visit the **Haus der Geschichte** (House of History; www. hausdergeschichte-dinkelsbue hl.de; Altrathausplatz 14; adult/ child €4/2; ⓧ9am-5.30pm Mon-Fri May-Oct, 10am-5pm Nov-Apr, 10am-4pm Sat & Sun year-round), in the same building as the tourist office.

✕ ⼞ p514

The Drive » Just 32km separate Dinkelsbühl from Nördlingen along the B25, accompanied by the Wörnitz River for the first part of the journey. A few kilometres short of Nördlingen is Wallerstein, a small market town with the beautiful Church of St Alban, also a Romantic Road stop.

⑥ Nördlingen

Charmingly medieval, Nördlingen lies within the Ries Basin, a massive impact crater gouged out by a meteorite more than 15 million years ago. The crater – some 25km in diameter – is one of Earth's best preserved, and has been declared a special 'geopark'.

WILLY WONKA'S NORDLINGEN

If you've seen the 1971 movie *Willy Wonka & the Chocolate Factory*, you've already looked down upon Nördlingen from a glass elevator – aerial shots of the town were used in the film's final sequences.

Nördlingen's 14th-century walls, all original, mimic the crater's rim and are almost perfectly circular: **Rieskrater Museum** (www.rieskrater-museum. de; Eugene-Shoemaker-Platz 1; adult/child incl Stadtmuseum €4.50/2.50; ⓧ10am-4.30pm Tue-Sun, closed noon-1.30pm Nov-Mar) tells the story. Next door is the **Stadtmuseum** (www.stadtmuseum -noerdlingen.de; Vordere Gerbergasse 1; adult/child incl Rieskrater Museum €4.50/2.50; ⓧ1.30-4.30pm Tue-Sun mid-May–early Nov), giving an interesting rundown of Nördlingen's story so far.

On a completely different note, the **Bayerisches Eisenbahnmuseum** (www. bayerisches-eisenbahnmuseum. de; Am Hohen Weg 6a; adult/ child €6/3; ⓧ noon-4pm Tue-Sat, 10am-5pm Sun May-Sep, 10am-5pm Sat & Sun Mar, Apr & Oct) near the train station is a retirement home for locos that have puffed their last. The museum runs steam trains up to Dinkelsbühl, Feuchtwangen and Gunzenhausen several times a year; the website has details.

✕ ⼞ p514

The Drive » The 18km drive to Harburg is along the arrow-straight B25.

⑦ Harburg

Looming over the Wörnitz River, the medieval covered parapets, towers, turrets, keep and red-tiled roofs of 12th-century **Schloss Harburg** (www. burg-harburg.de; Burgstrasse 1; courtyard admission €3, tour €4; ⓧ10am-5pm mid-Mar–early Nov) are so perfectly preserved they almost seem like a film set. Tours tell the Schloss's long tale and evoke the ghosts said to use the castle as a hang-out.

From the castle, the walk to Harburg's cute, half-timbered **Altstadt** takes 10 minutes, slightly more the other way (uphill). A fabulous village-and-castle panorama can be admired from the 1702 stone bridge spanning the Wörnitz.

The Drive » From Harburg follow the B25 15km to Donauwörth.

⑧ Donauwörth

Sitting pretty at the confluence of the Danube and Wörnitz Rivers, the small town of Donauwörth had its heyday as a Free Imperial City in the 14th century. WWII destroyed 75% of the medieval old

WHY THIS IS A GREAT TRIP
MARC DI DUCA,
WRITER

This 350km-long ribbon of historical quaintness is the Germany you came to see, but things can get crowded in the summer months, taking away a bit of the romance. Do the trip in winter when Bavaria's chocolate-box towns look even prettier under a layer of snow.

Above: Rothenburg ob der Tauber
Left: *Schweinshaxe* (pork knuckle) with sauerkraut and potatoes
Right: Würzburg Residenz, Würzburg

town but three gates and five town-wall towers still guard it today. The main street is Reichstrasse, which is where you'll discover the **Liebfraukirche**, a 15th-century Gothic church with original frescoes and a sloping floor that drops 120cm. Swabia's largest church bell (6550kg) swings in the belfry. The town's other major attraction is the **Käthe-Kruse-Puppenmuseum** (www. kaethe-kruse.de; Pflegstrasse 21a; adult/child €2.50/1.50; ☺11am-6pm Tue-Sun May-Sep, 2-5pm Thu-Sun Oct-Apr). In a former monastery, it's a nostalgia-inducing place of old dolls and dollhouses from world-renowned designer Käthe Kruse (1883–1968).

The Drive ›› Augsburg is 47km away via the B2 and the A8 motorway. The scenic route via back roads east of the A8 passes close to the pretty town of Rain, another minor halt on the Romantic Road.

- - - - - - - - - - - - - - - - - - - -

9 Augsburg

Augsburg is the Romantic Road's largest city and one of Germany's oldest, founded by the stepchildren of Roman emperor Augustus over 2000 years ago. This attractive city of spires and cobbles is an engaging stop, though far less quaint than others along the route.

Augsburg's top sight is the **Fuggerei** (🕿821-319 881 14, www.fugger.de; Jakober Strasse; adult/concession

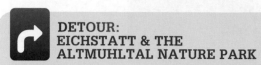

DETOUR:
EICHSTATT & THE
ALTMUHLTAL NATURE PARK

Start: ⑧ **Donauwörth**

A short 55km off the Romantic Road from Donauwörth lies the town of Eichstätt, the main jumping-off point for the serenely picturesque 2900-sq-km Altmühltal Nature Park, which follows the wooded valley of the Altmühl River. Canoeing is a top activity here, as is cycling and camping. The park is an ideal break from the road and a relaxing place to spend a few days in unspoilt natural surroundings. Eichstätt itself has a wealth of architecture, including the richly adorned medieval **Dom** (www.eichstaetter-dom.de; Domplatz; ◷7.15am-7.30pm), with its museum, the baroque **Fürstbischöfliche Residenz** (Residenzplatz 1; tour €1; ◷7.30am-noon Mon-Fri, 2-4pm Mon-Wed, 2-5.30pm Thu), where local prince-bishops once lived it up, and the **Willibaldsburg** (Burgstrasse 19; ◷9am-6pm Tue-Sun Apr-Oct, 10am-4pm Tue-Sun Nov-Mar), a 14th-century castle that houses a couple of museums.

€6.50/5.50; ◷9am-8pm Apr-Sep, to 6pm Oct-Mar), Europe's oldest Catholic welfare settlement, founded by banker and merchant Jakob Fugger in 1521. Around 200 people inhabit the complex today; see how the residents of yesterday lived by visiting the **Fuggereimuseum** (Mittlere Gasse 14; admission incl with entry to the Fuggerei; ◷9am-8pm Mar-Oct, to 6pm Nov-Apr).

Two famous Germans have close associations with Augsburg. Protestant Reformation leader Martin Luther stayed here in 1518 – his story is told at **St Anna Kirche** (www.st-anna-augsburg.de; Im Annahof 2, off Annastrasse; ◷noon-6pm Mon, 10am-6pm Tue-Sat, 10am-12.30pm & 3-5pm Sun May-Oct, slightly shorter hours Nov-Apr). The birthplace of poet and playwright Bertolt Brecht is now a museum, the **Brechthaus** (☎0821-454

0815; www.brechthaus -augsburg.de; Auf dem Rain 7; adult/concession €3.50/2.50; ◷10am-5pm Tue-Sun).

🍴 🛏 p515

The Drive ≫ Drive 43km to Landsberg am Lech along the B17. The route mostly follows the valley of the Lech River. Look out for signs to the saucily named town of Kissing!

- - - - - - - - - - - - - - - - - -

⑩ Landsberg am Lech

A walled town on the Lech, lovely Landsberg has a less commercial ambience than others on the route. Just like the Wieskirche further south, the small baroque **Johanniskirche** (Vorderer Anger 215) was created by baroque architect Dominikus Zimmermann, who lived in Landsberg and served as its mayor. **Neues Stadtmuseum** (www.museum-landsberg.de; Von-Helfenstein-Gasse 426;

adult/child €3/1.50; ◷2-5pm Tue-Fri, 11am-5pm Sat & Sun May-Jan, closed Feb-Apr) tells Landsberg's tale from prehistory to the 20th century.

The Drive ≫ The 28km drive along the B17 to Schongau should take 30 minutes. En route you pass through Hohenfurch, a pretty little town regarded as the gateway to the Pfaffenwinkel, a foothill region of the Alps.

- - - - - - - - - - - - - - - - - -

⑪ Schongau

One of the lesser-visited stops on the Romantic Road, attractive Schongau is known for its largely intact medieval defences. The Gothic **Ballenhaus** served as the town hall until 1902 and has a distinctive stepped gable; it now houses a cafe. Other attractions include the **Church of Maria Himmelfahrt**, with a choir by Dominikus Zimmermann.

The Drive » Take the B17 south until you reach Steingaden. From there country roads lead east and then south to Wies. This is where Bavaria starts to take on the look of the Alps, with flower-filled meadows in summer and views of the high peaks when the air is clear.

-----

⑫ Wieskirche

Located in the village of Wies, the **Wieskirche** (www.wieskirche.de; ⏰8am-8pm Apr-Oct, to 5pm Nov-Mar) is one of Bavaria's best-known baroque churches and a Unesco-listed site, the monumental work of legendary artist-brothers, Dominikus and Johann Baptist Zimmermann. In 1730, a Steingaden farmer claimed he'd witnessed his Christ statue shedding tears. Pilgrims poured into the town in such numbers that the local abbot commissioned a new church to house the

weepy work. Inside the almost-circular structure, eight snow-white pillars are topped by gold capitals and swirling decorations. The unsupported dome must have seemed like God's work in the mid-17th century, its surface adorned with a pastel ceiling fresco celebrating Christ's resurrection.

The Drive » Backtrack to Steingaden and rejoin the B17 to reach Füssen (32km). The entire

journey is through the Alps' increasingly undulating foothills, with gorgeous views of the ever-nearing peaks along the way.

-----

⑬ Füssen

Nestled at the foot of the Alps, tourist-busy Füssen is all about the nearby castles of Neuschwanstein and Hohenschwangau, but there are other reasons to linger. The town's **historical centre** is worth half a day's exploration and, from here, you can easily escape the crowds into a landscape of gentle **hiking trails** and Alpine vistas. Or take an hour or two in Füssen's very own castle, the **Hohes Schloss** (Magnusplatz 10; adult/child €6/free; ⏰galleries 11am-5pm Tue-Sun Apr-Oct, 1-4pm Fri-Sun Nov-Mar), today home to an art gallery.

✖ ⏚ p515

The Drive » To drive to King Ludwig II's castles, take the B17 across the river until you see signs for Hohenschwangau. Parking is at a premium in summer. However, as the castles

LANDSBERG'S DARK LITERARY CONNECTIONS

Landsberg am Lech can claim to be the town where one of the German language's best-selling books was written. Was it by Goethe, Remarque, Brecht? No, unfortunately, it was by Adolf Hitler. It was during his 264 days of incarceration in a Landsberg jail, following the 1923 beer-hall putsch, that Hitler penned his hate-filled *Mein Kampf*, a book that sold an estimated seven million copies when published. The jail later held Nazi war criminals and is still in use.

MUSEUM OF THE BAVARIAN KINGS

Palace-fatigued visitors often overlook the worthwhile **Museum der Bayerischen Könige** (Museum of the Bavarian Kings; www.museumderbayerischenkoenige.de; Alpseestrasse 27; adult/child €13/free; ⏰9am-5pm), installed in a former lakeside hotel 400m from the castle ticket office (towards Alpsee Lake). The big-window views across the beautiful lake (a great picnic spot) to the Alps are almost as amazing as the Wittelsbach bling on show, including Ludwig II's famous blue-and-gold robe. The architecturally stunning museum is packed with historical background on Bavaria's first family and is well worth the extra legwork. A detailed audioguide is included in the ticket.

TOP TIP: NEUSCHWANSTEIN & HOHENSCHWANGAU

The castles can only be visited on 35-minute guided tours. Buy timed tickets from the **Hohenschwangau Ticket Centre** (☎08362-930 830; www.hohenschwangau. de; Alpenseestrasse 12; ⊙8am-4pm Apr–mid-Oct, 9am-3pm mid-Oct–Mar) at the foot of the castles. In summer, arrive as early as 8am to ensure you get in that day.

are a mere 4km from Füssen's centre, it's probably not worth driving at all. RVO buses 78 and 73 (www.dbregiobus-bayern.de) run there from Füssen Bahnhof (at least hourly, tickets from the driver).

TRIP HIGHLIGHT

⑭ Neuschwanstein & Hohenschwangau Castles

The undisputed highlights of any trip to Bavaria, these two castles make a fitting climax to the Romantic Road.

Schloss Neuschwanstein (☎tickets 08362-930 830; www.neuschwanstein. de; Neuschwansteinstrasse 20; adult/child €13/free, incl Hohenschwangau, Linderhof & Herrenchiemsee €26/free; ⊙9am-6pm Apr–mid-Oct, 10am-4pm mid-Oct–Mar, ticket office opens 1hr before castle opening time) was the model for Disney's *Sleeping Beauty* castle. King Ludwig II planned this fairy-tale pile himself,

with the help of a stage designer rather than an architect. He envisioned it as a giant stage on which to recreate the world of Germanic mythology, inspired by the operatic works of his friend Richard Wagner.

It was at nearby **Schloss Hohenschwangau** (☎08362-930 830; www.hohenschwangau.de; Alpseestrasse 30; adult/child €18/free, incl Neuschwanstein, Linderhof & Herrenchiemsee €26/free; ⊙8am-5pm Apr–mid-Oct, 9am-3pm mid-Oct–Mar) that King Ludwig II grew up and later enjoyed summers until his death in 1886. His father, Maximilian II, built this palace in a neo-Gothic style atop 12th-century ruins. Less showy than Neuschwanstein, it has a distinctly lived-in feel, where every piece of furniture is a used original. It was at Hohenschwangau where Ludwig first met Wagner.

Schloss Neuschwanstein Castle in Bavaria

Eating & Sleeping

Würzburg ❶

✗ Bürgerspital
Weinstube · Franconian €€

(✆0931-352 880; www.buergerspital-weinstuben.de; Theaterstrasse 19; mains €13-38; ⏰10am-midnight; 📶) If you are going to eat out just once in Würzburg, the aromatic and cosy nooks of this labyrinthine medieval place probably provide the top local experience. Choose from a broad selection of Franconian wines (some of Germany's best) and wonderful regional dishes and snacks, including *Mostsuppe* (a tasty wine soup).

🛏 Hotel Rebstock · Hotel €€€

(✆0931-309 30; www.rebstock.com; Neubaustrasse 7; r €158-430; ❄️📶) Würzburg's top digs, in a squarely renovated rococo town house, has 126 unique, stylishly finished rooms with the gamut of amenities, impeccable service and an Altstadt location. Some rooms occupy a 2019 annex built on the site of a monastery garden and boast the city's most contemporary rooms. There's also a dramatic bistro and gourmet restaurant if you've got the cash.

Rothenburg ob der Tauber ❹

✗ Mittermeier · International €€€

(✆09861-945 40; www.villamittermeier.de; Vorm Würzburger Tor 7; 3-7-course menu €55-106; ⏰6-10pm Tue-Sat; 🅿️📶) Supporters of the Slow Food movement and deserved holders of a Michelin Bib Gourmand, this hotel restaurant pairs punctilious craftsmanship with top-notch ingredients, sourced regionally whenever possible. There are five different dining areas, including a black-and-white tiled 'temple', an alfresco terrace and a barrel-shaped wine cellar. The wine list is one of the best in Franconia.

✗ Zur Höll · Franconian €€

(✆09861-4229; www.hoell.rothenburg.de; Burggasse 8; mains €8-20; ⏰5-11pm Mon-Sat) This medieval wine tavern is in the town's oldest original buildings, with sections dating back to

the year 900. The menu of regional specialities is limited but refined, though it's the superb selection of Franconian wines that people really come for.

Dinkelsbühl ❺

✗ Haus Appelberg · Franconian €€

(✆09851-582 838; www.haus-appelberg.de; Nördlinger Strasse 40; dishes €8-18; ⏰6pm-midnight Mon-Sat; 📶) At this 40-cover wine restaurant, owners double as cooks to keep tables supplied with traditional dishes such as local fish, Franconian sausages and *Maultaschen* (pork-and-spinach ravioli). On warm days swap the rustic interior for the secluded terrace, a fine spot for some evening idling over a Franconian white.

🛏 Dinkelsbühler
Kunst-Stuben · Guesthouse €€

(✆09851-6750; www.kunst-stuben.de; Segringer Strasse 52; r €120-200; ♿@📶) Personal attention and charm by the bucketload make this guesthouse, situated near the westernmost gate (Segringer Tor), one of the best on the entire Romantic Road. Furniture (including the four-posters) is all handmade by Voglauer, the cosy library is perfect for curling up with a good read, and the suite is a matchless deal for travelling families. The artist owner will show his Asia travel films if enough guests are interested.

Nördlingen ❻

✗ Café Radlos · Cafe €€

(Löpsinger Strasse 8; mains €6-17; ⏰11.30am-2pm & 5pm-midnight Mon, Wed & Thu, 11.30am-midnight Fri, 10am-midnight Sat & Sun; 📶🅿️) More than just a place to tuck into tasty pizzas and pastas, this convivially random cafe, Nördlingen's coolest haunt, parades cherry-red walls that showcase local art and photography exhibits. Kids have their own toy-filled corner, while you relax with board games, soak up the sunshine in the beer garden or check your inbox.

Kaiserhof Hotel Sonne
Hotel €€

(📞09081-5067; www.kaiserhof-hotel-sonne.de; Marktplatz 3; s €55-75, d €80-120; P 📶) Right on the main square, Nördlingen's top digs once hosted crowned heads and their entourages, but it has elegantly gone to seed in recent decades. However, rooms are still packed with character, mixing modern comforts with traditional charm, and the atmospheric regional restaurant downstairs is still worth a shot.

Augsburg ⑨

August
International €€€

(📞0821-352 79; https://restaurantaugust.de; Johannes-Haag-Strasse 14; dinner €180-210; ⏰from 7pm Wed-Sat) Most Augsburgers have little inkling their city possesses two Michelin stars, both of which belong to chef Christian Grünwald. Treat yourself to some of Bavaria's most innovative cooking in the minimalist dining room, though with just 16 covers, reservations are essential.

Bauerntanz
German €€

(www.bauerntanz-augsburg.de; Bauerntanzgässchen 1; mains €8.50-19.50; ⏰11am-11.30pm) Belly-satisfying helpings of creative Swabian and Bavarian food – Spätzle (soft egg noodles) and more Spätzle – are plated up by friendly staff at this prim Alpine tavern with lace curtains, hefty timber interior and chequered fabrics. When the sun makes an appearance, everyone bails to the outdoor seating.

Dom Hotel
Hotel €€

(📞0821-343 930; www.domhotel-augsburg.de; Frauentorstrasse 8; s/d from €80/100; P 😊📶♿) Augsburg's top choice packs a 500-year-old former bishop's guesthouse (Martin Luther and Kaiser Maximilian I stayed here) with 57 rooms, all different but sharing a stylishly understated air and pristine upkeep; some have cathedral views. The big pluses here, however, are the large swimming pool and fitness centre.

Füssen ⑬

Zum Franziskaner
Bavarian €€

(📞08362-880 40 85; https://zum-franziskaner-fuessen.de; Kemptener Strasse 1; mains €6.50-20; ⏰11.30am-10pm; 📶) This traditional restaurant specialises in Schweinshaxe (pork knuckle) and schnitzel as well as other meaty Bavarian and Allgäu staples. There's some choice for non-carnivores such as Käsespätzle (rolled cheese noodles) and salads, and when the sun shines the outdoor seating shares the pavement with the 'foot-washing' statue.

Zum Hechten
Bavarian €€

(www.hotel-hechten.com; Ritterstrasse 6; mains €8-21; ⏰10am-10pm; 📶) Füssen's best hotel restaurant keeps things regional with a menu of Allgäu favourites like schnitzel and noodles, Bavarian pork-themed favourites, and local specialities such as venison goulash. Post-meal, relax in the wood-panelled dining room caressing a König Ludwig Dunkel, one of Germany's best dark beers brewed by the current head of the Wittelsbach family.

Hotel Sonne
Design Hotel €€

(📞08362-9080; www.hotel-fuessen.de; Prinzregentenplatz 1; s/d from €79/109; P 📶) Although traditional looking from outside, this Altstadt favourite offers an unexpected design-hotel experience within. Themed rooms feature everything from swooping bed canopies to big-print wallpaper, huge pieces of wall art to sumptuous fabrics. The public spaces are littered with pieces of art, period costumes and design features – the overall effect is impressive and unusual for this part of Germany.

German Fairy Tale Road

37

You might just live happily ever after! You'll certainly end this trip happy, having explored a beautiful swath of Germany and learned the real stories behind Grimms' fairy tales.

TRIP HIGHLIGHTS

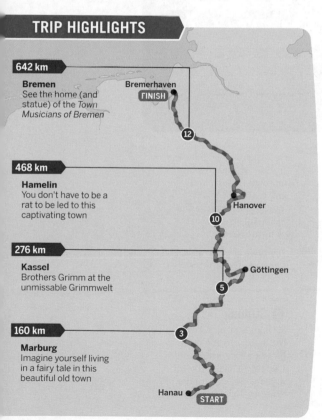

642 km

Bremen
See the home (and statue) of the *Town Musicians of Bremen*

468 km

Hamelin
You don't have to be a rat to be led to this captivating town

276 km

Kassel
Brothers Grimm at the unmissable Grimmwelt

160 km

Marburg
Imagine yourself living in a fairy tale in this beautiful old town

Bremerhaven
FINISH

Bremen

12

Hanover

10

Göttingen

5

3

Hanau
START

5 DAYS
707KM / 439 MILES

GREAT FOR...

BEST TIME TO GO

Enjoy this trip May to September when the weather is best for outdoor signtseeing.

ESSENTIAL PHOTO

Bremen's *Town Musicians of Bremen* sculpture.

BEST FOR FAMILIES

Grimmwelt, Kassel's popular attraction dedicated to all things Grimm and fairy-tale-worthy.

Marburg Altstadt (Old Town)

37 German Fairy Tale Road

Tirelessly roaming the villages and towns of 19th-century Germany, the Brothers Grimm collected over 200 folk tales that had been passed down for countless generations. The stories they published often bear little resemblance to the sanitised versions spoon-fed to kids today; rather, they are morality tales with blood, gore, sex, the supernatural, magic and much more. See the locations of the stories and learn about the remarkable brothers on this trip, which includes a few non-Grimm fairy-tale sights as well.

1 Hanau

A mere 20km east of Frankfurt on the Main River, Hanau is the birthplace of the Brothers Grimm (Jacob in 1785 and Wilhelm in 1786) and the perfect place to begin your trip. Strangely, their births are not overly com-memorated here...

Located within Philippsruhe Palace, dating from the early 18th century, the **Historisches Museum Schloss Philippsruhe** (✆06181-295 1799; www.museen-hanau.de; Philippsruher Allee 45; adult/ concession €4/3; ⊙11am-6pm Tue-Sun; P) has displays on town history, arts and crafts. The parks and gardens (free) are a beautiful stroll in snow or in summer.

The Drive » Hop on the A66 for a quick 50km run through the rolling hills to Steinau.

2 Steinau

Steinau is situated on the historic trade road between Frankfurt and Leipzig. (The town's full name is 'Steinau an der Strasse', an important

distinction when using your map app as there are several other Stein-aus in Germany.

The twin museums, **Brüder Grimm-Haus and Museum Steinau** (☎06663-7605; www.brueder -grimm-haus.de; Brüder Grimm-Strasse 80, Steinau; adult/concession €6/3.50; ⊙10am-5pm), inside the building where the Grimm family lived from 1791 to 1796, have exhib-its on the brothers, their work and the history of Steinau.

The Drive ≫ Head west on the L3196 for 18km to the B276, where you'll turn north. Weave through the valleys for 64km to the junction with the L3166 and follow the Marburg signs along the L3127, L3089, L3048 and L3125. Picnic spots abound along the route.

LINK YOUR TRIP

35 Romantic Rhine
Get your fill of castles and medieval villages: the end of the river trip is 65km east of Hanau.

36 The Romantic Road
Do one of the trips in reverse: the start of the quaint and historical Romantic Road is about an hour (110km) west from Hanau.

GERMANY 37 GERMAN FAIRY TALE ROAD

❸ Marburg

Hilly, historic and delightful, university-town Marburg is 90km north of Frankfurt. It's a delight to wander the narrow lanes of the town's vibrant **Altstadt** (Old Town), sandwiched between a palace (above) and a spectacular Gothic church (below). On the south side of the focal Marktplatz is the historic **Rathaus**, dating to 1512. At the base of the Altstadt's Reitgasse is the neo-Gothic **Alte Universität** (1891), still a well-used and well-loved part of Philipps-Universität – the world's oldest Protestant university. Founded in 1527, it once counted the Brothers Grimm among its students.

Perched at the highest point in town, a steep walk up from St-Marien-Kirche or the Marktplatz, is massive **Landgrafenschloss** (☎06421-2822 355; www.uni-marburg.de/uni-museum; Schloss 1; museum adult/concession €5/3; ☺museum 10am-6pm Apr-Oct, to 4pm Nov-Mar; ♿), built between 1248 and 1300. It offers panoramic views of bucolic hills, jumbled Marburg rooftops and the **Schlosspark**.

✕ 🛏 p528

The Drive » Head north on the B3; after 18km turn north on the L3073. Continue north for 37km through Gemunden and Frankenau to Edertal, where you'll find the park. Note how the forest gets thicker and darker as you go.

❹ Kellerwald-Edersee National Park

Nationalpark Kellerwald-Edersee (www.nationalpark-kellerwald-edersee.de) encompasses one of the largest extant red-beech forests in Central Europe, the **Kellerwald**, and the **Edersee**, a serpentine artificial reservoir 55km northeast of Marburg and about the same distance southwest of Kassel. A decade ago this national park, along with Hainich National Park in Thuringia and a cluster of other parks and reserves with large beech forests, became a Unesco World Cultural Heritage Site.

On a fairy-tale trip, it's fitting to wander into the deep woods, never forgetting that if your name is Grimm, nothing good is bound to happen. If you're lucky, you may see larger land animals like red deer; overhead, you might spot eagles and honey buzzards and, at night, various species of bat. (The brothers would surely approve.)

For information, head to the striking **visitors centre** (☎05635-992 781; www.nationalparkzentrum-kellerwald.de; Weg zur Wildnis 1, Vöhl-Herzhausen, off B252; exhibition entry €6.50/4; ☺10am-6pm Apr-Oct, to 4.30pm Tue-Sun Nov-Mar; ♿) at the western end of the Edersee.

The Drive » Drive east on the L3332, B485 and the B253 for 28km until you reach the A49 autobahn and zip along northeast until you reach Kassel.

❺ Kassel

Visitors to this culture-rich, sprawling hub on the Fulda River discover a pleasant, modern city.

Occupying a prime position atop the Weinberg bunker in the scenic **Weinbergpark** is the truly unmissable attraction on this trip, Kassel's **Grimmwelt** (☎0561-598 6190; www.grimmwelt.de; Weinbergstrasse 21; adult/concession €10/7; ☺10am-6pm Tue-Sun, to 8pm Fri; ♿). It could be described as an architect-designed walk-in sculpture housing the most significant collection of Brothers Grimm memorabilia on the planet. Visitors are guided around original exhibits, state-of-the-art installations and fun, hands-on activities, aided by entries from the Grimms' German dictionary: there was more to these brothers than just fairy tales, didn't you know?

Billed as 'a meditative space for funerary art',

DETOUR: FULDA

Start: ❷ Steinau

Although it's not quite on the Fairy Tale Road, photogenic Fulda is well worth a side trip for those interested in sumptuous baroque architecture, historic churches and religious reliquaries. A Benedictine monastery was founded here in 744, and today Fulda has its own bishop.

Inside the baroque **Dom zu Fulda** (☏0661-874 57; www.bistum-fulda.de; Domplatz 1; ☺10am-6pm Mon-Fri, to 3pm Sat, 1-6pm Sun Apr-Oct, to 5pm Mon-Fri Nov-Mar), built from 1704 to 1712, you'll find gilded furnishings, plenty of *putti* (cherubs), dramatic statues (eg to the left of the altar) and the tomb of St Boniface, who died a martyr in 754.

Fulda's history started in the **Michaelskirche** (St Michael's Church; Michaelsberg 1; ☺10am-6pm Apr-Oct, 10am-noon & 2-5pm Nov-Mar), one of Germany's oldest churches. A still-standing reminder of the abbey that made this town, this remarkable structure was the monastic burial chapel. Beneath classic witch's-hat towers, a Carolingian rotunda and crypt recall Fulda's flourishing Middle Ages, when the abbey scriptorium churned out top-flight illuminated manuscripts.

Don't miss Fulda's spectacular **Stadtschloss** (☏0661-102 1814; adult/concession €3.50/2.50; ☺10am-5pm Tue-Sun), built from 1706 to 1721 as the prince-abbots' residence. It now houses the city administration and function rooms. Visitors can enter the ornate **Historiche Räume** (Historic Rooms), including the grandiose banquet hall, and the octagonal **Schlossturm** (April to October) for great views of the town and magnificent **Schlossgarten** (palace gardens), where locals play *pétanque* (boules) and sunbathe.

The palace's fairy-tale qualities capture the era's extravagance. Don't miss the amazing **Speigelkabinett** (Chamber of Mirrors) and grandiose **Fürstensaal**, a banquet hall decorated with reliefs of tipsy-looking wine queens. There are also pretty views from the **Green Room** over the gardens to the Orangerie.

Fulda is 40km northeast of Steinau on the A66.

---

the **Museum für Sepulkralkultur**
(Museum for Sepulchral Culture; ☏0561-918 930; www.sepulkralmuseum.de; Weinbergstrasse 25-27; adult/concession €6/4; ☺10am-5pm Tue-Sun, to 8pm Wed) aims to bury the taboo of discussing death.

 p528

The Drive » The shortest leg of the trip takes you 6km west through Kassel's leafy suburbs. Take Wilhelmshöher Allee.

❻ Wilhelmshöhe

Wilhelmshöhe is the classy end of Kassel. You can spend a full day exploring the spectacular baroque parkland, **Bergpark Wilhelmshöhe** (☏0561-3168 0751; www.museum-kassel.de; Wilhelmshöher Allee 380, visitor centre; ☺9am-sunset, visitor centre 10am-5pm May-Sep, to 4pm Sat & Sun Oct-Apr; P ♿), which takes its name from **Schloss Wilhelmshöhe** (☏0561-316 800;

www.museum-kassel.de; Schlosspark 1; adult/concession €6/4, Weissenstein wing incl tour €4/3, audioguide €3; ☺10am-5pm Tue-Sun, to 8pm Wed; P), the late-18th-century palace inside its expanse. Amble through the forest, enjoy a romantic picnic and explore the castles, fountains, grottoes, statues and water features: the **Herkules** (☏visitor centre 0561-3168 0781; www.museum-kassel.de; Schlosspark Wilhelmshöhe 26, Herkules-Terrassen; adult/

WHY THIS IS A GREAT TRIP
RYAN VER BERKMOES, WRITER

Did they give us nightmares or fantasies? Or both? Who can forget hearing the wild stories of the Brothers Grimm as a child? Evil stepmothers, dashing princes, fair maidens, clever animals, mean old wolves and more. With every passing year, these stories become more sanitised. But the real fairy tales are far more compelling, as you'll learn on this trip.

Above: Kellerwald-Edersee National Park
Left: Weser Renaissance style houses, Hamelin
Right: Herrenhäuser Gärten, Hanover

concession €6/4; ⊙10am–5pm Tue-Sun mid-Mar–mid-Nov, daily May-Sep; [P] [♿]) statue and Löwenburg castle are also here.

The palace could star in any fairy tale. Home to Elector Wilhelm and later Kaiser Wilhelm II, the opulent complex today houses one of Germany's best collections of Flemish and Dutch baroque paintings in the **Gemäldegalerie** (painting gallery), featuring works by Rembrandt, Rubens, Jordaens, Lucas Cranach the Elder, Dürer and many others.

✕ 🛏 p528

The Drive » Retrace your 6km drive on Wilhelmshöher Allee back into Kassel and take the busy A7 up to Göttingen.

- - - - - - - - - - - - - - - -

❼ Göttingen

With over 30,000 students, this historic town nestled in a corner of Lower Saxony near the Hesse border offers a good taste of university-town life in Germany's north. Incredibly, since 1734, the Georg-August Universität has sent more than 40 Nobel Prize winners into the world. As well as all those award-winning doctors and scientists, it also produced the fairy-tale-writing Brothers Grimm (as German language teachers).

Stroll around the pleasant **Markt** and

GRIMM FAIRY TALES

In the early 19th century, the Grimm brothers travelled extensively through central Germany documenting folklore. Their collection of tales, *Kinder- und Hausmärchen,* was first published in 1812 and quickly gained international recognition. One thing you'll note about the 209 tales is that the original Grimm versions are much bloodier, more violent and earthier than today's ultra-sanitised, Disneyfied versions. It includes such fairy-tale staples as:

Hansel and Gretel A mother tries to ditch her son and daughter, a witch tries to eat them and Gretel outsmarts her. Kids and father reunited and all are happy (the evil mother had died).

Cinderella The story that gave step-sisters a bad name. Still, when the prince fits the shoe onto our heroine, all is good with the world, although in the Grimm version, the step-sisters are blinded by vengeful doves.

Rapunzel An adopted girl with very long hair, a prince who goes blind and some evil older women are combined in this morality play that ends with love when the prince stumbles upon an outcast Rapunzel and his sight is restored. In the first edition of the Grimms' book, Rapunzel had children out of wedlock.

Although best known for their fairy tales, it should be be noted that the Brothers Grimm were serious academics who also wrote *German Grammar* and *History of the German Language,* enduring works that populate reference shelves to this day.

nearby Barfüsserstrasse to admire the *Fachwerk* (half-timbered) houses. If you fancy, pop into a pub and make some new friends.

The city's symbol, the **Gänseliesel** (Markt), little goose girl, statue on the Marktplatz is hailed locally as the most kissed woman in the world – not a flattering moniker, you might think, but enough to make her iconic.

 p529

The Drive » Take the L561 22km west to the B80, then head northwest for another 27km to Bad Karlshafen. Enjoy the curving panoramas as you follow the Weser River, which links several of the Fairy Tale Road towns and cities.

⑧ Bad Karlshafen

Bad Karlshafen's orderly streets and whitewashed baroque buildings were built in the 18th century for local earl Karl by French Huguenot refugees. The town was planned with an impressive harbour and a canal connecting the Weser and the Rhine to attract trade, but the earl died before his designs were completed. The only reminder of his grand plans is the tiny **Hafenbecken** (harbour basin) populated by a gaggle of swans.

Take a stroll around the town centre, on the sinuous Weser's south bank, with the Hafenbecken and surrounding square, **Hafenplatz**, at its western end.

The interesting **Deutsches Huguenotten Museum** (German Huguenot Museum; 05672-1410; www.huguenot-museum-germany.com; Hafenplatz 9a; adult/concession €4/2; 10am-5pm Tue-Fri, 11am-6pm Sat & Sun mid-Mar–Oct, 10am-noon Mon-Fri Nov–mid-Mar) traces the history of the French Huguenot refugees in Germany.

The Drive » Stay on the B83 for the 58km to Bodenwerder. You'll enjoy Weser vistas for much of the journey – which might lure you to stop for a picnic.

⑨ Bodenwerder

If Bodenwerder's most famous son were to

have described his little hometown, he'd probably have painted it as a huge, thriving metropolis on the Weser. But then Baron Hieronymous von Münchhausen (1720–97) was one of history's most shameless liars (his whoppers were no mere fairy tales). He inspired the Terry Gilliam cult film, *The Adventures of Baron Munchausen* (1988).

Bodenwerder's principal attraction, the **Münchhausen Museum** (☎05533-409 147; www.muenchhausenland.de; Münchhausenplatz 5; adult/child €3/2; ⊙10am-5pm mid-May–Oct, by appointment Nov-Mar; P), tackles the difficult task of conveying the chaos and fun associated with the 'liar baron' – a man who liked to regale dinner guests with his Crimean adventures, claiming he had, for example, tied his horse to a church steeple during a snow drift and ridden around a dining table without breaking one teacup. It holds paintings and displays of Münchhausen books in many languages.

The Drive 》 The B83 again takes you north 23km to Hamelin, following the River Weser most of the way.

TRIP HIGHLIGHT

⑩ Hamelin

According to the Brothers Grimm's *Pied Piper of Hamelin,* in the 13th century *Der Rattenfänger* (Pied Piper) was employed by Hamelin's townsfolk to lure its rodents into the river. When they refused to pay him, he picked up his flute and led their kids away. Today the rats rule once again – fluffy and cute stuffed rats, wooden rats and tiny brass rats adorning the sights around town.

Rodents aside, Hamelin (Hameln in German) is a pleasant town with half-timbered houses and opportunities for cycling along the Weser, on whose eastern bank lies Hamelin's circular **Altstadt**. The town's heart is its **Markt**.

Many of Hamelin's finest buildings were constructed in the Weser Renaissance style, which has strong Italian influences. Learn more at the town's **Museum Hameln** (☎05151-202 1217; www.museum-hameln.de; Osterstrasse 8-9; adult/

concession €5/4; ⊙11am-6pm Tue-Sun; ✦).

 p529

The Drive 》 Drive 47km northwest on the B217.

⑪ Hanover

Known today for its huge trade shows, Hanover has an interesting a past: from 1714, monarchs from the house of Hanover also ruled Great Britain and the British Empire for over a century.

Let your hair down at the spectacularly baroque **Herrenhäuser Gärten** (☎0511-1683 4000; www.herrenhaeuser-gaerten.de; Herrenhäuser Strasse 4; ⊙9am-8pm May-Aug, shorter hours rest of the year, grotto to 7.30pm May-Aug, shorter hours rest of the year; U4, 5 to Herrenhäuser Gärten), the grandiose Royal Gardens of Herrenhausen, which are considered one of the most important historic garden landscapes in Europe. Inspired by Versailles' gardens, they're

THE FAIRY TALE ROAD

The 600km **Märchenstrasse** (Fairy Tale Road; www.deutsche-maerchenstrasse.com/en) is one of Germany's most-popular tourist routes, with over 60 stops along the way. It's made up of cities, towns and hamlets in four states (Hesse, Lower Saxony, North Rhine-Westphalia and Bremen), which can often be reached via a choice of roads rather than one single route. The towns are associated in one way or another with the works of Wilhelm and Jacob Grimm. While most towns can be easily visited using public transport, a car lets you fully explore the route.

a great place to slow down and smell the roses for a couple of hours, especially on a blue-sky day. With its fountains, neat flowerbeds, trimmed hedges and shaped lawns, the 300-year-old **Grosser Garten** (Great Garden) is the centrepiece of the experience.

The Drive » Take the A352 16km to the A7, then shoot northwest on that road and the A27 until you reach Bremen (127km).

TRIP HIGHLIGHT

⑫ Bremen

Bremen is well known for its fairy-tale character, a unique expressionist quarter and (it must be said, because Bremeners are avid football fans) one of Germany's most-exciting, if not overly successful, football teams.

With high, historic buildings rising up from this very compact square, Bremen's **Markt** is one of the most remarkable in northern Germany. The two towers of the 1200-year-old **Dom St Petri** (St Petri Cathedral; ☏0421-334 7142; www.stpetridom.de; Sandstrasse 10-12; tower adult/child €2/1, museum free; ⏱10am-5pm Mon-Fri, to 2pm Sat, 2-5pm Sun Oct-May, to 6pm Mon-Fri & Sun Jun-Sep) dominate the northeastern edge, beside the ornate and imposing **Rathaus** (Marktplatz), which was erected

in 1410. The Weser Renaissance balcony in the middle, crowned by three gables, was added between 1595 and 1618.

In front of the Rathaus is one of the hallmarks of Bremen, the city's 13m-high **Knight Roland statue** (1404). As elsewhere, Roland stands for a city's civic freedoms, especially the freedom to trade independently.

On the western side of the Rathaus you'll find the city's unmissable and famous symbol of the Grimm fairy tale: the **Town Musicians of Bremen** (1951) by the sculptor Gerhard Marcks. The story tells of a donkey, a dog, a cat and a rooster who know their time is up with their cruel masters, and so set out for Bremen and the good life. On the way they encounter a forest cottage filled with robbers. They cleverly dispatch the crooks and, yes, live happily ever after. The statue depicts the dog, cat and rooster, one on top of the other, on the shoulders of the donkey. The donkey's nose and front legs are incredibly shiny, having been touched by many visitors for good luck.

✕ 🛏 p529

The Drive » A quick shot up the A27 autobahn for 65km will bring you to Bremerhaven and the North Sea.

⑬ Bremerhaven

Anyone who has had the fairy-tale dream of running away to sea will love Bremerhaven's waterfront – part trade machinery, part glistening glass buildings pointing to a more recent understanding of the harbour as a leisure spot.

Bremerhaven has long been a conduit that gathered the 'huddled masses' from the verdant but poor countryside and poured them into the world outside. Of the millions who landed in America, a large proportion sailed from here; an enticing exhibition at the **Deutsches Auswandererhaus** (German Emigration Centre; ☏0471-902 200; www.dah-bremerhaven.de; Columbusstrasse 65; adult/child €15.80/9; ⏱10am-6pm Mar-Oct, to 5pm Nov-Feb), the city's prime attraction, allows you to share their history. The museum stands exactly in the spot where 7.2 million emigrants set sail between 1830 and 1974. Your visit begins at the wharf where passengers gathered before boarding a steamer. You then visit passenger cabins from different periods (note the improving comfort levels) before going through the immigration process at New York's Ellis Island.

Bremen Schnoor district

Eating & Sleeping

Marburg ❸

✖ Bückingsgarten   German €€

(📞06421-165 7771; www.bueckingsgarten
-marburg.de; Landgraf-Philipp-Strasse 6; mains
€7.50-24; ⏱ noon-10pm) Choose from two
separate menus at this venerable restaurant,
opened by G Dietrich Bücking in 1807 and now
offering German standards alongside lesser-
spotted international classics such as lentil
curry. Dine inside for the upscale experience,
or enjoy a sausage and pint in the beer garden:
both offer dramatic views from a hilltop position
next to the castle.

✖ Zur Sonne   German €€

(📞06421-171 90; www.zur-sonne-marburg.de;
Markt 14; mains €12.50-21.50; ⏱8am-2pm &
6-10pm; 🍴) In the heart of the Markt you'll find
'To the Sun', a delightful restaurant that feels
as though it's been serving meals to scholars
and students since the days of Martin Luther.
Sit in the handsome timbered dining rooms,
or al fresco in the square, to enjoy traditional
German fare and good fish dishes (a speciality,
as nets hanging from the rafters proclaim).

🛏 Vila Vita Rosenpark   Hotel €€

(📞06421-600 50; www.rosenpark.com;
Anneliese Pohl Allee 7-17; s/d from €120/130;
🅿❄@🛜🏊) Marburg's swankiest sleep
occupies a lovely spot on the Lahn River, a
short stroll from the station. If you're going to
splurge, superior double rooms and suites offer
better value at almost twice the size of singles.
There's an expansive wellness centre and two
restaurants on-site.

🛏 Welcome Hotel Marburg   Hotel €€

(📞06421-9180; www.welcome-hotels.com;
Pilgrimstein 29; s/d from €120/150; ❄@🛜)
Just below the Altstadt, this central hotel has
151 bright, spacious rooms with large windows,
desks and armchairs. Though windows are
soundproofed, you may want to ask for a quieter
room at the rear of the building.

Kassel ❺

✖ Lohmann   German €

(📞0561-701 6875; www.lohmann-kassel.de;
Königstor 8; mains €10-24; ⏱11.30am-2.30pm
Sun-Fri, 4.30-10pm daily) With roots that go back
to 1888, this popular, family-run *Kneipe* (pub)
has an old-style birch-and-maple-shaded beer
garden with an outdoor grill, while indoors is all
beery chatter and the happy tinkling of knives
and forks. Schnitzel (always pork) features
heavily on the menu.

🛏 Pentahotel Kassel   Boutique Hotel €€

(📞0561-933 9100; www.pentahotels.com;
Bertha-von-Suttner Strasse 15; r from €90;
🅿❄🛜) Spread over six floors, this welcoming
hotel has 137 compact, stylish rooms with
ambient lighting, arty design elements and free
high-speed wi-fi. There's a bar and restaurant
on-site, and you're nice and close to the
wonders of Bergpark Wilhelmshöhe.

Wilhelmshöhe ❻

✖ Matterhorn Stübli   Swiss €€

(📞0561-399 33; www.matterhornstuebli.de;
Wilhelmshöher Allee 326; mains €16-26; ⏱5.30-
11pm Tue-Sat, noon-2pm & 5.30-10pm Sun;
🍴) If you love cheese, fondue, schnitzel, or all
three, hotfoot it to this quaint Swiss restaurant.
If you like mushrooms as well, try the 'Original
Züri Geschnätzläts': veal escalopes served with
mushrooms and crispy rösti.

🛏 Kurpark Hotel
Bad Wilhelmshöhe   Hotel €€

(📞0561-318 90; www.kurparkhotel-kassel.de;
Wilhelmshöher Allee 336; s/d from €115/135;
🅿❄🛜🏊) In an excellent location near the
Unesco-listed Bergpark Wilhelmshöhe and
Kassel-Wilhelmshöhe train station, this stylish
hotel offers soothing rooms and common areas,
a restaurant, a cafe and an indoor pool, sauna
and spa.

Göttingen ❼

✕ Zum Szultenburger German €€

(📞0551-431 33; Prinzenstrasse 7; mains
€11-15; 🕑11am-3pm & 5-10pm Mon-Sat) This
traditional German pub does things to the
humble schnitzel that will make your mouth
water, while the *Rindergulasch mit Spätzle* (beef
goulash with hand-dropped noodles) is just the
ticket in cold weather. It's cosy and cheap and
the hearty food is delicious – no wonder it's
often described as the best place to eat in town.
Cash only.

Hamelin ❿

🛏 Komfort-Hotel
Garni Christinenhof Boutique Hotel €€€

(📞05151-950 80; https://christinenhof.de; Alte
Marktstrasse 18; s/d incl breakfast €93/130;
🅿🛜🏊) Olde-worlde on the outside, modern
within, this super-welcoming hotel boasts a tiny
swimming pool in the vaulted cellar, a sauna,
and compact (but pleasant and uncluttered)
rooms. The owners take particular care with
the generous buffet breakfast (almost entirely
homemade) and parking is free of charge.
Spread over two buildings, this is a great central
option.

🛏 Schlosshotel
Münchhausen Luxury Hotel €€€

(📞05154-706 00; www.schlosshotel-
muenchhausen.com; Schwöbber 9, Aerzen; s/d
tithe barn from €150/180, castle from €210/240,
apt €180; 🅿❄🛜) Palatial Schlosshotel
Münchhausen, 12km southwest of Hamelin,
occupies a baronial castle built in 1570. Stylish,
contemporary rooms in the main wing have
historic touches, the suites have tasteful period
furnishings and rooms in the tithe barn are
entirely modern. Two restaurants, lavish spa
facilities and two golf courses set in 8 hectares
of gorgeous parkland round off the luxury.

Bremen ⓬

✕ Engel Weincafe Cafe €

(📞0421-6964 2390; www.engelweincafe
-bremen.de; Ostertorsteinweg 31; dishes
€8.80-14.50; 🕑10am-11pm; 🛜📷; 🚊2, 6 to
Wulwesstrasse) On a sunny corner in Das Viertel,
this popular hang-out exudes the nostalgic vibe
of the old-fashioned pharmacy it once was. The
menu features breakfast, a hot lunch special,
crispy *Flammkuchen* (Alsatian pizza, with crème
fraîche), carpaccio, or just some cheese and a
glass of wine from the international list.

✕ Kleiner Olymp Seafood €€

(📞0421-326 667; www.kleiner-olymp.de;
Hinter der Holzpforte 20; mains €9.50-23.50;
🕑11am-11pm; 🛜) This homely kitchen in
Schnoor has a wonderful atmosphere, delicious
(and not too heavy) North German cuisine and
very reasonable prices. With a selection of
mouth-watering soups and starters, fish and
seafood feature predominantly on the menu:
bouillabaisse, North Sea crabs and plaice
cooked in a variety of ways.

🛏 Hotel Residence Boutique Hotel €€

(📞0421-348 710; www.hotelresidence.
de; Hohenlohestrasse 42; s/d from €75/95;
🅿@🛜) This century-old terrace, now
a charming hotel, also boasts some funky
apartments. The main building has rooms
facing the street, while the newer extension
backs onto the railway line but is still reasonably
quiet. Friendly staff and a sauna, bar and
dining room complete the package. Rooms and
apartments are furnished in differing styles.
Buffet breakfast is €10.

🛏 Dorint Park Hotel Bremen Hotel €€€

(📞0421-340 80; http://hotel-bremen.dorint.
com; Im Bürgerpark 1; s/d from €80/160;
🅿@🛜🏊; 🚊6 to Am Stern) Although its
exterior is certainly dated, this domed lakeside
mansion surrounded by parkland impresses
through its sheer extravagance and could be
considered Bremen's only true five-star, grand
hotel. It offers access to excellent spa, fitness
and beauty facilities, a heated outdoor pool and
views over the lake in a 'spa resort' ambience.

NEED ᵀᴼ KNOW

CURRENCY
Euro (€)

LANGUAGE
German

VISAS
Generally not required for stays of up to 90 days; some nationalities need a Schengen visa.

FUEL
Petrol stations are common on main roads and highways, and in larger towns. Unleaded costs around €1.30 per litre and diesel is €1.05.

RENTAL CARS
Auto Europe (www. autoeurope.com)

Avis (www.avis.com)

Europcar (www.europcar. com)

Hertz (www.hertz.com)

IMPORTANT NUMBERS
Europe-wide emergency covering police, fire and ambulance (📞 112)

Climate

Warm to hot summers, mild winters
Warm to hot summers, cold winters
Mild summers, cold winters
Cold climate

Hamburg
GO May–Sep

Berlin
GO May, Jun, Sep & Oct

Frankfurt
GO May–Sep

Munich
GO Apr, May, Sep & Oct

Freiburg
GO Jun–Sep & Dec

When to Go

High Season (Jul & Aug)
» Busy roads and long queues at key sights.

» Vacancies at a premium and higher prices in seaside and mountain resorts.

» Festivals celebrate everything from music to wine and sailing to samba.

Shoulder Season (Apr–Jun, Sep–Oct)
» Expect smaller crowds and lower prices, except on public holidays.

» Blooming, colourful flowers in spring and radiant foliage in autumn.

» Sunny, temperate weather ideal for outdoor pursuits and exploration.

Low Season (Nov–Mar)
» No queues but shorter hours at key sights, some of which may close for the season.

» Theatre, concert and opera season in full swing.

» Ski resorts busiest in January and February.

Daily Costs

Budget: Less than €120

» Hostel, camping or private room: €15–30

» Low-cost meal or self-catering: up to €8

» Day ticket on public transport: €5–7

Midrange: €120–200

» Private apartment or double room: €80–130

» Three-course dinner at a good restaurant: €30–40

» Couple of beers in a pub or beer garden: €9

Top end: More than €200

» Fancy loft apartment or double in top-end hotel: from €150

» Sit-down lunch or dinner at top-rated restaurant: €100

» Concert or opera tickets: €50–150

Eating

Cafes Coffee, drinks, snacks.

Bistros Light meals to full-blown dinners.

Restaurants Simple eateries to Michelin-starred temples.

Vegetarian Few wholly vegetarian places, limited choices on most menus.

Price categories indicate the cost of a main meal:

€	less than €15
€€	€15–30
€€€	more than €30

Sleeping

Hotels From budget to luxury; breakfast included unless indicated.

Pensiones Rates always include breakfast.

Hostels In cities and large towns; private or HI-affiliated.

Price categories indicate the cost of a double room with private bathroom in high season:

€	less than €80
€€	€80 160
€€€	more than €160

Arriving in Germany

Frankfurt Airport

S-Bahn €5; commuter rail lines S8 and S9 from Flughafen Regionalbahnhof to Frankfurt Hauptbahnhof, 4.30am to 12.30am (15 minutes).

Taxis €25–35; 20 minutes to the centre.

Mobile Phones

Most European and Australian phones function; turn off roaming to avoid data charges. If you are from outside the EU, buy a local SIM for cheaper rates.

Internet Access

Wi-fi (usually free) is available to guests in most hotels, B&Bs and hostels. Also offered by many cafes, bars, train stations and other public spaces.

Money

ATMs widely available in cities and towns, rarely in villages. While credit cards are increasingly accepted, Germany is still largely a cash-based society.

Tipping

Restaurant and bar prices include a service charge but locals still tip.

Useful Websites

Lonely Planet (lonelyplanet. com/germany) Travel tips, accommodation, recommendations and more.

Germany: The Travel Destination (www.germany. travel) German tourist board.

ADAC (www.adac.de) Driving info for Germany and neighbouring countries.

Opening Hours

Banks 9am–4pm Monday to Friday

Bars 6pm–1am

Cafes 8am–8pm

Clubs 11pm to early morning

Post offices 9am–6pm Monday to Friday, 9am–1pm Saturday

Restaurants 11am–11pm (food service often stops at 9pm in rural areas)

Major shops and supermarkets 9.30am–8pm Monday to Saturday (shorter hours outside city centres)

Language

German is easy for English speakers to pronounce because almost all of its sounds are also found in English. If you read our coloured pronunciation guides as if they were English, you'll have no problems being understood. Note that kh is like the 'ch' in 'Bach' or the Scottish 'loch' (pronounced at the back of the throat), r is also pronounced at the back of the throat (almost like a g, but with some friction), zh is pronounced as the 's' in 'measure', and ü as the 'ee' in 'see' but with rounded lips. The stressed syllables are indicated with italics.

GERMAN BASICS

Hello.	*Guten Tag.*	*goo·*ten tahk
Goodbye.	*Auf Wiedersehen.*	owf *vee·*der·zay·en
Yes./No.	*Ja./Nein.*	yah/nain
Please.	*Bitte.*	*bi·*te
Thank you.	*Danke.*	*dang·*ke
You're welcome.	*Bitte.*	*bi·*te
Excuse me.	*Entschuldigung.*	ent·*shul·*di·gung
Sorry.	*Entschuldigung.*	ent·*shul·*di·gung

Do you speak English?

Sprechen Sie Englisch? (pol)	*shpre·*khen zee *eng·*lish
Sprichst du Englisch? (inf)	shprikhst doo *eng·*lish

I don't understand.

Ich verstehe nicht.	ikh fer·*shtay·*e nikht

DIRECTIONS

Where's ...?

Wo ist ...?	vaw ist ...

How far is it?

Wie weit ist es?	vee vait ist es

Can you show me (on the map)?

Können Sie es mir (auf der Karte) zeigen?	*ker·*nen zee es meer (owf dair *kar·*te) *tsai·*gen

How can I get there?

Wie kann ich da hinkommen?	vee kan ikh dah *hin·*ko·men

Turn ...	*Biegen Sie ... ab.*	*bee·*gen zee ... ab
at the corner	*an der Ecke*	an dair *e·*ke
at the traffic lights	*bei der Ampel*	bai dair *am·*pel
left	*links*	lingks
right	*rechts*	rekhts

ACCOMMODATION

Do you have a ... room?	*Haben Sie ein ...?*	*hah·*ben zee ain ...
double	*Doppelzimmer*	*do·*pel·tsi·mer
single	*Einzelzimmer*	*ain·*tsel·tsi·mer
How much is it per ...?	*Wie viel kostet es pro ...?*	vee feel *kos·*tet es praw ...
night	*Nacht*	nakht
person	*Person*	per·*zawn*

Is breakfast included?

Ist das Frühstück inklusive?	ist das *frü·*shtük in·kloo·*zee·*ve

ON THE ROAD

I'd like to hire a ...	*Ich möchte ein ... mieten.*	ikh *merkh·*te ain ... *mee·*ten
4WD	*Allradfahrzeug*	*al·*raht·fahr·tsoyk
car	*Auto*	*ow·*to
motorbike	*Motorrad*	*maw·*tor·raht

Want More?

For in-depth language information and handy phrases, check out Lonely Planet's *German Phrasebook*. You'll find it at **shop.lonelyplanet.com**.

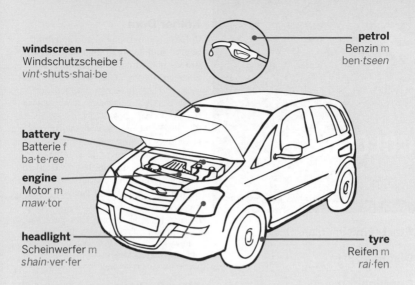

windscreen
Windschutzscheibe f
vint·shuts·shai·be

petrol
Benzin m
ben·*tseen*

battery
Batterie f
ba·te·*ree*

engine
Motor m
maw·tor

headlight
Scheinwerfer m
shain·ver·fer

tyre
Reifen m
rai·fen

How much is it per ...?
Wie viel kostet es pro ...?
vee feel *kos*·tet es praw ...

  day — Tag — tahk

  week — Woche — vo·khe

Does this road go to ...?
Führt diese Straße nach ...?
fürt *dee*·ze *shtrah*·se nahkh ...

(How long) Can I park here?
(Wie lange) Kann ich hier parken?
(vee *lang*·e) kan ikh heer *par*·ken

Where's a petrol station?
Wo ist eine Tankstelle?
vaw ist *ai*·ne *tangk*·shte·le

I need a mechanic.
Ich brauche einen Mechaniker.
ikh *brow*·khe *ai*·nen me·*khah*·ni·ker

My car/motorbike has broken down (at ...).
Ich habe (in ...) eine Panne mit meinem Auto/Motorrad.
ikh *hah*·be (in ...) *ai*·ne *pa*·ne mit *mai*·nem *ow*·to/*maw*·tor·raht

I've run out of petrol.
Ich habe kein Benzin mehr.
ikh *hah*·be kain ben·*tseen* mair

I have a flat tyre.
Ich habe eine Reifenpanne.
ikh *hah*·be *ai*·ne *rai*·fen·pa·ne

- -
EMERGENCIES

Help!
Hilfe!
hil·fe

I'm lost.
Ich habe mich verirrt.
ikh *hah*·be mikh fer·*irt*

Call the police!
Rufen Sie die Polizei!
roo·fen zee dee po·li·*tsai*

Signs
- - - - - - - - - - - - - - - - - - -

Einfahrt	Entrance
Ausfahrt	Exit
Einfahrt Verboten	No entry
Einbahnstraße	One way
Parkverbot	No parking
Mautstelle	Toll

STRETCH YOUR LEGS
COLOGNE

Start/Finish: Kölner Dom

Distance: 2km

Duration: 3 hours

Cologne's history is everywhere, as you'll see on this walk, which circles through the heart of the bustling city. You can view Roman or medieval ruins, and you'll always be near somewhere to pause for refreshments.

Take this walk on Trip

Kölner Dom

Cologne's geographical and spiritual heart – and its single-biggest tourist draw – is the magnificent **Kölner Dom** (Cologne Cathedral; ☎0221-9258 4720; www. koelner-dom.de; Domkloster 4; tower adult/ concession €5/2; ⏱6am-8pm, tower 9am-6pm May-Sep, to 5pm Mar, Apr & Oct, to 4pm Nov-Feb; ⛟5, 16, 18 Dom/Hauptbahnhof), with its soaring twin spires, art and treasures. Climb its south tower (533 steps) to the base of the steeple that dwarfed all European buildings until Gustave Eiffel built a certain tower in Paris.

The Walk » There are numerous large parking facilities around the Dom and the neighbouring Hauptbahnhof (follow the signs). After Kölner Dom, walk south across the Roncalliplatz to Am Hof, turn east past some good beer halls, then go south again on Bechergasse to Rathausplatz.

Altes Rathaus

Dating to the 15th century and much restored, the **old city hall** (Rathausplatz; ⏱8am-4pm Mon, Wed & Thu, to 6pm Tue, to noon Fri; ⛟5 Rathaus) has fine bells that ring daily at noon and 5pm. The Gothic tower is festooned with statues of old city notables.

The Walk » Head to the west side of the Rathaus.

Archäologische Zone

Cologne used the construction of the U-Bahn line to also build this grand **archaeological museum** (http://miqua.lvr. de; ⛟5 Rathaus) under the Rathausplatz. At the deepest level is the Praetorium, with relics of a Roman governor's palace. One level up are relics from the Middle Ages Jewish community.

The Walk » Cross the Marsplatz on the south side of the square to the museum.

Wallraf-Richartz-Museum

A famous collection of European paintings from the 13th to the 19th centuries, the **Wallraf-Richartz-Museum** (☎0221-2212 1119; www.wallraf.museum; Obenmarspforten; adult/concession €8/4.50; ⏱10am-6pm Tue-Sun; ⛟1, 7, 9 Heumarkt, ⛟5 Rathaus) occupies a postmodern cube designed by OM Ungers. Works are shown

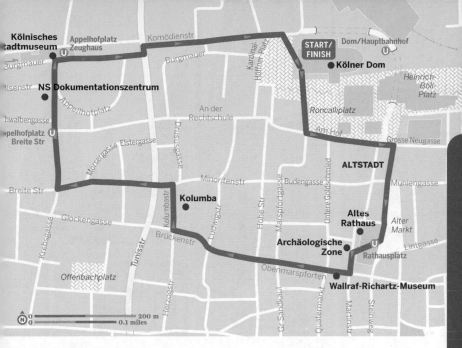

chronologically, with the oldest on the 1st floor. Standouts include brilliant examples from the Cologne School, known for its distinctive use of colour.

The Walk » Go west past oodles of shops on Obenmarspforten for four streets, then turn north on Kolumbastrasse.

Kolumba

Art, history, architecture and spirituality form a harmonious tapestry in this spectacular collection of religious treasures of Cologne's archdiocese. Called **Kolumba** (📞0221-933 1930; www.kolumba.de; Kolumbastrasse 4; adult/child €8/free; ⊘noon-5pm Wed-Mon; 🚊5 Rathaus), the building encases the ruins of the late-Gothic church of St Kolumba and layers of foundations dating to Roman times.

The Walk » Walk west on commercial Breite Strasse, then turn north on Dumont-Strasse.

NS Dokumentationszentrum

Cologne's Third Reich history is poignantly documented in the **NS Documentation Centre** (NS-DOK; 📞0221-2212 6331; www.museenkoeln.de/ns-dokumentationszen

trum; Appellhofplatz 23-25; adult/concession €4.50/2; ⊘10am-6pm Tue-Fri, 11am-6pm Sat & Sun; 🚊3, 4, 5, 16, 18 Appellhofplatz). In the basement of this otherwise mundane-looking building was the local Gestapo prison where scores of people were interrogated, tortured and killed.

The Walk » It's just a short jaunt north again along low-key Dumont-Strasse.

Kölnisches Stadtmuseum

The **Kölnisches Stadtmuseum** (Cologne City Museum; 📞0221-2212 2398; www.koelnisches-stadtmuseum.de; Zeughausstrasse 1-3; adult/concession €5/3; ⊘10am-8pm Tue, to 5pm Wed-Sun; 🚊3, 4, 5, 16, 18 Appellhofplatz), in the former medieval armoury, explores all facets of Cologne history. There are exhibits on Carnival, Kölsch (the local beer), eau de cologne and other things that make the city unique. An amazing model recreates the city of 1571; it's huge yet minutely detailed.

The Walk » Return to the Dom along Komödienstrasse, with the cathedral towers looming ever closer. Stop off for a much-deserved refreshment at Café Reichard, facing the Dom.

Switzerland

A place of heart-stopping natural beauty and head-spinning efficiency, Switzerland lies in the centre of Europe yet exhibits a unique blend of cultures. Dazzling outdoor scenery such as the ever-admired Alps, pristine lakes, lush meadows and chocolate-box chalets combines with local traditions, cosmopolitan cities and smooth infrastructure. In short, Switzerland makes it easy for you to dive deep into its heart: distances are manageable and variety is within easy reach. You can be perusing a farmers market for picnic provisions in the morning, then feasting on them on a mountaintop come lunchtime. At nightfall, try gazing at stars in the night sky from cosy digs, or revelling in the cultural offerings of one of Switzerland's urbane cities.

Geneva Cathédrale St-Pierre

Switzerland

38 **The Swiss Alps 7 Days**
The greatest of the great outdoors:
perfect peaks, gorgeous glaciers,
verdant valleys.

39 **Geneva to Zürich 7 Days**
Mountains, pastures, lakes and
small-town charm, book-ended by
Switzerland's biggest cities.

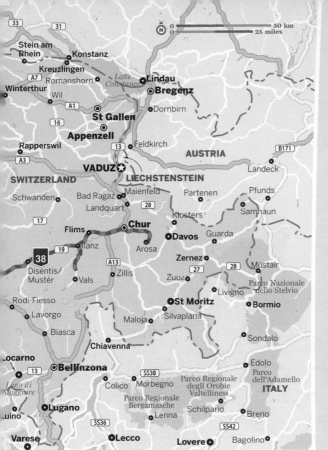

The Matterhorn

Symbol of Switzerland, this magical mountain demands to be photographed. See it for yourself on Trip **38**

Züri-West

Switzerland dispenses with its staid reputation in this hip neighbourhood in Zürich, full of great bars, clubs, cafes and restaurants. Explore it on Trip **39**

Interlaken

Wedged between alpine Thun and Brienz lakes and overlooked by the Eiger, Mönch and Jungfrau, Interlaken has one of the most enviable locations in Europe. See it all on Trip **39**

The Swiss Alps

38

From Arosa to Zermatt, this zig-zagging trip is the A to Z of Switzerland's astounding Alpine scenery, with gobsmacking panoramas, thrilling cable-car rides and local charm.

TRIP HIGHLIGHTS

612 km

Zermatt
Switzerland's Alpine heart beats strongest here

77 km

Vals
A modern architectural jewel, 7132 Therme embellishes this remote spa town

Grindelwald

Andermatt

Schilthorn (2970m)

Arosa
START

2

11

12
FINISH

Aletsch Glacier
A mesmerising marvel, viewed from on high

538 km

---

7 DAYS
537KM / 333 MILES

GREAT FOR...

BEST TIME TO GO

This trip can be done year-round, although certain mountain passes may be closed to vehicles in winter.

 ESSENTIAL PHOTO

The Matterhorn

 BEST FOR OUTDOORS

Whatever the season, the Alps offer activities galore.

38 The Swiss Alps

A natural barrier, the Alps are both a blessing and a burden when it comes to tripping around Switzerland. The soul-stirring views are stupendous, but you have to either get over or around the Alps, or go through them, to get to the next one. Starting in Graubünden's Arosa and finishing in Valais' Zermatt, this trip visits five cantons via hairpin bends, valley highways, tunnels, passes and cable cars to bring you the best.

❶ Arosa

Framed by the peaks of **Weisshorn**, **Hörnli** and moraine-streaked **Schiesshorn**, Arosa is a great Alpine all-rounder: perfect for downhill and cross-country skiing in winter, hiking and downhill biking in summer, and heaps of family activities year-round. Although only 30km southeast of Chur (Switzerland's oldest city), getting here involves 180-degree hairpin bends so challenging that Arosa cannot be reached

by postal buses. Once here, you may want to revel in the beauty of the Mario Botta–designed **Tschuggen Bergoase Spa** (Sonnenbergstrasse; www.ts chuggen.ch; Tschuggen Grand Hotel; nonguest morning/ evening pass Sfr65; ⊙8.30am-9pm), an architectural statement built at the foot of the mountains. The structure's recurring leaf-shaped motifs look particularly striking when illuminated at night.

✗ p551

The Drive » The trip from Arosa to Vals is 79km and takes 1¾ hours. Head back towards Chur, then take Rte 19 to Ilanz for the delightful road that passes through Uors and St Martin before arriving at Vals (1252m). About 2km short of the village, you emerge into Alpine pastures, liberally scattered with chalets and shepherds' huts.

TRIP HIGHLIGHT

❷ Vals

Shadowing the course of the babbling Glogn

(Glenner) stream south, the luxuriantly green Valsertal (Vals Valley) is full of sleepy hamlets and thundering waterfalls. Vals stretches 2km along its glittering stream. The secret of this chocolate-box village and its soothing waters is out since Basel-born architect Peter Zumthor transformed **7132 Therme** (☏081 920 70 70; https://7132therme. com; adult/child Sfr80/52; ⊙11am-8pm), formerly Therme Vals, into a temple of cutting-edge cool. Using 60,000 slabs of local quartzite, Zumthor created one of the country's most enchanting thermal spas. Aside from heated indoor and outdoor pools, this greystone labyrinth hides watery nooks and crannies, cleverly lit and full of cavernous atmosphere. Drift away in the bath-warm Feuerbad (42°C) and perfumed Blütenbad, sweat it out in the steam room, and cool down in the teeth-chattering Eisbad.

LINK YOUR TRIP

39 **Geneva to Zürich**
Arosa is a two-hour drive southeast (147km) on the A3 from Zürich, the end point of this bucolic ramble between Switzerland's biggest cities.

2 **The Graceful Italian Lakes**
A scenic two-hour drive (143km) across the Simplon Pass into Italy gets you to Stresa in the glorious Lake Maggiore region.

p551

The Drive ❯❯ Return to Ilanz, then continue on Rte 19 to Disentis/Mustér (50km, 55 minutes).

---

❸ Disentis/Mustér

Disentis/Mustér's Benedictine monastery, **Kloster Disentis** (www.kloster-disentis.ch; Via Claustra 1; museum adult/child Sfr10/5; ☺ museum 10am-5pm Mon-Sat, from 2pm Sun), rising like a vision above town, has a lavishly stuccoed baroque church attached. A monastery has stood here since the 8th century, but the present immense complex dates from the 18th century. Enter the **Klostermuseum**, crammed with memorabilia, left of the church entrance. Head left upstairs to the **Marienkirche**, a chapel with Romanesque origins now filled with ex-votos from people seeking (or giving thanks for) a miraculous intervention from the Virgin Mary. If you're peckish, a handy (and very good-value) on-site cafe-takeaway has soups, salads and specialities.

The Drive ❯❯ Disentis is an exhilarating (40 minutes, 32km) drive along Rte 19 and the twisting Oberalp Pass (2044m), which connects Graubünden and Uri cantons. In winter, the pass is closed to cars, but a car train connects Sedrun on Rte 19 and Andermatt (three daily services in winter, two in spring). See www.matterhorngotthardbahn.ch for reservations.

---

❹ Andermatt

Blessed with austere mountain appeal, Andermatt (Uri Canton) contrasts low-key village charm (despite a recent five-star development) with big wilderness. Once an important staging-post on the north–south St Gotthard route, it's now bypassed by the tunnel. It remains a major crossroads near four major passes (Susten, Oberalp, St Gotthard and Furka), making it a terrific base for **hiking** and **cycling**. The tourist office supplies free booklets.

One popular hike leads from the Oberalp Pass to sparkly **Lai da Tuma**, the source of the Rhine; the 11km round trip takes three to four hours, with 500m elevation gain. A walk around and along **Gotthardstrasse** reveals textbook dark-wood central-Swiss architecture, often weighed down with either geraniums or snow.

Skiers in the know flock to 2963m **Gemsstock** for the snow-sure winter slopes.

 p551

The Drive ❯❯ Take Rte 2 to Göschenen, then get on the A2/E35 and follow the signs for Lucerne. The road skirts the bottom of Lake Uri for lovely water views. Continue to exit 33 (Stans-Süd), then follow Rte 374 to Engelberg (one hour, 77km in total).

---

❺ Engelberg

Wonderful Engelberg (literally 'Angel Mountain') is divine, backed by the glacial bulk of **Mt Titlis** (www.titlis.ch), central Switzerland's tallest mountain, and frosted peaks, which feature in many a Bollywood production. After visiting the 12th-century Benedictine **Engelberg Monastery** (Kloster Engelberg; 🕿041 639 61 19; www.

🔘 LOCAL KNOWLEDGE: ZUMDORF

If the grand scale of this trip seems overwhelming, the antidote surely lies in a quick detour to Switzerland's smallest village, **Zumdorf**: little more than a cluster of small buildings on the Furkastrasse with a population counted on one hand. Despite its diminutive size, it has **Restaurant Zum Dörfli** (🕿041 887 01 32; www.zumdoerfli.ch; Furkastrasse; mains Sfr25-42), specialising in Swiss dishes (especially rösti) and venison (in season). You'll find it 6km southwest of Andermatt.

Andermatt Snow-covered village

kloster-engelberg.ch; church admission free, tours adult/child Sfr8/free; ☺1hr tour 4pm Tue, Thu & Sat), get closer to the heavens via the world's first revolving **cable car** (www.titlis.ch/en/tickets/cable-car-ride, adult/child return Sfr77/38.50; ☺8.30am-5pm). It pirouettes over the dazzling **Titlis Glacier**, peaks rising like huge spiky teeth ahead, before you step out onto Titlis station's **terrace** (3020m), with a panorama that stretches to Eiger, Mönch and Jungfrau in the Bernese Oberland. For even more thrilling views, take the adjacent **Cliff Walk** (www.titlis.ch/en/glacier/cliff-walk). Opened in 2012, this 100m-long, 1m-wide, cable-supported swinging walkway is Europe's highest suspension bridge.

There are some 360km of marked hiking trails in and around Engelberg. For gentle ambles and gorgeous scenery, head for **Brunni** across the valley. Its **cable car** (www.brunni.ch; cable car one way/return Sfr20/32, incl chairlift Sfr29/44) goes up to Ristis at 1600m, where a chairlift takes you to the Swiss Alpine Club's refurbished **Brunni Hütte** (☎041 637 37 32; www.brunnihuette.ch; dm adult/child Sfr26/14, incl breakfast & dinner Sfr65/41). From here, you can choose to watch a magnificent sunset before spending the night.

🛏 p551

The Drive >> Retrace your route to the A2, heading west, before turning onto the A8 (direction Interlaken), and continuing alongside bright-blue Brienzersee to Giessbachfälle. The journey is one hour and 10 minutes, or 71km.

- - - - - - - - - - - - - - - - - -

❻ Giessbachfälle

Illuminating the firs like a spotlight in the dark, the misty **Giessbachfälle** (Giessbach Falls; funicular one way/return Sfr5/10) plummet 500m over 14 rocky ridges. Europe's oldest **funicular** (one way/return Sfr6/9), dating to 1879, creaks up from the boat station, but it's only a 15-minute walk up to the most striking section of the falls.

The Drive >> Get back onto the A8 and follow it along the Brienzersee until exit 25 (Wilderswil/Grindelwald), then continue as the road winds its way through rural countryside up to Grindelwald (39km, 45 minutes).

- - - - - - - - - - - - - - - - - -

❼ Grindelwald

Grindelwald's sublime natural assets are film-set stuff – the chiselled features of **Eiger's** north face, the glinting tongues of **Oberer** and **Unterer Glaciers** and the crown-like peak of **Wetterhorn**.

WHY THIS IS A GREAT TRIP
SALLY O'BRIEN, WRITER

Even though I now call Switzerland home, the Alpine scenery still has an other-worldly effect on me. The abundance of snow-capped peaks, mountains with fairy-tale names that 'pop up' at numerous vantage points, time-defying glaciers, gravity-defying railways. And then there's the moment you catch sight of the Matterhorn...

Above: Aletsch Glacier
Left: Cable car, Grindelwald
Right: Zermatt

Skiers and hikers cottoned on to its charms in the late 19th century, making it one of Switzerland's oldest resorts. It has lost none of its appeal, with geranium-studded chalets and verdant pastures aplenty.

Turbulent waters carve a path through craggy **Gletscherschlucht** (Glacier Gorge; www. grindelwaldsports.ch; adult/ child Sfr19/10; ⏰9.30am-6pm Sat-Thu, to 10pm Fri), a 30-minute walk south of the centre. A footpath weaves through tunnels hacked into cliffs veined with pink and green marble. It's justifiably a popular spot for canyon and bungee-jumping expeditions.

Grindelwald is outstanding **hiking** territory, veined with trails that command arresting views to massive north faces, crevasse-filled glaciers and snow-capped peaks. Reach high-altitude walks by taking cable cars from the village.

🛏 p551

The Drive » Follow the signs to Lauterbrunnen, which is 20km (15 minutes) away by car.

----

8 Lauterbrunnen

Laid-back Lauterbrun-nen's wispy **Staubbachfall** (Staubbach Falls) inspired both Goethe and Byron to pen poems to their ethereal beauty. Today the postcard-perfect village, nestled in the valley of

AROUND GRINDELWALD: FIRST

From Grindelwald, a cable car zooms up to **First**, the trailhead for 100km of paths, half of which stay open in winter. You can trudge up to **Faulhorn** (2681m; 2½ hours), even in winter, via the cobalt **Bachalpsee** (Lake Bachalp). As you march along the ridge, the unfolding views of the Jungfrau massif are entrancing. Stop for lunch and 360-degree views at Faulhorn. You might like to continue to Schynige Platte (another three hours) and return by train.

Other great walks head to **Schwarzhorn** (three hours), **Grosse Scheidegg** (1½ hours), **Unterer Gletscher** (1½ hours) and **Grindelwald** itself (2½ hours).

First has 60km of well-groomed pistes, which are mostly wide, meandering red runs suited to intermediates. The south-facing slopes make for interesting skiing through meadows and forests. Freestylers should check out the kickers and rails at **Bärgelegg** or have a go on the superpipe at **Schreckfeld station**.

Faulhorn happens to be the starting point for **Europe's longest toboggan run**, accessible only on foot. Bring a sled to bump and glide 15km over icy pastures and through glittering woodlands all the way to Grindelwald via Bussalp. Nicknamed 'Big Pintenfritz', the track lasts around 1½ hours, depending how fast you slide.

Year-round, you can get your pulse racing on the **First Flyer**, a staggeringly fast zip-line from First to Schreckfeld. The mountains are but a blur as, secure in your harness, you pick up speeds of around 84km/h.

The **First Cliff Walk** is a summit trail with a 40m-long suspension bridge, climbing stairs and an observation deck, with suitably impressive views of the local landscape and the jaw-dropping mountains.

72 waterfalls – including the **Trümmelbachfälle** (Trümmelbach Falls; www.truemmelbachfaelle.ch; adult/child Sfr11/4; ☺9am-5pm Apr-Jun & Sep-Oct, 8.30am-6pm Jul & Aug) – attracts a less highfalutin crowd. Hikes heading into the mountains from the waterfall-laced valley include a 2½-hour uphill trudge to car-free **Mürren** and a more gentle 1¾-hour walk to **Stechelberg**. In winter, glide past frozen waterfalls on a well-prepared 12km cross-country trail.

The Drive » Head to Stechelberg (10 minutes, 6km), where you'll leave the car (paid parking available) and take the cable car to Schilturn (adult/child Stechelberg–Schilthorn return Sfr108/54).

- - - - - - - - - - - - - - - - - - - -

❾ Schilthorn

There's a tremendous 360-degree, 200-peak panorama from the 2970m **Schilthorn**, best appreciated from the **Skyline viewing platform** or the revolving restaurant **Piz Gloria** (☎033 826 00 07; www.schilthorn.ch; Höheweg 2; mains Sfr22.50-46; ☺8am-5pm). On a clear day, you can see from Titlis around to Mont Blanc, and across to the Black Forest in Germany.

Some visitors seem more preoccupied with practising their delivery of the line, 'The name's Bond, James Bond', because scenes from *On Her Majesty's Secret Service* were shot here in 1968–69. The **Bond World 007** interactive exhibition gives you the chance to pose for photos secret-agent style, and relive movie moments in a helicopter and bob sled.

The Drive » After you descend to Stechelberg, head to Kandersteg via the road down to Interlaken. Get on the A8/Rte 11, then take exit 19 (direction Spiez/Kandersteg/Adelboden). The 60km trip takes one hour.

- - - - - - - - - - - - - - - - - - - -

❿ Kandersteg

Turn up in Kandersteg in anything but muddy boots and you'll attract a few odd looks. Hiking is the town's raison d'être, with 550km of surrounding trails. An amphitheatre of spiky peaks studded with glaciers and jewel-coloured lakes – such as **Blausee** (www.blausee.ch) and **Oeschinensee** (www.oeschinensee.ch; cable-car one way/return Sfr22/30; ☺9am-5pm; ♿) – creates a sublime natural backdrop to the rustic village of dark-timber chalets.

In winter there are more than 50km of cross-country ski trails, including the iced-over Oeschinensee. The limited 15km of downhill skiing suits beginners while Kandersteg's frozen waterfalls attract ice climbers.

🛏 p551

The Drive 》 Take the BLS Lötschberg Tunnel, which

connects with Goppenstein (in Valais) at regular intervals daily; it takes 15 minutes. From Goppenstein, head east from Rte 9. Once past Brig, the deep valley narrows and the landscape switches to rugged wilderness, with a string of bucolic villages of timber chalets and onion-domed churches (47km).

- - - - - - - - - - - - - - - - - -

TRIP HIGHLIGHT

⓫ Aletsch Glacier

The **Aletsch Glacier** is a seemingly never-ending, 23km-long swirl of ice with deep crevasses that slices past thundering falls, jagged spires of rock and pine forest. It stretches from Jungfrau in the Bernese Oberland to a plateau above the Rhône and is, justly so, a Unesco World Heritage Site.

Picture-postcard riverside **Fiesch** on the valley floor is the best place to access it. From the village, ride the **cable car** (www.eggishorn.ch; Furkastrasse; adult/child return from Fiesch Sfr45/22.50) up to **Fiescheralp** and continue up to **Eggishorn** (2927m). Streaming down in a broad curve around the **Aletschhorn** (4195m), the glacier is just like a frozen six-lane superhighway. In the distance to the north rise the glistening summits of Jungfrau (4158m), Mönch (4107m), Eiger (3970m) and Finsteraarhorn (4274m). To the southwest of the cable-car exit, you can spy Mont Blanc and the Matterhorn.

🛏 p551

The Drive 》 It takes one hour (56km) to get to Täsch from Fiesch; first via Rte 19 to Visp and then the winding rural road to Täsch itself. Park the car here before boarding the train to car-free Zermatt.

LOCAL KNOWLEDGE: VALAIS WINE

The canton of Valais, which features so much of Switzerland's stunning Alpine scenery, is also the country's largest and best wine producer. Sampling it in situ at the end of a day's driving is a great idea.

Drenched in extra sunshine and light from above the southern Alps, much of the land north of the Rhône river in western Valais is planted with vines. Unique to the Valais are the *bisses* (narrow irrigation channels) that traverse the vineyards.

Dryish white Fendant, the perfect accompaniment to fondue and raclette, and best served crisp cold, is the region's best-known wine, accounting for two-thirds of Valais wine production. Dôle, made from Pinot noir and Gamay grapes, is the principal red blend and is full bodied, with a firm fruit flavour.

When ordering wine in a wine bar or restaurant, use the uniquely Swiss approach of *deci* (decilitre – ie a 10th of a litre) multiples. Or just order a bottle...

THE HIGH LIFE

Charming as Zermatt is, heading out of town and up to the mountains is a rush like no other. Europe's highest cogwheel railway, the **Gornergratbahn** (www.gornergrat.ch; Bahnhofplatz 7; return Sfr80-118), has climbed picture-postcard scenery to Gornergrat (3089m) – a 30-minute journey – since 1898. Sit on the right-hand side to gawp at the Matterhorn. Tickets allow you to get on and off en route; there are restaurants at **Riffelalp** (2211m) and **Riffelberg** (2582m). In summer an extra train runs once a week at sunrise and sunset – the most spectacular trips of all.

Views from Zermatt's cable cars are all remarkable, but the **Matterhorn Glacier Paradise** (www.matterhornparadise.ch; Schluhmattstrasse; return adult/child Sfr104/52; ⏱8.30am-4.50pm) is the icing on the cake. Ride Europe's highest-altitude cable car to 3883m and marvel at 14 glaciers and 38 mountain peaks over 4000m from the Panoramic Platform (only open in good weather). Don't miss the **Glacier Palace**, an ice palace complete with glittering ice sculptures and an ice slide to swoosh down bum first. End with exhilarating snow tubing outside in the snowy surrounds.

TRIP HIGHLIGHT

⑫ Zermatt

You can almost sense the anticipation on the train from Täsch. As you arrive in car-free Zermatt, the pop-up-book effect of the one-of-a-kind Matterhorn (4478m) works its magic. Like a shark's fin it rises above the town, with moods that swing from pretty and pink to dark and mysterious. Since the mid-19th century, Zermatt has starred among Switzerland's glitziest resorts. Today skiers cruise along well-kept pistes, spellbound by the scenery, while the style-conscious flash designer garb in the town's swish lounge bars.

Amble along the main-strip **Bahnhofstrasse** with its boutiques and stream of horse-drawn sleds or carriages and electric taxis, then head towards the noisy Vispa river along **Hinterdorf-strasse**. This old-world street is crammed with archetypal Valaisian timber granaries propped up on stone discs and stilts to keep out pesky rats. Look for the fountain commemorating Ulrich Inderbinen (1900–2004), a Zermatt-born mountaineer who climbed the Matterhorn 370 times, the last time at age 90.

A walk in Zermatt's **Mountaineers' Cemetery** (Kirchstrasse), in the garden of St Mauritius Church, is sobering. Numerous gravestones tell of untimely deaths on Monte Rosa, the Matterhorn and Breithorn. In July 2015 a **memorial** to 'the unknown climber'

was unveiled to mark the 150th anniversary of the Matterhorn's first ascent.

The **Matterhorn Museum** (📞027 967 41 00; www.zermatt.ch/museum; Kirchplatz; adult/child Sfr10/5; ⏱11am-6pm Jul-Sep, 3-6pm Oct–mid-Dec, 3-7pm mid-Dec–Mar, 2-6pm Apr-Jun) provides a fascinating insight into Valaisian village life, the dawn of tourism in Zermatt and the lives the Matterhorn has claimed. Short films portray the first successful ascent of the Matterhorn on 14 July 1865, led by Edward Whymper, a feat marred by tragedy on the descent when four team members crashed to their deaths in a 1200m fall down the North Wall. The infamous rope that broke is on display.

✕ p551

Eating & Sleeping

Arosa ❶

✖ Burestübli   Swiss $$

(☎081 377 18 38; www.burestuebli.com; Hotel Arlenwald, Prätschlistrasse; mains Sfr12-47; ⊙8am-midnight; 🛜) This chalet on the forest edge provides magical above-the-treetop views. Come winter, it's beloved by sledders who huddle around first-rate local produce.

Vals ❷

🛏 7132 Hotel   Design Hotel $$$

(☎058 7132 000; http://7132.com; Vals; d from Sfr650; P 🛜) At this 1960s colossus, renamed 7132 Hotel after Vals' postcode, rooms have been revamped under the design skills of world-famous architects Peter Zumthor from Switzerland, Andō Tadao and Kuma Kengo from Japan, and American Thom Mayne. The hotel also features three restaurants and a bar.

Andermatt ❹

🛏 River House Boutique Hotel   Design Hotel $$

(☎041 887 00 25; www.theriverhouse.ch; Gotthardstrasse 58; s/d from Sfr135/180; P 🛜) At this stylish eco-hotel in a 250-year-old building, the Swiss-American owners have used local materials to create unique and beautiful rooms with inlaid parquet floors and beams, some with river views. The on-site restaurant features local, eco-friendly produce, plus Swiss wines.

Engelberg ❺

🛏 Ski Lodge Engelberg   Hotel $

(☎041 637 35 00; www.skilodgeengelberg.com; Erlenweg 36; d from Sfr130; P 🛜) Run by hip Swedish skiers, this delightful, centrally located lodge fuses art nouveau flair with 21st-century comforts in smart rooms (including family rooms). Après-ski activities include steaming in a sauna, gazing at snowy peaks from an outdoor hot tub and dining on the excellent New Nordic cuisine.

Grindelwald ❼

🛏 Gletschergarten   Historic Hotel $$

(☎033 853 17 21; www.hotel-gletschergarten. ch; Obere Gletscherstrasse 1; s Sfr130-170, d Sfr240-330; P 🛜) The sweet Breitenstein family makes you feel at home in their rustic timber chalet, brimming with heirlooms. Decked out in pine and flowery fabrics, the rooms have balconies facing Unterer Gletscher at the front and Wetterhorn (best for sunset) at the back.

Kandersteg ❿

🛏 The Hayloft   B&B $

(☎033 675 03 50; www.thehayloft.ch; Altes Bütschels Hus; s/d/tr Sfr65/120/180; P) Picture a dark-wood, 500-year-old chalet snuggled against the hillside, flower-strewn meadows where cows graze placidly, views of waterfalls and glaciers. Guests at this former farm are welcomed like family and served delicious breakfasts and dinners.

Aletsch Glacier ⓫

🛏 Fiesch Youth Hostel   Hostel $

(☎027 970 1515; Sport Ferien Resort, Fiesch; dm with shared bathroom per person from Sfr35, d with private bathroom Sfr100; P 🛜) This complex plays host to lots of activities (and school groups). It's very well run, has spotless rooms and is an ideal spot to drop your bags for the night after a trip to Eggishorn and Aletsch Glacier.

Zermatt ⓬

✖ Chez Vrony   Swiss $$

(☎027 967 25 52; www.chezvrony.ch; Findeln; mains Sfr25-45; ⊙9.15am-5pm Dec-Apr & mid-Jun–mid-Oct; 🛜) Ride the *Sunnegga Express* funicular to 2288m, then ski down or summer-hike 15 minutes to Zermatt's tastiest slope-side address in the Findeln hamlet. Delicious dried meats, homemade cheese and sausage come from Vrony's own cows, grazing away the summer on the high Alpine pastures (2100m) surrounding it.

Geneva to Zürich

39

Connect the dots between Switzerland's two biggest cities as you drive through its enigmatic heartland, historic cities, spine-tingling ascents and a world-famous mountain trio.

TRIP HIGHLIGHTS

0 km

Geneva
Cosmopolitan city and old town grace galore

481 km

Zürich
Culturally vibrant city with a post-industrial edge

FINISH
9

Bern

Lucerne
8

Fribourg

1
START

Stanserhorn
An open-air cable car; the perfect Lake Lucerne panorama

402 km

7 DAYS
470KM / 292 MILES

GREAT FOR...

BEST TIME TO GO
Late spring, summer and autumn, when the light and weather are best.

 ESSENTIAL PHOTO

The verdant Emmental region exemplifies pastoral perfection.

✔ BEST FOR CULTURE

Zürich's mighty museums and relentless nightlife are intoxicating.

39 Geneva to Zürich

Rather than take a straight line from Geneva to Zürich, this trip gives you room to roam some of Switzerland's finest sights: small cities with charming Old Towns, heaven-sent lakes with dreamy views, winding roads through countryside bucolic and wild, an adventure capital with the perfect setting, a train ride to the top of Europe, and scenic ascents that will have you gasping – all book-ended by Switzerland's cultural capitals.

TRIP HIGHLIGHT

❶ Geneva

Cosmopolitan Geneva is a rare blend: a multicultural population chattering in every language under the sun, a distinctly French feel, one of the world's most expensive cities, a stronghold of the Protestant Reformation and a haven for dodgy bank accounts and humanitarian organisations.

With a whole day and night, schedule time for Geneva's magnificent **Old Town** (Old Town). For waterside attractions, head for the emblematic **Jet d'Eau** (Quai Gustave-Ador) and the egalitarian **Bains des Pâquis** (☎022 732 29 74; www.bains-des-paquis.ch; Quai du Mont-Blanc 30; pools adult/child Sfr2/1, sauna, hammam & Turkish baths Sfr20; ◷9am-8pm).

Plenty of museums will tempt you: among the best are the **Musée d'Art Moderne et Contemporain** (Museum of Modern & Contemporary Art, MAMCO; ☎022 320 61 22; www.mamco.ch; Rue des Vieux-Grenadiers 10; adult/child Sfr15/free; ◷noon-6pm Tue-Fri, 11am-6pm Sat & Sun; 🚇Musée d'Art Moderne), the **Musée International de la Croix-Rouge et du Croissant-Rouge** (International Red Cross & Red Crescent Museum; ☎022 748 95 11; www.redcrossmuseum.ch; Av de la Paix 17; adult/child Sfr15/free; ◷10am-6pm Tue-Sun

Apr-Oct, to 5pm Nov-Mar), and the lavish timepieces of **Patek Philippe Museum** (☎022 707 30 10; www.patekmuseum.com; Rue des Vieux-Grenadiers 7; adult/child Sfr10/free; ◷2-6pm Tue-Fri, 10am-6pm Sat). For a behind-the-scenes glimpse of the UN prebook a tour of the **Palais des Nations** (Palace of Nations; ☎022 917

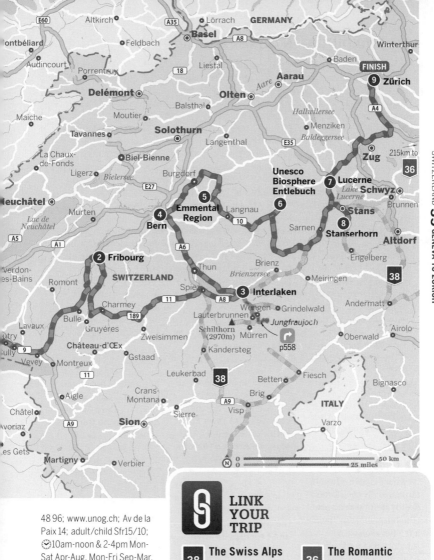

48 96; www.unog.ch; Av de la
Paix 14; adult/child Sfr15/10;
⊙10am-noon & 2-4pm Mon-
Sat Apr-Aug, Mon-Fri Sep-Mar,
guided tours 10.30am, noon,
2.30pm & 4pm).

✕ p561

The Drive » Head west via
the A1 until the A9 (follow signs
to Vevey/Montreux). Take exit
11 and follow signs for Lutry.
From Lutry, take Rte 9 (direction

LINK YOUR TRIP

38 The Swiss Alps
It's a two-hour
(147km) drive southeast
from Zürich to Arosa,
the starting point of the
Swiss Alps whirl.

36 The Romantic Road
From Zürich, drive east
via the A1 to Füssen in
Germany, and do the
gorgeous Romantic Road
trip in reverse.

ISLAND DINING IN GENEVA

Genevan living is easy in summer: a constant crowd throngs the lakefront quays to hang out in pop-up terrace bars such as **La Terrasse** (☏079 685 96 21; www.laterrasse. ch; Quai du Mont-Blanc 31; ☺8am-midnight Apr-Sep), the fashionista spot by the water to see and be seen. Meander away from Quai du Mont-Blanc to uncover a beloved trio of summertime shacks on the water's edge – al fresco and effortlessly cool.

The right-bank address is refreshingly casual: Rhône-side **Terrasse Le Paradis** (☏076 715 83 70; www.terrasse-paradis.ch; Quai Turrettini; ☺9am-11pm) is the type of cafe that practically begs you to pull out a book and stay all day in deckchairs arranged down steps to the water, while sipping beakers of homemade *citronnade* (lemonade). 'Paradise' does not serve alcohol, but green-mint tea flows and the wholly affordable sandwiches, salads and legendary tabbouleh hit the spot.

Le Bateau Lavoir (☏022 321 38 78; www.bateaulavoir.ch; Passerelle des Lavandières; ☺11am-midnight Mon-Thu, to 1am Fri, 5pm-1am Sat May-Sep) is an eye-catching boat with rooftop terrace moored between the old market hall and Pont de la Coulouvrenière. Its cabin-size dining area cooks fondue and basic local dishes, the crowd is hip and there is a 360-degree lake view. Its design and name evoke the wash-house boats – yes, where undies etc were washed – that floated here in the 17th century.

Then there's **La Barje** (☏022 344 83 56; www.labarje.ch; Promenade des Lavandières; ☺11am-midnight Mon-Fri, from 3pm Sat, from noon Sun Apr-Sep), not a barge at all but a vintage caravan with tin roof and candy-striped facade, parked on the grassy banks of the Rhône near the Bâtiment des Forces Motrices. The beer and music are plentiful, outside concerts and art performances pull huge crowds, and proceeds go towards helping young people in difficulty.

Vevey) until Cully, then head up Rte de la Corniche to Chexbres. Next follow Rte du Genevrex and get on the A9, followed by the A12 to Fribourg (143km total).

- - - - - - - - - - - - - - - - -

❷ Fribourg

Nowhere is Switzerland's language divide felt more keenly than in Fribourg (Freiburg, or 'Free Town'), a medieval city where inhabitants on the west bank of the river Sarine speak French, and those on the east bank (of the Sanne) speak German. Sights that merit a look-see include the bohemian **Espace Jean Tinguely – Niki de Saint Phalle** (☏026 305 51 40; www.mahf.

ch; Rue de Morat 2; adult/child Sfr7/free; ☺11am-6pm Wed & Fri-Sun, to 8pm Thu), the evocative **Old Town** filled with Gothic facades, the **Musée d'Art et d'Histoire** (Museum of Art & History; ☏026 305 51 40; www.mahf. ch; Rue de Morat 12; adult/child Sfr10/8; ☺11am-6pm Tue, Wed & Fri-Sun, to 8pm Thu). and the outsize **Cathédrale de St Nicolas de Myre** (St Nicolas Cathedral; ☏026 347 10 40; www.cathedrale -fribourg.ch; Rue des Chanoines 3; tower adult/child Sfr3.50/1; ☺7.30am-7pm Mon-Sat, 9am-9.30pm Sun, tower 10am-5pm Mon-Sat, 1-5pm Sun Apr-Oct) with its 74m-tall tower. Make time for a couple

of the city's bohemian cafe-bars, such as Le Port (p561) or **Café Culturel de l'Ancienne Gare** (CCAG; ☏026 322 57 72; www. cafeanciennegare.ch; Esplanade de l'Ancienne-Gare 3; ☺9am-11.30pm Mon-Wed, to midnight Thu & Fri, 1pm-midnight Sat, 9am-3pm Sun).

✖ ⊫ p561

The Drive » We've chosen a longish (103km, one hour and 50 minutes) scenic route along winding roads through lovely small towns and unspoiled countryside in Fribourg and Bern cantons. Head to the village of Charmey via Rte 189, then to Boltingen. Take Rte 11 to Speiz on Lake Thun, then follow Rte 8 to Interlaken.

❸ Interlaken

Once Interlaken made the Victorians swoon with mountain vistas from the chandelier-lit confines of grand hotels; today it makes daredevils scream with adrenaline-loaded adventures. Straddling the glittering Lakes Thun and Brienz and dazzled by the pearly whites of Eiger, Mönch and Jungfrau, the scenery is mind-blowing. Check out views from **Harder Kulm** (www.jungfrau.ch/harderkulm; adult/child Sfr34/17), or try daredevil activities with **Outdoor Interlaken** (☎033 826 77 19; www.outdoor-interlaken.ch; Hauptstrasse 15) – organised in advance. Leave the car in Interlaken after overnighting and head to the Top of Europe (Jungfraujoch) very early next morning.

🛏 p561

The Drive » From Interlaken it's a one-hour (54km) drive via Lake Thun's Seestrasse, past turreted Schloss Oberhoffen and art-nouveau-meets-neo-renaissance Schloss Hünegg. After Thun, you'll get to Bern quickly via the A6.

❹ Bern

Wandering through the picture-postcard **Old Town** (Bern Old Town), with its laid-back, riverside air, it's hard to believe that Bern (Berne in French) is the Swiss capital, but it is, and a Unesco World Heritage Site to boot. The flag-festooned, cobbled centre, rebuilt in grey-green sandstone after a devastating 1405 fire, is a delight, with 6km of covered arcades, cellar shops and bars, and fantastical folk figures frolicking on 16th-century fountains, such as the **Kindlifresserbrunnen** (Kornhausplatz). Be sure to visit Bern's

Münster (www.bernermuenster.ch; Münsterplatz 1; tower adult/child Sfr5/2; ◷10am-5pm Mon-Sat, 11.30am-5pm Sun Apr–mid-Oct, noon-4pm Mon-Fri, 10am-5pm Sat, 11.30am-4pm Sun mid-Oct–Mar), the famous **Bären-Park** (Bear Park; ☎031 357 15 15; www.tierpark-bern.ch; Grosser Muristalden 6; ◷8am-5pm), the architecturally daring **Zentrum Paul Klee** (☎031 359 01 01; www.zpk.org; Monument im Fruchtland 3; adult/child Sfr20/7; ◷10am-5pm Tue-Sun) and the well-endowed **Kunstmuseum** (Museum of Fine Arts; ☎031 328 09 11; www.kunstmuseumbern.ch; Hodlerstrasse 8-12; adult/child Sfr10/5; ◷10am-9pm Tue, to 5pm Wed-Sun).

✕ 🛏 p561

The Drive » Leave via the A6 and take Krauchthalstrasse (35 minutes, about 24km) through verdant countryside to Burgdorf. From Burgdorf to Affoltern im Emmental, 6km to the east, is a scenic drive past old farmsteads bedecked with flower boxes, neat woodpiles and kitchen gardens. Rte 23 between Affoltern and Langnau im Emmental is 21km (25 minutes).

❺ Emmental Region

After so much city time, the postcard-perfect landscapes of rural Switzerland beckon: time for the bucolic idyll of the Emmental region, where holey Emmental (Swiss cheese) is produced. To see the iconic cheese being made, head to

LOCAL KNOWLEDGE: FRIBOURG'S FUNICULAR

Nowhere else in Europe does a funicular lurch up the mountainside with the aid of sewage water (on certain days it smells as you'd expect). Constructed in 1899 and managed by the Cardinal Brewery until 1965 (when the municipality took over), the **Funiculaire de Fribourg** (Sfr3; ◷7am-8pm Mon-Sat, 9.30am-8pm Sun Jul & Aug, 9.30am-7pm Sep-Jun) links the lower town with the upper. It runs every six minutes, and the ride in one of two counterbalancing water-powered carriages from the lower Pertuis station (121m; Place du Pertuis) to the upper station (618m; Rte des Alpes) takes two minutes.

**Emmentaler Schau-
käserei** (Emmental Open
Cheese Dairy; 📞034 435 16
11; www.emmentaler-schau
kaeserei.ch; Schaukäsereis-
trasse 6, Affoltern; ⏰9am-
5pm) in Affoltern.

The region's gateway
towns of Burgdorf and
Langnau im Emmental
preside over a mellow
patchwork of quiet vil-
lages, grazing cows and
fabulous farm chalets
with vast barns and over-
hanging roofs, strung out
along the Emme's banks.
Burgdorf (literally 'castle
village') is split into an
Upper and Lower Town.

The natural highlight
of the Oberstadt (Upper
Town) is the 12th-century
Schloss (castle), with
its drawbridge, thick
stone walls and trio of
museums.

The Drive ≫ From Langnau
im Emmental, take Rte 10 for 30
minutes (23km), crossing from
Bern canton to Lucerne canton,
to reach Schüpfheim, the heart
of the Entlebuch biosphere.

----

6 Unesco Biosphere Entlebuch

The 39,000-plus-sq-km
Entlebuch area (www.
biosphaere.ch), a mixed

mountain-and-highland
ecosystem, was declared
a Unesco Biosphere
Reserve in 2001. Far
from being a lonely
wilderness outpost, the
reserve is home to some
17,000 people keen to
preserve their traditional
dairy-farming lifestyle.
The landscape of karst
formations, sprawling
moors (some 25% of the
area), Alpine pastures
and mountain streams,
which rise from 600m to
some 2350m above sea
level, makes for stirring
scenery. The park office is
in Schüpfheim.

DETOUR: JUNGFRAUJOCH: THE TOP OF EUROPE

Presided over by monolithic Eiger, Mönch and Jungfrau (Ogre, Monk and Virgin), the
crown jewels of Bernese Oberland's Alpine scenery will make your heart skip a beat.

The 'big three' peaks have an enduring place in mountaineering legend,
particularly the 3970m Eiger, whose fearsome north wall remained unconquered
until 1938. Today it takes only 2½ hours from Interlaken Ost by train to
Jungfraujoch (3454m), Europe's highest station.

From Kleine Scheidegg (the last stage of the journey), the train burrows through
the Eiger before arriving at the **Sphinx meteorological station**. Opened in 1912, the
tunnel took 3000 men 16 years to drill. Along the way, the Eigerwand and Eismeer
stops have panoramic windows offering glimpses across rivers of crevassed ice.

Good weather is *essential* for this journey; check beforehand on www.jungfrau.
ch and always take warm clothing, sunglasses and sunscreen. Within the Sphinx
weather station there's a nice sculpture gallery, restaurants, indoor viewpoints and
a souvenir shop. Outside there are views of the 23km-long **Aletsch Glacier** (p549).
On cloudless days, the views stretch as far as the Black Forest in Germany.

When you tire (as if!) of the view, you can zip across the frozen plateau on a flying
fox, dash downhill on a sled or snow disc, or enjoy a bit of tame skiing or boarding at
the **Snow Fun Park** (⏰11am-5pm early May–mid-Oct; 🎿).

If you cross the glacier along the prepared path, in around an hour you'll reach
the **Mönchsjochhütte** (📞033 971 34 72; www.moenchsjoch.ch; dm Sfr31, incl half-board
Sfr69; ⏰late Mar–mid-Oct) at 3650m, where hardcore rock climbers psych themselves
up to tackle Eiger or Mönch.

Lucerne Kapellbrücke (Chapel Bridge)

The Drive » Driving through Entlebuch from Schüpfheim, take the Panoramastrasse (which deserves to be more famous) to the town of Giswil (Obwalden canton; 50 minutes, 37km). Next, follow the signs to Lucerne (Luzern in German) along the A8 (30 minutes, 30km).

- - - - - - - - - - - - - - - - - -

❼ Lucerne

Recipe for a gorgeous Swiss city: take a cobalt lake ringed by mountains of myth (Pilatus, Rigi), add a well-preserved medieval **Old Town** (Altstadt), then sprinkle with covered bridges **Kapellbrücke** (Chapel Bridge) and **Spreuerbrücke** (Spreuer Bridge; btwn Kasernenplatz & Mühlenplatz), sunny plazas, candy-coloured houses and waterfront promenades. Legend has it that an angel with a light showed the first settlers where to build a chapel in Lucerne, and today it still has amazing grace.

One minute it's nostalgic, with its emotive **lion monument** (Löwendenkmal; Denkmalstrasse), the next it's highbrow, with concerts at acoustic marvel **Kultur und Kongresszentrum** (KKL; ☎041 226 79 50, www.kkl-luzern.ch; Europaplatz; guided tour adult/

EMPERORCOSAR/SHUTTERSTOCK ©

559

child Sfr15/9) and the peerless Picasso collection of **Sammlung Rosengart** ([📞]041 220 16 60; www. rosengart.ch; Pilatusstrasse 10; adult/child Sfr18/10; [🕐]10am-6pm Apr-Oct, 11am-5pm Nov-Mar). Crowd-pleasers such as **Verkehrshaus** (Swiss Museum of Transport; [📞]041-375 75 75; www.verkehr shaus.ch; Lidostrasse 5; adult/child Sfr32/12; [🕐]10am-6pm Apr-Oct, to 5pm Nov-Mar; [♿]) and the surrounding natural wonders never fail to impress, while balmy summers and golden autumns ensure this 'city of lights' shines constantly.

[🍴] p561

The Drive » A fast 15-minute, 15km journey along the A2 will get you from Lucerne to Stans' Stansstaderstrasse 19, for the journey up to Stanserhorn.

- - - - - - - - - - - - - - - -

TRIP HIGHLIGHT

8 Stanserhorn

Looming above the lake, 1898m **Stanserhorn** (www. stanserhorn.ch) boasts 360-degree vistas of **Lake Lucerne, Mt Titlis, Mt Pilatus** and the **Bernese Oberland**, among others. Getting to the summit is half the fun. The journey starts with a ride on a vintage 19th-century funicular from Stans to Kälti. From here, the nearly transparent **CabriO** ([📞]041 618 80 40; Stans-staderstrasse 19; funicular &

cable-car adult/child return Sfr79/23.50; [🕐]mid-Apr–early Nov), launched in 2012 as the world's first cable car with an open upper deck, takes you the rest of the way, offering amazing on-the-go views.

On sunny days or when many travellers are expected, book an online 'boarding pass' to confirm your time of departure and subsequent return.

At the summit there's the star-shaped **Rondo-rama**, the region's only revolving restaurant, which rotates 360 degrees every 43 minutes. Kids love the nearby **marmot park**, where the critters can be observed in a near-natural habitat.

The Drive » Retrace your route along the A2 and head toward Lucerne before changing to the A4 and following the signs to Zürich (50 minutes, 65km).

- - - - - - - - - - - - - - - -

TRIP HIGHLIGHT

9 Zürich

Culturally vibrant, efficiently run and set at the meeting of river and lake, Zürich is constantly recognised as one of the world's most liveable cities. It's a savvy, hard-working financial centre, yet Switzerland's largest and wealthiest metropolis has an artsy, postindustrial edge. Much of the Old Town, with its

winding lanes and quaint squares, is lovingly intact. Must-see sights include the glorious **Fraumün-ster** (www.fraumuenster.ch/ en; Stadthausquai 19; Sfr5 incl audioguide; [🕐]10am-6pm Mar-Oct, to 5pm Nov-Feb; [🚊]6, 7, 10, 11, 14 to Paradeplatz), with its Marc Chagall stained-glass windows, the **Grossmünster** (www. grossmuenster.ch; Grossmün-sterplatz; [🕐]10am-6pm Mar-Oct, to 5pm Nov-Feb; [🚊]4, 15 to Helmhaus) with its salt-and-pepper-shaker steeples, and the excellent **Kunsthaus** ([📞]044 253 84 84; www.kunsthaus.ch; Heim-platz 1; adult/child Sfr26/free; [🕐]10am-6pm Tue & Fri-Sun, to 8pm Wed & Thu; [🚊]5, 8, 9, 10 to Kunsthaus), which holds an impressive permanent art collection. For contemporary cool, walk around Züri-West. In summer, the fun revolves around lake and river pools like **Seebad Utoquai** ([📞]079 586 13 99; www.bad-utoquai.ch; Utoquai 49; adult/child Sfr8/4; [🕐]7am-8pm mid-May–late Sep; [🚊]2, 4, 10, 11, 14, 15 to Kreuzstrasse), **Frauenbad** ([📞]044 211 95 92; Stadthaus-quai; adult/child Sfr8/4; [🕐]7am-7.30pm May-Sep; [🚊]2, 5, 8, 9, 10, 11, 14, 15 to Bürkliplatz) and **Männerbad** ([📞]044 211 95 94; Badweg 10; [🕐]11am-6.30pm Jun–mid-Sep; [🚊]2, 8, 9, 13, 14, 17 to Sihlstrasse).

[🍴] p561

Eating & Sleeping

Geneva ❶

✕ Living Room — International $$

(📞022 909 6000; www.livingroombarand
kitchen.com; 11 Quai du Mont-Blanc, Ritz Carlton;
mains Sfr29-70, Sfr56-63; ⏱9am-3pm &
6-10pm) Tasteful decor, refined service, glorious
views of Lake Geneva, and a menu that puts
creative riffs on seasonal ingredients make the
Living Room a winner.

Fribourg ❷

Le Port — Arts Centre

(📞026 321 22 26; www.leport.ch; Planche-
Inférieure 5; ⏱10am-11pm Tue-Sun May-Oct; 📶)
No address better reflects Fribourg's creative
spirit. Squirrelled away in a former gas warehouse
on the banks of the Sarine, the Port bursts with
energy. On summer days Fribourgeois hang out
on its tree-shaded, riverbank terrace between
visits to pop-up ateliers, dining on seasonal
lunchtime platters (Sfr20) of locally cured meats
and homegrown veg.

🛏 Hotel Alpha — Boutique Hotel $

(📞026 322 72 72; www.alpha-hotel.ch; Rue
du Simplon 13; s/d from Sfr105/125; 🅿📶)
There's something wonderful about this simple
boutique hotel that's hard to put your finger
on. The compact, modern rooms may lack air-
conditioning but design smarts and incredible
staff have made excellent use of the building's
good bones to make it a quiet, cosy haven.

Interlaken ❸

🛏 Victoria-Jungfrau
Grand Hotel & Spa — Luxury Hotel $$$

(📞033 828 28 28; www.victoria-jungfrau.ch;
Höheweg 41; d Sfr479-749, junior ste from Sfr539,
ste from Sfr950; 🅿@📶♨) The reverent hush
and impeccable service at this landmark grand
hotel evoke another era. It's a perfect melding
of well-preserved art-nouveau features and
modern luxury, with plum views of Jungfrau, two
first-class restaurants and a fabulous spa.

Bern ❹

✕ Altes Tramdepot — Swiss $$

(📞031 368 14 15; www.altestramdepot.ch;
Grosser Muristalden 6, Am Bärengraben; mains
Sfr20-32; ⏱11am-11.30pm Sun-Thu, to 12.30am
Fri & Sat) At this cavernous microbrewery, classic
beer grub like schnitzel, *Bauernrösti* (fried
potatoes topped with an egg) and sausages with
sauerkraut compete against wok-cooked curries
and *tarte flambée* for your affection.

🛏 Hotel Landhaus — Hotel $

(📞031 348 03 05; https://albertfrida.ch;
Altenbergstrasse 4; dm/s/d from Sfr38/95/130;
🅿📶) Fronted by the river and Old Town spires,
this well-run boho hotel offers a mix of stylish
six-bed dorms, family rooms and doubles. Its
buzzing ground-floor cafe and terrace attracts
a cheery crowd.

Lucerne ❼

✕ Zur Werkstatt — International $$

(📞041 979 03 03; www.zurwerkstatt.ch;
Waldstätterstrasse 18; lunch/dinner menus
Sfr25/58; ⏱11.30am-1.30pm & 5pm-12.30am
Mon-Fri, 10am-2pm & 5pm-12.30am Sat; 🍴🚻)
This post-industrial restaurant revolves around a
show kitchen and hip cocktail bar. Menus are kept
simple, but the food is anything but, singing of the
seasons in dishes like hand-cut steak tartare with
crispy marrow and pumpkin chutney. Book ahead.

Zürich ❾

✕ Didi's Frieden — Swiss $$

(📞044 253 18 10; www.didisfrieden.ch;
Stampfenbachstrasse 32; 4-/5-course menu
Sfr89/99, mains Sfr25-50; ⏱11am-2.30pm &
5pm-midnight Mon-Fri, 6pm-midnight Sat; 🚃7,
11, 14, 17 to Stampfenbachplatz) Didi's Frieden
features among Zürich's top tables. The look is
understated elegance, service is discreet yet
attentive, and seasonal menus might include
venison steak with wild mushrooms and red
wine-shallot jus.

NEED TO KNOW

CURRENCY
Swiss franc (official abbreviation CHF, also Sfr)

LANGUAGE
German, French, Italian, Romansch

VISAS
Generally not required for stays of up to 90 days; some nationalities need a Schengen visa.

FUEL
Petrol stations are common on main roads and highways, and in larger towns. Unleaded costs around Sfr1.40 per litre and diesel is Sfr1.45.

RENTAL CARS
Auto Europe (www.autoeurope.com)

Avis (www.avis.com)

Europcar (www.europcar.com)

Hertz (www.hertz.com)

IMPORTANT NUMBERS
Europe-wide emergency covering police, fire and ambulance (☎112)

Climate

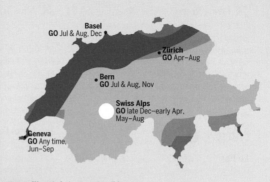

Basel
GO Jul & Aug, Dec

Zürich
GO Apr–Aug

Bern
GO Jul & Aug, Nov

Swiss Alps
GO late Dec–early Apr, May–Aug

Geneva
GO Any time, Jun–Sep

- Warm to hot summers, mild winters
- Warm to hot summers, cold winters
- Mild summers, cold winters
- Cold climate
- Polar climate, below zero year round

When to Go

High Season (Jul, Aug & Dec–Apr)
» In July and August walkers and cyclists hit high-altitude trails.

» Christmas and New Year see serious snow-sports action on the slopes.

» High season in ski resorts is late December to early April.

Shoulder (Apr–Jun & Sep)
» Look for accommodation deals in ski resorts and traveller hot spots.

» Spring is idyllic, with warm temperatures, flowers and local produce.

» Watch the grape harvest in autumn.

Low Season (Oct–Mar)
» Mountain resorts go into snooze mode from mid-October to early December.

» Prices are up to 50% lower than in high season.

» Sights and restaurants are open fewer days and shorter hours.

Daily Costs

Budget: Less than Sfr200
» Dorm bed: Sfr30–60

» Double room in budget hotel: from Sfr100

» Lunch out and self-catering after dark: from Sfr25

Midrange: Sfr200–300
» Double room in two- or three-star hotel: from Sfr200 (Sfr150 at weekends)

» Dish of the day (*tagesteller, plat du jour, piatto del giorno*) or two-course fixed menu: Sfr40–70

Top End: More than Sfr300
» Double room in four- or five-star hotel: from Sfr350 (Sfr250 at weekends)

» Three-course dinner in upmarket restaurant: from Sfr100

Eating

Cafes Coffee, drinks, snacks.

Bistros Light meals to full-blown dinners.

Restaurants Simple eateries to Michelin-starred temples.

Vegetarian Few wholly vegetarian places, limited choices on most menus.

Price categories indicate the cost of a two-course meal:

$	less than Sfr25
$$	Sfr25–50
$$$	more than Sfr50

Sleeping

Hotels From budget to luxury; breakfast included unless indicated.

Pensiones Chambres d'hôte in French-speaking Switzerland; rates always include breakfast.

Hostels In cities and large towns; private or HI-affiliated.

Price categories indicate the cost of a double room with private bathroom and breakfast in high season:

$	less than Sfr170
$$	Sfr170–350
$$$	more than Sfr350

Arriving in Switzerland

Zürich Airport

Trains Sfr3.40; run to Zürich centre, 6am to midnight, and take 13 minutes.

Taxis Sfr50–70; 20 minutes to centre.

Mobile Phones

Most European and Australian phones function; turn off roaming to avoid data charges. Those from outside Europe can buy a local SIM for cheaper rates.

Internet Access

Wi-fi (usually free) is available to guests in most hotels, B&Bs and hostels. Also offered by many cafes, bars, train stations and other public spaces.

Money

ATMs are on every second street corner in towns and cities; Visa, MasterCard and Amex widely accepted.

Tipping

Tipping is not necessary; hotels, restaurants, bars and even some taxis are legally required to include a 15% service charge in bills.

Restaurants You can round up the bill after a meal for good service, as locals do.

Hotels Hotel and railway porters expect a franc or two per bag.

Useful Websites

Lonely Planet (lonelyplanet.com/switzerland) Travel tips, accommodation, recommendations and more.

My Switzerland (www.myswitzerland.com) Swiss tourist board.

TCS (www.tcs.ch) Driving info for Switzerland.

Opening Hours

Most businesses shut on Sunday.

Banks 8.30am–4.30pm Monday to Friday

Museums 10am–5pm, many close Monday and stay open late Thursday

Restaurants noon–2.30pm and 6pm–9.30pm

Shops 10am–6pm Monday to Friday, to 4pm Saturday

STRETCH YOUR LEGS
GENEVA

Start: Jardin Anglais

Finish: Place du Bourg-de-Four

Distance: 2km

Duration: 3 hours

Geneva's beautiful Vieille Ville (Old Town) is the perfect spot for a charmingly edifying stroll, thanks to its mix of sights and a history lesson worthy of its status as one of the Protestant Reformation's key cities.

Take this walk on Trip

Jardin Anglais

Before strolling up the hill to the Old Town, visit the flower clock in Geneva's waterfront **garden** (English Garden; Quai du Général-Guisan), landscaped in 1854 on the site of an old lumber-handling port and merchant yard. The **Horloge Fleurie** (Flower Clock; Quai du Général-Guisan), Geneva's most photographed clock, is crafted from 6500 plants and has ticked since 1955. Its second hand, 2.5m long, is claimed to be the world's longest.

The Walk ≫ From the clock, cross Quai du Général-Guisan. Head south through the shopping district to Cour de St-Pierre, which faces the cathedral. It's about a seven-minute stroll.

Cathédrale St-Pierre

Begun in the 11th century, Geneva's **cathedral** (www.cathedrale-geneve.ch; Cour de St-Pierre; towers adult/child Sfr7/4; ⊙9.30am-6.30pm Mon-Fri, to 5pm Sat, noon-6.30pm Sun Jun-Sep, shorter hours rest of the year) is predominantly Gothic with an 18th-century neoclassical facade. From 1536 to 1564, Protestant John Calvin preached here; see his uncomfortable-looking seat in the north aisle. Inside the cathedral, 77 steps spiral up to the attic – a fascinating glimpse at its architectural construction – from where another 40 lead to the top of the panoramic **northern and southern towers**. Views of the Old Town and the Jet d'Eau are marvellous. In summer, free carillon (5pm) and organ (6pm) concerts fill the cathedral and its surrounding square with music.

The Walk ≫ Exit the cathedral and head for the Site Archéologique de la Cathédrale St-Pierre; a few dozen footsteps should cover it.

Site Archéologique de la Cathédrale St-Pierre

This small **archaeological site** (⌘022 311 75 74; www.site-archeologique.ch; Cour de St-Pierre 6; adult/child Sfr8/4; ⊙10am-5pm) in the basement of Cathédrale St-Pierre has 4th-century mosaics in the Roman

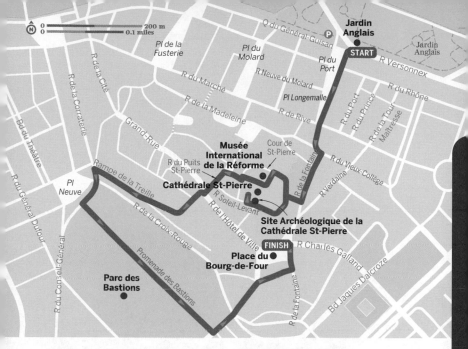

crypt, and the tomb of an Allobrogian chieftain. Its entrance is at the right of the cathedral's main portico.

The Walk » Head to the other side of the cathedral (a one-minute walk) to spend an hour at the Reformation Museum.

Musée International de la Réforme

This modern **museum** (Museum of the Reformation; ☑022 310 24 31; www.musee -reforme.ch; Rue du Cloître 4; adult/child Sfr13/6; ☉10am-5pm Tue-Sun) in an 18th-century mansion has state-of-the-art exhibits on the Reformation: printed bibles, the emergence of 16th-century Geneva as 'Protestant Rome', John Calvin and present-day Protestantism.

The Walk » From Cour de St-Pierre, walk down Rue Otto Barblan. Turn left onto Rue du Puits-St-Pierre and continue past Maison Tavel (the city's longest-standing private residence, now a museum) to the bottom of Rue Henri Fazy. It overlooks Parc des Bastions and has the world's longest bench. Turn down Rampe de la Treille and follow it to the park's gates.

Parc des Bastions

It's all statues – plus free life-size chess boards hosting lively games – in green **Parc des Bastions**. A laid-back stroll with locals along its tree-lined promenade reveals the 4.5m-tall po-faced figures of Bèze, Calvin, Farel and Knox on **Reformation Wall**, which stretches for 100m. There are play facilities for kids and a skating rink in winter.

The Walk » From Promenade des Bastion's eastern end, walk along Rue St-Léger. Continue under the bridge and continue until Place du Bourg-de-Four ends at the fountained terrace area.

Place du Bourg-de-Four

Eateries, bars and locals crowd Place du Bourg-de-Four, Geneva's oldest square. In summer it's filled to bursting with local denizens catching up. Stalwart **La Clémence** (☑022 312 24 98; www.laclemence.ch; Place du Bourg-de-Four 20; ☉7am-1am Mon-Thu, to 2am Fri, 8am-2am Sat, 8am-1am Sun) is a popular place to linger over a coffee.

Austria

AUSTRIA IS A ROAD-TRIPPER'S FANTASY LAND. Not only are there spectacular backdrops of spellbinding landscapes and story-book architecture, but opportunities abound to get out and experience them. Along these routes, you can scale soaring peaks, ski year-round, raft white-water rapids and pelt down toboggan runs. When you've had enough thrills and spills, Austria's multitude of cultural pursuits span medieval castles to monumental palaces, art-filled museums and magnificent churches. You can taste cheese at Alpine dairies, schnapps at distilleries, and beer and wine in monasteries where tipples are still made by monks. Or just hop aboard a horse-drawn carriage to clip-clop through cobbled, lamp-lit city streets.

Zillertal Alps Zell am Ziller

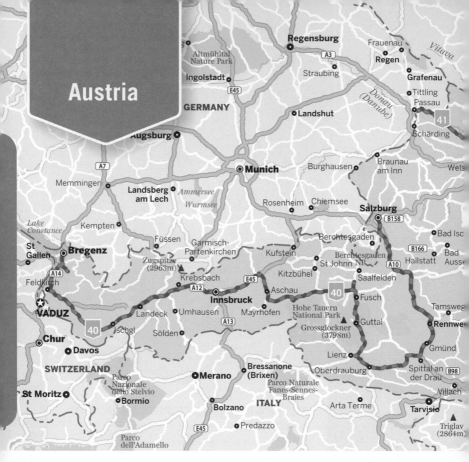

Austria

GERMANY

Regensburg

Altmühltal Nature Park

Ingolstadt

Straubing

Frauenau

Regen

Grafenau

Tittling

Passau

Donau (Danube)

Vitava

Scharding

Landshut

Augsburg

Munich

Burghausen

Braunau am Inn

Wels

Landsberg am Lech

Memmingen

Ammersee

Wurmsee

Rosenheim

Chiemsee

Salzburg

Bad Isc

Lake Constance

Kempten

Füssen

Garmisch-Partenkirchen

Kufstein

Berchtesgaden

Berchtesgaden NP

St Johann

Bad Ausse

Hallstatt

St Gallen

Bregenz

Zugspitze (2963m)

Krebsbach

Kitzbühel

Saalfelden

Feldkirch

Innsbruck

Aschau

Fusch

Tamsweg

VADUZ

Landeck

Umhausen

Mayrhofen

Hohe Tauern National Park

Grossglockner (3798m)

Guttal

Rennwe

Chur

Ischgl

Sölden

Lienz

Gmünd

Davos

Spittal an der Drau

SWITZERLAND

Parco Nazionale dello Stelvio

Merano

Bressanone (Brixen)

Oberdrauburg

Villach

St Moritz

Bormio

Bolzano

ITALY

Parco Naturale Fanes-Sennes-Braies

Arta Terme

Tarvisio

Parco dell'Adamello

Predazzo

Triglav (2864m)

40 Grossglockner Road 5–7 Days
Twist and turn along three of Austria's most spectacular mountain passes.

41 Along the Danube 2–4 Days
Follow the Danube River as it flows through forests and vineyards.

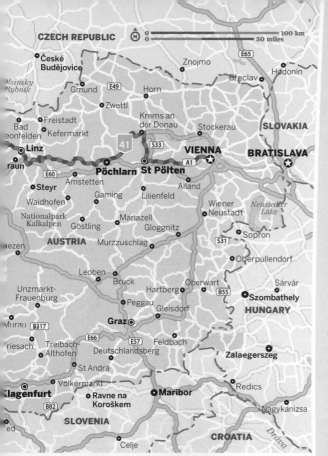

 DON'T
MISS

Lake Swimming

Many of Austria's
Alp-framed lakes reach
temperatures of up to
28°C in summer. Dive
into one on Trip 40

Salzburg

Famed for its starring
role in The Sound of
Music, Salzburg's
Unesco-listed Altstadt
(old town) is a treasure.
Visit on Trip 40

Hiking

Through forests, up
waterfall trails, down
gorges, along wildflower-
strewn meadows... You'll
find some of Austria's
best hiking on Trip 40

Vienna

With its resplendent
palaces, magnificent
museums and opera
house, Austria's capital
is the belle of the
country's ball. Waltz by
on Trip 41

Krems an der Donau

One of Austria's most
character-packed
towns, check out
the atmospheric old
town before taking
in the galleries of the
Kunstmeile (Art Mile).
It's all in Trip 41

Grossglockner Road

Austria's most exhilarating trip takes you on a wild roller-coaster drive over three legendary Alpine passes and packs in outdoor activities from year-round skiing to windsurfing.

40

TRIP HIGHLIGHTS

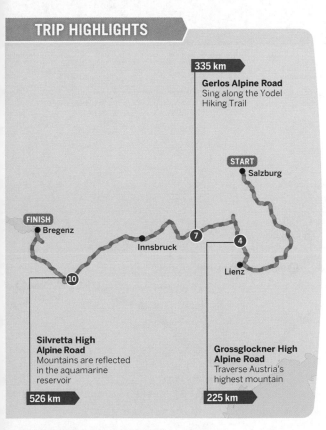

335 km

Gerlos Alpine Road
Sing along the Yodel Hiking Trail

START
Salzburg

FINISH
Bregenz

7

4

Innsbruck

Lienz

10

Silvretta High Alpine Road
Mountains are reflected in the aquamarine reservoir

526 km

Grossglockner High Alpine Road
Traverse Austria's highest mountain

225 km

5–7 DAYS
711KM / 442 MILES

GREAT FOR...

BEST TIME TO GO
The peak time to tackle this trip is midsummer.

ESSENTIAL PHOTO
Europe's highest waterfalls, the three-tiered Krimmler Wasserfälle.

BEST FOR DRIVERS
The Grossglockner's 36 heart-in-your-mouth hairpin bends.

Krimmler Wasserfälle Austria's highest waterfall

40 Grossglockner Road

Fair warning: if you're a faint-hearted driver (or passenger), this probably isn't the trip for you. But if you're up for a serious adventure, this Austrian classic provides an opportunity to experience epic scenery, invigorating alpine sports, and dizzying mountain passes with so many switchbacks they're used by high-performance car manufacturers and championship race drivers as test tracks.

❶ Salzburg

Salzburg's trophy sights huddle in the pedestrianised, Unesco World Heritage–listed **Altstadt** (old town). The tangled lanes are made for a serendipitous wander, leading to hidden courtyards and medieval squares framed by burgher houses and baroque fountains. You'll also see plenty of icons from the evergreen musical *The Sound of Music*.

Beyond city strolling, there are plenty of opportunities to get active, from swimming at **Freibad Leopoldskron** (Leopoldskronstrasse 50; adult/child €4/2; ⏲9am–7pm May–mid-Sep; 🚼), Salzburg's biggest lido, with diving boards, waterslides and volleyball, to hiking up Salzburg's rival mountains, the 540m **Mönchsberg** and 640m **Kapuzinerberg**. Both mountains are thickly wooded and criss-crossed by walking trails, with photogenic views of the

LINK YOUR TRIP

36 **The Romantic Road**

Strike north after Innsbruck to find a ribbon of historical quaintness running through Bavaria's western reaches.

39 **Geneva to Zürich**

Mountains, pastures, lakes and small-town charm, book-ended by Switzerland's biggest cities.

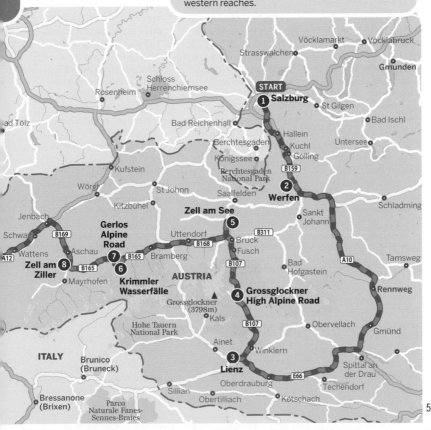

Altstadt's right bank and left bank respectively.

The Drive » It's 47km south from Salzburg on the B159 to Werfen, mostly along the Salzach River. After passing through a wide valley, you'll enter a tight, steep gorge; follow it until Werfen.

🛏 p579

The Drive » Take the A10 south to the Millstätter See (which you can visit on a trip through the Carinthian Lakes) and turn west onto the B100/E66 through the Drau Valley to Lienz (166km in total).

---

❷ Werfen

More than 1000m above Werfen in the Tennenge-birge mountains is **Eis-riesenwelt** (www.eisriesen welt.at; Eishohlenstrasse 30; adult/child €14/8, incl cable car €28/12; ⏱8.15am-4.30pm Jul & Aug, to 3.45pm May, Jun, Sep & Oct). Billed as the world's largest accessible ice caves, this glittering ice spectacle spans 30,000 sq metres and 42km of narrow passages burrowing deep into the heart of the mountains. A highlight is the cavernous **Eispalast** (ice palace), where the frost crystals twinkle when a magnesium flare is held up to them. Wrap up warmly for subzero temperatures. Photography is not permitted inside the caves.

On a wooded clifftop beneath the majestic peaks of the Tennenge-birge is the formidable fortress **Burg Hohenwer-fen** (Hohenwerfen Fortress; www.salzburg-burgen.at; adult/child/family €12.50/7/30, incl lift €16.50/9.50/39.50; ⏱9am-5pm May-Sep, shorter hours Mar, Apr & Oct), dating from 1077. Time your visit to be at the castle by 3.15pm for the falconry show.

❸ Lienz

Ringed by Dolomite peaks blushing reddish-pink at sunset, Lienz straddles the Isel and Drau Rivers, and lies just 40km north of Italy. An ancient **Ro-man settlement**, today it's a famed ski town (for its Zettersfeld and Hochstein peaks, and especially its 100km of cross-country trails), but it has an energetic vibe year-round.

If you want to get up into the mountains, **Berg-statt** (📞0664 516 5835; Kranewitweg 5; rock-climbing trips per adult/child from €80/60) has guides who can lead you on half-day, full-day and multiday rock climbing, via ferrata or summit trips.

The Drive » Take the B107 north, passing picturesque villages including Winklern – 17km from Lienz, with a wonderful alpine hotel – and Heiligenblut – look for the needle-thin spire of its pilgrimage church – to the Grossglockner High Alpine Road toll gates (43km in total).

TRIP HIGHLIGHT

❹ Grossglockner High Alpine Road

A stupendous feat of 1930s engineering, the 48km **Grossglockner Road** (www.grossglockner.at; day ticket car/motorbike €37/27; ⏱6am-7.30pm May, 5.30am-8.30pm Jun-Aug, 6am-7.30pm Sep & Oct) swings giddily around 36 switchbacks, passing jewel-coloured lakes, forested slopes and above-the-clouds glaciers as it traverses the heart of the Hohe Tauern National Park, peaking at the bell-shaped **Grossglockner** (3798m), Austria's highest mountain.

En route, flag-dotted **Kaiser-Franz-Josefs-Höhe** (2369m) has memorable views of Grossglockner and the rapidly retreat-ing Pasterze Glacier (best appreciated on the short and easy Gamsgrubenweg and Gletscherweg trails). Allow time to see the glacier-themed exhibition at the visitor centre and the crystalline Wilhelm-Swarovski observatory.

Get your camera handy for **Fuscher Törl** (2428m), with super views on both sides of the ridge, and **Fuscher Lacke** (2262m), a gemstone of a lake nearby. A small exhibition docu-ments the construction of the road.

A 2km side road cork-screws up to **Edelweiss Spitze** (2571m), the road's highest viewpoint. Climb the tower for staggering 360-degree views of more than 30 peaks topping 3000m.

Between toll gates, all attractions are free. Check the forecast before you hit the road, as the drive is not much fun in heavy fog, snow or a storm. It's often bumper-to-bumper by noon, especially in July and August; beat the crowds by setting out early.

The Drive » Descend the Grossglockner on the B107 to Bruck then take the B311 northeast to Zell am See.

TOP TIP: ALPINE ROAD TOLLS

Be aware that this trip's three top-draw drives – Grossglockner High Alpine Road, Gerlos Alpine Road and Silvretta High Alpine Road (p578) – incur hefty tolls. There's also a smaller toll on the detour to the Stubaital (p578). Toll booths accept cash and credit cards.

❺ Zell am See

Resort town Zell am See's brightly painted chalets line the shore of the deep-blue Zeller See, framed by the Hohe Tauern's snow-capped peaks.

Mountain breezes create ideal conditions for windsurfing on the lake; **Windsurfcenter Zell Am See** (📱0664 644 36 95; www.supcenter-zellamsee.at; Seespitzstrasse 13; 2hr beginner course €46; ☺dawn-dusk May-Sep) rents equipment and runs courses.

The Drive » From the lake, it's 54km to the Krimmler Wasserfälle. Head west on the B168 and B165 to Krimml; when you arrive in town the waterfalls come into view.

❻ Krimmler Wasserfälle

Europe's highest falls, at 380m, are the thunderous, three-tier **Krimmler Wasserfälle** (Krimml Falls; 📱06564-72 12; www.wasserfaelle-krimml.at; adult/child €4/1; ☺9am-5pm mid-Apr–Oct). The **Wasserfall-weg** (Waterfall Trail), which starts at the ticket office and weaves uphill through mixed forest, has up-close viewpoints. It's 4km one way (about a 2½-hour round-trip walk).

The Drive » From the falls, it's 7.7km (and eight hairpin bends) to the Gerlos Alpine Road toll gates.

TRIP HIGHLIGHT

❼ Gerlos Alpine Road

Open year-round, the **Gerlos Alpine Road** (www.gerlosstrasse.at; toll per car/motorcycle €10/7) winds 12km through high moor and spruce forest, reaching an elevation of 1630m. The lookout above the turquoise Stausee (reservoir) is a great picnic stop, with a tremendous vista of the Alps.

Take the 4.8km-long **Jodel Wanderweg** (Yodel Hiking Trail; www.jodelweg.at; Wald-Königsleiten) in Königsleiten. You can go it alone and practise your high notes at eight stops with giant cowbells, alpine horns and listen-repeat audio clippings. Alternatively, join a free guided sing 'n' stroll hike with trail founder Christian Eder. The three-hour downhill ambles begin at 10.30am every Wednesday from late June to mid-September at the Dorfbahn cable-car station; call the tourist office (📱06565 82 43) by 5pm the previous day to reserve a spot.

The Drive » Continue west on the B165, passing the reservoir Durlassboden, before descending to Zell am Ziller along six hairpin bends (63km in total).

❽ Zell am Ziller

At the foot of knife-edge Reichenspitze (3303m), Zell am Ziller is a former gold-mining centre and popular ski base.

Year-round, you can take a wild toboggan ride on the 1.45km-long **Arena Coaster** (www.zillertalarena.com; Zillertal Arena; adult/child coaster only €5.60/3.70; ☺9.30am-6pm late Jun-early Sep, shorter hours rest of year; 🚡), which incorporates both a 360-degree loop and a 540-degree loop. It's accessible by cable car, or a steep 1.5km walk.

Aktivzentrum Zillertal (www.aktivzentrum-zillertal.at; Freizeitpark Zell; 🚡) offers

WHY THIS IS A GREAT TRIP
CATHERINE LE NEVEZ, WRITER

Awe-inspiring mountainscapes and adrenaline-pumping activities abound on this alpine itinerary, but the ultimate draw is the drive itself, peaking with its trio of dizzying high-altitude switchback passes – the Grossglockner High Alpine Road, Gerlos Alpine Road and Silvretta High Alpine Road. This is a route that reminds you that the highlight of road-tripping isn't the destination but the journey.

Above: Innsbruck
Left: Skiing, Zell am Ziller
Right: Silvretta High Alpine Road

summertime paragliding, white-water rafting on the Ziller, canyoning, via ferrata climbing and – one for the kids – llama trekking.

🏠 p579

The Drive >> Zell am Ziller sits 60km from Innsbruck. Take the B169 north, then the A12 west to the city.

9 Innsbruck

Hit Innsbruck's cultural attractions, such as the Volkskunst Museum, then head up to its ski jump, the **Bergisel** (www. bergisel.info; adult/child €10/5; ⏰9am-6pm Jun-Oct, 10am-5pm Wed-Mon Nov-May), for a spectacular city and mountain panorama. Rising above Innsbruck like a celestial staircase, the glass-and-steel structure was designed by Iraqi architect Zaha Hadid.

Hadid also designed the space-age funicular **Nordkettenbahnen** (www. nordkette.com; single/return to Hungerburg €6/10, to Seegrube €19/32, to Hafelekar €21/35; ⏰Hungerburg 7.15am-7.15pm Mon-Fri, 8am-7.15pm Sat & Sun, Seegrube 8.30am-5.30pm daily, Hafelekar 9am-5pm daily), which whizzes from the Congress Centre to the slopes every 15 minutes. Walking trails head off in all directions from Hungerburg and Seegrube.

🍴 🏠 p579

The Drive >> Leave Innsbruck on the westbound A12 and veer southwest on the B188, passing a string of ski towns, to the

IMAGEBROKER/STEFAN SCHURR/GETTY IMAGES ©

DETOUR: STUBAITAL

Start: **9** Innsbruck

Slip out of sandals and into skis at year-round skiing magnet, **Stubai Glacier** (www.stubaier-gletscher. com). A one-day summer **ski pass** (adult/child €42.50/21.30) covers 26 lifts accessing 62km of slopes. Ski shops are plentiful; ski or snowboard and boot rental costs around €30/15 per adult/child. Summer skiing is between 2900m and 3300m and is dependent on weather conditions.

Lower down in the Stubai Valley, the **Wildewasserweg** waterfall trail wends for 9.2km (one way) to Sulzenau Glacier. En route, it passes the spectacular Grawa falls; there's a cafe with a panoramic viewing deck at its base.

The Stubai Glacier is just 38km south of Innsbruck. Take the A13 south to the toll gates (per car including passengers €3); keep right to take the B183 southwest along the valley.

Silvretta High Alpine Road toll gates (118km all up).

TRIP HIGHLIGHT

10 Silvretta High Alpine Road

Silhouetted by the glaciated Silvretta range and crowned by the 3312m arrow of Piz Buin, the Montafon Valley remains one of the most serene and unspoilt in the Austrian Alps.

The 23km-long **Silvretta High Alpine Road** (www.silvretta-bielerhoehe.at; car/motorcycle €16.50/13.50; early Jun-late Oct) twists and turns beneath peaks rising to well over 2500m before climbing over the 2036m Bielerhöhe Pass via 34 knuckle-whiteningly tight switchbacks. At the top of the pass, the **Silvretta Stausee** (2030m), a startlingly aquamarine reservoir, mirrors the surrounding peaks on bright mornings.

The Drive » It's 100km to Rappenlochschlucht. Continue on the B188 and join the A14 at aromatic Bludenz (home to the Milka chocolate factory; there's an outlet shop but, alas, no tours). Continue northwest to Dornbirn, from where Rappenlochschlucht is 4km southeast on Gütlestrasse.

11 Rappenlochschlucht

The **Rappenlochschlucht** (Rappenloch Gorge; www.rappenlochschlucht. at) was gouged out by the thundering Dornbirner Ache. From the car park, there's a 375m trail to the Staufensee, a turquoise lake ringed by forest.

At the bottom of the Rappenlochschlucht, a 19th-century cotton mill is the unlikely home of the world's largest collection of Rolls-Royces at the **Rolls-Royce Museum** (www.rolls-royce-museum. at; Gütle 11a; adult/child €6/3; 10am-6pm Tue-Sun Mar-Nov).

The Drive » Return to Dornbirn and head north on the B190 for 16km to Bregenz.

12 Bregenz

Bregenz sits on the shores of Lake Constance (in German, Bodensee), Europe's third-largest lake. The views here are extraordinary: before you the mirror-like lake; behind you, the 1064m-high Pfänder mountain, to the right, Germany, to the left, Switzerland.

A **cable car** (www. pfaenderbahn.at; Steinbruchgasse 4; adult/child one way €7.90/3.90, return €13.60/6.80; 8am-7pm) glides up the Pfänder. At the top, a 30-minute circular trail brings you close to deer, wild boar, ibex and whistling marmots at the year-round **Alpine Game Park Pfänder** (www.pfaender.at; Pfänder; sunrise-sunset).

Some 5km south of central Bregenz, where the Rhine flows into Lake Constance, is the nature reserve **Rheindelta** (www. rheindelta.org; Hard).

p579

Eating & Sleeping

Werfen ❷

🛏 Weisses Rössl   Pension €

(📞06468-52 68; www.weisses-roessl-werfen.at; Markt 39; s/d/tr €44/78/96; P 🛜) In the village centre, this good-value pension has great views of the fortress and the Tennengebirge from its rooftop terrace. Rooms are a blast from the 1970s, but all are large and cosy with sofas and cable TV.

Winklern

🛏 Hotel Tauernstern   Chalet €€

(📞04822-248; www.tauernstern.at; Winklern 24, Winklern im Mölltal; s €57-77, d €104-124, ste €134-144, half board €18; P 🛜) Sweeping valley views extend from the timber balconies of this mountain-set gem. Four-poster pine-and-stone beds, in-room fridges, a sauna and spa built from local wood and slate, and an exceptional gourmet restaurant using ingredients from local farms all make Tauernstern a fabulous pit stop before tackling the Grossglockner High Alpine Road.

Zell am Ziller ❽

🛏 Hotel Englhof   Boutique Hotel €€

(📞05282-31 34; www.englhof.at; Zellbergeben 28; s/d €76/122; 🛜) Beautiful blond-wood-panelled, white-linen-dressed rooms (many with balconies) and countless amenities make Englhof a superb place to stay. But what really seals the deal is its in-house gourmet restaurant and world-class cocktail bar with Austria's second-largest collection of spirits (over 1400 varieties), mixing incredible cocktails like a Bloody Mary with frozen cherry tomatoes and barbecued black-pepper seasoning.

Innsbruck ❾

🍴 Die Wilderin   Austrian €€

(📞0512-56 27 28; www.diewilderin.at; Seilergasse 5; mains €10-19; ⏱5pm-midnight Tue-Sun) Take a gastronomic walk on the wild side at this modern-day hunter-gatherer of a restaurant, where chefs take pride in sourcing locally and using top-notch farm-fresh and foraged ingredients. The menu sings of the seasons, be it asparagus, game, strawberries or winter veg. The vibe is urbane and relaxed.

🛏 Hotel Weisses Kreuz   Historic Hotel €€

(📞0512-594 79; www.weisseskreuz.at; Herzog-Friedrich-Strasse 31; s €66-105, d €100-180; P @ 🛜) Beneath the arcades, this atmospheric Altstadt hotel has played host to guests for 500 years, including a 13-year-old Mozart. With its wood-panelled parlours, antiques and twisting staircase, the hotel oozes history with every creaking beam. Rooms are supremely comfortable, staff are charming and breakfast is a lavish spread.

Bregenz ⓬

🛏 Schwärzler   Hotel €€

(📞05574-49 90; www.schwaerzler.s-hotels.com; Landstrasse 9; d from €135; P 🛜 🚿) This turreted, ivy-clad place is a far cry from your average business hotel. Contemporary rooms are done out in earthy hues and blonde wood, with comforts including bathrobes, flat-screen TVs and minibars. There's also a 400-sq-metre pool and a sauna area. Regional produce from organic farms features on the breakfast buffet.

Along the Danube

41

Follow the beautiful Danube River as it flows from the German city of Passau by the Austrian border through farmland, forest and vineyard-streaked hillsides to Austria's capital, Vienna.

TRIP HIGHLIGHTS

205 km

Dürnstein
Richard the Lionheart was imprisoned here in a now-ruined castle

293 km

Vienna
View Vienna by foot, horse-drawn carriage or Ferris wheel

Krems an der Donau

START
Passau

Linz   Melk   ⑦
         ④   ⑨   ⑩ FINISH

St Florian
Visit the abbey's exuberant basilica

92 km

Stift Göttweig
This Unesco-listed abbey serves its own monk-made wines

219 km

2–4 DAYS
320KM / 198 MILES

GREAT FOR...

BEST TIME TO GO
Aim for summer (June to September): many places close between November and March.

ESSENTIAL PHOTO

St Florian's dazzling interior.

BEST FOR ART

Linz' contemporary Lentos gallery.

Dürnstein Chorherrenstift, a former monastery

41 Along the Danube

Immortalised in the stirring Blue Danube waltz by Austrian composer Johann Strauss II, this magnificent river ripples with the reflections of dense green forests, hilltop castles, and ribbons of vineyards, particularly on its prettiest stretch, the Wachau, between Melk and Krems an der Donau. Along the river's course are plenty of surprises too, including the cutting-edge city of Linz, and two superb monasteries producing, respectively, sublime beer and wine.

❶ Passau

Just inside the German border, Passau's pastel-shaded Altstadt sits atop a narrow peninsula jutting into the confluence of three rivers: the Danube, the Inn and the Ilz. Christianity generated prestige as Passau evolved into the largest bishopric in the Holy Roman Empire, as testified by the mighty cathedral **Dom St Stephan** (Domplatz; ⏱6.30am-7pm).

Stroll the old town, which remains much as it was when the powerful

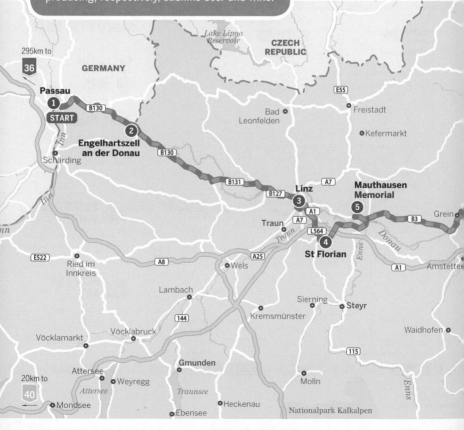

prince-bishops built its tight lanes, tunnels and archways with an Italianate flourish.

 p587

The Drive » Cross the Inn River where it joins the Danube and head east on ST2125 which, 3.3km later, becomes the B130 on entering Austria, and follows the Danube's southern bank. On your right, you'll pass Burg Krempelstein, built on the site of a Roman watch house. It's 26km all up to Engelhartszell an der Donau.

❷ Engelhartszell an der Donau

The little riverside village of Engelhartszell an der Donau is home to one of only eight licensed

LINK YOUR TRIP

36 **The Romantic Road**

Head west, skirting Munich, to this ribbon of historical quaintness running through Bavaria's western reaches.

40 **Grossglockner Road**

A hop and a skip south and you can twist and turn along three of Austria's most spectacular mountain passes.

Trappist breweries outside Belgium, and the only one in Austria. At the 1293-founded abbey **Stift Engelszell** (www.stift-engelszell.at; Stiftstrasse 6, Engelhartszell an der Donau; ⊙ church 8am-7pm Apr-Oct, to

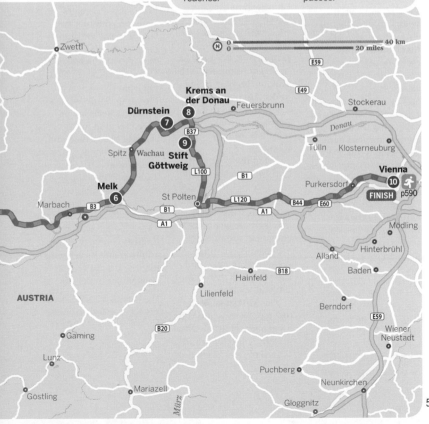

5pm Nov-Mar, shop 9am-5pm Apr-Oct, shorter hours rest of year), you can purchase monk-made brews (dark Gregorius, amber Benno and blond Nivard); the shop also sells liqueurs and cheeses produced here. Adjoining the shop is the abbey's gorgeous rococo church, completed in 1764.

The Drive » Take the B130; at Aschach an der Donau, cross the river on the B131, and continue east to Ottensheim to join the B127 to Linz (52km in total).

---

3 Linz

The Austrian saying *In Linz beginnt's* (It begins in Linz) sums up this technology trailblazer. Its leading-edge **Ars Electronica Center** (https://ars.electronica.art; Ars-Electronica-Strasse 1; adult/child €11.50/9; ☉10am-5pm Tue-Sun) has labs for interacting with robots, animating digital objects, converting your name to DNA and (virtually) travelling to outer space. After dark, the LED glass skin kaleidoscopically changes colour. Directly across the Danube is Linz' world-class contemporary-art gallery, the glass-and-steel **Lentos** (www.lentos.at; Ernst-Koref-Promenade 1; adult/child €8/4.50; ☉10am-6pm Tue, Wed & Fri-Sun, to 9pm Thu), with works by Warhol, Schiele and Klimt, among others.

But it's not all new in Austria's third-largest

city: the **Mariendom** (Neuer Dom; www.dioezese-linz.at; Herrenstrasse 26; ☉7.30am-7pm Mon-Sat, 8am-7.15pm Sun) is a neo-Gothic giant of a cathedral with a riot of pinnacles, flying buttresses and filigree traceried windows.

✕ 🛏 p587

The Drive » Take the A1 southeast to Ebelsberg, then continue on the L564 to St Florian (21km all up).

TRIP HIGHLIGHT

4 St Florian

Rising like a vision above St Florian is its magnificent abbey, **Augustiner Chorherrenstift** (www.stift-st-florian.at; Stiftstrasse 1; tours €10.50; ☉tours 11am, 1pm & 3pm May–mid-Oct). Dating to at least 819, it has been occupied by the Canons Regular, living under Augustinian rule, since 1071. Today its imposing yellow-and-white facade is overwhelmingly baroque.

Compulsory guided tours of the abbey's interior take in the resplendent apartments adorned with rich stucco work and frescos, including 16 emperors' rooms (once occupied by visiting popes and royalty) and a galleried library housing 150,000 volumes.

The **Stiftsbasilika** (open 6.30am to dusk) is an exuberant affair with an altar carved from 700 tonnes of pink Salzburg

marble, and a gold 18th-century organ.

The Drive » Head northeast on the L566 to join the B1. Follow it for 7.5km then turn east on the B123 to cross the Danube, before turning west on the B3. After 2.4km take the L1411 for 2.5 signposted kilometres to the Mauthausen Memorial (22km in total).

---

5 Mauthausen Memorial

Nowadays Mauthausen is a peaceful small town on the north bank of the Danube, but in WWII the Nazis turned the quarrying centre into the **KZ Mauthausen** concentration camp. Prisoners were forced into slave labour in the granite quarry and many died on the so-called *Todesstiege* (stairway of death) leading from the quarry to the camp. Some 100,000 prisoners perished or were executed in the camp between 1938 and 1945. The complex is now a **memorial** (☎07238-2269-0; www.mauthausen-memorial.org; Erinnerungsstrasse 1, Mauthausen; ☉9am-5.30pm Mar-Oct, to 3.45pm Tue-Sun Nov-Feb); English-language audioguides relate its sobering history. It's not recommended for under 14s.

The Drive » Travelling east for 76km brings you to Melk. Along the river at Grein, look out for the dramatic castle Greinburg rising to your left.

Wachau Valley Vineyards near Spitz village

6 Melk

Historically, Melk was of great importance to the Romans, and later to the Babenbergs, who built a castle here. In 1089 the Babenberg margrave Leopold II donated the castle to Benedictine monks, who converted it into the fortified **Stift Melk** (Benedictine Abbey of Melk; www.stiftmelk.at; Abt Berthold Dietmayr Strasse 1; adult/child €12.50/6.50, with guided tour €14.50/8.50; ⊙9.30am-5pm, tour in English 3pm). Fire destroyed the original edifice; today its monastery church dominates the complex with its twin spires and high octagonal dome. The baroque-gone-barmy interior has regiments of cherubs, gilt twirls and polished faux marble. The theatrical high-altar scene depicts St Peter and St Paul (the church's two patron saints).

The Drive » The Wachau is the loveliest valley along the mighty river's length: both banks here are dotted with ruined castles and terraced with vineyards. From Melk, follow the river northeast along the northern bank for 28km, passing medieval villages Spitz, Wösendorf in der Wachau and Weissenkirchen, to reach Dürnstein.

TRIP HIGHLIGHT

7 Dürnstein

Picturesque Dürnstein is best known for the **Kuenringerburg** – the now-ruined castle above the town where Richard the Lionheart (Richard I of England) was imprisoned from 1192 to 1193, before being moved to **Burg Trifels** in Germany.

Of the 16th-century buildings lining Dürnstein's hilly, cobbled streets, the **Chorherrenstift** (www.stiftduernstein.at; Stiftshof; adult/child €6.50/4; ⊙9am-6pm Mon-Sat, 10am-6pm Sun May-Oct) is the most impressive. It's all that remains of the former Augustinian monastery originally founded in 1410, and received its baroque facelift in the 18th century.

The Drive » Head east along the river on the B3 for 7.5km to reach Krems an der Donau.

⑧ Krems an der Donau

Against a backdrop of terraced vineyards, Krems has an attractive cobbled centre and gallery-dotted **Kunstmeile** (Art Mile; www.kunstmeile-krems.at). Its flagship is **Landesgalerie NÖ** (📞02732-908 010; www.landesgalerie-noe.at; Museumsplatz 1; adult/child €10/3.50; ⊙10am-6pm Tue-Sun), a futuristic structure from 2019 containing ever-changing exhibitions of edgy modern art and contemporary installations.

🛏 p587

The Drive » Leave Krems an der Donau on the B37 and cross the southbound L100.

Stift Göttweig is well signposted (9km altogether from Krems).

TRIP HIGHLIGHT

⑨ Stift Göttweig

Surrounded by grape-laden vines, Unesco World Heritage Site–listed **Stift Göttweig** (Göttweig Abbey; 📞02732-855 81-0; www.stiftgoettweig.at; Furth bei Göttweig; adult/child €8.50/5; ⊙10am-5.30pm Apr-Oct, shorter hours Nov) was founded in 1083, but the abbey you see today is mostly baroque. Highlights include the Imperial Staircase, with a heavenly ceiling fresco painted by Paul Troger in 1739, and the over-the-top baroque interior of the Stiftskirche (which has a Kremser Schmidt work in the crypt). Best of all is the opportunity to sip wine made here by the monks – including an exquisite Messwein rosé – on the panoramic garden terrace above the valley (you can also buy it at the abbey's shop).

The Drive » From Stift Göttweig, it's 79km to Vienna.

The most scenic route, through farmland and forest, is south on the L100 to St Pölten, then east on the L120 to join the eastbound B44 at Ebersberg. Continue through the Wienerwald (Vienna Woods) to the Austrian capital.

TRIP HIGHLIGHT

⑩ Vienna

Renowned for its imperial palaces, baroque interiors, opera houses and magnificent squares, Vienna is also one of Europe's most dynamic urban spaces. The best way to experience its blend of old and new is on a walking tour (p590).

A wonderfully atmospheric (if touristy) alternative is clip-clopping aboard a **Fiaker** (20min/40min/1hr tour €55/80/110; ⊙10am-9pm), a traditional-style open carriage drawn by a pair of horses. Drivers point out places of interest en route. Lines of horses, carriages and bowler-hatted drivers can be found at Stephansplatz, Albertinaplatz and Heldenplatz at the Hofburg.

You can also survey the city from Vienna's 65m-high, 1897-built Ferris wheel, the **Riesenrad**. It's located at the **Prater** (www.wiener-prater.at; 🚶; Ⓤ Praterstern), a sprawling park encompassing meadows, woodlands, and an amusement park, the **Würstelprater**, between the Danube and Danube Canal.

✗ 🛏 p587

TOP TIP: DANUBE CRUISES

Floating past vine-covered banks crowned by castles gives you a different perspective of the river. From Linz and Passau, **Wurm & Noé** (📞0851-929 292; www.donauschiffahrt.eu; Höllgasse 26) operates cruises between Regensburg, Germany and Vienna from March to early November. Ticket prices vary according to how many stops you stay on board.

Eating & Sleeping

Passau ❶

✖ Heilig-Geist-Stifts-Schenke   Bavarian €€

(📞0851-2607; www.stiftskeller-passau.de; Heilig-Geist-Gasse 4; mains €13-25; ⏱11am-11pm, closed Wed & Thu; 📶) Not only does this historical inn have a succession of walnut-panelled ceramic-stove-heated rooms, a candlelit cellar (from 6pm) and a vine-draped garden, but the food is equally inspired. Amid the river fish, steaks and seasonal dishes there are quite gourmet affairs such as beef fillet in flambéed cognac sauce. Help it all along with one of the many Austrian and German wines in stock.

⛏ Hotel Schloss Ort   Boutique Hotel €€

(📞0851-340 72; www.hotel-schloss-ort.de; Im Ort 11; s/d from €68/89; 🅿 📶) The most characterful place to sleep in Passau, this 800-year-old medieval palace by the Inn River conceals a soothingly tranquil boutique hotel, stylishly done out with polished timber floors, crisp white cotton sheets and wrought-iron bedsteads. Many of the 18 rooms enjoy river views and breakfast is served in the vaulted restaurant.

Linz ❸

✖ k.u.k. Hofbäckerei   Cafe €

(Pfarrgasse 17; dishes €3-6; ⏱6.30am-6.30pm Mon-Fri, 7am-12.30pm Sat) The Empire lives on at this gloriously frozen-in-time cafe in a timber-framed building dating from 1371. Here Fritz Rath bakes some of the best *Linzer Torte* in town – rich, spicy and with a wonderful crumbly lattice pastry. In summer, the best seats are in the shady courtyard.

⛏ Hotel am Domplatz   Design Hotel €€

(📞0732-773 000; www.hotelamdomplatz.at; Stifterstrasse 4; d/ste from €159/325; 🅿 ❄ 📶) Adjacent to the neo-Gothic Mariendom (ask for a room overlooking the cathedral), this glass-and-concrete cube filled with striking metal sculptures has 69 streamlined, Nordic-style

white and blond-wood rooms with semi-open bathrooms, as well as two suites. Wind down with a view in the rooftop spa. In fine weather, head to the cathedral-facing terrace for breakfast (€19), which includes a glass of bubbly.

Krems an der Donau ❽

⛏ Hotel Alte Poste   Hotel €€

(📞02732-822 76; www.altepost-krems.at; Obere Landstrasse 32; s €42-65, d €72-100; 📶) If you are on a budget and want to stay centrally, this historic 500-year-old post inn by the Steinertor (the medieval gateway into the old town) is for you. Basic but well-kept, the 23 rooms are gathered around an enchanting courtyard. Immaculate bathrooms are shared and rates include breakfast.

Vienna ❿

✖ Naschmarkt   Market €

(06, Linke & Rechte Wienzeile; ⏱6am-7.30pm Mon-Fri, to 5pm Sat; 🍴; Ⓤ Karlsplatz, Kettenbrückengasse) Stretching 500m along Linke Wienzeile between the U4 stops of Kettenbrückengasse and Karlsplatz, this is Vienna's biggest and best market. The western (Kettengasse) end has meats, fruit and vegetables (including exotic varieties), spices, wines, cheeses, olives, Indian and Middle Eastern specialities, and kebab and felafel stands. Altogether, there are 123 fixed stalls, including numerous sit-down restaurants.

⛏ Hotel Sacher   Historic Hotel €€€

(📞01-514 561 555; www.sacher.com; 01, Philharmonikerstrasse 4; d/ste from €400/700; ❄ 📶 🍴D, 1, 2, 71 Kärntner Ring/Oper, Ⓤ Karlsplatz) Stepping into Hotel Sacher is like turning back the clocks 100 years. The lobby's dark-wood panelling, original oil paintings, deep-red shades and heavy gold chandelier are reminiscent of a fin-de-siècle bordello. The smallest rooms are surprisingly large and suites are truly palatial. Extras include a taste of the cafe's famous *Sacher Torte* on arrival.

NEED ^{TO} KNOW

CURRENCY
Euro (€)

LANGUAGE
German

VISAS
Generally not required for stays of up to 90 days; some nationalities need a Schengen visa.

FUEL
Petrol stations are common on main roads and highways, and in larger towns. Unleaded costs around €1.07 per litre and diesel is €1.

RENTAL CARS
Auto Europe (www.autoeurope.com)

Avis (www.avis.com)

Europcar (www.europcar.com)

Hertz (www.hertz.com)

IMPORTANT NUMBERS
Europe-wide emergency covering police, fire and ambulance (112)

Climate

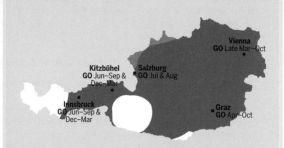

- Mild to hot summers, cold winters
- Warm to hot summers, mild winters
- Mild year-round
- Cold climate

Vienna
GO Late Mar–Oct

Kitzbühel
GO Jun–Sep & Dec–Mar

Salzburg
GO Jul & Aug

Innsbruck
GO Jun–Sep & Dec–Mar

Graz
GO Apr–Oct

When to Go

High Season (Apr–Oct)
» High season peaks from July to August.

» In lake areas, the peak is June to September.

» Prices rise over Christmas and Easter.

» Salzburg is busiest in July and August for the Salzburg Festival.

Shoulder (late Mar–May & late Sep–Oct)
» The weather's changeable, the lakes are chilly and the hiking's excellent.

» Sights are open and less crowded.

Low Season (Nov–Mar)
» Many sights are closed at this time of year.

» There's a cultural focus in Vienna and the regional capitals.

» Ski resorts open from mid-December.

» High season for skiing is mid-December to March.

Daily Costs

Budget: Less than €100

» Dorm beds or cheap doubles: about €25 per person

» Self-catering or lunch specials: €8–12

» Cheap museums: €4

Midrange: €100–200

» Doubles: €80–200

» Two-course meal with glass of wine: €30

» High-profile museums: €12

Top end: More than €200

» Plush suites and doubles in major cities: from €200

» Pampering at spa facilities: €40–100

» Fine dining and wine pairing: €70

Eating

Cafes Coffee, drinks, snacks.

Bistros Light meals to full-blown dinners.

Restaurants Simple eateries to Michelin-starred temples.

Vegetarian Few wholly vegetarian places, limited choices on most menus.

Price categories indicate the cost of a two-course meal, excluding drinks:

€	less than €15
€€	€15–30
€€€	more than €30

Sleeping

Hotels From budget to luxury; breakfast included unless indicated.

Pensiones Rates always include breakfast.

Hostels In cities and large towns; private or HI-affiliated.

Price categories indicate the cost of a double room with private bathroom in high season:

€	less than €80
€€	€80–200
€€€	more than €200

Arriving in Austria

Vienna Airport

Train & S-Bahn €4–12; to city centre every 30 minutes, 6am to 11.30pm (15 to 30 minutes).

Taxi €35–50; 30 minutes to centre.

Mobile Phones (Cell Phones)

Most European and Australian phones function; turn off roaming to avoid data charges. If visiting from outside the EU, buy a local SIM for cheaper rates.

Internet Access

Wi-fi (usually free) is available to guests in most hotels, B&Bs and hostels. Also offered by many cafes, bars, train stations and other public spaces.

Money

ATMs widely available. Maestro direct debit and Visa and MasterCard credit cards accepted in most hotels and midrange restaurants. Expect to pay cash elsewhere.

Tipping

Restaurant and bar prices include a service charge but locals still tip. Rounding up the bill to the nearest five euros or leaving a few coins usually suffices.

Useful Websites

Lonely Planet (lonelyplanet.com/austria) Travel tips, accommodation, recommendations and more.

Austria (www.austria.info) Austrian tourist board.

ÖAMTC (www.oeamtc.at) Motoring info for Austria.

Opening Hours

Banks 8am or 9am–3pm Monday to Friday (to 5.30pm Thursday)

Cafes 7am or 8am–11pm or midnight; traditional cafes close at 7pm or 8pm

Pubs and bars 5.30pm to between midnight and 4am

Restaurants Generally 11am–2.30pm or 3pm and 6–11pm or midnight

Shops 9am–6.30pm Monday to Friday (often to 9pm Thursday or Friday in cities), 9am–5pm Saturday

STRETCH YOUR LEGS
VIENNA

Start/Finish: Café Central

Distance: 3.4km

Duration: 4 hours

Vienna's grandeur unfolds in all its glory on this city stroll, from the timeless elegance of its *Kaffeehäuser* (coffee houses) to its monumental Hofburg palace, museums, parks and opulent opera house, as well as magnificent churches.

Take this walk on Trip

Café Central

Park just around the corner on Freyung and fortify yourself with coffee and a slice of chocolate-truffle *Altenbergtorte* at grand **Café Central** (www.cafecentral.wien; cnr Herrengasse/Strauchgasse; ⊙7.30am-10pm Mon-Sat, from 10am Sun; 🛜; ⓤHerrengasse).

The Walk >> Walk southeast on Herrengasse for 350m, then through the Michaelertor entrance gate to the imposing Hofburg.

Hofburg

Nothing symbolises Austria's culture and heritage more than the **Hofburg** (Imperial Palace; 📞01-533 75 70; www. hofburg-wien.at; 01, Michaelerkuppel; 🚌D, 1, 2, 71 Burgring, ⓤHerrengasse), seat of the Habsburgs from 1273 to 1918. Its oldest section is the 13th-century Schweizerhof (Swiss Courtyard).

The Walk >> It's a 750m stroll southwest through Heldenplatz, passing the twin museums Naturhistorisches and Kunsthistorisches on Maria-Theresien-Platz, to the MuseumsQuartier.

MuseumsQuartier

The **MuseumsQuartier** (Museum Quarter; MQ; 📞01-523 58 81; www.mqw.at; 07, Museumsplatz 1/5; ⊙information & ticket centre 10am-7pm; 🚌49 Volkstheater, ⓤMuseumsquartier, Volkstheater) is a remarkable ensemble of museums, cafes, restaurants and bars inside former imperial stables. With over 60,000 sq metres of exhibition space, the complex is one of the world's most ambitious cultural spaces.

The Walk >> Head southeast through the MuseumsQuartier's arched laneways to Mariahilfer Strasse. Turn left and continue 350m northeast to the Burggarten.

Burggarten

The **Burggarten** (Castle Garden; www. bundesgaerten.at; 01, Burgring; ⊙6am-10pm Apr-Oct, 7.30am-5.30pm Nov-Mar; 🚌D, 1, 2, 71 Burgring, ⓤMuseumsquartier) is a leafy oasis amid the city's hustle and bustle. The marble statue of Mozart is the park's most famous tenant, but there's also a statue of Emperor Franz Josef. Don't miss the **Schmetterlinghaus**

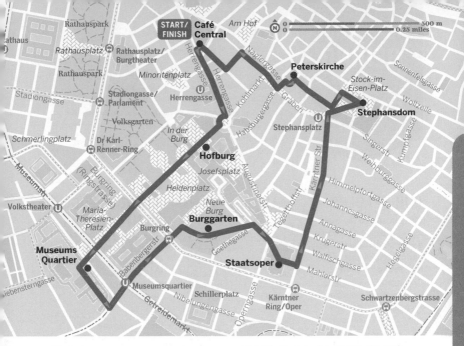

(butterfly house), and the **Palmenhaus** bar, housed in a beautifully restored *Jugendstil* (art nouveau) palm house.

The Walk » From the gardens' northeastern edge, walk southeast on Hanuschgasse for 200m to the city's resplendent opera house, the Staatsoper.

Staatsoper

The neo-Renaissance **Staatsoper** (www. wiener-staatsoper.at; 01, Opernring 2; tour adult/ child €10/5; [🚃]D, 1, 2, 62, 71 Kärntner Ring/ Oper, [U]Karlsplatz) is Vienna's foremost opera and ballet venue. Built between 1861 and 1869, it initially appalled the Viennese public, earning the nickname 'stone turtle'. You also can visit its museum and take a guided tour.

The Walk » Head north on Kärntner Strasse for 600m to the Stephansdom, and pause to check out the glorious tiled roof.

Stephansdom

Vienna's soaring, filagreed Gothic masterpiece, the **Stephansdom** (St Stephen's Cathedral; www.stephanskirche.at; 01, Stephansplatz; adult/child incl audio guide or guided tour

€6/2.50, all-inclusive ticket €15/4; ⊙9-11.30am & 1-4.30pm Mon-Sat, 1-4.30pm Sun, English tours 10.30am Mon-Sat; [U]Stephansplatz), is locally – and ironically – nicknamed Steffl (Little Stephan). A church has stood here since the 12th century; reminders include the Romanesque Riesentor (Giant Gate) and Heidentürme.

The Walk » Take Goldschmiedgasse northwest for 230m to Petersplatz and the domed Peterskirche.

Peterskirche

The **Peterskirche** (Church of St Peter; www. peterskirche.at; 01, Petersplatz; ⊙7.30am-7pm Mon-Fri, 9am-7pm Sat & Sun; [U]Stephansplatz) was built in 1733 according to plans by the celebrated baroque architect Johann Lukas von Hildebrandt. Interior highlights include a fresco on the dome painted by JM Rottmayr and a golden altar depicting the martyrdom of St John of Nepomuk.

The Walk » Head northwest on Graben and Naglergasse for 200m. Turn left onto Haarhof for 90m, then right onto Wallnerstrasse for 80m; Café Central is in front of you.

BEHIND THE SCENES

SEND US YOUR FEEDBACK

We love to hear from travellers – your comments help make our books better. We read every word, and we guarantee that your feedback goes straight to the authors. Visit **lonelyplanet. com/contact** to submit your updates and suggestions.

Note: We may edit, reproduce and incorporate your comments in Lonely Planet products such as guidebooks, websites and digital products, so let us know if you are happy to have your name acknowledged. For a copy of our privacy policy visit lonelyplanet.com/legal.

OUR READERS

Many thanks to the travellers who used last edition and wrote to us with helpful hints, useful advice and interesting anecdotes: Christopher Breddermann, Clément Borel, Sam Brooke, Andrea Carroll, Kirk Cassady, Betsy Chapman, Prisca Chiesa, Anne-Catherine Clerc, Rachel Day, Benoit Denis, Duane Dippon, Paul Erzinger, Jessica Ferrer, Amber Gret, Stephen Irlam, Erik Jacobsen, Brook Lameo, Wiebke Lösken, Timm Lotter, Chris Mence, Wessel Miedema, Sander Pelser, Anna Phillips, Zsuzsanna Remenyi, Jennifer Robertson, Meredy Slattery, Monika Smith, Daniela Stewart, Nicole Taskis, Gerbrich Wagenaar, Mirco Wilhelm, Nickos Yoldassis, Artem Zakharchuk, Barbara Zoccola

ACKNOWLEDGE-MENTS

Climate map data adapted from Peel MC, Finlayson BL & McMahon TA (2007) 'Updated World Map of the Köppen-Geiger Climate Classification', *Hydrology and Earth System Sciences*, 11, 1633–44.

Cover photograph: Schloss Neuschwanstein, Germany, Achim Thomae/Getty Images ©

Neuschwanstein shown courtesy of Bavarian Palace Department.

THIS BOOK

This 2nd edition of Lonely Planet's *Europe's Best Road Trips* guidebook was researched and written by Isabel Albiston, Oliver Berry, Stuart Butler, Jean-Bernard Carillet, Fionn Davenport, Marc Di Duca, Belinda Dixon, Peter Dragicevich, Duncan Garwood, Anthony Ham, Paula Hardy, Catherine Le Nevez, John Noble, Sally O'Brien, Josephine Quintero, Kevin Raub, Daniel Robinson, Brendan Sainsbury, Regis St Louis, Andy Symington, Ryan Ver Berkmoes, Kerry Walker, Nicola Williams and Neil Wilson. This guidebook was produced by the following:

Commissioning Editors Daniel Bolger, Kirsten Rawlings

Product Editors Kirsten Rawlings, Grace Dobell

Cartographers Alison Lyall, Julie Sheridan

Book Designers Ania Bartoszek, Fergal Condon, Gwen Cotter

Assisting Editors Joel Cotterell, Gabrielle Innes, Kate Kiely, Anne Mulvaney

Cover Researcher Fergal Condon

Thanks to Sonia Kapoor

INDEX

NICOLA WILLIAMS

Border-hopping is a way of life for British writer, runner, foodie, art aficionado and mum-of-three Nicola Williams who has lived in a French village on the southern side of Lake Geneva for more than a decade. Nicola has authored more than 50 guidebooks on Paris, Provence, Rome, Tuscany, France, Italy and Switzerland for Lonely Planet and covers France as a destination expert for the *Telegraph*. She also writes for the *Independent*, *Guardian*, lonelyplanet.com, *French Magazine, Cool Camping France* and others. Catch her on the road on Twitter and Instagram at @tripalong.

NEIL WILSON

Neil was born in Scotland and has lived there most of his life. Based in Perthshire, he has been a full-time writer since 1988, working on more than 80 guidebooks for various publishers, including the Lonely Planet guides to Scotland, England, Ireland and Prague. An outdoors enthusiast since childhood, Neil is an active hill-walker, mountain-biker, sailor, snowboarder and rock-climber, and a qualified fly-fishing guide and instructor. He has climbed and tramped in four continents, including ascents of Jebel Toubkal in Morocco, Mount Kinabalu in Borneo, the Old Man of Hoy in Scotland's Orkney Islands and the Northwest Face of Half Dome in California's Yosemite Valley.

REGIS ST LOUIS

Regis grew up in a small town in the American Midwest – the kind of place that fuels big dreams of travel – and he developed an early fascination with foreign dialects and world cultures. He spent his formative years learning Russian and a handful of Romance languages, which served him well on journeys across much of the globe. Regis has contributed to more than 50 Lonely Planet titles, covering destinations across six continents. His travels have taken him from the mountains of Kamchatka to remote island villages in Melanesia, and to many grand urban landscapes. When not on the road, he lives in New Orleans.

ANDY SYMINGTON

Andy has written or worked on more than a hundred books and other updates for Lonely Planet (especially in Europe and Latin America) and other publishing companies, and has published articles on numerous subjects for a variety of newspapers, magazines and websites. He part-owns and operates a rock bar, has written a novel and is currently working on several fiction and non-fiction writing projects. Andy, from Australia, moved to Northern Spain many years ago. When he's not off with a backpack in some far-flung corner of the world, he can probably be found watching the tragically poor local football side or tasting local wines after a long walk in the nearby mountains.

RYAN VER BERKMOES

Ryan has written more than 110 guidebooks for Lonely Planet. He grew up in Santa Cruz, California, which he left at age 17 for college in the Midwest, where he first discovered snow. All joy of this novelty soon wore off. Since then he has been travelling the world, both for pleasure and for work, which are often indistinguishable. He has covered everything from wars to bars – though he definitely prefers the latter. Ryan calls New York City home. Read more at ryanverberkmoes.com and at @ryanvb. His byline has appeared in scores of publications, and he's talked travel on the radio and TV.

KERRY WALKER

Kerry is an award-winning travel writer, photographer and Lonely Planet author, specialising in Central and Southern Europe. Based in Wales, she has authored/co-authored more than a dozen Lonely Planet titles. An adventure addict, she loves mountains, cold places and true wilderness. She tweets @kerrychristiani.

JOSEPHINE QUINTERO

Josephine first got her taste of not-so-serious travel when she slung a guitar on her back and travelled in Europe in the early '70s. In the mid '70s she moved to the US and launched her journalism career with a wine-and-lifestyle magazine in the Napa Valley. This was followed by a move to Kuwait, where she edited the Kuwait Oil Company magazine for six years, or until 1 August 1990 to be exact – the day Iraq invaded. After six weeks as a hostage and a hairy convoy escape route (via Iraq!) to Turkey, Josephine moved to the relaxed shores of Andalucía where she initially earned a crust as a ghostwriter, mainly on autobiographies for Marbella-based crooks and minor celebrities.

KEVIN RAUB

Atlanta native Kevin Raub started his career as a music journalist in New York, working for *Men's Journal* and *Rolling Stone* magazines. He ditched the rock 'n' roll lifestyle for travel writing and has written more than 95 Lonely Planet guides, focused mainly on Brazil, Chile, Colombia, USA, India, Italy and Portugal. Kevin also contributes to a variety of travel magazines in both the USA and UK. Find him at www.kevinraub.net or follow on Twitter and Instagram (@RaubOnTheRoad).

DANIEL ROBINSON

Over the past 25 years, Daniel has worked on dozens of Lonely Planet projects, including the first editions of *Cambodia* and *Paris* (co-authored with Tony Wheeler) and 12 of the 13 editions of France, researched in rain, sleet, snow and, when he's lucky, the kind of glorious sunlight that inspired the postimpressionists. Daniel's travel writing has appeared in *National Geographic Traveler,* the *New York Times* and the *Los Angeles Times,* and has been translated into 10 foreign languages.

BRENDAN SAINSBURY

Born and raised in the UK in a town that never merits a mention in any guidebook (Andover, Hampshire), Brendan spent the holidays of his youth caravanning in the English Lake District and didn't leave Blighty until he was 19. Making up for lost time, he's since squeezed 70 countries into a sometimes precarious existence as a writer and professional vagabond. In the past 11 years, he has written more than 40 books for Lonely Planet, about destinations from Castro's Cuba to the canyons of Peru.

PAULA HARDY

Paula Hardy is an independent travel writer and editorial consultant, whose work for Lonely Planet and other flagship publications has taken her from nomadic camps in the Danakil Depression to Seychellois beach huts and the jewel-like bar at the Gritti Palace on the Grand Canal. Over two decades, she has authored more than 30 Lonely Planet guidebooks and spent five years as commissioning editor of Lonely Planet's bestselling Italian list. These days you'll find her hunting down new hotels, hip bars and up-and-coming artisans primarily in Milan, Venice and Marrakesh. Get in touch at www.paulahardy.com.

CATHERINE LE NEVEZ

Catherine's wanderlust kicked in when she roadtripped across Europe from her Parisian base aged four, and she's been hitting the road at every opportunity since, travelling to some 60 countries and completing her Doctorate of Creative Arts in Writing, Masters in Professional Writing, and postgrad qualifications in Editing and Publishing along the way. Over the past decade-and-a-half she's written scores of Lonely Planet guides and articles covering Paris, France, Europe and far beyond. Her work has also appeared in numerous online and print publications. Topping Catherine's list of travel tips is to travel without any expectations.

JOHN NOBLE

John has been travelling for Lonely Planet since the 1980s. The number of LP titles he's written is well into three figures, on numerous countries scattered across the globe. He's still as excited as ever about heading out to unfamiliar destinations, especially off-the-beaten-track ones. Above all, he loves mountains, from the Pyrenees to the Himalaya. See his pics on Instagram: @johnnoble11.

SALLY O'BRIEN

Australian-born Sally has called Switzerland home since 2007. Swapping her surfboard for a snowboard, the beach for the lake and the barbecue for the caquelon, she loves exploring Switzerland's charming cities, the sublime Alps and lakes, and catching cable cars and trains to stunning vantage points. She lives with her husband, Denis, and their sons in the Lake Geneva region.

BELINDA DIXON

Only happy when her feet are suitably sandy, Belinda has been (gleefully) travelling, researching and writing for Lonely Planet since 2006. It's seen her navigating mountain passes and soaking in hot-pots in Iceland's Westfjords, marvelling at Stonehenge at sunrise; scrambling up Italian mountain paths; horse riding across Donegal's golden sands; gazing at Verona's frescoes; and fossil hunting on Dorset's Jurassic Coast. And all in the name of research. Belinda is also a podcaster and adventure writer and helps lead wilderness expeditions. See her blog posts at belindadixon.com.

PETER DRAGICEVICH

After a successful career in niche newspaper and magazine publishing, both in his native New Zealand and in Australia, Peter finally gave into Kiwi wanderlust, giving up staff jobs to chase his diverse roots around much of Europe. Over the past 15 years he's written more than 100 books for Lonely Planet on an oddly disparate collection of countries, all of which he's come to love. He once again calls Auckland, New Zealand his home.

DUNCAN GARWOOD

From facing fast bowlers in Barbados to sidestepping hungry pigs in Goa, Duncan's travels have thrown up many unique experiences. These days he largely dedicates himself to Spain and Italy, his adopted homeland where he's been living since 1997. He's worked on around 50 Lonely Planet titles, including guidebooks to Spain, Andalucía, Italy, Rome, Sardinia, Sicily and Portugal, and has contributed to books on world food and epic drives. He's also written on Italy for newspapers, websites and magazines.

ANTHONY HAM

Anthony is a freelance writer and photographer who specialises in Spain, East and Southern Africa, the Arctic and the Middle East. When he's not writing for Lonely Planet, Anthony writes about and photographs Spain, Africa and the Middle East for newspapers and magazines in Australia, the UK and US.

STUART BUTLER

Stuart has been writing for Lonely Planet for a decade and during this time he's come eye to eye with gorillas in the Congolese jungles, met a man with horns on his head who could lie in fire, huffed and puffed over snowbound Himalayan mountain passes, interviewed a king who could turn into a tree, and had his fortune told by a parrot. Oh, and he's met more than his fair share of self-proclaimed gods. When not on the road for Lonely Planet he lives on the beautiful beaches of Southwest France with his wife and two young children.

JEAN-BERNARD CARILLET

Jean-Bernard is a Paris-based freelance writer and photographer who specialises in Africa, France, Turkey, the Indian Ocean, the Caribbean and the Pacific. He loves adventure, remote places, islands, outdoors, archaeological sites, food and, of course Paris, his home. His insatiable wanderlust has taken him to 119 countries across six continents, and it shows no sign of waning. It has inspired many articles and photos for travel magazines and some 100 Lonely Planet guidebooks, both in English and in French.

MARC DI DUCA

A travel author for the past two decades, Marc has worked for Lonely Planet in Siberia, the Caribbean, Bavaria, England, Ukraine, Austria, Poland, Croatia, Portugal, Madeira and on the Trans-Siberian Railway, as well as writing and updating tens of other guides for other publishers. When not on the road, Marc lives near Mariánské Lázně in the Czech Republic with his wife and two sons.

FIONN DAVENPORT

Irish by birth and conviction, Fionn has spent the past two decades focusing on the country of his birth and its nearest neighbour, England, which he has written about extensively for Lonely Planet and others. In between writing gigs he's lived in Paris and New York, where he was an editor, actor, bartender and whatever else paid the rent. He posts his travel shots on Instagram – @fionndavenport.

OUR WRITERS

OUR STORY

A beat-up old car, a few dollars in the pocket and a sense of adventure. In 1972 that's all Tony and Maureen Wheeler needed for the trip of a lifetime – across Europe and Asia overland to Australia. It took several months, and at the end – broke but inspired – they sat at their kitchen table writing and stapling together their first travel guide, *Across Asia on the Cheap*. Within a week they'd sold 1500 copies. Lonely Planet was born.

Today, Lonely Planet has offices in the US, Ireland and China, with a network of more than 2000 contributors in every corner of the globe. We share Tony's belief that 'a great guidebook should do three things: inform, educate and amuse'.

ISABEL ALBISTON

After six years working for the *Daily Telegraph* in London, Isabel left to spend more time on the road. A job as writer for a magazine in Sydney, Australia was followed by a four-month overland trip across Asia and five years living and working in Buenos Aires, Argentina. Isabel started writing for Lonely Planet in 2014 and has contributed to 15 guidebooks. She's currently based in Ireland.

OLIVER BERRY

Oliver Berry is a writer and photographer from Cornwall. He has worked for Lonely Planet for more than a decade and has worked on more than 30 guidebooks. He is also a regular contributor to many newspapers and magazines and his writing has won several awards, including the Guardian Young Travel Writer of the Year and the *TNT Magazine* People's Choice Award. His latest work is published at www.oliverberry.com.

 MORE WRITERS

Published by Lonely Planet Global Limited
CRN 554153
2nd edition – Oct 2022
ISBN 978 1 7865 762 7 9
© Lonely Planet 2022 Photographs © as indicated 2022
10 9 8 7 6 5 4 3 2 1
Printed in China